Helena Augusta

WOMEN IN ANTIQUITY

Series Editors: Ronnie Ancona and Sarah B. Pomeroy

This book series provides compact and accessible introductions to the life and historical times of women from the ancient world. Approaching ancient history and culture broadly, the series selects figures from the earliest of times to late antiquity.

Cleopatra
A Biography
Duane W. Roller

Clodia Metelli
The Tribune's Sister
Marilyn B. Skinner

Galla Placidia
The Last Roman Empress
Hagith Sivan

Arsinoë of Egypt and Macedon
A Royal Life
Elizabeth Donnelly Carney

Berenice II and the Golden Age of
Ptolemaic Egypt
Dee L. Clayman

Faustina I and II
Imperial Women of the Golden Age
Barbara M. Levick

Turia
A Roman Woman's Civil War
Josiah Osgood

Monica
An Ordinary Saint
Gillian Clark

Theodora
Actress, Empress, Saint
David Potter

Hypatia
The Life and Legend of an
Ancient Philosopher
Edward Watts

Boudica
Warrior Woman of Roman Britain
Caitlin C. Gillespie

Sabina Augusta
An Imperial Journey
T. Corey Brennan

Cleopatra's Daughter
And Other Royal Woman of the
Augustan Era
Duane W. Roller

Perpetua
Athlete of God
Barbara K. Gold

Zenobia
Shooting Star of Palmyra
Nathanael Andrade

Eurydice and the Birth of Macedonian
Power
Elizabeth Donnelly Carney

Melania the Younger
From Rome to Jerusalem
Elizabeth A. Clark

Sosipatra of Pergamum
Philosopher and Oracle
Heidi Marx

Helena Augusta
Mother of the Empire
Julia Hillner

Helena Augusta

Mother of the Empire

JULIA HILLNER

OXFORD
UNIVERSITY PRESS

Oxford University Press is a department of the University of Oxford. It furthers
the University's objective of excellence in research, scholarship, and education
by publishing worldwide. Oxford is a registered trade mark of Oxford University
Press in the UK and certain other countries.

Published in the United States of America by Oxford University Press
198 Madison Avenue, New York, NY 10016, United States of America.

© Oxford University Press 2023

All rights reserved. No part of this publication may be reproduced, stored in
a retrieval system, or transmitted, in any form or by any means, without the
prior permission in writing of Oxford University Press, or as expressly permitted
by law, by license, or under terms agreed with the appropriate reproduction
rights organization. Inquiries concerning reproduction outside the scope of the
above should be sent to the Rights Department, Oxford University Press, at the
address above.

You must not circulate this work in any other form
and you must impose this same condition on any acquirer.

Library of Congress Cataloging-in-Publication Data
Names: Hillner, Julia, author.
Title: Helena Augusta : mother of the empire / Julia Hillner.
Description: New York, NY : Oxford University Press, [2023] |
Series: Women in antiquity | Includes bibliographical references and index.
Identifiers: LCCN 2022029976 (print) | LCCN 2022029977 (ebook) |
ISBN 9780190875305 (paperback) | ISBN 9780190875299 (hardback) |
ISBN 9780190875329 (epub)
Subjects: LCSH: Helena, Saint, approximately 255-approximately 330. |
Christian women saints—Rome—Biography. | Empresses—Rome—Biography.
Classification: LCC BR1720 .H4 H55 2023 (print) | LCC BR1720 .H4 (ebook) |
DDC 270.1092 [B]—dc23/eng/20220815
LC record available at https://lccn.loc.gov/2022029976
LC ebook record available at https://lccn.loc.gov/2022029977

DOI: 10.1093/oso/9780190875299.001.0001

Printed on demand

Comitibus
Kate, for believing in me
Julie, for laughing with me
Máirín, for asking all the right questions

Contents

Acknowledgments	ix
Abbreviations	xiii
Timeline of the Constantinian, Valentinian, and Theodosian Dynasties	xv
Dramatis Personae	xxi
Family Tree	xxvi
Maps	xxix

Introduction	1
The Case for (Chronological) Biography	2
Writing Helena's Life Forwards: Of Places, Gaps, and Relationships	6
Helena, Dynasty, and Power	9

PART I: EXTRA (C. 248–C. 289)

1. On the Frontiers	15
Demographics	15
Helena and the "Crisis of the Third Century"	22
Meeting Constantius	25
2. Weather Eye on the Horizon	34
Legalities	35
Helena at Naissus and Salona	39
Helena's Tetrarchy	49

PART II: OFF STAGE (C. 289–C. 317)

3. Sister Act	55
Lost Girl: Theodora	57
Fausta's Nose	65
Pruning the Tree	72
Waiting in the Wings, Becoming Christian?	75
4. The Necklace Affair	80
The Tomb at Šarkamen	82
Divine Mothers	87
The Augusta in the East	96
Fair Game: Empresses as Prey	106

viii CONTENTS

PART III: CENTER STAGE (C. 317–C. 329)

5. Keeping Up Appearances — 111
   The Road to Thessalonica: A Wedding, a Conspiracy, and a War — 113
   The Augusta Double — 122
   Fausta, Superstar — 132

6. Roman Holiday — 140
   Palace Life — 143
   Helena and the Constantinian Churches in Rome — 158
   New Look — 168

7. Four Deaths and an Anniversary — 178
   Murders in the Family — 182
   Becoming Genetrix — 194

8. From Here to Eternity — 204
   The Traveling Empress: Conflicting Portraits — 206
   Helena, the Pilgrim? — 208
   On the Road — 214
   A New Jezebel — 224
   Empresses in the Holy Land — 229

PART IV: CURTAIN AND ENCORES (C. 329–C. 600)

9. Burying an Empress — 247
   Final Honors — 250
   Rebranching the Tree — 262
   Coming through Slaughter — 266

10. Silence of the Empress — 274
    Extending Helena: Constantina — 277
    Burying Empresses, One More Time — 291
    Countering Helena: Justina — 298

11. New Model Empress — 309
    Ambrose's Helena — 309
    Reviving Helena's Look: Flaccilla and Thermantia — 317
    Reviving Helena in Action — 321
    Emulating Helena: Galla Placidia and Eudocia — 328
    A "New Helena" in Name: Pulcheria — 334
    Being Helena: Radegund — 339

Epilogue — 347
Ancient Sources — 349
Modern Studies — 355
Index — 383

Acknowledgments

In 2019–2020 I was lucky to have research leave and was planning to spend much of it in my study engaged with Helena. Little did I know that due to a global pandemic, it would become impossible to spend large parts of that year and many months of 2021 anywhere but in my study. Nonetheless, I talked to like-minded people every day, often several times per day, thanks to the wonders of Twitter. Although I am aware that this forum has many dark and distressing corners, I have found it full of generous and knowledgeable people who have patiently answered questions, imparted information, sent me reading and images, or simply shared my enthusiasm for Helena and all the other women of the Constantinian House. Thank you to every one of you for having kept me sane, because you really did. There are too many of you to mention, but special credit goes to Tadeus Calinca, aka @tadeuscalinca, whose tireless excavation of fourth-century women's lives has been an inspiration and who has become a dear virtual friend.

Of course, many colleagues and friends have done the same and more in "real" life. My long-standing LARGer community has given me numerous comments and sound critique on several chapters of this book: many thanks to Mattia Chiriatti, John Drinkwater, Rob Heffron, Simon Loseby, Máirín MacCarron, Kelsey Madden, Harry Mawdsley, Chris Mowat, Maik Patzelt, Alex Traves, Ulriika Vihervalli, Charles West, and Tianpeng Zhan. A very heartfelt further thank-you to Mattia for drawing my attention to Isabel Navarro Lasala's dissertation on Helena, and to John for gifting me a copy of *In Praise of Later Roman Emperors* and for simply being there. I am also deeply grateful to Rob for drawing all the maps, ground plans, reconstructions, and the Family Tree. I do not know how to repay my debt to Simon for reading the entire manuscript, saving me from many errors, and polishing my style. But I know what I owe you. All remaining errors are mine.

Further afield, I would like to thank the many colleagues who kindly shared published and even unpublished work with me: Klaus Belke, Alessandra Cerrito, Michael Fraser, Roy Gibson, Markus Löx, Christian Rollinger, Dennis Trout, Rebecca Usherwood, Belinda Washington, and Anthi Papagiannaki, whose work-in-progress on Constantinian cameos

I read in another reading group, at the University of Manchester, a very long time ago. Anna Francesca Bonnell-Freidin, Lucy Grig, Alice Leflaëc, and Andy Marsham provided me with precious source references and obscure literature. Lucy deserves a special thanks for having sent many empress-related opportunities my way, including inviting me to write two entries, on Constantia and Constantina, for the *Oxford Classical Dictionary* that set me on a path of true discovery. I would also like to thank audiences at the British School at Rome, the Department of Christian Archaeology at the University of Bonn, the Institute of Classical Studies in London, the International Medieval Congress, the Late Roman Seminar at the University of Oxford, the Seminar of Ancient and Medieval Studies at University College Cork, and at the conference *Mujeres imperiales, mujeres reales. Representaciones públicas y representaciones del poder* at the University of Alcalà (hosted by Margarita Vallejo-Girvès) for patient attention to and constructive criticism of my thoughts on Helena.

Before the pandemic curtailed such efforts, I took my research on what felt like a proper world tour, to visit as many places associated with Helena as possible. At several of these, experts stood ready to guide me through sites and materials. I would like to thank Vesna Crnoglavac and Stanislav Pavlović from the National Museum in Niš; Maria D'Onza from the Rheinische Landesmuseum and Winfried Weber from the Bischöfliche Dom- and Diözesanmuseum, both in Trier, and to Anja Busch for establishing those Trier contacts; Anna De Santis and Simona Morretta from the Soprintendenza Speciale Archeologia Belle Arti e Paesaggio di Roma, and, once again, Alessandra Cerrito, from the Sovrintendenza di Roma Capitale, as well as Stefania Peterlini from the British School at Rome for the initial correspondence with these experts in Rome. I would also like to thank Valeria Capobianco from the Deutsche Archäologische Institut in Rome for giving me access to their Cades Dactyliotheca ("der Große Cades") and to Daria Lanzuolo for explaining how to use the DAI's Fototeca. Unfortunately, the pandemic put a stop to my plans to visit sites related to Helena in Jerusalem and Bethlehem, but I would like to express my gratitude to Tom Holland who kindly shared astonishing memories of his trip to the Holy Sepulchre with me, even though "my" Helena isn't an Essex girl.

I was deeply honored and somewhat star-struck when Ronnie Ancona and Sarah Pomeroy invited me to write this book. I would like to thank them for their trust, Jill Harries for her enduring mentorship, and OUP's anonymous readers for their expertise and kindness. I profoundly appreciate my editor

Stefan Vranka's patient wait for me to deliver this book, well beyond agreed upon deadlines, and the calm and kind ways in which he guided me through the review process. The same is true for OUP's production team, especially Chelsea Hogue, Patti Brecht, and Nirenjena Joseph. I also owe much thanks to the staff at Sheffield University Library, at the Hellenic and Roman Library, and to Klara Wigger for procuring reading materials, to Azime Can for help with the index as well as to Agnes Crawford, Astrid Lehmberg, Dragana Mledanović, Silvia Orlandi, Lothar Schwinden, and Katja Soennecken for helping me obtain images. An enormous thank-you goes to Adam Blitz for having provided the cover image, which is a dream come true.

I slowly began collecting materials for this book while holding a Humboldt Fellowship at the Abteilung für Alte Geschichte of the Institut für Geschichtswissenschaft at the University of Bonn in the autumn of 2017. I would like to thank Konrad Vössing for hosting me; Imogen Herrad for many inspiring discussions; Jennifer Stracke for putting me in contact with Kornelia Kressierer from the Akademische Kunstmuseum, who kindly provided access to the Cades Dactyliotheca in Bonn (the "Kleine Cades"); and Erika Zwierlein-Diehl for giving me insight into the wonders of ancient gem research. By an amazing stroke of good fortune, I have now returned to Bonn for good. It has given me great pleasure to put final touches to the manuscript while holding a fellowship at the Bonn Center for Slavery and Dependency Studies named after the late Heinz Heinen, one of the foremost and humane experts on Helena. Most of this book, however, was researched and written while I was based in the Department of History at the University of Sheffield. My Sheffield colleagues remain unparalleled in creating the most amiable working atmosphere, and I would like to thank them all, and especially my fellow members of the Medieval and Ancient Section: Katherine Cross, Daniele Miano, Martial Staub, Casey Strine, and Danica Summerlin, in addition to those already mentioned; my heads of department Phil Withington and Adrian Bingham; and all the students who took my MA Module "Writing Late Antique Lives." A special thanks to Benjamin Ziemann for gifting me Thomas Etzemüller's *Biographien: Lesen—Erforschen—Erzählen* at the very early stages of writing this book. In Sheffield, I was also lucky to lead the Leverhulme Trust project "Women, Conflict and Peace: Gendered Networks in Early Medieval Narratives (RPG 2018–014)," of which this book is a major outcome.

This is a book about a woman who was connected to other women through men. I would like to imagine that she had many female friends as well, although information on this seems impossible to recover. I often think of the three women who were put to death in Nicaea sometime after 311 purely because they had been friends with the banished empress Valeria. They remained nameless and therefore tend to go unmentioned in modern scholarship. Fortunately, my own girlfriends are easy to name. This book is dedicated to three of them, Kate Cooper, Julie Gottlieb, and Máirín MacCarron, to thank them for their companionship during crucial stages of my career.

Julia Hillner
Bonn, September 2021

Abbreviations

ACO	Acta Conciliorum Oecumenicorum, ed. E. Schwartz, 4 tomes, Berlin, Leipzig: De Gruyter, 1914–1940
AE	L'Année epigraphique, Paris: Presses Universitaires de France, 1888–
AJA	American Journal of Archaeology
AnTard	Antiquité tardive
BABESCH	BABESCH Annual Papers of Mediterranean Archaeology
BHG	Bibliotheca Hagiographica Graeca, ed. F. Halkin, 3 vols., 3rd edn., Bruxelles: Société des Bollandistes, 1957
BZ	Byzantinische Zeitschrift
CBCR	Corpus Basilicarum Christianarum Romae
CIG	Corpus Inscriptionum Graecarum, 4 vols., Berlin: Reimer, 1828–1877
CIL	Corpus Inscriptionum Latinarum, Berlin: Reimer, 1862–
CJ	Codex Iustinianus, ed. P. Krüger, Berlin: Weidmann, 1877
CCSL	Corpus Christianorum Series Latina
CSCO	Corpus Scriptorum Christianorum Orientalium
CSEL	Corpus Scriptorum Ecclesiasticorum Latinorum
CTh	Codex Theodosianus, ed. Th. Mommsen, P. Meyer, Berlin: Weidmann, 1905
D	Digesta Iustiniani Augusti, ed. Th. Mommsen, Berlin: Weidmann, 1870
De Rossi, ICUR	G. B. De Rossi, Inscriptiones christianae urbis Romae, 2 vols., Rome: Società romana di storia patria, 1857–1888
DOP	Dumbarton Oaks Papers
G&H	Gender & History
GCS	Die griechischen christlichen Schriftsteller
ICUR	Inscriptiones Christianae Urbis Romae, Nova Series, Rome: Pont. Institutum Archaeologiae Christianae, 1922–
IG	Inscriptiones Graecae, Berlin: Berlin-Brandenburgische Akademie der Wissenschaften, 1873–
IGR	Inscriptiones Graecae ad Res Romanas Pertinentes, ed. R. Cagnat, 4 vols., Paris: Académie des Inscriptions et Belles-Lettres, 1901–1927

ILCV	Incriptiones Latinae Christianae Veteres, ed. E. Diehl, 3 vols., Berlin: Weidmann, 1925–1931
ILS	Inscriptiones Latinae Selectae, ed. H. Dessau, 3 vols., Berlin: Weidmann, 1892–1916
JAC	Jahrbuch für Antike und Christentum
JECS	Journal of Early Christian Studies
JEH	Journal of Ecclesiastical History
JHS	Journal of Hellenic Studies
JLA	Journal of Late Antiquity
JRA	Journal of Roman Archaeology
JRS	Journal of Roman Studies
JTS	Journal of Theological Studies (n.s. = New Series)
LCL	Loeb Classical Library
LP	Liber Pontificalis, vol. 1, ed. L. Duchèsne, Paris: De Boccard, 1955
LTUR	Lexicon Topographicum Urbis Romae, ed. E. M. Steinby, 6 vols., Rome: Quasar, 1993–2000
MAAR	Memoirs of the American Academy in Rome
MGH AA	Monumenta Germaniae Historica. Auctores Antiquissimi
MGH SRM	Monumenta Germaniae Historica. Scriptores rerum merovingicarum
MEFR	Mélanges de l'École française de Rome
NC	Numismatic Chronicle
PG	Patrologia Graeca
PLRE	A.H.M. Jones, J. Martindale, J. Morris, The Prosopography of the Later Roman Empire, 3 vols., Cambridge, UK: Cambridge University Press, 1971–1992
PO	Patrologia Orientalis
RE	Paulys Realencyclopädie der classischen Altertumswissenschaft, Berlin: Metzler, 1894–
RIC	Roman Imperial Coinage, London: Spink & Son, 1923–
SEG	Supplementum Epigraphicum Graecum, Leiden: Brill, 1923–
SLA	Studies in Late Antiquity. A Journal
TAPhA	Transactions of the American Philological Association
ZPE	Zeitschrift für Papyrologie und Epigraphik

Timeline of the Constantinian, Valentinian, and Theodosian Dynasties

c. 250	Helena is born, probably in Drepanon on the Propontis.
251	Defeat and death of Decius at Abritus in Thrace.
253–257, 266	Gothic sea-borne raids on the shores of the Black Sea and the Propontis.
257	Persecutions of Christians under Valerian.
260	Valerian is defeated at Edessa by Shapur and captured. Gallienus ends persecution of Christians.
267–268	Goths invade Greece and the Balkans and are defeated at Naissus by Claudius.
272–273	Aurelian's campaign against Zenobia of Palmyra. Helena meets Constantius.
c. 274	Helena gives birth to Constantine in Naissus.
275	Murder of Aurelian.
c. 282–284	Constantius becomes *praeses Dalmatiarum*. Helena in Salona?
284	Diocletian becomes emperor.
286	Diocletian appoints Maximian co-emperor.
Before 289	Constantius leaves Helena to marry Theodora, daughter of Maximian.
293	Constantius and Galerius appointed Caesars. Establishment of the Tetrarchy.
c. 295	Maximian's daughter Fausta is born in Rome. Constantine joins Diocletian's court at Nicomedia.
c. 300	Constantine's partner Minervina gives birth to Crispus.
303	"Great Persecution" of Christians begins in Nicomedia.
c. 304	Galerius' mother Romula dies.
305	Abdication of Diocletian and Maximian. Succession of Constantius and Galerius as Augusti. Severus and Maximinus Daza appointed Caesars.
306	Constantius dies in York. Constantine proclaimed Augustus by his troops. Galerius appoints Severus as Augustus. Usurpation of Maxentius in Rome and return of his father Maximian.

307	Severus invades Italy and is defeated by Maximian.
	Constantine marries Fausta.
308	Conference at Carnuntum.
	Maximian forced to abdicate a second time.
	Licinius appointed as Augustus, to succeed Severus.
	Galerius' wife Valeria is made Augusta.
310	Fausta reveals a plot by Maximian to Constantine and Maximian commits suicide.
311	Galerius ends Christian persecution with an edict of toleration.
	Galerius dies.
	Maximinus Daza banishes Valeria.
	Maximinus Daza renews persecutions.
	Lucian of Antioch is martyred in Nicomedia.
312	Constantine has a divine vision and defeats Maxentius at the Milvian Bridge.
	Death of Diocletian?
313	Constantine's sister Constantia marries Licinius in Milan.
	Constantine and Licinius renew commitment to Galerius' edict of toleration (so-called Edict of Milan).
	Licinius defeats Maximinus Daza near Adrianople. He commits suicide in Tarsos.
	Licinius kills Maximinus' wife, son, and daughter in Antioch, as well as Galerius' son Candidianus and Severus' son Severianus.
	A church council is held at Fausta's residence in Rome.
315	Constantine celebrates his Decennalia in Rome.
	Licinius executes Valeria and her mother Prisca in Thessalonica.
	Constantia gives birth to Licinianus in Sirmium.
316	Fausta gives birth to Constantine II in Arles.
	Constantine executes his brother-in-law Bassianus.
	Constantine declares war on Licinius and defeats him at the battle of Cibalae.
317	Crispus, Constantine II, and Licinianus appointed Caesars.
	Fausta gives birth to Constantius II in Sirmium.
c. 317–324	Helena arrives in Rome and repairs a bath outside the Sessorian Palace.
318	Helena's portrait appears on coinage minted in Thessalonica, alongside that of Fausta.
318–324	Fausta gives birth to Constantina, Constans, and perhaps one other child.
322	Crispus' wife Helena gives birth to Constantine's first grandchild.
324	Constantine defeats Licinius at the battle of Chrysopolis.

	Licinius is banished to Thessalonica.
	Constantius II is made Caesar and Helena and Fausta Augustae.
	Foundation of Constantinople.
325	Constantine kills Licinius.
	Council of Nicaea.
	Helena the Younger is born?
326	Constantine kills Crispus, Licinianus, and (perhaps, sometime later) Fausta.
	Constantine celebrates his Vicennalia in Rome.
326–328	Helena travels through the Eastern provinces, to Antioch and to Palestine.
c. 328	Helena dies and is buried in Rome on the Via Labicana.
330	Dedication of Constantinople.
333	Constans is made Caesar and perhaps betrothed to Olympias, daughter of Ablabius.
335	Flavius Dalmatius the Younger is made Caesar.
	Constantina marries her cousin Hannibalianus the Younger and is perhaps made Augusta.
	Constantine II marries an unnamed woman.
336	Constantine celebrates his Tricennalia in Constantinople.
	Constantine enslaves Licinius' remaining son.
	Constantius II marries his cousin, daughter of Julius Constantius.
337	Constantine dies and is buried in Constantinople.
	Massacre of Theodora's descendants in Constantinople.
	Constantine II, Constantius II, and Constans proclaimed Augusti.
337–340	Constantina arrives in Rome.
340	Constans defeats and kills Constantine II.
350	Magnentius kills Constans and is proclaimed Augustus in Gaul.
	Constantina promotes Vetranio to Caesar who later abdicates again.
	Magnentius marries Justina.
351	Usurpation of Nepotianus.
	Gallus made Caesar and married to Constantina.
353	Constantius II defeats Magnentius who commits suicide.
	Constantius II marries Eusebia.
354	Constantius II executes Gallus at Pola.
	Eusebia arrives in Rome.
	Constantina dies in Bithynia and is buried in Rome on the Via Nomentana.

355	Julian is made Caesar in Milan, married to Helena the Younger, and dispatched to Gaul.
357	Constantius II, Eusebia, and Helena the Younger in Rome.
360	Julian proclaimed Augustus by his troops in Paris.
	Helena the Younger dies and is buried in Rome on the Via Nomentana.
	Eusebia dies and Constantius II marries Faustina.
361	Constantius II dies.
363	Julian dies while on campaign against Persia.
	Jovian proclaimed Augustus.
364	Valentinian proclaimed Augustus and makes his brother Valens co-Augustus.
365	Usurpation of Procopius.
367	Gratian is made Augustus.
c. 368	Valentinian I divorces his wife Severa and marries Justina.
c. 372	Constantius II's daughter Constantia marries Gratian.
375	Valentinian I dies.
	Justina's son Valentinian II proclaimed Augustus by the troops on the Danube.
378	Valens is defeated by the Goths at the battle of Adrianople.
379	Theodosius I proclaimed Augustus in Sirmium.
381	Council of Constantinople.
383	Constantia dies and is buried in Constantinople.
	Theodosius I makes his son Arcadius Augustus and his wife Flaccilla Augusta.
	Gratian is killed.
386	"Basilica conflict" between Ambrose, Valentinian II, and Justina.
387	Magnus Maximus invades Italy, and Valentinian II and Justina flee to Thessalonica.
	Theodosius I marries Justina's daughter Galla.
	Theodosius I defeats Magnus Maximus.
392	Valentinian II is killed or commits suicide.
393	Theodosius I's son Honorius is made Augustus.
394	Theodosius I defeats Eugenius and Arbogast at the battle at the Frigidus.
395	Theodosius I dies in Milan.
404	Eudoxia, wife of Arcadius, dies.
408	Arcadius dies and is succeeded by Theodosius II.
410	Visigoths under Alaric sack Rome and take Honorius' sister Galla Placidia hostage.
414	Galla Placidia marries the Visigothic king Athaulf.

417	Galla Placidia marries the *magister militum* Constantius.
421	Constantius is made Augustus (Constantius III) by Honorius and dies.
423	Honorius dies.
425	Theodosius II proclaims Galla Placidia's son Valentinian III Augustus in the West.
431	Council of Ephesus.
438	Valentinian III marries Licinia Eudoxia, daughter of Theodosius II.
	Eudocia goes on a pilgrimage to the Holy Land.
442–443	Eudocia is banished or retires to the Holy Land.
450	Theodosius II dies and is succeeded by Marcian who marries Theodosius' sister Pulcheria.
451	Council of Chalcedon.

Dramatis Personae

Anastasia—Daughter of Constantius and Theodora; half-sister of Constantine; wife of Bassianus.
Basilina—Second wife of Julius Constantius; mother of Julian.
Bassianus—Probably a member of the Nummii family; husband of Anastasia; executed by Constantine in 316.
Constantia—Flavia Iulia Constantia; daughter of Constantius and Theodora; wife of Licinius.
Constantia (the Younger)—Posthumous daughter of Constantius II and his third wife Faustina; wife of Gratian; died in 383.
Constantina—Flavia Constantina; daughter of Constantine and Fausta; married Hannibalianus the Younger in 335 and Gallus in 351; died in 354.
Constantine—Flavius Valerius Constantinus; son of Constantius and Helena; proclaimed Augustus in 306; sole Roman emperor from 324; died in 337.
Constantine II—Flavius Claudius Constantinus; son of Constantine and Fausta; Caesar 317–337; Augustus from 337; killed in 340.
Constans—Flavius Iulius Constans; son of Constantine and Fausta; Caesar 333–337; Augustus 337–350; killed in 350.
Constantius—Flavius Iulius/Valerius Constantius; partner of Helena; husband of Theodora; father of Constantine, Julius Constantius, Flavius Dalmatius, Hannibalianus, Constantia, Anastasia and Eutropia; Caesar 293–305; Augustus 305–306; died in 306.
Constantius II—Flavius Iulius Constantius; son of Constantine and Fausta; Caesar 324–337; Augustus 337–361; died in 361.
Crispus—Flavius Valerius/Claudius/Iulius Crispus; son of Constantine and Minervina; born *c.* 300; Caesar 317–326; executed in 326.
Dalmatius—Flavius Dalmatius; son of Constantius and Theodora; father of Flavius Dalmatius the Younger and Hannibalianus the Younger; killed in 337.
Dalmatius (the Younger)—Flavius Dalmatius; son of Dalmatius; Caesar 335–337; killed in 337.

xxii DRAMATIS PERSONAE

Daughter of Julius Constantius—and of Galla; married Constantius II in 335; sister of Gallus and half-sister of Julian; died before 350.

Diocletian—Caius Aurelius Valerius Diocletianus; Augustus 284–305; abdicated in 305; died c. 311–312.

Eusebia—Probably daughter of the consul Fl. Eusebius of 347; married Constantius II c. 353; died before 361.

Eusebius of Nicomedia—Bishop of Nicomedia (c. 317–338) and then of Constantinople (338–341); acquainted with Constantia; maternal relative of Julian.

Eutropia—Born in Syria; wife of Maximian; mother of Theodora, Fausta, and Maxentius.

Eutropia (the Younger)—Daughter of Constantius and Theodora; mother of Julius Nepotianus; killed in early 351.

Fausta—Flavia Maxima Fausta; daughter of Maximian and Eutropia; married Constantine in 307; mother of Constantine II, Constantius II, Constantina, Constans, and Helena the Younger; Augusta in 324; perhaps killed in 326.

Galerius—Caius Galerius Valerius Maximianus; Caesar 293–305; Augustus 305–311; died in 311.

Galla—Sister of Vulcacius Rufinus and Naeratius Cerealis of the Naeratii family; first wife of Julius Constantius; died before 333.

Galla (the Younger)—Daughter of Valentinian I and Justina; married Theodosius I in 387; mother of Galla Placidia; died in 394.

Galla Placidia—Aelia Galla Placidia; daughter of Theodosius I and Galla; mother of Valentinian III; Augusta in 421.

Gallus—Flavius Claudius Constantius Gallus; son of Julius Constantius and Galla; Caesar 351–354; executed in 354.

Gratian—Flavius Gratianus; son of Valentinian I and Marina (Severa); Augustus 367–383; killed in 383.

Hannibalianus—Son of Constantius and Theodora.

Hannibalianus (the Younger)—Son of Flavius Dalmatius; king of kings and of the Pontic people 335–337; killed in 337.

Helena—Partner of Constantius, probably a concubine; mother of Constantine.

Helena, wife of Crispus—Married Crispus before 322; mother of at least one child, born in 322.

Helena (the Younger)—Younger daughter of Constantine and Fausta; married Julian in 355; died in 360.

DRAMATIS PERSONAE xxiii

Julian—Flavius Claudius Iulianus; son of Julius Constantius and Basilina; Caesar 355–360; proclaimed Augustus in 360; died in 363.

Julius Constantius—Son of Constantius and Theodora; married Galla before 326; married Basilina before 333; father of Gallus (with Galla) and Julian (with Basilina); killed in 337.

Julius Nepotianus—Son of Eutropia the Younger and (probably) Virius Nepotianus; proclaimed Augustus in Rome and killed in January 351.

Justina—Daughter of Iustus and a female member of the Constantinian family, probably a granddaughter of Julius Constantius; married Magnentius in 350–351; married Valentinian I *c.* 368; mother of Valentinian II and Galla the Younger; died *c.* 388.

Licinianus—Valerius Licinianus Licinius; son of Licinius and Constantia; Caesar 317–324; killed in 325–326.

Licinius—Valerius Licinianus Licinius; Augustus 308–324; deposed by Constantine in 324; killed in 325.

Magnentius—Flavius Magnus Magnentius; proclaimed Augustus in 350; defeated by Constantius II and committed suicide in 353.

Maxentius—Marcus Aurelius Valerius Maxentius; son of Maximian and Eutropia; usurped imperial power in 306; Augustus 308–312; defeated and killed by Constantine in 312.

Maximian—Marcus Aurelius Valerius Maximianus (Herculius); Caesar 285–286; Augustus 386–305 and 306–308; committed suicide in 310.

Maximinus Daza—Galerius Valerius Maximinus; son of Galerius's sister; Caesar 305–309; Augustus 309–313; defeated by Licinius and committed suicide in 313.

Minervina—Partner of Constantine, probably a concubine; mother of Crispus.

Mother of Maximinus Daza—Daughter of Romula and sister of Galerius.

Prisca—Wife of Diocletian; mother of Valeria; executed in 315.

Romula—Mother of Galerius and of a daughter, the mother of Maximinus Daza; died *c.* 304.

Theodora—Daughter of Maximian and Eutropia; married Constantius before 289; mother of Julius Constantius, Hannibalianus, Flavius Dalmatius, Constantia, Anastasia, and Eutropia; died before 337; posthumously awarded the title of Augusta in 337.

Theodosius I—Flavius Theodosius; Augustus 379–395; married Galla the Younger in 387 after the death of his first wife Flaccilla.

Valentinian I—Flavius Valentinianus; Augustus 365–374; married Justina *c.* 368 after divorcing his first wife Marina (Severa).

Valeria—Galeria Valeria; daughter of Diocletian and Prisca; wife of Galerius; Augusta in 308; executed in 315.

Valeria Maximilla—Daughter of Galerius and his first wife; wife of Maxentius; mother of Valerius Romulus and another son; possibly killed in 312.

Vulcacius Rufinus—Member of the Naeratii family; brother of Galla; Praetorian prefect of Illyria 347–353.

Wife of Maximinus Daza—Possibly a relative of Galerius; mother of a son and a daughter; executed in 313.

Family Tree

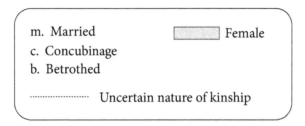

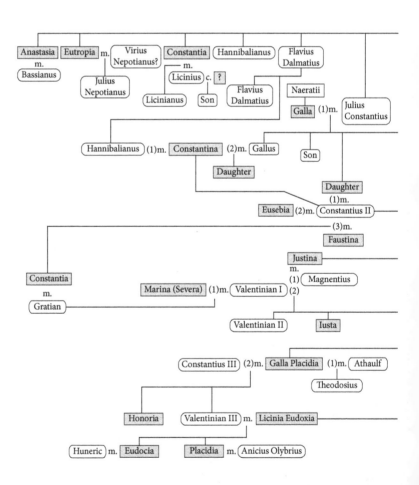

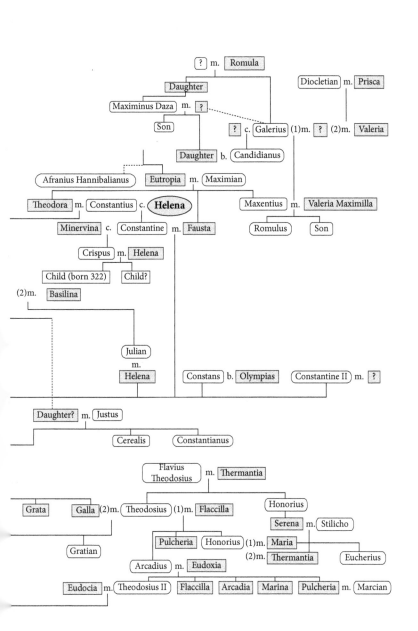

Maps

All maps and the family tree drawn by Robert Heffron.

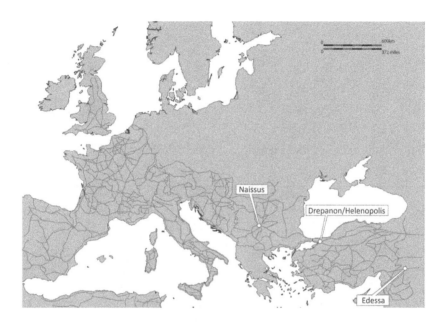

Map 1 Helena's "places of birth" (possible or imagined).

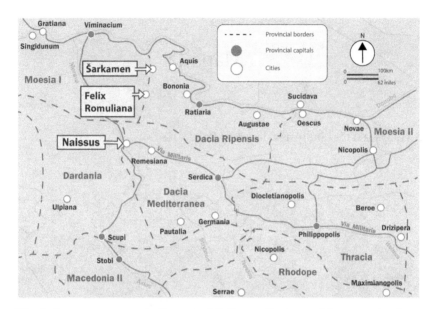

Map 2 Roman provinces in the central Balkans, after tetrarchic reorganization.

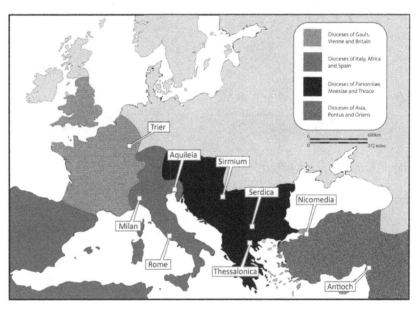

Map 3 Imperial residence cities during the tetrarchy.

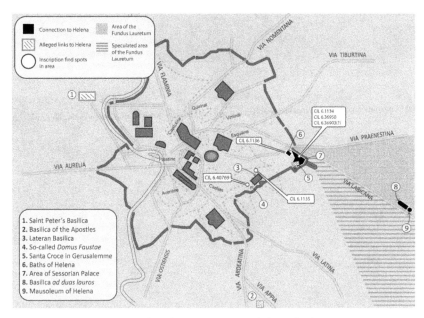

Map 4 Sites connected with Helena in Rome and the *suburbium*.

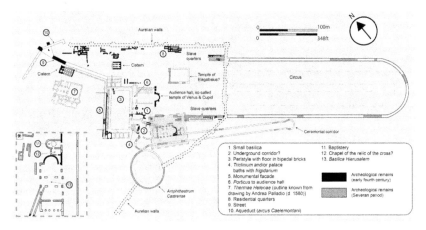

Map 5 Area of the Sessorian Palace.

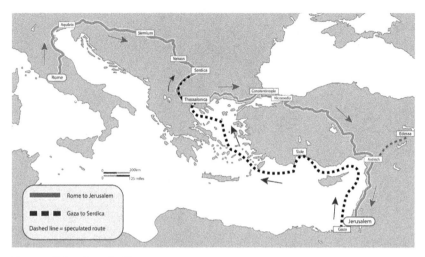

Map 6 Helena's probable itinerary 326–8.

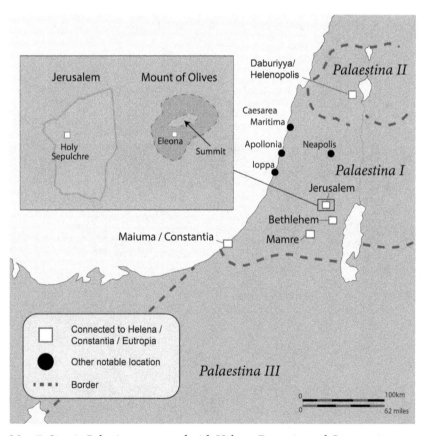

Map 7 Sites in Palestine connected with Helena, Eutropia, and Constantia.

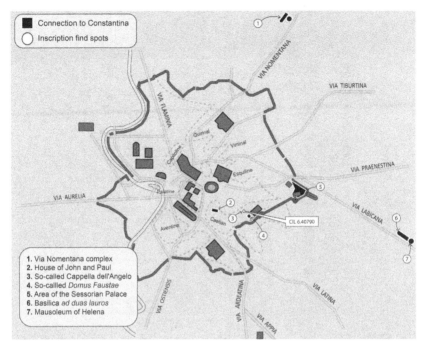

Map 8 Sites connected with Constantina in Rome and the *suburbium*.

Introduction

When I was asked to write a book about Helena, mother of the first Christian emperor Constantine, my immediate reaction was to decline politely. Helena is already the subject of stellar academic monographs, alone among the many fascinating women of the Constantinian dynasty.[1] True, these books deal, mostly, with Helena's enormous legendary afterlife, as the supposed founder of the True Cross. They do so because—so I was told—what we know about Helena's actual life would not fill a whole monograph. Helena did not leave what biographers call *ego-documents*, documents written by biographical subjects themselves. Like the lady on the cover of this book, sometimes believed to depict Helena, she is mouthless, and others speak for her. But almost everyone who wrote about her during late antiquity was writing after her death, on top of, mainly, being male and, in one way or another, opinionated.[2] What they wrote concerned only fragments of her life, above all, her travel to Palestine at the end of it. Moreover, Helena is best remembered for something she did not do, the discovery of the True Cross relic. Many shorter, often more biographical, discussions of Helena make similar observations.[3] I did not want to write another book about Helena's legend, reception, or route to sanctity and replicate work that can hardly be improved. A book-length biography, on the other hand, seemed nigh impossible.

The summer following my initial contact with Oxford University Press, I visited Trier, on a scorching hot day during our family holidays in Germany. Constantine, like his father Constantius and some of his fourth-century successors, frequently resided in the city on the Moselle, especially during the earlier part of his reign. We strolled around the various remains the presence of their courts had left behind. There are no historical sources that attest

---

[1] Drijvers (1992a); Pohlsander (1995); Harbus (2002). Navarro (2008) is an exception as she diligently assembles the sources on Helena's life rather than her legend.
[2] The exceptions during the period covered by this book are the pilgrim Egeria and the nun Baudonivia; see Chapters 8 and 11. On the cover image and its relation to Helena, see Chapter 4.
[3] Seeck (1912) 2820–22; Klein (1988) 355–75; Heinen (1998) 227–40; Consolino (2001) 141–59; Laurence (2002) 75–96; Heinen (2008) 9–29.

to Helena's presence here, only medieval legends.[4] Still, I was reminded of the wealth of material culture that originates from her lifetime, some of it, such as coinage with her portrait, from this very city. Watching my small daughter gaze upon the early modern statue of Helena holding the True Cross in the coolness of the city's cathedral, it dawned on me that a biography of Helena is possible if one pays attention to three additional factors beyond texts and objects. These are the gaps in her life course, the historically verifiable environments in which she moved or in which her portrait was displayed, and the female relationships surrounding her. These are the pillars on which this book is based.

The Case for (Chronological) Biography

It is said that writing a biography of an ancient person is a futile endeavor. Studies on ancient figures are often headed by the exclamation "This is not a biography" to express this sentiment.[5] Although rarely expanded on further, this common exclamation conveys a view that the ancient source base is too incomplete to trace an entire life cycle from childhood, that we do not have personal reflections to understand an "inner life," or, if we do, that we cannot surpass the barrier between modern and ancient expressions of emotion. These are all true statements, of course, but they do not explore the full scope of biography writing. As the doyenne of modern biography writing advises, there are many ways to write a biography and there are no definitive rules.[6] An enlightened practitioner of the craft has recently observed that the rules of *modern* biography writing are not sufficient to capture what was important to an *ancient* person anyway. We look in vain for clues about an individual's "quirky" uniqueness, contradictions, inner journeys, or changes of character due to life circumstances in ancient texts. Ancient writers were interested in socially "integrated," not psychologically "fragmented," personalities, and in presenting their own personality as such.[7] Seen from this perspective, it does not matter very much that we do not have Helena's ego-documents. They may have told us very little about "what she was really like." As we know from

---

[4] It is, at a stretch, possible that Helena died in Trier; see Chapter 9. On the medieval legends, see later in this chapter.
[5] See, for example, Barnes (1981) v, on Constantine; Leadbetter (2009) 1, on Galerius; both studies are much used in this book.
[6] Lee (2009) 18.
[7] Gibson (2020) 14–16.

other late antique imperial women's writing, they would have been largely performative if written personally by her at all.[8]

This is a biography because it seeks to understand the characteristics of Helena's life and to test the limits of our knowledge about them. For all our supposed inability to know much, Helena ghosts through literature on the Constantinian period, not to mention popular imagination. She does so with two personal qualities that are usually taken for granted and therefore often remain unexamined: her loving relationship with Constantine and her immense Christian piety. In a recent biography of Constantine, we discover that he would not have changed the world if Helena "had not given him the strength to face the uncertainty of his future" and that "his relationship with Helena was a potent force that transformed his life." From another, we learn that Helena must have been a Christian before Constantine and Constantius, because their "actions are what one would expect of the husband and son of a Christian woman."[9] Other, although generally older, scholarship sees Helena molding Constantine's attitudes toward his kin. Her concerns for the succession of her grandsons allegedly kept his stepfamily banished from court, and her protectiveness of her oldest grandson Crispus, whom she supposedly helped to raise, led to the death of her unloved daughter-in-law Fausta.[10] For others again, she was, if not a relic hunter, an enthusiastic church founder and "more than a symbolic partner" to Constantine, shaping the persona of Christian imperial women, from that of her granddaughter Constantina to the women of the Theodosian dynasty and beyond.[11] All these views operate on the premise that Helena's relationship with Constantine, her personal religious disposition, and her role at his court gave her agency, the ability to make independent choices, and power—the ability to control and influence the behavior of people. Some of these views are purely speculative, others take their lead from the ancient sources. They deserve scrutiny.

This is also a biography because it starts with Helena's birth and follows her lifespan and her legacy during late antiquity in chronological fashion. "Cradle to grave" biography is not the most fashionable form of life writing these days. It has been argued that it gives the distorted impression that human lives are linear and gapless. Some of the most exciting biographies of

---

[8] Hillner (2019c).
[9] Potter (2014) 34, 298; Stephenson (2009) 3, who echoes Rufinus, Hist. eccl. 10.7.
[10] See, for example, Klein (1988) 356; Pohlsander (1984) 106; but also van Dam (2007) 110 n.34; and Chapter 7 in this book.
[11] Angelova (2015) 120 and passim; Brubaker (1997).

ancient figures that have appeared in recent years are organized differently. They study themes that cast light on how these individuals themselves ordered their lives or on how their lives "reflected and shaped" their times.[12] It would be possible to do this for Helena also, embedding her in contexts of significance to late antique historiography. Readers of this book are certain to look for themes such as motherhood, conversion, pilgrimage, or church patronage in connection with Helena's life. They will find them, but they are not used as an explanatory model of her life.[13]

Forgoing a chronological approach has downsides and not just for narrative reasons.[14] It has downsides specifically for a subject like Helena, who was only written *about*. We do not have the luxury of scouring her own writing to deduce what she herself would have found meaningful. A thematic approach therefore reduces Helena's life to aspects and events that the late antique men who left us the most extensive testimony reduced it to. These are, above all, her Christianity and her visit to Palestine when she was the most senior imperial woman in the empire, but when she was also already around 80 years old. Such an approach bears the risk of introducing anachronisms into our understanding of her life. Helena's position and activities at Constantine's court at the end of her life do not necessarily supply proof for why he brought her to his court in the first place. To avoid the collapsing of time, we must accept that the majority of Helena's long life was lived in the third century and during the period of the tetrarchy. These earlier contexts provide more persuasive reasons for Constantine's promotion of his mother than her Christian piety alone. Concentrating on what late antique authors claimed happened at the end of her life also potentially exaggerates the importance of such testimony. Eusebius of Caesarea's *Life of Constantine*, which contains the most detailed account of Helena's travels, was not widely read in the fourth century and remained virtually unknown in the Western part of the empire. It also has distinctive qualities that tell us more about Eusebius than the subjects he wrote about.[15] This does not mean that it cannot be used as information on Helena's life if carefully handled, especially since Eusebius was, by all

---

[12] Jacobs (2016) 27, who coins the term *cultural biography* for this approach. Gibson (2020) organizes his biography of Pliny around the landscapes in which Pliny moved and about which he wrote.

[13] For motherhood, see pp. 40–43; conversion, pp. 75–79; church patronage, pp. 158–67, 234–37; for pilgrimage, pp. 234–243.

[14] Kinkead-Weekes (2002), from whom I also borrow the phrase *writing lives forwards*.

[15] For a discussion of Eusebius' aims of writing the so-called Helena-excursus in the *Life of Constantine*, see Chapter 8. Eusebius' *Life of Constantine* was little read in the fourth century even in the East, because Eusebius himself was considered doctrinally suspect; see Lieu (1998) 155.

accounts, an eyewitness of Helena. But we should not take his interests as the analytical lens through which to approach earlier evidence on Helena's life, or, for that matter, later evidence on her commemoration.

Most importantly, a chronological approach highlights precisely that Helena's life and her legacy were not linear affairs. The most significant feature of both her life and her legacy was that they were interrupted. While this is not a novel insight in itself, at least for her life, it invites us to reflect on Helena's specifically female experience, both as an individual and as a subject of historical study. Of course, men's lives were and are also not gapless or linear. But the fiction that human life can be told in a linear way was developed with respect to the lives of men, who over centuries have been the subject of biographical writing. This fiction could be upheld because a reasonable number of men throughout history have led public lives that left behind enough historical records, including, of course, their own writings, to make their lives presentable as a continuum. Less public female lives, even of high-status women who wrote, on the whole developed along a different trajectory, with long documentless spells of supposedly "doing nothing" and more time spent in obscurity without leaving a trace in the historical archive. If women had set the norm for biography writing, perhaps a linear idea of a life would never have taken hold.[16]

While all of this has been true for historical female life cycles generally, interruptions and nonlinearity were a particular feature of Roman women's lives at all social levels. Many high-status women and especially imperial women were pawns in volatile and changing alliances between families. At the same time, the immense social and gender inequalities of Roman society also allowed high-status men to pursue temporary companionship, transitory sexual gratification, and alternative family planning with low-born women. Well-attested and legally regulated elite family customs such as divorce, remarriage, and concubinage created and sustained complex domestic situations in which different women appeared in and disappeared from the more stable lives of men.[17] Of course, many Roman men were affected by these social practices, too, but male public lives were not defined by them. Women tend to appear in Roman sources in relation to men and interruptions in these relationships also lead to their disappearance from

---

[16] On the issues attention to gender creates for the genre of biography writing, see Etzemüller (2012) 136–40; von Zimmermann (2005) 21–22; Ní Dhúill (2020) 11–41.

[17] The historiography on the social dimensions of Roman family law is vast. Examples that underpin many discussions in this book are Arjava (1996) and Evans Grubbs (1995).

historical documentation.[18] Helena is a case in point. She disappeared from the public record after Constantine's father Constantius decided to leave her to marry another woman, Theodora, who then, but only then, comes to our attention. Later, when Constantine had become emperor and promoted his mother, Theodora disappeared again. This book takes the ruptures created by the circulation of women seriously and uses them as a way to recover the roles they played in the lives and, in this case, imperial politics of men.

Writing Helena's Life Forwards: Of Places, Gaps, and Relationships

The sources on the historical Helena are roughly of three types, with each providing information about a particular period of her life. Helena's early life makes a fleeting appearance in a good number of texts that are, despite their variety, mostly focused on chronicling imperial history and therefore interested in explaining Constantine's rise to power. Some, although by no means all, are products of a pagan tradition hostile to Constantine. Second, Helena appears on or in objects of imperial self-display presenting her as a member of the imperial family. These range from epigraphy, sculpture, coinage, and imperial monuments to cameos, intaglios, and other carved gemstones. Although these are the only sources contemporary to Helena's life, they are often treated separately from texts.[19] This book integrates them into the narrative, paying particular attention to sometimes microscopic changes to Helena's representation in terms of titulature, epithets, and iconography to chart Constantine's changing attitude toward his mother's role in his dynastic program. The third type of sources are Christian authors' more expansive but increasingly legendary treatments of Helena's pious activities in Palestine at the end of her life. This book will not argue that Helena found the True Cross but will try to wrestle back some of her scope of action from this material.

Even where objects or epigraphy derive from Helena's lifetime, their frequent separation from original contexts means that we face many difficulties in interpreting their commission, production, and use. Problems of interpretation, if of a different type, also surround the textual sources on Helena's life,

---

[18] Dixon (2001) 20–21.
[19] Drijvers (1992a) and Pohlsander (1995) each have separate chapters or appendices entitled "Portraits of Helena" and "Image in Roman Art," which provide extremely useful catalogues of objects.

and not just the legendary ones. Chronologically arranging the events they describe provides us with narrative time, but this is often at odds with the time of their composition, invariably much later, and their relation to each other. It is possible to explore, illuminate, and sometimes overcome these epistemological fault lines by introducing a fourth body of evidence: natural and human geography. Such data can be recovered from the ancient sources themselves; from material remains; from today's landscapes; or from mapping distances, reconstructing visibility lines, or timing ancient travel. A spatial perspective is important because Helena's world was one of developing regionalism. For various reasons, throughout the late third and fourth centuries, members of imperial families had diverse provincial backgrounds and therefore multipolar experiences. Furthermore, different imperial courts moved between many different places, each generating their own material culture, including objects or texts referencing Helena and other imperial women. Confronting textual sources not only with each other, but also with insights from regional and environmental contexts, frequently allows us to strip them of their elements of hindsight and therefore strengthen their validity. Situating portraits of Helena, where possible, within their regional settings allows us a glimpse of whom Constantine wished to take notice of his mother. Attention to space helps us to determine the scope and limits of Helena's actions and the quality of her interactions with relatives, officials, bishops, or subjects, and even the reasons for her appearances in the historical record.

What spatial data cannot do is bridge the gaps in the documentary record. During the thirty years between Constantius' departure from Helena's life and her reemergence as a member of Constantine's court, we are almost completely left in the dark about her situation. Another gap, after her death, is significant, too. We have, at most, hostile views about Helena in the sixty-odd years between her last imperial portrait on coinage and her reemergence as the finder of the True Cross. Such gaps have frequently invited scholarly speculation or even inventions by hagiographers and novelists. Helena's very first hagiographer, the ninth-century monk Almann of Hautvillers, took this route. In his *Life of Saint Helena*, written on the occasion of the translation of what he believed to be her relics from Rome to the monastery of Hautvillers in 840–842,[20] Helena is a noble lady of nearby Trier and resides in that city

---

[20] Another relic translation occurred in Rome in the twelfth century, when further alleged remains of Helena were removed from her mausoleum to S. Maria in Ara Coeli; see Pohlsander (1995) 159–60. On her burial, see Chapter 9.

for the majority of her life until relocating to Rome in her old age.[21] Evelyn Waugh's Helena, in his eponymous novel of 1950, leads a rather happy British expat life on the Dalmatian coast during her historically obscure years, in addition to being the daughter of a Celtic king. "The novelist," so Waugh, chooses "the picturesque in preference to the plausible."[22] Although extrapolation and contextualization are necessary methods when dealing with fragmentary ancient sources, I have taken this axiom as a warning against filling the voids in Helena's life with too much picturesque imagination. The same is true for the gaps in her commemoration. Based on what the sources tell us, her immediate influence on the behavior of the next generation of Constantinian women cannot be taken for granted and should not be simply insinuated. It is more productive for our understanding of Helena to investigate the reasons for her absence from the historical record than to smooth them over.

Gaps in a life cycle can be clues about a life, but so can be the moments when individuals become visible to us. We also need to look closely at the circumstances of Helena's returns from obscurity. Helena returned twice, each time in a startling new costume. The sexualized low-born woman turned into the majestic power-dressing Augusta and then, in her legendary incarnation, into the humble imperial relic hunter. To get from one to another without falling back onto unsubstantiated claims of filial devotion, intense piety, and immediate notoriety is possible if we consider Helena's life (or any human life[23]) not merely as an individual venture. Her life was a web of changing relationships to which she was sometimes central, sometimes marginal, and sometimes ancillary, including after her death. Even during her absence from our sources, we have enough evidence to trace this web through the men Helena was related to by kinship. We also have enough evidence to investigate how this web changed through the appearance and departure of other women in these men's lives. Most importantly, we can establish when, how, where, and for whom emperors tried to shape the composition of the imperial family, and the role of women within it. Late antique emperors and authors had a choice of which woman to mention, and the foregrounding of other women over Helena still tells us much about her role

---

[21] Almann of Hautvillers, Vita seu potius homilia de S. Helena, 13. Almann also switches around Constantius' two relationships: he leaves Theodora for Helena.
[22] Waugh (1950), ix–x. Waugh draws on Anglo-Norman legends of Helena, especially those popularized by Geoffrey of Monmouth, that postulate her as the daughter of the legendary Celtic king Cole, based in Colchester; see Harbus (2002) 65–66.
[23] Ní Dhúill (2020) 16.

while alive and her reception while dead. Furthermore, dynastic display, imperial competition, and the ways in which these were adapted by late antique writers go a long way in explaining why Helena became visible when she did.

The structure of this book reflects this premise. It is divided into four parts. The first and third deal with periods of Helena's life that appear in the available sources (*c.* 248–*c.* 289; *c.* 317–*c.* 329). The second part covers the time of her first absence from the historical record, which coincides with the complex and changing dynastic politics of the tetrarchy. It reconstructs the exchange, promotion, deaths, and survivals of the imperial women in whose steps Helena followed upon her return. The final part considers the ebbs and flows of Helena's emergence as an exemplary Christian empress, up to the divergence of this model into clear Eastern and Western traditions around the year 600. It shows that Helena's commemoration as a significant figure of Constantinian and Christian history took a long time to take shape. While she was almost ignored by her immediate descendants, it took the advent of a new dynasty, the Theodosian, for her rediscovery.

Helena, Dynasty, and Power

This book does discuss not only Helena, but also an astonishing historical experiment. In 324, Constantine awarded his mother the Augusta title. She was not the first woman so honored. Forty-two imperial women had been before her.[24] She herself received the tribute together with her daughter-in-law Fausta. Yet, Helena was different from all of them. Although some imperial sons had conferred the title on their mothers beforehand, these had all been either wives of emperors themselves or came from aristocratic backgrounds, connecting emperors to important stakeholders. Modern historians often call Helena a dowager empress, but she was nothing of the sort.[25] She had never been the wife or widow of an emperor. What is more, her background was provincial, even murky.

Constantine took the unprecedented decision to make Helena a visible member of his court for several reasons, but one of the most significant was dynastic. These motivations are not entirely separable from his religious

---

[24] Kolb (2010b) 23–35 offers a list of sixty women (from Livia to Theodora, wife of Justinian) for whom the title is attested or postulated.

[25] For example, Holloway (2004) 58; De Blaauw (2014) 139. For the Augusta title and previous mothers who received it, see Chapters 4 and 5.

program. After all, in 324 Constantine had just defeated his pagan co-emperor Licinius and he soon sent his mother to project the Christian nature of his dynasty and rule to Licinius' former territories. It is not impossible that Constantine wanted to blur the boundaries between his mother and the humble mother of his new God incarnate, although it was left to churchmen, many of them writing much later, to fully connect these dots. But it would be wrong to attribute to Constantine an unchanging vision when it came to the role of his mother within his dynasty. Helena's appearance as a member of Constantine's court, her later promotion to Augusta, and her even later travel around the Eastern provinces each followed a dynastic crisis that thinned out the different lines of succession created by Constantius' decision to leave Helena for Theodora decades before. These activities also followed the different stages of Constantine's conquest of the Eastern part of the empire and his gradual discovery that inhabitants of these lands remembered what the wives of his imperial rivals had done, looked like, and how they had died. The complicated makeup of Constantine's family and his progressive erasure of other imperial households meant that his own absorbed a notable number of imperial women and refashioned them as "Constantinian." For some time, Helena was only one among these, outshone especially by her daughter-in-law Fausta. She only slowly grew into the role for which she is now remembered best, as the senior woman of the Christian empire furnished with remarkable competencies. All of this tells us much about the specifics of Constantine's reign and style of rule.

It is from the uniqueness of Helena's position, relative to other Constantinian women, but also relative to previous empresses, that we can grasp some particulars of her existence and, perhaps, the extent of her power. For it is clear that Helena came a long way, both in the physical and the figurative sense. She had experiences that many women of her background without a doubt did not even dream of, although she was also the beneficiary of social, regional, and political changes that made such dreams not entirely impossible. Her life can be told as a gradual widening of spatial, social, cultural, and religious horizons. In its course, she lived in small settlements on the margins of the empire as well as in imperial palaces at its center, got to know many of its roads, and managed a lap around the Eastern Mediterranean at least once in her life. She also had experiences that were unmatched even among high-elite women of her time. Although Helena shared with many of them the common fate of ruptures to her family life, few women faced a return in old age to the very same family circles from which they had been previously removed, and even fewer were then used to defuse the conflicts created by such ruptures and returns. All of this tells us much both about the opportunities for women at the turn of the fourth century, and the constraints they nonetheless faced.

Does all this mean that Helena had power? To answer this question, it is useful to reflect on different kinds of power that Roman imperial women had.[26] Although there was no formal position of "empress" in the Roman empire, imperial women were frequently endowed with titles, symbols, and sometimes even competencies that institutionalized their roles.[27] Helena was as well, to the extent that later observers considered her to have been a "partner in reign" with her son. The visibility of women in imperial self-display did, however, not necessarily equate with their power, or to put it simply, ideology is neither identity nor experience.[28] We need to remember that Constantine remained the source of Helena's official image, including its timing and location, and (as recognized by Eusebius) the ultimate authority behind her recorded deeds.

Visibility did advertise to the inhabitants of the Roman empire an imperial woman's closeness to the emperor. It has long been acknowledged that such closeness and its acceptance by Roman subjects lend imperial women, as well as other members of the imperial household, informal or "personal" power.[29] Helena clearly accrued agency from this position, especially since she was often in direct contact with populations at key imperial locations. In this way, she may well have steered imperial decisions, including on matters of Christian policy such as church building, although from the sources we have, we cannot be entirely sure. If she did have opinions about her faith, or any opinions, they remain indistinguishable from those of Constantine.

This resemblance may be a result of a documentary and literary culture that subsumed all imperial action into a universal or "integrated" whole. But it was also the result of Helena's decisive lack of a third kind of power often connected with Roman empresses, perhaps the most important of all. This power derived from the reach of networks in which empresses operated

---

[26] As laid out by Späth (2010) 293–308. See also James (2001) 1–7 who underscores the increasing institutionalization of the empress's role in the Byzantine empire, although the Theodosian dynasty played a greater role in this development than the Constantinian one; see Chapter 11.

[27] For this reason, the very term *empress* is ambiguous in the Roman context; see Brennan (2018) 1–16. In this book, I have used it for wives of emperors and women who received the title of Augusta. I have also used it for Helena from the time of her appearance at Constantine's court to reflect her unique position.

[28] Langford (2013) 5.

[29] Kolb (2010b) 19.

and the quality of their resources. The more empresses could fall back on their own families, property, education, and clientele, the more influential they were, and the better they could exploit their visibility and the proximity to the emperor for their own interests.[30] Helena did not, unlike most of her predecessors, come from an aristocratic family or another imperial household, so she had little of these resources. Constantine entrusted his mother with sensitive political missions far beyond what may be expected of a woman of her age and background. We may be able to deduce from this Helena's personal qualities of diplomacy, tact, and mediation.[31] It mostly reflects that Constantine trusted her to be loyal, but her loyalty cannot have entirely been the result of true choice. If Constantine needed Helena, in the absence of the collective power just described, Helena needed Constantine even more. She needed his support to become part of the imperial family, to have access to funds, and to maintain an aspect of respectability. She even needed him to be remembered, for her commemoration by her descendants ceased almost as soon as Constantine was dead. She even, at least in the Eastern empire, needed him to become a saint. If there is another overarching theme to Helena's life, it is dependency.

Another recent biographer of a fourth-century figure, of the intransigent heresiologist bishop Epiphanius of Cyprus, reminds us that his subject "is late antiquity." For this modern scholar, the life of Epiphanius serves as a window into the intersections of theology, politics, and personalities that shaped the early church and, in turn, the modern field of "Patristics."[32] I hope readers of this book will be able to deduce from its pages that it is possible to write imperial history of the fourth century through the lens of imperial women, and that these women "are late antiquity," too. Nonetheless, I also agree with the Master's students who took my course "Writing Late Antique Lives" at the University of Sheffield in the spring of 2018. After a lengthy and abstract discussion on the relationship between the biographical genre and the great questions of late antique historiography, they reminded me that the primary goal of biography writing is "to keep it human." In this spirit, let us raise the curtains on Helena.

---

[30] Kunst (2010); Späth (2010) 305–7; Levick (2014) 19–39. Seen from this perspective, perhaps the most powerful empress in the Constantinian period was Eusebia, the wife of Constantius II, one of the few imperial women with an independent family background and, perhaps not coincidentally, remembered as supremely influential. See Tougher (2020).
[31] Heinen (2008) 23.
[32] Kim (2015) 1; see also the review by Reed (2017). Kim uses the term *critical biography*.

PART I
EXTRA (C. 248–C. 289)

1
On the Frontiers

When Helena was born, the Roman empire had around 50 million inhabitants.[1] The vast majority of them remain to us just part of that statistic. By contrast, we have a substantial amount of information about Helena's early life: an indication of social status, a name perhaps given at birth, a possible place and an approximate date of birth. Given what these early data prefigure, Helena—female, non-elite, and non-urban—could easily have lived an equally forgotten life. People of her kind were not only among the most marginalized and vulnerable, but also the most "muted" inhabitants of the Roman empire, rarely talked about in our sources and rarely leaving a trace of themselves.[2]

The survival of Helena as a historical figure is therefore an astonishing feat, which of course derives from her later role as the mother of the first Christian emperor. That she could assume this role, however, comes down not only to her personal qualities, but also to being at the right place at the right time in her youth. Helena's luck was to be young at a time when Roman social boundaries were dramatically shifting, and to hail from a region of the Roman empire of pivotal importance to Rome's military and political survival in this very period.

Demographics

Traditional Roman social norms favored the adult freeborn male, the urban, the educated, and those with inherited landed wealth and hence ancestry. Roman society—as described in legal and moralizing literature—can be imagined as a pyramid of decreasing access to the rights and privileges of a group at the top who enjoyed all these advantages.[3] These principles were

---

[1] The population of the Roman empire has been estimated as 64 million in the second century, but it probably thereafter fell by around 10 percent due to diseases and economic hardship: Potter (2014) 17.

[2] Scheidel (1995) 203.

[3] See the helpful diagram in Alföldy (2014) 146.

being tested in the third century, but were very much still in place at the time Helena was born. From what we can recover, the infant Helena was positioned toward the bottom end of this pyramid. This is not only because she was born a girl, although in the deeply patriarchal Roman world this in itself put her at a disadvantage. Even among the elite, the social roles afforded to girls centered almost exclusively around their body's sexual availability and their ability to reproduce.[4]

But Helena was not even born into the elite. Perhaps the first account of Helena's origins, the *Origo Constantini*, written as early as the 340s and fairly objective on this subject, describes her as "very common," *vilissima*. This is a term that also appears in Roman legal discourses discussing judicial treatment of lower-class people, elsewhere called *humiliores*. In the third century, this category encompassed vast swathes of inhabitants of the empire, both free and unfree. The importance of class distinctions, rather than distinction by free, freed or enslaved status, had increased since the granting of citizenship to all free people residing in the Roman empire in 212. With citizenship being universal, it had lost its value, with the effect that free people at the lower end of society found themselves gradually amalgamated with slaves in the eyes of the law. Although the term itself is equivocal, *vilis* could therefore even mean that Helena was born into slavery.[5] There is other, albeit slim, evidence to that effect. Apart from Helena's reported later profession and marriageable status, to which we will return later on, this evidence revolves around her name.

Helena's full name, at least at the end of her life, was Flavia Iulia Helena. She carried the same family, or gentile, names *Flavius* and *Iulius* that are attested for Constantine's father, Constantius.[6] This could imply that she had been his slave and acquired his names when he freed her from slavery, according to the conventions of the formal legal procedure of manumission that also conferred citizenship.[7] Onomastics, however, are only a loose guide to social origin, particularly at a time when Roman naming customs were in flux, as was the case in the third and early fourth century. Names such as Flavia and Iulia

---

[4] Caldwell (2015) 2.
[5] Origo Const. 2.2. As a generally Constantine-friendly text [see Barnes (2014) 4], it must be objective on this point. On the legal and social meaning of the term *vilis*: Heumann, Seckel (1971) 624–25. On *humiliores* and lower classes in the third century in general, see Alföldy (2014) 173–76.
[6] Helena's full name is attested on CIL 6.1134, CIL 6.36950 (restored on a missing fragment) and on posthumous coins: RIC VIII Constantinople 33–35, 38, 48, 49; Roma 27, 53; Treveri 42, 47, 55, 63–64, 78, 90. On Constantius' original name, Barnes (1982) 36 and n. 34.
[7] On manumission of female slaves, Perry (2014) 59–67.

were extremely common and had by this point lost their strict function as family names. Furthermore, Helena's full name is attested only after she had been given the title Augusta by her son in 324 and mostly on posthumous coinage. It could also have been the product of her son's or grandsons' efforts to align her more tightly with the Constantinian imperial line after she had become a public figure.[8] Either way, of her three names, Helena was probably the only one that she carried throughout her life and that her parents therefore gave her. It was another very popular name all over the Roman world, although before the reign of Constantine, it was very rarely used among the aristocracy. This is another indication that Helena's origins were, at the very least, as common as the *Origo Constantini* suggests.[9]

Due to its wide dissemination, Helena's name cannot give us any clues about her regional background. It can reasonably be assumed, however, that the world she was born into was that of the provincial settlements along the military highways on the Northeastern margins of the Roman empire. Within this vast area between the Balkans and Mesopotamia lie several possible candidates for her birthplace. It may indeed be simplest to assume that Helena did not venture far to come to Naissus (today's Niš in southern Serbia), where she gave birth to Constantine and which is the first securely attested location connected with her life. This would make her a native of the militarized province of Upper Moesia (modern Serbia), and more specifically that province's Eastern border with Thrace.[10] Yet, a number of late antique authors, of varying reliability, place Helena's origin beyond Thrace, out in the semi-urban milieus on the Southern stretch of the trunk road between the Danube and the Roman frontier with Persia.

According to the earliest mention of her birthplace in an early-fifth-century legendary text ascribed to Marutha, the bishop of Maïpherqat in Mesopotamia, Helena was from the district of Kfar Fahār (the "pottery quarter") of Edessa (modern Urfa in southeastern Turkey). Edessa was the capital city of the frontier province of Osrhoëne in northern Mesopotamia, which formed a buffer zone with Sasanian Persia.[11] This legend erratically associated events from the beginning of the Christian empire with the

---

[8] Salway (1994) 139. Constantine and his children all carried the name Flavius/Flavia; Crispus, Constans, and Constantius II were also Iulius (Constantine II was Claudius, a name that Constantine briefly adopted after 312, when he shed the tetrarchic Valerius). See PLRE I, Constans 3, 220; Constantinus 3, 223; Constantius 8, 226; Crispus 4, 233.
[9] Kajava (1985) 52.
[10] On Constantine's birth and Naissus, see further discussion in Chapter 2.
[11] Canons Ascribed to Maruta of Maipherqat, pp. 16, 24, 103–5.

contemporary struggles of Edessene Christians during the Christological disputes of the time it originated from, the early fifth century. It described Helena as an intrepid combatant of heretics.[12] The story is nonetheless remarkable for its insistence on the modesty of Helena's birthplace, defined by manual work and disrepute. Due to the need for clay and kilns, and the ensuing heat, risk of fire, and smell, the work of potters took place on the margins of ancient cities and hence in proximity to the polluting presence of human burials. Little wonder that a biblical story, of which the authors of this tale were doubtless well aware, calls the burial ground of the poor, strangers, and criminals "the potter's field."[13]

Like any Christian account of humble and marginalized origins, the Edessene tale served a didactic purpose. But the knowledge that Helena was from inconspicuous, even non-urban surroundings—and not from one of the great cities of the Roman empire—was also widespread in late antiquity outside the ecclesiastical sphere. It was repeated by the sixth-century historian Procopius in his *Buildings*, written to praise the emperor Justinian's building projects. He tells us that Helena came from Helenopolis, a formerly unremarkable village (*kṓmē ouk axiólogos*) on the Southern shore of the Propontis, elevated into a city of that name by Constantine in honor of his mother (today's Hersek in Turkey).[14] This settlement, previously called Drepanon or Drepana ("sickle"), was situated on a peninsula of that shape guarding the entrance to the gulf of Nicomedia, the metropolis of Bithynia and Pontus in northern Asia Minor.[15]

Procopius is cautious about Helenopolis' identity as Helena's birthplace, which he reports as a rumor (*phásis*). It was, however, a rumor that was most probably true. Admittedly, other and earlier authors who mention Drepanon's name-change do not explain it in this way. Most give no explanation at all,[16]

---

[12] On the story and its fifth-century context, see Drijvers (2001) 51–64; on its afterlife, Wood (2017). Edessa was also the origin of other legends related to Helena or to the discovery of the True Cross (see Chapter 11). The story is also preserved by a number of medieval authors writing in Arabic: Hamza ibn-al-Hasan (Hamza al-Isfahani), Annales 2.4; al Mas'udi, Tanbih, transl. in Carra de Vaux (1896) 198; Eutychius of Alexandria (Sa'id ibn Batiq), Annales 1.409. The Chronicle of Seert, Hist. Nest. 15, names Helena's birthplace as Nisibis (modern Nusaybin), further East from Edessa, but on the same road.

[13] Matthew 27:3–8. On the existence of "potter's fields" and their marginality in Roman towns in general, see Kyle (1998) 163–68.

[14] Procopius, De aed. 5.2.1–5. On the geography, see Mango (1994) 143–46.

[15] Belke (2020) 595–98. Malalas, Chron. 13.12, knows a different tradition that made Helenopolis the former village of Suga (otherwise unknown). Burgess, Witakowski (1999) 203 argue that Helenopolis' original name was Drepana.

[16] Eusebius, Vita Constantini 4.61.1; Ammianus Marcellinus 26.8.1; Socrates, Hist. eccl. 1.17; Sozomen, Hist. eccl. 2.2; Justinian, Nov. 28.1 (535).

but some link it with Helena and Constantine's veneration for the martyr Lucian, whose relics were kept there. Lucian had suffered martyrdom at Nicomedia during emperor Maximinus Daza's persecution of Christians in 312. A dolphin was believed to have brought his body, thrown into the gulf, to Drepanon, which was only 35 kilometers west from Nicomedia. The story of how Lucian's relics led to the foundation of Helenopolis is given in most detail by the heterodox church historian Philostorgius. He wrote at the beginning of the fifth century and claimed that Helena herself awarded Drepanon city status. The story was in circulation even earlier, since it appears in Jerome's Chronicle of 380, although this church father credits Constantine and not Helena with veneration for the martyr.[17]

It is, however, impossible that the renaming of the city as Helenopolis primarily honored the martyr, rather than Helena herself.[18] The tradition involving Lucian was dear to some authors, especially Philostorgius, due to this martyr's alleged "Homoian" beliefs, which this church historian shared. But it clearly and incongruously omits any explanation of the name, which presumably derived from the location of the martyr's remains at a place of personal interest to Helena. Constantine renamed many cities, including for their Christian credentials, but usually chose a toponym derived from his own name. His deviation from this pattern indicates that Drepanon's relationship with Helena went beyond the place's Christian history.[19]

Matters are further complicated by the existence of at least one other city named by Constantine after his mother, in Palestine. Constantine also renamed the province of Diospontus as Helenopontus to honor Helena, probably after her death. Although this province was in the same region as Drepanon, it lay further east along the Black Sea coast.[20] Again, Helena may have had a personal relationship with these places. Perhaps she visited the town in Palestine, prompting the inhabitants' conversion to Christianity in a stronghold of Judaism. The same could apply to Drepanon, but another, later imperial renaming of a city, by Constantine's nephew Julian, provides solid

---

[17] Philostorgius, Hist. eccl. 2.12–14; Jerome, Chron. 327; see also Chronicon paschale 327 (Dindorf, p. 527), which claims the city was renamed on January 7, Lucian's feast day, and Theophanes, Chron. AM 5818.
[18] Pohlsander (1995) 4.
[19] On Constantine's renaming of cities and provinces after imperial family members, see Lenski (2016) 131–64 and further discussion here, p. 259.
[20] Palestine: Sozomen, Hist. eccl. 2.25; Hierocles, Synecdemus 54. The city is not named, but see Chapter 9. Helenopontus: Justinian, Nov. 28.1 (535); Hierocles, Synecdemus 38. Constantine's son Constans was murdered in a town (*oppidum*) called Helena in the Pyrenees in 350: Epitome de Caesaribus 41.23. There is no indication that Constantine renamed it.

evidence that the latter's change of name to Helenopolis was due to the site having been the birthplace of the emperor's mother. In 362, Julian elevated a neighboring village in Bithynia to city status and named it after his own mother, Basilina, who undoubtedly came from Bithynia. Julian was famously disgruntled with Constantine and Helena on account of Helena's grandsons' complicity in the murder of his father and generally keen on stressing his own lineage. He must in this way have been seeking to allow his mother's birthplace, now Basilinopolis, to rival nearby Helenopolis.[21] For Procopius, at least, the tradition that Drepanon was Helena's birthplace seemed credible, for he repeated it twice in his short paragraph about Helenopolis, explaining that Constantine sought to repay the place for the "rearing" (*tropheîa*) of Helena and describing Helena as its "nursling" (*trophímē*).

Of the three possibilities mentioned in our sources, Drepanon, then, remains by far the most likely candidate for Helena's place of origin. If so, Helena was originally Greek-speaking, as her name also suggests. She may also have been bilingual (or even trilingual), since the Propontis region was ethnically and culturally very close to the more Latin-speaking Thrace, and in general a hub of interregional exchange.[22] While such skills would have been useful to Helena, especially in her later life, it is debatable whether they were any more than oral, at least in her youth. Given the combination of her gender, background, and non-urban upbringing, Helena was almost certainly illiterate, a feature that made her additionally dependent on others, perhaps throughout her life.[23]

Illiteracy and the scarcity of written life data for the lower levels of society explain the widespread custom among ordinary inhabitants of the empire to only roughly estimate their age, on those occasions when Roman imperial bureaucracy required them to produce such information.[24] For Helena's age, certainly, all we have are estimates. A few years after her death, Constantine's biographer Eusebius, bishop of Caesarea, wrote that Helena had been "more or less perhaps about eighty years" old when she passed away.[25] This is by ancient standards an unusually advanced age, although by no means abnormal.

---

[21] ACO 2.1.3; Belke (2020) 452. On Basilina, Julian, and the death of his father, see Chapter 9. On Julian's attitude toward his family, Malosse (2001).

[22] Bouzek, Graninger (2015) 13–15. Historically, the Southern shore of the Propontis had belonged to the city-state of Byzantion; see Robert (1949) 39–40.

[23] Woolf (2000) 876–77, on the intrinsic relationship between writing and cities in the Roman world; 881 on dependency.

[24] Parkin (2003) 31–35; Duncan Jones (1977) on age estimates and illiteracy specifically.

[25] Eusebius, Vita Constantini 3.46: σχεδόν που τῆς ἡλικίας ἀμφὶ τοὺς ὀγδοήκοντα ἐνιαυτοὺς διαρκέσασα.

For that reason, it may have derived from official sources, unless Eusebius chose it to underscore Helena's impressive, almost biblical lifespan.[26] If we believe it, we can calculate that Helena was born between 248 and 250, or roughly around the middle of the third century, since imperial coins ceased to be struck in her name from 329, indicating this as the approximate date of her death.[27] Eusebius' extreme vagueness of "more or less perhaps about" should also remind us that no one, not even Helena herself, may have known her precise birthdate.

It has been suggested that Constantine and his sons felt keen embarrassment about Helena's origins, and this explains the silence about it by pro-Constantinian authors, such as Eusebius.[28] Such censorship may well have been real, in a world where knowledge of Helena's humble origins was potentially harmful to the emperor's claims of legitimacy. Nonetheless, gossip about Helena's low status did make the rounds, perhaps already in the 280s, when Constantius left her to further his political career with an advantageous marriage into the imperial family.[29] Basic facts about Helena's very early life, such as the identity of her birthplace and an approximate idea of her age, we may however owe to the empress's own memories, unless we choose to consider them all as fabrications. We need to remember that when Constantius left her, Helena was already middle-aged, and she was at least into her sixties by the time she joined her son's court a couple of decades later. Interested observers may still have been able to discover some details of Constantius' relationship with Helena, but few people who knew anything about her very early youth would have been around at either stage, and chances that written records of her early life survived are negligible.

These various gaps in our knowledge of Helena's early life should hardly surprise us. Instead, whether created by deliberate silence or simply by obliviousness, they can be taken as confirmation of the obscurity of her background. The basic facts we have tell us that Helena was fortunate to survive her childhood at all. To understand how it was possible that she then embarked on a startling journey to the top of society, we need to turn to the turbulent events and related landscapes of the mid-third century.

---

[26] Parkin (2003) 36–56 on Roman age expectancy.
[27] On the date of Helena's death, see Chapter 9. Note that Seeck (1912) dates her death and therefore also that of Helena's birth incorrectly.
[28] Harbus (2002) 10.
[29] See Chapters 2 and 3.

Helena and the "Crisis of the Third Century"

At the time of Helena's birth, the Roman empire was on the verge of rapid and dramatic transformation. The previous two decades had already seen serious political instability after the last multigenerational dynasty that had ruled Rome, the Severans, had ended with the murder of the teenaged Severus Alexander and his mother Julia Mamaea in 235. The founder of that dynasty, Septimius Severus (d. 211), had been the last emperor to expand the Roman empire East into Mesopotamia, partly by turning client kingdoms, like Osrhoëne, later one of Helena's imagined home regions, into Roman provinces. The emperors who succeeded the Severans were embroiled in intense power struggles between the senate, the army, the people of Rome, and the Praetorian Guard (an elite military unit acting as imperial bodyguard), and regularly faced civil war. In addition, they were battling with fiscal difficulties and unprecedented pressure on Roman frontiers, particularly in the East and Northeast. In the East, recent Roman successes were quickly reversed after a regime change in Persia that saw the Sasanians take power. Meanwhile, Goths and Carpi were persistently raiding the lower Danube region throughout the 240s. The man who ruled the empire when Helena was born *c.* 250, Decius, was the eighth emperor in the fifteen years since Severus Alexander had been killed.[30]

Decius' reign, which itself lasted only two short years from 249 to 251, was trendsetting in many respects and in ways that would decisively shape Helena's life.[31] His reign had started conventionally enough for the mid-third century, with Decius' usurpation of the previous emperor, Philip the Arab. Decius was proclaimed emperor by his troops, the legions of Pannonia and Moesia, in the Danubian provinces to which Philip had sent him to put down a revolt and deal with the Gothic incursions. For Decius, this was a homecoming. He had been born in the area, in a village near the city of Sirmium in Pannonia Inferior (modern Sremska Mitrovica in Serbia). From now on, the Danubian legions would play a key role in the making and unmaking of emperors. Due to the exposure of the Balkans to Gothic invasion, the deteriorating situation on the Persian frontier, and the loss of territory elsewhere, the extensive frontier zone between the Danube, the Black Sea, and the Propontis started to become the military epicenter of the empire and the

---

[30] For background, see Drinkwater (2005).
[31] On the fundamental political and cultural changes in the mid-third century, Potter (2013) 12–14.

army's main recruiting ground. As a result, political fortunes were now being made very close to Helena's home. Many emperors would continue to hail from the Illyrian and Thracian provinces throughout the rest of the century, and increasingly they came from obscure, military backgrounds.

Although Decius was himself still of senatorial background, he recognized the geopolitical significance of the Northeastern sector of the empire. He adopted the name Trajan, the emperor who over a century earlier had extended Roman territory in these parts beyond the Danube and Euphrates frontiers. In fact, Decius harbored groundbreaking universalist ideas, epitomized by his promulgation, right at the beginning of his reign, of a general edict that ordered all inhabitants of the empire to sacrifice to the Roman state's divine protectors and to collect a certificate to that effect. The edict was meant as a traditionalist gesture to appease the gods in the face of mounting problems, rather than an attack on specific sectors of society deemed resistant to such religious consensus. The gesture nonetheless created entirely new realities. The edict defined Roman religion as a universal and mandatory community, rather than a conglomeration of local cults, and as such visibly excluded those who did not want to submit to common public ritual. Most prominent among such refuseniks were Christians. Decius' edict not only set the precedent for subsequent Christian persecutions, such as that of emperor Valerian just a few years later. It also laid the foundations of the concept of imperial religion on which Christianity thrived after its adoption by Constantine.[32] Helena would experience soon enough what this meant.

Whatever Decius' motives, in the short term his pious strategy did not have the desired effect. In June 251 he and his son were killed in battle against the Goths at Abritus in Thrace (modern Razgrad in Bulgaria). This event ushered in a period of existential threats to the empire that was to last throughout Helena's childhood and teenage years. We have no way of knowing to what extent Helena was directly affected by the disastrous events that rapidly unfolded: Gothic, Alemannic, and Sasanian invasions; military defeats; losses of territory; separatist movements; Christian persecutions; economic downturns and bouts of plague. There is no reason to assume that for Helena emperors and their families represented anything more than ever-changing portraits on coins, if she ever happened to see one. Little did Helena know that she would once be portrayed in the same way as those mid-third-century empresses, who, in an attempt to distinguish them from their

---

[32] Rives (1999).

Fig. 1.1 Obverse of Antoninianus showing Otacilia Severa, wife of Philip the Arab (d. 249). Found in Naissus/Niš, now at the National Museum in Niš. © Julia Hillner.

Severan predecessors, were the first to sport an intricate hairstyle that Helena would herself wear many years later, a reverse plait pulled back to front over the head (Fig. 1.1).[33]

It is abundantly clear that the so-called crisis of the third century did not affect everyone in the empire equally and that there were regions that continued to be peaceful and prosperous.[34] But Helena's home region was not one of them. Whether we locate Helena in Naissus or Drepanon, she is likely to have been acutely affected by the turmoil.[35] It is from the province of Bithynia and Pontus, where Drepanon was located, that we get the deepest sense of how invasions impacted on lives, and especially female lives, in these years. Strengthened by their defeat of Decius, Gothic groups who had settled north of the Black Sea took up piracy, haunting the northern shores of Asia Minor.[36] In 257, they sailed unhindered through the Bosphorus, and raided around the Southern coast of the Propontis. The Goths largely shunned prolonged sieges of walled cities, plundering the countryside and abandoned settlements instead.[37] The unfortified village of Drepanon, at the delta of the river Dracon and on a flat and marshy peninsula protruding into the gulf of

---

[33] On the hairstyle: Schade (2003) 13. On Helena's own hair, see Chapter 5.
[34] See for the debate around the "crisis" Liebeschuetz (2007).
[35] On the following, see also Wilkes (2005).
[36] Zosimus, Hist. nea 1.27 and 1.31–6, describes these successive raids in detail.
[37] Kulikowski (2006) 18–20. On Drepanon's environment, see Belke (2020) 597.

Nicomedia, must have presented a prime target. A pastoral letter of Bishop Gregory of Neocaesarea in neighboring Pontus, dealing with the aftermath of a Gothic raid only a couple of years earlier, tells us in no uncertain terms that their booty regularly included human captives. Gregory's letter reminds us that for women and girls caught up in such events, the danger was not only to be captured, but also to be abused and raped. Gregory considered the question of whether such violated women had committed a sin and whether it was therefore inadvisable for Christian men to hold communion with them. He decided they were innocent, but his chilling contemplation shows that for women in these areas rape by Gothic invaders could mean not only battered bodies, but subsequent social stigmatizing by their fellow Romans, too.[38] Even if we assume that Helena had already made her way to Naissus by the 250s, similar risks would have caught up with her there. A Gothic foray reached this city in 268. The Goths were defeated outside it a year later by emperor Claudius, who subsequently adopted the title Gothicus.[39]

Gothic captivity was clearly not Helena's fate, but certainly in a place like Drepanon she would have lived in constant fear of it. Bishop Gregory's letter is also testimony to the spread of Christianity in Bithynia and Pontus, where the presence of Christian communities can be traced back to the early first century and where we have evidence in the third for their recent persecution under Decius. As later authors made abundantly clear, Helena was not born a Christian. This is not surprising, as the majority of people living in Bithynia and Pontus were still pagan in the mid-third century. Yet, chances are that she knew Christians, and perhaps even witnessed some of their suffering, in her youth. The thought that she would one day be a leader of their faith would have been inconceivable to her then.[40]

Meeting Constantius

If life was dangerous in Helena's part of the world at this time, it also provided opportunities. The military operations on the Danube, the Euphrates, and the Black Sea necessitated significant and regular Roman troop movements across Thrace and Asia Minor, not only in reaction to emerging conflicts,

---

[38] Gregory Thaumaturgus, Epistola canonica 1.
[39] Ferjančič (2013) 24.
[40] On the Decian persecution in Bithynia, McKechnie (2019) 215–16. On Helena's religion, see Chapter 3.

but also because these regions served as key land connection between the Western and Eastern parts of the empire. It is probably in this context that Helena, at around 20 years of age, met Constantius, Constantine's father. The fifth-century story from Edessa mentioned before, our earliest account of Helena's origins, claims that a man of imperial descent from Rome, Valentinianus bar Qustus, visited the Eastern regions of the empire and fell in love with Helena, who was already a Christian. With her father's consent, he married her before being promoted to Caesar. The author was clearly confusing Constantius here with a subsequent emperor, Valentinian (probably I). Later Arabic authors who transmit the story correct his name to Constantius or Constans and describe him as an imperial envoy.[41] While the geographical, religious, and social aspects of the Edessene tale are legendary, it is not unlikely that Constantius chanced upon Helena during his travels.

Constantius was one of the men who had profited from the increased significance of the Danubian provinces and their armies in the third century. He was born no later than 250, probably in the Eastern part of Moesia (modern Serbia), which under Aurelian (270–275) would become Dacia Ripensis, or, according to a different tradition, in Dardania in Southern Moesia.[42] Constantine would later claim that his father was the product of a marriage between a Dardanian nobleman and the niece or daughter of emperor Claudius Gothicus (d. 270), who was himself from Moesia. This descent was a dynastic fabrication, but all the available clues do locate Constantius' origin in the area of Naissus, which was situated between Dardania, of which it was culturally a part, and (the later) Dacia Ripensis (see Map 2).[43]

In terms of social background, it is probable that Constantius came from a military family, of a type that was numerous in the historically highly militarized central Balkan regions, where Roman veterans dominated society.[44] But the career he carved out was different from that of his ancestors and more in tune with the times. His first recorded post was one that had been created only recently. After the emperor Valerian had lost a large amount of troops in battle against the Sasanians in 260, which had also seen him captured, his son

---

[41] Chronicle of Seert, Hist. Nest. 17; Eutychius of Alexandria (Sa'id ibn Batiq), Annales 1.409.

[42] A native of Illyricum: Aurelius Victor, Caes. 39.26; Julian, Misopogon 348D, implies Dacia Ripensis, as he mentions the banks of the Danube as his family's origin; Dardania: Historia Augusta, Divus Claudius 13. On Constantius' birthdate, see Barnes (1982) 35.

[43] On Constantius being Claudius' grandson through his mother: Eutropius, Brev. 9.22; the son of Claudius' niece and a nobleman (*nobilissimo gentis Dardanae viro*): Historia Augusta, Divus Claudius 13, and see Origo Const. 1.1. Constantine styled himself *nepos divi Claudii*, see, for example, ILS 699. On Naissus being in Dardanian territory, Vasić (2013) 91.

[44] Mirković (2007) 44.

and successor Gallienus had rebuilt his army mostly with Danubian recruits, among them a new mobile unit of soldiers, the *protectores*. They accompanied the emperor on his campaigns and could be flexibly deployed. Constantius served in that unit, also known as the *comitatus*, probably during the time of the emperor Aurelian. It was in this capacity that, between the spring of 272 and winter of 273, he seems to have escorted the emperor along the military highways from the Balkans—where Aurelian had chosen to abandon the province of Dacia to the Goths—to the East along the military highways. Their aim was to challenge the queen of the separatist kingdom of Palmyra, Zenobia, who had advanced into southern Asia Minor. Their journey took them through Thrace, over the Bosphorus, past Nicomedia and through Bithynia.[45] It is reasonable to assume that somewhere on the way Constantius met Helena.

Later stories of Helena's and Constantius' encounter would claim that they met at an inn. The most fantastic of these is told in a medieval Latin romance, usually dated to the thirteenth century. Here, Helena is described as an aristocratic girl from Trier in Gaul on a pilgrimage to Rome. The emperor—Constantius—is taken by her beauty and decides to rape her in the inn (*hospicium*) at which she is staying, unknowingly siring a son, Constantine, in the process. Despite the brutality of his act, Constantius takes pity on Helena, leaving her a golden ring. Amid the many complications that follow, Constantine is kidnapped and brought to Constantinople where he falls in love with a Byzantine princess and Helena opens her own inn to secure her livelihood. Eventually, Constantius recognizes his ring and son, who in the end inherits both his Western Roman empire and the Byzantine empire.[46]

Similar, although less fanciful, stories already circulated in earlier Byzantine hagiographies of Constantine. The first written record of these texts dates from the ninth century, but oral or lost written versions may have existed much earlier. In these accounts, Helena is the daughter of an innkeeper in Drepanon.[47] A *tribunus* named Constans, an imperial envoy to the Persians (or in other versions Sarmatians), comes to stay and asks for a woman with whom he can spend the night. The innkeeper sends him his

---

[45] Constantius' early career: Origo Const. 2: *protector primum, inde tribunus, postea praeses Dalmatiarum*; see Barnes (1982) 36–37, (2014) 27. On the *protectores* and the *comitatus*: Potter (2014) 253–54.
[46] Libellus de Constantino Magno eiusque matre Helena.
[47] The most popular one was BHG 364 (which names Drepanon), ed. in Guidi (1908), while the earliest are BHG 365z, 366, and 366a; see further Lieu (1998) 153–54. For their dates, Winkelmann (1987).

own daughter. They have sex, for which Constans pays with a purple dress. Helena is left pregnant, as is revealed to Constans in a dream, so he orders her father to care for the child. Many years later, by which time Constans is emperor, he sends further envoys to Persia, who on their way discover the child Constantine, by means of the purple dress Helena is able to produce. As a result, Constantine is reunited with his father and goes on to become the first Christian emperor. The conventional novelistic topoi of these medieval tales—the context of travel, the hidden identities, the family separations, the unexpected rediscovery through symbolic tokens—is clear enough. So, too, are the elements of Christian edification, in particular Helena's sexual humiliation, which turns out to be a salvation story instead. Even so, such stereotyped tales may contain some underlying truths, particularly if we consider the inherent mobility of Constantius' profession, which they capture very well.

The idea that Helena was working at an inn when she met Constantius was, in fact, already current a few decades after her death. In his funerary speech on the emperor Theodosius delivered in 395, Ambrose, the late-fourth-century bishop of Milan, developed the image of Helena as a model Christian empress: humble, pious, and orthodox.[48] His Helena started out as a *stabularia*, a woman working in an inn or tavern (*stabulum*). Upon her encounter with Constantius, she experienced a spectacular transformation "from dung to royalty" (*de stercore ad regnum*), or, in the expression of Psalm 113.7 that Ambrose cites, she was lifted "from dust ... and dung" (*de terra ... de stercore*). Ambrose's words are wrapped in layers of exegesis invoking the biblical precedents of the innkeeper who hosted the holy family in Bethlehem and of the one who tended to the robbed and wounded man brought in by the good Samaritan (Lk 2.7 and 10:35). These various allusions strongly suggest that Ambrose envisaged Helena in a roadside inn, and of the type where one could get a change of horses.

Modern scholars have sometimes imagined the inn that Ambrose was alluding to as a publicly funded station of the *cursus publicus*, the imperial post, at which Constantius would have stayed when on his assignment. Some have also understood Ambrose's term *stabularia*, the feminine of the more commonly attested *stabularius*, and therefore Helena, as the respectable landlady of such a post station, or alternatively the landlord's daughter.[49]

---

[48] Ambrose, De ob. Theod. 42. For further discussion, see Chapter 11.
[49] Barnes (2014) 31–33. Note that such post stations existed from the late third century on and were commonly called *mansio* or *statio* in Latin (*stathmoi* in Greek), but this is not a term Ambrose chose to describe Helena's inn; Di Paola (2016) 9–18.

Imperial post stations could indeed be luxuriously equipped places, designed to host important visitors. In 275, the emperor Aurelian would die in one on a Thracian highway, as, many years later, would Helena's granddaughter Constantina, while traveling through Bithynia.[50] Whether post stations were widely considered respectable places is doubtful, however, particularly as most of them catered to all travelers. The young Helena's contemporary Cyprian, bishop of Carthage (d. 258), warned a correspondent of the risks of theft at imperial post stations, while the later fourth-century rhetorician Libanius thought them seedy places, where, intriguingly, in light of the later legends surrounding Helena's meeting with Constantius, prostitutes were furnished to lodgers on demand.[51]

For all his biblical referenes, Ambrose must have known that any mention of the term *stabularia* would have reminded his audience of sexual promiscuity and commercial sex. All inns, whether post stations or humbler venues, were habitually associated in Roman writing with prostitution. Elite men considered these establishments places of excess due to the free mingling of men and women.[52] This is clear, for example, in a law issued by Helena's son Constantine many years later, in 326, in which he clarified the distinction between a landlady (*domina tabernae*) and her female staff who served the drinks (*ministerium*). The latter, Constantine explained, were so removed from any sexual honor, and so base (embodying *vilitas*), that they could not even be charged with adultery. The landlady, however, could be expected to act with modesty (*pudicitia*). Since she had honor, it would have been a crime if she were to sleep with a man who was not her husband.[53]

As this law was issued in response to an official's specific query about the validity of adultery charges, it is unlikely that Constantine was trying to set the record straight about his mother and her honor here. Her past as a landlady, rather than a mere waitress, is also by no means confirmed. The use of the term *vilis* in Constantine's law with reference to the waiting staff even speaks against it, since Helena was also from this class.[54] In addition, Constantine's law shows that, even if technically a landlady was

---

[50] Aurelian was murdered at such a place; see Historia Augusta, Divus Aurelianus 35.4–5 (the inn is called a *mansio*). For Constantina Ammianus Marcellinus 14.11.6; Passio Artemii 14 (*statio* at Caeni Gallicani) and Chapter 10.

[51] Cyprian, ep. 66.3; Libanius, Or. 46.19.

[52] See Leyerle (2009) 117–18: the connection between inns and prostitution was taken "utterly for granted."

[53] CTh 9.7.1 (326).

[54] Evans Grubbs (1995) 206–8.

to be considered respectable, in practice people were unclear about this so they needed reminding. More often than not, they thought about landladies as procuresses, as Libanius did in the speech mentioned above.[55] As for waitresses, they were simply beyond morality, not least because the majority of the workforce in inns and taverns—and therefore perhaps also Helena—was enslaved.[56] All of this testifies to the complex relationship between lower-class women, lower-class professions, and commercial sex in the Roman world.

It is remarkable then that Ambrose chose to emphasize Helena's profession. Like the later Byzantine hagiographers, it seems he was attracted by the potential for her life to be layered so neatly onto a Christian story of humility, salvation, and charity. Nevertheless, he went to great lengths to package the information about her early life in a way that did not allow for misunderstanding, by repeatedly prefacing the term *stabularia* with the qualifier "good" (*bona*). Helena's past as a *stabularia* must therefore have been too well known to be passed over in silence. Ambrose was looking for a way to make it palatable to his audience.

In fact, other authors allude to Helena's dishonorable profession, too. The historian Zosimus, writing around the year 500, calls Helena a "truly ignoble woman" (*gynè ou semnê*) and "indecent" (*ásemnos*). In Philostorgius' Church History, she appears as a "common woman no different from a prostitute." Although these authors post-date Ambrose, behind their words lurk earlier fourth-century lost texts, the fiercely pro-Julian history of Eunapius, and, in Philostorgius' case, a speech given by Julian himself.[57] Stories similar to those implicit in Ambrose were therefore already circulating, although their accuracy may be limited, given their authors' anti-Constantinian outlook. Less loaded evidence that Ambrose was dealing in facts comes from one of Libanius' orations, written a few years before Ambrose's, in 390. It deals with Helena's past only in an indirect way, by way of making an example. Libanius mocked Flavius Optatus, the first *patricius* Constantine ever nominated and consul of 334, who had been originally a grammarian. This man had been married to an innkeeper's daughter from Paphlagonia, with whom he had

---

[55] See for such an attitude, for example, D 23.2.43.9 (Modestinus); Grossmark (2006) for a rabbinic perspective on female innkeepers as prostitutes.

[56] D 3.2.4.2 (Ulpian) and CJ 4.56.3 (225), for example, imply that innworkers were usually slaves (and also prostituted).

[57] Zosimus, Hist. nea 2.8.2, 2.9.2; Philostorgius, Hist. eccl. 2.16a: φαύλης τινὸς γυναικὸς καὶ τῶν χαμαιτύπων οὐδὲν διαφερούσης. On Eunapius as a source for Zosimus, see Paschoud (2003) xlvi–xlvii.

fallen in love while on a trip to that region. Libanius claimed that this unsuitable match had held back Optatus' career until Constantine came along, implying that under this emperor, for reasons of family history, love affairs with daughters of innkeepers were no big deal at all.[58]

None of this means, of course, that Helena was a prostitute or, to use a less moralizing term, sex worker. We should note the ease with which being female and low-born could be conflated with prostitution or at least sexual promiscuity in the ancient mindset, particularly where such women's labor involved contact with men outside their family. Even the selling of merchandise in a public place or work in a mill carried the whiff of sexual debauchery.[59] Nonetheless, if we accept that Helena worked in an inn, we cannot exclude the possibility that she was prostituted as well. However much we are dealing with ancient prejudice against the women employed in Roman inns, the evidence overwhelmingly suggests that coerced sex work was still practiced in such places.[60] If Helena was enslaved, she will have been among those who provided such services, for female slaves were always prone to sexual exploitation by their owners.[61] But even if Helena was freeborn, and her father still alive, she would not have been immune from that fate. The audiences of the Byzantine hagiographies dealing with Constantine's conception were expected calmly to stomach the news that Helena was casually prostituted by her father, the innkeeper. Parents prostituting their children, boys and girls, are similarly recorded in earlier Roman times. Until the fifth century, when Christian emperors started to legislate against the practice—in itself an indication that it was widespread—this was a perfectly legal thing to do.[62]

Late imperial laws often connect sex work to impoverished circumstances. Roman female poverty could be due to structural reasons. Freeborn women had relatively limited opportunities to find employment in the Roman labor market, which was often seasonal anyway, and earned low wages if they did. Many jobs employing women in other historical societies, such as in domestic service, in the Roman world were performed by slaves or freed people of both sexes, or by free men.[63] Moreover, Roman poverty rates, as in all societies,

---

[58] Libanius, Or. 42.26 (For Thalassios).
[59] Pauli Sententiae 2.26.11. Here, the point was again that such women were exempt from charges of adultery, that is, not respectable women. On mill workers, McGinn (2004) 28.
[60] McGinn (2004) 19.
[61] On slaves and prostitution, Perry (2014) 29–37.
[62] CTh 15.8.2 (428).
[63] On prostitution of children, see McGinn (2004) 61–68; Laes (2011) 204–6. For a law connecting prostitution with poverty see, for example, Justinian, Nov. 14.1 (535). On women's lower wages,

went up in times of unusual social pressures, such as famines, war, and population displacement.[64] We need to remember that the young Helena lived in uncertain times, and in a region that, due to repeated invasions, suffered considerable economic instability. It would not be surprising if she, or her family, tried to make ends meet by all possible means, including supplementing meager incomes through the occasional selling of family members' bodies.[65] Seen from this perspective, it does not matter much whether Helena had been born a slave or not, or whether she ever formally worked as a prostitute or not. At this level of society (as the law recognized), few women were in full control of their bodies, making them vulnerable to commercial sexual abuse. Even if the latter did not actually happen, this vulnerability formed their experience, and it would have been part of Helena's upbringing.

We do not know where within the vast swathe of imperial territory between the Danube and the Euphrates Constantius and Helena first met. Somewhere in the larger region around the Propontis is most likely, if not perhaps in Drepanon itself, despite the Byzantine hagiographers' testimony. Although the village was positioned at the narrowest point of the Gulf of Nicomedia, which would have made it an easy maritime route via which to bypass Nicomedia, it was not a traffic hub in the third century.[66] In any case, Aurelian's *protectores*, of whom Constantius was one, did not sidestep Nicomedia, since some of them are attested in the city at the time that Aurelian's army was passing through.[67] Depending on how long these men stayed in the Bithynian capital, it is not inconceivable that they also traveled around the surrounding region. This could have taken some of them through Drepanon, if only to reach the thermal baths of Pythia some 30 kilometers further west along the coastal route (today's Termal/Yalova Kaplıcası). Coincidentally or not, in 337, Helena's son Constantine traveled on this very route. Having fallen ill in Constantinople, the emperor sailed across

---

Groen-Vallinga, Tacoma (2017) 110; on freewomen's exclusion from domestic service, the most common occupation for women historically, Joshel (1992) 127, Table 5.2.

[64] Prell (1997) 65.
[65] See Åshede (2016) 933 on the point that most Roman prostitution was occasional.
[66] Belke (2020) 266. Frequent flooding of the river Dracon turned inland roads from Drepanon unviable. It was only in the sixth century that new connections to the South were built from here. Even Constantine did not improve on Drepanon's connectivity, making it more likely that he honored it as the place where his mother was born, rather than to improve "the network of communications" with Constantinople, as argued by Mango (1994) 150. Today, Drepanon's (or rather Hersek's) logistical advantages are fully recognized by the Osman Gazi bridge spanning the Gulf of İzmit at exactly this point.
[67] CIL 3.327; see Barnes (2014) 37.

the Propontis to the hot baths in the vicinity of Helenopolis, which can only be those of Pythia. Finding no solace either there or in the city's church, he proceeded along the shore to Nicomedia, where he soon passed away in a suburban villa.[68]

It is attractive to think of the dying emperor journeying in the opposite direction from that taken by his father when he met his mother more than sixty years earlier, perhaps even in Pythia itself. As a thermo-mineral bath resort to which people traveled for medical or recreational reasons, it would have been teeming with hostelries of both the upmarket and the shadier sort. But poor women from villages like Drepanon would also have drifted to work, or been trafficked there, in the post stations along the main military highways throughout Bithynia and up into Thrace, or to the great metropolis of the region, such as Nicomedia itself or Byzantium, where Aurelian's army wintered in 273.[69] If they were full-time sex workers, such mobility did not lend them more freedom, for most were forced to live and work in controlled and confined spaces.[70] In any of these uncompromising situations, Helena's world was one of narrow horizons, with little scope for imagining another reality and every prospect of a short future.

---

[68] Eusebius, Vita Constantini 4.61; Socrates, Hist. eccl. 1.39; Sozomen, Hist. eccl. 2.34. On Pythia and Constantine's visit see Belke (2020) 963–64.

[69] Roman thermo-mineral resorts attracted a fair amount of criticism for the life-styles they encouraged, see Yegül (1992) 94. Aurelian in Byzantium: Drinkwater (2005) 52; on female trafficking McGinn (2004) 27.

[70] McGinn (1998) 70.

2
Weather Eye on the Horizon

Helena opened a new chapter of her life when she started to live with Constantius, but her past still had the power to shape the nature of their relationship. Constantius did not make Helena his legal wife, or at least not in the eyes of later observers. The majority of sources mentioning their union are either silent or vague about its quality or describe it openly as different from a legal marriage.[1] Only very few endeavor to make the relationship look more legitimate, by using the technical term for a legal wife, *coniunx*. Among them is an inscription erected by the governor of the province of Lucania et Bruttii in southern Italy, Alpinius Magnus, in honor of Helena after she had been made Augusta in 324. The erection of statues to imperial women required imperial permission, so we can assume that the wording of the inscription reproduced official uses of language, possibly aiming to obscure Helena's background.[2]

If so, such official uses did not stick. Other sources, including further honorary inscriptions from Helena's lifetime, employ the much less precise term *uxor*. *Uxor* was widely used to denote the female partner in any form of lasting union between a man and a woman, whether this was a "proper marriage" (*matrimonium iustum*) or not.[3] The legal term for monogamous and lasting unions falling short of the status of marriage was *concubinatus*. *Concubina* is what a majority of authors call Helena when describing her relationship with

---

[1] Socrates, Hist. eccl. 1.17–18; Sozomon, Hist. eccl. 2.1.2, 2.2.1 mention the union without further qualification. Eusebius, Hist. eccl. 8.13 does not mention Helena, but insists Constantine was Constantius' lawful son, which suggests there was doubt about it known to him, see Harbus (2002) 10.

[2] CIL 10 517. See also Aurelius Victor, Caes. 39.25 who uses the term *coniugium* to describe the relationship, although this term refers both to Constantius and his co-emperor Galerius' former relationships, the latter of which was probably a legal marriage; see Chapter 4 for further insights. On the wording of inscriptions, refer to Schade (2016).

[3] CIL 10.1483; Origo Const. 1; Eutropius, Brev. 9.22; Epitome de Caesaribus 39.2; Jerome, Chron. 292; Prosper Tiro, Ep. chron. 942; Chronica Gallica a. 511, 445. For CIL 10.678, often taken as referring to Helena as *uxor*, see p. 195. See Heumann, Seckel (1971) 611 on the term *uxor*. Drijvers (1992a) 17 considers the Greek term γυνή used for Helena by some Greek authors as equivalent to *uxor*, throwing further doubt on its meaning of "legal wife," particularly since it is not used in this way by Philostorgius, Hist. eccl. 2.16 and Theophanes, Chron. AM 5796 and 5814. See Rawson (1974) 304 about the use of the linguistic "trappings" of *matrimonium iustum* to describe other forms of unions.

Constantius, sometimes alternating it with *uxor*.[4] Their information may have been tainted by the gossip put into circulation about Helena by people hostile to her son Constantine. While the authors using the term *concubina* were by no means also all hostile, they were nonetheless happy to perpetuate the ambiguity surrounding Helena's and Constantius' relationship. It is very doubtful that they would have degraded Helena in this way had it been accepted that she had really been a legitimate wife.[5] They were, therefore, correct, at least from the point of view of their time, the fourth century or later, when marriage restrictions had become more severe. Whether Constantius and Helena themselves would have described their union in these terms at the time they began it is far less certain, as we shall see now.

Legalities

In Roman custom, concubinage was a bond between a free or freedman and a free or freedwoman of lower social standing. At least on the level of morality, it was differentiated from another, even more fragile, relationship, *contubernium*, between a free, freed or enslaved man and an enslaved woman. In terms of legal consequences, however, it similarly meant that any issue was excluded from a father's inheritance and assumed the social status of their mother. Concubinage could be the result of legal bans on certain types of unions. The scope of marital prohibitions was ever shifting, but in the mid-third century included relationships between men of senatorial rank and freedwomen, between freeborn men and sex workers, and between all men and female slaves. But not all unions with lower-class women were banned. For example, senatorial men could marry poor freeborn women, men below senatorial rank freedwomen, and freedmen could even marry sex workers.[6]

Nonetheless, some men still chose to keep their partners as concubines, for motivations of respectability, rather than legal reasons. At the elite level,

---

[4] Jerome, Chron. 306; Orosius, Hist. adv. pag. 7.25.16; Prosper Tiro, Ep. chron. 976; Chronica Gallica a. 511, 445; Cassiodorus, Chron. 308; Bede, Hist. eccl. 1.8 and Chron. 411. Zosimus, Hist. nea 2.8.2 does not use the term *concubine*, but says Constantine was the son of illegal intercourse; see also Chronicon Paschale 304 (Dindorf p. 517): Constantine was born from "another sexual intercourse" with Helena; Suda, s.v. Konstantinos: οὗτος ἐξ ἀφανῶν τίκτεται τῷ βασιλεῖ Κωνσταντίῳ ("he was born from obscurity to the emperor Constantius").

[5] Consolino (2001) 144.

[6] McGinn (1991); McGinn (2002) 49–57; Arjava (1996) 205–08; Evans Grubbs (1995) 294–96.

Roman men customarily married rather late in life, and then generally to women of a much younger age. Some of these men often took coetaneous concubines beforehand as an easily discardable outlet for their sexual desire and as housekeepers while awaiting a "proper" marriage match with a woman of their own status who would also bring a dowry. In the later fourth century, Augustine, a town councilor's son who subsequently became bishop of Hippo, famously lived for fourteen years with a concubine, perhaps a freedwoman, while he was a bachelor. Lower down the class scale, men were less socially endogamous, and many married freedwomen, although generally their own, as the alternative meant having a wife who had potentially already been sexually exploited by someone else. Those with social aspirations nevertheless avoided "marrying down" too much. The most commonly attested form of concubinage was between a freed slave and her former master, which shows how unions with their own freedwomen did not seem respectable enough for marriage even among many non-senatorial men.[7] One sector of society where concubinage was widely practiced was the Roman military. While soldiers were no longer banned from marrying in the third century as they had previously been, many still settled down to family life only after completing their service, if they married at all. But during active service, some soldiers still maintained sexual relationships, often with their own slaves or freedwomen, whom they sometimes married after retiring.[8]

Constantius was, as far as we know, freeborn, but, in the early 270s, he was not of senatorial status. There were no legal impediments to his marrying Helena, unless she was a slave or a sex worker. The evidence that Helena was Constantius' concubine implies that she was free or freed, but does not make it inconceivable, again, that she had at some point been a sex worker. But other scenarios are possible, too. As a *protector*, Constantius was already in the imperial orbit and upwardly mobile. A desire to mimic elite endogamy may have discouraged Constantius from making Helena his legal wife if she was his own freedwoman and certainly if she had been someone else's, and perhaps even if she was freeborn but poor.[9] Equally, it may not have seemed practical to Constantius to marry at this point of his life, even if he was genuinely fond of Helena and looking for a long-lasting relationship with her. When he met Helena, Constantius was only in his early twenties, not much

---

[7] McGinn (2002) 74–80 (on status endogamy). On Augustine Power (1992). On marriage restrictions in Augustine's day, see below n. 12.
[8] Phang (2004).
[9] Leadbetter (1998) 79–80.

older than Helena herself. Like other military men from his Danubian homeland—where soldiers typically only married in their thirties—and as a young man in active military service, and in a mobile unit besides, a less formal union may have suited him.[10] He may still have planned to marry Helena upon retirement. In either case, if Helena's and Constantius' union was a concubinage, Helena must have been extremely lowborn, that is to say, poor, even if she was not a slave or freedwoman. Any woman deemed "respectable," that is, propertied, had legal grounds to bring a case of *stuprum* (sexual violence against a woman of marriageable status), so discerning men would have thought twice about making such a woman their concubine only.[11]

It is also possible, indeed probable, that Constantius and Helena simply assumed they were married. Our knowledge about concubinage derives mostly from the writings of Roman jurists, eager to protect members of the elite against any unwanted legal consequences of their sexual behavior, and from inscriptions erected in the city of Rome and Italy, not the far-flung Danubian provinces. The difference between marriage and concubinage was not a matter of different documentation, for Roman marriage did not require a legal certificate. The difference lay exclusively in the wide social gap between a man and his partner, and was as such rather ill-defined. Even where the law in theory allowed for marriage, such divides in status were taken more seriously at the center of the empire than at the provincial periphery, as another law issued by Constantine in 336 demonstrates. In that year, Constantine expanded marriage prohibitions both downward and upward. He banned not only senators, but also equestrians, town councilors, and priests of the official cults from marrying not only freedwomen and female slaves, and their daughters, but also actresses and their daughters, tavern workers (*tabernaria*) and the daughters of innkeepers, daughters of pimps and gladiators, female marketers, and "lowborn and degraded" women (*humilis et abiecta*) generally.[12]

This law was part of Constantine's wider attempts during these years to create a respectable aristocracy in the East whose behavior would correspond to the higher moral standards of their Western counterparts. As such, it also provides evidence that the marriage habits of the provincial and local

---

[10] Scheidel (2005) 6–7 on the marriage age of Danubian soldiers.
[11] McGinn (1991) 346.
[12] CTh 4.6.3 (336).

elites whom the emperor was promoting for that purpose were not always up to scratch from a Western senatorial perspective.[13] Lactantius, the Christian rhetor who was tutor of Constantine's son Crispus, wrote that the officials of the tetrarch Maximinus Daza, one of Constantine's predecessors in the East, had all married "the daughters of ordinary people." His disdain helps to explain Constantine's attempts to rectify this situation.[14] One of Constantine's consuls of 334, Flavius Optatus, was, as we have seen, married to an innkeeper's daughter from Paphlagonia.[15] When he married his wife under what may have been perfectly legal circumstances, it would not have been something that Optatus, then only a grammarian, anticipated as problematic or shameful, even though such women, as we have seen, were considered decidedly seedy in higher social circles. In the same way, it was unknowable to Constantius in the early 270s—a long time before he became a public figure—that his relationship with Helena, perhaps another daughter of an innkeeper or even a tavern worker, would come under this kind of moral scrutiny. It is unlikely, again, that Constantine was targeting the relationship of his own parents, which he believed or at least claimed to have been legitimate anyway, with this tightening of marriage regulations. Even so, and ironically, his own legislation contributed to casting doubt over the nature of their relationship. After Constantine's law, even if Helena had been a poor but freeborn woman, her relationship to a man like Constantius—now known as a former emperor—would have raised eyebrows, because that law of 336 made all poor women not only morally but also legally unsuitable marriage matches for vast swathes of men. The historian Eutropius, writing in the second half of the fourth century, duly describes Helena and Constantius' relationship as a "shadier sort of" marriage (*matrimonium obscurius*). By this he may be expressing the view that, even if Constantius and Helena thought they were married, by the moral standards of the Roman elite, later enshrined in law by her own son, they were not really wed.[16]

All of this, of course, matters for the legitimacy of Constantine's birth. However, the legitimacy of his birth mattered much less than other factors, above all military support, in making him acceptable, much later, as legitimate emperor.[17] The nature of Helena's relationship with Constantius is far

---

[13] Evans Grubbs (1995) 287–88; McGinn (1997) 78.
[14] Lactantius, De mortibus pers. 38.5: *mediocrium filias*.
[15] On Optatus, see pp. 30–31.
[16] Eutropius, Brev. 10.2.
[17] Corcoran (2012) 9.

more significant for our understanding of her experiences during these early years of her life. If Constantius treated Helena as a placeholder to provide sexual services until a more marriageable woman came along, her situation would have been rather unstable. This was not the case if she was waiting for marriage, and possibly freedom, upon his retirement from service, or if, indeed, she thought of herself as already married. Given the military and provincial contexts of Constantius' life in this period, the latter two scenarios are more plausible. Helena must have hoped she had entered a monogamous and long-lasting bond with Constantius.

Helena at Naissus and Salona

By the time Helena gave birth to her son Constantine, she was residing in Naissus.[18] Although both Bithynia, her likely home region, and Naissus were on the periphery of Thrace, they were still about 500 miles apart. It was rare for women in the ancient world, at least for those below the level of the elite, to migrate so far independently. Long-distance female mobility usually happened in male company, either of family members, or of the army, slave traders, or, even more bleakly, sex traffickers. A man must therefore have brought Helena to Naissus. This is likely to have been Constantius, given that the city was in his home region.[19]

Constantine was born on February 27. While his birthday was recorded, possibly for astrological reasons, as in the case of his mother we lack direct information about his birth year. Again, we can recalculate it from estimates by late antique authors of his age at the time of his death in 337. These vary between 60 and 65 years, placing Constantine's birth in the mid-270s.[20] If this is accurate, Constantine was born during a period when Constantius was on active military service, which lasted at least throughout the reign of Aurelian (270–275). At some point, Constantius progressed to the position of tribune, with equestrian rank, a rather typical promotion from the post of *protector*.[21] As tribune, he commanded a cavalry unit, either mobile or provincially based. The latter may have been stationed in Naissus, where the presence of a

---

[18] Constantine's birthplace: Firmicus Maternus, Math. 1.10.13; Origo Const. 2.
[19] Tacoma (2016) 111.
[20] Barnes (1982) 39–40. Barnes correctly dismisses attempts to date Constantine's birth to the mid-280s on the basis of references in several panegyrics to the emperor's youthfulness in the years 300–310.
[21] Southern (2007) 129–30.

military battalion (the *cohors I Aurelia Dardanorum*) is attested until late antiquity.[22] This would explain why Constantius settled his family here, but so would his command of a mobile unit. While some concubines, most notably Augustine of Hippo's, accompanied their partners on their travels, this would not have been feasible in the context of military campaigns. Instead, it seems logical to think that Constantius established a pregnant Helena close to his own family while he pursued his military commitments elsewhere. Patrilocal residence habits, where couples moved in with or close to the male partner's family, were common throughout the empire.[23]

Constantine's birth was followed by a stable and relatively long-lasting family life at Naissus. He spent his childhood years in the town in the company of his mother, and—presumably at times—his father, who stayed together for at least a decade after his birth.[24] In a concubinage, children were normally avoided, for procreation was not its point, so the arrival of Constantine could indicate that Constantius and Helena had looked differently upon their relationship all along. But, of course, given the unreliability of ancient methods of contraception, the avoidance of children was seldom accomplished, as again the example of Augustine, who fathered a son with his concubine, demonstrates.[25] If his parents' union was a concubinage, Constantine could then well have been an accident. He would in any case have been an illegitimate child, though Constantius may still have tried to redress this. Such was a not an uncommon procedure, but not altogether easy, as in the provinces the emperor himself had to approve the process, called *arrogatio*.[26] In the later fourth century, Libanius of Antioch tried in vain to get such imperial dispensation for his illegitimate son born in concubinage. In this case, the mother was an enslaved woman. This made the situation even trickier, as the son was in consequence also enslaved and in the meantime Constantine, characteristically, had tightened the law around the legitimization of children in 336. On the other hand, Constantine also issued a law that retrospectively legitimized children from concubinages where the woman had been freeborn, as long as she and the father had subsequently legally married and the man had no other children outside this relationship.

---

[22] Vasić (2013) 91; Jeremić, Filipović (2016) 1743–44.

[23] Augustine's concubine accompanied the later bishop of Hippo to Rome and Milan, where he held teaching positions, Conf. 6.15. On stay-at-home wives, see Lee (2007) 142. On patrilocal residence patterns, see Huebner (2013) 31–35.

[24] Origo Const. 1.2: Constantine was "raised" at Naissus, *eductus*.

[25] Augustine, Conf. 6.15. On concubinage and children, see Arjava (1996) 208–09.

[26] Jerome, Ep. 69.5 on the frequency of petitions for arrogatio.

These laws acknowledged the fuzziness around marriage and legitimacy, and reflect the understandable ignorance about its legal context outside the elite proper.[27] Constantius and Helena may well have thought of Constantine as legitimate, only becoming mindful of potential issues when Constantius' awareness of his social status grew. In any case, historical events suggest that it would not have been difficult for Constantius to get—or even dispense—imperial approval of his son's legitimization at some point, if needed.[28]

Whatever his status at birth, Constantine was clearly loved by his father, who showed an unfailing interest in him. In consequence, his presence must have made the bond between Constantius and Helena stronger, resulting in further children. Even if Constantine was her only child to reach adulthood, Helena must have had multiple pregnancies during her long relationship with Constantius, especially if she and Constantius considered their union legitimate. Statistics show that most women in Roman antiquity had between five and ten pregnancies during their lifetime, with all the medical dangers that this entailed, although just one or two children, on average, survived into adulthood. It is therefore possible that Helena suffered the loss of one or more unborn or born babies, all the while caring for at least one small child. How this felt is hard to measure, in an age where bereavement over children was a common occurrence. But numerous funerary inscriptions for infants from across the Roman empire tell of deep parental grief's existence.[29]

There is also further, if dubious, evidence that Constantius and Helena had other children. It concerns Constantine's sisters Constantia and Anastasia, and a possible brother, Constantius.[30] The girls are usually held to be Constantine's half-sisters, the products of Constantius' later marriage to the woman he left Helena for, Theodora, which produced six children. In truth, the names of only three of these children, all boys, are directly linked with Theodora. Several sources identify Constantia and Anastasia as Constantine's sisters, but none identifies their mother.[31] A note in the *Origo Constantini*, an early source, instead implies they were Constantine's full sisters. The passage in question describes Constantine's embassy in 315, headed by a man called Constantius, to his fellow emperor Licinius, who had married Constantia, to

---

[27] Constantine's laws are CTh 4.6.2, 3 (336) and the law mentioned in the later CJ 5.27.5 (477). On Libanius and the legal context, see Arjava (1996) 211–15.
[28] Constantine's co-emperor Licinius later legitimized a son born from a concubine; see p. 265.
[29] Sessa (2018) 177 for statistics. On grief, see Carroll (2018) 212–15.
[30] On Anastasia and Constantius, see Chausson (2002) 137–46; Tougher (2011) 184.
[31] Eutropius, Brev. 9.22; Orosius, Hist. adv. pag. 7.25.5. For Theodora's children, see further pp. 61–62. For sources on Constantia and Anastasia, see PLRE I Anastasia 1, 58; Constantia 1, 221.

persuade him to accept Anastasia's husband Bassianus as his Caesar.[32] Here, Constantia is mentioned as Constantine's sister (*soror*) and Anastasia as his "other" sister (*altera soror*). Since Constantine undoubtedly had a half-sister, Eutropia the Younger, this phrasing, which clearly excludes Eutropia the Younger from sisterhood, is at least curious. The identity of the ambassador Constantius is also unclear. He may have been Constantine's half-brother Julius Constantius, a son of Theodora, or another Constantius and therefore possibly a son of Helena. This man's name in any case implies a blood relation with the emperor, if not necessarily brotherhood.[33]

Two further late antique texts also identify at least Constantia as Helena's daughter. One is the *Passio Gallicani*, a hagiographical tale from Rome, possibly written in the fifth or sixth century, in which Helena and a Constantia appear as a mother and daughter pair living in the imperial palace in Rome. The other is Ps.-Gelasius of Cyzikus's *Church History*, written c. 475, which calls Constantia Helena's daughter (*thygátēr*) and describes Constantine and Constantia's shared grief over the death of their mother, Helena. The *Passio Gallicani* is a confused account, as it also depicts Constantia as Constantine's daughter, which would make Helena her own son's wife or partner. Ps.-Gelasius, meanwhile, was embellishing a story inherited from earlier church historians, Rufinus, Socrates, Sozomen, and Theodoret, all of whom describe Constantia as Constantine's sister, but without any reference to Helena.[34] Neither of these texts is entirely reliable on facts, therefore, but they both fed on a memory, widespread in both East and West and possibly some factual basis, that Constantia was Constantine's favorite sister or at least the sister to whom he gave most prominence.[35]

None of this, however, offers any conclusive proof that Constantia, or Anastasia, or Constantius, was Constantine's full, rather than half-sibling. In addition, our interpretation of this data is complicated by the fact that we have no knowledge of the birthdates of any of these individuals. Dating the birth

---

[32] Origo Const. 1.13.

[33] PLRE I, Constantius 1, 224. Chausson (2002) 138–40, 145–46 suggests brotherhood and identifies this Constantius as Flavius Constantius, Constantine's Praetorian Prefect in the years 324–327: PLRE I, Fl. Constantius 5, 225. One would assume, however, that a full brother of Constantine would have left more traces in the source record. Barnes (2014) 212 n. 14 identifies this Constantius with Julius Constantius.

[34] Passio Gallicani 7–8: *Helena cum filia sua Constantia*. For a discussion of the author's confusion, Diefenbach (2007) 107 n. 105. See also Conti, Burrus, Trout (2020) 7 for manuscripts of the Passio Gallicani that have "Constantina" (Helena's granddaughter). Ps.-Gelasius of Cyzikus, Hist. eccl. 3.7.6, who follows Rufinus, Hist. eccl. 10.12; Socrates, Hist. eccl. 1.25; Sozomen, Hist. eccl. 2.27; Theodoret, Hist. eccl. 2.3.

[35] On Constantine and Constantia, see also Chapter 7.

of Constantia and Anastasia within the period of Helena and Constantius' relationship, which ended in the late 280s if not beforehand, would make at least Constantia a rather old bride, at least in her mid-twenties, when she married Licinius in 313, though this would not necessarily have been unusual.[36] Still, as we shall see, the behavior of Constantine's half-brothers with regard to this marriage implies that Constantia was closer to them than to Constantine himself. Constantia's later prominence and apparent importance to Constantine probably derived less from their close blood kinship than from her status as the wife of a previous emperor.

In addition to frequent pregnancy, whether to term or not, Helena may also have shared some of the other difficulties facing young wives, and even more so concubines, and above all the stress of being transplanted far from her home. If Helena was from the Propontis, she exchanged a Mediterranean coastal life for the mountainous landlocked world of the central Balkans, where winters, during one of which Constantine was born, were bitterly cold and where she had to get accustomed to a new idiom, for this was predominantly Latin-speaking territory. Contemporary female letters that survive from Roman Egypt vividly describe the loneliness of uprooted women, especially with partners like Constantius who were frequently away, which also often left them to the mercies of their partner's not always supportive family.[37] The presence of a paternal relative in Constantine's orbit, as suggested by the ambassador Constantius mentioned previously, shows that Constantine's paternal family, into which Helena now entered, was a close-knit group.

Nonetheless, living in Naissus may have been a happy time for Helena. Helena and Constantius were of a similar age, which made their partnership more egalitarian. Being the mother of a living son, a precious asset in a patriarchal society faced with high infant mortality, gave Helena authority. Her relationship with Constantius provided her with personal security and economic stability that would have been the envy of many a transient female worker in the ancient world. At the very least, she knew that her son would be well cared for, whatever happened to her. When, many years later, Augustine of Hippo left his concubine behind, he took their son Adeodatus with him, who was deeply loved not only by him, but also by his paternal grandmother, Monnica.[38]

---

[36] Constantine's daughter Helena was in her thirties when she married; refer to Chapter 10.
[37] Huebner (2013) 144–49; for a letter example, see Bagnall, Cribiore (2006) 282.
[38] Augustine, Conf. 6.15; 9.16.

Above all, Helena's spatial surroundings should have allowed her to enjoy a quiet, provincial existence. Naissus, a Roman *municipium* (self-governing city) since at least the second century, was a peaceful town in the later 270s and 280s, benefiting from Aurelian's decision to give up Dacia, which had calmed the Danube frontier. Its strategic location near a confluence of two navigable rivers, the Nišava and the Moravia, and at the junction of significant trans-Balkan roads leading to the Danube, the Adriaticum, the Aegean, the Black Sea, and the Bosphorus meant that Naissus was well connected to long-distance trade networks. This occasionally brought foreign goods, people, and a breeze of cosmopolitan lifestyles into town. At the same time, Naissus was a very small city, situated on a plateau above the Nišava that was later occupied by an Ottoman fortress and is now the site of a municipal park. Helena could walk around the walls that enclosed the city in less than an hour. This was a close-knit urban community, where people encountered each other on a daily basis in the city's forum and civilian basilica situated at the heart of the city, or the main city baths just outside town. The surrounding countryside was barely Romanised, and in some rural stretches Thracian was still spoken, a language perhaps known to Helena from the Propontis. Christianity does not seem to have arrived in Naissus before the fourth century.[39]

While Naissus was renowned for some of its inhabitants' specialist skills in both base and fine metalwork—owing to the proximity of imperial mines in the central Balkans—its rhythms of life were dominated by the agricultural calendar. The Nišava and Moravia flowed through vast fertile valleys farmed, particularly in the city's vicinity, by the descendants of the veterans who settled here from the second century on. For the young Constantine, his childhood years were unhampered by formal education, scarce in any case in a town like Naissus, but Helena and Constantius may also have not yet seen the need for it.[40] Constantine clearly had fond memories of Naissus. After he had become emperor and retaken the territory in which his birthplace was situated from his rival emperor Licinius in 317, he built an enormous imperial villa just outside the city, about a mile down the road toward Serdica. The site, known later in the fourth century as Mediana, incorporated several earlier third-century farming estates that exhibit residential features testifying to

---

[39] On Naissus's topography, see Mirković (2007) 58–60; Vasić (2013) 91–93. On Christianity in Naissus, Jeremić, Filipović (2016).
[40] Origo Const. 1.2: Constantine was "raised" at Naissus, *eductus*, but "less versed in letters," *litteris minus instructus*.

Fig. 2.1 Third-century semi-circular geometrical floor mosaic in *opus tessellatum* with white, red, and ocher stones, from the area later occupied by Constantine's imperial villa at Mediana. © Julia Hillner.

modestly prosperous tastes, such as porticoed courtyards and dining rooms with apses and geometrical floor mosaics (see Fig. 2.1). One of these may well have belonged to Constantine's paternal family. These are the material surroundings in which we might best imagine Helena as a young mother.[41]

In the early autumn of 275, the Praetorian Guard assassinated the emperor Aurelian, who was once again en route to the Eastern frontier, at the imperial post station of Caenophrurium near Byzantium. The confusion around Aurelian's murder, instigated by his private secretary over a personal grievance, may have paved the way for the brief rule of his wife, Ulpia Severina, a unique occurrence in Roman imperial history. Soon, however, another former Danubian general, Tacitus, succeeded to Aurelian's throne.[42] If Helena took any notice of these momentous events, and of an empress's role within them, it was only because they must have brought Constantius home. Yet, they did not end his career. It was, in fact, just about to take off, with a critical effect on his relationship with Helena.

[41] On Mediana: Milošević (2013) 118–25; Vasić (2007) 96–107.
[42] Drinkwater (2005) 53; on the role of Ulpia Severina, see Bleckmann (2002) 333–39.

Less than a decade after Aurelian's death, Constantius became what was later described as *praeses Dalmatiarum* or *Dalmatiae*. This post, usually dated to the reign of emperor Carinus (282–284), was probably the civilian governorship of the province of Dalmatia, an equestrian position since the time of Gallienus. As such, it represented a considerable step up for Constantius in terms of an administrative career.[43] If this was indeed the case, he will have moved his household and family, including Helena, to Salona, the buzzing provincial capital of Dalmatia, situated at the mouth of the river Jadro on a wide bay of the Adriatic coast (today's Solin in Croatia on the bay of Kaštela).[44]

Compared to Naissus, Salona was of venerable antiquity. Having attracted settlers from Italy since at least the second century BC, it was established as a Roman colony by either Julius Caesar or Augustus. It was, by ancient standards, a sizable city, the largest in Dalmatia. It housed around 50,000 inhabitants within its extensive walls, and dominated a city territory that stretched 30 miles in both directions along the coast, as well as incorporating numerous offshore islands. For Helena, with her experiences of semi-rural life, unstable frontiers, grubby female labor, and small-town motherhood, coming to Salona in the company of the city's highest-ranking imperial official must have been an overwhelming and startling experience. Even though she had been exposed to imperial power throughout her life, from the governor's urban villa in the upper city of Salona, she would have been able to grasp the full extent of Rome's impact on the Mediterranean, well beyond the more austere contexts to which she was accustomed.

Within touching distance of Italy, the empire's ancient center, and with a natural harbor protected by islands that facilitated control over the shipping routes in the Adriatic and trade into the Dalmatian interior, Salona was enormously prosperous. The invasions and military operations that had taken place earlier in the century had barely affected it. In sharp contrast to Naissus, the army played a negligible role in Salona's urban life. The largely civilian residents enjoyed all the lavish trappings of a Roman lifestyle. The city's monuments included large public baths and an amphitheater with space for about a quarter of Salona's population, which was renovated at around the time of Helena's likely residence in the city (Fig. 2.2).[45] As a

---

[43] Origo Const. 2. Historia Augusta, Carus et Carinus et Numerianus 17: *praesidatum Dalmatiae administrabat*. See Barnes (2014) 28 who thinks this was a military command.
[44] Wilkes (1969) 220–38, 354–91, 416–17; Sanader (2007) 67–72, also on the governor's villa.
[45] Excavations published by Dyggve, Weilbach (1933).

Fig. 2.2 Remains of the amphitheater in Salona. The governor's box was situated above the arch in the center of the picture. © Julia Hillner.

magistrate, Constantius would have attended, or even organized, spectacles here, generating collective identity, showcasing social hierarchies, and displaying for entertainment in the arena those who were excluded from the civic community.[46] Given her background, Helena, for whom such displays may have been a new experience, can be counted lucky for having been able to sit among the audience on their stone benches, or perhaps even to look on from the governor's viewing box.

As a cosmopolitan place, Salona offered scope for diversity, too. Judging by the explosion of monumental Christian building there in the fourth century, some of which was dedicated to martyrs who had allegedly died during the persecutions of the early fourth century, the city must already have housed a substantial and visible Christian community by the late third century. These Christians were enjoying more peaceful times for their religion now that the persecutions of the mid-third century had ended, for the time being, with Gallienus' edict of toleration in 260. Funerary inscriptions suggest that many of them came, like Helena, from around the Eastern Mediterranean. Witnessing Christianity in a confident, organized, and urban form may have been another new experience for Helena.[47]

---

[46] Kyle (1998) 7–10.
[47] Christianity in Salona: Wilkes (1969) 427–535; Cambi (2007) 121–36.

48 EXTRA (C. 248–C. 289)

Just at this moment, when Helena was expanding her horizons, her life was fatefully interrupted. It is unclear exactly how Constantius had advanced his career so successfully, although his talent for military and administrative efficiency must have been a crucial factor. But what is certain is that over the next few years, he became ever closer to the imperial center; so close indeed for one emperor to desire him as a kinsman, leading Constantius to leave his life with Helena behind. As both ancient and modern authors laconically put it, sometime in the late 280s, Helena was "cast aside" to make room for a more expedient match.[48] This language is fitting as under Roman law of the time, it was relatively easy to separate from a wife, especially if she had come without a dowry, but even easier to discard a concubine. Concubines were not protected by the law at all, as such unions did not involve the transmission of property.[49] Even though Constantius may have felt pressured to leave Helena, as some sources suggest, he did not forego his chance of further social advancement that, whether known to him at the time or not, paved his way to imperial rule. Since Constantine seems to have been aware of his mother's whereabouts later, it would appear that she had continued to receive some kind of support from Constantius. Nonetheless, she probably lost direct access to her son, especially if Constantius had acknowledged him, for Roman fathers had much greater rights over their children than mothers.[50] Despite modern historians' wish to believe that Helena remained close to Constantine, we can in truth only speculate about their relationship over the next thirty years. It is not directly recorded in any source.

How Helena felt about all of this is unknown, and perhaps even unknowable to a modern observer. As even the most cursory look at Roman marriage law testifies, relationships between men and women were fragile, and their rupture was to the latter's disadvantage, especially if conducted across the Roman world's status barriers. Despite the hopes they may have had, women like Helena must have known that they were living on borrowed time.

---

[48] Origo Const. 1.2: *relicta*; Eutropius, Brev. 9.22: *ambo* [= Constantius and Galerius] *uxores, quas habuerant, repudiare conpulsi*; Epitome de Caesaribus 39.2 *abiecta*; Aurelius Victor, Caes. 39.25: *diremptis prioribus coniugiis*; Prosper Tiro, Ep. chron. 942 *[Diocletianus] . . . ambos . . . repudiare uxores suas (sic) quas prius habebant coegit*. Although *repudiare* is a technical term that denotes a legal divorce, each time it is used, it is in reference to both Constantius and Galerius' partners, so cannot be taken as full evidence that Constantius' was a legal marriage. For modern authors who use the term *cast aside*, see, for example, Cooper (2013) 131.
[49] On divorce, see Arjava (1996) 177–83.
[50] On Roman custody law, Arjava (1996) 86–87.

Helena's Tetrarchy

For the following three decades, Helena disappears from the public record. When she returned, she was a Christian empress, unrecognizable perhaps even to herself. The man who changed Helena's life was the emperor Maximian. He was the father of the woman Constantius married, Theodora. Since 286 Maximian had co-ruled the empire with his senior partner, Diocletian. Diocletian, another career soldier of modest origins, from the environs of the very same Salona, famously initiated the most experimental period of Roman imperial rule. By 293 he had established what modern historians call the tetrarchy (four-men rule), an imperial "college" composed of two senior (Augusti) and two junior emperors, or "heirs" (Caesars). One of these Caesars was Constantius, by now also Maximian's son-in-law. The second was another military man called Galerius.[51]

Emperors before Diocletian had appointed co-rulers. Unlike most of these, Diocletian insisted on merit, not blood. Power was in theory shared not between family members, but between men distinguished by their military abilities. Bonds were sanctioned through divine associations with Jupiter and Hercules as patrons or even fictive ancestors, turning the senior Augustus Diocletian and his Caesar Galerius into *Iovii*, and Maximian and Constantius into *Herculii*.[52]

These principles of divinely revealed merit also had an effect on the role of imperial women in tetrarchic self-promotion. Even though Roman imperial rule was never a hereditary regime, the patrilineal nature of Roman society had conventionally led to the anticipation that Roman imperial wives would produce heirs. Even if they had only daughters, a dynastic line could still be forged through the husband and children of an emperor's daughter. This, in turn, had given imperial women dynastic potential, making them carriers of imperial legitimacy.[53] The wives of tetrarchs were, at least publicly, not expected to produce heirs, however, so their dynastic value was diminished. As a result, the visibility of imperial women and their customary celebration through titulature, on coinage, in official architecture, artwork, and literature decreased remarkably in the first decade of the tetrarchy.[54]

---

[51] For developments: Harries (2012) 27–33.
[52] On the concept of the tetrarchy, see Hekster (2015) 277–341. For Maximian's paternity of Theodora see Chapter 3.
[53] On the concept of "dynastic potential" of imperial women, which, even though it varied in strength, can be observed throughout the Roman imperial period, see Priwitzer (2010) 238; Busch (2015) 214–17.
[54] Hunnell Chen (2018).

These principles soon collided with the reality that tetrarchs had wives, and other female family members, such as mothers, sisters, nieces, and daughters. At times, the latter were still employed to forge marital bonds between individual tetrarchs, if not necessarily in a strategic way. Such marriages were also arranged to exclude other men from aspiring to power through marriage to imperial relatives, showing that the idea of imperial daughters as potential carriers of imperial legitimacy had not disappeared. Some of the tetrarchs and their emerging rivals had concubines, too. Since there now existed, at any given time, four tetrarchs, and often a number of usurpers, this increased the number of imperial women dramatically and, it must be stressed, in a wholly unprecedented way. Between Diocletian's ascent to the throne in 284 and the downfall of the last tetrarch Licinius in 324 (by now only a diarch with Constantine), we know of the existence, if not necessarily the names, of twenty-three imperial women, many of whom were related to each other due to marriage alliances (see the Family Tree at the beginning of this book).[55] After Helena's disappearance, and not unrelated to it, the imperial landscape therefore filled with an expansive, messy, and often brutalized network of women.

By the time that we can reconnect with Helena thirty years later, marriage and blood ties linked many of these women to her son's own imperial household. What is more, the second generation of tetrarchs who assumed power from 306 had resumed a more conventional promotion of their female relations and had also tried either to exploit or suppress the dynastic potential of their colleagues' women. Constantine did, too. Upon her eventual reappearance as an imperial woman, Helena was thus thrust into an entirely new and unfamiliar circle of female relatives, at a court that was seeking to establish a balance between continuity and rupture with the immediate imperial past, including its dead and still-living empresses.

When Constantius left her, Helena was a middle-aged woman. Normally, she would have disappeared from historians' view forever. It is to Constantine's credit that Helena did not. Still, her promotion by her son also meant that, extraordinarily and awkwardly, she would go on to meet some of the women who had earlier replaced her. She was drawn into the domestic

---

[55] The twenty-three women are, in alphabetical order: Anastasia, Constantia, Constantina, Eutropia, Eutropia the Younger, Fausta, Galla, Galerius' concubine, Galerius' first wife, Galerius' sister, Helena, Helena (wife of Crispus), Helena the Younger, Licinius' concubine, Maximinus Daza's wife, Maximinus Daza's daughter, Minervina, Prisca, Romula, Severus' wife, Theodora, Valeria, Valeria Maximilla.

conflicts created by their motherhood of different dynastic lines. She moved in their spaces, above all in the city of Rome. Her public image responded to their public images and would eventually replace them. While Helena is waiting in the wings, we should therefore spend time with some of the imperial women who decisively shaped her later life.

PART II
OFF STAGE (C. 289–C. 317)

3

Sister Act

Sometime in the first quarter of the fourth century, a sumptuous town house was redecorated in the Lateran area of the city of Rome (see Map 4, n. 4). Like much of this neighborhood, the house in question, situated just west of the site where soon Rome's first bishop's church would rise, was imperial property. It may have been refurbished by the usurper Maxentius just a few years before. A loggia running alongside the residence's internal garden was now further embellished with a monumental program of wall paintings showing a family procession of larger than life-sized men and women. These painted figures, clad in purple and illuminated by the natural light filtering in from the garden, solemnly towered over anyone moving through this corridor toward its focal point, a large curved space enclosing a sculptural display of uncertain nature. The paintings' integration with the loggia's architectural features was designed to give onlookers a ceremonial yet intimate encounter with their hosts' significance.

The patron of this artwork was probably Constantine himself. This is not only because of its date, based itself on the dating of the brickwork beneath the corridor's wall plaster, or because Constantine succeeded to Maxentius' ownership of imperial property in Rome. The loggia's original excavation in the 1970s also revealed painted inscriptions along the porphyry-colored strip below the figures' feet, interpreted as transcriptions of popular acclamations to Constantine, his family, and Licinius, which would date them to before 324. While this interpretation has been met with caution—not the least because the inscriptions are now almost indiscernible—with these paintings we may still be looking at the way in which Constantine wanted visitors to this residence to experience his family, shortly after he took control of Rome. They align well with what we know about other decorated imperial spaces of the time. The iconography of the images, especially the figures' purple clothing and quasi-divine appearance, is strongly reminiscent of tetrarchic representation. Furthermore, some of their attributes, such as the small

Fig. 3.1 Wall paintings from the *domus* under the Istituto Nazionale della Previdenza Sociale in Rome, Museo Nazionale Romano Palazzo Massimo. Figures identified from the right as Constantius, Theodora, Constantine (the figure identified as Fausta to the left of Constantine is still in situ). Foto n. 588519: S. Sansonetti, su concessione del Ministero della Cultura—Museo Nazionale Romano.

statuette representing *pietas* held by the leading male figure, reflect virtues promoted in Constantinian propaganda.[1]

The procession of painted figures is now sadly rather damaged, but within it we can make out two women, in the second and fourth places, respectively, each following a man (Fig. 3.1). The disputed inscriptions identify the first pair as Constantius, Constantine's father, and his wife Theodora, the woman for whom he left Helena, and the second pair as Constantine himself and his wife Fausta. Even where we disregard the epigraphic evidence, these identifications make a lot of sense, especially given the corridor's date. As we shall see in this chapter, during the early years of Constantine's reign, it was these two couples—rather than Helena—who were at the heart of the Constantinian dynastic agenda, and particularly in Rome.

The two pairs of figures on the monumental frieze in the Roman residence are separated from each other and from the following figures by a pole, possibly a spear, distinguishing them as two spousal groups. Assuming these

---

[1] The house is now situated under the Istituto Nazionale della Previdenza Sociale (INPS) on Via Amba Aradam. For the inscriptions: CIL 6.40769. On the paintings, see Guarducci (1972) 386–92; Scrinari (1991) 162–222; McFadden (2013); Hillner (2017a) 81–85. See Liverani (2004) for caution regarding the inscriptions, but note that Simona Morretta of the Soprintendenza Speciale Archeologia Belle Arti e Paesaggio di Roma has orally confirmed Scrinari's interpretation to me and that it is accepted by CIL.

show Constantius and Theodora and Constantine and Fausta, respectively, this marital representation obscures close ties between the women. Theodora and Fausta, married to a father and his son, were not only in-laws, but, more importantly, both were daughters of the tetrarch Maximian and sisters to the usurper Maxentius, each of whom Constantine had just deposed. The masking of these ties, here and elsewhere in Constantinian propaganda, was deliberate. As we shall see throughout this book, Constantine was continuously preoccupied with shaping his family tree in such a way as to keep it focused on himself. While this led to the actual removal of male relatives, where his female relations were concerned, it predominantly involved publicly presenting them as directly linked to himself. This strategy was important, because Constantine's intricate kinship network meant that many of his female relations had intimate connections, as daughters, wives, or mothers, to rival men, with all the conflicting loyalties, or perceptions thereof, that this entailed (see Family Tree). As Constantine's rivalries, and their locations, changed over time, so did the women he foregrounded.

Eventually, Constantine would include Helena in these strategies. He only did so, however, from the mid-310s, when, after his children with Fausta had been born, he started to contemplate sole imperial rule and also a single dynastic line. At the time the paintings in the Roman residence were commissioned, Constantine's main concern was how to reconcile the fact that his wife and his mother-in-law, but even more importantly his stepmother and her sons, were related to the imperial men he had just killed and who had ruled the city he had just taken. He resolved this issue by incorporating them into his dynasty, iconographically and politically.

Lost Girl: Theodora

Late antique authors, all writing after her death, disagree about Theodora's exact relationship with the emperor Maximian. Some call her his daughter, others his stepdaughter. Modern historians have unwittingly muddied the waters around Theodora even further. They generally run with the latter suggestion, adding the speculation that she was the daughter of Maximian's wife Eutropia from an earlier marriage to a man called Afranius Hannibalianus, who became consul in 392. This assumption is based on prosopographical grounds and relies entirely on Theodora and Constantius naming one of their sons Hannibalianus.[2]

In arguing for Theodora's stepdaughter status, modern historians, like ancient authors before them, may have fallen into a trap laid by a Constantinian version of events. Maximian's son Maxentius presented Theodora as a sister, and later in the fourth century, Constantine's nephew Julian, a grandson of Theodora, and his supporters also had no trouble claiming imperial descent from Maximian for himself.[3] Given Constantine's habits of severing links between the women of his dynasty and his rival emperors, it is therefore more likely that Theodora was Maximian's biological daughter and that this relationship was later rewritten as step-daughterhood to accommodate changing political circumstances. Early in his reign, it was important for Constantine to promote Theodora as the wife of his imperial father, not as Maximian's daughter, in order to build up a genuine Constantinian dynasty. Later on, when Theodora's children and their offspring grew into imperial rivals, especially for Constantine's sons born from 316 on, the story was convenient to diminish the extent of their imperial ancestry.

Theodora herself was born around the same time that Helena gave birth to Constantine, or just a few years later, making her coetaneous with her stepson.[4] At this point, Maximian, who allegedly came from a family of "shopkeepers" in the Pannonian countryside near Sirmium (today's Sremska Mitrovica), must still have been a simple soldier. Theodora's mother Eutropia was from Syria.[5] Her encounter with Maximian could have occurred during one of the military operations that brought the future emperor to the East,

---

[2] Daughter: Origo Const. 2; Philostorgius, Hist. eccl. 2.16a; Theophanes, Chron. AM 5814; stepdaughter: Aurelius Victor, Caes. 39.25; Eutropius, Brev. 9.22; Jerome, Chron. 292; Epitome de Caesaribus 39.2, 40.12. The theory about Afranius Hannibalianus' paternity of Theodora goes back to Seeck (1901), but has taken on almost primary source authority, see, for example, PLRE I, Theodora 1, 895. Barnes (1982) 33–34 disputes it, although does not explain the origin of the stepdaughter story. He argues Theodora was the daughter of Maximian and his first wife, Afranius Hannibalianus' daughter, but this, in turn, does not explain why one of Theodora's daughters was named Eutropia, unless we take seriously the claims in the Historia Augusta that Constantius' father was called Eutropius (Historia Augusta, Divus Claudius 13). See also Vanderspoel (2020) 39 for a supposed connection between Afranius Hannibalianus and Constantine's nephews Gallus and Julian based on their common geographical connection to Tralles in Asia Minor. Vanderspoel postulates that Afranius Hannibalianus was Eutropia's brother, which seems more plausible (see also Family Tree).

[3] Maxentius called Constantius his brother-in-law: RIC VI, Rome 245, 252. Maxentius is clearly emphasizing imperial kinship via Maximian, rather than kinship through his mother Eutropia alone. Julian and supporters: Philostorgius, Hist. eccl. 2.16a; Passio Artemii 41. See also Zonaras, Epit. hist. 13.1 (generally drawing on pro-Julian sources) who calls Theodora and Fausta sisters.

[4] Theodora's birthdate is calculated on the basis on the date of her marriage, which must have taken place before 289, see the discussion that follows, and after she was 12. On the age of marriage in law and custom of elite Roman girls, see Caldwell (2015) 94–133.

[5] Epitome de Caesaribus 40.10; 40.12.

the earliest of which came during his service under Aurelian.[6] As we shall see, Eutropia stayed in the orbit of Constantine's court even after her husband and son had been eliminated, and she and Helena may well have met.[7] For all their differences, not the least because she had been an emperor's legitimate wife, Eutropia's early life experiences were not dissimilar from those of Helena. Scooped up by a soldier on campaign, she was transported to an ever more dazzling new life, motherhood far from home, and ultimately residence in Rome, the ancient capital of the empire.

Like all tetrarchs, Maximian was constantly on the move. Between the late 280s and early 290s, he had his hands full with raids by people living beyond the Rhine–Danube frontier and with suppressing the usurpation of Carausius, who had taken control of northwestern Gaul and Britain. Several Western cities emerged as imperial residences during this time, to house the itinerant emperor: Trier in northeastern Gaul, and Milan and Aquileia in Italy. This was in keeping with general developments during the tetrarchy, when many cities, chosen for strategic or personal preferences, were actively built up as permanent residences, so imperial power could be performed outside Rome (see Map 3).[8] Meanwhile, the relationship between the senior tetrarchs and Rome itself was an ambiguous one. Rome and its people had to be respected, even revered, as the symbolic heart of the empire, the embodiment of its history and unity, and the seat of the Roman state's most ancient institution, the Senate. Even so, at least Diocletian and his Caesar Galerius were suspicious of the old Italian senatorial aristocracy and their republican traditions.[9]

Maximian, who was the senior tetrarch active in the Western empire, was more aware of the profound imperial importance of Rome, and the necessity to keep the senatorial aristocracy on side, since its members were also the major landowners in his key Western regions of Italy and North Africa.[10] He visited the city several times, and seems to have spent increasingly lengthy periods there, especially toward the end of his reign when he was in charge of major tetrarchic building projects, including the massive Baths of Diocletian on the Esquiline Hill. Above all, he resumed the habit of earlier third-century

---

[6] For Maximian's service under Aurelian: Aurelius Victor, Caes. 39.28. If Eutropia was Theodora and Fausta's mother, we must assume she had a long childbearing period, from the mid-270s to the 290s, although this would not be unusual; see Chapter 1 on Roman women's fertility rates.
[7] On Eutropia's continuing relations with Constantine, see Chapter 8.
[8] Harries (2012) 40.
[9] Diocletian's disdain for Rome is detailed in Lactantius, De mortibus pers. 17.
[10] On Maximian and the senatorial aristocracy, see Potter (2010) 30.

emperors, who, to ensure continuity of the imperial presence, had always made sure to leave family members resident in the city while they were on campaign.[11]

At some point, therefore, Maximian installed his family in the imperial capital. It was in Rome that Eutropia, by now also mother of a son, Maxentius, gave birth to her youngest child, Fausta, sometime in the 290s. And it was also in Rome that she spent the subsequent years, together with her youngest daughter, at least.[12] To mark the event, Maximian may even have emulated Diocletian's strategy of anchoring female imperial presence in the urban landscape. Diocletian named palaces (*domus*) after his wife Prisca and his daughter Valeria in Nicomedia. A "palace of Fausta" (*domus Faustae*) large enough to house an assembly of bishops is known from the period immediately after Constantine took Rome. Unless we assume Constantine instantly renamed a residence in the city after his wife, its origin may well date back to Maximian's control of the city.[13]

Despite their display of companionship on the Roman wall fresco, Theodora may have never met her baby sister, at least not during Fausta's childhood. For when Fausta was born, Theodora was already married to Constantius. At some point Constantius had resumed his military career under Maximian, distinguishing himself during the emperor's campaign across the Danube against the Alemanni in 287. By 289, he was not only Maximian's son-in-law. He had also attained a "most powerful office," probably a military command, as Maximian's court orator, Mamertinus, called it in one of the flowery but unspecific speeches that characterized tetrarchic court ceremonials.[14]

Mamertinus delivered his praise speech in Trier, which would become Constantius' and Theodora's main residence after Constantius had joined the imperial college in 293 as the senior of the two Caesars. The capital of Gallia Belgica, had long been an important administrative center, but

---

[11] For Maximian's visits to Rome: Barnes (1982) 58–60 and Enßlin (1930) 2509–10. On third-century emperors' family members residing in Rome, see Davenport (2017) 30.

[12] Julian, Or. 1.5d. Fausta's birth has been linked to Maximian's visit to Rome in 298 or 299. See, for example, Rougé (1980) 7–10, but this provides feeble evidence, as his presence was not required for the event; Nixon, Saylor Rodgers (1994) 198 n. 19. If age requirements were met at her wedding in 307, she must have been born at least in 295, although it should be noted that it took Fausta nine years subsequently to become a mother, so she may have been younger; see Drijvers (1992b) 502 n. 12.

[13] On the *domus Faustae*, see Chapter 6. On Nicomedia, Lactantius, De mortibus pers. 7.

[14] Panegyrici Latini 10.11.4, *potissimo officio*. The reference of this passage to Constantius is now generally accepted [see Barnes (2014) 40–42] even if it remains unclear what the office exactly was. For the Alemanni campaign, see Nixon, Saylor Rodgers (1994) 110.

entered its most remarkable urban phase in the later third century when it became the seat of the Gallic separatist emperors, who were later defeated by Aurelian. Trier was a good-sized Roman city, encompassing nearly 3 square kilometers within its walls. The new imperial building projects initiated by Constantius in the eastern part of the city, a palace with a monumental facade toward the city and sprawling (but never completed) baths, now came to occupy more than a seventh of that intramural area. They transformed the city's topography, razing former administrative buildings and a residential neighborhood, and dominating the urban landscape through their sheer monumentality. The still standing palace basilica, heated, decorated with gold-glass mosaics, and furnished with a large apse, rose over 30 meters high and was probably the tallest brick building in the whole of Gaul. In 310, another court orator praised the new buildings as "close to the stars and the heavens."[15]

All of this must have made a profound impression on the inhabitants of Trier, as did the arrival of a continuously growing imperial household to populate these buildings. It served to generate many local memories connected with imperial women in this city, above all Helena, although she herself may never have resided here. This household also did not include the young Constantine, or at least not for long. Theodora's marriage had made her his stepmother, to the romantic delight of much later Byzantine authors who suspected Theodora of being so jealous that Constantine had to be hidden from her. In one particularly vicious version, Theodora is the mother of a disabled son, which prompted Constantius to search for another child to adopt, before fortuitously rediscovering the biological son he had fathered with Helena some time earlier.[16] In reality, Theodora's relationship with Constantine during the time of her marriage was transient, for at some point in the 290s he soon departed to the East to receive more formal education at Diocletian's court than he had gained at Naissus. He then took up military service in Mesopotamia, Egypt, and on the Danube.[17]

Theodora was also mother not just to one child, whether disabled or not, but to at least six who survived into adulthood, three sons and three daughters. Of this offspring, only the names of her sons Flavius Dalmatius,

---

[15] Panegyrici Latini 6.22: *in tantam altitudinem suscitari ut se sideribus et caelo digna et vicina promittant*. On Trier, Goethert, Kiessel (2007). A coin finding dates the beginning of the basilica's construction to 305.

[16] This version is told in the so-called Patmos legend, on which see Kazdhan (1987) 212.

[17] On the education, Eutropius, Brev. 10.7.2; on Constantine at Diocletian's court, Potter (2013) 63–81.

Hannibalianus, and Julius Constantius are directly known.[18] From passages that mention Constantine's "sisters," modern historians have reconstructed the names of her three daughters as Constantia, Anastasia, and Eutropia the Younger.[19] Like her own mother before her, Theodora was remarkably fertile.

The dynastic connections between Maximian and Constantius would under different circumstances have raised the potential of Theodora's sons for imperial succession. This was in part because of their double imperial ancestry, with an emperor for father and one for grandfather. Some late antique authors further imply that Maximian had adopted Constantius upon becoming Caesar.[20] If the adoption story referred to a concrete legal process rather than just a symbolic gesture, it turned Constantius into not only the eldest brother of his wife and her siblings Maxentius and Fausta, but also, under Roman law, positioned him and his sons under Maximian's paternal power, his *patria potestas*. Maximian would have had to release Theodora from this power, but extended it over her and Constantius' children (including Constantine, unless he remained Constantius' illegitimate child or had been emancipated[21]). As we shall see in the next chapter, these adoption and marriage arrangements were mirrored in the relationship of Diocletian, the other senior tetrarch, with his Caesar Galerius. They may have been meant more to exercise tight legal controls over the junior team in the imperial college, rather than to establish inheritance rights.

What was not matched on Diocletian's and Galerius' side, however, and complicated things, was the profusion of male children. This complicated matters because it transformed Maximian, uniquely within the tetrarchy, into a *paterfamilias* presiding over a large pool of diverse heirs: his own son Maxentius, his possibly adopted son Constantius, his grandsons by Theodora, and perhaps even Constantine. Such an abundance of male heirs would have been the envy of earlier Roman emperors. Still, this fecundity ironically came at a time when imperial children were not officially supposed to have any

---

[18] Barnes (2014) 41–42. The three boys are named in that order by Philostorgius, Hist. eccl. 2.16a. Other authors just mention that Constantius and Theodora had six children: Eutropius, Brev. 9.22; Origo Const. 1.2; Orosius, Hist. adv. pag. 7.25.5; Prosper Tiro, Ep. chron. 942; Chronica Gallica a. 511, 445; Jordanes, Getica, 298. Suda s.v. Konstantinos just says they had sons; Eusebius, Vita Constantini 1.18 that Constantius had an unspecified number of sons and daughters.

[19] See Chapter 2 for arguments that Constantia or Anastasia, or both, were Helena's children.

[20] Panegyrici Latini 7.3.3: *iure adoptionis nepotem* (with reference to Constantine); see also 7.14.4. On the adoption story's historical authenticity, Hekster (2015) 278. Late antique observers also noted the parallel with Rome's second emperor Tiberius, Augustus' adoptive son and husband to his daughter Julia: Eutropius, Brev. 9.22.

[21] On adoption and *patria potestas*, see Kaser (1971) 66; Huebner (2007) 35–36.

currency. Indeed, among this pool, it was the imperial candidates not biologically related to Maximian who eventually prevailed. As had been established in the system set up by Diocletian, the Caesar Constantius succeeded Maximian as Augustus when the latter and Diocletian famously abdicated in 305. Although Lactantius retrospectively claims that Constantine and Maxentius had been groomed for imperial succession as Caesars, new men were chosen: Maximinus Daza, the other Augustus Galerius' nephew, and Severus, Galerius' long-standing army friend.[22]

The death of Constantius at York in Britannia, where he was campaigning against the Picts, just over a year after he had become Augustus, on July 25, 306, promptly reopened the succession question. Following the abdication of Diocletian and Maximian, Constantine had left the East, allegedly to avoid being eliminated by Galerius, and had rejoined his father. According to his biographer Eusebius of Caesarea, writing in the late 330s after Constantine's death, the dying emperor now appointed his eldest son his successor, upon which he was acclaimed as Augustus by his father's troops. If there had been any doubts about the legitimacy of his birth, they were irrelevant to Constantine's receipt of this military backing, which was all that mattered at the time.[23] Nonetheless, Eusebius describes in vivid terms how not only Constantine, but also Constantius' wife and his other children, lined up at Constantius' deathbed. The dying emperor—according to Eusebius already a Christian—blessed this "great band" of sons and daughters, and his wife.[24] But Eusebius also takes great pains to assure us that within this great band Constantine was Constantius' eldest son, and that imperial succession therefore had passed naturally to him. Eusebius' efforts show that, even though they may not have mattered at the time, questions around the imperial legitimacy of Theodora's offspring mattered over thirty years later. The harmonious picture he painted was designed to quell concerns that Constantine's half-brothers had a claim to the throne or that his half-sisters imparted imperial pretensions to their husbands or sons. This was important, because, as we

---

[22] Lactantius, De mortibus pers. 18.12–15; Barnes (2014) 50–51. Lactantius uses the name *Daia*, but Daza (an Illyrian name) is the correct form of his name; see Mackay (1999) 207–09.

[23] Eusebius, Vita Constantini 1.17–18, 22; see also Lactantius, De mortibus pers. 24. See Omissi (2018) 103–16 on the question of whether Constantine was a legitimate emperor or an usurper (as argued by Omissi).

[24] Vita Constantini 1.17, 1.21.

shall see, Constantine's sons, Helena's grandsons, considered these relatives as real rivals.[25]

Eusebius also set up another smokescreen to cloud political realities by failing to name the wife of Constantius present at this deathbed. It is doubtful that he did not know about her, because during the time he wrote, Theodora's portrait appeared on imperial coinage for the first time, to mask the violent struggles over imperial succession between her and Helena's descendants.[26] It is therefore more likely that Eusebius wanted to obscure Theodora's identity in order to blur it with Helena's, who assumes a prominent place in his *Life of Constantine* as the Constantinian dynasty's prime female ancestor.

Eusebius' presentation of Constantius' wives followed Constantine's lead in redrawing the dynastic map. It is important to remember, however, that Eusebius did so only after Helena had become a visible public figure, and after many events that had driven apart the two branches created by Constantius' two sexual relationships. It is also important to remember that, as far as his female relatives were concerned, erasure was not Constantine's own technique for redrawing the dynastic map. He was less in the business of eliminating women than in refashioning them as Constantinian, and reinserting them into his own story. With Theodora, this was a relatively easy thing to do, because for the majority of people in the Roman empire, outside the places where she had resided, Rome and Trier, Theodora had remained invisible throughout her life. Although there were portraits for more domestic settings, Constantius, as far as we know, adhered to the principle of not publicly advertising his wife in art form.[27] The appearance of Theodora's image in Rome only, as discussed at the beginning of this chapter, is therefore particularly pertinent.

The situation with Constantine's own wife Fausta was very different, because she acquired public visibility early on. More importantly, this visibility occurred on the initiative of her father Maximian, who, as we have seen, may even have named a palace in Rome after his daughter. This created a different dynastic problem for Constantine.

---

[25] See Chapter 9.
[26] See Chapter 9.
[27] See Bergmann (1989) who identifies three copies of the same portrait in Oslo, Munich, and Rome as a head of Theodora, possibly commissioned for a domestic context on the occasion of her wedding.

Fausta's Nose

Constantine and Fausta married in the late summer of 307, in Trier. Politics had somersaulted since Constantine's proclamation as Augustus by his father's troops the year before. Constantius' colleague Galerius had not accepted it, appointing Constantius' former Caesar Severus as Western emperor. Meanwhile, since 305 Maximian had assumed the lifestyle of a retired senator, doubtlessly with his wife Eutropia and Fausta, by perambulating between his southern Italian properties. Theodora and her children, who, as we have seen, were possibly under Maximian's paternal power, may have joined them after Constantius' death. Her brother Maxentius had been residing as a senator in a villa just outside Rome, the ancient Maximianic family base.

It is therefore not surprising that in the autumn of 306, when a revolt against the senior Augustus Galerius' attempt to tax the city broke out in Rome, the rioters turned to nearby Maxentius. He took the opportunity to proclaim himself emperor, while only adopting the title of *princeps*. Faced with aggression from Severus, the Augustus now leading his father's former army, Maxentius recalled Maximian, upon which the troops deserted Severus, who surrendered. In order to fend off the arrival of Galerius from the East, Maximian and Maxentius struck an alliance with Constantine. Against Galerius' wishes, the rebel Western emperors offered Constantine the title of Augustus. The alliance was sealed with Constantine's marriage to Fausta.[28] If Constantius had really been adopted by Maximian, an event invoked by the orator who delivered his wedding speech, Constantine might also have felt obliged to keep on good terms with his *paterfamilias*.

Despite its political convenience, Constantine and Fausta's marriage perhaps also made good on a betrothal agreed upon several years earlier, before Constantine left for the East, and designed to strengthen his loyalty to the tetrarchic project.[29] The wedding orator vividly describes this engagement, which Constantine's nephew Julian also later claimed had been arranged by

---

[28] For these developments, see Corcoran (2017) 62–63. One of Maximian's properties may have been the villa del Casale at Piazza Armerina in Sicily, where some have also identified a mosaic representation of Eutropia, although all this is now considered doubtful; see Wilson (2018) 205. For Fausta's wedding: Panegyrici Latini 7.4; Lactantius, De mortibus pers. 27.1; Eutropius, Brev. 10.3; Zosimus, Hist. nea 2.10.6. For date and place, see Nixon, Saylor Rodgers (1994) 180–84. Others think it took place in Arles, for example, Longo (2009) 25.

[29] On Constantine's engagement to Fausta: Panegyrici Latini 7.6; Julian, Or 1.7d. Maxentius was certainly betrothed to Galerius' daughter Valeria Maximilla around this time, possibly to sweeten the pill of being overlooked for succession to Caesar in favor of Constantius in 293; see Cullhed (1994) 16.

Constantius and Maximian as emperors. The orator invoked a wall painting that decorated a dining hall in Maximian's imperial palace in Aquileia, which showed Fausta as a girl (although older than she could have been at the date of the betrothal), but "already venerable through her divine grace" (*iam divino decore venerabilis*). This figure was depicted as handing the youthful Constantine a plumed helmet encrusted with precious gems as a betrothal gift, a *munus sponsale*. Not unusual for a wedding speech, which after all celebrated an imminent sexual act, the orator invoked an erotic image. He insinuated, perhaps frighteningly for the young Fausta, that the painting prophesized a form of love between the couple that their "modesty denied" them at the time of their betrothal (*vobis verecundia negabat*).[30]

Whether this engagement had really occurred is debated, but it is not unlikely.[31] Admittedly, Constantine in the meanwhile had maintained a relationship with another woman, Minervina, before he married Fausta. Around 300 Minervina became the mother of his eldest son, Helena's grandson and Fausta's later stepson, Crispus. Late antique authors without fail present Minervina as Constantine's concubine.[32] Although this may reflect such authors' hostility toward Crispus or Constantine, it would not have been extraordinary for Constantine to keep a concubine while he was waiting for an underage Fausta to reach marriageable age, as many other young Roman men also followed the same practice. Our understanding of this process is complicated, however, by the assertion of Constantine's wedding orator that Constantine had delivered himself to the "laws of marriage" (*matrimonii legibus*) as a young man, to form a "marital mind" (*animum maritalem*).[33] This could allude to a marriage with Minervina, but it is very uncertain testimony and could equally refer to Fausta and Constantine's betrothal.[34] Such betrothal, much more than the actual wedding itself, created the marriage's contractual obligations through establishment of the bride and groom's

---

[30] On wedding speeches, Hersch (2010) 3–5.
[31] Engagement as historical: Barnes (1981) 31; less so (2014) 55–56. For a critique, see, for example, Drijvers (1992b) 501–02.
[32] Epitome de Caesaribus 41.4: *concubina*; Zosimus, Hist. nea 2.20.2: παλλακίς; Zonaras, Epit. hist. 13.2 describes Crispus as illegitimate. Julian, Or. 7.227C–234C claims Constantine had many children with many women, γυναῖκες. He implies some were bastards. For the historiography of Minervina as a concubine, see Hunnell Chen (2018) 49 n. 23. Barnes (2014) 49 and Potter (2013) 96–99 believe it was a legal marriage, and that Minervina was an aristocrat from Antioch or a relative of Diocletian, respectively, but this is conjecture. PLRE I Fl. Iulius Crispus 4, 233; Minervina, 602–03, dates the birth of Crispus to 305; see also Pohlsander (1984) 81–82. Barnes (1982) 44 dates it to no later than 300; Potter (2013) 98 to 303.
[33] Panegyrici Latini 7.4.1.
[34] Callu (2002) 112 n. 12.

consent and dowry negotiations.[35] As we have seen, this is also how the speech later frames it. The orator may have wanted his audience to appreciate that engagement to Fausta had focused Constantine's mind upon preparing for marriage by developing a "marital mind" and the right "uxorious" (*uxorius*) attitude. This is all the more so as the orator explicitly references Fausta in this passage as well, as the wife whom Constantine would marry after "having schooled himself in all the observances of modesty with a prophetic mind." "Modesty" (*verecundia*) is the term to which the orator again resorts later, when describing Fausta's attitude during the betrothal scene.[36] The orator did not have to suppress knowledge of Constantine's concubinage with Minervina, which his audience must have known about due to Crispus' existence. Concubinage, and its benefits of channeling and containing the sexual desires of young men before respectable marriage, were such an accepted part of the Roman cultural fabric that the orator may have even been obliquely referencing it as one of the ways in which Constantine had prepared for marriage.[37]

What speaks most against the orator alluding to a legal marriage between Constantine and Minervina—and therefore also for a historical betrothal with Fausta—is that a Roman wedding speech referring to the groom's previous marriage would not only have been unusual, but, in this case, downright shocking. This is because such a relationship would have involved the breaking of the betrothal between Constantine and Fausta, which the same orator clearly described as a legal transaction only a few moments later, with all the damage to a woman's reputation that this entailed. It would have slighted not only the woman who was now being celebrated as a bride, Fausta, but also, most importantly, her father, Maximian.[38] It is inconceivable that the orator risked such offense, especially since he presented

---

[35] See Hersch (2010) 39–42 on the financial transactions that made a betrothal.

[36] Panegyrici Latini 7.4.1: *Sed, ut res est, mente praesaga omnibus te verecundiae observationibus imbuebas, talem postea ducturus uxorem*, transl. Nixon, Saylor Rodgers (1994) 194–95.

[37] For similar literary references, highlighting the groom's previous sexual activity as a quality for making a good husband, see Caldwell (2015) 146–47; see also Libanius, Or. 14.61, presenting bachelor sexual activity with lowborn women as upholding the marital order. Cf. Drijvers (1992b) who argues that Maximian and Fausta would have been offended by Constantine keeping a concubine while betrothed.

[38] For the legal connotation of the term *munus sponsale*: Heumann, Seckel (1971) 551 and the legal consequences of broken betrothals Evans Grubbs (1995) 142–44. Constantine himself legislated that the party who had broken an engagement had to return all gifts, CTh 3.5.2 (319). For a girl a broken engagement often resulted in rumors around the intactness of her virginity; see Caldwell (2015) 131, Sardella (2016) 84–85. Mac Cormack (1976) 57 stresses that panegyrists had the choice to omit uncomfortable information, so there was no need for an orator to draw attention to such details.

Maximian as the superior emperor, who "decides the fate of human affairs," while Constantine, who received the title of Augustus from him, was to "send frequent laurels of victory to [his] father-in-law." This hierarchy of power reflects the awe in which Maximian was still held in the Western part of the empire.[39]

Similarly, Fausta herself is presented very much as Maximian's daughter, rather than Constantine's wife. According to the orator, it was Maximian who chose Constantine to be his son-in-law as well as his adopted grandson. The betrothal, whether it really happened or not, is portrayed as happening at Maximian's initiative. It was Maximian's palace that was decorated with the painting of the betrothal scene, allowing him to gaze upon "this little girl and this growing boy" (*illam parvulam et hunc intuendo crescentem*) in delightful anticipation of their union. It was by giving Maximian grandchildren that Constantine was expected to strengthen the Roman state, providing it with "everlasting roots" (*perpetuis radicibus*).[40] Hearing, however indirectly, of her future motherhood may have made Fausta listen up, but everyone else would have gasped: the expression of such sentiments was a radical departure from the familiar tetrarchic propaganda of succession by merit. While biological ties always privately mattered to the tetrarchs, their significance had not been officially mentioned since 289, when the court orator Mamertinus had drawn attention to Maxentius as Maximian's heir.[41]

The wedding speech of 307 was very much in tune with the redirection of imperial succession plans toward family ties at this time, as is also apparent among the Eastern tetrarchs, especially Galerius, as we shall see in the next chapter. In the insecure years ushered in by the abdication of 305, something fundamental shifted and a supra-dynastic imperial collective began to lose its appeal. Emperors lucky enough to still be in power, and their court orators, returned to a celebration of their own individual families and their dynastic ties to bolster their legitimacy.[42] This also meant that they returned to celebrating their women publicly. Maximian's embellishment of a reception area in his palace with a painting of his daughter and son-in-law's betrothal—or more likely, the reinterpretation of an existing painting as showing this scene—was clearly widely advertised, since the wedding orator expected his

---

[39] Panegyrici Latini 7.14.1, transl. Nixon, Saylor Rodgers (1994) 209 and 187 on the predominance of Maximian in this panegyric.
[40] Panegyrici Latini 7.2.2; 7.7.1.
[41] Panegyrici Latini 10.14.1. On the scene in 289, Cullhed (1994) 15.
[42] Hekster (2015) 287–96.

Fig. 3.2 Half-argenteus with portrait of Fausta and caption *Faustae nobilissimae feminae* on the obverse (RIC VI Treveri 756). © The Trustees of the British Museum.

audience to know about it. Fausta soon appeared in official imagery outside the palaces, too. Silver coins with the value of a half argenteus (a short-lived type of coin to be replaced by the half-siliqua) were minted in Trier, probably on the occasion of her wedding and dedicated to her (Fig. 3.2). Their obverse shows a very young Fausta wearing a hairstyle reminiscent of that sported by Severan empresses a hundred years earlier, with the hair waved around the face and plaits coiled on the back of the head into a flat bun. On the reverse appears either Juno or Venus, as they did on many coins of Roman empresses.

Together, these crowned goddesses lay out a panorama of female imperial roles. Juno, the supreme female deity, here with the epithet "queen" (*regina*), holding scepter and *patera*, a shallow libation bowl, and accompanied by a peacock, stood for the good fortune of the empire generated by the empress's piety, fertility, and motherhood. Venus, the divine ancestress of the Roman people, signaled how the empress's marital love and the offspring it produced would bring prosperity to the Roman empire, here represented by the globe and palm branch held by the goddess. Her presence on this coin may have referenced the wedding speech's erotic imagery, or vice versa. Her epithet *felix* (propitious) recalled the meaning of Fausta's own name (auspicious).[43]

---

[43] Fausta's name appears in the dative. On this iconographic program, Longo (2009) 85–95, Angelova (2015) 90–92. See Temeryazev, Makarenko (2017) 10, 12–13 on the motifs of Juno and Venus. The coin with Venus on the reverse is RIC VI Treveri 756. The coin showing Juno is published

Amidst all this reversion to tradition, there were also new elements, above all Fausta's title, "noblest of women" (*nobilissima femina*), minted onto the silver coins. As we shall see in the next chapter, this imperial female title, ultimately borne by Helena, too, was a tetrarchic innovation.

Fausta's half-argenteus marked the first time that an imperial woman had appeared on imperial coinage for nearly twenty-five years.[44] Its distribution was small and aimed at impressing the arrival of a new empress in Trier on the imperial residence's inhabitants, used to the presence of an older empress, her sister Theodora. But even if its target was only local, this coinage marked, nonetheless, a decisive change of policy.

It is uncertain again, however, how far this new iconographic program designed around his wife can be traced to Constantine alone. In the same way as Fausta's wedding speech praised the Augustus Maximian, and not Constantine, as the head of the house created by her marriage, Fausta's wedding coinage emphasized the link to her father. She is clearly represented as Maximian's daughter, recognizable as such through her button nose that mirrored Maximian's representation on coins.[45] In the dynastic triad of Constantine, Fausta, and Maximian, it was the old emperor who still held the balance of power. Even though the mint was Constantine's, as was the palace in which his wedding was held, the alliance with Maximian, advertised through his wife's looks, gave him, the newcomer in Gaul, a substantial degree of authority. During this early period of his reign, it was beneficial to Constantine to play the role of Maximian's son-in-law, or even son.[46]

This filial relationship was not to last. Roman marriage always created a complicated relationship between father-in-law and son-in-law. Women did not legally pass into their husband's family, but stayed closely connected to their birth family, creating tension with public discourses around the harmony of the conjugal couple and the subordination of wife to husband.[47] At the imperial level, as signified by the iconography of coinage among other things, an empress's loyalty to the emperor bolstered his claim to care for the

---

in Gilles (1986), 44–47; images of both in Longo (2009) tav. II 23–24. For Severan women's similar hairstyle on coins, see, for example, Temeryazev, Makarenko (2017) 16.

[44] The last empress to appear on coinage was Magnia Urbica, wife of Carus or Carinus, in 283–84; see Chapter 4.
[45] Delbrueck (1933) 18–19; Bergmann (1977) 184–85; Bergmann (1989); Schade (2003) 58; see, for example, RIC VI Siscia 87 for Maximian's button nose.
[46] Van Dam (2007) 83–84.
[47] Cooper (2007b) 96–114.

state. Yet, in her wedding speech and on her coinage, Fausta was promoted as both a "Maximianic" woman and a wife of another emperor, which, in the increasingly fraught context of the second tetrarchy, could have raised questions about where her loyalty really lay.

Matters soon became even more complex when Constantine and Maximian fell out politically. Following a failed attempt to depose his own son Maxentius in Rome in 308, Maximian returned to his son-in-law in Gaul. Not much later, after he had been forced to abdicate for a second time by the imperial college at a conference held at Carnuntum on the Danube in November 308, Maximian attempted to also oust Constantine. While residing in Arles, Constantine's favored base when in southern Gaul, he tried to take control of the treasury and parts of the army while Constantine was away campaigning on the Rhine. The plan was soon thwarted and Maximian committed suicide in July 310.[48]

When he wrote about these events a few years leater, Lactantius inserted a remarkable element into his story. He claimed Constantine had at first spared Maximian, but the old emperor soon tried his hand at treachery again. He attempted to persuade his daughter Fausta to assist him in an assassination plot against Constantine. She was to leave the door to their bedroom open and lightly guarded, so Maximian could kill Constantine in his sleep. Lactantius describes Fausta as a young impressionable girl on whom Maximian worked with flattery and promises of a new, more suitable husband. It is true that Fausta was still a teenager, but this portrait of her was designed more to allow Lactantius to underscore the shock of what came next: Fausta decided to put her allegiance to her husband over that to her father, and told Constantine of the plan "straight away" (*protinus*). On the night in question, Constantine placed a eunuch in his bed and succeeded in catching Maximian red-handed. Constantine then gave him the choice of suicide or execution.[49]

Fausta's role in the unraveling of Maximian's final conspiracy is also mentioned by other authors, and there may therefore be some truth to it.[50] Still, Lactantius' unique framing of the story around decisions of what was to happen in the imperial couple's bedroom, and Fausta's subordination to her husband rather than her father in this regard, marks this as an attempt to show that Fausta had truly become a "Constantinian" woman.[51] It was following

---

[48] Harries (2012) for some background.
[49] Lactantius, De mortibus pers. 30; see Rougé (1980) 9 on what the story tells us about Fausta's age.
[50] Jerome, Chron. 308 (sic), Eutropius, Brev. 10.3; Zosimus, Hist. nea 2.11; John of Antioch frg. 195.
[51] On the bedroom (*cubiculum*) as a site of authority struggles in Roman literature, see Sessa (2007). On the story's meaning, also James (2013) 107.

Maximian's downfall that Constantine also began to put out tales of his father Constantius' descent from the emperor Claudius Gothicus, thereby creating a separate line of imperial inheritance that bypassed Constantius' relationship with Maximian.[52] It is not inconceivable that the story of how Theodora, Constantius' wife, was merely Maximian's "stepdaughter" also began circulating around this time. This possibly also arose in response to Maxentius, who was still ruling in Rome, promoting Constantius as his "brother-in-law" (*adfinis, cognatus*) and divine ancestor around this time. Such appropriations equally necessitated creating stricter boundaries between the Constantinian and Maximianic family groups.[53] Maximianic women, whatever their noses looked like, were slowly streamlined into a purer Constantinian dynasty.

Pruning the Tree

All of these issues were important in 310, when the stories of Fausta's betrayal and possibly of Theodora's stepdaughter status were put into circulation. They continued to be so also at the time of Lactantius' writing in 313–316, for Constantine had meanwhile wiped out Fausta's and Theodora's brother, Maxentius, too. In the spring of 312, the man Galerius had chosen to replace Severus as Augustus of the West, another long-standing army comrade called Licinius, was marching against Maxentius from the East to claim his territory. Constantine realized that if Licinius took Italy, he would have a greater rival for rule in the West on his hands than Maxentius presented. Overtaking Licinius and occupying Italy for himself became Constantine's key concern. This meant also attacking and defeating his brother-in-law and step-uncle, who was holed up in Rome. Constantine did so at the battle of the Milvian Bridge just outside Rome on October 28, 312. It was on the eve of this battle that he allegedly had the fateful vision of a cross-shaped sign in the sky that ushered in his conversion to Christianity.[54]

With his victory over Maxentius, Constantine took Rome, a city of great symbolic significance, in both traditional Roman and in emerging Christian terms. But it was also, as we have seen, a city that had for nearly twenty years

---

[52] Potter (2013) 125–26 (the Claudius connection is mentioned in Panegyrici Latini 6.2.1–4, delivered in 310).

[53] On this promotion, see Corcoran (2017) 64; Hekster (2015) 295.

[54] Barnes (2014) 74–83, with a bibliography. The vision had possibly already taken place much earlier.

been intimately connected to the Maximianic dynasty he had just eliminated. The last years of Maxentius' reign had witnessed an ambitious building program in Rome that advertised Maxentius as protector of the Roman people and the city's glorious, even mythical past. Constantine moved swiftly to appropriate this material legacy for his own purposes, condemning the memory of the "tyrant" Maxentius and setting himself up as the "liberator" of Rome, while combining this with the promotion of his new divine allegiance.[55]

Still, Constantine had to tread more carefully around the memory of Maximian, a legitimate emperor, whose close connections with and promotion of the Roman senatorial aristocracy had facilitated the rise of Maxentius in the first place. What is more, a number of Roman noble families whose members all had held public offices under Maximian or Maxentius were or were about to be tied to the old emperor by marriage. These arrangements involved three of Theodora's children, Constantine's half-siblings. Her eldest son Julius Constantius, born around 290, married Galla, a member of the Naeratii family, while her daughters Anastasia and Eutropia the Younger married into the Nummii and Virii Nepotiani families, respectively. These unions are difficult to date. Anastasia's marriage took place before 315, while Julius Constantius and Galla had a daughter of marriageable age in 335, who must therefore have been born before 323. The unions for his underage grandchildren may have already been planned by Maximian himself in the years following Constantius' death. Alternatively, they could have been orchestrated by Constantine to build his own ties to the senatorial aristocracy after victory over Maxentius, as he knew he needed this group to run matters in Italy and North Africa at least.[56] Either way, they turned Maximian and the Maximianic women who for some time had dwelled in their midst into the kin of Roman noble families. We can expect these families, and their networks, to have been watching attentively how the new and unfamiliar emperor dealt with this fact.

Constantine's response, predictably, was to rewrite family history by simultaneously excluding some of his Maximianic kin while co-opting others.[57] Maxentius' mother, Eutropia, apparently still living in Rome, had to declare publicly that Maxentius was the son not of Maximian, but of "a

---

[55] Curran (2000) 76–90. See also Chapter 6.
[56] Hillner (2017a) 79. On Anastasia, see also Chapters 5 and 7; Julius Constantius and Galla's daughter married Constantine's son Constantius in 335, PLRE I Anonyma 1, 1037. On the birthdate of Julius Constantius, see Barnes (2014) 4, although he thinks Julius Constantius was Theodora's second eldest son.
[57] Van Dam (2011) 249–50.

Syrian."[58] It is unlikely that she had any choice in the matter, although it is notable that Constantine let her live, probably because she was also the mother of his wife. Her startling admission of adultery did not prevent Eutropia from continuing to reside at Constantine's court. But it made her dependent on the emperor's mercy in the face of apparently blatant criminality and severed the links between the disgraced Maxentius and Maximian. At the same time, it enhanced Constantine's own relationship to Maximian, as he was married to his and Eutropia's daughter, who, with Theodora's stepdaughterhood also established, was now the only carrier of his dynastic potential. This became particularly important once Fausta had children, from 316 on. By 318, the old Augustus was not only rehabilitated, but even hailed as a divine ancestor of the Constantinian house in 318, alongside Constantius and Claudius Gothicus.[59] Finally, Constantine even contemplated elevating Bassianus, a scion of Maximian's old allies, the Nummii family, and the senatorial husband of Maximian's granddaughter, Constantine's half-sister Anastasia, as his Caesar.[60] The survival and reasonable treatment of all these various Maximianic women are all the more striking when we consider that Constantine hunted down and killed Maxentius' wife Valeria Maximilla and her small younger son, and mutilated her portraits. Maximilla, who was also the daughter of Galerius, held no dynastic value for Constantine and was, therefore, disposable.[61]

At the same time, attempts to prune Constantine's jumbled family tree into a tidier shape also continued. Both in North Africa and Italy, former Maximianic territories, Constantine instituted colleges of priests for the cult of his family, the *gens Flavia*, presented as descended from Claudius Gothicus.[62] It is with this context in mind that we need to return to the paintings in the imperial residence in the Lateran area of Rome with which we began this chapter. If their interpretations are correct, these show an idealized ceremonial procession of the Constantinian family into which Theodora

---

[58] Origo Const. 1.4. See also the cryptic statement in Epitome de Caesaribus 40.3 that Maxentius was "substituted through female cunning" (*suppositum arte muliebri*); Panegyrici Latini 12.4.3: a "changeling" (*suppositus*).

[59] See Barnes (1982) 35 on Constantine declaring Maximian divine.

[60] See further discussion in Chapter 5.

[61] The knowledge of a panegyrist in 313 that Maxentius had moved his wife and son from a palace to a private house (*domus privata*; Panegyrici Latini 12.16.5) shortly before battle suggests Constantine had found and killed her. On the mutilation of Maximilla's portraits, see Varner (2001) 56. The head is now in the Musei Capitolini, Magazzino, inv. 1063. On Maximilla PLRE I, Valeria Maximilla 2, 576.

[62] Aurelius Victor, Caes. 40.15 and ILS 705.

and Fausta were inserted as Constantinian wives. What is more, the procession was headed by Constantius and Theodora, holding, respectively, a statuette resembling *pietas* (family loyalty) and, like the goddess Juno on Fausta's wedding coins, a libation bowl. This procession was, therefore, a ritual domestic occasion presided over by a Constantinian *paterfamilias* to whom not just the men, but also the women were subordinated, in a domestic space that may have still belonged to Maxentius until recently. It erased these women's Maximianic past.[63] Of course, this was the imperial family, so there were general lessons emanating from the walls of this corridor about the connection between domestic propriety and the welfare of the empire. But lessons were also to be learned close at hand, in the grand residences of Rome's aristocratic families, many of which were situated on the Caelian hill stretching west and north from the Lateran toward the center of the city. Some of these neighbors may have visited the residence and its ceremonial hallways, while others would have heard about their iconography. News about the magnificent decorations of imperial houses traveled far and their dynastic messages were suitably conveyed by court orators, as we have seen in the case of Fausta's betrothal scene in the palace of Aquileia. For the eyes and ears of audiences in Rome and beyond, the sprawling female branches of the Western tetrarchy were also being pruned back to a more Constantinian family tree.

Waiting in the Wings, Becoming Christian?

During the early years of his reign, Constantine, as yet lacking any legitimate heirs, hence probed a dynastic experiment that focused on his stepfamily and his in-laws, simultaneously chasing away male Maximianic connections while trying to profit from female ones. In all of this, Helena, an outsider to these networks, was nowhere to be seen. Nonetheless, as we will see later, the dynamics engendered by the existence and representation of Theodora and Fausta would affect not only how Constantine presented his mother to the world, but also where he did so.

This is not to say that Constantine was out of contact with his mother during this period. There is little evidence, however, that she was already by

---

[63] The original excavator of the site, Valnea Maria Scrinari (1991), identified the house with the *domus Faustae* mentioned in Optatus, Against the Donatists 1.22–24, and above in this chapter. This identity is unlikely.

his side then, either in Trier or in Rome, as some have imagined.[64] The only and very indirect evidence about Helena's life during her long absence from the historical record derives not from the West, but puts her back to where she began, on the shores of the gulf of Nicomedia.

Here, Helena may have witnessed a martyrdom. As we have already seen, in the fifth century, it was reported that Helena had venerated Lucian of Antioch, whose relics were kept in Drepanon. Lucian was a Christian priest who came originally from Samosata on the Euphrates. He had led an enormously successful school in Antioch where he taught theology and the interpretation of scripture and edited a famous recension of the Greek bible. According to Eusebius of Caesarea writing not long afterward, he was apprehended in Antioch and brought to Nicomedia, where he defended himself for his faith in front of Maximinus Daza, to no avail. He died in Nicomedia in January 312, perhaps by public beheading, perhaps from injuries sustained during torture in prison.[65]

Lucian was a late victim of the so-called Great Persecution initiated by Diocletian in the same city of Nicomedia nearly a decade earlier, in February 303. The decision to persecute Christians followed the tetrarchic emperors' renewed emphasis on the relationship between Roman ancestral religion, public expressions of religious loyalty, and the welfare of the state, combined with an anxiety over the growing institutionalization of the church over the previous decades. Four edicts were issued between 303 and 304, targeting church property and services, the legal rights of Christians, the freedom of clerics, and, finally, ordering Christians to sacrifice to the traditional gods, although perhaps only in Rome. Galerius called the persecutions off just before his death in 311, with an edict that reverted to the toleration of all Christians introduced by Gallienus in 260. But his nephew and successor in the East, Maximinus, renewed repression, including and especially in the city of Nicomedia that he had occupied after Galerius' death. It was this final spasm of the pagan Roman empire that led to Lucian of Antioch's demise.[66]

Historians have long wondered what the connection between Helena and Lucian could have been, assuming the story of her veneration for the

---

[64] Rome: for example, Drijvers (1992b) 30–34; Barnes (2014) 42. Historians have also speculated that Constantius brought Helena to Trier [see, e.g., Klein (1988) 356], but her presence in the Gallic city, well attested in medieval sources, is an invention of tradition in the ninth century. See Drijvers (2011) 134–35 and the introduction to this book.

[65] Eusebius, Hist. eccl. 8.13.2 and 9.6.3; Philostorgius, Hist. eccl. 2.12–14; Vita Luciani 20. See Slusser (2003). See also Chapter 1.

[66] Potter (2014) 329–32, 346–47, 357–58.

Christian professor was not a later invention. Such an invention would, however, have been curious—and dangerous—for Lucian's memory subsequently acquired an aura of heresy, as he had been the teacher of several opponents to the Council of Nicaea in 325.[67] It is therefore more likely to be true. Had Helena heard Lucian preach or in some way witnessed his death? Or, was she simply fascinated, much later, that the body of a famous martyr had been brought to Drepanon, as this was her place of origin?[68] We cannot be sure, but if it was the former, her acquaintance with Lucian must have occurred in Nicomedia in the autumn of 311, since it is unlikely that Helena had somehow ended up in Antioch after her separation from Constantius.[69] It is more plausible that she had returned to her home region around Nicomedia, a city where, at times, her son resided during his stint at Diocletian's court. While Constantine returned to the West in 305, the Lucian story could suggest that his mother may have stayed there a lot longer, at a time when the Eastern tetrarchs were becoming increasingly hostile to Constantine.[70]

The Lucian story also raises the question of the origins of Helena's Christian faith. Eusebius tells us she was converted by Constantine, which following his narrative must have been after 312.[71] Some fifth-century church historians, however, claim Helena was a Christian before Constantine. Both versions affirm that Helena had at some point been a pagan, but none of these authors had direct knowledge of Helena's spiritual journey. In both cases, their interest lay in Constantine, not Helena, whether to illuminate how the faith radiated from the emperor or to claim, improbably, that his Christian roots reached back into his childhood. If the name of Constantine's sister Anastasia, referencing the resurrection, is anything to go by, it may be an indication that Constantius, at least, had Christian sympathies at the time of this girl's birth. But while it has sometimes been argued that Anastasia was Helena's daughter, she is far more likely to be Theodora's, which in turn opens up an entirely new set of questions about the religiosity of Helena's successor in Constantius' affections.[72]

---

[67] On Lucian's disciples, see Chapter 7.
[68] Barnes (1981) 194 suggests Helena had heard Lucian preach (but not that she witnessed his death as he imagines Helena with Constantine in 311); Pohlsander (1995) 4 argues that her interest stemmed from his relics in Drepanon.
[69] For the date of Lucian's martyrdom, see Barnes (2004).
[70] For the return of abandoned women to their birth families, see Huebner (2013) 78. On Constantine in Nicomedia, see above in his chapter.
[71] Eusebius, Vita Constantini 47.2: οὕτω μὲν αὐτὴν θεοσεβῆ καταστήσαντα οὐκ οὖσαν πρότερον.
[72] Theodoret, Hist. eccl. 1.18.1: Helena brought Constantine the "nurture" (τροφήν) of piety; see also Ps.-Gelasius of Cyzikus, Hist. eccl. 3.6.1; and for the West: Fredegar, Chron. 2.42. Malalas, Chron. 13.2 claims Constantine and Helena embraced Christianity simultaneously, influenced by

It would be attractive to imagine that Helena became a Christian because she witnessed a martyrdom, especially of a man who was also known as having had female admirers, passionate enough to be prepared even to die with him.[73] Yet, the relationship between persecution and conversion in early Christianity was complex. It would be naïve to think that in a world as structurally violent as that of the Romans, discrimination against Christians, or their repression and execution, shocked onlookers into sympathy or even admiration by default. Still, the Roman spectacle of death was designed to instill a privileged in-group with a sense of entitlement, which could be shattered if those dying in front of them had only recently been members of the spectators' in-group themselves.[74] In the early fourth century, Christian communities undoubtedly comprised men and women who, like Lucian, were regarded as respectable citizens in other circumstances. This made the injuries inflicted upon them troubling and outrageous, as authors like Eusebius of Caesarea did not cease to emphasize.

Nonetheless, rather than the deaths themselves, it was the constant telling and retelling of such martyr stories (a process that also inflated the numbers of those actually persecuted) that played a bigger role in engaging people with Christianity. So did the growing presence of Christian communities in cities. It is entirely possible that Helena, wherever she lived, was drawn into the emerging pastoral care of ecclesiastical institutions, like other abandoned women of the time.[75] Few late antique Christians had a conversion "moment" as Constantine perhaps did, and most grew gradually into a new faith.[76] Helena's mobility in her early life must have brought her into contact with thriving Christian communities, as we have seen earlier, for example, in a city like Salona, which unsurprisingly also became a locus of martyr stories from the "Great Persecution."[77] Such personal experiences may have then

---

the Actus Silvestri; on this point, see Chapter 11. See Drijvers (1992a) 35–36, who also discusses and rightly dismisses the theory that Helena was originally Jewish. I will not repeat this antisemitic scholarly tradition here. On Anastasia, see Potter (2013) 63–64 who finds it unlikely that her name was given to Anastasia at birth. For the argument that Anastasia was Helena's daughter, see Chapter 2.

[73] Vita Luciani 9–10.
[74] See also Potter (1993) about Roman authorities' fears of such effects.
[75] Bremmer (1999), although note that the women mentioned in early Christian texts are generally widows who had been legally married, perhaps a requirement for such charity.
[76] On the "constructed" nature of conversion moments, and the role of teaching, preaching, storytelling, and practice in early Christian conversions, see Papaconstantinou (2015). Attempts to track numbers of and patterns for conversion in the first three centuries have been largely unsatisfactory, mainly due to the artificial nature of conversion stories.
[77] On Salona's martyrs, Yasin (2012) 69–72.

been reinforced through events or stories Helena heard at Nicomedia, where Christian influence may have even reached into the imperial household before being severely repressed through the destruction of life, livelihoods, and buildings.[78] Given that mother and son lived apart for long periods of time, it is all the more likely that Helena's Christianity developed at first independently from Constantine's. We cannot know what being a Christian meant to her, but we should note that it is unclear whether Helena was ever baptized, even on her deathbed.[79]

It was, of course, Constantine who, after defeating Maxentius in the autumn of 312, ostentatiously, publicly, and forcefully embraced Christianity, albeit equally remaining unbaptized. He used his first winter in Rome to legislate in favor of Christian clergy and to lay the groundwork for the Christian basilicas that would eventually encircle the city like a protective shield.[80] For now, Helena still remained in the shadows. It would be almost another six years until she publicly reappeared. In anticipating that moment, we need to keep our attention on the East, where, following the abdication of 305, a new generation of Eastern tetrarchs had also been busy shaping the image of imperial women. They did so in ways that would create headaches and opportunities for Constantine in equal measures and would deeply determine Helena's appearance.

---

[78] On Christian Nicomedia, Belke (2020) 842–43.
[79] On Helena's potential deathbed baptism, see Chapter 9. For more about the unreliable fifth-century Actus Silvestri's claim that Helena was baptized in Rome, see Chapter 11.
[80] Barnes (2014) 84–85. On the Roman basilicas Chapter 6.

4
The Necklace Affair

Not long after Constantine took Rome, a reception hall in Trier was also decorated with impressive paintings.[1] Like the painted corridor in Rome, the hall opened up to a garden and is usually thought to have formed part of an elevated and conspicuous space within Trier's imperial palace. Situated under the crossing of today's cathedral, the earliest incarnation of which terminated its use in 335, the hall featured frescoed walls and a coffered ceiling (Fig. 4.1). Fifteen panels of this ceiling, framed by red and green borders and ornamental golden ribbons, are extant. Among depictions of cupids and bearded men, four panels, including the central one, display the busts of women, although the female gender of one of them is difficult to determine with certainty. Each woman's head, painted in vivid, plastic style, is surrounded by a halo (circle of light). They all hold different objects, a jewelry box with a pearl necklace, a mirror, a drinking cup (*kantharos*), and, in the case of the less clearly gendered one, a flute. While the latter also wears a few ornaments, especially bracelets, and seems to be dressed in a purple mantle, the other three women are veiled and richly bejeweled.

The orator at the Trier court in 307 who evoked Fausta and Constantine's painted portraits at Aquileia amply confirms the role of paintings in imperial self-representation.[2] The four female figures have consequently often been identified as women of the Constantinian family, especially due to their haloes, conventionally an imperial or divine attribute, and the purple of their clothes or veils. But suggestions as to their specific identities have differed. The lady in the central panel, for example, has been named both as Helena and as Fausta, Constantine's wife (see cover image).

---

[1] Coin findings date this structure to between 315 and 332; Kempf (1977) 155. Panels of the ceiling, reconstructed from many thousand plaster fragments between 1946 and 1993, are now in the Bischöfliche Dom- and Diözesanmuseum Trier. The original excavations were published in Kempf (1950).

[2] See Chapter 3, also McFadden (2013) 98 on other examples of and textual references to painted imperial spaces in late antiquity. See also Merobaudes, Carm. 1.5–6, with Clover (1971) 11, 17 for a fifth-century reference to a painted ceiling at the palace in Ravenna that showed the emperor and his wife in the center.

Helena Augusta. Julia Hillner, Oxford University Press. © Oxford University Press 2023.
DOI: 10.1093/oso/9780190875299.003.0005

Fig. 4.1 Konstantinische Deckenmalerei (painted Trier ceiling), © Rudolf Schneider, Museum am Dom Trier.

The interpretation of the paintings as portraits has also been questioned. This is partly due to the ladies' informal, sometimes even coquettish appearance. According to an alternative reading, the women, accompanied by the philosopher-style men, are allegorical embodiments of virtues or personifications of elements of ancient education (*paideia*), of the honorable use of wealth, and, symbolized by the women's veils, of domestic harmony. Some of these readings also query whether the hall was an imperial space at all, rather than part of the house of a provincial or imperial aristocrat who was keen to display his culture.[3] There is, however, a consensus that the central image, of the woman with the *kantharos*, has a special place in the composition, as her appearance significantly disturbs the ceiling's gender symmetry. She is the only one who is presented frontally, and with a diagonally folded *palla* (mantle). Her gestures are less informal than those of the others, with the lifting of her veil signifying "chastity" (*pudicitia*). She is also the only one who wears a contemporary imperial hairstyle, the so-called

---

[3] Interpretation as portraits, for example, Alföldi (1955); Alföldi (1959–1960); Kempf (1978) 4–6. Interpretations as allegories: Brandenburg (1985); Rose (2006). The allegorical interpretations could also apply in an imperial space, of course.

spherical hairstyle, with small ripples framing the face and the rest of the hair bundled at the neck, pulled up and then tucked down under a headband from the back. This woman has therefore been variously explained as both an imperial portrait and an epitome of Youth (*Iuventas*) or Welfare (*Salus*).[4]

The questions of whether the images are imperial portraits or allegories, and whether they were installed in an imperial or an aristocratic context, should therefore not distract from the painters' adaptions of current female imperial fashion to shape their subjects' appearance.[5] Such adaptations suggest that local artists were well aware of imperial sartorial styles, jewelry, and trends in coiffure, which is not surprising given the presence of an imperial court in Trier. This also means that the Constantinian women resident in the city may have appeared to some of its inhabitants or visitors in similar outfits, perhaps even in this very hall. The outfits themselves thus deserve closer scrutiny, especially so since some of their elements decidedly mirror what we now know about the attire of Eastern tetrarchic imperial women. The ceiling in Trier hence provides us with a first glimpse of the connection between late tetrarchic and Constantinian representations of women, which, as we shall see, would profoundly shape Helena's public image. To understand this connection more accurately, we need to return to the material culture of the Danubian provinces, where not only Constantine hailed from, but also the majority of his tetrarchic rivals, their women, and, most crucially, their mothers.

The Tomb at Šarkamen

In the autumn of 1996, a team of archaeologists from the University of Belgrade discovered the site of an imperial villa near the village of Šarkamen.[6] It had been known for some time that Roman remains from the tetrarchic period were situated in this area of eastern Serbia, part of the former Roman province of Dacia Ripensis. This was not least because fragments of a deliberately destroyed porphyry statue representing a seated emperor, which resembled other tetrarchic sculpture, had been found here two decades earlier.

---

[4] Simon (1986) 39–46, also Weber (2000), 37–42 for a survey of the different positions. For the hairstyle, see Weber Della Croce (2016) 1510. For imperial female hairstyles, see also Chapter 5.
[5] Weber (2000) 41–42; James (2001) 37.
[6] Popović, Tomović (2005); Tomović (2009).

The team from Belgrade now showed that these archaeological remains did not belong to a military fortification, as had been believed, but to a monumental fortified residential complex that was the twin of emperor Galerius' rural palace Felix Romuliana at Gamzigrad, only 40 kilometers away (see Map 2). Both imperial residences had been built by the same craftsmen and were abruptly abandoned in 311, with the one at Šarkamen left unfinished.

At the top of a slope a short distance west of the fortified complex stood a mausoleum, which overlooked the site from a small plateau. Underneath the plateau a burial pit had been cut into the mountain, containing ashes and human bones gathered from a funerary pyre. The mausoleum, originally completely sealed from the outside, had at some point been plundered. Even so, at one side of the burial pit, in a small niche, the excavators made a spectacular find of something the tomb raiders had overlooked: a collection of a woman's golden jewelry, consisting of twenty-nine pieces, including earrings, finger rings, fasteners for hair braids, a pendant, and three necklaces. They had doubtlessly belonged to the woman who had been buried here and were only part of a larger ensemble, the majority of which was robbed. Nine gold foil plaques complemented the find; some of them folded, others crumpled up. Several of them bear imprints of coins with the portraits of Diocletian and Constantius. Still bearing traces of soot, these grave goods had clearly played a sacral role in the funerary ritual.

The proximity to and the striking architectural similarity with Felix Romuliana suggest the imperial villa at Šarkamen belonged to the tetrarch Maximinus Daza, Galerius' nephew, who, like his uncle, hailed from this region. After Galerius' death in 311, Maximinus became preoccupied with a protracted civil war against his co-emperor, Licinius, who took over the Balkans, including this region, and eventually defeated Maximinus in 313. This explains the desertion of the site at Šarkamen after 311.

Given its environment and the nature of the grave goods, the mausoleum must have housed one of Maximinus' deceased female relatives. When the site was abandoned, Maximinus' wife and daughter were still alive, as we shall see. It is therefore most likely that the mausoleum contained the remains of Maximinus' mother, just as a mausoleum at Felix Romuliana had been erected for Galerius' mother, Romula. In fact, Maximinus' mother was Galerius' sister and, therefore, Romula's own daughter (see Family Tree).[7]

---

[7] Srejović, Tomović, Vasić (1996) 231–43; Popović (1998) 287–312; Vasić, Tomović (2005), 257–305; Tomović (2009) 463–66; Johnson (2009) 82–86. On Galerius and Maximinus' mothers PLRE I, Romula, 770; Anonyma 24. Maximinus' wife and daughter are not listed in PLRE.

84　OFF STAGE (C. 289–C. 317)

The evidence from both Šarkamen and Felix Romuliana reflects the imperial dynasty building carried on by and around Galerius, originally Diocletian's Caesar. Galerius was also Diocletian's son-in-law, having married his daughter Valeria. As we have seen, after Diocletian and Maximian's abdication in 305, he became Augustus, ruling the East with his nephew Maximinus as his Caesar, while Constantius reigned as Augustus in the West. Although again much of the evidence is obscured by later Constantinian literature, it is clear that Galerius capitalized on his special connection to Diocletian from relatively early on. He promoted himself and his own family, while staying faithful to an idea of a fourfold imperial college that also included men external to his kinship group.

The women around Galerius—his mother Romula, his unnamed sister, his daughter Valeria Maximilla (married to Maxentius), his mother-in-law Prisca, and his wife Valeria—played a crucial role in creating imperial links through which Galerius would seek to exert influence among this college, albeit in a somewhat haphazard way.[8] This is clear, above all, from the account of Lactantius in his *On the Deaths of the Persecutors*, whose principal villains are Galerius and his nephew. A remarkably large number of imperial women appear in this work, most of whom are connected to Galerius.[9] In writing a polemical and providential piece of Christian writing, Lactantius used female characters and their actions mostly to provide a moral comment on the character and behavior of imperial men. But he did not invent these women. He recorded their names and the places in which they operated, with many details on aspects of their lives and deaths. Lactantius had lived in some of these places at the same time and was writing in the East *c.* 315–316. Before 303, he had been employed as a panegyrist at Diocletian's court in Nicomedia, so he knew some of these women personally. Their details were also still verifiable at the time he wrote, just a few years after the events, so while embellished, they could hardly have been entirely fabricated.[10] These women were clearly remembered after their deaths, which is not surprising, because, as the tetrarchy multiplied their imperial residences, many inhabitants of the Roman empire experienced living in proximity to

---

[8] See Corcoran (2012).

[9] Imperial women appear either directly or indirectly in Lactantius, De mortibus pers. 7, 9, 11, 15, 18, 27, 30, 35, 39–41, 43, 45, 47, 50–51. On Lactantius' purpose and why it means reading his passages on women with caution, see James (2013) 104–5.

[10] On Lactantius' time and place of writing and familiarity with Diocletian's court, Barnes (2014) 176–78.

imperial women for the first time, too. Such memorability of these women was precisely what made them useful for Lactantius' purposes.

The visibility of these women was also due to their increasing public representation, especially toward the end of Galerius' reign. Amidst the disintegration of the tetrarchy, Galerius rediscovered the ceremonial value of his women, just as Maximian and Constantine did in the West around the same time, as we saw in the last chapter. The finds at Šarkamen reflect this value. What remained of the grave goods of Maximinus' mother were locally made adornments, not all of the highest quality. Some featured inlays made of glass paste, for example, instead of precious stones. Some object types, such as the hair fasteners, have otherwise only been found in non-Roman burial contexts (Fig. 4.2). All of this is not surprising. Based on what we know of Galerius' family, his sister came from this border region and was not from a high social background. We also have to take into account that other, more precious pieces of her jewelry did not survive. The collection also displays the same empire-wide changes in decorative tastes, especially through Eastern Mediterranean influences, that are observable in many places from the later third century. These include a predilection for polychromy and for intricate ornamental metalwork. Among such objects is a remarkable piece that

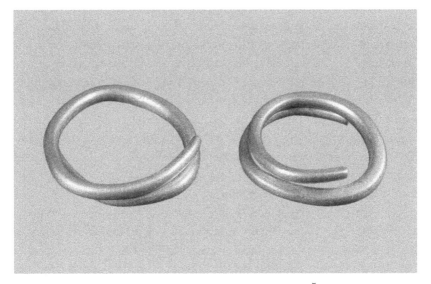

Fig. 4.2 Golden hair fasteners; found in the mausoleum at Šarkamen. From the collection of the Krajina Museum, currently on long-term loan to National Museum Belgrade. © National Museum Belgrade.

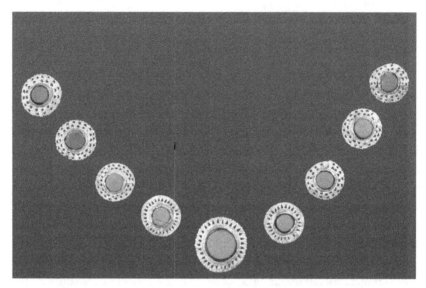

Fig. 4.3 Polychrome necklace with nine medallions; found in the mausoleum at Šarkamen. From the collection of the Krajina Museum, currently on long-term loan to National Museum Belgrade. © National Museum Belgrade.

does not follow previous local goldsmithing repertoires: a necklace created by nine large medallions with filigree gold frames around circular pieces made of blue glass in imitation of two-layered opal (nicolo) (Fig. 4.3).[11] This necklace is an exact likeness of the necklaces depicted on the collar of the Constantinian women of the ceiling in Trier, especially the one in the central panel (Fig. 4.1 and cover image). We know that goldsmiths from an imperial workshop in nearby Naissus, the likely place where Maximinus Daza's mother's jewelry was produced, worked for Constantine after he had taken over his hometown from Licinius in 317. They could well have created similar necklaces for his women, or craftsmen closer to the emperor could have done so after an exchange of prototypes with the workshop at Naissus, a connection clearly attested for other items, such as gold rings.[12]

As we shall see, similar necklaces are also portrayed around the necks of other imperial women in the East during this period of the tetrarchy. Together with the facts that the jewelry belonging to Maximinus' mother had played a performative role in a ceremonial cremation, and that her and

[11] Popović (2013a) 188–95.
[12] Popović (1998) 304; (2013b) 171.

Romula's bodies were buried in monumental, commemorative tombs, this indicates that Galerius and Maximinus were developing a public persona for their female relatives.[13] We will trace this process that established the latter years of the 310s as a formative period for the subsequent representation of Constantinian women. A few years later, when Constantine took over the Eastern part of the empire and began displaying his female relatives, including Helena, he very much responded to these developments.

Divine Mothers

All the men who considered themselves to be emperors during the period of the tetrarchy were born into relative obscurity. This is true even for Constantine and Maxentius, who were sons of emperors, but not "born into the purple." Their fathers were still mere soldiers at the time of their respective births. Diocletian was said to have been the son of a scribe, even a freedman, from Dalmatia, Maximian of shopkeepers near Sirmium, Licinius of peasants in Dacia. Galerius and Maximinus allegedly started out as cattle shepherds in Dacia Ripensis. Severus was of low birth (*ignobilis*) from Illyria.[14] Admittedly, the information we can glean about these men from late antique sources is clouded by polemics, but given their military and regional background, these assertions of their humble origin seem neither unusual nor, therefore, entirely without foundation.

It also then follows that these men's mothers would have been of obscure origins, quite similar to those of Helena. It may even have been the case that their relationships with the fathers of their sons did also not always meet legal or at least elite moral standards of marriage. We know little of these women's lives, and much of what we know is murky. Of Diocletian's mother, it was said that her name was *Dioclea*, the same name as the place in which he was born. Dioclea may be an alternative name for the city of Doclea in southern Dalmatia (today's Dukljia). Since Diocletian's father was reportedly a freedman, his mother may have been born enslaved and, as such, named after her place of origin, as was not uncommon.[15]

---

[13] On the importance of depositing grave goods for the confirmation of the deceased's and their family's social status among the living, see Halsall (1998) 331. On Maximinus' interests in jewelry that he used to outfit his "satellites," see also Lactantius, De mortibus pers. 37.

[14] PLRE I Diocletianus 2 253–54; Licinius 3, 509; Maximianus 8, 573; Maximianus 9 (= Galerius), 574; Maximinus 12, 579; Severus 30, 837.

[15] Epitome de Caesaribus 39.1. Cambi (2004) 38–39.

Among the mothers of the tetrarchs, apart from Helena, only two stand out: Galerius' mother Romula and her daughter, Maximinus Daza's mother. They stand out because Galerius and Maximinus drew attention to them, at least in death. The mausolea at Gamzigrad and Šarkamen drew a sacred landscape over the hills of Dacia Ripensis. The two rural palaces constructed by the emperors here were similar projects to Diocletian's retirement palace at Spalatum (today's Split) outside Salona. The only buildings used—and in Šarkamen's case completed—were the burial sites, however, both constructed to the east of the fortified palaces. Romula's mausoleum at Gamzigrad, on a ridge overlooking the palace, is now situated next to her son's, where he was buried following his death in 311 (Fig. 4.4). It had initially stood alone, having been built during the earliest construction phase of the palace, between 303 and 305. The erection of Maximinus' palace, and his mother's mausoleum, must have begun after he became Caesar in 305, or more likely Augustus in c. 309. Both mausolea were accompanied by their respective funerary mounds nearby, where cremation supplemented by the offering of precious objects had taken place. Some of these had melted in the fire; others,

Fig. 4.4 Mausoleum of Romula at Gamzigrad. © Dragana Ehrismann Mladenović.

like Maximinus' mother's grave goods, were only placed nearby, as was customary for imperial funerary pyres.[16]

The preservation of the funerary pyres, which in both cases formed an architectural unity with the mausolea, strongly suggests that they had been used for the divine consecration of these women.[17] By the time of the tetrarchs, the role of the Senate in granting divine status to deceased emperors or imperial family members was long gone. The tetrarchic emperors were associated with the divine already during their life, and they and their relatives could therefore also be considered divine (*divi*) after death. Nonetheless, ritual cremation to confirm the elevation to divine status of imperial individuals (*apotheosis*) continued.[18] In Maximinus' mother's case, her body was cremated, while in the case of Romula, who may have been inhumed, an effigy would have taken its place.[19] The palace of Felix Romuliana in itself underscored Romula's new divine status, reflected not only in its name, inscribed in its brickwork, but also in decorations found all around the site, including of peacocks that usually accompanied depictions of female imperial apotheosis. A temple built inside the palace area may have been dedicated to her cult, although some evidence also points to the worship of Magna Mater here, a mother goddess venerated all over the Roman world and also strongly associated with Roman imperial women.[20]

The two mausolea and their respective mounds were, moreover, both positioned toward the rising of the stellar constellation of Orion on winter solstice day (December 25 in the calendar of the time). The axis of orientation of the mausoleum in Šarkamen was hence erected on an almost parallel line, 40 kilometers apart, to that of its earlier counterpart at Gamzigrad. The symbolism around this cosmological scheme cannot be fully deciphered. It may reflect beliefs around the soul's salvation concurrent in the worship of the god Mithras, which was followed by some tetrarchs, including Galerius. Mithraism was widespread in the Balkan regions, where it often merged with worship of the Sun (Sol). Women were, however, commonly excluded from this cult. The astronomical orientation of their burial may therefore more

---

[16] On the two mausolea, Johnson (2009) 74–86; on imperial funerary procedure, 11–14. Romula's mausoleum has been robbed. On Gamzigrad, see also Leadbetter (2009) 236–40.

[17] Srejović (1994), 123–41; Johnson (2009) 14.

[18] Johnson (2009) 180–81. On the role of the Senate in granting apotheosis to imperial women, see Price (1987) 87, and on its diminution, 92–93.

[19] Johnson (2009) 80–82.

[20] Srejović (1994) 149–56; Srejović (1995) 302, 304–5. On the peacock, Juno's bird, as soul carrier and symbolic imagery for the apotheosis of empresses, see Gradel (2002) 307–10. On Magna Mater and Roman empresses, Langford (2013) 107.

simply represent the immortality of Romula's and her daughter's souls, for at the time of their burial the winter solstice was commonly regarded as the gate toward the human soul's reunification with the divine. The mausolea's strongly cosmological architectural arrangement, in both cases a rotunda with a domed octagonal upper level, also points in this direction.[21]

Given their locations, Romula's and her daughter's deification would have been visible above all to the rural population of Dacia Ripensis. Both women's lives were intrinsically interwoven with this region. Romula was originally from the larger province of Dacia north of the Danube, which had been part of the Roman empire since the early second century. Around the same time as Gothic raiders swept through Helena's home region in the 250s and 60s, trans-Danubian Dacia suffered incursions by the Carpi, an ethnic group that had previously lived to the east of the Roman province. Undoubtedly in order to escape a similar fate of rape and captivity as that inflicted on some women on the Black Sea area by the Goths, as described in a letter by bishop Gregory of Neocaesarea, Romula took flight and crossed the Danube.[22] Although this was surely a traumatic experience for Romula, her sudden departure was probably less due to a cloak-and-dagger escape and more the result of a military operation moving communities out of this war-torn zone across the river and resettling them in more peaceful territory. Such official internal population movement is rarely documented, but must have been quite frequent in the dying days of Roman Dacia.[23]

Lactantius makes many snide remarks about Galerius' and Maximinus' "barbarian" identity, linking this directly to Romula's origins.[24] In reality, Romula, if she had been born free, was a Roman citizen, as most inhabitants of Dacia had been since the early third century. Whatever her status had been in Dacia, she was resettled among peasants in Dacia Ripensis (at that time, a region still split between Moesia Superior and Inferior, and Thrace), perhaps even in the vicinity of Galerius' later palace at Gamzigrad. Here, she gave birth to at least two children, Galerius and his sister. We hear little about their father other than that he was "of the land" (*agrarius*), so possibly a dependent tenant, a rather oppressed social group. Resettled groups were

---

[21] Mladenović (2009). On imperial mausolea's architectural design and cosmology, see also Johnson (2009) 182.
[22] Lactantius, De mortibus pers. 9.1. On Gregory's letter, see p. 25.
[23] Better documented are the Roman army's frequent involvement in moving and resettling non-Roman groups within the empire: on these, see Halsall (2014). Leadbetter (2009) 18–21 dates Romula's escape to 251–255.
[24] Lactantius, De mortibus pers. 9; 18; 27.

regularly classed among such "humiliores" by our sources.[25] Given that the background of Romula's grandson Maximinus was allegedly also rural before he embarked on his military career, it seems that the family continued to live and intermarry within a peasant community for three generations.

Lactantius does not mention Galerius' father at all. Instead, he concentrates on his mother, dwelling on her devotion to "the gods of the mountains" (*deorum montium cultrix*), another way of suggesting that she, and by proxy Galerius and Maximinus, were somehow less than Roman. Of course, in hailing from the Roman empire's periphery, Romula and her family may well have worshipped indigenous gods and followed local cult practices, as rural folk did all over the Roman empire. The burials under her daughter's funerary mound at Šarkamen reflect an autochthonous tradition, as does the presence of those local-style hair fasteners among her grave goods.[26] More important is the remarkable religious authority that Romula wielded among her community, gained from becoming the resident mother of an emperor. Lactantius describes her organizing cult activities for these mountain gods, including almost daily sacrificial banquets whose sumptuous leftovers were donated to the villagers. These were the people who would be living in the vicinity of her palace, former neighbors now gazing in awe at her new status and, later, at her divine tomb towering over the landscape.[27]

Nonetheless, Galerius ensured his mother's place in his imperial project also became known far beyond his home region. Not only did contemporary and later authors writing elsewhere know her origin and name, but also about her residence, religious activities, and last resting place. They also circulated the story that Galerius was the product of Romula's sexual intercourse with a divine being, "in the fashion of Olympias, the mother of Alexander the Great," who was believed to have conceived the legendary Macedonian leader by coupling with Zeus. The anonymous source of this latter quote, from the end of the fourth century, venomously adds that Olympias was also suspected of having had sex with a snake. In an earlier version of the story that Lactantius transmits, the divine father claimed by Galerius is identified

---

[25] Epitome de Caesaribus 40.15: *ortus parentibus agrariis*. Eutropius, Brev. 9.22.1 reports that Galerius was born "in Dacia not far away from Serdica" (today's Sofia), so further south, although measures of distance in ancient authors are arbitrary. For the social status of the resettled on the Roman frontier, see Whittaker (2004) 212.
[26] Vasić (2007) 85–86 and (2013) 99.
[27] Lactantius, De mortibus pers. 11. Lactantius mentions this to underscore Romula's hatred for the Christians of the region who chose to stay away.

as Mars.[28] This was fitting, given Romula's name, though that name, in fact, testifies more to her Dacian parents' absorption of Roman culture.[29] Even so, it also connected Galerius more directly with the origins of Rome and the imperial regime than did his membership of Diocletian's divine "Iovii" family. Mars was both the father of Rome's founder Romulus and claimed as divine patron by the first Roman emperor, Augustus. It is therefore not impossible that Galerius himself was behind this claim, associating himself with both a Roman founding god and with Alexander the Great through his mother, although perhaps not as explicitly as Lactantius contends.

There is, of course, a conceptual difference between Romula's apotheosis and her supposed sexual intercourse, as a mortal, with a god. Galerius' divine filiation and Romula's divine status were chronologically distinct claims, and at least at first they were broadcast to different audiences, respectively, global and local. The story of divine filiation, not incompatible with tetrarchic self-representation, seems to have originated earlier, after Galerius' victory against the Persians in 298.[30] It was meant primarily for the consumption of an empire-wide audience, not the least because the community at Felix Romuliana knew his real father. Indeed, Lactantius sarcastically remarked that by telling this story, Galerius had damaged his mother's sexual reputation.[31] As for Romula's apotheosis, Galerius may not have celebrated it beyond his local community and his home region, at least not at first. When she died, around 303–304, Galerius was still Caesar and imperial women were still sidelined in order to highlight the divinely associated brotherhood between the tetrarchs. Galerius never minted consecration coins for Romula, although this is not unusual. Dead female relatives very rarely appeared on imperial coinage and had not appeared on provincial coinage since the second century.[32] Still, the two traditions of divine affiliation and maternal apotheosis at some point converged, at the very latest at the time when Galerius chose to be buried and consecrated next to his mother at Felix Romuliana. They proved so powerful that his nephew Maximinus soon adopted a similar

---

[28] Epitome de Caesaribus 40.17: *more Olympiadis, Alexandri Magni creatricis*; at 16, he also mentions Felix Romuliana and that it was named after Romula. Lactantius, De mortibus pers. 9. For Olympias and Zeus: Plutarch, Life of Alexander, 2–3. Olympias was also known as being fond of the snake worship associated with the cult of Dionysus.

[29] The capital of Dacia Malvensis, a Roman colony, was called Romula.

[30] For a similar chronology, Srejović (1995) 299–300.

[31] Lactantius, De mortibus pers. 9: *maluitque Romulam matrem stupro infamare*. On Mars as imperial ancestor, see Hekster (2015) 261–66. Note that the palace of Felix Romuliana was decorated with images of semi-divine sons of mortal mothers: Srejović (1994) 153; (1995) 303.

[32] Hekster (2015) 136–38.

strategy, capitalizing on his connection to Romula and Galerius. He was less successful, however, as he lacked the time to broadcast his mother's apotheosis more widely. As a result, we do not even know her name.

Romula, however, gained a notoriety that could be exploited by writers like Lactantius, for whom she became a convenient rhetorical device to explain Galerius' hatred of Christians. Describing the "womanly complaints" with which she "incited" her son against the Christians, he turned her into the inspiration behind the so-called Great Persecution of Christians that began on February 23, 303, when Diocletian ordered the church at Nicomedia to be destroyed. Neither Romula nor perhaps even Galerius was behind this, but the passage shows that she was familiar enough to Lactantius' audience to be used to embody the time-honored trope of the irrational woman as the source of evil.[33]

This conventional appearance of Romula in our textual tradition should not mask that the ways in which Galerius and Maximinus made use of their mothers was nothing short of extraordinary. Of course, the celebration of motherhood was an important element of Roman imperial ideology, as it was in Roman society generally. In epigraphy and iconography, Roman imperial women were regularly associated with mother goddesses, if to varying degree. They were praised for their matronal qualities of piety, fertility, and chastity, as well as, of course, their actual motherhood of heirs. They were at times styled as maternal protectors of the army, the people of Rome, the Senate, or even the empire.[34] Emperors had also deified imperial women before.

Among the women revered either by titles and epithets or through apotheosis, however, we rarely see mothers of emperors who had not also themselves been the wife or at least a relative of an emperor. This is striking, because due to the lack of heredity in imperial succession and the biological difficulties of raising male heirs, many emperors, especially in the second and third centuries, had mothers from outside the imperial sphere. They may have paid them respects, and, when of noble background, these women often played a role in the aristocratic society of Rome. But they usually remained unacknowledged

---

[33] Lactantius, De mortibus pers. 11.2: *filium suum non minus superstitiosum querelis muliebribus ad tollendos homines incitavit*. On Romula's non-role in this matter, Leadbetter (2009) 130–31. On the female influencer, especially in Christian literature, Cooper (1992). On the persecution, see Chapter 3.

[34] Langford (2013) 73–75, 106–7, who notes the "megalomania" of such connotations under Septimius Severus. Also Angelova (2015) 83–84.

at the imperial level.³⁵ Emperors before Galerius who had not been born to previous emperors commonly celebrated their horizontal or descending female relations, above all imperial wives (who may have become mothers), but also sisters, daughters, and nieces, rather than non-imperial female ancestors. If their female relatives' past was non-imperial, emperors looked toward the present, in the sense of making dynastic alliances, and the future, in the sense of producing heirs. The only exceptions were Julia Soaemias, the mother of Elagabalus; Julia Mamaea, the mother of Severus Alexander; and their mother Julia Maesa, who after 224 became one of the last women before Romula to be deified. But even these, as relatives of the former empress Julia Domna, were already part of the Severan dynasty through maternal kinship. No deified imperial woman had therefore ever been as devoid of an imperial background as Romula, who was also the first imperial woman deified after a fifty-year gap.³⁶

Nor had any imperial mausoleum ever been built for the sole occupancy of a Roman imperial woman before Romula received hers. Imperial relatives, male and female, had been usually laid to rest in collective imperial mausolea. These often began by being restricted to a particular imperial family, but soon came to house unrelated imperial successors, like the mausoleum of Augustus or the mausoleum of Hadrian in Rome. The only imperial women recorded as buried separately from their male relatives before Romula were those who had died in disgrace, such as Agrippina the Younger, mother of Nero, but even her body was later transferred to the mausoleum of Augustus.³⁷ Single occupancy of a mausoleum by just one dead emperor only became much more the norm in the course of the third century. Still, the wives and other female relatives of these later emperors would also usually be buried with the emperor, not elsewhere. Diocletian, who built himself a mausoleum within his retirement palace, now Split's cathedral of St. Domnius, expected to share his final resting place with his wife Prisca, at least judging from its decorations, which featured carved portraits of the couple.³⁸

---

³⁵ Aristocratic rather than imperial mothers of some Julio-Claudian emperors are an exception here (Agrippina the Elder and Antonia the Younger), but they were related to Augustus, and they were not formally deified, although worshipped in the provinces. On emperor's mothers, see Hekster (2015) 111–60.

³⁶ Varner (2001) 43 lists seventeen deified women; Price (1987) 57 lists twenty-seven "family members," but without references. The last deified woman before Romula was Mariniana, Valerian's wife (died c. 253).

³⁷ See the list in Johnson (2009) Appendix A.

³⁸ Johnson (2009) 69–70. As it turned out, Prisca was killed and her body thrown into the sea; see discussion to follow.

Galerius may have planned something similar for his own wife, Valeria, but reserved Romula's mausoleum for her exclusive use, building his own next to it. Maximinus may have wanted to also copy this plan at Šarkamen, but did not finish the project. The astronomical links and parallel orientations of the two structures for mother and daughter were also unmatched in the Roman world, although more common in the Near East.[39] So, too, was Galerius' claim of direct divine affiliation, which no Roman emperor before him had dared to make. Previous emperors had made only vague allusions to divine ancestry, although these were then often picked up and magnified in the provinces.[40]

Romula and her daughter are examples of the remarkable social mobility that some Roman women enjoyed during this period. Like Helena, this advancement was due to their origins in the imperial laboratory of the later third and early fourth century, the Northeastern parts of the empire in the Balkans and Asia Minor. Here, quite common women could become the divine mothers of emperors, at least in this period in time. However much he was building on existing traditions around imperial women, such as deification, Galerius' focus on his unassuming mother as ancestress was entirely novel. It reflects his personal ambition within the tetrarchy, also amply attested elsewhere, which intensified after Diocletian's abdication.[41] The provincial focus of such commemorations should not surprise us, for Galerius had little time for the old capital, and the cult of imperial women had always been more popular and innovative in the provinces than in Rome.[42] Galerius capitalized on the blank canvass of his lineage by using the tested method of writing a woman into his origin story.[43] It was this that, in turn, induced some late antique authors, like Lactantius, to take a closer look at his "barbarian" background.

But Galerius' experiment foreshadows not only the efforts of his nephew Maximinus, but also those of Constantine. To be sure, Constantine's promotion of his own mother was not an exact copy of what Galerius' actions were, as we shall see. He neither deified Helena, nor openly claimed she had

---

[39] See Beck (1999) 10–34 on the astronomic orientation of the peripheral columns surrounding the mausoleum built by Mithridates II of Commagene for his mother, Iseis, in the first century B.C.E.

[40] On the divine ancestry of emperors, Hekster (2015) 239–75. Mars was a divine patron (not ancestor) for some third-century emperors, which may explain Galerius' choice.

[41] Corcoran (2012).

[42] Hemelrijk (2015) 70. Some imperial women were worshipped in the provinces without having been deified in Rome.

[43] See Geary (2006) 4–5 who notes a shift in late antiquity from origin stories in which women die violently to those where women were life-giving.

had sex with a god (even though Christian observers alluded to parallels between Constantine and Helena and Christ and the Virgin Mary). And although Helena did end up as the sole occupant of her mausoleum in Rome, Constantine may not have planned this from the start, as Galerius did. Still, like Galerius, Constantine styled his unassuming mother ancestress of his dynasty, next to whom he originally planned to be buried. In many ways, he was even more radical than Galerius. Despite her very modest background, he minted coins for his non-imperial mother, something no emperor had done before, and laid her to rest in the very heart of the empire.[44] Even if Constantine himself was not directly influenced by Galerius (although their common regional and imperial background suggests he was), we may detect in Lactantius an uneasy feeling that people thought his situation was comparable. Constantine was beginning to move his humble mother onto the imperial stage at the time when Lactantius was writing. His depiction of Romula as the "evil and persecuting imperial mother" from the Balkans may well have been meant as a counterweight to Helena, "the good and pious imperial mother" from these regions.

The Augusta in the East

On November 11, 308, Galerius assembled the men who, in his opinion, could lay claim to imperial authority past and present at Carnuntum on the Danube, where he was campaigning against the Carpi. Carnuntum, about 40 kilometers down the river from Vienna, was an important military base at the western entrance to the Carpathian Plain, as well as the capital of Pannonia Superior. The imperial men probably met in the large governor's palace situated on the banks of the Danube between the civilian city and the legionary camp. They included Galerius, his Caesar Maximinus, Constantine, the retired Diocletian, and Maximian, who had just joined Constantine in Gaul. Maxentius was not invited. The main aim was to reconstitute this somewhat dysfunctional group into the four-man imperial college. Galerius accomplished this by co-opting his old army friend Licinius as a new Augustus of the West, to replace the dead Severus, and announcing Constantine as his Caesar. Their task was to defeat Maxentius. Galerius also compelled Maximian to retire once again, but he and Diocletian were honored as

---

[44] See Chapters 5 and 9.

"senior" Augusti. Subsequently, both Maximinus and Constantine refused to call themselves mere "Caesars," and Galerius eventually acknowledged their claims so that from 310 the imperial college consisted of four Augusti and two honorary ones.[45]

Around the time of the conference, a statue was erected in the headquarters building at the center of Carnuntum's legionary camp, near or in the camp's main temple, portraying a female figure holding a small child (Fig. 4.5). Made of the local limestone, the now sadly headless woman is clad in an overgarment (*palla*) with a richly embroidered and originally multicolored border. That border's loose right-hand end is draped diagonally across the wearer's torso and over her extended left arm. Around her collar the female figure wears two necklaces. One of these is made of large medallions, not dissimilar to the necklace found among the grave goods of Maximinus Daza's mother at Šarkamen.

The sculpture is now conventionally believed to represent an empress as a real or symbolical mother, set up in the camp to convey a message of maternal care for the army and the empire, or to thank her for such nurturing. The sculpture has been dated to between the end of the third and early fourth century, and its likeness has been connected with a number of imperial women, including Aurelian's wife Ulpia Severina, Fausta, and Helena.[46] But the tetrarchs' presence here in 308 that also manifested itself in material culture—they famously restored a Mithraeum near the legionary camp— suggests another potential candidate: Galerius' wife Valeria, who may have accompanied the emperor to Carnuntum.[47]

Valeria was the daughter of Diocletian, whom Galerius had married around the same time that Constantius had married Theodora. For this to happen, he had also been compelled or chose to abandon his previous partner.[48] We hear little of Valeria while Galerius was Caesar or during the early years of his time as Augustus. However, even then she was not as invisible as sometimes thought. In one of the places where she resided during her life, Nicomedia, a palace stood that her father Diocletian had ordered the construction of and then named for her. In Nicomedia, he also commissioned another palace named for her mother Prisca, thereby cementing his women's

---

[45] Barnes (2014) 70–71; Leadbetter (2009) 200–5. On Carnuntum, Humer (2014).
[46] Schade (2003) 29–30; for a detailed discussion, see Landkron (2006).
[47] For the Mithraeum CIL 3, 4413.
[48] Eutropius, Brev. 9.22; Aurelius Victor, Caes. 39.25; Jerome, Chron. 292. On the dating of these marriages, see Chapter 3.

Fig. 4.5 Headless portrait statue of an imperial woman, made from limestone; found at Carnuntum. © Landessammlungen NÖ, Archäologischer Park Carnuntum (Foto: N. Gail).

virtual presence in the minds of Nicomedians, even if the two women were physically shielded from public life.[49] Lactantius insinuated that, within this domestic sphere and with their eunuchs and servants (*domestici*), Valeria and her mother practiced Christianity, supported by Nicomedia's numerous Christian ministers. The authenticity of this claim is unclear, although it

---

[49] Lactantius, De mortibus pers. 7. On the concept of "presence in absence" with regard to the concealment of late antique women, Lindblom (2019) 240.

is not entirely unbelievable, given the growing presence of Christianity in urban communities, especially in the East.[50] But it mainly served Lactantius to question Diocletian and Galerius' authority, as they did not even appear to be in control of their own households. Nonetheless, it gives a glimpse of the court apparatus sustaining tetrarchic empresses' lifestyle and its links with certain demographics. Later, Lactantius also mentions Valeria's ladies-in-waiting, recruited from the empire's senatorial aristocracy, one of whom was even from Rome itself, with a daughter among the Vestal Virgins. This is a rather surprising detail, given Galerius' alleged animosity toward the old Roman elite, and casts some doubt on whether it was as fierce as supposed.[51]

Knowledge about Valeria's sexual life also circulated, in accordance with the customary public interest in the intimacy of a female imperial body and its ability to produce heirs. It was discussed how she could not have any children on her own and therefore had to adopt Galerius' illegitimate son Candidianus.[52] Candidianus was born c. 296, the product of a relationship that Galerius had with a woman Lactantius calls a "concubine." Since Galerius was at this point already married to Valeria, Lactantius cannot have used this term in its legal sense, as a monogamous partnership with a woman of lower social standing. Like all Roman husbands, Galerius could have extra-marital sexual partners with impunity, as long as they were not themselves respectable women. Like many Roman wives, Valeria would have been accustomed to this behavior, as would, more tragically, the unnamed "concubine," who also stood to lose her son in a very public manner.[53]

Valeria's original title may have been *nobilissima femina*, "noblest of women." At least, this is the title carried by her mother, Diocletian's wife Prisca, Galerius' daughter Valeria Maximilla, and, as we have seen, Maximian's daughter Fausta. This designation, not attested before the tetrarchy, may have been reserved for women directly related to the Augusti. It was a way to acknowledge their status, on a par with the Caesars who

---

[50] See pp. 47–48.

[51] Lactantius, De mortibus pers. 15. The passage also implies that Valeria lived with her mother in Nicomedia, while married to Galerius. On authority and household control, see Cooper (2007a). Valeria's ladies in waiting: De mortibus pers. 39–40.

[52] Lactantius, De mortibus pers. 50.2. This is one of the reasons why Galerius' daughter Valeria Maximilla is commonly believed to have been the daughter of his previous partner. See PLRE I, Valeria Maximilla, 575; yet also see Leadbetter (2009) 61, 78 n. 123 and Barnes (1982) 38, who dismisses the existence of a first wife of Galerius altogether.

[53] PLRE I Candidianus 1, 178. On Roman husbands' frequent and accepted sex with slaves and other women not deemed "marriageable," and the immense sexual power imbalances this created, see Arjava (1996) 202–5. On concubinage, see Chapter 2.

were also *nobilissimi*, without conferring the more recognizable honor that came with the title Augusta.[54] But in 308, perhaps even before the conference in Carnuntum, Galerius did just that. He promoted Valeria to Augusta, the first empress to receive the title since 283, although before the tetrarchy and since Augustus' wife Livia had been granted the title by her son Tiberius after Augustus' death in 14 C.E., it had been a standard honor for an imperial woman.[55] It was possibly also at this point that Valeria adopted Galerius' name and became known as Galeria Valeria on coinage and epigraphy, a more unusual move.[56] She also received the title of *mater castrorum*, "mother of the camps." This was another, although much less frequent epithet bestowed on Roman empresses since the second century, and Valeria would be the last to bear it. Perhaps awarded to women who accompanied their husbands on military campaigns, the title associated the vitality of a dynasty with the prosperity of the army. Its bestowal on Valeria could well be the context for the Carnuntum statue.[57] Valeria was hailed as *augusta* and *mater castrorum* in at least three inscriptions accompanying public statuary erected after the conference in Carnuntum in Asia Minor and Greece, testifying to the fact that inhabitants of the empire took notice of her elevation.[58]

Galerius indeed advertised Valeria's new name and status widely by minting her portraits on his coins. Although he only had three short years to do so, coins showing Valeria make up 8 percent of the total volume of Galerius' known issues, more than, for example, Trajan or Aurelian had minted for their wives.[59] All imperial mints in Galerius' Eastern half of the empire issued her portrait: six on gold aurei, gold multipla, and bronze folles (Siscia, Serdica, Thessalonica, Nicomedia, Antioch, Alexandria) and two just on bronze (Cyzikus, Heraclea). All these coins' reverse sides show, without fail, the goddess Venus holding an apple, labeled as *Victrix* (victorious). Like the reverse of Fausta's half-argenteus in the West (Fig. 3.2) and much previous coinage showing Roman empresses, this underscored Valeria's love for

---

[54] Maximilla: CIL 14.2826; Prisca's title is recorded on an inscription from Salona. See Jeličić-Radonić (2009) 312–15; Corcoran (2017) 61.

[55] Kolb (2010b) 14–17.

[56] On the name change: Kajava (1985) 42 n. 4. On the date of the Augusta title, Sutherland, Carson (1967) 15.

[57] Schade (2003) 12; see also Langford (2013) 31–48, who however argues it was the civilian population, not the military, who was the audience for this honor.

[58] CIL 3.13661 = ILS 8932, from Apamea, erected by Valerius Diogenes, the governor of the province Pisidia between 309 and 311; IGR 4.1562, from Teos in Asia Minor, in Greek (μητέρα κάστρων); IG 7.2503 erected by the city of Thebes in Boeotia, also in Greek. See also Lactantius, who calls her Augusta, De mortibus pers. 39.1, 40.2, 41.1.

[59] Hekster (2015) 136.

her husband as love for the empire, here linked explicitly with military victory and safety.[60]

Again, as with Fausta's coin portrait in the West, Valeria's featured innovations, and of a much starker and sustained nature. The empress's portrait included several elements that had rarely or never been seen on a coin before, but are not dissimilar to the outfit of the Carnuntum statue (Fig. 4.5). Valeria was often portrayed wearing a richly embroidered mantle (*palla contabulata*), folded diagonally over her chest but presented frontally to the viewer, rather than sideways. Around her neck frequently appeared a necklace, either a single string of pearls, a broader collar necklace with inlaid stones, or a triple necklace with strings of pearls framing larger stones or medallions. Her hair was usually bound into the reverse plait that third-century empresses had already sported, held in place by a diadem of the "stephane" type (a metal arc; see Fig. 1.1). On occasion, however, it was depicted differently. Sometimes Valeria wears the so-called spherical hairstyle, with small ripples framing the face and the rest of the hair bundled at the neck, pulled up, and then tucked down under a headband from the back. This is more rare, but can already be seen on coins showing Aurelian's wife, Ulpia Severina.[61] On other coins, Valeria sports an entirely new hairstyle. It involved a plait wound around her head like a laurel wreath or headband, sometimes studded with jewels and sometimes accompanied with a string of pearls or a stephane (Fig. 4.6).[62]

In the past, female relatives of Roman emperors had been depicted soberly on coinage and official statuary, without ornaments, except for the stephane, an originally divine attribute. Earrings, necklaces, hair decoration, brooches, finger rings, or bracelets were absent from these earlier public images, and women's clothes were plain (albeit, on statuary, probably colored). The official representation of the early imperial empresses reflected an archaizing moral discourse in which respectable Roman women were not to draw attention to their bodies, even when, in reality, they often wore jewels and outlandish clothes in public as well as in private.[63]

---

[60] Schade (2003) 10. See Carlà (2012) 74 on whether Valeria's coins responded to Fausta's.
[61] For example, RIC VI Thessalonica 34. On Severina Schade (2003) 13; Bergmann (1977) 182.
[62] RIC VI Alexandria 128A, 129; Nicomedia 53, 57, 58; Serdica 34, 41, 42, 43; Siscia 196, 204 (with ribbon, bound at the back), 210, 211; Thessalonica 29, 33, 34, 35, 36. Maurice (1908) 81 cautiously calls this headgear a diadem. Note that the head of a girl now at the Louvre, sometimes identified as a young Fausta, also sports a pearl-studded braid; see Schade (2003) 167–68 and Taf. 22.
[63] On the discourse around jewels and imperial women, see, for example, Pliny, Hist. nat. 9.117 on Caligula's wife Lollia Paulina; on early imperial Roman women and the display of jewelry, generally see Stout (1995) 77–100; Schade (2003) 31–34; Fejfer (2008) 347; Batten (2009) 484–501.

Fig. 4.6 Bronze follis (AE2) showing Galeria Valeria Augusta on the obverse; Venus Victrix on the reverse (RIC VI Thessalonica 36). Courtesy of the American Numismatic Society.

With her coin portrait, Valeria defied all these norms. To be sure, she was not the very first imperial woman pictured like this. The last emperor before Diocletian took power, Carinus, had minted portraits of his wife, the Augusta Magnia Urbica, c. 284 that are similar, with frontal bust (resting, as Valeria's also sometimes does, on a crescent moon), embroidered robe, and triple-layered necklace. The reverse also showed Venus Victrix. The similarity in appearance of the two women suggests that some aspects of Valeria's outfit had already become part of the empress's standard public image by the end of the third century. This also implies that Valeria and perhaps also other tetrarchic women may have made ceremonial public appearances, as the necklace found in the mausoleum of Maximinus' mother, so similar to some of the pieces depicted on the coins, also suggests. The late-third-century change in attitudes toward the public representation of the empress's embellished body was possibly in response to an increase in jewelry and sumptuous clothing as accepted markers of the status of aristocratic and other elite women. But the embroidered mantle also mirrors elite men's clothing, in particular the consul's *trabea triumphalis*, often worn by the emperor himself, which again hints at the formal context in which such a new female costume was worn.[64]

---

[64] On the increase of jewelry in public portraits, see Fejfer (2008) 350; Berg (2003) 15–73. On the *trabea triumphalis*, Schade (2003) 15. On Magnia Urbica's coin portrait, Bergmann (1977) 183.

Unlike Magnia Urbica's festooned coin image, which was confined to one small issue from a single mint, Ticinum in Northern Italy, Valeria's circulated more widely. The majority of the coins featuring this iconography derived, however, from only three mints: Siscia in Pannonia Savia, and above all Serdica in Dacia Mediterranea (which ceased to mint after 308) and Thessalonica in Macedonia. Thessalonica was also the mint that most enthusiastically produced portraits of Valeria with the entirely novel wreathlike and often pearl-decorated plait or headband, which broke the very long tradition of the reverse plait as the main imperial female coiffeur.[65] Most of the other mints, with the exception of Nicomedia, continued to portray Valeria in a conventional plain style, including those under the Caesar Maximinus' control, Antioch and Alexandria.

Although the logic behind the artwork produced at imperial mints can be difficult to decipher, this regional pattern can hardly have been a coincidence, especially since the minting of female imperial portraits was an honor carefully controlled by the imperial administration.[66] Coins with Valeria's distinctive bejeweled look emerged fully only in Galerius' heartlands, and above all in Thessalonica, his favorite residence, where she must also have lived in this period.[67] It is also from Thessalonica that another possible stone portrait of Valeria derives, this time from a palatial context. She looked down on the goings-on in the palace from a *tondo* on Galerius' small triumphal arch in the peristyle, mirroring the emperor's portrait on the opposite side.[68] Once again, as with his mother Romula, it was his home region between the Danube and Thrace that was Galerius' main audience when it came to the representation of his women. It was also here where, after 308, and not far from Carnuntum, he renamed a province in honor of his wife, Pannonia Ripensis, where he ordered territory cleared for agriculture. It was henceforth known as Valeria.[69]

---

[65] Bergmann (1977) 184; Schade (2003) 18–19. The Serdica and Thessalonica coins feature the mint mark SM (*sacra moneta*), which indicates that the minting of coins was palace-directed; see Delmaire (1989) 505–6.

[66] Schade (2003) 8; Brubaker, Tobler (2000) 12, James (2013) 100. If there was scope for choice at the local mint, it was limited to the reverse (in Valeria's case, always the same). On the peculiar geographical pattern of Valeria's portrait, see also Bergmann (1977) 184. Siscia was Licinius' mint and exhibited some confusion on how to adopt the new features of female imperial portraiture.

[67] On Thessalonica and Galerius' substantial building program, Leadbetter (2009) 233–36. On his residence there, Barnes (1982) 62.

[68] Calza (1972) 151 n. 64; Wegner (1984) 151.

[69] Aurelius Victor, Caes. 40; Ammianus Marcellinus, 19.11.4. Waldron (2018) 191 for the date.

What did Galerius want to achieve through this marked and often unusual promotion of his wife? His main aim was to cement his position as senior Augustus among a group of men who all now claimed this title. For he was the only one with an Augusta, not a mere *nobilissima femina*, at his side. That fact was suitably advertised on imperial monuments, such as milestones, where Valeria's name appears alongside that of Galerius, but the wives of the other men of the imperial college go unmentioned (Licinius may not have had a wife yet, but the other men named on such objects all did). Her relative equality within this college was also recognized elsewhere in epigraphy through her evocation as "our mistress" (*domina nostra*, déspoina hēmôn), echoing how imperial men were addressed under the tetrarchy (in Latin *dominus noster*). Valeria was a daughter of Diocletian, which was important, but she was also redefined as very much Galerian, most explicitly through her change of name. She was now part of an imperial conjugal entity with Galerius, the two sides mirroring each other, as on the arch at Thessalonica or even in dress, with the female side augmenting the male, in a manner beyond the reach of his competitors.[70]

Galerius may also have attempted to make a more dynastic statement. Not every emperor had awarded the Augusta title, which did not describe an empress's legal or official position, but referenced her honor. The pattern of the title's distribution over the preceding centuries suggests it was used to make a statement about the strength of a dynasty and its link with the imperial founding couple, Augustus and Livia. This was especially so when a dynasty was new or there was no immediate agnatic male heir.[71] On a more subtle note, changing an empress's hairstyle had likewise almost always served as a sign of dynastic branding.[72] Valeria was not a biological mother, but she had adopted Galerius' illegitimate son Candidianus, whom Lactantius suspected Galerius of fostering as an imperial heir as early as 305. At some point, but possibly after Galerius had become senior Augustus, Candidianus, then in his early teens, was betrothed to Maximinus Daza's daughter, a very young girl. With this betrothal, Galerius was consolidating his links to Maximinus,

---

[70] On this aim, see Leadbetter (2009) 205. Milestones: AE 1979.602a from Hermokapeleia in northwestern Lydia; Mouterde (1908–1909) 538–39 no. 3, from Beirut, in Maximinus' territory. *Domina nostra* title: ILS 8932; SEG 54.638, possibly a monumental building inscription. On the title "our mistress" as mirroring male address: Schade (2003) 52. If Galerius had been adopted by Diocletian, Valeria would also have been emancipated, weakening her link to her father, at least in the legal sense. See Chapter 3.
[71] Kolb (2010b) 16–17; Washington (2015) 27; Angelova (2015) 83.
[72] Schade (2003) 13.

perhaps with the aim of building up Candidianus as a future Caesar, either Maximinus' or Licinius' (in the case of the latter, the marriage link would have bought Maximinus' loyalty).[73] The award of the title Augusta to his adoptive mother would only have strengthened Candidianus' imperial claims. In addition, Galerius may have hoped that by making Valeria a highly visible and physically distinctive presence in the Balkan provinces, he might win Candidianus support from his troops recruited from this region should it be needed. As a man raised in the provinces, Galerius looked on bodily adornment, for men and women, as a sign of status, and his audience would have agreed.

As in the case of Romula and her daughter, Galerius' publicity around his wife anticipated many aspects of Constantine's promotion of his own women. The female portraits on the ceiling in his palace in Trier, with which we began this chapter, already give us ample evidence for this dialogue. Seen in the context of iconographic developments prior to and especially during Galerius' reign, the bejeweled demeanor of the ladies portrayed here is not a reason to doubt their imperial connotations. On the contrary, it precisely points in this direction. But more specific elements indicate this, too, and not merely just the necklaces with medallions. Each of the women on the Trier ceiling wears in her hair a stephane and a string of pearls, while two of them also sport a wreath. The central lady wears a spherical hairstyle. The lady with the mirror wears a *palla contabulata* with an embroidered rim, which she pulls over her head.[74] Even though they appear on the bodies of different women, these elements variously echo Valeria's depiction on her coins. Of course, the portraits in Trier may be allegories. Nonetheless, we will rediscover many of these elements in the representation of Constantine's wife, and especially of his mother, from the title of *nobilissima femina* through her address as *domina nostra*, and down to the pearl-studded hair wreath, which would become Helena's signature coiffure.

---

[73] Candidianus destined to be Caesar: Lactantius, De mortibus pers. 20; betrothal of Candidianus: De mortibus pers. 50. Since Maximinus' daughter was only 6 or 7 in 313, the betrothal cannot have happened earlier than 306. On Galerius' dynastic plans, see Barnes (1982) 6–7 ns. 18, 23; Leadbetter (2009) 204, 241–42; Corcoran (2012) 8–9.

[74] For the mantle as a *palla contabulata*, Weber Della Croce (2016) 1510.

Fair Game: Empresses as Prey

In his succession plans, Galerius oddly disregarded Maximinus, who was, of course, his nephew, whose daughter was betrothed to Candidianus, and who was possibly also related to Galerius through his unnamed wife, who may have been another female relative. Despite all this, at the conference in Carnuntum, Licinius, no relative of Galerius, had been promoted over his head.[75] In consequence, Maximinus started to erect statues of his children, who included a son, "in every city" of his territory (Syria and Egypt), and to mention their names in his imperial announcements. Lactantius also made a dark allusion to Maximinus' involvement of their mother in judicial processes against Christian women at his residence in Antioch. This need not be true, but it does suggest he afforded his wife with some kind of publicity.[76] Although Maximinus dutifully minted coins for the Augusta Valeria, as we have seen, these did not adopt her new and distinctive look. Maximinus was certainly capitalizing on his proximity to Galerius, celebrated also in the commemoration of his mother at Šarkamen, but he had his own dynastic plans.

Whatever Maximinus' or Galerius' longer-term schemes may eventually have been, they made these emperors' wives and children visible, but ultimately also very vulnerable. When Galerius died in 311 en route from Thessalonica to Felix Romuliana, Maximinus regarded Valeria's dynastic and legitimizing value so highly that he even contemplated leaving his wife to marry her. Lactantius gives a running commentary on the events that ensued. He shows Valeria emerging as a woman who was courageous, resourceful, and well networked, but ultimately unable to counter the imperial machinery when it was set against her.[77] Assessing her situation after Galerius' death and burial at Felix Romuliana, she decided she would be safest with his nephew, at that time residing in Nicomedia. In making this choice, she defied the wishes of Galerius who had recommended her and her son to Licinius and placed them in his *manus*, a legal term that denoted the imposition of formal paternal power. Since Valeria had not been under Galerius' power, however, she was free to make her own choices.[78] After she had arrived at Nicomedia (presumably with Candidianus), she had to turn

---

[75] On Maximinus' wife, see Barnes (1999). Lactantius, De mortibus pers. 18 calls Maximinus an *affinis* (in-law) of Galerius. On Maximinus' son, Lactantius, De mortibus pers. 50.

[76] Eusebius, Hist. eccl. 9.11.2 and 7; Lactantius, De mortibus pers. 50. Eusebius says Maximinus' relatives oppressed his subjects.

[77] On the following, Lactantius, De mortibus pers. 35, 39–41, 50–51.

[78] She was probably *sui iuris*, that is, independent from her father also; see prior n. 70.

down Maximinus' unwanted marriage request, using a number of forceful arguments. They included the killer line that if he divorced a loyal wife (*fidam coniugem*), she could hardly trust him to also not leave her in turn. In response to this rejection, Maximinus confiscated her property, took away the eunuchs and companions (*comites*) Galerius had assigned to her, and exiled her, alongside her mother Prisca.[79] Maximinus also allegedly persecuted and even executed women of her entourage, falsely charging them with adultery. It is notable, however, that Maximinus let Valeria, Prisca, and even Candidianus live, perhaps out of family piety or perhaps fearing public outrage, for Valeria, Lactantius tells us, was exceedingly popular.

The next emperor Valeria had to face, Licinius, who defeated Maximinus in April 313, was not so lenient. She had probably anticipated this when choosing Maximinus over him. Licinius, not bound by family either to Galerius, Maximinus, or indeed the former Augustus Severus, decided to eliminate any remaining family members of these men still surviving in the Eastern provinces. By autumn 313 he had hunted down and killed Maximinus' wife, son, and daughter, who had fled from Nicomedia to Antioch after Maximinus had committed suicide at Tarsus. Licinius ordered the empress to be drowned in the river Orontes. She was perhaps thrown from the famous loggia in the palace of Antioch, situated on an island in the river facing the city, from which emperors customarily showed themselves to the population.[80] Her very public death also added to the condemnation of Maximinus' memory, while his children were disposed of to suppress their potential provision of imperial legitimacy to a future rival. Licinius similarly executed Severus' now adult son Severianus, who had served under Maximinus.[81]

All the while, Licinius was looking for Valeria, who, Lactantius tells us, was spending her exile from Maximinus' court "in the deserted solitudes of Syria." We should not imagine this as being as strenuous as it sounds; like other banished imperial women before her, Valeria was probably living on an imperial estate with her entourage.[82] She was unguarded, could receive correspondence, including from her father, and move around easily. This she now

---

[79] On the contradictory dates of the death of Diocletian, see Barnes (1982) 42. He may have died in 312. Prisca, we learn from this, lived with her daughter, rather than with Diocletian near Salona, who was apparently still alive.
[80] On the palace in Antioch, see Wulf-Rheidt (2007) 63 with bibliography. The loggia is mentioned in Libanius, Or. 11.205–7.
[81] See Varner (2001) on different motivations for killing the family members of former emperors.
[82] Stini (2011) 203–6.

did, to check, rather poignantly, whether Candidianus, who had been with Maximinus, was alright. Hatching an astonishingly enterprising ploy, she donned common clothes (with the implication that she usually did not) and mingled with Licinius' court in Antioch. Here, she learned to her dismay that Candidianus had already been killed when Licinius had been at Nicomedia in June. She understandably fled and managed, with her mother and, we must assume, her household, to hide from Licinius for fifteen months. They were sustained by the "popular adoration" (*plebeio culto*) Valeria enjoyed in the provinces, no doubt in part in consequence of her husband's manipulation of her public image.

In the end, this popularity also led to her downfall. In early 315, she was, not surprisingly, recognized at Thessalonica, where she may have brought her small group of women to benefit from her friendships in the city. Arrested together with her mother Prisca, both were beheaded in front of a large crowd full of compassion (*miseratio*), and their bodies were thrown into the sea to prevent any continuing veneration at their place of burial and to commit their souls to eternal wandering. Afterward, some of Valeria's public statuary may have been defaced.[83] Lactantius tells this tale as the logical conclusion of how the pagan persecutors met their deserved ends, punished not only by their own gruesome deaths but also by those of their entire households. For him, Valeria's and Prisca's virtue served to highlight the depravity of Licinius and Maximinus. Even Lactantius was not able to fully detach himself from Valeria's impressive appeal, which he may have once personally witnessed.[84]

In their brutality, Maximinus and Licinius were only mimicking Constantine's behavior after he had taken Rome in the autumn of 312; he had likewise killed members of the imperial family not related to him—Maxentius' wife and child—while sparing those who were. For the inhabitants of the Roman provinces, these were extraordinary years. Never before had not one, but four empresses, been publicly murdered in a short space of time, both in and, even more strikingly, away from Rome. As we shall now see, this violence and its regional contexts determined Helena's appearance, both in person and in iconography.

---

[83] Jeličić-Radonić (2009) 314–15 on two marble heads from Salona now in the Museum at Split. See p. 119 on the fate of Valeria's portrait on the arch of Galerius. On Valeria's recognizability, see also Waldron (2018) 194. On the spiritual beliefs around deposing of a body into water, Johnson (2009) 9.

[84] James (2013) 105. See also Lactantius, De mortibus pers. 51: *Ita illis pudicitia et condicio exitio fuit*, "Their ruin was their virtue and their situation."

ated by bestiality, by a woman's lamentation over her dead husband. In the background, a fortress looms — dark, angular, unmistakably Teutonic. The air is heavy with the smell of smoke and iron.

PART III
CENTER STAGE (C. 317–C. 329)

5
Keeping Up Appearances

In 318 or 319, the mint in Thessalonica issued two coins showing profiles of Helena and Fausta, describing them as "noblest of women," *nobilissimae feminae*.[1] The two women were displayed in plain *palla*, without any jewelry. Their hair was pulled back in an elegant chignon, a coiffure made fashionable by Faustina the Younger, wife of Marcus Aurelius (Figs. 5.1 and 5.2).

This was how Helena, by now around 70, finally came into the view of her son's subjects and shifts into ours: with a classicizing, austere demeanor of stern authority, her angular head with its muscular neck, full cheeks, small mouth, large eyes, and pronounced eyebrows resembling those of contemporary male emperors, especially Constantine.[2] Fausta's features were slenderer and more feminine, although she was also depicted in a more mature guise than on the silver coin minted for her wedding, with a soft matronal chin. Helena's aquiline nose clearly identified her as a Constantinian woman, for a similar feature also graced Constantius' portrait and continued to distinguish Constantine's. While Fausta did not acquire a curved nose, her portrait had by now lost her father Maximian's button nose (as still shown in Fig. 3.2). Clearly, these portraits do not reflect Helena's or Fausta's real looks, which are irrecoverably lost to us, nor simply conventional ideals of beauty. They were carefully curated dynastic branding.[3]

The coins' reverse show an eight-pointed star inside a laurel wreath fastened by a ribbon, the tail ends of which frame the mint mark TSA. It set out a programmatic statement. The laurel wreath referenced Constantine's qualities as a military victor and (through the ribbons) civic leader. The single star, which had already featured prominently on his father's coinage, implied

---

[1] RIC VII, Thessalonica 48, 49, 50, 51 (the latter two without mint mark, but according to RIC VII, p. 493–94 minted in Thessalonica, in 318). The coins are generally dated to 318–319, but see Drijvers (1992a) 40 for a discussion. Cf. Alföldi (1959–1960) who argues that the Helena coin features Helena, the wife of Crispus (on whom, see Chapter 7). This has been rightly dismissed; see Longo (2009) 63.

[2] The mint at Thessalonica now also created a new portrait of Constantine similar to Helena's, with large eyes, small mouth, a curved nose, and a strong neck; see Bruun (1961) 19 and tav. IV, n. 235.

[3] Schade (2003) 53–54; Longo (2009) 62. On "Constantinian looks," especially the aquiline nose: Smith (1997) 184–85. On "similitudo" and "normative styling" of family members as dynastic branding: L'Orange (1984) 3–6. Similitude of features signified similitude of character.

Fig. 5.1 Bronze follis (AE2) showing Helena, with caption *n(obilissima) f(emina)* on the obverse; eight-pointed star in laurel wreath on the reverse (RIC VII Thessalonica 48). Courtesy of the American Numismatic Society.

Fig. 5.2 Bronze follis (AE2) showing Fausta, with caption *n(obilissima) f(emina)* on the obverse; eight-pointed star in laurel wreath on the reverse (RIC VII Thessalonica 49). Courtesy of the American Numismatic Society.

the polar star and signified stability and eternity. Placing the star within the wreath promised an auspicious future for the empire.[4] By linking these

---

[4] Longo (2009) 90–91; for the meaning of the star and the wreath (both rare on previous empresses' coins), Temeryazev, Makarenko, vol. 1 (2017) 12, 14. In 317–318 Constantine made another dynastic statement on coinage minted in Thessalonica, issuing a bronze series that included portraits of his "divine" ancestors Constantius, Maximian, and Claudius Gothicus: RIC VII Thessalonica 24, 25, 26.

prospects to his own mother as well as to the mother of his sons, Constantine situated his family and his heirs at the beginning of a glorious time for the Roman empire.

This was a colossal message, but—like Fausta's wedding coin in 307—it was broadcast to a rather select audience. The coins were only minted in Thessalonica, in the smallest denomination available, the bronze follis, which would have been used frequently in day-to-day transactions. This suggests they were designed to reach predominantly this city's inhabitants. When we left Constantine, he had just become sole ruler of the Western part of the empire. At that time, Thessalonica, like the entire Balkans, were still outside his territory, contested ground between his co-emperors Licinius and Maximinus Daza. To understand how and why the city became the locus of Helena's reappearance, at least in portrait form, we need to trace the moves Constantine made after his triumph at the Milvian Bridge in 312 to consolidate his supremacy and cement his dynasty.

The Road to Thessalonica: A Wedding, a Conspiracy, and a War

Constantine left Rome in early 313, moving his court and army north along the Via Cassia, and then across the snowy Apennines in the direction of Milan. The occasion that brought the emperor to Maximian's old residence at this unseasonal time of year was the marriage between his half-sister Constantia and his co-emperor Licinius, who traveled down from his base at Sirmium in Pannonia.[5] According to Lactantius, Constantia had been betrothed to Licinius prior to Constantine's invasion of Italy a year earlier. This news had prompted Licinius' rival in the East, Maximinus, to ally himself with Maxentius.[6] With Maxentius out of the way, Constantine was prepared to lend his support to Licinius' campaign against Maximinus for overall control of the East, or rather, pledge not to attack his pending brother-in-law as well. Alongside various administrative reforms, the alliance also entailed a shared commitment to Galerius' edict of toleration of Christians and to

---

[5] Origo Const. 5.13; Epitome de Caesaribus 41.4; Zosimus, Hist. nea 2.17.2. The marriage is also mentioned, but not the location of the wedding, by Eusebius, Hist. eccl. 10.8.3; Eusebius, Vita Constantini 1.50; Aurelius Victor, Caes. 41.2; Orosius, Hist. adv. pag. 7.28.19; Socrates, Hist. eccl. 1.2.8; Sozomen, Hist. eccl. 1.7.5; Theodoret, Hist. eccl. 2.3.

[6] Lactantius, De mortibus pers. 43; Zosimus, Hist. nea 2.17.2.

114 CENTER STAGE (C. 317–C. 329)

the return of their confiscated property (the so-called edict of Milan), which Licinius was to implement in his present and future territories.[7]

In return, Licinius renounced his claims to Italy and received Constantia as his bride, in the splendid environs of Milan's imperial palace. The event would undoubtedly have been marked by another wedding oration, delivered in the audience hall discovered recently in the area of Via Gorani. Afterward, the couple would have retired to the more intimate chambers in the northern part of the palace, which featured a banquet hall and several bedrooms arranged around a circular peristyle.[8] As in the case of Fausta's wedding in Trier six years before, Constantia herself may have played only a subordinate role in the celebrations, which once again were focused on the relationship between the new imperial brothers-in-law, who also held a joint consulship that same year. Licinius and Constantine displayed their unity ceremonially in the city through a procession and games in the circus adjacent to the palace, where they may have presented their wives to the public.[9] As Theodora's daughter, Constantia was also the granddaughter of Maximian, whose body may by now have been interred in his mausoleum in Milan, just a short stroll west from the imperial palace. The public appearance of Constantia might therefore have served both emperors as they looked to establish good relations with a Milanese audience.[10]

Very shortly after the wedding, Licinius departed from Milan with his new wife by the same route along which he had come, across the Dinaric Alps, rapidly installed her at his residence in Sirmium, and went off with his army to face Maximinus, who had meanwhile been advancing West. Licinius' defeat of Maximinus only a couple of months later at the battle of Adrianople left him in charge of the entire East, from Siscia to Alexandria.[11] Sirmium, on the left bank of the Save, became Constantia's main home for the next three years of her life. Here, she would give birth to her son Licinianus in the summer of 315, presenting Licinius' son from an earlier relationship to an

---

[7] Barnes (2014) 90–97. Despite the name, there was no public declaration to that effect, but the agreement is mentioned in a letter by Licinius to the governors of his provinces and those he conquered from Maximinus: Lactantius, De mortibus pers. 48.2; Eusebius, Hist. eccl. 10.5.4.

[8] See Sannazaro (2016). Remains of the space with the circular peristyle survive in Via Brisa.

[9] On Constantine and Licinius' procession (*adventus*), see RIC VII, p. 411 (gold medallions struck with *Felix Adventus Augg NN*, minted in Ticinum). On the customary elements of an imperial adventus, Cioffi (2016).

[10] See Chapter 3 on Maximian.

[11] Barnes (1982) 81 for Licinius' movements in 313–314. For the return first to Sirmium: Origo Const. 5.13.

enslaved concubine with a younger half-brother.[12] Sirmium was another city where the installation of a tetrarchic residence had engendered a huge transformation of the urban landscape. It was located at a road junction between Dalmatia in the south and the Danube in the north, which formed the nearby Roman frontier. This river frontier was close, but a mountain range, today's Fruška Gora hills, stretching along its southern side conveniently sheltered the city from it.

Several emperors of the third century, including Maximian, had hailed from the city or its environs. Some relatives of Maximian may still have been living here, as he had built an imperial villa in his birthplace, the remains of which have been discovered at Glac, 4 kilometers from Sremska Mitrovica.[13] Again, Constantia's family connections to this city would have benefited Licinius' relations with its inhabitants. Although emperors had frequently chosen to base themselves in Sirmium when on campaign on the middle Danube, Licinius' reign featured the most expansive building projects in the city's history.[14] The imperial palace in the southern part of the city, facing the river, was lavishly decorated and considerably expanded, as still surviving remnants of mosaic-floored audience halls show. To its northern side was added a large circus, the largest unexcavated building of its kind in the Roman empire. It seated double the population of Sirmium and must therefore have been designed to attract an audience from across the region. Further north, near the Forum, Licinius built public baths and grain stores. Since Sirmium was surrounded by marshes, there were limits on its growth, so the imperial buildings had to spread into the city, razing earlier residential quarters. Like the locals in other tetrarchic residence cities, therefore, Sirmium's inhabitants were abruptly and directly confronted with the monumentality of an imperial court. From 313 on, this court was mainly represented by Constantia and Licinius' children, for in the early years of their marriage Licinius was frequently on campaign in the East. It was they who would have been facing the crowds from the palace's purposely built loggia looking onto the circus.[15]

---

[12] Epitome de Caesaribus 41.4; Zosimus, Hist. nea 2.20.2; PLRE I, Licinius 4, 509–10. See also Hillner (2017b).

[13] Maximian's villa near Sirmium is currently being excavated under the direction of Richard Miles (glac-project.sydney.edu.au/; last accessed 1/26/2021). The villa is mentioned in Epitome de Caesaribus 40.10.

[14] Marcus Aurelius had died here.

[15] Popović (2007) 21–27. On the imperial box in the circus at Sirmium, see Humphrey (1986) 612–13.

Constantia's motherhood created a headache for Constantine. To consolidate his power, Licinius naturally regarded his new son as an imperial heir, who was both the grandson and the great-grandson of emperors. Meanwhile, Constantine's own marriage to Fausta, now fast approaching a decade, had so far remained childless. Of course, Constantine did have an older, by now teenaged son, Crispus, although doubts surrounded the legitimacy of his birth. Constantine's dynastic strategies in the years 315–316 suggest that, in consequence, he worried about losing control over long-term imperial succession plans.

The evidence is obscure, but Constantine seems at first to have proposed a further expansion of the imperial college to embrace his other half-sister Anastasia's husband Bassianus. As we have seen, Bassianus was a descendant of the old senatorial family of the Nummii, previous allies of the emperor Maximian, but the idea of his promotion was perhaps primarily inspired by his equal relations with Constantine and Licinius as the brother-in-law of both of them. He was to become Caesar with responsibility for Italy. It seems likely that Crispus was to be another Caesar, although it is unclear with which of the senior Augusti the new Caesars would be paired. In the autumn of 315 Constantine used a man named Constantius, probably his half-brother Julius Constantius, to offer this plan to Licinius, but his co-emperor, at least according to Constantinian sources, rebuffed it.[16]

At this difficult juncture, a momentous event in the summer of 316 dramatically transformed the dynamics of dynastic planning. Fausta finally gave birth to her first living child, a son who was soon named Constantine after his father, in the imperial palace at Arles in southern Gaul.[17] Like Licinius, Constantine now had a direct heir "born into the purple," that is, during his reign. For the first time he contemplated sole rulership and imperial succession to his immediate descendants only. At the same time, this birth opened up another problematic dimension. As his plan of the previous autumn shows, so far Constantine had been partly relying on his half-siblings to build his dynasty, who were moreover, unlike himself, also of double imperial ancestry.

---

[16] Origo Const. 1.13. On Anastasia and Constantius, sometimes held to be Helena's children, see also Chapter 2; on the marriage between Anastasia and Bassianus, possibly already arranged by Maximian, and on Crispus' legitimacy, Chapter 3.

[17] Epitome de Caesaribus 41.4; Zosimus, Hist. nea 2.20.2. PLRE I, 223, Constantinus 3 maintains that this son was not Fausta's, but that of a concubine; this seems incorrect and based on the vague remarks by Zosimus that he had been born "a few days" before being made Caesar; see Barnes (2014) 212 n. 19. Julian, Or. 1.9d refers to Constantine (II) as the son of Fausta, and the events of 315–316 would not make any sense if he had not been a legitimate son.

In addition, they were not only tightly networked with each other and with the senatorial aristocracy, but also, through Constantia, with Licinius himself. Any role for these half-siblings in Constantia's marriage arrangements is not recorded, but it may nevertheless have existed. Given that Constantia had by this time at least one grown-up full brother, Iulius Constantius, it is not immediately obvious why it should have been Constantine—after all, only a half-brother—who had sole power to arrange this girl's marriage, unless of course by virtue of being emperor.[18] Furthermore, if Valeria's entourage as described by Lactantius followed a standard form, Constantia's ladies-in-waiting in Sirmium would have included female members of the senatorial aristocracy, and perhaps even her sister Anastasia herself.[19] In fact, Anastasia's husband Bassianus and his brother Senecio for a time lived at Licinius' court. This alone is a sign that Constantine's siblings and their aristocratic kin though marriage were pushing their own agendas.

These connections now gave Constantine a pretext to advance against Licinius and the opportunity to quell any hopes for a share in imperial power his siblings may have harbored. The *Origo Constantini* claimed that Licinius, at the instigation of Senecio, sent Bassianus to assassinate Constantine. This may have been a story put into circulation to justify Constantine's next steps, but in any case Bassianus was executed and Constantine's half-brothers Julius Constantius and Flavius Dalmatius removed from court, as were some leading Roman aristocrats, including possibly the former urban prefect Rufius Volusianus and his relative, the poet Optatianus Porfyrius.[20] We do not know precisely what happened to Anastasia, although she may have continued living in Rome.[21] Constantine further demanded that her brother-in-law Senecio, who was still with Licinius, be surrendered to him, but Licinius refused. In response, Constantine declared war on Licinius.[22]

---

[18] After Constantius' death, Constantia would have been either legally independent, or, if Constantius had been legally adopted, within the power of Maximian until 310, by which time at least her two eldest brothers Flavius Dalmatius and Julius Constantius may have been around 20; see Chapter 3. On Constantine's half-siblings as "partisans" of Licinius, see Kent (1981) 4.

[19] On Valeria's ladies-in-waiting. see p. 99.

[20] They are attested in Toulouse and Corinth in subsequent years; see Chapter 6 that follows. On Volusianus, Barnes (1981) 66–67.

[21] See Chapter 6.

[22] The entire story around the advancement and conspiracy of Bassianus is told only in the pro-Constantinian Origo Const. 5. 13–15, but may also be alluded to in Eusebius, Vita Constantini 1.47 and 50. The story is rather garbled. Given the connections between Licinius and Bassianus, it is also possible that the former proposed the latter as Constantine's Caesar. Barnes (1981) 66 and (2014) 100–103 believes Constantine proposed Crispus as Licinius' Caesar and Bassianus as his own. See also Chausson (2002) 137–38; van Dam (2007) 110 n. 34; Stephenson (2009) 164–65; Potter (2013) 169–70.

Within a few weeks, Constantine had defeated Licinius at the battle of Cibalae on October 8, 316, less than 100 kilometers west of Sirmium. Licinius fled from the battlefield to his city of residence, but only to collect Constantia, the children, and his treasure from the palace, perhaps mindful of his previous treatment of Maximinus' family and of Galerius' widow Valeria. They then retreated to Licinius' native lands, Dacia Ripensis, where Licinius appointed a co-emperor named Valens from among his generals. Licinius' army was defeated by Constantine's forces again in Thrace, but managed subsequently to lead Constantine into a trap by staying in his rear as he advanced toward Byzantium, thereby blocking his escape route to the West. The two emperors reached a peace agreement at Serdica (today's Sofia) in the early spring of 317, on which occasion Valens was executed and, on March 1, a new imperial college constituted. It was based for the first time in more than thirty years openly and unashamedly on the principle of biological succession and included, as Caesars, Licinius' and Constantine's baby sons Licinianus and Constantine (II), but also Crispus.[23] Constantine's sons were hence in the majority, and since Crispus was on the cusp of adulthood, he had an effective delegate at his side.

The peace settlement at Serdica also ceded all the Balkan provinces except Thrace to Constantine. For the first time in his reign, Constantine was in control of his homeland, while Licinius and Constantia took up residence beyond the Bosphorus, in Nicomedia.[24] In June 317 Constantine moved his court to Sirmium for the summer, where on August 7, in the imperial palace just vacated by Constantia's young family, Fausta gave birth to her second son, Constantius (II).[25] The court then wintered at Galerius' palace in Thessalonica in 317–318, probably to enjoy the milder seaside climate.[26] It was at this moment, with a dynastic future even more firmly established, the descendants of his stepmother Theodora sidelined, and in a region much marked by the lives and deaths of tetrarchic empresses, that Constantine decided to promote his mother.

The decision to do so specifically in Thessalonica may well have been designed to dispel the ghosts of the past that haunted this urban landscape. As we saw in the previous chapter, Thessalonica's mint had less than a decade

---

[23] Origo Const. 5.17–19. Eutropius, Brev. 10.6.3; Epitome de Caesaribus 41.4; Jerome, Chron. 317; Orosius, Hist. adv. pag. 7.28.22.26; Consularia Constantinopolitana 317; Zosimus, Hist. nea 2.20.2.
[24] Barnes (1982) 80.
[25] Julian, Or. 1.5d states that Constantius was born in Illyricum; CTh 11.30.7 confirms Constantine was in Sirmium in the summer of 317.
[26] Barnes (1982) 73.

ago issued coin after coin with the Augusta Valeria's portrait, during the period when she was resident there with Galerius. Less than four years previously, Thessalonicians had witnessed the decapitation of this woman and her mother Prisca, possibly in the city's circus built by her husband next to his palace, after which their headless bodies were dragged to the sea wall and flung into the Aegean.[27] Valeria's face had then been scratched from the city's surfaces. Still, at some point her portrait on the "small arch" of Galerius was recarved as the city's Tyche (Patron of Fortune) with a characteristic turreted crown, perhaps acknowledging her deep connection with her former residence.[28]

Now Constantine proceeded to insert his own women into these spaces of memory. Helena and Fausta's tetrarchy-era title—*nobilissima femina*—harked back to the immediate and also local past (the same title had been carried by Prisca, at least). Their sober, un-bejeweled looks were reminiscent of an even earlier, golden republican age. Nonetheless, Constantine's decision to put not only his wife, as Galerius had done, but also his mother on a coin was revolutionary and heralded in a new era. Portraits of imperial mothers, and certainly living ones, had never been a standard numismatic choice for Roman emperors (see Fig. 5.3). They were most popular during the latter days of the Severan dynasty, but thereafter avoided by subsequent third-century emperors, possibly as an "oriental" custom. In addition, no emperor who founded a dynasty had ever put his mother on a coin. It was the Balkan provinces, which had recently seen Galerius' lowly mother Romula celebrated and consecrated as an ancestress, that again provided the regional context for Constantine's momentous step.

The coins of Helena and Fausta minted in Thessalonica, perhaps distributed while Constantine was in residence here, may reflect that they also interacted in person with their subjects. It is unclear whether Helena was with Constantine at this time—as we shall see, she may have been in Rome—but Fausta was. Another object that dates from this time, the late 310s to early 320s, seems to place Helena and Fausta in a public context. This is the so-called Ada Cameo, a large, 11-centimeter-high three-layered sardonyx (white and brown agate gem) carved in relief (Fig. 5.4).[29] Cameos were decorative items, in Roman times often inset into jewelry. They were

---

[27] On the topography of Thessalonica, see Mentzos (2010).
[28] On this process, Kiileric (2014) 63–64.
[29] Now in the Stadtbibliothek in Trier. By the early ninth century, this cameo had been placed as a central decoration on a gospel book belonging to Ada, sister of Charlemagne; hence the name. See Bruns (1948) 29–31; Demandt, Engemann (2007), III.19.1. The cameo had originally been dated to an earlier time, the period of Claudius, but it is now generally accepted that it was made or

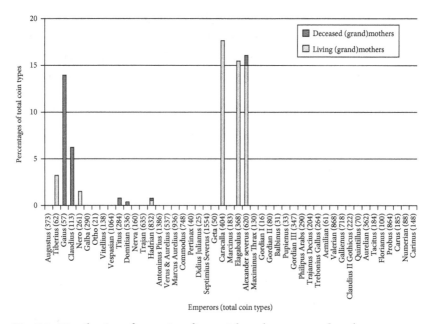

Fig. 5.3 Distribution of portraits of imperial mothers or grandmothers on Roman imperial coinage. Courtesy of Olivier Hekster and Liesbeth Claes. The table first appeared as Table 3 in Hekster (2015).

popular throughout the imperial period, but Constantine in particular was fond of this art form. Such objects not only transmitted dynastic statements through their iconography, but also showcased the emperor's far-reaching connections, wealth, and control of specialist craftsmen. Sardonyx was hard to procure and extremely difficult to carve.[30]

Five members of the Constantinian family appear on the Ada Cameo, two female and three male or three adults and two children. They look out at the observer from behind a balustrade decorated with large eagles, a view usually taken to depict the rim of a carriage or of an imperial circus box (*kathisma*), in line with the key role that horse-drawn ceremonial processions and the circus played in ruler–subject communication during this period.[31]

---

adapted under Constantine. See Drijvers (1992a) 191–92; Zwierlein-Diehl (2007) 202–4 for further discussion.

[30] Krug (2011) 188–91.
[31] Weber Della Croce (2010) 21–33. For a comparison, see the representation of the Theodosian family on the obelisk in Constantinople.

Fig. 5.4 The so-called Ada Cameo. Courtesy of Wissenschaftliche Bibliothek der Stadt Trier/Stadtarchiv Trier. Foto: Anja Runkel; Ru Nr. 093 2021.

The women are generally identified as Helena (far left, veiled) and Fausta (second from right), while the largest male figure (second from left) presents Constantine himself. The conjugal couple of Fausta and Constantine are of the same size and therefore identified as the most important figures depicted. The precise dating of the object hinges on the identity of the children. It has been suggested that they are Constantine II and Crispus and that the cameo therefore celebrated their appointment as Caesars in 317. Alternatively, they have been seen as Fausta's two older sons Constantine II and Constantius II, which would mean the cameo was made before her youngest son Constans was born in the early 320s.[32]

The Ada Cameo's original function cannot be fully determined anymore, but it was probably a gift from Constantine to a loyal supporter, most likely a member of the senatorial aristocracy. This person would have worn the carved gem about their person or, given its size, on objects in their possession, as a token of the imperial favor they enjoyed, mediating the imperial presence to their friends and visitors.[33] Its iconography has to be read in such a context of commissioning, gift giving, and display, as it drew on the multiple dimensions of spectacle and gaze. The imperial family are perhaps shown sharing in a circus spectacle with their subjects from their box, but at the same time they themselves become a sight for the cameo's viewer, who stands in for the crowd.[34] This dynamic only worked through the viewer's understanding of this image as a likeness of how the emperor appeared in public, at least for some of the time and to some of his subjects. This suggests not only that Helena was and appeared at least sometimes with Constantine in these years, but also, once again, that Constantine's mother and wife were increasingly thrust into the public sphere, beyond the purely local context of Thessalonica.

The two women were not, however, in full view of all Roman subjects as yet. For example, Eusebius of Caesarea's *Church History*, completed around 325, does not mention them, although he does refer to Constantia.[35] Fausta and Helena's public presence increased dramatically only when Constantine became sole emperor in 324. But even then, it initially remained the strict double act between the two women that had been set up on their Thessalonica coins and the Ada Cameo, with Fausta taking the more prominent role.

The Augusta Double

Constantine and Licinius did not remain at peace for very long, as Constantine had probably always intended. A first indication that relations

---

[32] On Constans' birth PLRE I, Constans 3, 220.
[33] Zwierlein-Diehl (2007) 17.
[34] See Lim (1999) for an analysis of this dynamic underpinning elite objects with circus scenes.
[35] Constantia: Eusebius, Hist. eccl. 10.8.

had soured was their appointment of different sets of consuls in their respective territories from 321, a year in which Licinius and his son held the office in the East, and Constantine's sons Crispus and Constantine in the West. They were further strained by Licinius' renewed clampdown on Christians, or at least this is what was claimed by Christian authors, especially Eusebius of Caesarea. In any case, such stories gave Constantine another opportunity to style himself as a "liberator" of Christians, as he had done in opposition to Maxentius, when he eventually attacked Licinius again in the summer of 324. Licinius was defeated twice, once at Adrianople in Thrace, after which he fled to Byzantium, and then again, on September 18, on the other side of the Bosphorus at Chrysopolis, near Chalcedon. Licinius then retreated to Nicomedia.[36]

Throughout these hostilities, Constantia had remained steadfast at Licinius' side, perhaps mindful that her marriage had been arranged as a guarantor of friendship between the two men. After Licinius' first defeat in 316, it may have been this dynastic connection that induced Constantine to continue power-sharing with his brother-in-law.[37] But it did not take long for Constantine to be ready to give up on the arrangement, even in the certain knowledge that this made Constantia's life more unsafe. In continuing the relationship, Licinius, for his part, must still have regarded Constantia as an asset. It is notable, however, that he never responded to Constantine's promotion of his women by striking coins with his own wife's portrait, although he may have erected a statue of her in Byzantium.[38] Of course he knew that making imperial women visible also made them vulnerable in an unstable political situation.

Licinius was not to be disappointed by Constantia's loyalty, courage, and commitment to her wifely duties of peacemaking. After deliberating in Nicomedia's palace for up to two months, Constantia eventually paid her brother a visit in his camp. She pleaded with Constantine for the life of her husband and that of her 9-year-old son, the Caesar Licinianus. In one version of this story, Constantia spread Licinius' purple mantle in front of her brother. Unlike Valeria Maximilla, Valeria, Prisca, or Maximinus Daza's wife, Constantia had the advantage of a blood relationship with her husband's vanquisher, but she also had the gift of persuasion. Constantine

---

[36] For background see Harries (2012) 113.
[37] As noted by Aurelius Victor, *Caes.* 41.6: *affinitatis gratia refectum consortium* ("an agreement restored thanks to kinship").
[38] See Schade (2003) 232, n. II 30.

did not only let her live, but also, at least at first, Licinius and Licinianus, and even the man Licinius had hastily appointed Caesar after Adrianople, Martinianus. Constantine then entertained his in-laws at a banquet, presumably at Nicomedia, and afterward allowed them to retire to the palace at Thessalonica, albeit probably under guard. In this way a humiliated Licinius, who owed his survival to his own wife, returned to the scene of his brutal murder of other emperors' wives, and the more recent triumph of Constantinian women.[39]

Even before Constantine decided to grant his dethroned sister her wish for the lives of her loved ones, Constantine bestowed the ancient title of Augusta on both Helena and Fausta. These awards were announced at the same time as the appointment of Constantine's second son with Fausta, Constantius II, as Caesar on November 8, 324. He replaced the disgraced Licinianus, taking his place alongside his brothers Constantine and Crispus. Taken together, these acts unmistakably signaled that there was now one sole Augustus, supported solely by his biological kin, at the helm of the Roman empire.[40]

This was not the first time that more than one imperial woman had simultaneously held the title of Augusta. Under Trajan, for example, his wife Plotina, his sister Marciana, and his niece Matidia had all been Augustae. Then, as now, this served to underscore the unity and cohesion of the imperial family and, hence, the empire. Ruling a harmonious household had always qualified Roman men for political rulership.[41] Nonetheless, Constantine's elevation of his un-imperial mother to Augusta was, again, unprecedented. More specifically, therefore, Helena's and Fausta's titles were designed to strengthen Constantine's branch of the Constantinian family, against his stepmother Theodora's descendants. To highlight his own line, Constantine's younger daughter, born around this time, was named Helena after her grandmother.[42]

---

[39] Origo Const. 5.28, Epitome de Caesaribus 41.7 (mantle story); Zosimus, Hist. nea 2.28.2, Zonaras, Epit. hist. 13.1; Jordanes, Getica 21. Martinianus was sent to Cappadocia. For Constantia's peacemaking mission possibly taking place only in December, see Potter (2013) 213. It is sometimes assumed that Constantia was accompanied by the bishop Eusebius of Nicomedia, but this seems to be an erroneous assessment. See Bleckmann (2003a). On Eusebius' relationship with Constantia, see Chapter 7. On the wifely duty of peacemaking, see Cooper (2007b) 149.

[40] For a possible iconographic commemoration of the event on the so-called Hague Cameo, see Stephenson (2015) and Chapter 7, n. 1 in this chapter.

[41] Temporini (2002a) 193–95. On the political importance of the serene multigenerational imperial household, see Hutmacher (2010).

[42] Drijvers (2011) 137. See Leadbetter (1998) 81 on Constantine's continuous worries about his half-brothers' "better claims of dynastic propinquity," despite his imperial authority being ultimately based on his undoubted military success. For the date of Helena the Younger's birth, see Barnes (1982) 43. She may have been too young to marry in 335 (see Chapter 9), so was probably born 324–325.

Fig. 5.5 Bronze follis (AE 2/3) showing Helena on the obverse, and caption *Fl(avia) Helena Augusta* and Antioch mint mark on the reverse (RIC VII Antioch 61). Courtesy of KHM—Museumsverband.

The speed with which all these titles were awarded, immediately after Constantine had defeated Licinius, suggests this scheme had been planned before Constantine commenced his second war against his brother-in-law.[43] If we are to believe Eusebius, Helena's new status was announced in all provinces and to all army units (as presumably was Fausta's, but Eusebius does not mention her).[44] Coins bearing portraits of the two new Augustae were again issued, steadily increasing in volume over the next two years. By 326 every current imperial mint produced such coinage, predominantly on bronze.[45] Once again, Constantine wanted to make sure that his message reached all parts of the population, and this time across the empire.

The very first coins showing Fausta and Helena as Augustae were, however, minted in Antioch, and not accidentally. Constantine visited the city on the Orontes in December 324, making a ceremonial entry. His wife's and mother's portraits appeared as part of a dynastic bronze series, a form of propaganda Constantine had not used before (Figs. 5.5 and 5.6). The series also featured himself, and the three Caesars Crispus, Constantine the

---

[43] Bruun (1966) 69; Drijvers (1992a) 41; Barnes (1982) 9 and (2014) 43 date the award of the Augusta title to November 8, 324, but cf. Alföldi (1963) 144 who postulates a later date, on the occasion of Constantine's Vicennalia in 325.
[44] Eusebius, Vita Constantini 3.47. He calls her "august empress" (αὐγοῦστα βασιλίδα).
[45] Helena's and Fausta's coins are collected in RIC VII. For a full list of these entries, see Waldron (2018) 198 n. 79. Coins were minted in 324–325 in Antioch, Cyzikus, Nicomedia, Thessalonica, Sirmium, Ticinum, Siscia, Trier, Arles, Lyon, London, and Rome; and in 325–326, in addition also in Heraclea and Alexandria. Only Nicomedia, Thessalonica, Sirmium, and Ticinum issued gold coins with portraits of Helena (for Fausta there are multipla from Trier; see text that follows).

Fig. 5.6 Bronze follis (AE 2/3) showing Fausta on the obverse, and caption *Flav(ia) Max(ima) Fausta Aug(usta)* and Antioch mint mark on the reverse (RIC VII Antioch 62). © Salem Alshdaifat, courtesy of Athena Numismatics.

Younger, and Constantius. Their obverses showed an imperial portrait without a legend, while the reverses displayed matching name and title in the center, with only a very small symbol above. In the case of Fausta and Helena, this was an eight-pointed star, recalling their earlier coins from Thessalonica (Figs. 5.1 and 5.2), above a crescent moon. The moon was the supreme symbol of the empress, faithful companion to the emperor's sun and brilliant only due to him. For the first time, these coins also used the nomenclature of Constantine's "gens Flavia" for his women, designating them as Flavia Helena and Flavia Maxima Fausta. Dynastic series were also minted elsewhere at the same time, but only those of Antioch included the two Augustae.[46] Their appearance here must therefore have had a special significance. Once again, as in Thessalonica in 318, these coins were intended to address an urban audience that not long before had witnessed the murder of a resident empress, Maximinus Daza's widow, at the hands of Constantine's defeated enemy, Licinius.

The peculiar backs of the Antiochene coins appeared only on the initial issue of Augustae coinage and would not be repeated. All remaining coins with a regular monetary value[47] from the years 324 to 326 that bear portraits

---

[46] Bruun (1966) 70, on the visit, and RIC VII pp. 669–70 on the unusual dynastic series; see also Drijvers (1992a) 41; Navarro (2009a) 80; Ramskold (2013) 418–19. On the moon, Longo (2009) 211.

[47] That is, excluding medallions and multipla, gold coins with varying multiple values of the standard solidus.

of Helena and Fausta followed a remarkably similar iconography on their reverse (Figs. 5.7 and 5.8). This combined the Augusta in question with a very narrow set of allegorical attributes, although one that, unlike that of Valeria not long before, avoided any overt religious connotations. Helena's bust was always accompanied by a figure representing the "Security of the State" (*securitas reipublicae*), a usually veiled lady holding a palm branch, sometimes laden with dates as a sign of peace, and wearing the end of her mantle draped over her left arm. She was similar to earlier numismatic representations of *pax* (Peace). For her part, Fausta was paired with either the "Hope of the State" (*spes reipublicae*) or, less frequently, the "Welfare of the State" (*salus reipublicae*). Either concept was depicted as a woman, also often veiled, clutching two small children to her chest who raise their hands to her face, in a style resembling earlier embodiments of fertility (*fecunditas*). The two children were an allusion to Fausta's own, although she was, by then, a mother of four or five.[48] Fausta's coins thus signaled how fertility and the imperial motherhood of heirs instilled hopes for the future well-being of the Roman empire, which was rather conventional imagery for the emperor's wife. The meaning of Helena's visual design was altogether more inventive. *Securitas* and *pax* were not notions usually associated with the Roman empress, but with the emperor, especially one who, like Constantine, had just saved the empire from (civil) war. Whereas Fausta's motherhood signified the future, Helena was celebrated for securing tranquility and peace in the present, through having delivered Constantine, Licinius' conqueror, to the world.[49]

Not only the backs of their coins started to differ from 324 on, but Helena and Fausta's obverse portraits also now substantially diverged from one another, unlike on the earlier coins from Thessalonica where the two women had been presented as mirror images. This trend was already apparent in the coinage from Antioch and developed further over the next two years (Figs. 5.7 and 5.8). Fausta kept her relatively youthful looks, her waved hair, and the chignon, which now often came with a visible hair fastener, sometimes

---

[48] Fausta may have had at least one more, sixth pregnancy, resulting in the birth of a son around 320 who died soon afterward. See Vanderspoel (2020) 36.

[49] On the iconography of Fausta's and Helena's coinage, see Maurice (1914); Drijvers (1992a) 42; Pohlsander (1995) 180–83; Brubaker, Tobler (2000) 576, Schade (2003) 53–58; Longo (2009) 49–50, 62–66, 97–98, 107–15; Navarro (2009a) 80–82; James (2013) 503–4. On the iconography of the reverse on Fausta's coins, see also Vanderspoel, Mann (2002). Washington (2015) 275 lists the distribution of metals/types among the extant coin issues—Fausta: 7 gold (solidus)/14 medallions and multipla/86 bronze; Helena: 5/8/135. On *Securitas*, see also Chapter 9.

Fig. 5.7 Gold solidus showing Helena with caption *Fl(avia) Helena Augusta* on the obverse, with spherical hairstyle, double pearl necklace fastened in the middle, and headband; *Securitas reipublicae* on the reverse (RIC VII Ticinum 183). © The Trustees of the British Museum.

Fig. 5.8 Gold solidus showing Fausta with caption *Flav(ia) Max(ima) Fausta Aug(usta)* on the obverse, with decorated chignon and single-string pearl necklace; *Salus reipublicae* on the reverse (RIC VII Ticinum 182). © Museum of Fine Arts, Boston.

decorated with pearls. She also acquired a necklace, usually a single string of pearls.

Helena's coiffure, by contrast, was transformed into a much more complicated style. She was mostly depicted with a so-called spherical hairdo, with small ripples of hair around the front, and the rest of the hair brushed from the neck over the head in a way that almost resembles a helmet. As we have seen, this style had already been evident on Valeria's coins, and is worn by the woman on the central image of the painted ceiling in Constantine's palace in Trier (see Fig. 4.1 and cover image). It became Helena's primary look during these years, although sometimes she was also portrayed with the more traditional reverse plait. Her face was also smoother than on the Thessalonica coin, but she retained a hint of the Constantinian curved nose. She always wore a necklace, again usually of pearls and sometimes with multiple strings. In Sirmium, however, notably the recent residence of Licinius' wife Constantia, the mint artists preferred to depict her with a necklace with inlaid stones or medallions, as they did with Fausta. Both women, but more often Helena, were also sometimes pictured with pearl pendant earrings, like the women on the Trier ceiling.[50] Above all, Helena was frequently portrayed with a metallic headband with inlaid jewels.

Around the time that Helena appeared on Constantine's coins with a headband, Constantine's own portrait began to feature a diadem, with him becoming the first Roman emperor ever to bear one. His adoption of this headgear came shortly after he had defeated Licinius to mark his sole rulership in a characteristically bold and unprecedented stylistic move. Originally the ornament of Hellenistic kings, the diadem referenced Alexander the Great, another divinely favored ruler of all the known world. By the later 320s and 30s, the diadem appeared on Constantine's coins as a string of rosette-shaped jewels or a pearl-bordered band, with a central stone on the forehead. By this time, Constantine was sporting a diadem also in real life, and contemporaries considered it part of his imperial regalia, similar to purple clothing. The jewel-studded diadem with a central stone continued to be worn by later Roman emperors and, from the later fourth century, by empresses, too.[51]

Due to its simultaneous appearance with Constantine's diadem, it has been suggested that Helena's headband was another feature of the newly developing imperial insignia of the mid-320s. If so, it could have marked Helena as sharing in her son's power and, in addition, ranking in the dynastic hierarchy

---

[50] Helena with earrings, for example, RIC VII Cyzikus 54, Antioch 61, Nicomedia 79, Sirmium 66, Rome 270. Necklace with inlaid stones: RIC VII Sirmium 60 and 61.

[51] On Constantine's diadem and its changing shape: Delbrueck (1933) 56–62; Alföldi (1963) 93–99, dating the introduction of the diadem to 326; Smith (1997)177. Eusebius, Vita Constantini 4.66 comments on Constantine's diadem as part of the royal ornaments; also Epitome de Caesaribus 41.14. Sometimes the diadem was just a simple band.

above her co-Augusta Fausta, who usually appeared bare-headed.[52] The much later, ninth-century chronicler Theophanes thought that Helena had been formally crowned.[53] It should, however, be noted that he believed this of Fausta, too, and, overall, was probably projecting customs of his own time back into the imperial past. There are indeed several stylistic elements that speak against Helena's headband being an official "diadem." To begin with, it featured significant differences from Constantine's diadem, above all an absence of the ribbons that tied it at the neck, as was traditional for Hellenistic headgear. These ribbons also associated Constantine's diadem with the more customary laurel wreath of Roman emperors, which had never been featured on empresses' coins. Earlier empresses wore the stephane instead, which in turn never appeared on either Helena's or Fausta's coins, perhaps due to its association with female divinity. Helena's headband was always covered by hair at the neck and also never acquired the central forehead jewel, which later on during the Constantinian period characterized the "official" imperial diadem. Furthermore, instead of a metallic headband Helena also often wore just a simple string of pearls in her hair.[54] Finally, Fausta is sometimes portrayed with a similar metallic, jewel-inlaid headband, too, but only on the rare occasions that she wore a spherical hairstyle on her coins.[55]

These somewhat erratic patterns in the headdress of the Augustae indicate that Helena's headband was primarily a decorative accessory, especially connected with the construction of the spherical hairstyle, where the hair was pushed under the band from behind, with only one lock pulled over it above the forehead.[56] This coiffure, if worn in real life, certainly needed to be sustained somehow to prevent it from collapsing, so the headband's appearance may have been as much practical as symbolic. It was unusual, given the customary avoidance of the portrayal of any artificial hair props on portraits of earlier Roman empresses, that this one was depicted on Helena's and some of Fausta's coins. But even this may not have been a radical statement, so much as a simple reflection of fashion. As we have also seen, Valeria Galeria was already shown with a headband or pearled hair strings on her coins, probably

---

[52] Modern scholars who interpret Helena's diadem as official insignia: Maurice (1908) 90; Delbrueck (1933) 63–64 (with reservations); Bleckmann (1994) 24.
[53] Theophanes, Chron. AM 5816.
[54] See, for example, RIC VII Alexandria 38, Heraclea 79.
[55] RIC VII Thessalonica 162, Trier 482.
[56] Alföldi (1963) 144–45; Holum (1982) 33; Drijvers (1992a) 42–43; Drijvers (1992b) 503–4; Schade (2003) 56; Longo (2009) 62–63.

incorporating female provincial trends in the imperial portrait. In fact, some mints may have used Valeria as a model for Helena.[57]

Still, Helena appeared more richly adorned with jewels than Fausta on her coins, even if she was not wearing "official" imperial insignia. Her abundance of pearls is especially remarkable, and even exceeded what had previously been depicted on Magnia Urbica's and Valeria's coins, who were never presented as wearing earrings, let alone pearl earrings. Pearls were among the most highly valued precious objects in the Roman empire, and symbolically associated with energy and light. They were immediately recognizable and therefore reflected status like no other jewels. This was especially so on two-dimensional, monochromatic coin images where it was otherwise difficult to convey the splendor of jewelry.[58]

All this does not have to mean that Helena had more authority than her daughter-in-law, but rather that Helena and Fausta's portraits were designed to reflect differently on Constantine. Fausta, the mother of Constantine's heirs, was modeled, in appearance and attributes, on earlier imperial wives, especially Faustina the Younger. Her presentation signaled the continuity of tradition and was therefore relatively sober. For Helena, as the non-imperial mother of an emperor, the mints had few prototypes for coin portraits. Galerius, as we have seen, did not mint coins for his mother Romula, the only visible imperial woman comparable to Helena (although one who was, notably, associated with Alexander the Great). The closest parallels are third-century coins struck for Julia Maesa, the grandmother of Elagabalus and Severus Alexander, and her daughters, the young emperors' mothers, Julia Soaemias and Julia Mamaea. These coins presented the women as unadorned, however, and evoked, again rather conventionally, virtues such as piety (*pietas*) or fertility (*fecunditas*), sometimes personified by the goddesses Venus or Juno.[59] This can be explained by that imperial center's attempt to insert these Syrian women into a transfer of Roman imperial power from earlier Severan ancestors to their younger male relatives, and to downplay their influence perceived by hostile commentators as "foreign."[60] This consideration did not apply to Helena who could and would not be presented as a conduit between imperial men.

---

[57] On Valeria's looks, see Chapter 4. For the similarities between Helena and Valeria, see also Maurice (1914) 317. On the reluctance to portray artificial aids in imperial women's hairstyles in earlier Roman art, despite their clear need for supportive frameworks, see Bartman (2001) 13–14.

[58] Longo (2009) 66; Kalavrezou (2012) 362–63. Pearls were even more highly priced than gold.

[59] Termeryázev, Makarenko, vol. 2 (2017) 56–65, 68–72.

[60] See Bleckmann (2002) 279–96.

For Helena, the imperial mother without a background, an entirely new image was developed. It borrowed some of the fashionable elements already apparent on Valeria's coins, as well as underscoring, especially through the pearl jewelry and the intricate hairstyle, her wealth, taste, respectability, and civility, and thereby also Constantine's legitimacy. Above all her portrait, and hence also these qualities, were closely aligned with that of Constantine, through their similar physiognomy. Helena's appearance reflected on her son's superior personality as a civic ruler bringing prosperity to the empire, but at the same time confirmed his, and therefore also her, status.[61]

Fausta, Superstar

Coinage was the main means by which the Roman imperial center projected its values onto subjects. Based on the extant numismatic evidence, it was Fausta, not Helena, who was at the center of Constantine's dynastic program in the mid-320s.[62] This is not immediately obvious from the frequency of their portraits, with Helena's being estimated at 5 percent, while Fausta's stands only at 3 percent, of Constantine's total coinage output (notably, both are lower than the percentage of Valeria's coinage among that of Galerius, which stood at 8 percent). The slightly larger volume of Helena's coinage can, however, be explained by the fact that Helena's portrait as Augusta was minted for five years and Fausta's only for two.[63] In any case, Fausta appeared much more frequently than Helena on high-value coinage, especially multipla of gold solidi, that is to say, coins of multiple value of the standard gold denomination.[64] The iconographic scheme involving Fausta on some of the reverses of these coins is remarkable and unprecedented (Figs. 5.9 and 5.10).

A multiplum minted in Trier between 324 and 326 bears the portrait of Fausta on the obverse, with her usual delicate countenance and exquisite details in the rendering of her pearl-studded tunica and hair, testifying to the care that had gone into engraving the die. But the reverse is even more

---

[61] For these differences between Fausta's and Helena's portraits, also see Longo (2009) 62–63.
[62] See also Woods (1991) 243–45; Potter (2009).
[63] On percentages, see Hekster (2015) 112. McClanan (2002) 17 argues that Helena appeared on 20 percent of Constantine's coinage. I could not verify her figures, derived from a paper delivered by Andrew Carriker to the American Numismatic Society in 1993. According to RIC VII, Helena appears on sixty-six of Constantine's emissions and Fausta on sixty-two.
[64] On the comparative ratios of gold solidi, multipla, and medallions with portraits of Fausta and Helena, see Washington in n. 49 in this chapter. Multipla with Fausta: RIC VII Nicomedia 69a, Ticinum 178, Trier 443, 444, 445. Helena: RIC VII Ticinum 177.

Fig. 5.9 Reverse of gold multiplum showing Fausta sitting on a throne (RIC VII Treveri 443). © The Trustees of the British Museum.

striking (Fig. 5.9). It shows a central haloed female figure—most likely Fausta herself—on a throne while nursing a child. The occasion commemorated may have been the birth of Fausta's youngest son, Constans. Fausta is flanked by two smaller women, allegories that may represent Felicity, Piety, Fertility, or Good Fortune, and two further children holding wreaths. These latter appear as *genii* (family spirits), but were probably also a reference to Fausta's two older sons. With the coin's caption reading *pietas Augustae*, "Piety of the Empress," it broadcast the predictable message that imperial procreation and motherhood were a duty the empress owed to the Roman people for their safety and well-being. The way in which the coin did so was, however, wholly unusual, for never before had imperial coinage presented an empress sitting frontally on a throne, let alone in the act of breastfeeding. The mixture of the domestic with the official gave this image an almost sacral aura.[65]

Whereas Fausta was here framed in the context of biological reproduction, another multiplum minted in Trier referenced her wider role in the fortunes of Constantine's dynasty, again employing unusual iconography (Fig. 5.10). This issue was minted for her stepson, the Caesar Crispus, son of Minervina, perhaps even early in 324, before Constantine set out against Licinius for the second time. On the reverse appeared a group of three figures. In the

---

[65] RIC VII Treveri 443, 444, and 445. On the unusual iconography, see Schade (2000), (2003) 48. On the coin, also Longo (2009) 114–15; Potter (2013) 242–43. Julia Domna was depicted as sitting on a throne, but not frontally: RIC IV Caracalla 588.

Fig. 5.10 Gold multiplum of Crispus, with Fausta between two male figures on the reverse (RIC VII Treveri 442). © The Trustees of the British Museum.

foreground two men of different sizes in tunicas and mantles shake hands in a gesture known as *dextrarum iunctio* (the joining of the right hands), while a woman stands between them, embracing them both while facing the viewer of the coin. Around the group runs the caption "Fortunate Offspring of Constantine Augustus" *(felix progenies Constantini Aug(usti))*. This image is commonly interpreted as representing Fausta with Crispus (the larger figure on the left) and his co-Caesar, her oldest son Constantine, although it has alternatively been postulated that the two men on the reverse stand for her own sons, Constantine and Constantius.[66] Either way, together with the obverse showing the portrait of Crispus, this was an image conveying and emphasizing the peace that ruled the Constantinian dynasty, despite the different lineages created by Constantine's relationships with Minervina and Fausta. This reflects Constantine's continued anxieties around succession, but it was also an image that afforded Fausta a central and quasi-official role. She was portrayed as indispensable for the maintenance of harmony and the stability of imperial power. This can be seen not only because she appears between the two men, in a manner reminiscent of earlier iconography of, for example, Julia Domna between her two sons.[67] It is also because Fausta wears a full-length embroidered mantle that resembles Galeria Valeria's garments.

---

[66] Longo (2009) 109–11; for identification of the male figures as Fausta's sons, Filippini (2016). Potter (2009) 142 for the date.
[67] RIC IV Septimius Severus 886.

Faint traces of embroidered costume also appear on some of Helena's coins from the mid-320s, especially those minted in Sirmium.[68] However, such dress was never as pronounced as it had been on Valeria's and was now on Fausta's portrait. Furthermore, none of the issues for Helena comment on the link between the role of an empress and male imperial power as explicitly as does this coin reverse from Trier. Fausta's robe is, in fact, a mirror image of the *trabea triumphalis* that Crispus himself sports on the obverse. This assimilation between male and female imperial appearance can also be seen on a Constantinian bronze portrait bust from Arles, sometimes identified as Fausta because of the woman's chignon. The lady pictured is attired with a pearl necklace, a stephane that is similar to those worn by the women on the Trier ceiling, and, crucially, a pearl-stringed diadem. Unlike Helena's diadem, this one features a central jewel above the forehead, just as Constantine's diadem often did.[69] On the Ada Cameo, the lady identified as Fausta also seems to wear such an oval-shaped ornament, while the headdress of "Helena" (on the left) takes the form of a band of evenly shaped stones (see Fig. 5.4).

The extant media that promoted Fausta as playing a constitutive part in imperial power, if not exactly sharing in it, were broadcasting to elite audiences. The bust from Arles probably derived from the imperial palace and would only have been seen by a select group of people. Multipla were hardly everyday coins, but were, like cameos, used as gifts to dignitaries and as payment to high military officials. Even so, the prominent role of Fausta may also have been perceived more widely. Fausta's and Helena's portraits might have featured on other gifts Constantine gave to his loyal followers, such as intaglio gemstones mounted onto signet rings and used as seals.[70] Although the evidence for such objects is difficult to interpret precisely as it derives mostly from plaster casts or glass paste copies produced in the early modern period, it seems again that Fausta was the more prominent subject of such portrayals. The only such extant gemstone portrait that survives, a jasper intaglio (Fig.

---

[68] RIC VII Sirmium 54. On Fausta's dress on Crispus' multiplum, see Schade (2003) 29, 55; Longo (2009) 109–11. Apart from the Sirmium coins, Helena appeared with an embroidered robe only after Fausta's death. See Chapter 7, Fig. 7.2; Chapter 9, Fig. 9.4. Delbrueck (1933) tav. 10.12, 11.14 erroneously claimed the latter posthumous portrait of Helena is the first example of an imperial woman being depicted as wearing a *dalmatica* with an embroidered border.

[69] Delbrueck (1933) 166; Calza (1972) 252; Wegner (1984) 153. Image at laststatues.classics.ox.ac.uk LSA-572 (last accessed 1/30/2021). The object is now at the Musée de l'Arles et de la Provence antiques.

[70] On types of imperial gifts (usually identified by the imperial portrait), see Marsden (1999) 89–103; Beyeler (2011) 31–37. Marsden (p. 90) speculates that objects with female portraits were gifted by empresses themselves, perhaps even to other women.

Fig. 5.11 Red jasper engraved with a portrait interpreted as that of Fausta. © The Trustees of the British Museum.

5.11), is possibly of her, while plaster casts of such objects have also been attributed with more certainty to Fausta than to Helena.[71]

Of course, intaglio gifts with imperial portraits were also given only to select individuals, who were allowed to seal their correspondence with Constantine in this way to ensure that the emperor prioritized the reading of their letters. Still, seals, doubling as signatures, had a wide range of further usages, from the validation of documents and acting as passports to the safeguarding of stored goods.[72] Like coinage, they were a significant channel for imperial portraits' dissemination to a wider public, and due to their infinite reproducibility, their dissemination was less susceptible to the control of the imperial center than coins. Inhabitants of the Roman empire therefore had ample opportunity to come face-to-face with their empress Fausta. For some of them, it may have involved just popping down to their city's

---

[71] On the jasper intaglio, see Walters (1926) 211 n. 2010, tav. 25. It has been identified as Fausta by Delbrueck (1933) 168–69 on the basis of its similarity to her coin portrait, as has a plaster case with a possible portrait of Fausta taken from a carnelian gem (Cades, Impronte gemmarie, 41.628). Spier (2007) 121 has expressed doubts on both, but such are far less pronounced than those about two plaster casts of intaglio portraits that Delbrueck (1933) 165–66 identified as Helena (Cades, Raccolta di ritratti, 2.70 and Cades, Impronte gemmarie, 41.619). The first piece, which also exists in an early modern glass paste copy, is the cast of an ancient gem, but it has now been firmly dated to the second century: Zwierlein-Diehl (2007) n. 832. The second Helena piece is now considered a modern fabrication: Spier (2007) 172. For a portrait of Helena on an aquamarine gem "in the round" probably produced after the death of Fausta, see Chapter 6.

[72] On Constantine gifting seals and further usage, Zwierlein-Diehl (2007) 6–9, 17.

market to buy or sell quantities of goods measured by an imperially authenticated steelyard. After the third century, the counterpoise weights on such steelyards usually came in the form of imperial busts, most commonly of empresses. Although most of these date to the fifth century or later, at least one bronze weight featured the bust of Fausta, who as such lent official imperial sanction to any business transaction conducted with the accompanying steelyard.[73]

In these different ways, Fausta's image seeped into everyday lives and popular imaginations. It is therefore not surprising that Fausta's portrait also frequently appeared on some of the most ordinary, but also most vital, objects that people possessed, terracotta lamps. Around twenty lamps displaying Fausta survive, found on sites all around the Mediterranean and all of them dating from the late fourth or early fifth century. The lamp producers may have therefore been inadvertently using a template from the Constantinian period for this product, rather than creating an entirely new design. Helena's portrait appears, too, but by contrast only one lamp depicting her is known.[74] It was Fausta's image, with her characteristic chignon and necklace, circulating on official and unofficial objects that, at least in the mid-320s, embodied the persona of the Constantinian empress.

* * *

Constantine's eastward territorial expansion between 317 and 324, and his progress toward sole imperial power, were charted by gradual and regionally distinct displays of the female imperial body. Fausta's and Helena's first localized appearances on coinage in Thessalonica in 318, and then on the dynastic issues at Antioch in late 324, are evocative, as both cities had seen the bodies of previous empresses mangled by Constantine's twice-defeated rival Licinius. By 325, however, there was an empire-wide and very disciplined representation of Constantinian women, with mother- and daughter-in-law embodying discrete spheres within the dynasty.

Helena's reappearance may testify to the deep bond forged during those early years at Naissus between Constantine, who clearly had monitored her

---

[73] Hartley, Hawkes, Henig, Mee (2006), 184 no. 155: steelyard weight found in Gloucestershire now at Corinium Museum at Cirencester, identified as Fausta by Martin Henig. On empresses as steelyard weights (over seventy are known), see also McClanan (2002) 29–35.
[74] Gualandi Genito (1975) 79–95. The lamp with Helena's portrait is in the Museo Civico Archeologico di Bologna. Although Fausta's reputation was tainted in 326, her memory was rehabilitated later (see Chapter 10), so it should not be a priori excluded that the craftsmen knew who they were portraying.

whereabouts during their separation, and his mother. But filial love alone is not sufficient to explain Helena's unusual resurgence. Later commentators were quick to interpret the public mother–son relationship between Helena and Constantine within a Christian framework of pious motherhood and remarkable sonship. Eusebius specifically highlighted that Constantine had minted Helena's portrait on coins. It should be stressed, however, that Christianity was not the primary motivation for Helena's promotion to Augusta in 324. No direct reference to the emperor's new Christian faith appears on her coinage, unless perhaps through the disappearance of the stephane.[75] It is far more likely that Constantine was inspired by Galerius' promotion of his mother Romula, which he adapted into a more sustained dynastic program. Helena served Constantine by allowing him to shape a cohesive family group against his stepfamily's claims and as a useful reminder to subjects that Constantinian empresses lived where tetrarchic empresses had died. Displaying his mother as a woman of status, bedecked in pearls, would also have helped Constantine to dispel rumors about his own legitimacy, an implicit confirmation of the doubts surrounding Helena's background.

In her portraits, Helena appears if not exactly youthful, then with a vigorous attractiveness that must belie her actual looks at the time. Already in 318 she was, even by modern standards, an old woman. Imperial portraits were not about individuals and personality, but about ideals and typecasting. This is not to say that Helena's new status did not also shape her experience. After a lifetime of ordinariness and obscurity, her propulsion into a public celebrity, and one that was intimately and visibly linked with the supreme ruler of the Roman empire, undoubtedly gave Helena an authority that was breathtaking, not the least for herself. The title of Augusta, in particular, conferred recognizable honors, even if Helena still stood in her daughter-in-law's shadow.[76] Fausta was also, of course and awkwardly, the sister of the woman who had earlier taken Helena's place at Constantius' side. Still, despite their relentless public depiction in tandem, it is unclear how much time the two women—or any of the women within the Constantinian family—actually spent together. For while Helena may have been with Constantine and Fausta

---

[75] See Eusebius, Vita Constantini 3.47.2 who claims Helena was made Augusta because she was a good Christian, and elaborates on Christian motherhood; see Chapter 8. An even more direct association of Helena with the Virgin Mary is presented by Ambrose of Milan; see Chapter 11.
[76] James (2001) 125, on the power that came with the Augusta title.

in Thessalonica in the winter of 317–318, or in Antioch, when Constantine entered the city in December 324 and coins with her portrait were distributed to the delighted population, much firmer historical evidence situates Helena elsewhere around this time. At last, we find her in Rome, the old imperial capital on the Tiber.

6
Roman Holiday

Constantine never considered residing in Rome for any length of time. Initially, his military campaigns against Licinius during the decade after the battle at the Milvian Bridge ruled this out in any case. But Rome still mattered to Constantine as the site of his conversion to Christianity and, inextricably linked to that, of his victory over his brother-in-law Maxentius, which had given him uncontested power in the West. The city's historic role also mattered a great deal to the Western senatorial elites based in Rome. Constantine's relationship with these men and women was not as fraught as has sometimes been argued, but they were predominantly still pagan, and some had been loyal to Maxentius, and before him, to Maximian.[1] The subtle reinsertion of his Maximianic wife and stepmother into a Constantinian family story after 312, as described in previous chapters, shows that Constantine believed this audience required careful handling.[2]

It is therefore not surprising that Constantine thought he needed a representative in the city, as Maximian had provided in the person of his wife Eutropia. He, too, needed someone to provide an imperial presence, to oversee the monumentalization of his victory and new faith in Rome's material fabric, and to act as a mediator between the old Roman aristocracy, Rome's people, Rome's clergy, and the imperial center. In early 313, when he left the city, Constantine had options as to whom he could appoint for these tasks. The holding in October 313 of a Western church council, chaired by the Roman bishop Miltiades, at a residence in the Lateran area named after the empress, Fausta, may indicate that his wife, of course a Roman by birth, had stayed behind. But Constantine could not spare Fausta for long, for he also badly wanted heirs.[3] Several of his half-siblings, however, were presumably

---

[1] On Constantine's relationship with Rome, see Harries (2012) 124; Salzman (2016); Moser (2018) 13–44, with a bibliography of earlier scholarship postulating hostility or indifference.

[2] See Chapter 3.

[3] Optatus, *Against the Donatists* 1.22–24. For doubts that the Fausta in question was Constantine's wife, see, for example, Liverani (1990) 28, Liverani (2020) 18–19. He argues that Fausta's memory was banned, but see pp. 294–295 for a more nuanced picture. It would seem too much of a coincidence that Constantine called a council into a space named after another Fausta. See also prior p. 60. On the council, see the text that follows.

also resident in Rome, married to members of the senatorial aristocracy. It was probably during the emperor's own second visit to the city, in 315, that he contemplated the elevation to Caesar of his brother-in-law Bassianus, husband to his half-sister Anastasia.[4]

As we have seen, Constantine brutally canceled this plan within a year. The fall-out ended in the removal of his half-siblings from Rome, and possibly even of their mother Theodora, if she was still alive. Constantine's nephew Julian, son of his half-brother Julius Constantius, would lament that his father was forced for his own safety to roam the empire like Odysseus after the fall of Troy.[5] Some historians have seen Helena's jealous mind behind Constantine's ostensible exclusion of Theodora's children from power, and it is true that the latter were apparently never directly involved in imperial government again during Helena's lifetime.[6] Given Helena's experience of being first abandoned and then restored into a dynastic network expanded by her former partner's subsequent family, we may not want to judge her too harshly for harboring feelings of resentment. Even by Roman standards, this was a unique, and perhaps uniquely stressful, situation. Yet, apart from a dark allusion by Julian that Helena was his father's "wicked stepmother" (mētryiá)—a twisted claim, as it was his grandmother Theodora who had become Constantine's stepmother—there is little evidence of Helena's agency in the events of 316.[7]

Nonetheless, as we have seen, Helena's public appearance as a dynastic figure on Constantine's coins was clearly connected to these events, which were soon followed by Constantine's first victory over Licinius. The same is true for her arrival in Rome, where the senatorial aristocracy would have been badly shaken by Bassianus' downfall and its consequences. To be sure, our only relatively secure date for Helena's residence in Rome is as late as July 326, when Constantine assembled his family in the old capital to celebrate the twenty-year anniversary of his imperial rule (*vicennalia*).[8] But Helena's

---

[4] For the marriages of Constantine's half-siblings, see Chapter 3; for Bassianus as Caesar, Chapter 5. For Constantine's visit to Rome in 315, Barnes (1982) 72.

[5] Julian, Letter to Corinthians (where his father resided for a while) frg. 4, quoted in Libanius, Or. 14.29–30. Julius Constantius and Flavius Dalmatius are also attested as having resided in Toulouse; see Barnes (2014) 164. Theodora was certainly deceased by 337; see Chapter 9.

[6] See, for example, Klein (1988) 356. Note, however, that CTh 12.17.1 (321 or 324) may be addressed to Flavius Dalmatius.

[7] Julian's view is quoted in Libanius, Or. 14.30. For doubts about Helena's involvement in the removal of Constantine's half-siblings from court, see Drijvers (1992a) 52.

[8] See Chapter 7 for more on the Vicennalia celebration in 326. Cf. Barnes (1981) 220–21 who believes that Helena arrived in Rome shortly after 312.

name, and memories of her patronage of individuals, civic and Christian urban institutions there, are so intimately connected with parts of the city's topography that it is safe to assume she spent a reasonable amount of time in Rome.[9] More importantly, the first record of Helena's activities in Rome dates from 317 or shortly thereafter. This takes the form of an inscription commemorating her restoration of a bathhouse in the vicinity of Constantine's imperial palace in the eastern part of Rome, the Sessorium. Although this object in itself is no proof that Helena was present in Rome, the specificity of the benefaction and its location suggests Helena's intervention had been triggered by firsthand knowledge of the site.[10] Another inscription from around this time, accompanying an honorary statue of Helena "mother of the greatest victor Constantine" erected by "the council and people" of Saepinum in central Italy, gives us a direct clue not only to when but also why Helena started to reside in Rome. Saepinum, an otherwise unassuming provincial town, was particularly famous for being the ancestral home of the senatorial Naeratii family, into which Constantine's now banished half-brother Julius Constantius had married. The statue (which does not survive), commissioned before Helena became Augusta, seems likely to reflect a benefaction or even visit by Helena shortly after she arrived in Rome, to assure this city of imperial favor despite the disgrace of their important local patrons.[11]

Constantine therefore had recourse to his aging, obscure mother as an imperial delegate in the area of Rome only a few years after his conquest of the city and under very specific circumstances. In Rome, Helena stepped into a political gap to provide damage control and stability—*securitas*, the very ideal promoted on her coins—to Constantine's projects and social relations in the city, and to strengthen the dynastic superiority of her son's side of the Constantinian family tree. It would not have been Helena's own choice to reside in Rome and to take up an awe-inspiring assignment in a city hitherto entirely unfamiliar to her.

---

[9] Drijvers (2016) 151. The architecture of the new imperial palace buildings that Constantine had constructed in Rome indicates in any case that he envisaged a durable imperial presence in Rome. I would like to thank Markus Löx for this observation. For the palace, see the discussion that follows.

[10] CIL 6.1136. Helena is referred to without the title Augusta, but as a grandmother of Caesars, dating the inscription to 317–324. Johnson (2005) also deduces the date of 317 as the beginning of Helena's stay in Rome from this. For discussion of the inscription, see Drijvers (1992a) 47; Pohlsander (1995) 73; and the text that follows here, also on Helena's palace.

[11] CIL 9.2446: *Helenae matri domini nostri Constantini maximi victoris semper Aug(usti) ordo et populus Saepinatium* (dated to before 324 due to the absence of the Augusta title). On the Naeratii and Saepinum, Gaggiotti (2010; see p. 24 for more on the statue of Helena at Saepinum) and Chausson (2007) 123.

In today's popular and devotional imagination, Helena is invariably connected to Rome's Christian landscape, into which, eventually, her body would be laid to rest. When tracing Helena's sphere of activity in the city, we will however not begin here. As we shall see, the contours of her Christian faith and patronage continue to remain decidedly vague also in Rome, at least during her lifetime. We gain a much stronger sense of Helena as a historical individual—including her ability to skillfully mediate imperial presence—when turning to palatial topographies and evidence for civic patronage within the walls of Rome. Judging by her portraits extant from the city, the living Helena was presented in Rome in a classicizing way, and based on the evidence of her philanthropic acts, she behaved like a traditional Roman empress. This was perhaps expected by and necessary for the conservatively minded elites and populace of the city and in accordance with the reasons why she resided in Rome.

Palace Life

When Helena traveled around the Eastern provinces following her sojourn in Rome, she was greeted by the inhabitants of the cities she visited and distributed gifts to them. We can assume that she also received a ceremonial entry into Rome, even if she came there without Constantine. An episode involving Eusebia, the wife of Helena's grandson Constantius II, demonstrates how an arriving empress could be afforded certain ceremonial trappings. In 354, Eusebia visited Rome on her own. In his panegyric on the empress, Julian described her entry into Rome in a way that strikingly resembled that of an imperial *adventus*, featuring a delegation of the Senate and the people to greet her, a visit to the Forum, popular acclamations, and the distribution of largesse to "the leaders of the tribes and the centurions of the commons," surviving relics of the republican political organization. This was all according to Rome's "custom to receive an empress," implying that there was an existing procedure that dated back to the time of Helena and before. By the time of Flaccilla, wife of Theodosius I (d. 386), there was certainly "imperial protocol" regulating the empress's arrival in Constantinople, which may have built equally on earlier precedent from Rome.[12] The usual milestones

---

[12] Julian, Or. 3.129C: ὁπόσα τε ἔνειμε τῶν φυλῶν τοῖς ἐπιστάταις καὶ ἑκατοντάρχαις τοῦ πλήθους ἀπαριθμήσασθαι. He also uses the term *epidēmía*, the Greek equivalent of *adventus*. On the official trappings of this visit, see also Di Mattia (2003) 331. For the date, see PLRE I, Eusebia, 300.

of an emperor's *adventus* were a procession with much largesse through the Porta Flaminia and along the intramural stretch of the Via Flaminia toward the Forum, where he would deliver speeches to the Senate and people. The emperor would then traditionally offer a sacrifice at the Temple of Jupiter on the Capitol and preside over games at the Circus Maximus before retiring to the Palatine.[13] From the description of Eusebia's *adventus*, we can deduce that Helena skipped certain elements of this. Christian emperors did not sacrifice anymore, but the empress as a woman would never have done so anyway. It is also uncertain whether Helena would have given speeches or launched circus games. We also know that she did not retire to the Palatine, but to a palace in the southeastern part of Rome. Still, such topographical change does not mean that her presence did not affect the rhythms of urban life.

Helena resided at the southern end of Rome's green belt, an area of garden estates (*horti*) that extended over the top of the Quirinal, Viminal, Esquiline, and Caelian hills (Map 4). Most of the Esquiline and eastern part of the Caelian was imperial property in the early fourth century, although the boundaries of previous property units often continued to be observed and estates were owned by various members of the imperial family. This region was also where the residence with the painting showing the Constantinian family was situated, and where Constantine's wife Fausta owned her house.[14] While this home was located further west toward the summit of the Caelian hill, Helena's residence was in Rome's easternmost corner, in the garden estate known as the Horti Spei Veteris in the third century (Map 4, n. 7).[15] Part of it had once belonged to the philosopher Seneca whose property had been confiscated by Nero. It extended from the double gate opening to the Via Labicana and the Via Praenestina (now Porta Maggiore), where eight of Rome's aqueducts entered the city, for about 1 kilometer along the southern side of the Via Caelimontana.

In the earlier third century, members of the Severan dynasty had used these gardens as a residence. In particular, Elagabalus had lived here,

---

On Eusebia in Rome, also Chapter 10. On Helena in Eastern cities, Chapter 8. Flaccilla: Gregory of Nyssa, In Flaccillam 481–82.

[13] Humphries (2007) 30–33.
[14] For the residence with the paintings, see Chapter 3. For the "house of Fausta," see pp. 148–149. The two are sometimes held to be identical, but the evidence is inconclusive.
[15] The name derived from an ancient Temple of *Spes* (Hope) in this area. For the following, see Colini (1955); Colli (1996); Guidobaldi (1999); Borgia, Colli, Palladino, Paterna (2008a, 2008b); Fraioli (2012) 330–38; Barbera, Magnani Cianetti (2016).

building a temple on the gardens' grounds dedicated to the Syrian god who was his namesake.[16] Other structures from this time included an amphitheater and an enormous circus, connected to each other by a long corridor, as well as baths and a large rectangular hall. After the tragic end of the Severans, the palace fell into disuse, exemplified by emperor Aurelian's decision in the 270s to build his new city wall right through the middle of its circus. Now Constantine revived the residence and perhaps even united its grounds with the area north of the Via Caelimontana, the Horti Lamiani and the Horti Tauriani, making them as sizable as Hadrian's suburban villa at Tivoli. It is also possible that the palace now came to be known as "Sessorium," a reference to its stature as an imperial residence (*sedes*), although the toponym may also already have been slightly older.[17]

It is not difficult to see why this site appealed to Constantine. To begin with, it was exceedingly lovely. Centuries of wealth in aristocratic and imperial hands had turned the hills of Rome into beautifully groomed private parks, with an array of lawns, tree arrangements, pastures, and water features that allowed the privileged few a taste of nature at the heart of the city.[18] Just north of the Sessorian Palace itself, possibly built during the course of its enlargement by Constantine, stood a large domed octagonal room, lavishly decorated and heated, which is now erroneously known as the *tempio di Minerva Medica*. It was probably a dining space where a select group of urban guests could be entertained in the midst of greenery. A nearby hall was furnished with a mosaic showing hunting scenes echoing the elite pastimes conducted in the forests and fields beyond Rome's walls.

It was not leisure alone, or even predominantly, that attracted the imperial court here. The area around Porta Maggiore was one the highest points in Rome, the reason why several aqueducts entered the city here. The palace buildings, especially the huge audience hall that Constantine erected here at 21 meters high, were visible from afar, while also being segregated from the city by the intramural stretch of the Aqua Claudia (the Arcus Caelemontani; Map 5, n. 10). Between the palace and the civic center of Rome, only 2 kilometers downhill along the intramural Via Labicana, stretched aristocratic residential areas. At its western border, in the area known as the Lateran, Constantine was building a grand church for the Roman community and its

---

[16] Historia Augusta, Elagab. 13.5 and 14.6.
[17] Orlandi (2016) 278–79.
[18] On the *horti Romani*, see Frass (2006).

bishop Miltiades (Map 4, n. 3). Building had commenced immediately after Constantine had entered the city, in November 312, and the place chosen had a clear Maxentian connotation. Rather than selecting a site connected to the previous history of Christianity in Rome, the new church rose over the razed barracks of Maxentius' horse guard, the *equites singulares*, many of whom had died with him at the Milvian Bridge.[19]

The Sessorian Palace was therefore at the same time conveniently set apart, underscoring the sacral aura of the emperor and his family, and a conspicuous reminder to its senatorial and clerical neighbors of the imperial presence in the city. The complex shifted imperial gravity to this southeastern corner of Rome, away from the Palatine where Maxentius had resided, both as usurper and before that, presumably, as a child with his mother Eutropia and his siblings. It is notable that Constantine did not revive the Severan circus here, perhaps to highlight that circus games were for the enjoyment of the entire populace in the middle of the city. Maxentius had famously built a circus in his villa on the Via Appia, an exclusive affair for the entertainment of the emperor and his private guests only. Constantine was keen to distance himself from such behavior of the "tyrant" from whom Constantine had just "liberated" the Roman people. He also increased the number of seatings in the Circus Maximus itself.[20]

The Sessorian Palace therefore meant imperial business. Its architecture reflected the importance of the ceremonial in imperial self-representation, emphasizing imperial legitimacy, closeness to the divine, and the natural character of the deeply hierarchical social order that saw the emperor at the top.[21] On its city-facing side, the complex had, like other tetrarchic palaces, a monumental, possibly colonnaded facade (Map 5; n. 5). Behind it lay the representative areas where official visitors would be formally received and the amphitheater. The more intimate, residential rooms of the court stretched out to the rear, to the east and north of the current church (Map 5, n. 13), connected to the more "public" areas through an easily policed corridor. It is here, adjacent to the Aurelian wall which functioned as the palace's northern enclosure, that two self-contained domestic spaces have been discovered, decorated with monochrome mosaics, walls painted in red and gold,

---

[19] On the date of the Lateran basilica and its construction history, see Krautheimer, Corbett, Malmstrom (1977); Curran (2000) 94–96; Holloway (2004) 57; Liverani (2020).

[20] Aurelius Victor, De Caes. 40.27; Panegyrici Latini 4.35.5. See Curran (2000) 83–86. *Tyranny* and *liberation* are key terms of the inscription on Constantine's arch, dedicated by the Senate in 315: CIL 6.1139.

[21] Kolb (2007).

Fig. 6.1 Residential area of the Sessorian Palace: so-called *domus dei ritratti*.
© Julia Hillner.

open courtyards with water features, and upper floors. These are usually interpreted as the homes of higher-ranking imperial court members (Fig. 6.1; Map 5, n. 8). Nearby, the abandoned intramural part of the circus was transformed into a service area and slave quarters at around this time.

As was customary, the palace's layout allowed for selective and gradual access to the late antique emperor, who, in this instance, happened to be generally represented by his mother. Constantine himself visited Rome only three times: in 312, 315, and 326. The public appearances of Constantinian women in the increasingly elaborate imperial ceremonials of the day are obscured by the topos of informal "female influence" on imperial decision making beloved of late antique authors. Imperial women were often portrayed as being susceptible to a network of court lackeys promoting the interests of contacts in the outside world. For instance, Constantine's sister Constantia was described as influencing her brother Constantine in favor of the "Arian" heresy on the instigation of an "Arian" presbyter who was part of her household. Later in the fourth century, such supposed intrigue was often traced to the empress's eunuchs, as in the case of Constantius II's wife Eusebia who was allegedly close to the villainous chamberlain and eunuch Eusebius. Such stories show that court outsiders suspected imperial women to be powerful due to their proximity to the emperor, but also placed this power emphatically within the domestic sphere and the sphere of intrigue and female gullibility. This was one of the ways in which an emperor's decisions could then be legitimately questioned.[22]

In reality, much government business at the Roman court was at all times conducted through personal connections and the persuasion of the emperor. Within this system, it had long been acceptable to approach imperial women and their entourages for support. Their accessibility was expected and access to them much competed over, and some empresses at least also held formal audiences. When their own interests were not at stake or the emperor was considered "good," commentators could observe this behavior quite neutrally or ignore it completely. For example, when Eusebius of Caesarea described Helena's later travels around the East, he cheerfully referenced her "private" meetings with subjects.[23] In Rome, we find a somewhat muted trace of a successful case of female imperial patronage in the holding of the aforementioned church meeting at Fausta's residence in the Lateran area in October 313. Constantine called this meeting to sort out a schism in the church of Carthage that had arisen from divergent views on the correct behavior of clerics during the recent persecution. Although this synod is usually described as having been instigated by the bishop Ossius of Cordoba, one of Constantine's clerical advisors who was in contact with one of the parties, the location of the meeting place suggests that Fausta was also involved and that the parties concerned had pursued a multilateral strategy of petition.[24] Fausta had her own connections in Rome, which may have extended to the clergy, but more importantly, she was also a relative of Maximian and Maxentius, who had until recently ruled Africa. In 311 Maxentius had restored church property seized during previous persecutions in these provinces, and for that reason he would have been remembered as a benefactor. It is therefore not inconceivable that a delegation of clerics had approached his sister to advocate their cause with her more unfamiliar husband, perhaps while she was in Rome with Constantine in the winter of 312–313.[25] In any

---

[22] On the stories surrounding Constantia, see Hillner (2019a). On Eusebia and Eusebius: Socrates, Hist. eccl. 2.2; Theodoret, Hist. eccl. 2.16. Another example from Constantinian times is Athanasius, Historia Arianorum, 5, who claimed heretics got access to Constantine "through women,": παρα τῶν γυναικῶν σύστασιν. See also Chapters 7 and 8 here.

[23] Eusebius, Vita Constantini 3.44; James (2001) 83–84; Busch (2015) 224–26 for the Theodosian period. For the earlier empire, see Späth (2010) 293–308. Saller (1982) 57 and n. 98 for the personal nature of imperial rule. On empresses' audiences, for example, Cassius Dio, Historiae 78.18.2 (Julia Domna); Julian, Or. 3.123A–B (Eusebia); Mark the Deacon, Vita Porphyrii 39–43 (Eudoxia).

[24] See n. 3 in this chapter.

[25] This is the so-called Donatist schism that would rumble on throughout the fourth century; on the details, see Potter (2013) 401–2. On Maxentius and Africa, see Rosen (2013) 68.

case, the fact that the synod's location at an empress's house was recorded without further comment implies that neither Constantine nor those who kept the meeting's records were concerned about the visibility of Fausta's patronage. Even during the Constantinian period, imperial women therefore engaged with different sections of the population in a publicly accepted way.

For Helena, it means that we need to place her as much in the representational areas of the Sessorian Palace as in the more residential ones. Nonetheless, she indubitably had gatekeeping courtiers around her who regulated her representational activities; those who populated the residential spaces described earlier. In the case of the previous Augusta, Galerius' wife Valeria, such courtiers had included noble women, male "companions" chosen by the emperor from civil or military palace officials (*comites*), and eunuchs.[26] We know that Constantine also employed the latter, often enslaved individuals, in his household and around his women.[27] When his father-in-law Maximian plotted to murder him in the palace at Arles, Constantine allegedly deceived him by putting a eunuch in his and Fausta's bed who was duly assassinated in his stead. Eunuchs were useful, not only because they were considered sexually "safe" attendants of women, but also because their inability to have their own families and their often foreign origins ensured a relative social isolation that increased their dependency on and hence loyalty to the imperial family. Eunuchs' role as gatekeepers could render them very powerful indeed, which accounts for the depictions of them as schemers. It was nonetheless a perilous position, for their role was also to absorb the criticism of the emperor himself (and sometimes to become "fall guys"). One of Helena's courtiers may have been the chamberlain Festus, a position later usually occupied by eunuchs, who before 324 donated revenue from a landed estate that he owned near Rome in the territory of Praenestina to the Lateran baptistery. Another may have been the eunuch Eutherius who served emperors from Constantine to Julian and finally retired to Rome, because here "he was cherished and loved by everyone," which implies he had previously visited the city at a time when a court was in residence.[28]

---

[26] Lactantius, De mortibus pers. 39.
[27] On Constantine and eunuchs, Tougher (2020) 191-92; more generally on imperial eunuchs: Tougher (2008) 36-53.
[28] On the assassination story, see Chapter 3. Festus: LP I 174. On Eutherius Ammianus Marcellinus 16.7.7: *colatur a cunctis ordinibus et ametur*; PLRE I, Eutherius 1, 314-15. Given his biographical data, Eutherius may also have been in Rome with Helena's granddaughter Constantina in the 340s (see Chapter 10), especially as he served Constans during this time, the emperor of the West.

150 CENTER STAGE (C. 317–C. 329)

Not all of Helena's courtiers were eunuchs, however. The Sessorian and Lateran areas were dotted with statues of the empress erected by faithful men who had probably been in her service (see Map 4 for find spots). A "very devoted" equestrian official, the *praepositus rerum privatarum* (supervisor of imperial property) Flavius Pistius, erected an honorary statue for Helena in Rome after 324, perhaps to repay some personal favor he had received. Its inscribed pedestal was found on the eastern side of the Lateran complex, not far from an area that has been identified as an administrative and storage space connected with the *res privatae*. Another fragment of a marble object dedicated by Pistius was found near the Sessorian Palace.[29] Pistius' job title suggests that he was in charge of leasing out imperial land, collecting its revenues and overseeing its tenants.[30] As such, he may have been responsible for land allocated to Helena from the *res privatae*, of which, as we shall see, some was located just outside Rome's walls. After Helena had left Rome for the East, another honorary statue was erected by the senator (*vir clarissimus*) and *comes* Iulius Maximilianus, this time in the vicinity of the Sessorian Palace, where the corresponding inscription was found. Maximilianus also dedicated a marble plaque to Helena, perhaps attached to a further statue and again found at the Sessorium. His title of *comes* indicates that he was a member of the imperial service, too, assigned as a personal companion to Helena's court, similar to the officials that had surrounded the Augusta Valeria.[31]

These courtiers, especially the chamberlains, were tasked with sorting visitors into those who were granted more formal audiences, those who were allowed more intimate get-togethers, and those who would be denied access altogether. Bribery played a customary role here.[32] A caller lucky enough to have cleared the hurdle of such gatekeepers and merit a formal audience with Helena at the Sessorian Palace had to traverse a large peristyle in heading toward the audience rooms lined along its eastern side (Map 5, n. 3). Among them were either baths or a ceremonial dining hall, decorated with bluish-green cipollino marble, as well as a smaller audience room, all serviced by

---

[29] CIL 6.1135 (lost); CIL 6.36903; on the service area near the Lateran, Scrinari (1989) 2213 and Chapter 10. On honorary inscriptions for Helena found in the area of S. Croce and the Lateran, Orlandi (2016).
[30] Delmaire (1989) 214, 217.
[31] CIL 6.1134 (now at S. Croce in Gerusalemme) and the very fragmentary CIL 6.36950 (now mostly lost); dated to after 326, because they mention the Caesars Constantine and Constantius, but not Crispus.
[32] Gerontius, Vita Melaniae 11 records that the the early fifth-century ascetic Melania took precious objects for the eunuchs and chamberlains when visiting Serena, the emperor's sister.

Fig. 6.2 Remains of the Constantinian audience hall in the Sessorian Palace (later erroneously called the "Temple of Venus and Cupido"). © Julia Hillner.

an underground tunnel (cryptoporticus) running under the peristyle that hid the grubby side of slavery from sight (Map 5, ns. 1, 2, 4). The largest of these rooms was the aforementioned audience hall that in size and layout recalled that of the palace in Trier and the huge apse of which still survives (Fig. 6.2). In the fifth century a "basilica Heleniana which is also called the Sessorium" is reported to have hosted an assembly of the Senate, clergy, and fifty bishops in the presence of the emperor Valentinian III and his mother Galla Placidia. This is usually taken as a reference to the adjacent church, the later S. Croce in Gerusalemme, but at this point this church was commonly called "Hierusalem." Given the equation of the basilica Heleniana with the palace, it may instead refer to this audience hall, a more natural environment in which the emperor would have interacted with a large crowd. If so, memories of Helena at this place ran deep and beyond association with explicitly Christian space.[33]

Within late antique palatial architecture, apsed audience halls were the material manifestation of the emperor's increasingly sacral aura. The one in Rome was separated from the peristyle by a porticus that served as an antechamber in which guests were made to wait, certainly sometimes for hours (Map 5, n. 6). Upon entering, they would have been overwhelmed by the height of the space and the green and red marble inlays (*opus sectile*) on the floor and high walls, but their eyes would swiftly be drawn to the apse beyond, light-flooded and painted in gold, which in the Sessorian Palace was 10 meters deep, deeper still than the one in Trier. When in 325 the assembly of bishops met in a similar palace hall at Nicaea, Constantine took his seat on a golden throne in the middle of the apse's raised floor that emphasized his near-divine status.[34] We have no record of whether Helena ever did the same at the Sessorian Palace. But many years later an imperial woman, the emperor Honorius' sister Serena, did use this palace hall at the Sessorium for audiences, where she received the Roman noble and Christian holy woman Melania. On this occasion, Serena came to meet Melania in the peristyle, embraced her, accompanied her through the hall, sat on her throne, and urged Melania to sit as well. An even later Roman saint's life story, the *Passio Gallicani* written in the sixth century, remembers Helena herself coming out of the palace to greet the story's legendary protagonist, the converted Roman general and later martyr Gallicanus, and welcome him inside. In both cases, the imperial women were presented as humbling themselves out of respect for their visitors' Christian piety and asceticism. The inversion of procedure in these scenes gives us a glimpse of how hierarchies would normally have been observed during real visits to Helena in this space.[35] Indeed, some late antique empresses were recorded as conducting their audiences from behind

---

[33] Gesta de Xysti purgatione 4: *sederunt in uno conflicu in basilica Heleniana quod dicitur Sessorium*. This document is an early-sixth-century text describing the occasion, which may be fictitious, but the text was still drawing on knowledge and understanding of the Sessorian Palace. The early-sixth-century bishop Symmachus was called to a church council in *Hierusalem basilica palatii Sessoriani* in 501, which must in contrast refer to the church (Acta Synhodi a. DI, 438).

[34] Eusebius, Vita Constantini 3.10.5. On the role of audience halls in late Roman palatial architecture, see Ellis (2000), 170–73. A reconstruction of the decorations of the hall at the Sessorian Palace, with a floor decorated in red and green, and a golden triumphal arch framing the apse, see Bottiglieri, Colli, Palladino (2016).

[35] Gerontius, Vita Melaniae 12; Passio Gallicani 6.

curtains or surrounded by bodyguards, to emphasize the gulf between them and imperial subjects.[36]

Who might Helena's visitors have been? In the 380s, the Christian priest and ascetic Jerome reported that it was the noble women of Rome who eagerly waited outside the empress's door every day, similar to Melania's visit to Serena not long afterward.[37] According to Jerome, the aristocratic ladies of Rome spent their time on such rounds of visits in order to cement their husbands' positions within the networks of power. It would have been imperative for the female forebears of these women to see the aging Augusta Helena, however lowborn, too, and repeatedly. This must especially have been the case after the mysterious events surrounding the death of Constantine's brother-in-law Bassianus, which may have also seen some of these women's husbands exiled.[38] Furthermore, as we shall see, Constantine's half-sister Eutropia the Younger continued to live in Rome. The same may have been true for Anastasia. At some point before 365, baths in Constantinople were named after her, but, of course, this does not have to mean she was present in the city on the Bosphorus. There is slight evidence that she was buried at St. Peter in the Vatican.[39] These "Theodoran" sisters certainly paid Constantine's mother respect, dispensing with any distaste or embarrassment they may have felt for the woman their mother had replaced and who had now so extraordinarily arrived in their life. Some of these relatives and other elite visitors may also have graduated into becoming Helena's more intimate courtiers, just like Galerius' wife Valeria had included her mother Prisca and senatorial women among her ladies-in-waiting. Senatorial women also appear among the courtiers of Serena.[40]

We may be able to see a reflection of Helena's influence in furthering senatorial careers in the erection of statues in her honor by senatorial men at their posts. Among these were the *vir clarissimus* Alpinius Magnus, who around

---

[36] See Gregory of Nyssa, In Flaccillam 483–84 on Flaccilla, wife of Theodosius I. On curtains in imperial ceremonies involving women, see also Wieber-Scariot (1999) 116–21.

[37] Jerome, ep. 22.16, written 384: *Si sibi solent adplaudere mulierculae de iudicibus viris et in aliqua positis dignitate, si ad imperatoris uxorem concurrit ambitio salutantium, cur tu facias iniuriam viro tuo*? It is unclear whether he is referring to a specific empress, or just making a general point. If the former, he may be referring to Gratian's widow Laeta, who was a Roman aristocrat and resided in Rome after his death in 383; see PLRE I Laeta 1, 492.

[38] Moser (2018) 15–28. On Bassianus, see Chapter 5. On Eutropia the Elder, see Chapter 8 and Eutropia the Younger Chapters 9 and 10.

[39] On Anastasia's burial at St. Peter, possibly in the mausoleum later reused for the Western Theodosian dynasty, Schumacher (1986). On the baths named after her, see Chapters 9 and 11.

[40] Lactantius, De mortibus pers. 39–40. On Serena: Gerontius, Vita Melaniae 11 (she sends the wives of senators to visit Melania).

325 sponsored a statue of the empress at Salerno, and the *vir clarissimus* and *curator rei publicae* (imperial urban envoy) Valerius Gypasius, who did the same at Sicca Veneria in Africa Proconsularis (El Kef near Tunis) sometime after 326. It is notable that both these men did not belong to the oldest families in Rome; possibly an indication that Helena was directing her patronage toward those slightly less well connected. Alpinius Magnus was originally from Sicily and of equestrian rank. After 324, and perhaps due to Helena's patronage, he is attested as a senator, and with postings to senatorial governorships, first in Sicily and then in Lucania et Bruttii (today's Calabria). Both Magnus and Gypasius declared themselves on the surviving statue pedestals as "devoted" to Helena, and to her "excellence and piety" and her "divine will and majesty," respectively.[41]

Another group of men Helena must have engaged with, whether in formal audience, at more informal gatherings, or indirectly through her courtiers, were those involved with Constantine's many ongoing building projects in Rome. While Helena was in residence here, the city was in the grip of enormous building activity, both inside and outside its walls. Constantine sought to dismantle Maxentius' reputation by completing and rededicating some of the monuments his brother-in-law had built. These included the grand basilica at the Forum's northeastern corner and the adjacent building, where Maxentius had tried to promote a cult around his family, merged with the veneration of Rome's founder, Romulus, a dynastic link that Constantine was anxious to sever.[42] In addition, Constantine styled himself as the patron of the Roman people and protector of their rights, including the receipt of imperial largesse. Although Maximian and Diocletian had just presented the people with a vast bath complex at the northeastern end of the Quirinal hill, Constantine added another one, at the southern end of that same hill.[43] The emperor's most radical intervention in the city's topographical makeup were his church foundations.[44] Never before had a Roman emperor sponsored

---

[41] CIL 10.517: *devotus excellentiae pietatique eius* and CIL 8.1633: *devotus numini maiestatique eius*. On Alpinius Magnus, see Drijvers (1992a) 50–51.

[42] Curran (2000) 80–84; Johnson (2005) 280. On Maxentius' aims, Cullhed (1994) 52–55. Dedication of the basilica to Constantine is mentioned in Aurelius Victor, De Caes. 40.26.

[43] Aurelius Victor, De Caes. 40.27; Johnson (2005) 281 who argues that they may also have been an original project by Maxentius.

[44] In the sixth-century Book of Pontiffs (LP I: 172–83), seven churches are attributed to Constantine: The Constantinian basilica, now S. Giovanni in Laterano with its baptistery; the basilica "at the two laurel trees" on the Via Labicana dedicated to Sts. Peter and Marcellinus; the basilica in the Sessorian Palace, now S. Croce in Gerusalemme; the basilica of St. Laurence on the Via Tiburtina; the basilica of St. Peter at the Vatican; the basilica of St. Paul on the Via Ostiensis; and the basilica of St. Agnes on the Via Nomentana. St. Peter, St. Paul, and St. Agnes were built by Constantine's children or at the very least remained uncompleted during his lifetime [on St. Agnes, see Chapter 10; on St. Peter

a Christian building, and never before had the Christian community of Rome been able to worship in surroundings as safe and as monumental as Constantine's churches. Constantine clearly felt compelled to repay his personal debt to his new God quickly, but his new faith also generated a new vision of popular patronage, one that encompassed the formerly persecuted Christians and their liturgical need for places to pray and to be buried.

This focus of Constantine's building activity may have brought Helena into contact with the Roman bishop, who after 314 and throughout the time that Helena spent in Rome was a man called Silvester. Although the involvement of this bishop in Constantine's church projects in Rome is only documented in the sixth century, it can be assumed to have existed, especially since Constantine also communicated directly with the bishop of Jerusalem Macarius about church building in his city. On that occasion, Constantine directed the bishop to his imperial officials, including the governor of Palestine, to obtain building materials and labor. He also encouraged Macarius to liaise with him personally about decorative items, such as marble and precious metals. The emperor had a monopoly on the use of such items and also needed to give his approval for the reuse of ornaments from other public and sometimes even private buildings (so-called *spolia*). Later, Constantine also sent his mother to Jerusalem, as a mediator on the ground, where he granted her access to the imperial treasury (*basilikôn thēsaurôn*) "to manage at her discretion" probably partly for the supply of luxury building furnishings. It is therefore quite likely that she had previously fulfilled this role in Rome also, especially since Constantinian churches in Rome employed a large quantity of *spolia*, such as marble columns.[45]

The building industry in Rome was, however, on a different scale than it was in a province such as Palestine, which helps to account for the rapid completion of many of Constantine's projects in the old capital. Many of its constituent parts, such as the brick and mortar industries, had been in imperial hands since the time of Caracalla and had latterly been revived under Diocletian for his massive urban projects. At Rome, there were regularly appointed urban officials to oversee the building process, who would

---

and St. Paul, Logan (2011) 44–49]. The same may be true for St. Laurence and S. Croce (on the latter, see the discussion that follows). Constantine may have built a church not mentioned in the Book of Pontiffs, the basilica of the Apostles on the Via Appia, now S. Sebastiano, see p. 159.

[45] Eusebius, Vita Constantini 3.30 and 47. On the correspondence with Macarius, Curran (2000) 91–92, and see Chapter 8 here. On imperial approval for *spolia* and their heavy use in Constantinian buildings, Brenk (1987) 103–7. On imperial monopoly of precious stone and metal, Hirt (2015).

commission architects, solicit cost estimates, manage an enslaved workforce, and hire additional free laborers through the builders' guild. These previously independent and senatorial posts were becoming centralized under the urban prefect at the time of Constantine.[46] If we consider Helena to have been involved with construction projects in Rome, we need to imagine her engaging not only with the bishop or imperial administrators, but with the holders of these urban posts also, especially the urban prefect, the highest imperial representative in Rome and usually a member of an old senatorial family. It is perhaps not a coincidence that later memory connected Helena with the saint Gallicanus previously mentioned here. The man who is believed to have inspired this fictive hagiographical figure was Ovinius Gallicanus, donor of a Christian church to Ostia, but also the urban prefect at around the time when Helena first arrived in Rome.[47]

We should envisage that Helena's contacts with such men involved more than just ecclesiastical construction projects. The only building in Rome that the historical Helena can unequivocally be connected with is not a church, but the aforementioned public thermal complex that stood just outside her palace (Map 4, n. 6; Map 5, n. 7). Helena did not build it, for it had stood here since Severan times, too. Its surviving mosaic decorations, showing athletes, resemble those found in the Baths of Caracalla, and the design of its central hall was a smaller-scale copy of the one in the greater imperial baths. At some point, possibly because the area had been abandoned after the demise of Elagabalus, these baths had been damaged by a fire. Helena restored them, and a monumental inscription, framed by a border of acanthus leaves and dovetail handles emphasizing its official character, was affixed, probably to its facade, to commemorate her intervention. Helena's renovation works may have extended to the cistern itself, situated next to the baths on slightly higher ground, the brickwork of which attests to attempts to regulate the flow of water between its different compartments in the early fourth century (Fig. 6.3).[48] By 330 Helena's courtier Iulius Maximilianus, mentioned earlier, had become a *consularis aquarum* (overseer over the aqueducts). While this postdates Helena's restoration of the baths and his dedication of her statues, Maximilianus' connection with the water supply still suggests that

---

[46] Chastagnol (1960) 30–63.
[47] PLRE I Ovinius Gallicanus 3, urban prefect 316–17. See Champlin (1982).
[48] CIL 6.1136, now in the Vatican Museums, affixed to the wall behind Helena's sarcophagus in the Sala a Croce Greca: *D(omina) n(ostra) He[lena venerabilis do]mini [n(ostri) Constantini A]ug(usti) mater e[t] avia beatis[simor(um) et flore]ntis[simor(um)] [Caesarum nostr]oru[m] therm[as incendio de]stru[ctas restituit]*. On the baths, Palladino (1996); Borgi, Colli, Palladino, Paterna (2008a) 12.

Fig. 6.3 Remains of the cistern of the "Baths of Helena." © Agnes Crawford.

his promotion stemmed from the empress's actions in improving thermal provision in this area of Rome.[49]

Helena's very visible patronage of baths from almost the moment of her arrival in Rome is curious. In the earlier empire it was unusual for empresses to sponsor such facilities in Rome. Baths at least named after imperial women are recorded in Constantinople for the later fourth, fifth, and sixth centuries, including one named for a Helena (which may, however, also refer to the emperor Julian's wife); one for a Anastasia; one for Eudoxia, the wife of Arcadius; and one for Sophia, the wife of Justin II. Here again, Helena may have been the model for such patronage, especially at a time when bathing was becoming increasingly connected to Christian ideas of healing and care for the sick.[50] Helena's restored baths in Rome, of a type popular all over the empire with small hot and cold facilities and a *palaestra* (open-air gym),

---

[49] On the connection between Maximilianus' statue dedications and the Baths of Helena, see Drijvers (2016) 149 and Merriman (1977), although his argument that Helena also sponsored an aqueduct feeding the baths is not entirely convincing. They were probably supplied by the Aqua Alexandrina.

[50] For the baths named after empresses in Constantinople, see Angelova (2015) 140–41, 173–80 who takes Helena's as referring to Constantine's mother. On the Baths of Anastasia, see Chapter 10. For Rome, the only previous example of baths named after imperial women is the Lavacrum Agrippinae on the Viminal; see Richardson (1992) 234. Provincial baths were sometimes named after earlier empresses, for example, the Baths of Faustina Minor at Miletus; Yegül (1992) 291.

were, however, still wedded to more classical ideas of urban leisure time, as were Constantine's baths on the Quirinal. Their proximity to her palace was key, as this cemented bathers' impression of this area of Rome as the center of imperial power. Even more important was their location near one of the busy main gates of Rome, which made the baths convenient for the many travelers arriving or departing on the Labicana and Praenestina roads. They carried with them the memory of imperial patronage by the "mother of the emperor and grandmother of the Caesars," as Helena's building inscription proudly proclaimed. Helena's benefactions were closely linked with the wider promotion of the imperial family.

Although popular patronage was therefore within Helena's brief, it is less clear whether she would have ventured beyond the confines of the palace and out into the city, except for making further ceremonial entries or departures when traveling to places outside Rome. One such place may have been Campania, where the local city council of Naples erected an honorary statue for her. But while this may have commemorated a visit, it is equally possible that such honors, which similarly included statues for Fausta in Surrentum and Privernum, were court-directed strategies to transfer a local population's loyalty to the Constantinian dynasty, in a region that had been the emperor Maximian's favorite not long before.[51] In Rome, Helena may have engaged with sections of the population in the amphitheater attached to her palace, which was still in use as late as the sixth century.[52] She may also have interacted with the Roman people in a Christian context, although the evidence for this is slim, as we shall now see.

Helena and the Constantinian Churches in Rome

Although there are several churches in Rome that claim foundation or at least endowment by Helena, her actual involvement with these remains elusive, if to a varying degree. In Rome, as elsewhere, Helena's Christian legend grew to supervene over her life, and the consequences of this can be felt up to the present day. Sometimes, this has led to decidedly tenuous associations.

---

[51] CIL 10.1484; 10.1483; 10.678; AE 2007, 354. On Campania as Maximian's residence, see Chapter 3.

[52] Anonymus Valesianus 12.69 situates an execution, of the count Odoin *in palatio quod appellatur Sessorium* under Theodoric in the year 500, which may have taken place in the amphitheater as a customary place for executions.

This is certainly the case for the church now known as S. Sebastiano, and in late antiquity as the Basilica of the Apostles (*basilica Apostolorum*), situated on the Via Appia outside Rome's walls, about 3 kilometers southeast of the city (Map 4, n. 2). Constantine's foundation of this church is not mentioned in any text, but has been postulated among others on the basis of a monogram discovered on the side of a threshold leading to the church's courtyard that may represent a contraction of his name. For reasons of symmetry, some modern scholars have further hypothesized about the existence of a second monogram on the other side of the threshold, one bearing Helena's name. This hypothesis lacks any material support and owes more to what later generations thought they knew about Helena, her Christianity, her relationship to her son and to the city of Rome, than actual fact.[53]

In the cases of two other churches, we move closer to the historical Helena, but her agency nonetheless escapes us. A sixth-century text, the Book of Pontiffs, a serial biography of the Roman bishops, claims that Constantine founded a church in the area of the Sessorian Palace. The Book of Pontiffs further states that upon its foundation the emperor gifted the church a relic of the True Cross and chose its name, "Hierusalem." This is the church known since the twelfth century as S. Croce in Gerusalemme (Fig. 6.4; Map 4, n. 5; Map 5, n. 13). Notably, the Book of Pontiffs does not mention Helena herself in conjunction with this foundation, although another sixth-century document does note the existence of a *basilica Heleniana* within the Sessorian Palace. As we have seen, this latter structure may or may not be identical with the church of "Hierusalem." Although it is not inconceivable that Helena had been given a relic of the cross during her trip to Jerusalem, as we will find out shortly, the story that it had been Helena herself who discovered the cross would not develop until some years after her death. Nor did she ever return to Rome after her visit to the East. It is therefore impossible for Helena to have been involved in person in the donation of a cross relic, or even, because the two do seem to have been connected, in the church's foundation. Some archaeologists have in any case dated the church, which transformed a third-century hall of the palace, to the mid-fourth century. Perhaps Constantine or one of his sons who built the church deposited a cross relic here after Helena's death. It is equally possible that this story only became attached to this site,

---

[53] The hypothesis of the Helena monogram is expertly demolished by Dirschlmayer (2015) 49, with the relevant bibliography. The extant monogram may also contract the name of Constans or of Constantius II. For the church: Brandenburg (2004) 63–69. There are also doubts that this church was an imperial foundation at all; see Thacker (2007) 28.

Fig. 6.4 The northern wall of S. Croce in Gerusalemme, reusing a wall of the third-century palace in this area. © Julia Hillner.

recorded as being called "Hierusalem" only in the fifth century, after the rise of the legends around Helena's discovery of the True Cross.[54]

A similar fog envelops the church of St. Peter at the Vatican (Map 4, n. 1). The Book of Pontiffs also claims that Constantine and Helena had donated a golden cross to this church, erected above the tomb of the apostle. It bore the inscription "Constantine Augustus and Helena Augusta. A glittering hall surrounds the royal house with similar brilliance."[55] The completion of St. Peter's has been dated to the 330s, however, or even to the reign of Constantine's sons Constans or Constantius, in either case again after Helena's death.[56] It has therefore been suggested that the cross was an object originally deposited at the church of "Hierusalem" in the Sessorian

---

[54] LP I 179. For problems regarding Helena's involvement, see Drijvers 34 (1992a); Dirschlmayer (2015) 44–46. On the date of the building based on archaeological evidence, Krautheimer (1937) 191–92 ("verso il 350"); Colli (1996) 779 ("avanzata età costantiniana"), although see Brandenburg (2004) 106 who dates the church to before 324 as the Book of Pontiffs only lists endowments from lands in the Western empire. Restaino (2017) 457–503 provides the most recent archaeological and architectural overview. On the *basilica Heleniana*, see the earlier discussion in this chapter. On Helena in Jerusalem, the story of the True Cross, and the emergence of the name "Hierusalem," see Chapters 8 and 11; on Constantine's possible gift of a cross relic to the Sessorian church, De Blaauw (1997) 62–63; (2014) 139–43.

[55] LP I 176: *Constantinus Augustus et Helena Augusta hanc domum regalem simili fulgore coruscans aula circumdat*. The inscription is often translated as "Constantine Augustus and Helena Augusta. He surrounds this house with a royal hall glittering with equal splendor" [see, e.g., Davis (2010) 18], but this does not follow the Latin grammar.

[56] Constans or Constantius: Bowersock (2002). Liverani (2015) argues the church was begun by Constantine, but may have been completed after his death.

Palace (the "royal house" referenced in the rather enigmatic inscription) and only later transferred to St. Peter.[57] This raises the same issues as were just described, since we cannot be sure either that the church of "Hierusalem" was founded under Constantine, or that it focused from the outset on the veneration of the cross. Again, it may be the case that this second sixth-century report about a cross was retrojected from later tales that emerged around Helena's Christian patronage.

The most conspicuous connection between Helena and a Constantinian church relates to a third church in Rome's *suburbium*, the basilica *ad duas lauros* ("at the two laurel-trees") on the Via Labicana (today's Via Casilina; Map 4, n. 8). It was situated at nearly 4 kilometers beyond the walls, on a slight elevation on the northern side of the road that stood roughly in the center of a vast imperial estate of about 4860 hectares. This estate's boundaries can be reconstructed from an entry in the Book of Pontiffs, which describes the revenues of this Christian complex, including those derived from the surrounding land. According to this account, the estate bordered on the intramural area occupied by the aforementioned Sessorian Palace, with which it had formed a physical unit until the Aurelian wall had separated the two in the later third century. Afterward, it extended from the double city gate of Praenestina and Labicana (in the Book of Pontiffs called Porta Sessoriana) some 10 kilometers eastward along the Via Labicana. To the north and south it was framed, respectively, by the Via Praenestina and, perhaps, the Via Latina, making it triangular in shape, with an eastern boundary that, again, ran about 10 kilometers from north to south. The estate, which must have cultivated wine, fruit, flowers, and vegetables for the urban market, seems to have been managed from a site close to the aqueducts that ran along the Via Labicana (the Anio Vetus and Novus and the Aqua Marcia), called the Fundus Lauretum. It was this site, which also featured a bath complex, that may have given the entire estate its name.[58]

---

[57] Bowersock (2002) 35.

[58] LP I 183 lists as revenue for the basilica *ad duas lauros: fundum Laurentum iuxta formam cum balneum et omnem agrum a porta Sessoriana usque ad uia Penestrina a uia itineris Latinae ad montem Gabum, possessio Augustae Helenae, praest. sol. Ī CXX* ("the fundus Laurentus [usually corrected to Lauretum], next to the aqueduct with a bath and all the land from the Porta Sessoriana up to the Via Praenestina from the way of the Latina route up to the Mons Gabus, the possession of the Augusta Helena, which delivers 1120 solidi"). For the topography, see Deichmann, Tschira (1957) 66–68; Vendittelli (2011a) 8–9 with a map. The area *inter duas lauros*, also mentioned in LP I 199, was known as imperial property already to Tertullian, apol. 35. Coarelli (1986) 35–38 argues that the Fundus Lauretum did not cover the entire area between the Via Praenestina and Latina, but was concentrated around the length of the Via Labicana (approximately 2020 hectares).

The Book of Pontiffs describes the Fundus Lauretum as the *possessio* (possession) of Augusta Helena. Among the further endowments of the church, consisting of land revenues and liturgical vessels, it goes on to list a substantial goblet of fine gold inscribed with the name "of the Augusta." In both cases, doubts surround the authenticity of these claims. The former, on Helena's *possessio*, is sometimes regarded as a later addition to an original fourth-century revenue list, presumably made, as in other cases, to strengthen the site's connection to Helena. As for the goblet, some manuscript variants of the Book of Pontiffs give the inscription as the name "of the Augustus" (*Augusti*).[59] But even if we accept these assertions of Helena's connection with the church as historical, it would be wrong to believe that all of this was simply a reflection of Helena's personal piety. The complex on the Via Labicana had multilayered purposes and was part of Constantine's larger monumental vision for a Christian Rome. In fact, the church "at the two laurel trees" was the second Christian construction project that Constantine began after the Lateran basilica and should therefore be regarded as part of a scheme that encompassed both sites.

The land surrounding the basilica had been imperial property long before Helena took possession of it. The basilica that now rose up here was, in part, built above catacombs dating to the second half of the third century, an underground labyrinth of tunnels with burial slots in their walls. Both pagan and Christian communities had extensively used these prior to Constantine's reign and would continue to do so into the later fourth century through an entrance situated in the courtyard on the south side of the church. But the bodies of ordinary Christians or pagans had not been the only ones interred in this area. Due to its proximity to their barracks in the Lateran area, a necropolis dedicated to the imperial bodyguard, the *equites singulares*, had overlain the warren of catacombs since the second century.[60]

Providing burial on one's land was an established act of personal patronage in the Roman world in the absence of systematic state-sponsored care for the dead. Use of the catacombs on this imperial property had probably been leased out to various religious or professional associations that provided

---

[59] LP I 183: *scyphum aureum maiorem purissimum, ubi nomen Augustae designatur, pens. lib. XX*, with list of MSS variants. On the *possessio Helenae* possibly being a later addition to the original text, Diefenbach (2007) 179 n. 373.

[60] See Deichmann, Tschira (1957) 46–66; Krautheimer (1959); Guyon (1987); Rasch (1998) 25–43; Curran (2000) 99–102; Holloway (2004) 88–93; Brandenburg (2004) 55–60; Johnson (2005) 110–18; Venditelli (2011b) 30–50; Dirschlmayer (2015) 47–51; also for the following archaeological and architectural details of both the basilica and mausoleum.

their members with burial in return for a membership fee.[61] In the case of members of the imperial horse guard, their burial on imperial land at the Via Labicana had been granted as a special privilege. Constantine now not only abolished this privilege, but also destroyed the entire necropolis altogether, in combination with his elimination of the horse guard itself for its support of Maxentius. Its brickwork and headstones were used as building material for the Christian edifice. The orientation of the church, set at an odd angle to the road, followed the former graveyard's enclosure, which had possibly been built under Maxentius. Once again, Constantine's act of Christian charity was interwoven with his desire to epitomize his victory over Maxentius. The Lateran basilica, atop the troops' barracks, together with the basilica "at the two laurel trees," over their burial ground, provided this message in stereo parallel.

Constantine also redirected his patronage of this site toward his new fellow Christians. Some of these received preferential treatment by no longer having to seek burial in the catacombs, but above ground in the unusual liturgical surroundings of the basilica. Underneath its floors and that of its courtyard archaeologists have discovered rows upon rows of tightly stacked graves. The primary purpose of the basilica, a massive building of over 65 meters length, was thus to serve as a funerary space. Its outline was circus-shaped, with the exterior naves curving around the central one at the western end. This ambulatory design allowed for funerary processions and other ceremonial visits to tombs, including the anniversary banquets that were still common among fourth-century Christians.

Although from the later fourth century onward, burial in the cemeterial basilicas of Rome was coveted for its proximity to the tombs of Christian martyrs, this was not the primary motivation for the creation of this church, probably the very first one of its type. It is true that by the sixth century, the basilica "at the two laurel trees" was dedicated to two Roman martyrs, Peter and Marcellinus, members of the Roman clergy who had allegedly died during Diocletian's persecution. There is, however, no trace of their veneration at the time of Constantine, let alone by the emperor or his mother, despite their general respect for martyrs as publicized by Eusebius and others. For Peter and Marcellinus' tombs in the catacombs, which were only monumentalized later in the fourth century, lay outside the perimeters of the

---

[61] Rebillard (1999).

church, at an oblique angle to the apse, without direct access from the basilica.[62] Of course, this does not exclude the possibility that a diffuse adoration of the saintly dead motivated those who sought to inter their relatives here. However, quite apart from the martyrs, the church "at the two laurel trees" was initially meant more to reward devotees with burial close to another set of extraordinarily special dead: the deceased of the imperial family.

Shortly after the start of the construction of the basilica itself, a large circular mausoleum with a dome, still partly extant today, was erected opposite its eastern end (see later Figs. 9.1 and 9.3; Map 4, n. 9). As coin finds and brick stamps show, it, too, was completed before 326. Both structures were connected by a sizable narthex (antechamber) that opened to the church and to the vestibule of the mausoleum through arcades on either side. Numerous graves were sunk into this narthex's floor already in the Constantinian period. On the basilica's southern side, a portico provided entrance to the entire complex. Stairs lead up from the street level to a covered passage along the eastern side of the portico. Visitors climbed these to arrive at the southeastern corner of the basilica, from where they then had the opportunity to either turn right toward the narthex and mausoleum or left into the basilica.

It was here, in the mausoleum opposite the basilica, that Helena would find her final rest a few years later, becoming its first and perhaps only occupant.[63] At the time of its construction, however, the mausoleum was planned as a dynastic burial chamber to house, in its seven niches, multiple members of the Constantinian family, including Helena, but also Constantine himself. Eusebius of Caesarea called the site the "imperial tombs" (*eríois basilikoîs*).[64] As we have seen, a mausoleum designed solely for a female member of the imperial family would have been unusual and certainly in Rome. At a time before he took over the East, it is unlikely that Constantine wanted to echo in the ancient capital the tetrarchs Maximinus Daza and Galerius' experimental posthumous treatment of their respective mothers, even if he knew about it by then.[65] At this stage, moreover, Helena had not yet been singled out as the

---

[62] On Peter and Marcellinus: LP I 182. On the precedence of the imperial cult over that of martyrs here, and possibly elsewhere in the Constantinian basilicas, see Guyon (1987) 262; Diefenbach (2007) 165–75; Hellström (2016); Oosten (2016). A liturgical calendar (Depositio martyrum, LP I 12) from the first half of the fourth century mentions another martyr venerated in the catacombs *ad duas lauros*, Gorgonius, but again he did not seem to have had a cult site within the basilica. On Constantine and martyrs, see Eusebius, Vita Constantini 3.48, 4.61, and Chapter 1 and 3 on Helena and Lucian of Antioch.

[63] See further discussion in Chapter 9.

[64] Eusebius, Vita Constantini 3.47; Guyon (1987) 256–58; Brandenburg (2004) 59; Diefenbach (2007) 178–79; Delogu (2011) 18; Dirschlmayer (2015) 47; Angelova (2015) 136.

[65] See Chapter 4.

most important woman of his dynasty, whose special status might warrant such an unusual recognition. Instead, and following the example of other imperial mausolea in Rome, Constantine was looking to build a commemorative dynastic complex here, in his city of victory. It uniquely combined elements of Christian funerary liturgy and large assembly space with features of the imperial cult through a bipolar architectural design combining a cemetery basilica and mausoleum. The complex's significance was also reflected in its large endowment, the scale of which, an annual income of 3,754 solidi, was surpassed only by that of the Lateran basilica.[66] In these well-furnished surroundings, the emperor hoped to lie close to the saints among the bodies of his relatives, and beyond them of his Christian people at large, all united in death and faith.

Again in response to the exponential growth of her legend, by the seventh century the church was considered Helena's foundation, an *ecclesia Helenae*, where she rested among the martyrs in her "rotunda."[67] We can certainly imagine that the historical Helena took a keen interest in a burial complex destined also for her. She contributed to its endowment, although, as we shall see, this most likely happened after her death and it is unclear whether she had been the Fundus Lauretum's actual owner.[68] Even here, as elsewhere in the Roman Christian landscape, we cannot postulate that this ecclesiastical project was undertaken on her initiative.[69] This should not surprise us. It is true that independent female patrons are well attested, both as donors to and founders of Christian institutions, in Rome and elsewhere, although only from the later fourth century onward. Aside from the date, one difference between many of these benefactors and Helena was, however, access to funds. Securely attested female church founders in late antiquity were usually wealthy heiresses of the Roman elite.[70] Although Helena, as we shall see later, was given control of the imperial treasury and allocated income from it, it was, given her background, unlikely that she had sufficient property independent from her son to sustain and endow major construction work of her own choosing. This was different even from her daughter-in-law Fausta,

---

[66] LP I 182–83.
[67] Notitia Ecclesiarum urbis Romae 16: *in sua rotunda*.
[68] See Chapter 9.
[69] As done, for example, by Deichmann, Tschira (1957) 77 or Angelova (2015) 138 who maintains that the Book of Pontiffs "glosses over Helena's building initiative."
[70] For Rome, see the cases of Vestina and Demetrias (LP I 221, 238). The financial relationships between wealthy women and the Christian church were of increasing concern to late antique law givers; see Kuefler (2015).

who, we must assume, had received an inheritance upon her imperial father's death.[71] It is again Fausta, not Helena, who may have had more scope to act as an independent patron of Christians at this time, despite later authors claiming she remained a pagan throughout her life.[72] In Milan, a "church of Fausta" (*basilica Faustae*) was mentioned later in the fourth century, located outside the walls between the palace and the mausoleum built by Fausta's father Maximian.[73] Even if conclusions about ownership from toponyms are always difficult, and we have less information about Fausta's religious beliefs than those of Helena, the association of Fausta's name with a church in the city of her father's main residence is suggestive, particularly given that church's location.

The patronage of churches by empresses also stood apart from that of other women on account of their special status, quite beyond the question of whether they had their own means to fund it.[74] Empresses owed their official position to the emperor. Their actions reflected on the values of the imperial household as a whole and were therefore usually carefully curated. This had also been true for earlier empresses' civic or religious building patronage, despite their frequent access to independent wealth. Their activities had already been part of and complemented the emperor's program of self-representation. It is often difficult therefore to ascribe precise acts of patronage to earlier empresses, too, and evidence for their personal agency is rare and elusive.[75] Such absorption of empresses' deeds into those of the court continued in the case of Christian patronage. Of course, some things did change. In parallel with the rising role of Christian piety as an important and, at some point, perhaps the central imperial virtue, empresses' church foundations become more discernible over the course of late antiquity. Imperial women could partake in performance of this virtue more directly than in other acts of a traditional nature, such as military leadership. This opened spaces for agency unavailable to earlier empresses. Although Helena would become the model for some of these later female imperial church founders, in her own time all this lay far into the future, however.[76]

---

[71] Constantine may have confiscated Maximian's property after his suicide, but political suicide was usually chosen to allow for the customary transmission of property to descendants; see Plass (1995) 93.

[72] Zonaras, Epit. hist. 13.1. Zonaras' comments owe to Fausta's bad reputation on account of her death, see Chapter 7.

[73] Ambrose, Ep. 22. For its location, Sannazaro (2016) 411.

[74] For the following, James (2001) 148–63; Dirschlmayer (2015) 5–17.

[75] Stephens Falcasantos (2017) 115; Washington (2015) 37–40.

[76] On these developments and Helena as a model for later empresses, see Chapter 11.

In early-fourth-century Rome, the emperor's main aim was to give his new community spaces to worship and to be buried, and to make a dynastic statement about his new faith that presented the imperial family as a converted collective.[77] There is little evidence that anything Helena did deviated from this aim or that she played more than a secondary role in realizing it.

All of this is not to say that Helena did not personally care about Christian worship. There is, in fact, evidence that, even if we could not connect the current basilica of S. Croce in Gerusalemme in the Sessorian Palace with Helena, she maintained her own palace chapel in the form of a room at the southeastern corner of the church, which was itself established within a rectangular transitional area of the palace between the amphitheater and the residential areas (Map 5, n. 12). From epigraphic evidence, we know that in the fifth century Valentinian III, his mother Galla Placidia, and his sister Honoria developed this cross-vaulted room in some way, perhaps decorating it with a mosaic. This space may have become the nucleus of the later church "Hierusalem," and it was perhaps here where Constantine deposited a cross relic after Helena's death. If this had been Helena's chapel, however, we must envisage her venerating the Christian God in the privacy of her palace, rather than in one of the brand-new churches about town. This is hardly surprising, as even for emperors imperial visits to churches outside the palace are only recorded from the later fourth century on.[78] Whether the church of S. Croce or only this chapel can be dated to the period of Helena's residence in Rome, either may also have been serviced by her personal priests. As we know from the aforementioned episode involving Constantine's sister Constantia, Constantinian women had or were expected to have such men attached to their households. The peculiar architecture of S. Croce itself, which included transverse arcaded walls that divided the nave into three oblique compartments (see Map 5, n. 13), was in any case designed to shield the imperial court, or at least its female members, from those members of the congregation coming in from the city.[79] If the lay-out of the church dated from

---

[77] Another ecclesiastical space where Constantine may have presented his family in this way according to Kähler (1962) was the patriarchal basilica in Aquileia. He maintains that the extant portraits in the church's mosaic floor (seven women and nine men) portrayed members of Constantine's family, including himself, Fausta, and Helena. This suggestion has not found agreement among scholars.

[78] McLynn (2006).

[79] On the possibility that the cross-vaulted space (the still existing partially subterranean chapel in S. Croce now called S. Elena) was Helena's chapel, and on the transversal walls of the basilica: Colli (1996) 779–82; Restaino (2017) 488–94. The room behind this chapel sometimes referred to as a baptistery was almost certainly not used as such at the time of Helena. On Galla Placidia's intervention, see Chapter 11. On private priests, especially those serving elite women, Bowes (2008) 80–82.

Helena's time, it offers a microcosm of the palace and, on a larger scale, the nature of Helena's life in Rome: one of benign accessibility to the urban community but, simultaneously, one of otherworldly, even gendered segregation.

New Look

Imperial spaces were not only awe-inspiring through their architecture. A court orator in 321 claimed that those approaching the emperor would be dazzled by his brilliant appearance. The bright purple colors of the emperor's silk clothes, and the glistening jewelry on his head and elsewhere on his body, such as his belt and shoes, furthered such impressions of otherworldly superiority.[80] If her coin portrait reflects her ceremonial appearance, Helena was similarly bedecked in jewels on such occasions. She would have worn a purple *palla* over a silk tunic with sleeves, the *dalmatica*, perhaps girded with a bejeweled belt. The *palla*, with a high collar covered by a necklace, had a gold-stitched border and, as the posthumous coins of Helena suggest, pearls along the hems. Eusebius of Caesarea, who saw Helena in the East, described her garments as simultaneously "majestic" and "decent." The clothes shown on her coins were designed to fully cover and hide the female body, but in their bulkiness, weight of fabric, and luxurious decoration, they also allowed for imposing power dressing designed, like the emperor's, to impress an audience. Helena's convoluted hairstyles that seemed to defy the laws of gravity signified her civility, wealth, authority, and, ultimately, Roman-ness, for loose hair was worn only by "barbarians" and slaves. Above all, the elaborate styling of jewels, clothes, and hair sent the message that their wearer had time and labor to spend on perfecting their public appearance. If Helena dressed as she appeared on her coins, she would have had to spend hours in the company of slaves trained in hairdressing (*ornatrices*), the draping of clothes, and the many other skills of female beautification, at least for ceremonial occasions. Given the tediousness of the process, which involved the use of hair pieces, glue, and sewing techniques, she may also have worn the same hairdo for several days in a row.[81]

---

[80] Panegyrici Latini 4 (10).5.1–4; Kolb (2007) 174. Male imperial ceremonial dress in Constantinian times is known above all from the so-called Missorium of Kerch, showing, possibly, Constantius II.

[81] On Helena's coin portrait, see Chapter 5. On Helena's posthumous coins, see Chapter 8. Eusebius, Vita Constantini 3.45: ἐν σεμνῇ καὶ εὐσταλεῖ περιβολῇ. On the messages transported by late antique female clothing: Clark (1993) 111–18. On the techniques and time it took to dress up Roman elite women's hair: Stephens (2008).

Fig. 6.5 Bronze medallion showing Helena with caption *Flavia Helena Augusta* on the obverse; on the reverse, a standing female figure with an apple and two children and the caption *Pietas Augustes* (RIC VII Rome 250). © The Trustees of the British Museum.

Not many coins struck in Rome between 324 and 326 for Helena and Fausta survive. Those that do largely follow the empire-wide numismatic style, showing Helena with a spherical hairstyle, necklace, and diadem and Fausta with her chignon, and *securitas* and *spes reipublicae* slogans on the reverse.[82] However, there is one series of coins from Rome that bucks the trend. This is an issue of bronze medallions, probably minted for the distribution of largesse, again between 324 and 326. Alongside the portraits of Constantine and his three Caesar sons, Crispus, Constantius, and Constantine, those of Helena and Fausta appear, too.[83] Helena is featured here with what for her was a novel hairstyle. A thick braid is wound crownlike around her head, while the hair framing her face is stiffly undulated, covers the ears, and ends in a loop of hair at the neck (Fig. 6.5).

This was, again, not an entirely new style, even for empresses. Valeria Galeria had previously been portrayed with a crownlike braid, although hers had been thinner, flatter, and positioned closer to the top of her head. Nonetheless, we can assume that this was a fashionable hairdo adopted by imperial women and now adapted further to suit Helena. On the medallion's

---

[82] RIC VII Rome 270, 271, 291, 292, 293. On Helena and Fausta's usual coin portraits, see Chapter 5.
[83] RIC VII Rome 248 (*felicitas Augusta*); 250 (*pietas Augustes*); 251 (Fausta's portrait, the caption on the reverse is worn away toward the end).

reverse appears either a female figure with an olive branch and scepter, or a woman wearing the same hairstyle worn by Helena on the obverse. She is holding a child and extending a hand with an apple or globe to another one standing beside her. The latter image is also shown on the reverse of Fausta's medallion, although here the figure wears a veil. The caption around the woman with the olive branch reads *felicitas Augusta*, while that surrounding the woman with the apple and children is *pietas Augustes*, an erroneous spelling of *Augustae*. *Felicitas* (Happiness) and *pietas* (Love for the gods, the emperor, and the Roman people) were standard reverse slogans of Roman empresses' coins, but during the time of Constantine only appeared on medallions.[84]

The emergence of Helena's new hairstyle on coin issues from Rome gives the impression that a distinctive look was created for the old Augusta in her city of residence, although it is not one that would have been any less time-consuming to perfect. This new look predated her promotion to the most senior woman of the Roman empire in 326, and underscores the importance that Constantine conferred on Helena's presence in Rome.[85] The extant examples of her three-dimensional image also suggest this, although they are, of course, much harder to date, or even to verify. There are numerous sculptures in modern museum collections that have, at one time or another, been identified as depictions of Helena.[86] Only four marble portraits can reasonably be assumed to actually be of Helena, due to a combination of their similarity with the medallion portrait we have just described and with each other and their outsized scale. They all probably originate from Rome and are dated to the 320s and 30s.[87] Two—the most secure attributions—are seated statues that are effectively replicas despite some minor differences between them, such as the tilt of the head (Figs. 6.6 and 6.7). They originally date from the second century, but their heads were recarved to represent Helena. A third example takes the form of a bust (Fig. 6.8), and the fourth and last one

---

[84] On the reverse types, see Longo (2009) 55 and 112. RIC VII Rome 250 is sometimes described as minted in Nicomedia. On Valeria Galeria's hairstyle, see Chapter 4.

[85] The crownlike braid also appears on posthumous coins of Helena; see Chapter 9. On her promotion, Chapter 7.

[86] Wegner (1984) 143–48 lists nineteen heads, statues, or statuettes; not listed by Wegner are: two heads, in the National Museum in Athens, Stathatos Collection, and in the Archaeological Museum Istanbul, inv. 5318 [both mentioned by Pohlsander (1995) 178]; a head in Kassel, Staatliche Kunstsammlung, Inv. Ge 236 [Prusac (2011) n. 483]; a statue at S. Croce [Lavin (1967)], on which see Chapter 7; and a head found in the catacombs of S. Callisto [Pontificia Commissione di Archeologia Sacra inv. 69; Ramieri (1989)]. See also Calza (1972), 168–80; Drijvers (1992a) 189–91.

[87] This dating is based on the upward gaze of the eyes, a characteristic of imperial portraiture at the time, expressing stately detachment, rather than religious spirituality as formerly thought.

Fig. 6.6 Marble seated statue, Musei Capitolini, Rome. Courtesy of Roma, Musei Capitolini. Archivio Fotografico dei Musei Capitolini. © Roma, Sovrintendenza Capitolina ai Beni Culturali. Photo: Julia Hillner.

Fig. 6.7 Marble seated statue, Galleria degli Uffizi, Florence. Courtesy of the Gabinetto fotografico, Galleria degli Uffizi.

is a marble head, again recarved from an earlier portrait and now affixed to a standing statue possibly of different origin (Fig. 6.9).[88]

---

[88] On the methodologies of establishing whether a sculpted portrait was imperial, see Schade (2003) 75–77. Schade 65, 173–77 establishes Figs. 6.6 and 6.7 as Helena, and cautiously also Fig. 6.8. On Figs. 6.6 and 6.7, see also Arata (1993) and Paolucci (2012–2013). The provenance of Fig. 6.8 from Rome can be assumed, but is not fully confirmed. On Fig. 6.9 (where the crownlike braid is slightly different) as presenting Helena: Prusac (2011) n. 485. On all four, see also Calza (1972)

Fig. 6.8 Marble bust. © Antikensammlung, Staatliche Museen zu Berlin, Foto: Universität zu Köln, Archäologisches Institut, CoDArchLab, 53243_FA-SPerg-000097-01_Gisela Geng.

Like the bronze medallion, each of these four portraits depicts Helena with a thick double hair braid wound around her head clockwise, at times secured with visible, pearl-studded hair pins. They all also feature stiff hair ripples around the face and, originally, hair loops at the neck, though these are only extant on the bust (Fig. 6.8). However, unlike the medallion portrait, the ears are left exposed. The faces are similar, both to each other and to that on the medallion. Helena appears here with an aquiline nose (as shown by Fig. 6.6; in the other examples, the nose was restored in modern times), fleshy cheeks,

170–73, 174–75 (who was the first to identify Fig. 6.6 as Helena) and Fittschen-Zanker (1983), 34–36. Two further heads, one in Vienna (Kunsthistorisches Museum inv. I 1497) and one in Copenhagen (Ny Carlsberg Glyptotek inv. 1938), are also often discussed as part of this "Helena group," but the attributions are very insecure. See Alföldi (1963) 133 n.1; Giuliani (2016). The head at the Palazzo del Governatorato, inv. 19152, previously identified as Helena is now considered a modern forgery; see Schade (2003) 92.

Fig. 6.9 Marble head mounted on a body possibly of different origin, Villa Borghese, Rome. © Julia Hillner.

a protruding matronal chin, a hint of wrinkles around the eyes, and a small mouth with the intimation of a smile. The complicated turbanlike hairstyle—which, in reality, would have required thigh-length hair and prolonged sessions with curling irons—adds to the note of benign and majestic authority that is also expressed in the face. The physiognomy clearly marks Helena's dynastic affiliation to the Constantinian house. At the same time, the head's smoothness and harmonic proportions emphasize Helena's femininity.

In the case of the two seated statues (Figs. 6.6 and 6.7), ideals of beauty and womanhood are also expressed through Helena's body, which remains that of the earlier sculptures originally portraying an Antonine empress as Aphrodite. Again, the statues' assimilation of the empress with Venus recalls Helena's representation on the medallion from Rome. Here, Helena appears therefore anachronistically attired in the intricately folded clothes of the Hellenistic age, an ankle-length and belted undergarment (*chiton*) pinned along the sleeves to create delicate star-shaped patterns, and a light mantle (*himation*) draped over the knees. The almost transparent fabric is at the same time voluminous, indicating prosperity, and tightly clad to the body, accentuating its feminine curves. Together with the relaxed pose and the coquettishly protruding sandaled foot, the statues exude a sensuality that seems at odds with the maturity of the recarved head, let alone Helena's real age at the time of around 80, or, indeed, with her Christianity. It is also a far cry from Helena's heavy and decent ceremonial clothes as described by Eusebius and shown on her coinage. It is unlikely she ever wore such Hellenistic garb in real life. While this combination of old and new, young and matronal may seem incongruous to us, it offers a further example of the Constantinian aesthetics of blending a golden past with a glorious present.[89]

Since the seated statues, like all the other extant sculptural depictions of Helena, hail from Rome, we can assume that their appearance was court-directed and tailored toward audiences in the imperial capital where she was residing. Although we know from inscriptions that statues were erected for Helena outside Rome, too, it is not known whether she was portrayed elsewhere with the same classicizing elegance and with this striking coiffure.[90] Her seated statues will in any case have been displayed in the imperial palace rather than in a public area, as was customary for the representation of the empress in this form. Judging from their less accomplished backs, they had

---

[89] On this assimilation, Varner (2020) 112.
[90] For Helena's inscriptions outside Rome, see Chapter 7.

probably stood inside niches.[91] Such objects can therefore only have been seen by a select group of people, who were privileged enough to gaze upon the empress in this eroticized form, but could also be expected to grasp the semi-divine metaphor. Nonetheless, as had been the case with Fausta's portrait in the palace of Aquileia discussed in an earlier chapter, knowledge of this Roman image traveled. A tiny aquamarine three-dimensional gemstone, now at the Museo Archeologico Nazionale in Venice, and again recarved from an earlier portrait, this time of Sabina, wife of Hadrian, bears a striking resemblance to the head of the Capitoline statue (Fig. 6.6). While developed for Rome, Helena's new looks were also consumed elsewhere.[92]

* * *

From her time in Rome, Helena finally emerges to us with a more defined personal profile, stepping out of Fausta's shadows. She had arrived at the top, with as much authority, status, and comfort as any woman, bar Fausta, could have in the Roman empire. Her accessibility to subjects in Rome and ability to mediate their concerns to the emperor also clearly gave her the power to shape some decisions, although we have no clear sense of quite how she used it.

Still, Helena's splendid surroundings at the Sessorian Palace which we can plausibly reconstruct should not mask the fact that, as an individual, she must have been on a steep personal learning curve. Our last record of Helena's environment was of her life in Naissus, Salona, and Nicomedia, where her outlook had expanded from the provincial to the imperial, but still gazed upon the center of power rather than from it. Ceremonial palace life in Rome, without Constantine and as the senior member of the imperial family in charge, would have been poles apart, not the least in terms of restrictions on her mobility. What is more, Helena was given the difficult political task of visually promoting her branch of Constantine's family, in the face of a potentially diffident Roman aristocracy. We can only speculate how far and in what ways she was trained for such public engagements.

All evidence suggests that despite her advanced age Helena fulfilled her mandate impressively. The honorary statues erected for her during this period were all dedicated by senators, and not the most obvious ones, by imperial officials, sometimes of the lower ranks, or by urban institutions, rather than by members of her

---

[91] Fejfer (2008) 333. Note that Varner (2020) suggests that the statues stood in the Castra Peregrina, based on the interpretation by Paolucci (2012) 431 that they symbolized "Securitas."
[92] Gagetti (2011).

family. They must therefore be taken as a sign of direct favors she had dispensed and that were duly repaid. If the speed of Constantine's Roman building projects had anything to do with her presence in the imperial capital, then Helena must also have been an efficient director of works. She was clearly admired by male administrators who worked in and beyond Rome. Although we cannot be sure if the restoration of the baths outside her palace resulted from her own initiative, it was completed quickly, at the beginning of her sojourn in Rome, doubtlessly after an assessment of how best to start making her presence in the city known. In any case, Helena would have collected vital experience during this period on how to deal with subjects' needs by engaging with a wide circle of constituents, from the elites to the Roman population and, perhaps, the Roman bishop. Helena would need this experience, for in 326 a profound family crisis enhanced her relevance to her son even further and propelled her into a new sphere of action.

7
Four Deaths and an Anniversary

Given Constantine's emphasis on dynastic legitimacy and the hope it gave for the empire's future, the emperor's was a family that was often portrayed. Among the earliest of such portraits is the so-called Hague-Cameo (Fig. 7.1), which was produced at around the same time as the Roman paintings possibly depicting a Constantinian family procession that we discussed earlier (Fig. 3.1). The cameo, which seems to reference Constantine's victory over Maxentius, may have been commissioned to commemorate the emperor's Decennalia of 315 (the tenth anniversary of his rule), which he celebrated in Rome. Cut into a large layered agate gemstone, it is commonly believed to show Constantine and his wife, a veiled Fausta, facing each other in a mythologized embrace that recalls the divine characters of Zeus-Dionysos and Hera-Demeter-Ariadne. They are positioned sideways on a triumphal chariot rumbling over a fallen *krater*, and pulled by centaurs trampling young men, one dressed in tunica, an allusion to victory in civil war. Victory herself hovers above the scene, extending a laurel wreath toward the already laureate central male figure. The woman behind Constantine's right shoulder is sometimes identified as Helena, but has also been interpreted as Constantine's fictional grandmother Claudia, niece of Claudius Gothicus. Given the cameo's probably early date and, as we shall see, its focus on legitimate inheritance, she may alternatively and more plausibly represent Theodora, Constantine's stepmother.[1]

If the dating is correct, the little boy in military gear standing in front of Constantine must be Constantine's first-born and at this point only son, Crispus, the offspring of his earlier relationship with Minervina. Crispus'

---

[1] The cameo, named after the Dutch king's residence, is also known as the Great Cameo or Gemma Constantiniana; see Henig (2006), 138–39, no. 76; Drijvers (1992a) 192–93. For the interpretation of the smaller female figure as Claudia, Zadoks-Josephus Jitta (1966). Bastet (1968) believes her to be Livia and dates the cameo earlier, to 310. Halbertsma (2015) believes the women to be Helena and Fausta, with a date of 315 and a recut in 324 to add their laurel wreaths, partly based on the assumption that Helena had raised Crispus, for which there is no evidence. Stephenson (2015) also argues for Fausta and Helena, but the boy is identified as Constantius II. In his view, the cameo commemorated their elevation to Augustae and Caesar, respectively, in 324.

Helena Augusta. Julia Hillner, Oxford University Press. © Oxford University Press 2023.
DOI: 10.1093/oso/9780190875299.003.0008

Fig. 7.1 So-called Hague Cameo, or Gemma Constantiniana. © National Museum of Antiquities, Leiden.

frontal depiction, to which both women conspicuously point, made him the focus for the cameo's viewer. The women's gesture, including that of his childless stepmother Fausta, highlight how, at this moment in time, Crispus was Constantine's heir apparent.[2] Consciously or not, this arrangement echoed one of the earliest examples of a dynastic cameo, a sardonyx carving commissioned by Nero's mother Agrippina, showing Augustus and his wife Livia, looking at each other from either side of their great-great-grandchild, a very young Nero who is himself confronting the viewer.[3]

As we have seen, the makeup of the Constantinian family changed rapidly over the next decade, for Fausta gave Crispus three half-brothers and two half-sisters. It is also possible to trace these shifts through the changes in dynastic iconography, ranging from the Ada Cameo showing Crispus and Constantine the Younger, appointed Caesar in 317, in front of Constantine, Fausta, and Helena (Fig. 5.4), to the golden multiplum from Trier c. 324, with

---

[2] Crispus (and Theodora) may also have appeared in the family procession on the Roman fresco from the house near the Lateran from around the same time; see Scrinari (1991) 164–65.

[3] This cameo is at the State Hermitage Museum in St. Petersburg, inv. ГР-12537.

Fig. 7.2 Bronze medallion, after 327 (?). © C. Hémon/Musée départemental Dobrée—Grand Patrimoine Loire-Atlantique.

its striking image of harmony between Fausta, her son Constantine, and Crispus (Fig. 5.10). Despite Fausta's belated motherhood, these portraits still recognized her stepson Crispus, therefore, as a fully fledged member of the expanding Constantinian dynasty.

At some point, however, Constantine's family iconography acquired a new veneer, which would have been utterly unrecognizable to a viewer of the Hague Cameo in 315, despite the similarities in composition. A bronze medallion now at the Musée Dobrée in Nantes, dated by the Christogram it features to the later 320s or even 30s, depicts yet another dynastic scene, with another couple gazing at each other above a group of three children (Fig. 7.2).[4] Once again Constantine is facing a woman, but this time it is not his wife Fausta, but his mother Helena, identifiable by the characteristic hairstyle with which she had often been portrayed in Rome, featuring the stiff ripples around the face and a braid wound around her head.[5] Albeit

---

[4] On the Christogram (the Chi-Rho) appearing on Constantine's coins from 327, Bruun (1997).
[5] Identification as Helena: L'Orange (1984) 123; Lançon, Moreau (2012) who argue that the far left of the three smaller portraits in the foreground shows Constantine's sister Constantia. Although

probably posthumously, Helena appeared here, for the first time, in the heavily embroidered robe that mirrored the emperor's *trabea triumphalis*, as previously worn by the imperial wives Magnia Urbica, Valeria Galeria, and Fausta on coins (Fig. 4.6 and Fig. 5.10). The medallion thus promoted the idea that the couple at the helm of the empire, by God's providence, were the emperor and his mother, rather than the emperor and his wife. What is more, Crispus had now disappeared. Although the imperial couple's facing busts once again frame the heirs apparent, the children depicted here are very likely to represent Constantine's three younger sons, Constantine, Constantius, and Constans, the last of whom was elevated to Caesar in 333.[6] The Constantinian family tree had been pruned again, into a slenderer shape consisting of Helena, Constantine, and her three grandsons.

Dynastic portraits from the Constantinian period are precious objects, not only for their materials, craftmanship, and antiquity, but also for their historical value. Their beauty and their insistent messages of loyalty, harmony, peace, and faith cannot mask the fact that, in reality, the Constantinian family engaged repeatedly in the replacement of its women and its heirs. So far we have witnessed Helena's substitution by Theodora, Theodora's sons by Constantine, Minervina by Fausta, Bassianus by Constantine the Younger, and Licinianus by Constantius II. Finally, we reach Helena's extraordinary replacement of Fausta and of Crispus by Fausta's sons. This was a pattern that had started at a domestic level, with Helena's fateful "casting aside" in the late 280s, but it increasingly followed the brutal logic dictated by public events and the pursuit of power. As such, behind their harmonious facade, Constantinian family portraits reveal a persistent anxiety about the dynastic fragility that derived from the complex sexual relationships entertained by Constantine and his father before him. This anxiety always had the potential to swerve into conflict, violence, and death. Perhaps inevitably, it did. It is true that some members of the family—such as Helena and Constantine's half-siblings—were not removed altogether. But many were not so lucky. Between the carving of the Hague Cameo and the minting of the bronze medallion from Nantes, at least five of Constantine's relatives lost their lives. The

---

Constantia assumed a certain role at Constantine's court in the later 320s (see pp. 183–187), this attribution does not seem likely on an iconographic level. Wegner (1984) 153 identifies the woman facing Constantine as Fausta, although Fausta is never portrayed with a hair braid. On Helena's portrait in Rome, see Chapter 6. The period of Nero once again provides an early example of an emperor and his mother facing each other, on a gold aureus minted in 54: RIC I Nero 1.

[6] See Chapter 9.

execution of Constantine's brother-in-law Bassianus in 316 had only been the beginning. It was during this period that one quality of Helena forcefully emerged. While she did have an interrupted life, she was also a serial survivor of family ruptures.

Murders in the Family

In early 325, Constantine seemed in full control, both of his empire and of his family. After raising his dynasty's profile through the award of new titles to his nearest relatives, he set out to transform the territory conquered from Licinius and to connect with its Christian inhabitants. Residing in Nicomedia, Diocletian's former headquarters, Constantine sent letters to the Christian churches and the inhabitants of the Eastern provinces to announce a string of measures that reversed the results of Licinius' recent persecutions. The banished were recalled and restored to their former status, those that had been sent to work in the mines or state factories were released, and confiscated property was returned, either to the original owner, their kin, or their local church. Unlike in 313, when Constantine and Licinius had similarly pronounced property restitutions, those who had benefited from these confiscations were not compensated. In addition, Constantine promoted Christians to administrative roles, and prohibited the consultation of oracles and traditional cult practices during the course of holding public office. Instead, he began a campaign of church building, and for this purpose gave bishops access to imperial funds and to the officials who administered them.[7]

However, trouble was brewing for Constantine on both the religious and the dynastic front. At some point the emperor became aware of a theological dispute disturbing Christian communities in the East. It concerned the teaching of an Alexandrian presbyter called Arius about the relationship between God the Father and Christ the Son. As far as we know—for the evidence is muddled and Arius' position was also far from fixed—he had postulated that Christ was not co-eternal with God the Father. This position was considered heretical by Arius' own bishop Alexander and by other, but by no means all, Eastern bishops. During the winter of 324–325 and into the spring, Constantine tried to end this disagreement through diplomacy, but

---

[7] Copies of Constantine's letters are reproduced in Eusebius, Vita Constantini 2.24–42, 46, and 48. The appointment of Christian governors and prohibition of sacrifice is mentioned in 2.45–46. On all of this, Barnes (2014) 107–11.

to no avail. Eventually, he called all Christian bishops to a universal council to settle the matter, to be held in his presence in Nicaea in May 325.[8]

Before the council met, Constantine found time to kill Licinius. As we have seen, the former emperor had been allowed to live in Thessalonica, presumably with his wife, Constantine's sister Constantia, and his sons. As in the case of other conflicts within Constantine's kinship group, it is difficult to understand what really happened here. The spin put out by the imperial court was that Licinius had tried to rebel against Constantine by inciting barbarian troops who served in the Roman army to revolt, whereupon other soldiers resisted and demanded his death. In one version of the story, Constantine even brought in the Senate to publicly condemn him, after which Licinius was allowed to commit suicide, a story suspiciously similar to reports of Maximian's fate in 310. In truth, there may have still been some support for Licinius in some quarters, both in the East and in the West. Although Christians were more numerous in the Eastern Mediterranean, they did not constitute a majority and the emperor's assertive actions in their favor intervened in many non-Christians' daily lives and livelihoods in unsettling ways. There may also have been sympathy for Licinius within the pagan aristocracy in Rome.[9] It is unlikely that resentments stretched to outright conspiracy, but Constantine may have been fearful that it might, so decided it was time for Licinius' removal. Other authors report that Licinius was secretly strangled, a shameful sort of death. These authors also highlight the role of an imperial woman in the affair. They remembered that Constantine had given his sister an oath (*sacramentum*/hórkos) that he would spare her husband's life. Now they found the emperor's behavior wanting or, in the case of the pagan Zosimus, writing around the year 500, went so far as to deem it a repellent sacrilege.[10]

Whatever happened to Licinius, Constantine let his widow live and even received her back in honor at his court. Unlike Licinius, she was, of course,

---

[8] On the so-called Arian controversy that emerged from these events (but evolved from Arius' original theology), Hanson (1988).

[9] Barnes (1981) 214 who notes that the original consul of 325, Valerius Proculus, possibly a pagan senator, seems to have been abruptly removed.

[10] Origo Const. 5.29; Orosius, Hist. adv. pag. 7.28.20 (both note the parallel to Maximian); Socrates, Hist. eccl. 1.4; Theophanes, Chron. AM 5815; Codex Angelicus, Vita Constantini 23 [in Opitz (1934)]: Licinius prepared a rebellion; Zonaras, Epit. hist. 13.1: involvement of the Senate. Constantine breaks his oath: Eutropius, Brev. 10.6.1; Jerome, Chron. 323; Zosimus, Hist. nea, 2.28. Eusebius, Vita Constantini 2.18; Consularia Constantinopolitana 325; Epitome de Caesaribus 41.7–8; Sozomen, Hist. eccl. 1.7.5 just record that Licinius as well as his former Caesar Martinianus, banished to Cappadocia, were killed.

a blood relation, which might have saved her. Constantine may also have remembered the upheaval caused by Licinius' own earlier killings of imperial widows, not least in Thessalonica. Furthermore, Constantia, who had previously resided at Nicomedia for almost a decade, was valuable to her brother for her Eastern connections. She indeed used her new position to further the careers of men who had been active at Licinius' former court. Among them was the tutor of her son Licinianus, the grammarian Flavius Optatus, who, as the orator Libanius later bemoaned, made a stellar career under Constantine despite having an unsuitable wife.[11]

Constantia's usefulness was a two-edged sword for Constantine. On the upside, it manifested itself almost immediately on the ecclesiastical front. After the Council of Nicaea got underway in May, Constantia managed to convince three leading attendees, the bishops Eusebius of Nicomedia, Theognis of Nicaea, and Maris of Chalcedon, to subscribe to the definition of the relationship between God and Christ decided by the council and promoted by her brother, to which they had initially objected. This was the so-called homoousian formula, which postulated that God and Christ were "of one substance." Constantia had long been acquainted with the prominent Eusebius, who had arrived to preside over the church of Nicomedia around the same time that Licinius had moved his residence there, in 317. Now, her intervention ensured that the council could almost unanimously (save for two Libyan bishops who supported Arius) agree on the doctrine backed by Constantine.[12]

However, the fragile ecclesiastical unity achieved at Nicaea began to unravel as soon as the council was concluded. By October 325, Constantine had to banish Eusebius, Theognis, and Maris to Gaul for continuing to agitate against the assembly's sentences of ex-communication of Arius, to which they had not subscribed, and for communicating with malcontent parties in Alexandria. In the letter Constantine wrote to the church of Nicomedia, the emperor among other matters drew attention to Eusebius' close links to Licinius, his complicity in Licinius' persecutions, and his spying on Constantine for the "tyrant," all of which supposedly served as proofs of his criminal mind.[13]

---

[11] On Optatus and Libanius, see Chapter 1.
[12] Philostorgius, Hist. eccl. 1.9. On Eusebius of Nicomedia, see Barry (2019) 132–53. For Constantia's acquaintance with Eusebius, see also Chapter 8. Eusebius, Vita Constantini 3.10 may allude to the presence of three members of Constantine's family at the council, among whom may have been Constantia; see Ridley (1980) 256.
[13] Urkunde n. 27.9, ed. Opitz.

Under such circumstances it was a difficult predicament for his credibility that, in the eyes of his Eastern subjects, Constantine himself had dangerously close links with Licinius, too, as personified by his sister and Eusebius of Nicomedia's friend Constantia. This also had repercussions for his standing among the supporters of the Council of Nicaea, who still remembered Constantia's role in these theological disputes even many generations later.[14] Furthermore, for some of his pagan subjects and supporters of Licinius in the East, Constantia offered a link to the past. This was all the more so because at first, Constantia returned to Constantine's court and her former palace in the company of her children, her 10-year-old son Licinianus, the former Caesar, and possibly also her stepson, Licinius' offspring from an enslaved concubine.[15]

To offset any attempt by enemies to capitalize on lingering popular sentiments, Constantine decided visibly to detach Constantia from Licinius. He chose a variant to the strategy of promoting the face of a Constantinian woman in a space vacated by a former empress, which he had applied before with Helena and Fausta in Thessalonica and Antioch. The difference was that this time he promoted the very woman who had operated in the same space before. She was simply given a different, Constantinian costume, similar to the treatment of Theodora and Fausta in Rome after the victory over Maxentius. When the mint in Constantinople opened in early 326, a series of dynastic bronze coins was struck, the only such issue ever from this mint. On this series, Constantia's portrait appeared next to Fausta's and Helena's (as well as Constantine's, and those of the three Caesars Crispus, Constantine, and Constantius). The caption of Constantia's coin proclaimed her to be the "sister of Constantine Augustus," while a wreath-enclosed legend almost menacingly prophesized her "Love for the State" (Fig. 7.3).[16] The coinage paralleled Constantine's likely insertion of a statue that Licinius had erected for his wife in Constantinople into a dynastic group featuring himself, his sons Constans and Constantius alongside Constantia.[17]

Constantia's coin caption directly invited the viewer to consider her biological relationship with the emperor. Constantine had presented Constantia

---

[14] Hillner (2019a) 383–93 and Chapter 8.

[15] Origo Const. 5.29 reports that Licinius was survived by his wife and son. On Licinianus, see text that follows; on her stepson, Chapter 9.

[16] RIC VII Constantinople, 7–15. On the Constantinopolitan mint opening with this series, see Ramskold (2011) and (2013) 421. Helena and Fausta are accompanied by their usual *securitas* and *salus*. On Constantia's coin and the meaning of *pietas publica*, see also Longo (2009) 209.

[17] Schade (2003) 232, n. II 30.

186 CENTER STAGE (C. 317–C. 329)

Fig. 7.3 Bronze follis showing Constantia *n(obilissima) f(emina)* on the obverse, with captions *soror Constantini Aug(usti)* and *pietas publica* enclosed in a wreath on the reverse (RIC VII Constantinople 15; scan from *The Roman Imperial Coinage, Volume 7: Constantine and Licinius, AD 313–337* by Bruun, Patrick M, Sutherland, CHV (eds.) and Carson, RAG (ed.), with kind permission of Spink & Son Ltd, London).

as his "sister" before, on a milestone in the West, in Gallia Narbonensis, erected between 317 and 324 that described the Caesar Licinianus as "son of the Augustus Constantine's sister." At that time, Constantine felt the need to emphasize to the subjects in his territory that this Eastern Caesar was nonetheless a Constantinian. Constantia's coin from Constantinople now drew attention still further away from her former status as Licinius' empress and the mother of his heir. Those remembering this link will have registered it as another humiliation of the former emperor.[18]

Within the dynastic series of 326, the coin not only reappropriated Constantia, but also visualized her new status within the hierarchy of the Constantinian dynasty. This status was decidedly junior to that of the other women. Constantia had never been proclaimed Augusta by Licinius, and now she would never be. The title afforded to her at her brother's court was one from which Helena and Fausta had long graduated, the old tetrarchic dignity of *nobilissima femina* (noblest of women). All three women were depicted with pearl necklaces on the issues in this dynastic series, but while Helena and Fausta wear their customary spherical hairdo and chignon, respectively, Constantia was portrayed with a thick pearl-studded braid around her head, similar to the style that had been developed for Helena in Rome. This was to create a gallery of distinguishable and distinctive Constantinian women within the context of this series, much as Helena's new look in Rome was meant to make her distinctive, but not superior. More suggestive is Constantia's inclusion in the coinage of the new mint of Constantinople, the city that Constantine was building up as his new residence during these years. Constantine thought that it was the population of this city, whose walls Licinius had recently fortified and outside which he had been defeated, that needed reminding that, at least symbolically, Licinius' empress was no more.[19]

If Constantine's mercy had given Constantia a feeling that she and her children were now safe, it must soon have evaporated. With the Council of Nicaea concluded in July, Constantine turned his mind to the celebration of his Vicennalia, the twenty-year anniversary of his reign. Festivities began in Nicomedia, but were to culminate in Rome the following year, in July 326, where his entire family was to assemble. In the spring of 326 Constantine started to move his court (perhaps including Constantia and her son) through Thrace and the central Balkans, passing Serdica, Naissus, and Sirmium on the way, before arriving in Italy in April.

Here, disaster struck. Intelligence reached Constantine that critically shattered his trust in his oldest son, Crispus. Crispus, now normally resident in Trier, had probably always intended to join his father in Northern Italy to complete the last leg of the journey to Rome and the Vicennalia celebrations

---

[18] CIL 17.2.183.
[19] On the foundation of Constantinople as a "victory city," see Stephenson (2009) 194–96.

together. Now, this would become his life's final trip. After a trial conducted by Constantine who acted both as emperor and as Crispus' *paterfamilias* with power over his children's life and death, Crispus was transported to a town near Pola in Istria. Here, he was executed or forced to commit suicide, possibly by poison. Throughout the empire, but especially in Italy, his name was erased from imperial monuments to subject him to *damnatio memoriae* (condemnation of his memory). One such erasure occurred on the base of a statue dedicated to his grandmother Helena, which stood in the city of Salerno.[20]

News of Crispus' violent death must have come as a shock to the inhabitants of the empire. Although (or because) Crispus' mother may have been merely a concubine, Constantine had so far always stayed loyal to his eldest son, as his own father had done with him. As we have seen, even after Fausta's sons were born, Crispus continued to be included in Constantine's imperial college of Caesars and was styled as a "Iulius," implying strong links to his imperial grandfather Constantius. When in 322 Crispus provided Constantine with his first grandchild, probably a boy, this happy dynastic event had been publicly announced in the city of Rome.[21] What is more, Crispus, by now in his mid-twenties, had grown into Contantine's trusted collaborator, and not merely in administering Gaul, where he was primarily based. He was a gifted military leader, and decisively contributed to Constantine's victory over Licinius through the defeat of his admiral Abantes. His achievements and importance to his father ensured that he had not only been prominently displayed in imperial iconography and epigraphy, but also heaped with honors—he was appointed consul no less than three times—and celebrated by poets and writers in search of imperial favor. Most poignantly, Eusebius of Caesarea had conspicuously associated Constantine and Crispus as godfather and godson in the edition of his church history written in 324. In the later version published after 326, the passage was quietly removed. Eusebius would never mention Crispus again.[22]

---

[20] On Constantine's and Crispus' whereabouts and journeys in 326, see Barnes (1982) 77 and 84. On Crispus' execution at Pola Ammianus Marcellinus 14.11.20. On poison as the means of death: Sidonius Apollinaris, Ep. 5.8.2; Gregory of Tours, Decem Libri Hist. 1.36. Aurelius Victor, Caes. 41.11 calls Crispus' trial a *iudicium patris*, alluding to Constantine's power as a *paterfamilias*. On Crispus' *damnatio memoriae*, see Usherwood (2022), who argues it was popular reaction to Crispus' death rather than centrally managed; Helena's inscription is CIL 10.517.

[21] CTh 9.38.1 (October 30, 322).

[22] On Crispus' career, Pohlsander (1984). On Eusebius and the passage in his church history, Barnes (1981) 150.

Although the killing of Crispus was clearly public knowledge, the motivation behind it was not. Some authors, generally those earliest in date, were cautious about advancing any opinions, with one directly stating that the reason was uncertain.[23] But rumors inevitably circulated and they also embroiled Helena in the affair, by connecting Crispus' death with further, even more mysterious developments within the Constantinian family. According to one version of events, it had been his own wife Fausta who had provided Constantine with the initial evidence that made him doubt his son, by claiming that he had raped her. This was a crime that—when it involved a respectable woman, let alone the empress—carried the death penalty. This story further asserted that having dealt with his son, Constantine was confronted by his mother, presumably in Rome where he had proceeded for the celebrations of his anniversary. Here, Helena allegedly presented him with information that Fausta's accusations against Crispus had been false. Fausta had been in love with her stepson, but when he rejected her advances, she had sought revenge by concocting the rape story. Now believing his mother, Constantine punished Fausta by suffocating her in an overheated bath.[24]

But other stories circulated, too, describing Fausta and Crispus as accomplices, rather than antagonists. They had supposedly been adulterous lovers and had even plotted against Constantine. The adultery version was peddled with particular enthusiasm by Zosimus, the late-fifth-century pagan historian hostile to Constantine, who also reported that Constantine killed Fausta in the bath to console Helena for the death of her grandson. Plagued by his guilty conscience, he then converted to Christianity, once he learned from a mysterious "Egyptian" introduced by the "women of the palace," presumably again Helena, that this religion offered redemption for his sins.[25]

Some of these lurid scenarios painted by late antique authors are not entirely implausible, although to a varying degree. To begin with, we should

---

[23] No reason given: Consularia Constantinopolitana 326; Ammianus Marcellinus 14.1.20; Jerome, Chron. 325 (sic); Jerome, Vir. ill. 80. The reason is uncertain: Aurelius Victor, Caes. 41.11.

[24] Fausta's rejected advances and false accusation of rape: Passio Artemii 45.12–18; Zonaras, Epit. hist. 13.2 (neither mention Helena). Unspecified slander by Fausta: Epitome de Caesaribus 41.11 (who mentions Helena's distress) and Philostorgius, Hist. eccl. 2.4 (who does not mention Helena, but alleges Fausta had an affair with an errand boy). Fausta's murder in the bath: Epitome de Caesaribus 41.12; Philostorgius, Hist. eccl. 2.4; Zosimus, Hist. nea 2.29; Sidonius Apollinaris, Ep. 5.8.2; Gregory of Tours, Decem Libri Hist. 1.36; Suda s.v. Kriskos (sic). On stuprum: Arjava (1996) 217–20. See Rocco (2013) 244 n. 5 for a comprehensive bibliography on the affair.

[25] Crispus and Fausta plotting: Gregory of Tours, Decem Libri Hist. 1.36; affair with Crispus: Zosimus, Hist. nea 2.29; Suda s.v. Kriskos (sic). See also John Chrysostomus, Homiliae XV in Epistolam ad Philippenses 4.15.5: Fausta exposed naked on a mountain top for adultery.

not a priori exclude the possibility that Crispus raped Fausta and that she was simply not believed, but accused of adultery herself.[26] We could alternatively assume a romantic relationship between Fausta and Crispus, who, after all, were close in age and had almost grown up together. They may have contemplated Crispus' usurpation of power from his father. It has even been suggested that Fausta may have become pregnant by Crispus and that her death was the tragic consequence of trying to abort the child with hot fumes. However, it is difficult to see how Fausta and Crispus could have conducted an affair in the years preceding their deaths, given that they were hundreds of miles apart. An equally significant objection against a plot between Crispus and Fausta, with or without any sexual overtones, is that she would have been working against her own children's interests.[27] Therefore, if we want to follow the literary accounts that connect Crispus' fate with that of Fausta, we might more reasonably imagine that Fausta was worried precisely about her own sons' prospects of succession and intrigued against Crispus accordingly, either by accusing him of rape or simply of plotting against his father. When her machinations were subsequently exposed, Fausta would then either have been killed, or forced to commit suicide.[28]

In either case, Helena may have acted out of devotion to her grandson, or of long-held resentment against her daughter-in-law, the sister to her old rival Theodora. Helena's deep devotion to Crispus, the corresponding depth of her grief at his death, and her anger at Fausta are indeed often assumed. One historian has recently even argued that Helena had Fausta killed without consulting Constantine.[29] Such assumptions of Helena's devotion to Crispus, however, rely entirely on the stories about her intervention after his death, in a rather circular fashion, for we have no evidence of Helena's interaction with Crispus (or with Fausta, for that matter) otherwise. Some historians have further pointed to the possibility that Crispus may have been married to a relative of Helena. This woman was, curiously, also called Helena, as announced, unusually, in the imperial law that celebrated the birth of Crispus' child in 322, in a reference that suggests a certain kind of prominence. It has therefore

---

[26] Rocco (2013) 251 and (2018) warns us against not taking ancient accounts of rape seriously.

[27] See Woods (1998) 77 for the suggestion about a botched abortion; also Stephenson (2009) 223. For doubts, especially for practical reasons, see Barnes (2014) 147.

[28] Suicide: Barnes (2014) 148. Fausta's intrigue in the interest of her children is usually considered more plausible than an affair between Fausta and Crispus: Rougé (1980); Barnes (1981) 220, (2014) 144–50; Drijvers (1992a) 60; Pohlsander (1995) 23; Evans Grubbs (1995) 36; Harries (2012) 260.

[29] See, for example, Pohlsander (1984) 106 for Helena's devotion to Crispus. Helena independently killed Fausta: Olbrich (2010). Woods (1998) 79 also assumes the involvement of Helena, but only because he credits her with typically female knowledge of how to conduct abortions.

been argued that this Helena was the daughter of one of Helena's other children by Constantius. This would mean that Crispus had married his cousin, in keeping with dynastic habits. We hear nothing more of this woman and her child or children after Crispus' death. His downfall may therefore have dealt a double blow to Helena. The theory about the existence of an otherwise unknown full brother of Constantine, let alone one with children, seems however very difficult to sustain in view of the importance afforded to dynastic succession in many texts about the Constantinian era and in relation to Constantine's own dynastic strategies.[30] It is, of course, also possible that this Helena had been a more distant relative. But it seems far more likely that Crispus' wife had assumed the name Helena for dynastic reasons, given the ease with which imperial names were changed and added during this period. Her existence alone, in any case, can hardly be said to serve as any proof of the elder Helena's vengeful emotional state after Crispus' death.

Meanwhile, there exist other versions of Crispus' death that complicate this rather neat and romantic story of Helena's indignation about her daughter-in-law's behavior toward her favorite grandson. Several sources mention another murder in connection with that of Crispus, that of Constantia's young son Licinianus. The ecclesiastical historian Orosius, writing in the early fifth century, darkly alluded to the possibility that Crispus and Licinianus died because they were both predisposed toward the "Arian" beliefs just refuted at the Council of Nicaea. Perhaps Orosius' interpretation offers some distorted echo of a real plot between Crispus and the Licinian faction. But it seems more likely that Constantine had come to regard his legitimate nephew, the son of a former emperor and grandson of at least one, if not two, as a continued threat.[31] More significantly, the texts that highlight the death of Crispus in conjunction with that of Licinianus were written earlier than those associating it with Fausta's demise, which some of them do not even mention. And even when they do, they separate her death from that of the two male figures, both textually and in time. Jerome, in his chronicle written c. 380, dates Fausta's death to the year 328, two years later than those of Crispus and Licinianus. All of this raises further questions about whose death was connected with whose, if any.[32]

---

[30] Imperial law: CTh 9.38.1 (322). On Helena as possible grandmother of Crispus' wife, see Chausson (2002) 145–46, but see also Chapter 2. Frakes (2005) 95 speculates that this Helena was Licinius' daughter. On Crispus' possible second child: Barnes (1981) 220.

[31] Orosius, Hist. adv. pag. 7.28.

[32] Jerome, Chron. 325 and 328; Eutropius, Brev. 10.6: "[Constantine] killed his son, a splendid man, and the son of his sister, a young man of agreeable quality, soon also his wife, and later many

It was certainly the case that Fausta vanished from public view in the later 320s. Coins ceased to be minted with her portrait after early 327, although again later than coinage with Crispus' portrait disappeared.[33] There is evidence that her name was also erased from official media, hinting that she had, indeed, committed an offense or was widely understood to have done so by the inhabitants of the empire. One such erasure may have occurred in the heart of Rome, in the splendid residence decorated with frescoes of the Constantinian family in the Lateran area discussed in an earlier chapter, where Fausta's name appears to have been painted over at some point. Similarly, on an inscribed statue base that had been erected in her honor by the Southern Italian city of Surrentum, her name, as well as her attributes of being "wife," "mother," and "stepmother," were chiseled out. This ritual act, attacking her not only as an individual, but also severing her links to the Constantinian family, clearly highlights that local people believed her offense had somehow been directed against the emperor and the dynasty. Crispus' name was excised from this inscription, too. However, since his name was removed in this way from a vast range of imperial media following his downfall, this again does not necessarily signify that his and Fausta's *damnatio memoriae* derived from a crime they had committed together.[34]

Numerous questions therefore still surround the events of 326: When exactly did Fausta die, and were her death and that of Crispus really connected? And if not, why did she die? Was she really suffocated in a bath? Why would Constantine, after having found out about Fausta's alleged slander, not rehabilitate his son's memory, if only for the sake of his grandchildren, at this stage the only ones he had? And why, if Fausta and Crispus had been having an affair, should Helena have felt able to object to Crispus' punishment?[35] Her son, after all, had only a few months previously legislated against adultery, reinforcing previous emperors' distaste for this capital crime.[36] Was

friends" (*egregium virum filium et sororis filium, commodae indolis iuvenem, interfecit, mox uxorem, post numerosos amicos*). Orosius does not mention Fausta. See Potter (2013) 245–47 for doubts that the deaths of Fausta and Crispus were related to each other.

[33] Potter (2009) 144–45.

[34] Rome: CIL 6. 40769; Scrinari (1991) 173; Surrentum: CIL 10.678; and see for another case of Fausta's erasure in Privernum in Campania AE 2007, 354.

[35] On the illogical sequence of events in Zosimus, see Paschoud (2003) 236.

[36] CTh 9.7.1 (April 326), and see also CTh 9.40.1, 11.36.1 (313, 314). Given the arbitrary workflow and reactive nature of Roman legislation, it is improbable that there was a causal relationship between Constantine's adultery legislation and Fausta's death; see Evans Grubbs (1995) 350–51. The law of 326 is, in any case, hard to reconcile with Fausta's case. Its aim was to restrict the ability to bring adultery charges to close male relatives and suppress "informers" outside this group, but if events were true as reported in 326, Constantine had relied on informers.

Helena really as devoted to Crispus (or his wife) or as resentful of Fausta as is often assumed? And how, if at all, does Constantia's son Licinianus—who was surely doomed to die sooner or later because he constituted a dynastic threat—fit into this?

Most of these questions must remain unanswered due to the aura of secrecy created by the imperial court. Late antique authors faced the same problem. The fantasies that sprung up around these deaths show how observers were scrabbling around for explanations, but also for ways to integrate events into their own assessment of Constantine's reign. These attempts gathered pace as the years went by and were fueled by the benefit of hindsight about other aspects of Constantine's reign. Orosius' musings that Crispus and the child Licinianus were similar to "Arian blasphemers" seem misguided, but fit his interest in Constantine's alleged promotion of Nicene Christianity. Zosimus' account of Constantine's killing spree as the trigger to his hypocritical Christian conversion can be traced back to the more generic grievances of disgruntled pagans, supporters of Licinius or slighted members of the Constantinian family of the fourth century.[37] Many accounts also borrowed elements from the mythical, biblical, and imperial past to make sense of what had happened. They variously and at times simultaneously alluded to the tales of the Greek hero Theseus' wife Phaedra who fell in love with her stepson Hippolytus, to the patriarch Joseph's rejection of the advances by the wife of Potiphar, Joseph's master during enslavement in Egypt, and to Nero's murder of his wife Octavia in a hot bath. It is also notable that the story about Fausta revealing Crispus' offense to Constantine subversively echoed her earlier actions that led to the suicide of her father Maximian.[38]

Above all, many of our authors, especially those further removed in time from the events, fell back onto one of the most trusted justifications for supposedly irrational male decision making known to mankind, that of female influence. A whole host of well-known gendered stereotypes—the slighted female lover, the sexually promiscuous young wife, the wicked stepmother, the resentful abandoned woman, the spiritually gullible mother, the

---

[37] On Zosimus' sources here (including Eunapius, Nicomachus Flavianus, and Julian), see Paschoud (2003) 236; Harries (2012) 260; see also Sozomen, Hist. eccl. 1.5.1–2; Evagrius, Hist. eccl. 3.41 who reject this account of Constantine's conversion as "pagan" yarn. On the inconclusive evidence for the events in 326 in general, Drijvers (1992b) 505–6.

[38] Sidonius Apollinaris, Ep. 5.8.2, mentions satirical verses by the consul of 331, Ablabius, that supposedly described the Constantinian age as "Neronian." It is not clear if already Ablabius (if he had written such verses at all) linked this assessment to the death of Fausta, as Sidonius did. See Harries (2012) 259. On Ablabius, see also Chapter 9. On Fausta and Maximian's suicide, see Chapter 3.

interventionist mother-in-law, the indulgent grandmother—were deployed in these stories (and in their retelling by modern historians who tend to augment them even further). From a chronological perspective, these more stereotypical explanations form the latest narrative layer surrounding the death of Crispus. But they comprehensively obscure further what really happened, including Helena's true involvement. Reports of the latter seem to stem from gendered imaginations based on a hazy memory of a few facts: that Helena had originally been replaced by Fausta's sister Theodora, that she had been in Rome with the emperor at the time in question, that she had restored a bath damaged by a fire in the city, but above all that, after Fausta's demise, she became the most important woman in the Roman empire.[39]

Becoming Genetrix

What is certain is that when Constantine arrived in Rome on July 18 or 21 of 326 for the climax of the celebrations of his Vicennalia, the profile of his dynasty had already been brutally changed, even if Fausta disappeared only later. On July 25 he held his traditional *adventus* with the usual pomp and procession, but was heckled by the populace, possibly in the circus where he presided over the games associated with the arrival of an emperor. It has been suggested that these insults were related to pagan senators' supposed dismay, as reported by Zosimus, that Constantine eschewed the customary sacrifice at the Temple of Jupiter on the Capitol before the games. The veracity of Zosimus' account has, however, also been doubted and, even if such refusal happened, it is more plausibly dated to the aftermath of Constantine's triumph over Maxentius in 312. In 326, we can imagine that the Roman populace and aristocracy were delighted about the presence of an emperor in their city, but also disturbed and confused by the recent violent events.[40] After all, they—like everyone else around the empire—had become accustomed to the public expressions of the emperor's love for this eldest son and of the

---

[39] See for similar gendered stereotypes ruling ancient assessment of Julio-Claudian events, Ginsburg (2006) 106–32 (she identifies the stereotypes "wicked stepmother," "bossy woman," and "sexual transgressor," especially in terms of incest and adultery). For the Constantinian period, see James (2013). For Helena's bath building in Rome, see Chapter 6.

[40] Insults by people: Libanius, Or. 19.19, 20.24. See also John Chrysostom, Homiliae XXI de statuis 21.3, on an attack of one of Constantine's statues with stones. See Moser (2018) 18 on dating these incidents to Constantine's presence in Rome in 326. At n. 20 Moser also lists copious literature discussing the date and veracity of Zosimus's account of Constantine's refusal to sacrifice, in Hist. nea 2.29.2–5.30. On the date of Constantine's arrival in Rome, Barnes (1982) 77.

importance of Fausta Augusta for the stability of his government. If we are to believe reports about Licinius' conspiracy, we can also imagine that hope for the return of this rival dynasty in the form of Licinius' son, the former Caesar, existed in some quarters of the city.

To offset any dangerous bewilderment, Constantine was, once again, intent on demonstrating the unity of his now reconfigured (if somewhat disfigured) family. Some historians have claimed that Helena's name was superimposed on the aforementioned inscription in Surrentum from which Fausta's name had been erased. Yet, the extant inscription bears no trace of any such intervention.[41] Instead, Constantine found more subtle ways to manipulate the memory of recent disagreeable events, geared once again toward advertising harmony and concord in his family and among his women. He proceeded to devise another brazen rewrite of his genealogy.

It is notable that it was just around this time that Constantine's half-brothers, at the same time the sons of Constantius and Theodora, brothers of Constantia and nephews of Fausta, reappear in the imperial orbit (for these connections, see this book's Family Tree). At least two of them, probably Julius Constantius and Flavius Dalmatius, joined the emperor in Rome for his Vicennalia. Julius Constantius' presence in Italy in 326 is further confirmed by his son Gallus' birth that year in Etruria, perhaps in a villa belonging to his aristocratic wife Galla. A short while later, these men's grandmother Eutropia, also Fausta's mother, re-emerged within his imperial circle, too. Although we cannot verify her whereabouts after the dark days following Maxentius' defeat in 312, she was reportedly in contact with her son-in-law after 326, even though he was by now responsible for the deaths of not one but two of her children.[42] During Constantine's Vicennalia celebrations in Rome, Julius Constantius and Dalmatius allegedly advised Constantine on how to deal with the insults the people of Rome had leveled at him. Constantine wisely followed Julius Constantius' recommendation to react with clemency and humor.[43] The reunion with his half-brothers had probably always been planned, but at this turbulent moment Constantine may particularly have

---

[41] CIL 10.678. Superimposition with Helena's name is claimed by, for example, Drijvers (1992a) 49; Van Dam (2007) 303. I would like to thank Rebecca Usherwood for sharing the results of her personal inspection of the stone with me. For another "replacement" incident, that of Helena's name for Theodora's at the residence under INPS in the Lateran area, see Scrinari (1991) 167, but again due to the state of the inscription the name cannot be verified anymore.
[42] On the birth of Gallus: Ammianus Marcellinus 14.11.27; on Eutropia, see Chapter 8.
[43] Libanius, Or. 19.19, also mentioned in Or. 20.24 but without the brothers.

appreciated their unique links to the city of Rome, publicized by their appearance with him in the imperial circus box.

But Constantine was also anxious to send another message to the Roman public. This message concerned the loyalties of his half-sister, the recently twice-bereaved Constantia, and the status of his own mother of obscure background, resident in their very midst, but suspected of meddling in Fausta's disappearance or death.

Sometime after 326, an honorary statue was erected for Constantia in Rome (Fig. 7.4). Due to the inscription's fragmentary state, we do not know who dedicated this statue nor exactly where it was displayed, but without a doubt it expressed or at least reflected imperial sentiment.

The inscription on the marble statue base mentioned two Caesars only, so was composed after Crispus' disgrace. Even more significant was

Fig. 7.4 Inscription on a marble statue base erected for Constantine's sister Constantia in Rome (CIL 6.1153). Courtesy of Roma, Musei Capitolini. Archivio Fotografico dei Musei Capitolini. © Roma, Sovrintendenza Capitolina ai Beni Culturali. Photo: Julia Hillner.

Constantia's introduction. She appeared, for the first time, with her father's Constantius' gentile name *Iulia*. Constantius had changed from Iulius to Valerius (Diocletian's gentile name) upon becoming Caesar in 293, a name Constantine had also used for himself and his older sons Crispus and Constantine, alongside that of his fictitious ancestor Claudius. After 317, Constantine had reintroduced his father's original *gentilicium* for his two younger sons and occasionally for Crispus, in a clear dynastic move that now also encompassed Constantia.[44] Furthermore, Constantia's inscription in Rome echoes the coin minted with her portrait a few months before in Constantinople. She is described as "sprung from an illustrious and divine family," as the "sister" of Constantine Augustus, and, most significantly, as the "aunt" of the "most blessed Caesars" (Constantine and Constantius).[45] As with the Constantinopolitan coin, the inscription ignored any links between Constantia and Licinius, and of course also between Constantia and her own son Licinianus, a previous Caesar. As had happened so often during Constantine's reign, another woman was being reclaimed for his version of history.

Constantia's inscription, with its attention to kinship relations, echoed well-established formulas on inscriptions erected previously for Helena and Fausta. Public epigraphy of Constantinian women (but not, generally, coin legends) from all places and periods stressed their family relationships to Constantine and his sons. Helena was usually described as the "mother" of Constantine (*mater, procreatrix*), "grandmother" of the Caesars, and sometimes even "wife" (*coniunx*) or "partner" (*uxor*) of Constantius, while Fausta was "partner" of Constantine (*uxor*) as well as "stepmother" (of Crispus) and "mother" of the Caesars. This sustained focus on kinship was in line with Constantine's promotion of his dynasty from the mid-320s. Both Helena and Fausta were also commonly addressed as "our mistress" (*domina nostra*), as Galeria Valeria had already been, and as "venerable" (*venerabilis*) and "most pious" (*piissima*). In one instance, Helena was called "most clement" (*clementissima*), which was a virtue that had hitherto been largely reserved for emperors. This is another sign that the presentation of her public persona

---

[44] See PLRE I Constans 3, 220; Constantinus 3, 223; Constantius 8, 226; Crispus 4, 233.
[45] CIL 6.1153: *Inlustri et divinae prosap[iae] / genitae venerabili soror[i] / d(omini) n(ostri) Constantini Aug(usti) et / amitae / dd(ominorum) nn(ostrorum) b{a}eatissimorum Ca[es(arum)] / d(ominae) n(ostrae) Fl(aviae) Iul(iae) Constantiae nob[iliss(imae)] / [feminae.* PLRE I Constantia 1, 221 maintains that Constantia's name was erased, but this is wrong; see laststatues.classics.ox.ac.uk, LSA-1385 (last accessed 2/12/2021).

was always particularly aligned with that of Constantine, as is also apparent in her coin portrait and her allegorical virtue of *securitas*.[46]

However, in a diversion from public epigraphy for Constantinian women before 326, Constantia's inscription also signaled clear hierarchies, as her coin from Constantinople had also done. She was styled once more as a junior *nobilissima femina*. Since the Augusta Fausta had now disappeared from the scene, this left Helena as the most senior woman in the Constantinian family, ahead of Constantia and replacing Fausta. After 326, and on inscriptions from Rome, Helena was now not only presented as the sole Augusta of the Roman world, but as a near-mythical foremother of its emperor and his offspring. To begin with, Helena was, like Constantia, described with Constantius' gentile name. Her full name, Flavia Iulia Helena, appeared in public communication for the first time in Rome and only in or after 326. This was all the more unusual in her case, since Constantia as Constantius' daughter naturally wore his *gentilicium*, whereas Helena would not have. Of course, for various reasons Helena may have been referred to by this name before, for example, because she had been Constantius' freedwoman. But the timing of its first public usage implies that *Iulia* was now added to the rest of her name to link her even more tightly to Constantine's imperial family lineage.[47]

Even more astonishingly, Helena was now hailed as the "creator" (*genetrix*) of the Constantinian house, a term that again appears only on inscriptions dated to 326 or afterward, and only on those erected in Rome (e.g., Fig. 7.5). The label *genetrix* both emphasized Helena's role as ancestress and associated her with the divine. It recalled the goddess Venus and her role as the divine ancestress of the Roman people through the city's founder Aeneas, her son. The first Roman emperor Augustus, through his adoptive father Caesar, had also claimed descent from the goddess. Augustus' wife Livia, in particular, had been associated with Venus Genetrix, but the goddess had been a feature of most Roman empresses' coins up to Valeria Galeria and the young Fausta. Venus Genetrix was usually depicted holding an apple, just as the female figure did on the obverse of the Roman medallion of Helena discussed in the

---

[46] Inscriptions for or mentioning Helena: CIG 3.4349, Nollé (1993) nos. 47 and 49, CIL 6.1134 (*genetrix*), CIL 6.1135 (*genetrix*), CIL 6.1136, CIL 6.3373 (probably inauthentic), CIL 6.36950 (*genetrix*), CIL 6.40769, CIL 8.1633, CIL 9.2446, CIL 10.517 (*procreatrix*), CIL 10.1483 (*clementissima*), CIL 10.1484 (probably inauthentic, see Drijvers (1992a) 51–52), CIL 13.1023 (probably inauthentic); possibly also CIL 6.31400. For Fausta: CIL 10.678, AE 2007, 354, CIL 6.40769, CIL 12.668. On Helena as the "wife" of Constantius, see Chapter 2. On the label "clementissima," Schade (2003) 52. On Helena's epigraphy, see also Navarro (2009a) 59–78, (2009b); Orlandi (2016).

[47] On Helena's name, see Chapter 1.

Fig. 7.5 Inscription on a marble statue base erected for Flavia Iulia Helena, *genetrix* of Constantine, and "grandmother" of the Caesars Constantine and Constantius, dedicated by the *comes* Iulius Maximilianus, after 326 (CIL 6.1134; found in the area of the Sessorian Palace, now at S. Croce in Gerusalemme). © Julia Hillner.

previous chapter, and, perhaps not coincidentally, as the Venus Victrix on Valeria Galeria's' coin reverses had done.[48] The epithet turned Helena even more directly into the originator of Constantine's dynasty, in a way that mirrored the mythical foundation story of Rome itself.

---

[48] Angelova (2015) 12–14, 24, 77, 88–90. On Valeria's coins, see Chapter 4.

By concentrating on Helena as the beginning, the *genetrix*, of his dynasty, and adding Constantia, Constantine was publicly rearranging his family tree yet again, reshaping it both vertically and horizontally. It is notable that even his father Constantius was relatively absent from this post-326 epigraphy of Constantinian women from Rome, other than indirectly through his gentile name, now oddly carried by his partner, Helena. Constantius is also conspicuous by his absence from the Nantes medallion, equally minted after 326 (Fig. 7.2).[49] In the process of his efforts to dispel or rectify memories of recent events, Constantine's genealogy had become a rather matriarchal tree, consisting of his mother, himself, her grandsons, and their aunt. It curiously recalled Galerius' celebration of his mother Romula, another ancestress without a background or earthly husband, and his sister, Maximinus Daza's mother. However, Constantine projected this image far wider than the old tetrarchs had ever done, by inscribing it into the heart of the empire.[50]

The material arrangement of Helena's and Constantia's public statues may well have matched the wording of their inscriptions in material form. At least in Helena's case, there is evidence that her statues were at times gathered with those of her son and grandsons into dynastic group portraits, a veritable physical family tree, similar to the one depicted on the Nantes medallion. There are literary references to the erection of such groups in Constantinople, and they existed in Rome, too.[51] In the sixteenth century, a marble base for a statue of Helena with the epithet *genetrix* (Fig. 7.5) was found behind the church of S. Croce in Gerusalemme, the area of Helena's former palace. At the same time, the remains of statues for Helena, Constantine, and his sons Constantine and Constantius were also discovered. All these men were also mentioned on the inscription on the base of Helena's statue. In the report on these findings, the statue itself was described as clad in a foot-length "stola" and a mantle, while Constantine and his sons appear "in armor." Attempts have been made to match this written record of Helena's statue with existing objects, such as the statue now at the Villa Borghese (see Fig. 6.9, on the assumption that the body is original, too) or a statue now standing on the

---

[49] Angelova (2015) 115 argues this may be because Constantine wanted to highlight the Christianity of his family, as exemplified by his pious mother, but not his pagan father. Yet, Helena's inscriptions do not make any reference to the Christian faith. Constantine could also have presented his father in a Christian light, had he so wished. Stories to such effect did circulate not much later; see Eusebius, Vita Constantini, 1.13, 16, 17.

[50] See Chapter 4.

[51] For Constantinople: Parastaseis 58 for a group showing Constantine, Helena, and his sons in the Philadelphion in Constantinople; see also Schade (2003) 231 and Chapter 9. For dynastic family groups in general, Alexandridis (2000).

altar in the Cappella di S. Elena at S. Croce that depicts Helena holding the cross. The latter, an ancient statue originally representing the goddess Juno, is assumed to have been reused for Helena already in late antiquity. In both cases, the identifications are rather hypothetical. Nonetheless, the sixteenth-century finds imply that Helena's status as "ancestress" of Constantine's family branch and as "mother" and "grandmother" of emperors was expressed not only through inscriptions and medallions, but also visualized through the spatial combination of her portrait with the images of the male imperial lineage she had engendered. Based on the epigraphic record, we could readily imagine that statues of Constantia were sometimes featured among such groups in Rome, too, as they were in Constantinople.[52]

When Constantine arrived in Rome in July 326, it turned out to be a very different visit from the one he must have envisaged for the celebrations of his Vicennalia. Much has been written about the "fall-out" between the emperor and the Roman aristocracy on this occasion, allegedly leading the emperor to turn his back on the old capital and concentrate on his new foundation of Constantinople, and to populate it with a new aristocracy. But his abandonment of Rome was not as pronounced as it has been claimed, not even after 326. Although Constantine and his sons would take up residence elsewhere, their links to the city remained strong, not least on account of the continuous presence of imperial relatives in the city even after Helena's death. As a matter of fact, when the imperial court left Rome again in September, Constantine's Praetorian prefect Flavius Constantius, very likely another of his relatives, stayed behind, and some of his half-brothers may have done so, too.[53] Nonetheless, the contemporaneous promotion of the imperial family through new statues for its previously underrepresented female members such as Constantia, as well as through new titles, new epithets, and new female genealogies, shows that Constantine thought some damage control was needed in the old capital. The dynastic nature of this publicity suggests it was not the emperor's religion that had been the main problem, but the recent bloodshed in his family. This is not surprising, given the close entanglement between Fausta's family and Rome over the past thirty years.

* * *

[52] For the Villa Borghese statue: Guglielmi (2016). She cites from Pirro Ligorio, Codice Torino, libro XV, folio 119 who described the discovery of the statues in the "garden" of S. Croce in Gerusalemme. For the statue of Helena holding the cross now at S. Croce: Lavin (1967).

[53] On Constantine's alleged abandonment of Rome following his visit in 326, see, for example, van Dam (2011) 150–52. On Flavius Constantius (who became consul in 327) remaining in Italy, see PLRE I Fl. Constantius 5, 225.

Many people had to die before Helena could attain the exalted status of what the early-fifth-century church historian Rufinus would call "queen of the world and mother of the empire."[54] But her direct complicity in this advancement remains shadowy. Her peculiar position does warrant speculation about her possible resentment of Fausta, but there is no ultimate proof. What we do know is that Fausta's death lifted Helena up to dizzying heights that she would otherwise not have reached. Still, unlike some of his tetrarchic rivals, most notably Licinius, Constantine was not an emperor who killed off imperial women lightly. This makes Fausta's disappearance even more harrowing, and was a powerful warning to those who were ultimately spared the emperor's wrath. While Constantine's clemency may have been partly inspired by Christian teaching, it stemmed largely from the fact that he was related to a great many of these widows, who consequently held dynastic value for him. This clemency meant that Helena was not the only survivor of Constantine's killing spree prior to and during his Vicennalian year. Among the others were his sister Anastasia, the former empresses Constantia and Eutropia, and possibly even Crispus' widow Helena. But Constantine's generosity did not necessarily stretch to their children.

We can only imagine how these widows carried their personal grief during their continued presence at this imperial court. The Antiochene priest John Chrysostom's observation, in the early 380s, of the imperial widow with a son who "trembles that one of those now ruling should kill him out of fear for the future," may hold true here as well.[55] We can also only imagine how these women interacted with each other, and with Helena. But what we can see are Constantine's recurrent attempts to present at least some of them as quintessentially Constantinian, and to reshape their identities by emphasizing their relationship with himself. This strategy began in Rome, partly because Constantine visited the city shortly after the family crisis and partly because the imperial image had always been particularly important here. It was in Rome that Helena was first presented as the origin of the Constantinian house, even obscuring Constantius' contribution.

The connotations of this special mother–son relationship, as promoted in Roman epigraphy, were couched in pagan "genetrix" language. Their Christian theological potential was to be realized elsewhere and later. As

---

[54] Rufinus, Hist. eccl. 10.8: *Regina orbis ac mater imperii*.
[55] John Chrysostom, Ad viduam 4. On the passage, see also Washington (2015) 214. The widow described here may be Charito, widow of Jovian, or Justina, widow of Valentinian I, on whom see Chapter 10.

Constantia's coin from Constantinople shows, careful dynastic branding also mattered to Constantine in the East, and perhaps even more so, given this had been his former co-emperor's territory and he was espousing deeply interventionist policies, especially on the Christian doctrinal front. Unfinished government business therefore awaited Constantine in the Eastern half of the empire, and it was there he swiftly returned once his Vicennalia celebrations in Rome had been concluded. This time, he took his mother with him, despite her now being around 80 years of age. For what lay ahead, it seems that Constantine deeply valued Helena not only for her potential to be promoted as the pious mother of the most Christian emperor and female originator of his dynasty. He probably also prized the loyalty, diplomatic skills, energy, and diligence she had demonstrated in Rome as well as her prior knowledge of the East.

8
From Here to Eternity

All the indications are that Helena began her tour of the Eastern provinces, including, famously, Palestine, from Rome, and in the late summer of 326. Most accounts place this trip after the Council of Nicaea, which ended in July 325. Constantine's interest in biblical sites also only followed this council, as we shall see, making it logical that his mother would have visited Jerusalem, in the early fourth century an unassuming provincial city, only afterwards. Since Helena was in Rome earlier than 326, as described in previous chapters, and still there at the time of Constantine's Vicennalia, which ended in August 326, she would have had little opportunity to squeeze in a lengthy trip around the Eastern provinces during the previous year. Imperial travel was a slow affair.[1]

What happened during Helena's tour is the best documented part of her life. Many authors who remembered Helena in the centuries following her death focused on her activities in Palestine, and they often extrapolated from this information to make general points about her status and powers. For example, when writing to his friend Sulpicius Severus in 402 to send the Gallic ascetic a relic of the cross, Paulinus, a Roman senator turned bishop of Nola in southern Italy, called Helena Constantine's "co-regent with the title of Augusta." Sulpicius Severus duly repeated this observation in his chronicle, completed the year after, claiming that Helena "reigned along with her son as Augusta."[2] The two men based this assumption purely on what they knew about the empress's actions in the Holy Land, where they believed—mistakenly, as we shall see—she had also discovered the True Cross.

As we have discussed, and as this chapter will confirm, Helena never "co-reigned" with Constantine, if the phrase implies that she made independent

---

[1] In Eusebius, Vita Constantini the affairs of Nicaea end with chapter 3.24, after which he details Constantine and Helena's activities in Palestine; this is followed by Socrates, Hist. eccl. 1.17; Sozomen, Hist. eccl. 2.1; Theodoret, Hist. eccl. 1.17. Rufinus, Hist. eccl. 10.7 says the trip was "at the same time" as the Council of Nicaea (*per idem tempus*). Helena cannot have departed earlier than late 324, after the defeat of Licinius.

[2] Paulinus of Nola, Ep. 31.4: *nomine conregnans Augustae*, Sulpicius Severus, Chron. 2.33: *cum filio conregnabat*.

decisions on government. Any power and resources she had were directly derived from her son, and any official order she gave on military or legal matters only reinforced ones he had already given. It should also be noted that Constantine no longer minted gold coins bearing Helena's portrait after the death of Fausta. Helena's status at the end of her life was awe-inspiring and distinct, but it was not higher than Fausta's had been. Nonetheless, Paulinus and Sulpicius Severus can be forgiven for thinking in terms of co-regency (a perspective that in their case, as we shall see later, was also influenced by the status of empresses of their own time). On her voyage, Helena was presented as Constantine's delegate, becoming the face of imperial rule for local communities and at this level she did influence some decisions he made, such as lending support to some church foundations in Palestine.

Modern historians have generally followed late antique leads by also declaring the last two years of Helena's life as her most "memorable."[3] Whether this was as true on a personal level as it is on the historiographical is, of course, hard to tell. We should not forget that Helena was, by this point, over 80 years old and her profound experiences of migration were already well behind her, including the crossing of linguistic and status boundaries, and of public service. We may imagine that, after all this, she found her imperial duties on this journey no more challenging than others she had performed, but also that she found the spiritual aspects of her trip to be fresh and rewarding. But we do not know whether Helena prioritized these memories or experiences over others she had accumulated during her long life and should not presume that she did because we do.

Despite the importance afforded to this period of Helena's life in ancient, medieval, and modern historiography, it is not necessarily the clearest. We do not have direct information about the exact purpose, length, and route of Helena's trip, her means of transport, or her companions, although it is possible to make plausible inferences about all these matters from what we otherwise know about aspects of ancient imperial travel. What is also not clear is the exact impression her trip left on contemporary observers. Let us therefore begin with them.

---

[3] Drijvers (1992a) 55; Pohlsander (1995) 96.

The Traveling Empress: Conflicting Portraits

Traces of Helena's tour in the Eastern empire may be found in the writing of two leading churchmen contemporary to her: Eusebius of Caesarea and Athanasius of Alexandria. From these, we can reconstruct many factual details. Nonetheless, the depiction of Helena in these writings—the aim of which was not an objective study of the empress—is contradictory. Eusebius has left us a lengthy report, in the form of an excursus in the *Life of Constantine*. It has to be considered in the context of his changing aims in writing the *Life* itself.[4] This work had started out as a speech of praise for Constantine, when the emperor was still alive. One of its purposes was to stress the alignment between Eusebius' theological position and the emperor's. This was important, because Eusebius had given only half-hearted support to the doctrine on the relationship between God and Christ formulated at the Council of Nicaea and continued to be suspected of heresy in some quarters. After Constantine's death, however, the text morphed into a wider rationalization of Constantine's reign, following the violent succession of his sons to imperial rule over the summer of 337. We will return to these bloody dynastic events in the next chapter. Here, it is important to bear in mind that at the time Eusebius was writing, there were three newly minted emperors, Helena's grandsons. He was keen to present them as Constantine's rightful heirs, ruling the Christian empire in harmony, like a Trinity (ch. 4.40). Eusebius accordingly stressed that the imperial line descending from Helena was of a preordained nature, which explains her prominent appearance, out of all proportion to the other imperial women Eusebius mentioned.[5] A further predicament for Eusebius was that he could not mention Fausta, the new emperors' mother, who gave them their double imperial ancestry.[6] Finally, it should also be noted that the *Life* was left unfinished and unrevised when Eusebius himself passed away in May 339.

The excursus on Helena bears signs of this difficult writing process. It is made up of two discernible sections, one of which deals with her activities in Palestine (chs. 3.42–43), while the other details her voyage through the Eastern provinces in more general terms (chs. 3.44–47). Both sections end

---

[4] See Cameron (1997) on the need to look at the *Life of Constantine* as a literary text before using it as a historical source.

[5] Eusebius mentions Constantine's stepmother (as Constantius' wife), sisters, mother-in-law (Vita Constantini 1.18, 21; 3.51–52), but only Helena and Constantia are named, the latter because Constantine names a city after her; see more on this in this chapter.

[6] On the background of the *Life of Constantine*, Cameron, Hall (1999) 3, 9, 12, 28.

with Helena's death, which is thus described twice. This duplication suggests that the two sections represent two different stages of composition that Eusebius failed to harmonize before he died. It is probable that the more microscopic section on Palestine was part of a more advanced draft intended to enhance Helena's relevance, fully Christianize her trip, and underscore the new regime's relationship with Christianity's Holy Land.[7]

Eusebius' Helena is extensively described. By contrast, the traveling empress only made a passing appearance in the writings of Athanasius, the combative bishop of Alexandria, who as a young deacon had attended the Council of Nicaea and made it his life's mission to defend its creed. Following this council, as we have seen, Constantine had banished the Alexandrian presbyter Arius and his supporters. However, Constantine then convened another council, at Nicomedia in the winter of 327–328, which recalled Arius after accepting a written statement of his belief that avoided the contentious term *homoousios* settled on by the Council of Nicaea. Not everyone among the clergy agreed, least of all Athanasius, who had just become bishop of Alexandria and now refused to readmit Arius to his Alexandrian church. This initiated a long drawn-out battle over the Christian church's definition of faith. For the rest of his reign, Constantine sometimes turned against Arius (banished again in 333), and sometimes against Athanasius (banished in 335). But the conflict became particularly intense when, upon becoming emperor, Constantine's son Constantius took the side of Athanasius' adversaries. He eventually sponsored an anti-Nicene theological formula (ratified at the Council of Rimini in 359), which postulated the similarity (*homoios*) rather than consubstantiality (*homoousios*) of God and Christ. Amid these disputes, Athanasius had to vacate and returned to his see another four times.[8]

Less than twenty years after her appearance in Eusebius' *Life of Constantine*, and thirty years after her voyage through the Eastern provinces, Athanasius of Alexandria recalled Helena's role in these ongoing theological disputes, in his *History of the Arians*, written in exile in 357.[9] As we shall see, Athanasius' Helena was not the pious, almost saintlike, "thrice-blessed" empress that Eusebius had described. She was more akin to the scheming, manipulative women of power that populate classical and biblical literature, but who gained

---

[7] Heinen (1995) 101–5; Destephen (2018) 48–50.
[8] For background, see Barnes (1993), 14–8; Potter (2013) 224–44. On the Council of Nicaea and subsequent banishments, see also Chapter 7.
[9] Athanasius, Historia Arianorum 4.

particular traction during the fourth-century battles over Christian orthodoxy, in which heresy sometimes quite literally "became a woman."[10] This less favorable portrait should caution us against retrospectively exaggerating the significance of Helena's trip for contemporary Christian communities.

For both Eusebius and Athanasius, then, Helena was a foil to highlight the worth of imperial and ecclesiastical men. Nonetheless, it is from the discrepancies in her portrait between, but also within, their writings that we are able to glimpse the real Helena, too. Both men afforded her an agency not seen in any other contemporary source, even if they judged it differently. This agency must therefore have been very visible. In this regard, it is remarkable how Helena emerges, especially from Eusebius' pages, not only as spectacularly pious, but also as full of energy and curiosity, despite her age. These may, of course, be conformist tropes to describe a mother and grandmother of emperors. However, we should not forget that we owe to Eusebius the first and only literary portrait of Helena by a contemporary who had actually seen her in action. One cannot help thinking that some of his descriptions of her personality derived from the deep impression Helena left on the bishop of Caesarea during the days she spent on his turf. But before we look at Eusebius's contacts with the empress, let us reflect on the nature of her trip and follow her trail to Palestine.

Helena, the Pilgrim?

Since Helena's trip followed the disturbing family crisis of the summer of 326, modern historians have often connected her voyage to these events.[11] At the more outspoken end of such explanations, it has been suggested that she may have either gone into a punitive "exile," sought an escape from court due to disaffection with her murderous son, or embarked on a penitential quest to atone for her complicity in the demise of Crispus and Fausta. The latter claim is largely based on Eusebius' statement that Helena sought, through prayers of thanks for her son and grandchildren, to "repay a debt."[12] However, seen

---

[10] Humfress (2020) 39.

[11] For example: Hunt (1982) 32–33; Barnes (1981) 221. Drijvers (1992a) 67 is more skeptical.

[12] Eusebius, Vita Constantini 3.42, χρέος. Escape from court: see, for example, Lenski (2004) 114–15. Penance: Chadwick (1948) 33. Exile for having killed Fausta: Olbrich (2010). Another passage sometimes cited in this context is Ambrose, De ob. Theod. 41, and his description of Helena in the Holy Land as "anxious." Given the time distance, it is difficult to take this as evidence of her real emotional state.

in the overall context of the *Life of Constantine*, Eusebius' remark was simply geared toward exalting the ruling dynasty's piety, exemplified by the care for the Christian empire that flowed from Helena's maternal disposition.[13] In addition, given that Constantine did his level best to suppress concrete details about Crispus' death and Fausta's disappearance, it would be surprising if he had broadcast his mother's role in the affair in this way, if indeed she had one at all. Even in a Christian context, public expressions of repentance were a serious matter with wide-ranging reputational consequences that an emperor could ill-afford.[14] It is also unlikely that Helena would have defied Constantine on this point. Nothing else we know about Helena's life gives any indication that she would have disobeyed her son, on whom her entire status and livelihood depended, to pursue her own personal quest for redemption. As we shall see, she was in any case not traveling incognito, but in the public manner of a Roman empress, charted by the award of official honors at the places she visited. Constantine would hardly have wanted to raise doubts on such occasions about whether he or Helena were guilty of murdering his son and wife.

While they might not go as far as claiming that Helena sought forgiveness for a specific sin, many historians still call her journey a "pilgrimage," noting her personal religious experience and "intense" piety, especially during her visit to the "Holy Land," and her "urging" of her son to build churches.[15] Of course, among contemporaries, we only have Eusebius' word for Helena's religious feelings, and these are not necessarily presented as any more "urgent" than Constantine's. But even if these feelings were real, it can be doubted that Helena conducted a "pilgrimage," as understood in the Christian sense. At the beginning of the fourth century, there was as yet no clear concept of nor even a term for Christian pilgrimage. There is little evidence that Helena, or her contemporaries, understood the physical burden of long-distance travel as embracing the human condition of the wandering sinner in search of a lost eternal homeland. There is also no evidence that they hoped for divine mercy for their sinful state through the dispensation of charity at specific sacred places within a Christian landscape, especially where these still lacked any built environment.[16]

---

[13] See also Borgehammar (1991) 133–34.
[14] See Hillner (2015) 73–74. See also Holum (1990) 71 for doubts with regard to Helena specifically.
[15] For use of the term, see, for example, Walker (1990) 17; Odahl (2004) 187–95; Smith (2007) 10; Drbal (2014); Barnes (2014) 43 ("official pilgrimage"). For Helena's "intense" piety, Pohlsander (1995) 28; for her "urging" of Constantine, Johnson (2005) 293.
[16] On the development of the concept of Christian pilgrimage, McGowan, Bradshaw (2018) 33–39.

Rather than viewing Helena's journey through the prism of anachronistic concepts, it is more useful to note the intriguing parallels or even continuities between Helena's journey and those of previous emperors who toured the provinces, above all Hadrian, who had also visited Jerusalem, for unclear reasons. Aspects of Helena's trip recall those undertaken by the well-traveled emperor of the second century, especially her wish, as Eusebius describes, to "inspect" or "behold" regions and peoples "with imperial concern." The verb Eusebius chooses, *ephorân*, combines a degree of ethnographic search for knowledge, likewise evident in Helena's quest to, in his words, "research" the "wondrous places," with an element of administrative oversight and scrutiny. Hadrian had been similarly described as showing a keen investigative interest in the cultural sites he encountered on his travels. As in Helena's case, and that of many other ancient travelers who came before her, such interest was often religious in nature. But the main purpose of Hadrian's trips was, undoubtedly, political, to broadcast imperial power throughout his territory in a personal, tangible way, which naturally included the patronage of buildings and the distribution of gifts. None of this was unusual behavior for an emperor, even though Hadrian made more use of this "tool of government" than most.[17]

It is indeed reasonable to assume that Helena's trip also had a political purpose and was engineered to distract from or placate any concerns inhabitants of the empire may have had about recent events. Although these concerns might have arisen from Crispus and Fausta's demise (as they did in Rome), it is perhaps more relevant to remember the topographical parameters of Helena's voyage. In the second section of his Helena excursus, which was probably the earlier one, Eusebius himself makes it quite clear that Helena undertook a general tour of the East, to "visit districts and peoples" with "imperial authority" (*basilikês exousías*). The Eastern empire was a region that was still healing from a recent civil war and was now confronted with profound religious reform. Several of Helena's actions during her travels had a peacemaking quality that addressed this specific situation, despite Eusebius' attempt to give them a more universal, Christian meaning. Among these were the release of prisoners, support for those oppressed by the "greedy," and the recall of those condemned to forced labor and exile.[18]

---

[17] Eusebius, Vita Constantini 3.42. For the parallels between Helena and Hadrian and travel as a "tool of government", see Holum (1990) 66–81, 72. The political nature of her trip: Drijvers (1992a) 65; Hunt (1997).
[18] Eusebius, Vita Constantini 3.42, 3.44.

The ability to announce an imperial amnesty—something that was the prerogative of the emperor and an act of clemency outside the rule of law—would have been an unprecedented power for an empress, dangerously crossing into the legal, and therefore male, sphere.[19] We do not have to assume, however, that Helena issued new or independent orders, for what she did echoes Constantine's announcements after the defeat of Licinius, as also reported by Eusebius and described earlier. Similarly, Helena's church patronage in Palestine, discussed later on in more detail, can be interpreted as part of the general church building scheme initiated by Constantine at this point.[20] In light of such duplications, Helena's trip has sometimes been dated to 325, due to doubts that she would have repeated the same orders issued by her son shortly beforehand.[21] But quite apart from the difficulty of reconciling Helena's known movements with such an early date, this repetition should not surprise us. Imperial administration was a slow process, and ineffective local response to government announcements was a constant complaint of both imperial legislators and individual observers. Even if Constantine had demanded the release of prisoners, the return of property, and the banished, and the erection of churches everywhere already at the end of 324 (which cannot in any case be verified with certainty), we should not expect that these tasks, or anything else he had mandated afterward, would have been fully and smoothly executed by the autumn of 326.[22] Nor may Constantine have expected it. What can look to us like the dysfunction of the Roman bureaucratic system effectively acted in an emperor's favor, as it increased the value of his personal intervention. Sending an imperial representative would ensure not only that the emperor's will was accomplished, but also that his subjects would see that he personally cared.[23] Rather than controversially painting Helena as an empress acting above her station, therefore, Eusebius wanted to remind his readers of Constantine's personal care, anchored in his dynasty and personified in his mother.

---

[19] On the legal nature of amnesties, Waldstein (1964).
[20] See Hunt (1982) 35 for Helena's actions being a mirror of Constantine's announcements. Eusebius' claim that Helena released some from oppression by the greedy (ἠλευθέρου τε πλεονεκτουμένους) is vague, but needs to be linked to Constantine's announcement on the return of confiscated property (Vita Constantini 2.35-41). For Constantine's announcements in the aftermath of Licinius' defeat, see Chapter 7.
[21] Fortner, Rottloff (2000) 86. See also Borgehammar's dating discussed in n. 93 in this chapter.
[22] Heinen (2008) 23. See CTh 11.39.1 (325) for a potential case of confusion that had arisen from Constantine's edicts; also Potter (2013) 217–18 for the long process of establishing Constantine's rule in the East, Millar (1971) 15 for the slowness of communication during the Constantinian period.
[23] Kelly (2006) 228–31.

It was not only unfinished business in the aftermath of Licinius' defeat that made the design of an imperial tour of the East appealing to Constantine in late 326. Since late 324, new and disturbing events had materialized that threatened the stability of his reign, as described in the previous chapter. For at least some of his Eastern subjects, the clandestine killing of their former emperor Licinius and then his son would have been just as troubling as the death of Crispus and the disappearance of Fausta. Soldiers in particular may have become restless upon hearing this news, or it was feared they might, as they had sworn an oath of loyalty to the young Caesar (and to Crispus) at the time of his promotion. Eusebius describes Helena as distributing donatives to the army during her trip, something emperors usually did only on the occasion of accession, victories, birthdays, or anniversaries. This was certainly one of the reasons why Helena had access to the imperial treasury, again an unusual power for an empress, which is why Eusebius reported it as remarkable. Perhaps Helena's donatives were connected with Constantine's Vicennalia, as there was often a time delay in the actual payment of such gifts. But they may also be attributable to Constantine's worries about morale among vitally important Eastern troops.[24]

Beyond these political issues, there were other reasons why a more sustained imperial presence in the Eastern provinces was warranted. Here, the theological disputes that had led to the Council of Nicaea had not been quelled and continued to threaten Christian unity. As Eusebius describes, Helena made sure that she was repeatedly seen entering and donating to churches in the cities she visited, which implies a sustained diplomatic mission to tie Eastern Christian communities to the imperial project in these tense and disunited times.[25] It should also be noted that, at least during part of her trip many bishops were away from their sees in the winter of 327–328, attending Constantine's aforementioned church council at Nicomedia. With the bishops absent, his mother's ostentatious distribution of alms to the poor served to deepen the image of the emperor as a Christian benefactor.[26] Finally, on a more local level, there may have been recent unrest in Palestine. Many decades later, John Chrysostom intimated that there had been a Jewish

---

[24] Eusebius, Vita Constantini 3.44, 3.47. On donatives on anniversaries, the fact that these were not always paid on the actual occasion, and on extraordinary donatives, see Delmaire (1989) 555–56. On oaths by soldiers on the accession of Caesars, Lee (2007) 52–54.

[25] Eusebius, Vita Constantini 3.45. See also Drijvers (1992a) 59–69 for the situation in the East, rather than the events in the West, as reason for Helena's travel.

[26] Eusebius, Vita Constantini 3.42, 44. On the Council of Nicomedia, see Barnes (1981) 229. Exactly 250 bishops attended.

revolt at the time of Constantine, although the details he gives are unspecific and hard to date. One might equally imagine that they occurred in consequence of the momentous interventions in the city's sacred topography triggered by Helena's visit.[27]

The context of the amnesties and the donatives shows, therefore, that Helena acted as a true imperial delegate. In other times, this role would almost certainly have been taken on by the emperor himself or by another male member of the imperial family. Why did Constantine not undertake this journey himself? It may have been because he was busy with other aspects of government during the period that Helena spent on her travels, such as, for example, the Council of Nicomedia. It has also been suggested that he had "a guilty conscience" after the events of 326 and feared "divine disapproval" were he to visit holy sites. But if so, he could have chosen a male delegate, for example, from among his half-brothers whom he had just started to bring back into the imperial fold, a process he would accelerate in the coming years.[28]

Appointing his aging mother must once again therefore have been a conscious decision. It is a sign that Constantine trusted his mother, both in terms of her loyalty, and in terms of her personal qualities, including, possibly, her ability to speak Greek. We can also imagine that Constantine chose an imperial woman to represent him precisely due to her gender. Sending a woman, and one who through her coin portrait was known to subjects as a symbol of the empire's security, would strike a supremely conciliatory note. Furthermore, both the disappearance of Fausta and the continuing presence of Licinius' widow Constantia at Constantine's court could have caused confusion among his subjects about unity within the imperial household. It cannot be ruled out, as we shall see, that Constantia accompanied Helena on her trip, in which case she would have added to the dynastic "front" the emperor wished to project. It was hardly the first time that Constantine used his women in this way. But in the East, he could also reasonably expect a receptive audience for such a move. As we have seen, due to the characteristic decentralization of imperial residences during the tetrarchy, the Eastern empire was a region that was used to or even anticipated the presence of

---

[27] John Chrysostom, Adversus Iudaeos 5.11.
[28] On the brothers' reappearance, see Chapter 7. Flavius Dalmatius did get a military commission in the East, based in Antioch, a few years later; see PLRE I Fl. Dalmatius 6, 240–41. On Constantine's guilty conscience, Holum (1990) 76 (with skepticism). Barnes (1982) 77 on Constantine's occupations in 327–328.

empresses, even those traveling alone, as, for example, Valeria had done.[29] In fact, Helena's trip did not raise any eyebrows. With the exception of Eusebius and Athanasius, contemporary and mid-fourth-century commentators on Constantine's reign do not bother to mention it at all, which must mean that Helena's voyage was not considered particularly controversial.

Although political considerations outweigh reasons of personal piety as explanations for Helena's trip, the distinction between sacred travel, educational sightseeing, and a state visit is not particularly helpful.[30] To be sure, there is a danger that we might cast Helena as a pilgrim mainly because she was a female traveler, replicating ancient discourses that presented women as more invested than men in the physical and tangible side of religion and less in its intellectual, let alone its political aspects.[31] Eusebius may have framed Helena's activities in Palestine against this tradition, and was in any case interested in them mainly for how they reflected on Constantine and his sons as Christian emperors. On the other hand, to emphasize Helena's role as Constantine's political or diplomatic ambassador only bears the risk of underplaying her own experience. Her trip could well have assumed pious qualities, even if it had begun primarily as a "simple" tour of inspection and appeasement. In other words, Helena may have developed spiritual interests in the sacred sites of Palestine once she had seen them firsthand, and with knowledgeable guides, for the first time in her life.

On the Road

At the beginning of the fourth century, a traveler from Rome could have taken several routes to reach the Eastern Mediterranean. The fastest would have entailed embarkment in Rome's harbor city of Portus or the Bay of Naples and either sailing across the open sea to Alexandria and then north along the coasts of Egypt, Palestine, and Syria, or, less dangerously, through coastal navigation via ports in southern Italy, Greece, southern Asia Minor, and Cyprus. Under auspicious weather conditions and with continuous

---

[29] Holum (1990) 76 also speculates that Helena was less threatening to subjects because she traveled without soldiers, but see the discussion that follows. On Valeria's travels, Chapter 4.
[30] See Elsner, Rutherford (2005).
[31] Stephens Falcasantos (2017) 91 and passim.

means of transport and no stops, either voyage took around twenty days to reach a port in Palestine, such as Gaza.[32]

There is a small amount of epigraphic evidence that may suggest Helena traveled to the East on a vessel that navigated the northern shores of the Mediterranean, embarking at the Bay of Naples in Campania and progressing along the coasts of Greece and Asia Minor. These derive from honorary statues dedicated by cities, the erection of which can sometimes be connected to the imperial honorand's presence in a given place, either in preparation for their visit or in subsequent appreciation of having been granted one.[33] At least two statues were erected to honor Helena by the city council and people of Naples that postdate the death of Crispus. Four more are known from Side in Pamphylia Prima on the southern coast of Asia Minor, again dedicated by the city's municipal authorities and set up along the main colonnaded street or in the theater.[34] These statues do not, however, provide a precise date for Helena's potential presence.[35] Since the Bay of Naples was a favorite summer destination for the Roman elite, Helena may have visited it from Rome on another occasion.[36] It is also more likely, as we shall see, that she came to Side on her return from Palestine.

There are other reasons that speak against Helena taking this route, or indeed for her going by ship at all, at least for her outward journey. One of these is climatic. A coastal voyage eastward through the Aegean in late August or September had to battle the prevailing Etesian winds, which made maritime progress in that direction very difficult.[37] More significantly, Helena left Rome at the same time as Constantine who also traveled back to the East after his Vicennalia, but overland. It would be surprising if the emperor had let his mother take on a maritime trip, rather than her joining the safer, morally more decorous and more comfortable surroundings of his trek at least

---

[32] Route descriptions, including on time and distance, are based on information available at orbis.stanford.edu. On navigation in the Mediterranean, see Arnaud (2005). A later female, and possibly imperial, traveler, the Lady Poemenia, sailed across the open sea from Italy; on her, see further discussion here.

[33] Ward Perkins (2016) 39 and Lenski (2016) 326, with reference to Helena's statues in Side.

[34] Naples: CIL 10.1483, 1484; Side: Nollé (1993) nos. 47, 48; Onur (2006) 198, n. 4. A fourth unpublished statue of Helena, currently standing "on the stage of the theatre" of ancient Side, is listed at laststatues.classics.ox.ac.uk LSA-2098 (last accessed 2/16/2021). Odahl (2004) 187 postulates a sea journey.

[35] For doubts on the usefulness of honorary statues to ascertain the whereabouts of emperors, see Munk Højte (2000). There is no full study on the correlation with the itineraries of empresses, but see Brennan (2018) 79 on Sabina.

[36] Drijvers (1992a) 53. See also p. 158.

[37] Andreau (2005) 207–11.

as far as Nicomedia. Taking all of this into account, it is safest to conclude that Helena set out in one of the carriages of the emperor and his entourage. Again, there were two regular overland routes to the East. The faster one involved a crossing of the Adriatic to Dyrrachium in Macedonia to meet the Via Egnatia that ran via Thessalonica toward the Bosphorus and beyond through Asia Minor. An imperial messenger using the horses of the imperial post (*cursus publicus*) in the height of summer could cover the distance between Rome and Constantinople in as little as ten days in this way, although it would have taken a passenger carriage a few weeks longer.[38] In 326, however, Constantine chose to return to the East by the route on which he had come, the entirely landlocked military highway across the Balkans, via northern Italy, Pannonia, Moesia, and Thrace, where in its turn it connected with the Via Egnatia.[39] When one adds her onward journey to Palestine, Helena's journey by this circuit would have stretched some 4,000 kilometers and, as we shall see, taken almost eighteen months (Map 6).

Traveling in Constantine's train for at least some of her eastward journey returned Helena to the spaces of her past with Constantius. At first, however, her stations were along a memory lane of a different, more awkward nature. In late October, the court halted in Milan, the burial place of Maximian, whom his daughter Fausta had betrayed to protect the life of Constantine, or so the Constantinian story went. By late November, they had reached Aquileia, where the palace had once been decorated with pictorial celebrations of Constantine and Fausta's union, and the new Christian basilica had just been paved with a mosaic that may have featured this imperial couple in happier times. A month later, the court arrived at Sirmium, where less than a decade before Fausta had given birth to her second son Constantius, who had later adopted the title of Caesar in place of another little boy born in Sirmium, Constantia's tragic son Licinianus. Toward the end of February 327, finally, Constantine's presence is attested in Thessalonica. This was, of course, the city where Helena and Fausta had been first publicly presented as the female face of the Constantinian dynasty.[40]

---

[38] Lolos (2007) 273–93.
[39] On Constantine's travel, Barnes (1982) 77. For Helena taking this route, also Hunt (1982) 35; Destephen (2018) 44.
[40] Maximian's death and the decoration of the palace in Aquileia: Chapter 3; mosaics in the basilica of Aquileia: Chapter 5, n. 77: Constantius and Licinianus' births and Fausta and Helena in Thessalonica: Chapter 5.

From this itinerary it is clear that Constantine moved exceptionally sedately, more than twice as slowly as he had on his way to Italy earlier in 326.[41] He hence spent a good deal of his time engaging with the populations of these residence cities that had grown so accustomed to the presence of the former Augusta, both in the symbolic and in the physical sense, for, of course, Constantine had visited these same cities in the company of Fausta just a few months before. Having Helena (and possibly Constantia) by his side would have helped him to uphold or reassert an image of household control. Indeed, it was perhaps only during these interactions with his subjects that the utility of his mother taking a further, more extended trip around Licinius' former territories became fully clear to him.

On their way from Sirmium to Thessalonica, Constantine's entourage passed Naissus. Given that several months elapsed before they reached the city on the Macedonian Gulf, it is reasonable to assume that the emperor and his mother paused for some time in his hometown. It is uncertain how long it had been since Helena was last there. Constantine had visited at least once before, in 319, but at that time Helena was probably in Rome.[42] The urban landscape had been substantially transformed since the distant days of her more tranquil life as a young mother. An imperial palace had been built within Naissus' walls in the northern part of the city. An imperial factory for the manufacture of weapons had also been established. The population had grown and suburban neighborhoods were developing. Christianity was slowly arriving in Naissus, too. The earliest church, erected just east of the city, dates to the Constantinian era. Most significantly, Constantine had started to build his grandiose imperial villa on the road to Serdica. It was here that later emperors resided when they came to Naissus. They enjoyed the lavishly decorated heated audience hall accessed through a massive peristyle fronted by a monumental gate, the large bath complex, and the summer and winter dining rooms, where luxurious mosaic floors with intricate ornamental designs had replaced those on which Helena as a young mother may have walked (Fig. 2.1 and Fig. 8.1). Behind them sprawled administrative and military quarters capable of housing large entourages of civil servants and soldiers needed for the transactions of a court on the move. We can assume that Constantine and Helena also resided here in early 327, interacting with

---

[41] Ramskold (2013).
[42] CTh 2.15.1 and 2.16.2 were both issued from Naissus in July 319.

Fig. 8.1 Mosaic floor in the winter dining room (stibadium B) at Constantine's imperial villa at Mediana. © Julia Hillner.

their former neighbors through awe-inspiring ceremonies.[43] It is tempting to think that it was here that the emperor and his mother sketched out the map of her further travels.

Unless Helena and Constantine parted ways at some point and Helena traveled ahead, they reached Nicomedia together in June or July 327. For Constantine, this was, for now, the end of the road. For Helena, it was only the beginning of the first leg of the journey that she would cover on her own, and that would bring her, eventually, to Jerusalem and Bethlehem. Despite now being in her home region, she probably set out straight away. This is not only because we find her as far South as the imperial residence city of Antioch in the latter half of 327, but also because the later in the year, the more difficult it became to traverse the Anatolian peninsula. Many years afterward, in February 437, another female traveler, the ascetic Melania the Younger, had a very difficult time crossing this region to get back to her monastery in Palestine from Constantinople. She even had to get off her mule and

---

[43] The imperial palace within Naissus was partly excavated on the site called Gradsko Polje in 1987–1988, but the results have not been fully published. For the urban development of Naissus in the fourth century, see Vasić (2013) 93 and Jeremić, Filipović (2016). For Mediana: Milošević (2013). For later emperors in Naissus, see Chapter 10.

walk through the Cilician Gates (Gülek Pass) due to the deep snow. As her companion and biographer Gerontius says, she embraced this journey as an ascetic exercise, even though the emperor and empress, Theodosius II and his wife Eudocia, had tried to prevent her from traveling due to the expected hardship.[44] The empress Helena may likewise have admired Christian suffering, but would not have willingly undertaken it.

Even if Helena had taken the straightest route to Jerusalem, her stations would have included important landmarks of the Eastern empire. Before reaching Antioch, she would have touched on the Anatolian cities of Nicaea, host to the recent church council, and Ancyra, capital of the province of Galatia Prima. Further South she must have proceeded through Caesarea, capital of Palaestina Prima, given that Eusebius witnessed her visit. Eusebius may have regarded this linear route alone as a tour of what he calls the "Eastern provinces" (*heōa*), since it did indeed cross the entire administrative district of the "Eastern diocese" created under the tetrarchy, except for Egypt and Libya, that Helena did not reach. Yet, Eusebius also claimed that Helena stayed over even "in the smallest towns."[45] If this is more than a simple exaggeration, this may be a reference to towns in Palestine, where he observed the welcome given to the empress. The church historian Sozomen further reports that Constantine renamed a town in Palestine in honor of his mother, which could have been in commemoration of her visiting it. The town may have been Daburiyya (today's Kfar Kama) in Galilee, which had biblical connotations. A Byzantine biography of Constantine in any case reported that Helena visited towns in southern Galilee.[46] There were also many other smaller towns lining the highway from Nicomedia to Jerusalem, especially along the coast of Syria, Phoenice, and Palestine, where Helena may well have stayed overnight out of simple necessity.

There are, however, signs that Helena made some detours from this direct itinerary. At some stage, as mentioned previously, she distributed gifts to the Eastern troops. While she could, of course, have done this through a delegate, this act would then hardly have been remembered, as it was, as an empress's patronage. But to do this in person, Helena would have had to travel away from the coast. The majority of the Eastern army were stationed in the

---

[44] Gerontius, Vita Melaniae 56. See text that follows on Helena in Antioch.
[45] Eusebius, Vita Constantini 3.42, 45: ἐν ταῖς βραχυτάταις πόλεσι. There is a tradition that Helena visited Mount Sinai, founding a monastery, two churches, and a garden around the site of the burning bush, still kept alive today at St. Catherine's monastery, but this is wholly legendary; see Pohlsander (1995) 96–98.
[46] On Daburiyya as Helenopolis, see Lenski (2016) 159–60; Byzantine biography: Guidi (1908) 646.

frontier provinces of Mesopotamia and on the Euphrates in Osrhoëne, as a bulwark against Persia.[47] Could the early-fifth-century claim of Osrhoëne's capital Edessa to have been Helena's birthplace stem from a memory of her visit to this city for this purpose? Several decades later, yet another female traveler named Egeria, who undertook a long pilgrimage to the holy sites of the Eastern Mediterranean in the early 380s, also diverted East from the main road at Antioch to visit Edessa, in order to see the tomb of the apostle Thomas, and Carrhae, the city of Abraham. While her extant travel memoir makes no mention of Helena on this occasion, Egeria does remark that "there is no Christian who has arrived at the holy places, that is, in Jerusalem, who does not <also> head [to Edessa] to pray."[48] Perhaps Helena's detour had popularized the holy sites of Mesopotamia for later female religious travelers as well as those in Palestine.

Even the straightest route from Nicomedia to Jerusalem required Helena to cover about 1,600 kilometers. During late summer and early autumn, one could have made this journey in less than a month if frequently changing horses at the imperial post stations. But a few years after Helena's visit to Palestine, another traveler from Constantinople to Jerusalem and back, the famous "Bordeaux Pilgrim" (perhaps a woman), took a whole seven months to complete the roundtrip.[49] Unlike the Bordeaux Pilgrim, Helena was a privileged traveler, probably using a high-speed, four-wheeled, and suspended covered wagon, the *carruca*, which may even have contained a sleeping cot. Still, it is unlikely that she could have traveled much faster, and due to her imperial status, her progress was probably even slower. On their earlier imperial trip to the East between 128 and 133, the emperor Hadrian and his wife Sabina took about six months just to cross Anatolia (starting from Ephesus, rather than Nicomedia). They then also spent the winter months of 128–129 in Antioch, from where Hadrian visited the Persian frontier at Palmyra, before progressing on to Jerusalem, which they reached sometime in the year 130.[50]

This slowness was, of course, due to the many ceremonial and administrative events that were inevitably bound up with imperial visits to provincial cities. From the time that Roman emperors first began traveling around

---

[47] See Destephen (2018) 51 for these topographical considerations, although he believes Helena sent a delegate. Eastern troops: Isaac (1997) 457–58. On Edessa as Helena's birthplace, see Chapter 1.
[48] Egeria, Itinerarium 17: *nullus Christianorum est, qui non se tendat illuc gratia orationis, quicumque tamen usque ad loca sancta, id est in Ierusolimis, accesserit.*
[49] Hunt (1982) 56–57.
[50] Brennan (2018) 98–99. On the *carruca*, see Tilburg (2007) 52.

their territory, these were designed and refined to make the imperial presence and Roman rule manifest to the provincial public and temporarily to transform the periphery into the imperial center. With festivities taking place both outside a city and inside—involving speeches, processions, choirs, crowd acclamations, donations, dedications of buildings, games, and sacrifices—these rituals could last for days.[51] Afterward, such visits were also often inscribed into a city's material fabric, through the erection of statues, of which Helena's at Naples and Side may be examples. When Eusebia, the wife of Helena's grandson Constantius, traveled to court for her wedding, "folk in each place came to meet her with welcome and rejoicing," as happened again when she visited Rome in 354. A fifth-century empress, Eudocia, even gave a speech to the town council when visiting Antioch in 438.[52] We do not know whether Helena spoke publicly to local dignitaries in like fashion, but she certainly distributed gifts to whole cities and also to individuals in private audience. From Eusebius' description of Helena's travels in Palestine, it is clear that visits to churches also formed part of her ceremonial calendar. On such occasions, she engaged with crowds, surely arranged, in accordance with tradition, to give a snapshot of society, with all ages, sexes, and now even the urban poor present.[53]

Eusebius here made a point that one could see Helena on foot, mingling with the crowd. With this he emphasized her splendid humility, a familiar sentiment among late antique Christian authors who frequently comment on high-status individuals' getting down from their carriages, or exhort them to do so.[54] Walking during an imperial visit to a city was, nevertheless, an extraordinary thing for an empress to do. In the earlier Roman empire, an imperial woman did not even ride on the emperor's uncovered chariot (*biga*), but, in response to expectations of female modesty, in a two-wheeled covered carriage known as the *carpentum*. At least in Rome, this was how empresses customarily participated in imperial processions, and while Constantinian iconography does also show them standing with the emperor on open

---

[51] Cioffi (2016). See also Holum (1990) 72–73.
[52] Eusebia: Julian, Or. 3.112A and 3.129C. Eudocia: Evagrius, Hist. eccl. 1.20. Eudocia was also honored with statues following her visit; Busch (2015) 151–52.
[53] Eusebius, Vita Constantini 3.44, 3.45. On the composition of the crowd during imperial welcome rituals in provincial cities, see, for example, Ammianus Marcellinus 22.2.4. On private audiences, see Chapter 6.
[54] On walking as a form of Christian humility, see, for example, Palladius, Lausiac History 55.2.

chariots, it is unclear how far these images are merely allegorical.[55] Eusebius' comment on Helena's habit of walking may therefore imply a new, Christian transformation of arrival rituals, where the Christian empress made an ostentatious gesture of being at eye level with her fellow believers, or simply an adaptation of *adventus* ceremonials to the fact that the empress was traveling alone.[56] Either way, seeing an empress—usually a shielded or at least a distant figure—up-close was a breathtaking experience for Constantine's subjects, as is reflected in Eusebius' star-struck account. Even if she did meet subjects on foot, such events were also strictly choreographed. Helena wore simple but "majestic" clothes, as Eusebius also tells us, making sure her humility was highly visible.

Imperial visits to provincial cities were enormous and, for local communities, costly affairs also because accommodations had to be found for extensive retinues. The example of Helena's grandson's wife Eusebia shows how imperial women would sometimes travel with "chariots and horses and carriages of all sorts, decorated with gold and silver and copper of the finest workmanship."[57] As we shall see, some of Helena's carriages may have accommodated Constantine's mother-in-law Eutropia and his sister Constantia. A traveling group of imperial women satisfied Constantine's desire to show dynastic harmony, but these two women also had invaluable knowledge of the Eastern provinces, with one having been their empress and the other born in Syria. In addition, we can imagine that Helena's party consisted, at the very least, of her eunuchs and other slaves, as well as male and female members of the senatorial aristocracy appointed as special companions. It has been suggested that Helena did not travel with a military escort, but sources from both the earlier and the later empire show that empresses were routinely assigned a bodyguard. For instance, Helena's granddaughter, Helena the Younger, had one with her while in Paris with her husband Julian. In any case, while on her voyage, Helena needed a military escort, for personal protection as well as to project a sense of imperial status and, given that Helena was a woman traveling on her own, decorum. As the memoirs of Egeria show, even

---

[55] Latham (2016) 119–20. On Constantinian iconography, see Figs. 5.4 and 7.1. See Gregory of Nyssa who suggests that either a covered carriage or chariot was suitable for empresses entering cities, In Flaccillam 481–82.

[56] On an empress walking on ceremonial occasions, see John Chrysostom, Homiliae dictae postquam reliquiae martyrum 2.2 (referring to Eudoxia).

[57] Julian, Or. 3.110D describing Eusebia's bridal train from Macedonia to Milan (taking the military road through the Balkans in reverse): ἁρμάτων καὶ ἵππων καὶ ὀχημάτων παντοδαπῶν χρυσῷ καὶ ἀργύρῳ καὶ ὀρειχάλκῳ μετὰ τῆς ἀρίστης τέχνης εἰργασμένων.

women below the imperial level preferred to travel with one, at least in some regions.[58]

Helena would also have been accompanied by secretaries and imperial officials whose task it was to manage petitions, orders to governors, building projects, donatives to soldiers, and other distribution of largesse. Among the latter were surely officials attached to the treasury, to which, we might recall, Eusebius said she had unlimited access. Eusebius uses the term *thēsaurós*, which suggests that the office involved here was that of the finance minister known as the "Count of the Sacred Largesses," an office created by Constantine not long before. Its holder was in charge of the emperors' movable property (such as jewelry), the production of precious raw materials through mining and quarrying, mints, and, outside Rome, imperial building projects (as well as exclusive projects, such as the production of purple fabrics)—in short, everything needed to luxuriously outfit the emperor and the imperial family, and to supply their patronage and gift giving.[59] Constantine himself may have had a movable treasury, in the sense that, when he was on the move, his train transported quantities of gold and silver, and even artists who designed coin templates. As soon as he arrived in a city with a mint, it would be put to work to produce gold and silver coinage for his largesse, leaving bronze coinage to local production.[60] If Helena's train likewise transported ingots, Antioch was the last city where these could have been minted into coins. But there is little in the pattern of coin issues from Antioch to suggest increased minting around the time of Helena's voyage.[61] To comply with her patronage brief, therefore, she must have carried with her a reasonable amount of currency; another reason to have a military escort.

In Antioch, where, like Hadrian two centuries earlier, Helena may have spent the winter of 327–328, she and her companions would have stayed in the sprawling imperial palace overlooking the Orontes. Perhaps the three imperial women remembered how not so long ago a more unfortunate empress, Maximinus Daza's widow, had been drowned in the river below. It is also possible that from time to time, Helena stayed at one of the imperial post

---

[58] Julian, Epistula ad Athenienses 284B. On bodyguards of earlier empresses, see Rollinger (forthcoming). Also Holum (1990) 76 on Helena's alleged lack of military escort. Military escorts of people below imperial level: Egeria, Itinerarium 7.

[59] Delmaire (1989) 37 on the creation of the post (perhaps on the occasion of Constantine's Vicennalia), 64, 69 on the remit.

[60] Delmaire (1989) 505, 527; Ramskold (2013).

[61] Between 326 and 328 Antioch seems to have produced only bronze coins: RIC VII, 689–691, albeit two series with the portrait of Helena.

stations (*mansiones*), as other emperors and female members of the imperial family are recorded to have done. If so, Helena may well have been driven to recall her less gilded youth.[62] In provincial capitals and certainly even in smaller towns, Helena would have had to quarter her staff in any available domestic spaces, while she and selected companions stayed in the governor's palace or a leading citizen's residence. In addition to food rations, at least a third of private houses could by law be requisitioned for government business, which surely included the needs of a traveling empress. Many owners would have been only too delighted to provide this favor. Imperial visits were such an honor to subjects that sometimes delegations went out to welcome their esteemed guest, as happened in 438 when inhabitants of Jerusalem met the empress Eudocia already at Sidon in Syria.[63] But not everyone was always pleased. Later in the fourth century, the traveling Lady Poemenia, perhaps a member of the Theodosian dynasty, had a nasty experience when she appeared with a large entourage—consisting of eunuchs, priests, and even bishops—in the small community of Nikiupolis in the Nile delta. Her companions got into a brawl with locals who injured some of them and even insulted Poemenia herself. There may have been resentment over the obligation to provide hospitality for traveling members of the imperial court, an issue that is often discussed in late Roman laws.[64] It is unlikely that the mother of the emperor was treated in a similar way, but even Helena would not find everything on her trip smooth sailing.

A New Jezebel

According to Athanasius' *History of the Arians*, Helena had an unpleasant run-in with the bishop of Antioch, Eustathius, supposedly one of the staunchest supporters of the Nicene creed. His "Arian" opponents brought him before Constantine on a false charge that he had insulted the emperor's mother. Eustathius was banished for the crime, together with his priests and deacons.[65] The episode involving Eustathius allows us to roughly date a

---

[62] On imperial post stations, see Chapter 1.
[63] Gerontius, Vita Melaniae 58.
[64] Palladius, Historia Lausiaca 35. On Poemenia as a member of the imperial family with entitlement to hospitality: Fortner, Rottloff (2000) 146–48. On the obligations of hospitality Goffart (1980) 41–42. Holum (1990) 73 on the housing of the emperor during his travels. On the death of an empress at Antioch, see Chapter 4.
[65] Athanasius, Historia Arianorum 4–5.

stage of Helena's Eastern trip, as his banishment is now commonly dated to early 328. Whether the story of the insult is true or not, Athanasius and his readers regarded it as plausible, because Helena had been in Antioch around this time. Before being sent on to Constantine, Eustathius was allegedly first tried in Antioch by a council of bishops, who were either on their way to or from the council at Nicomedia held in the winter of 327–328, as already mentioned.[66] Their meeting was presided over by Eusebius of Caesarea, so, if Helena personally witnessed this council at Antioch, she would have already met Eusebius on this occasion.

It is unclear whether Eustathius had actually insulted Helena. The fifth-century church historians list different reasons for his banishment, ranging from a charge of Sabellianism (a doctrine that envisaged the Trinity as an expression of divine aspects, rather than distinct persons) to one of sexual behavior inappropriate for a priest.[67] These sources were all written at a time when Helena's image was untouchable, and when it was unwise to draw her into an affair that had seen a defender of Nicaea—by then the established orthodoxy—persecuted. In the 350s, Athanasius had felt no such qualms yet. Still, it seems unlikely he pulled a claim of such resonance about the grandmother of a reigning emperor out of thin air, especially since, as we shall see, the emperor of the time, Constantius II, may not have wished to be reminded of unpleasant aspects of Helena's life.[68] An insult to the empress may very well have been among the package of accusations against the Antiochene bishop, therefore, especially when the case was brought to the emperor who would have been less interested in Eustathius' failings in matters of ecclesiastical discipline.

But what was the insult? It has been suggested that Eustathius suspected Helena, or her son Constantine, of having "Arian" sympathies. This suggestion is based not only on Athanasius' testimony, but also on reports that Helena venerated the martyr Lucian whose relics were held in Drepanon. Lucian had been the teacher of Arius, Eusebius of Nicomedia, and other leading opponents to the decisions made at the Council of Nicaea.[69] Before

---

[66] Barnes (1978); Chadwick (1948) 27–35; Gwynn (2007) 141. See also Pohlsander (1995) 85–87 and Parvis (2006) 100–101, although she believes Helena traveled to Palestine in the autumn of 326, which can be excluded for reasons described earlier.

[67] Philostorgius, Hist. eccl. 2.7; Socrates, Hist. Eccl. 1.24.2; Sozomenus, Hist. eccl. 2.19.1; Theodoret, Hist. eccl. 1.22.

[68] See Chapter 10.

[69] Drijvers (1992a) 71; Lenski (2016) 268. On Lucian's teaching of Arius, Eusebius, and others: Philostorgius, Hist. eccl. 2.3. On Helena and Lucian of Antioch, see also Chapter 1, 3, and 9 here.

we hasten to imagine an epic public clash between bishop and empress over a matter of theology, however, we should take note of the fact that Athanasius said the charge of insult was an invention, one concocted by Eustathius' "Arian" opponents. Even so, Athanasius still makes Helena complicit in this conspiracy, thereby implying her "Arian" sympathies. Just before he turned to Eustathius' case, Athanasius had compared the orthodox heroes of his *History* to the biblical Naboth who had falsely been accused of blasphemy in front of the king of Samaria, Ahab, by Ahab's wife, the wicked queen Jezebel. This had led, ultimately, to Jezebel's banishment of the prophet Elias who had reprimanded the queen for her part in the affair (1 Kings 21). Although Athanasius mentions only Naboth, not Jezebel, his biblically versed readers, Egyptian monks,[70] would have immediately seen the parallel with the false charge involving Helena. What is more, Athanasius then compounded this implication of her involvement by enumerating the names of other Nicene bishops who had been banished through the influence of imperial women: Eutropius of Adrianople, persecuted by Basilina, the second wife of Constantine's brother Julius Constantius, and Marcellus of Ancyra, banished on the instigation of Eusebius of Nicomedia, who allegedly had access to Constantine "through his women."[71]

In Athanasius' version of events, then, Helena was surrounded by "Arians" who exploited her and other imperial women's natural wickedness and privileged access to the emperor to further their causes. Athanasius implies that the leader of these "Arians" was Eusebius of Nicomedia. With regard to Helena, and the episode in Antioch, Eusebius' direct influence can however be doubted, since he was still in banishment in Gaul at this time. To give the impression of a cohesive conspiracy, Athanasius was, in fact, collapsing time here, for the banishments of Eutropius and Marcellus also happened somewhat later. Basilina would have been too young in 327 to take any political action (she died, still at a young age, c. 333), and Marcellus' exile occurred only in 336, long after Helena's and Basilina's deaths.[72] What we see in Athanasius' account above all is his desire to explain Constantine's puzzling deviation, by recalling Arius and the bishops who supported him, from the decisions made at the Council of Nicaea. Athanasius chose a cautious but well-trodden

---

[70] Barnes (1993) 126.
[71] Athanasius, Historia Arianorum 4–5: παρα τῶν γυναικῶν σύστασιν. Basilina is described as "most active in the proceedings against him" (Βασιλίνα γὰρ ἦν ἡ πάνυ κατ'αὐτοῦ σπουδάζουσα).
[72] On Basilina, also the mother of Julian, see PLRE I, Basilina, 148, and further in Chapter 9. On Marcellus, Gwynn (2007) 143.

route to do so, by showing that Constantine had been tricked by an alliance between "Arians" and women, who should, of course, have stayed well out of ecclesiastical affairs. Athanasius was a regular exponent of the narrative power of the topos of "womanly influence" on male decision makers widespread in ancient literature.[73]

This is not to say that Athanasius' account lacks elements of truth. In the first place, his story was convincing because everyone knew that Constantine's court was always full of women. Among these were his mother, daughters, the wives of his brothers, and in time, of his sons and nephews, as well as the widows remaining from his purges of his male relatives. As we have seen before, it was also common for political agitators to approach these women for patronage when it suited their cause. Indeed, even Athanasius himself had done so before writing the *History of the Arians*, for his patron, as we shall see, had at one point been Constantine's sister Eutropia the Younger.[74] It is therefore not inconceivable that others, like Eusebius of Nicomedia, had operated through similar channels, too, although not yet against Eustathius. Eusebius had a network far more superior than that of many of his rivals. Not only was he acquainted with Constantine's sister Constantia, but he also became the emperor's kinsman. He was related to Licinius' former Praetorian prefect, Julius Julianus, whose daughter was the very Basilina who married Julius Constantius, after the death of his first wife Galla sometime after 326. Julianus' transition from Licinius' to Constantine's court, where he was appointed consul in 325, had probably been facilitated by Constantia, too. Eusebius clearly made use of these connections and, after his recall from banishment, progressed toward an intimate relationship with Constantine, to such an extent that he was the bishop who baptized the emperor on his deathbed in May 337.[75]

Although Athanasius does not mention Constantia, later authors who recounted the early days of the Nicene struggles focused particular attention on her supposed influence. Constantine's recall of Eusebius of Nicomedia and his fellow bishops from exile allegedly came down to a dream Constantia had about his orthodoxy. Constantia also supposedly kept an "Arian" presbyter in her household, planted there by Eusebius, who spread false beliefs both to Constantine and later to his son Constantius.[76] It may have been Constantia's

---

[73] Cooper (1996) 11–12.
[74] Chapter 9. For access to imperial women, see also Chapter 6.
[75] PLRE I, Iulius Iulianus 7, 478–79. Kinship with Eusebius of Nicomedia can be deduced from Ammianus Marcellinus 22.9.4, who reports that Eusebius of Nicomedia was a relative of Julian. Constantine's baptism at the hands of Eusebius of Nicomedia is first reported by Jerome, Chron. 337.
[76] On these stories, see Hillner (2019a).

companionship with Helena on her travels—and therefore her potential presence at Antioch, too—that caused Helena to become wrapped up in such stories, alongside her association with the tainted Lucian of Antioch.

None of this proves, however, that any of these imperial women had "Arian" leanings. Constantia is known to have had theological interests, but these make her out more as a recent convert from paganism than as an expert on inner-ecclesiastical debate.[77] According to a letter that either Eusebius of Nicomedia or Eusebius of Caesarea wrote to Constantia while she was still empress, she attempted to acquire or even commission a painting of Christ.[78] Whichever Eusebius this was, he rebuked her, pointing out that the veneration of images of gods and heroes was a pagan practice, and unorthodox for Christians. For her part, Basilina also appeared interested in church affairs, to the extent that she left funds for the church of Ephesus in her will, to store up "treasures in heaven."[79] Helena's interest in Lucian, in turn, may have stemmed primarily from the fact that his relics were kept in her place of origin, Drepanon, unless we want to imagine that she witnessed his martyrdom in Nicomedia in 311. Lucian's own doctrinal views are, in any case, extremely unclear.[80] From what we know about these women's religious interests, then, they extended more to aspects of popular devotion and religious practice, than to specialized and highly contentious Trinitarian questions.

More importantly, there was no clear theological position that could be labeled "Arianism," certainly not in the late 320s or 30s. There were intellectual, social, and increasingly political networks that floated a range of ideas about the nature of the relationship between God and Christ that became more polarized over time. It has even been doubted whether the "Arian" opposition to the decisions taken at the Council of Nicaea was organized by a single ringleader, Eusebius of Nicomedia, as Athanasius would like us to believe. To blur matters even further, many bishops, such as Eusebius of Caesarea, continued to change their stance.[81] Significantly, Constantine himself changed position, as he seems to have cared more about the unity of the church, which would be blemished by the existence of banished clerics and endless wrangling, than he did about theological precision or consistency. The emperor's

---

[77] Barnes (2010) 313–17.
[78] The letter is edited in Thümmel (1992) 283–87. The historical authenticity of the letter or at least of some parts is debated by Sode, Speck (2004) 113–34, but see Gero (1981) 460–70, Thümmel (1984) 210.
[79] Palladius, Dialogue 13.
[80] Gwynn (2007) 202–5.
[81] Gwynn (2007) passim.

female relatives may have been part of bishops' networks and facilitated access to the emperor, and naturally favored those churchmen with whom they were personally acquainted. But there is no real evidence that their position was any different from that of Constantine. We should not follow incensed churchmen in blaming women for decisions about ecclesiastical politics that were made by Constantine. Instead, it is far more likely that imperial women deemed it safest to change their views in accordance with the emperor's.

On this reading, Helena had probably been insulted by Eustathius of Antioch, but it is more questionable whether it was on a matter of doctrine. Perhaps the bishop had made an unwise remark about her low origins and their connotations of dubious sexual morals. It is telling that one of the fifth-century church historians, Theodoret, replaced Athanasius' story of a false accusation fabricated by Helena with that of a false accusation of Eustathius' sexual promiscuity fabricated by an Antiochene prostitute. In his adaptation of the story, Eusebius of Nicomedia and his cronies bribed this nameless woman to declare, under oath, that the bishop had fathered her child. Perhaps Theodoret still knew a version of the insult of Helena, too dangerous to repeat at his time, and reworked it in this way.[82] Helena's humble background remained an aspect of her life that made her vulnerable and Constantine was sensitive to that fact. Beneath the rhetorical layers we therefore may see, for once, Helena's chilling readiness to use her power when needed. Whatever the insult had been, it quickly became ammunition in the escalating conflict over the Nicene creed and the person of Athanasius, turning Helena into a veritable Jezebel. It puts into perspective the resounding success she had with the next bishop she encountered, Eusebius of Caesarea.

Empresses in the Holy Land

If we have tracked Helena's movements correctly, she arrived in Palestine in early 328. As she approached from the north along the coastal road, the so-called Via Maris, the first city she reached in that province was Caesarea Maritima, Eusebius' see and the prosperous capital of Palaestina Prima. Helena would have stayed in the governor's palace at its southern edge, dramatically situated on a promontory extending into the sea, with panoramic

---

[82] Theodoret, Hist. eccl. 1.22. Theodoret's attitude to the power of empresses was ambiguous at best.

views over the city and its harbor. Eusebius would have undoubtedly regaled his imperial visitor with stories about the city's Christian martyrs who had been held in the prisons under the palace less than twenty years before, then executed in the circus just outside, their dead bodies unceremoniously disposed without proper burial at the gates she had just passed through. These cruel events had allegedly brought the pillars of the city's porticoes, its streets, and the whole ground on which it stood to tears.[83] It was surely not the first inspiring martyr story Helena would have heard on her long journey in the aftermath of a persecution, at a time when many of the empire's bishops were looking to position their sees within the grand sweep of Christian history.[84] But in Palestine this history had deeper material and spiritual roots than anywhere else. Encountering Eusebius, who more than anyone "theologically branded" Palestine, initiated Helena into the knowledge that she had truly touched sacred ground.[85]

Eusebius presided over a city more famed for its imperial, civic, and pagan heritage than its biblical identity, unlike his counterpart in the other major see of Palestine, Bishop Macarius of Jerusalem. It was to Macarius that Helena headed next. From Caesarea, Helena would have continued down the coast, touching the towns of Apollonia and Ioppa, before then turning inland for the ascent to Jerusalem through the Ayalon Valley, passing Emmaus, mentioned by Eusebius in his compendium of biblical sites and therefore possibly noted as well by the empress.[86] Shortly afterward, Jerusalem came into sight, perched on the Judaean hills. Some 150 years before, Hadrian had established the Roman colony Aelia Capitolina here, on occasion of his visit in 130. The colony had destroyed the city's last remnants of the Second Temple period, gutted its sacred Jewish topography by erecting Roman temples throughout the urban landscape, including one to Venus on the northern side of the Forum, and laid out the city on a grid plan, thereby extinguishing Jewish life that had still persisted in the city. When Helena visited, its inhabitants were Latin- and Greek-speaking pagans and, increasingly, Christians. It is unclear where she stayed, as no governmental or residential buildings have been excavated within the Roman city, although there existed substantial villas in the immediate countryside to the southeast.[87]

---

[83] The story is told in Eusebius, Martyrs of Palestine 9.12. See Sivan (2008) 302–3.
[84] Constantine's letter to the Eastern provincials (see Chapter 7) had specifically mentioned "tombs of the martyrs" to be restored to churches.
[85] For the quote, see Kalleres (2005) 432.
[86] Eusebius, Onomasticon, Section E: The Gospels.
[87] Weksler-Bdolah (2019) 51–60, on the temples: 116–26; residential buildings: 130.

In the early fourth century, the ancient center of the Jewish world was therefore a political, administrative, and even military backwater, for the legion that had been stationed in the adjacent camp had been withdrawn in the late third century. It is, accordingly, not immediately obvious why a traveling empress would visit. The answer lies in Constantine's discovery, following his conquest of the Eastern territories, of the geographical origins of his new faith.[88] Soon, this interest extended to the monumentalization of specific biblical sites. The most well-known and earliest of these is the ecclesiastical complex built over the locations of Christ's passion, now known as the Holy Sepulchre, in the area formerly occupied by the Temple of Venus. Eusebius tells us that Constantine had ordered the temple to be destroyed, upon which a spectacular discovery was made, of Christ's tomb in the ground below. Although Eusebius claims that Constantine acted on divine inspiration, it is reasonable to assume that the bishop of Jerusalem, Macarius, had asked the emperor for permission to remove the temple, as he would have needed to, either at or following the Council of Nicaea, where the two men had met. There had been a local belief since at least the second century that the temple stood on the place where Christ had been crucified, Golgotha, which at the time of Jesus' death had lain outside the city. Eusebius' goal in the *Life of Constantine* was to praise the Christian emperors, so he may have wanted to downplay Macarius' role, particularly as there may have been political and theological rivalry between the two men.[89]

After the temple had been destroyed, the area successfully excavated, and the surprising find of the tomb made, Constantine commanded a richly decorated Christian church to be erected on the site. It is possible that the idea to build a church here came to Constantine only after he had been informed of the tomb's discovery. Macarius' interest may have only been in securing access to a holy place, Golgotha, and now also the tomb, since his own bishop's church was situated elsewhere, on Mount Zion. Eusebius quotes the emperor's letter to Macarius announcing his decision about the church, which can be dated to 326. It described the discovery of the tomb and offered the bishop every possible support for building a church over it through the

---

[88] Hunt (1997) 407.
[89] Eusebius, Vita Constantini 3.26–40. On local knowledge of the sites connected with Christ's life, Irshai (2006) 99. On Macarius' role, including his attempt to promote the see of Jerusalem at the council, see Hunt (1982) 9; Drijvers (1992a) 64 n. 45; Hunt (1997) 411; Heid (2001) 44.

232 CENTER STAGE (C. 317–C. 329)

agency of the Praetorian prefect's deputy Dracilianus and the governor of Palestine, especially in procuring labor and building materials.[90]

The ecclesiastical complex, which would in time become the episcopal church, was eventually dedicated in 335 in the presence of a large assembly of bishops. It consisted of a basilica, which was accessed through a monumental gateway and atrium from the street running to the east of it, the colonnaded *cardo maximus* (main street) of Aelia Capitolina. This edifice with double side-aisles, upper galleries, marble-faced walls, and a gilded ceiling stretched out toward the covered tomb cut into the rocky hill to the west, which was at first enclosed by a large courtyard. The courtyard itself was believed to incorporate the foot of the Golgotha hill (which became a kind of shorthand for the church itself, also often just called "Martyrium"). During the reign of Constantine's son Constantius, the tomb would be encased in the domed structure that still exists, the Anastasis (Resurrection).[91]

When Helena arrived in Jerusalem, the city was therefore in the grip of a profound transformation, as Rome had been upon her arrival there a decade earlier. Constantine's letter to Macarius expressed the emperor's deep concern for the splendor of the church he was building and encouraged Macarius to get in touch with him personally about the supply of precious ornaments from imperial domains. Helena's visit, in the company of officials of the Sacred Largesses, helped to make sure that all the bishop's needs were fulfilled. The memoirs of the female pilgrim Egeria—the first source that mentions Helena in connection with this church—recorded that the basilica was decorated "in the presence of Helena."[92] Egeria picked this information up through local gossip, but it is not at all inconceivable that Helena's visit to Jerusalem coincided with this phase of the construction project.

Since the church was already in an advanced state of construction in early 328, Helena cannot, however, have been involved in the event for which she is most remembered, the discovery of the True Cross and its nails, allegedly unearthed from the rubble generated by the excavations of Christ's tomb. She can also not be considered the founder of the Holy Sepulchre.[93] This is

---

[90] Eusebius, Vita Constantini 3.32. Eusebius mentions the Holy Sepulchre also in his Tricennalian Oration/Laus Constantini 9.17 held in 336. On the sequence of events: Drake, Orlandi, Pearson (1980) 132–39; Heid (2001) 44–45. On Macarius' church, Mimouni (1990) 215–34. On the date of the letter to Macarius, Barnes (1989) 120.

[91] The archaeological remains (also of the other Constantinian foundations) were first described by Vincent, Abel (1914–1926); see also Taylor (1993); Biddle (2000); Garbarino (2005); Losito (2010).

[92] Egeria, Itinerarium 25.9: *sub praesentia matris suae* [=Constantine's].

[93] Hunt (1982) 37–38; Drijvers (1992a) 64, 148; Pohlsander (1995) 101–3; Heid (2001) 44; Dirschlmayer (2015) 40–41. Note that Borgehammar (1991) 133–39 assumes that the excavations, in

a chronological inconsistency that our sources for the cross discovery, none of which date from earlier than the late fourth century, missed, especially Theodoret, who has Helena carrying the letter that already described the excavations during which her discovery was supposedly made.[94] The many sources written closer to the time that refer to relics of the cross in Jerusalem or elsewhere, including Egeria's travel memoirs, do not mention Helena as the discoverer.[95] Even so, the sources do suggest that an object identified as a relic of the cross had been found during the reign of Constantine. At least this was being claimed by Macarius' successor Cyril around a decade after Eusebius wrote, at a time when the cross was displayed in Jerusalem and many pieces of this object were apparently already in circulation around the Mediterranean. In 351 Cyril mentioned the happy occurrence of their discovery to Helena's grandson, Constantius II. In this letter he remembered that "divine grace granted him who was rightly seeking piety the discovery of the hidden holy places," which implies a male relic hunter, perhaps Macarius, who would in any case have been responsible for the ceremonial framing of such an event. On the other hand, Eusebius himself, who covers the building of the Holy Sepulchre complex so extensively, does not even seem to mention the cross. This may have been because he envied Macarius, or because he was theologically opposed to the veneration of such a relic, or because it distracted from his literary scheme.[96] If what was believed to be the True

the spring of 325, were conducted in Helena's presence. For reasons detailed at the beginning of the chapter, it is unlikely that Helena's trip can be dated so early.

[94] Rufinus, Hist. eccl. 10.7–8; Paulinus of Nola, Ep. 31; Sulpicius Severus, Chron. 2.33; Socrates, Hist. eccl. 1.17; Sozomen, Hist. eccl. 2.1.2–2.2.4; Theodoret, Hist. eccl. 1.18; Ps.-Gelasius of Cyzikus, Hist. eccl. 3.6.2. Ambrose, Ob. Th. 44–48 claims the cross was recovered from the excavations of Golgotha, not the tomb, which could mean the discovery was made later during Helena's presence [Garbarino (2005) 246–47], although it is not clear how familiar he was with local spatial details. The current chapel of St. Helena, the legendary finding spot of the cross, is indeed under the basilica, but its relationship to the fourth-century spaces is unclear. See Heid (1989) 47, with a bibliography.

[95] These are: Cyril of Jerusalem, Catecheses 4.10; 10.19; 13.14 (c. 348–350); L'épître de Cyrille (351) in Bihain (1973); CIL 8.20600 (359; cross relic mentioned on a North African reliquary box; see also CIL 8.9255, on which more is revealed in Chapter 11); Gregory of Nyssa, Vita Macrinae (370) 30; Egeria, Itinerarium 25.9 (380s); John Chrysostom, Homiliae LXXXVIII in Iohannem, 85.1 (c. 390); Jerome, Ep. 46. 12 (388–392). John Chrysostom also mentions cross relics worn on necklaces in Contra Iudaeos et Gentiles 10 (386–387).

[96] L'épître de Cyrille 3, Bihain (1973) 287: ζητοῦντι τὴν εὐσέβειαν τῶν ἀποκεκρυμμένων ἁγίων τόπων παρασχούσης τὴν εὕρεσιν. On the possibility that the "evidence of his most sacred passion," mentioned in Constantine's letter as having been found in the tomb (Vita Constantini 3.30: τὸ γνώρισμα τοῦ ἁγιωτάτου ἐκείνου πάθους) may be an allusion to the cross, see Borgehammar (1991) 106; Heinen (1995) 96; contra: Hunt (1997) 415; Cameron, Hall (1999) 279–81; Drijvers (2011) 158. Eusebius suppressed information about the discovery of the cross due to politics: Rubin (1982) 79–105; to theology: Walker (1990) 127–30; Borgehammar (1991) 116–88; Drake (1985); to literary reasons: Heid (2001) 50–51. It should be noted that if a cross was found, it did not leave an impression on the Bordeaux Pilgrim who visited in 333 but does not mention this relic.

Cross had been found during the excavations under the Temple of Venus, it is not inconceivable that Helena was presented with relics of it on her arrival shortly afterward. She could then have taken them back to the emperor, giving rise to the story that Constantine kept pieces of the cross in his diadem, his horse's bridle, in his palace, his column in Constantinople, and the church in the area of the Sessorium in Rome.[97]

The period during which Helena visited Palestine was, in any case, an age of discovery. It is plausible, therefore, that the emperor hoped his mother's visit would engender even more such dramatic finds, or, more likely, that local communities sought to exploit her visit in this way.[98] If so, they were not disappointed. While it is impossible to associate Helena with the most important ecclesiastical institution in Jerusalem, the Holy Sepulchre, Eusebius describes the empress herself as "dedicating" or "establishing" two additional temples at biblical locations, "adorning" them (*katekósmei*) and giving them "wonderful monuments" (*thaumastoîs mnḗmasi*). One was built over the cave or grotto of the Nativity in Bethlehem, a village 9 kilometers south of Jerusalem, and one on the "mountain of the ascension," that is, the Mount of Olives east of the city, at the cave where Christ had taught his disciples (Matthew 24–25).[99]

These two monuments must be the Church of the Nativity in Bethlehem and the so-called Eleona ("Olive grove") church 50 meters below the summit of the Mount of Olives (Map 7). Both were mentioned as Constantinian foundations already in the fourth century and their origins are archaeologically dated to the early fourth century. Like the church at the Holy Sepulchre, they were laid out on a basilica-with-atrium plan, but in both cases the holy sites, or caves, were more directly integrated into the basilical architecture. This was perhaps because these two churches were not required simultaneously to serve as bishop's churches with separate liturgical needs and could therefore allow for a less segregated flow of pilgrims. The Eleona, of which foundation trenches and walls partly survive, consisted of a simple three-aisled nave, an apse to the east, and an atrium to the west, with the sacred grotto situated under a raised platform extending into the central nave from

---

[97] On the possibility that Helena received relics, Heinen (1995) 94–97; Heid (2001) 43. On the church in the Sessorian Palace, see Chapter 6. On the various places where the relics were supposedly kept, Chapter 11.
[98] Heid (2001) 46.
[99] Eusebius, Vita Constantini 3.43. For an interpretation of these two churches as foundations during Helena's visit to Palestine, see Drijvers (1992a) 64; Hunt (1982) 14, 37; Hunt (1997) 417; Pohlsander (1995) 92; Heinen (1995) 112; Heid (2001) 50.

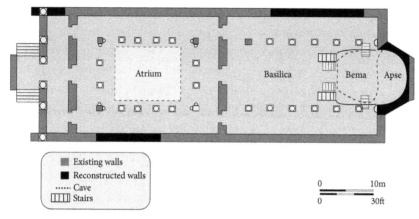

Fig. 8.2 Groundplan of the Eleona. Drawn by Robert Heffron, based on Tsafrir (1993) 33.

the apse (a bema, as also known from synagogue architecture) (Fig. 8.2). In Bethlehem, an octagonal structure rather than an apse was attached to the eastern side of the five-aisled nave, over the cave of the Nativity and with a hole in the ground that allowed visitors to gaze down on the site of Christ's birth. The octagon also recalled the concentric layout customary of imperial palatial and funerary architecture of the period.[100]

Other fourth-century observers—the Bordeaux Pilgrim and Egeria—who describe the Church of the Nativity and the Eleona do not mention Helena as their founder. The Bordeaux Pilgrim ascribes these churches to Constantine, proving, incidentally, that they had been completed by 333. Elsewhere, Eusebius does so, too. In his Tricennalian Oration, given in Constantinople in 336 in praise of Constantine, Eusebius claimed that the emperor had discovered the three sacred caves—of the Nativity, of the tomb, and at the site of the Ascension—and built a church at each. Helena is ignored.[101] The silence of both the Bordeaux Pilgrim and Egeria is easily explained by their understanding of these foundations as imperial. Whatever contribution Helena may have made would simply have been subsumed into a larger imperial project, funded with imperial money, as we have already discussed in

---

[100] Patrich (2006) 368–69. On the Eleona, also Tsafrir (1993) 33; Bloedhorn (1995). The church was destroyed in 614 during the sack of Jerusalem by the Sasanians. In Bethlehem, the church was replaced by a new structure under Justinian, which still stands.

[101] Itinerarium Burdigalense 594.2, 595.6, 598.7, 599.5; Eusebius, Tricennalian Oration/Laus Constantini 9.17.

relation to churches in Rome.[102] Meanwhile, Eusebius had reasons in his different works to prioritize either Constantine or Helena. In the Tricennalian Oration, delivered in the presence of a living emperor in his thirtieth year of reign, he presented the three foundations over three caves as part of a unified plan by Constantine, revealed to him by divine inspiration, to honor the three theophanies (visible manifestations of God): the Nativity, the Resurrection, and the Ascension. Above all these triads hovers, of course, the concept of the Trinity, which, in 336, Eusebius, given his mixed reputation in this regard, was keen to be seen as endorsing. Soon afterward, however, when writing the *Life of Constantine*, Eusebius was keener to give credit to Helena instead.

The Helena excursus in the *Life of Constantine* begins with an echo of the threefold scheme of the Tricennalian Oration. It follows on directly from Eusebius' discussion of the "cave" of the tomb and starts with the declaration that Constantine "after learning of two more places venerated for their mystic caves," honored these with embellishments.[103] This focus on the emperor was a remnant of the original text Eusebius had intended as a simple encomium to Constantine. But, as mentioned at the beginning of this chapter, the brutal dynastic events of the summer of 337 induced Eusebius to foreground Helena's role in the version that has come down to us. Over the course of the excursus, Constantine recedes into the background, until his only action lies in the offer of gifts to the churches (including gold and silver objects and carpets) in Helena's memory, that is, after her death. As we have seen, Eusebius specifically mentioned Helena's three grandsons—now the three reigning emperors—as the subjects of Helena's prayers in the Holy Land, and he subsequently refers to them again in relation to her death. He intended to give the impression that Constantine's succession plan had already taken threefold form in the late 320s, even though this was not really the case, as we shall see. Since in the late 330s it was now Helena's value as the founder of this most Christian tripartite dynasty that had assumed paramount importance, her value as a church patron had increased, too, warranting more visibility of her performance of this role.[104] At the same time, the mere mention of Helena in this context indicates that she really had exercised such patronage. Although she was the new emperors' grandmother, Eusebius would not have

---

[102] See Chapter 6. Dirschlmayer (2015) 32–34.
[103] Eusebius, Vita Constantini 3.41: Ἀπολαβὼν δ'ἐνταυθοῖ χώρας ἑτέρας δυσὶν ἄντροις μυστικοῖς τετιμημένας.
[104] Heinen (1995) 100–105; Heid (2001) 50. See also for Eusebius' association of Constantine's sons with the Trinity, Vita Constantini 4.40.2. For the events of 337, see Chapter 9.

reascribed these churches' foundation to her and in this way diminished the emperor's role, if it had been Constantine alone who had founded them.

All of this also shows that, despite Eusebius' insistence on a unified church building program, the history of the Constantinian foundations in Palestine was pragmatic, piecemeal, and not even theologically coherent. Eusebius' evolving agenda as a writer, but also his attempt to paper over such incoherence, led to further confusion over the exact location of Helena's church on the Mount of Olives, whether at its summit or over the cave where Christ had taught. The *Life of Constantine* is unclear on this point, but it is more likely that the church was at the latter spot and not only due to the archaeological discoveries of the Eleona. The only known church on the summit, commemorating the Ascension, was built later, by the aforementioned Lady Poemenia (this was the so-called Inbomon, a circular church that is now a mosque).[105] Eusebius perhaps kept this information deliberately opaque in order to suit his account of three churches marking the three theophanies of the Nativity, Resurrection, and Ascension.[106]

In reality, Helena's interest seems to have been focused on sites connected with various stages of Christ's life, theophanic or not, because they were presented to her as places in which the local Christian community were already interested. As in the case of Christ's tomb, the locations of the cave in Bethlehem and the teaching cave at the Mount of Olives had long been enshrined in tradition. Although we should not give credence to Eusebius' assertion that Helena came to Palestine already filled with an ardent desire to walk in Christ's footsteps (Psalm 132:7), Bible in hand, it is not hard to imagine that her interest was roused once she was shown these sites and learned their history. The key figure here may, once again, have been Macarius, ignored by Eusebius, but encouraged by the success of the Holy Sepulchre to try and claim other sites, too. It is also possible that Helena encountered Joseph of Tiberias during this trip, a convert from a prominent Jewish family, who would go on to build several churches in Galilee with Constantine's help.[107]

---

[105] On the Inbomon church, Hunt (1982) 161–62. Later this church was also retrospectively associated with Helena; see Paulinus of Nola, Ep. 31.4.

[106] Walker (1990) 204–5. Eusebius' own Demonstratio Evangelica 6.18.23 shows that Eusebius knew perfectly well that the cave and the spot from where Christ ascended were two different places, as was also believed later in the fourth century. See Alliata, Pierri (2002) 314.

[107] Walker (1990) 275–81 suggests Eusebius as Helena's guide, but this seems unlikely given his silence about it; see also Borgehammar (1991) 125. On Joseph of Tiberias, Lenski (2016) 154–55.

The fortuitous process by which a Constantinian church foundation in Palestine could come to pass through the intervention of an imperial woman is described by Eusebius himself in the *Life of Constantine*, four chapters after the excursus on Helena. Eusebius here turns to the foundation of another basilica in Palestine, at the Old Testament site of Mamre, 40 kilometers south of Jerusalem near Hebron (Map 7). It was here, at the oak tree where he had pitched his tents, that three angels had allegedly appeared to the patriarch Abraham to announce the pregnancy of his wife Sara (Genesis 18:1–15). Eusebius cites a letter he, Macarius, and the other bishops of Palestine had received from Constantine that described how a woman the emperor calls "related to me by marriage" (κηδέστρια) had discovered pagan idols and an altar for sacrifices at the site and how she had written to inform him of the matter. Constantine, in turn, informed the bishops that he had commanded the *comes* Acacius to destroy all these structures and to build a church there. We know from other sources and archaeological remains that this was accomplished before 333, in the form of yet another basilica, which incorporated within its atrium the sacred well, the oak tree, and Abraham's altar.[108]

Due to the emperor's reference to his marriage, the mystery imperial woman was probably Constantine's mother-in-law Eutropia.[109] This identification has led some scholars to assume that Eutropia's presence in Palestine must have occurred before 326, after which, it is assumed, her daughter's disgrace would have prevented her from communicating with the emperor and receiving the positive response described here.[110] However, such an early date is unlikely, because it would make Eutropia, the widow of a pagan emperor, the first imperial person to have visited a Christian site in Palestine, at a time when even the first Christian emperor had not yet shown interest in this remote province. The reference to the *comes* Acacius further suggests Constantine's letter to the bishops dates from after 326, as we know from other sources that he was active in the region during the period of 327–328.[111] This later dating has, in turn, led some scholars, again wedded to the idea that Eutropia could not have had friendly relations with the emperor after 326, to

---

[108] Eusebius, Vita Constantini 3.51–52; Hunt (1982) 15–16.
[109] The fifth-century church historian Sozomen, Hist. eccl. 2.4 does indeed identify her as Constantine's mother-in-law, although he also does not give her name.
[110] For example, Rubin (1982) 87–91. On the family crisis of 326, see Chapter 7.
[111] Eusebius, Vita Constantini 3.62.1, which sees Acacius in Antioch in 327 or 328; see Barnes (1981) 143 and PLRE I Acacius 4, 6.

argue that the unnamed woman must instead have been the mother of a new, third wife of Constantine.[112]

There is, however, no need to believe that Eutropia was in disgrace (or even to invent a third marriage of Constantine). On the contrary, it was entirely in keeping with Constantine's track record in dealing with imperial women after a family crisis for him to demonstrate that Eutropia was still working in his interest and for the greater imperial good. Her anonymity in his letter does not speak against this, as for reasons of modesty, it was good practice in ancient letter writing to leave female family members unnamed.[113] Even after 326, Eutropia remained the grandmother of Constantine's sons and also of his half-brothers, who became more visible after the deaths of Licinius, Crispus, and Fausta. Rather than highlighting disgrace, Constantine's strategy was always to stress dynastic harmony and to suppress knowledge of palace affairs. Since Eutropia's outing to Mamre must date from after 326, the chances are that it coincided with Helena's presence in the East and that the two empresses' trips to Palestine were somehow connected.[114] It seems inconceivable that Constantine allowed the maternal grandmother of his sons to roam independently around the same province that their paternal grandmother had just honored or was about to honor with an official visit. As the widow of a defeated emperor (and someone who had already once before admitted to adultery), Eutropia was reliant on Constantine's favor and resources, so he was well able to control her movements, just like Maximinus Daza had done with Valeria.[115]

Eusebius' silence about all this stemmed from several motives. He may have stuck to the facts, because even if the empresses traveled together, this does not have to mean that Helena was also present at the site of Mamre. Her group may well have broken up into different parties to spread imperial presence more widely, or Eutropia may have stayed on in Palestine after Helena departed.[116] As we have seen, Helena herself went north from Jerusalem to visit Galilee, which some its inhabitants took as an opportunity to express their loyalty to the Christian emperor. Eusebius was also keen to separate this fourth church foundation at Mamre from the others, because it challenged his triad-scheme and betrayed the truth: how Constantine's foundations

---

[112] See Destephen (2018) 41–43; for doubts, Barnes (2014) 150.
[113] See Hillner, MacCarron, Vihervalli (2022).
[114] Drijvers (1992a) 71.
[115] On Valeria, see Chapter 4. On Eutropia and adultery, Chapter 3.
[116] Hebron was among the destinations of day excursions from Jerusalem for Egeria: McGowan, Bradshaw (2018) 18.

in the Holy Land were, in fact, a lot more haphazard (even where Mamre memorialized yet another theophany).[117] Eusebius was equally anxious to separate the anonymous reference to Eutropia from his reports of Helena and her grandsons. This was because in the *Life of Constantine* he tried, as has long been recognized, to avoid not only the subject of Fausta, but even more importantly any mention of Constantine's stepfamily, who were Eutropia's grandchildren and great-grand-children.[118] It is notable that, in the accompanying gloss to Constantine's letter about Mamre, Eusebius does not draw any further attention to the anonymous imperial woman mentioned by the emperor himself.

Nonetheless, Constantine's letter gives good insight into how an imperial church foundation proceeded when the emperor was not present. The meaning of the site was discovered during a visit by an imperial woman. Again, it is unlikely that Eutropia was led here simply by her diligent reading of Scripture, so she must have had a local guide. This was apparently not one of the bishops to whom Constantine wrote, for they are sternly rebuked for their neglect of the site and outshone by his relative's piety (*eusébeia*).[119] However, Eutropia could do little more than alert the emperor to the situation. After that, the site had to be desecrated, imperial officials had to get involved, bishops informed, imperial funds mobilized, and architects appointed. Eutropia did not have the authority to do any of this. Helena may have had some such power, but we can still imagine her engaging in a similar correspondence with her son, especially when it came to the consecration, and in some cases surely also confiscation, of terrain.[120]

As in the case of Rome, it would therefore be wrong to hail Helena, or indeed Eutropia, as independent church founders. All four of the new Palestinian churches were imperial, whoever had initiated their construction. There is no evidence that Helena had any input into the design of the Church of the Nativity or that of the Eleona, and in any case, they were decorated and completed after she had died. However, unlike in Rome, we do gain some understanding of an empress's agency in religious matters however blurred this is by Eusebius' changing rhetorical strategies. Above all, Helena

---

[117] The three angels at Mamre were also often used to reference the Trinity: Maraval (2002) 67.
[118] On Eusebius' avoidance of these tricky subjects due to the dynastic developments in the late 320s and 30s, see Cameron, Hall (1999) 200–201, 273, 300–301.
[119] Eusebius, Vita Constantini 3.51–52.
[120] The necessity for an empress to ask for permission to deconsecrate ground is acknowledged by Paulinus of Nola, Ep. 31.4 ("[Helena] asked [Constantine] to give her the authority... to clear all the sites there" *eum rogabat, ut sibi facultatem daret cuncta illic loca... purgare*).

and her entourage were on the ground in Palestine, while Constantine was far away. Even if they were steered by local traditions, they were in control of bringing such sites to the emperor's attention. It is therefore doubtful whether the Constantinian churches in Bethlehem, on the Mount of Olives and at Mamre, would have been built without the empresses' intervention.

During their travels, both empresses doubtlessly experienced their Christian faith in new, spatial, and tactile ways, and learned how these related to the sacred traditions and their own salvation. It seems that they understood Christianity above all in opposition to traditional Greco-Roman cults, even in Palestine. They found pagan, rather than Jewish, marks on the holy sites repellent, or focused on these because they knew the emperor would find them repellent. This is not surprising given their very recent conversions and Constantine's own, well-documented concerns about pagan trappings around holy places.[121] This is evident from Eutropia's actions at Mamre, but perhaps also applied to Helena's churches in Bethlehem and on the Mount of Olives. The cave at Bethlehem was inaccessible due to its location in a sacred wood dedicated to Adonis. The Eleona was erected in the midst of a pagan cemetery, which the church building terminated.[122]

Conversely, it is unclear whether the empresses had any special interest in female elements of Christian devotion, and specifically the Virgin Mary, much patronized by later empresses. Eusebius evoked a parallel between Helena and Mary in the *Life of Constantine* when he called Constantine Helena's "only begotten son" (*monogenḗs*). He also said that Helena "embellished the pregnancy of the God-bearer" with her Church of the Nativity, using the term *theotókos*. The bishop of Caesarea may have been picking up here on the imperial representation of Helena as an almost divine ancestress of the Constantinian house and on the gossip around her humble origins, both of which he could exploit for his own agenda. His focus was, however, decidedly on Constantine, artfully eliding, as Constantine himself had often done, the distinction between the emperor and Christ. There is little sign that Eusebius sought to build up the Virgin Mary as a model of virtue or a special intercessor for the Roman empress. This was in keeping with contemporary theological attitudes, for opinion on Mary's own sanctity

---

[121] On Constantine's relative disinterest in the Jewish history of Palestine, see Hunt (1997) 422–23. For Eusebius' efforts to nonetheless inject anti-Jewish sentiments into the emperor's actions, Sivan (2008) 192–94.
[122] On the history of the two caves: Maraval (2002) 64–65. On the tombs discovered in the area of the Eleona, see Sebag, Nagar (2007) 427–46. Jerome, Ep. 58.3 mentions the sacred wood in Bethlehem.

was still divided in the early fourth century. Whether Helena herself had Mary on her mind when visiting Bethlehem is therefore unknown.[123]

This is not to say that Helena's interventions at the Nativity cave did not give popular and imperial female devotion to the Virgin a significant boost in the long run. Her imperial visit and the resulting arrival of imperial patronage in any case transformed the sacred landscape of Palestine generally and elevated its sites to a far grander, super-regional status. Of course, some early Christian travelers had previously visited Palestine in search of the physical locations of scriptural places. The idea of mapping a Christian "holy land" onto Jewish and Roman geographical realities had also emerged before Helena set foot in Palestine, not least through Eusebius' writing.[124] The emperor's recognition of these ideas and approaches, through visible and monumental support of his female relatives' activities, accelerated their development, however. Concrete changes in behavior within local communities may also have resulted from the personal appearance of imperial women in the region. This is suggested by Constantine's award of city status to Gaza's port of Maiuma for its inhabitants' mass conversion to Christianity. The new city was renamed Constantia, as Eusebius tells us, after Constantine's "pious" sister. This may be a sign that Constantia had some particular role in the events that had occurred here, perhaps because she had visited this harbor town when accompanying Helena.[125]

The Bordeaux Pilgrim, arriving in Palestine only five years after Helena, already had an unchallenged understanding of the "holy land" as the geographical center of the Christian world. A whole flood of Christian pilgrims followed in the coming decades, and many more late antique Christians traveled to the "holy land" in their imaginations. With imperial patronage came an economic uplift, too. Pilgrimage brought investment to Palestine, and Jerusalem's population quickly outgrew the confines of the old Aelia Capitolina.[126] Even though Helena was not the first Christian pilgrim,

---

[123] Eusebius, Vita Constantini 3.46; Vita Constantini 3.43: τῆς θεοτόκου τὴν κύησιν... κατεκόσμει, see also van Dam (2007) 304–5; Angelova (2015) 212. On devotion to and understanding of Mary in pre-Constantinian and Constantinian times, Limberis (1994) 101–7; Limor (2014).

[124] On visits of earlier Christians to biblical sites, many of which are mentioned by Eusebius: Maraval (2002) 65–66; Smith (2007) 7–8.

[125] Eusebius, Vita Constantini 4.37; Socrates, Hist. eccl. 1.18. See also van Dam (2007) 114 n. 38 who believes Constantia also "retired" to Maiuma.

[126] On Helena's visit as a watershed event, Stephens Falcasantos (2017) 98, 113. On the population of Jerusalem in the fourth century, Weksler-Bdolah (2019) 131. The city expanded particularly toward the south.

she and her companions can therefore safely be called the originators of Christian pilgrimage.

Gradually, this image became hugely influential, not least for imperial women who came after her. By the fifth century, Helena set the standard for correct female imperial behavior. By the Byzantine period, Helena was believed to have founded more than thirty churches in the "holy land."[127] Still, it is notable, especially in our early pilgrim testimonies, that she was not immediately remembered as the most important driver of the Constantinian building program in Palestine, just as she also had not been in Rome. In each case, it was Constantine himself who got the credit. The commemoration of Helena as a devout pilgrim, church founder, and relic hunter took time to take shape. We should not, therefore, overestimate the impact that Eusebius' account of Helena's efforts on its own made. Even more strikingly, authors writing outside Palestine at first hardly remembered her at all. This shows that a traveling empress was not as unusual a sight in the early fourth century as we might think. And when Helena was remembered, it was not in a positive way, not even by Christian authors. Athanasius' description made her the first imperial woman clashing with a bishop over a question of theology. As such, Helena foreshadows not only the righteousness of later empresses, but also their antithetical image as the sidekick of heretics and threats to episcopal authority. It is to these conflicting legacies and how they shaped the lives of the next generation of Constantinian women that we now turn.

---

[127] Nikephoros, Hist. eccl. 8.30.

PART IV
CURTAIN AND ENCORES
(C. 329–C. 600)

9
Burying an Empress

Helena spent the spring of 328 in Palestine. According to Eusebius, she attended the consecration ceremonies of the new churches in Bethlehem and on the Mount of Olives. Since Christian consecration ritual involved the very first celebration of the Eucharist, the building process had been speedy, and confirms that the "discovery" of the caves and the two churches had already been envisaged locally before Helena's arrival. Here, we might usefully compare the visit of the later emperor Theodosius II's wife Eudocia to Jerusalem in 438, during which we can note a similarly swift church founding procedure. Eudocia founded a church outside Jerusalem's Damascan Gate dedicated to St. Stephen, whose relics had been discovered in 415. Although she had only arrived in the spring, Eudocia attended the church's consecration already in May. Due to her activities in Palestine, Helena's return from her travels cannot have occurred before the summer of 328. This would make the length of her trip again comparable to that undertaken by Eudocia, whose travel to the Holy Land took place between early 438 and, after a stay in Antioch, early 439.[1]

Eusebius tells us that shortly after returning from her travels, Helena passed away peacefully, at around 80 years of age. Constantine ceased minting coins with Helena's portrait from early 329, which means that her death occurred between the summer of 328 and the following spring. Eusebius does not mention a cause of death, but, given her age, she may have been simply exhausted after so many journeys over such a long period. He does note that Helena died in the presence of Constantine, who "looked after her and held her hands." For the Roman elite, being surrounded by family members was the ideal way to end one's life, as it allowed the dying to settle their affairs with the living. Helena therefore died a Roman matrona's death.

---

[1] Eusebius, Vita Constantini 3.43: Helena "consecrated" the two churches (ἀφιέρου), a term Eusebius uses also for the consecration ceremony of the Holy Sepulchre in 336 (4.40–41). On early Christian church consecration ceremonials, see Birkedaal Bruun, Hamilton (2016). On Eudocia's presence at the dedication of St. Stephen: John Rufus, Life of Peter the Iberian 49. The length of her trip: Holum (1982) 184–89.

It is less clear whether Helena also died the death of a Christian, after being baptized, though this is perhaps implied by Eusebius' declaration that upon death Helena's soul "was transformed into the permanent essence of an angel." It is nevertheless notable how vague Eusebius remains on this point, especially as he insists on Constantine's deathbed baptism in the same work. It is, of course, possible—if unusual—that Helena had already been baptized at some point during her life and that Eusebius simply did not mention it. But Helena may also not have been baptized at all, perhaps because she died so quickly that no rituals could be arranged in time.[2]

In the summer of 328 Constantine was, once again, on route to the West. At first, he spent a few months strengthening the Danubian frontier against Gothic aggression, while residing at Serdica in Western Thrace. By late September, he was in Trier. He then passed the autumn and winter quelling an invasion of the Alemanni on the Upper Rhine.[3] On this evidence, it is most probable that Helena had caught up with Constantine in Serdica (today's Sofia). It is possible that she had done so by sailing first along the coast of Asia Minor to Thessalonica, the nearest Mediterranean port to Serdica. Helena's honorary statues in Side, on the southern coast of Asia Minor, suggest that at some point she visited this town. The most plausible time for this would have been during her return from Palestine, on which she may have embarked with her entourage from Gaza's port of Maiuma, either on this occasion or subsequently renamed as Constantia. The Etesian winds that would have hindered her outward voyage by boat in the summer of 326 made the return journey from Palestine toward the Aegean via Cyprus a very popular excursion during the summer season (Map 6). A coastal route would also have allowed Helena to visit Seleucia, as Egeria did later in the fourth century to pray at the famous shrine of Thecla, the follower of the Apostle Paul.[4]

Having reconnected with Constantine, it is unclear whether Helena traveled on with him to Trier and died there, passed away en route, or died in the

---

[2] On the date of Helena's death, Drijvers (1992a) 73; Pohlsander (1995) 146–47. On the coins: Bruun (1966) 72–73. Eusebius, Vita Constantini 3.46: θεραπεύοντός τε καὶ τῶν χειρῶν ἐφαπτομένου... ἐπὶ τὴν ἄφθαρτον καὶ ἀγγελικὴν οὐσίαν. Helena's death, at 80 years old, is also mentioned by Socrates, Hist. eccl. 1.17; Sozomen, Hist. eccl. 2.4; Theodoret, Hist. eccl. 1.17. On dying in the presence of family: Noy (2011). Heinen (1995) 106–7 on the possibility that Helena did not die a baptized Christian. Constantine's baptism: Vita Constantini 4.62. Deathbed baptism as a common form of baptism at the time: Nathan (2000) 135.

[3] Barnes (1982) 77. On Constantine's perhaps preemptive campaign against the Alemanni, Drinkwater (2007) 198–99.

[4] On Side and navigational routes, see p. 215; on the Etesian winds when sailing from the East, also Leyerle (2009) 118. It is notable that Cyprus has a strong legendary connection to Helena; see Pohlsander (1995) 99–100. Egeria in Seleucia: Itinerarium 23.1–5.

imperial palace of Serdica, which sprawled out into the southeastern area of the "old city" that had been walled in the late second century. If the latter is true, she breathed her last in the region where she had passed the formative years of her early motherhood and in one of Constantine's favorite cities.[5]

This reconstruction of events based on chronological and geographical data could explain why Constantine did not attend Helena's funeral, as he was called to urgent military matters on the German frontier. Even so, if she died before he reached Gaul, he traveled with her coffin for at least some of his progress West, before sending it on for burial to the old capital of Rome, which housed the only imperial mausoleum Constantine had thus far built.[6] Helena's final resting place was, then, partly a pragmatic choice. Perhaps it had also been Helena's wish to be buried in the city where she had resided at length. But it is also entirely possible that in the late 320s Constantine still intended to be buried in Rome himself and considered the mausoleum he had erected there as the "imperial tombs," to use Eusebius' phrase. In 328–329, he had not begun to build the Apostoleion in Constantinople in which he would eventually be buried, and even on Constantine's death, the inhabitants of Rome were still fully convinced they would receive his dead body. In any event, this did not happen, which may have generated more disappointment among Rome's citizens in their emperor than any of his previous absences or potentially neglected sacrifices.[7]

In any case, Constantine's entrusting of his mother's body to the old capital shows that Constantine still valued Rome highly at this point and was keen on enshrining an eternal imperial presence in its midst. Conversely, it also shows how highly he valued his mother, as ancestress of his dynasty, the way in which she had been presented to the inhabitants of Rome in particular. The honors Constantine afforded to the dead Helena were numerous,

---

[5] On the imperial palace in Serdica that may have extended over an area of approximately 30,000 square meters, see De Sena (2014). Constantinople, Nicomedia, Rome, and Palestine have also been proposed as Helena's place of death; see Pohlsander (1995) 147–48. These cannot be easily or at all aligned with Helena's death in the presence of Constantine in 328–329.

[6] Eusebius, Vita Constantini 3.47: "to the imperial city" (βασιλεύουσαν πόλιν) by which he here, as elsewhere, must mean Rome (3.7; 4.69). Socrates, Hist. eccl. 1.17 erroneously misunderstood the term as referring to Constantinople, leading to further faulty Byzantine traditions; see Pohlsander (1995) 153–56.

[7] Eusebius, Vita Constantini 3.47: ἡρίοις βασιλικοῖς; 4.69 on Roman expectations around Constantine's burial; also Aurelius Victor, Caes. 41.18 who may have witnessed Roman reaction, Diefenbach (2007) 151. The earliest record of the Apostoleion is in Eusebius' Vita Constantini 4.58–60 in connection with Constantine's death. It may not have been begun before 330, and perhaps as late as 334; see Johnson (2009) 120. On the mausoleum in Rome see Chapter 6 and the discussion that follows.

glorious, and in part unprecedented. It is therefore all the more astonishing that soon after her death, Constantine abandoned the matriarchal family tree he had been shaping, replacing it with a new dynastic context in which Helena's position was, once again, uncertain.

Final Honors

Eusebius indicates that Helena received a funeral with full imperial honors. Although Eusebius referred to dead bodies elsewhere in the *Life of Constantine*, he reserved the same term, *skênos*, exclusively for Helena and Constantine's corpses. He thereby linked Helena's funeral to the emperor's at the Apostoleion in Constantinople about a decade later, which he described in detail. Constantine gave Helena's body a "very large military guard of honour" for its progress to Rome.[8] If Constantine's own funeral can be taken as a guide, upon arrival, her body would have then lain in state for some days, wrapped in linen studded with herbs and spices, probably at the Sessorian Palace.[9] Markets and places of entertainment would have closed. A contingent of soldiers, followed by a procession of mourning senators and common people solemnly holding candles and incense, would have then carried her bier through the Porta Labicana and along the 4 kilometers to the mausoleum Constantine had built next to the basilica "at the two laurel trees" (Map 4; n. 8, 9; Fig. 9.1). The bier would have been covered with golden and purple fabrics and possibly also a painted or wax image of the deceased Helena.[10]

Upon arrival at the mausoleum, a funeral oration would have been given. Some decades later, in 386, Gregory, the bishop of Nyssa, delivered the funeral oration for the empress Flaccilla, wife of Theodosius I, in which he praised her piety, humility, philanthropy, and modesty. We have no indication of whether Helena was eulogized in comparable fashion during her funeral or, if so, by whom. There are, however, echoes of similar female virtues in Eusebius' résumé of her life at the end of his Helena excursus, alongside an enumeration of Constantine's honors for her, which may well originate from the text of an oration that circulated after her death. At Constantine's funeral,

---

[8] Eusebius, Vita Constantini 3.47 and 4.60; bodyguard, 3.47: πλείστη γοῦν δορυφορίᾳ τιμώμενον...ἀνεκομίζετο.
[9] Angelova (2015) 138 speculates that, with Helena's body, Constantine also sent a relic of the cross to be deposited here.
[10] On the ceremony and trappings of imperial funerals in late antiquity, Johnson (2009) 8–16.

Fig. 9.1 Remains of the Mausoleum of Helena, Via Labicana, Rome. © Julia Hillner.

the traditional rites were followed by a Christian ceremony, with prayers and the Eucharist celebrated by "priests." Eusebius' silence about any similar occurrence at Helena's funeral in Rome is again notable, and another indication that Helena may not have died a baptized Christian. On the other hand, her mausoleum was intimately attached to a Christian space. One might argue that she would have not been buried there unbaptized, although given imperial control over this site, it is unlikely that anyone would have dared to object.[11]

Whatever the character of her funeral ceremonies, Helena's body was then transported into the mausoleum. Helena's last resting place was decidedly beautiful, luminous, and full of color. The interior of the mausoleum,

---

[11] Eusebius, Vita Constantini 4.65–73, on Constantine's funeral. On embalming techniques Effros (2002) 72–74. Flaccilla's funerary oration: see Chapter 11. Helena's list of honors (Augusta title, gold coins): Vita Constantini 3.47. Heinen (1995) 106–8 on whether Helena received a Christian burial.

a 26-meter-high and 20-meter-wide circular space covered by a dome, was flooded with light from seven large windows in the upper elevation. They illuminated its sparkling cipollino marble floor; its walls decorated with a geometrical scheme of green, red, and yellow marbles from Greece, North Africa, and Egypt; and the seven niches studded with gold, blue, and green mosaics that ran around its perimeter below the windows. The mosaics may have displayed biblical motifs.[12]

Unlike Maximinus Daza's mother back at Šarkamen in Dacia Ripensis, Helena was not cremated. It was a practice considered un-Christian, and one that had also long fallen out of use in Rome itself, although more slowly for emperors.[13] Instead, her body was placed in a stone sarcophagus that stood in the mausoleum's largest rectangular niche, opposite the entrance. That Helena received this form of burial is first attested by the sixth-century Book of Pontiffs, which records a list of gifts that Constantine made to furnish the mausoleum. They included a "pure silver altar, weighing 200 pounds, in front of the tomb (*sepulchrum*) of the blessed Helena Augusta, which is sculpted from precious stone with little figures of porphyry."[14] This description fits the massive sarcophagus of Egyptian porphyry that was retrieved from the mausoleum in the twelfth century for Pope Anastasius IV's burial at the Lateran (d. 1154) (Fig. 9.2). It was heavily repaired in the eighteenth century, when the two busts on either side of its front were restored as female portraits, presumably to represent Helena, although they may also signify divinities.[15] However, it is clear that the coffin had entertained a military theme from the beginning, since it is dominated by depictions of rows of mounted Roman soldiers riding dynamically over fallen barbarians or leading them into captivity. For this reason, it is often assumed that the sarcophagus had not originally been intended for Helena, or was not hers at all.

---

[12] See Chapter 6 on the architecture of the ecclesiastical complex at the Via Labicana. On the interior of the mausoleum: Vendittelli (2011b) 41–48; Paparatti (2011) 92–99, with a reconstruction of the color scheme and catalog of fragments of decoration (made of serpentine, *giallo antico, pavonazzetto, rosso antico, verde antico*, porphyry).

[13] Johnson (2009) 15. For pagan emperors' apotheosis ritual, which demanded cremation, an effigy was burned. Price (1987) 101 maintains that Constantine was the first emperor not cremated.

[14] LP I 182: *altarem ex argento purissimo, pens. lib. CC, ante sepulchrum beatae Helenae Augustae, qui sepulchrum est ex metallo purphyriticus exculptus sigillis*. The Latin is rather garbled. A possible correction based on manuscript variants (see LP I 182) is *ex metallo purphyritico/purpureo exculptis sigillis*. A "porphyry sarcophagus" is also mentioned by Bede, *Chron.* 420, and by a Greek *vita* of Constantine and Helena, possibly in its earliest form dating to the fifth century [Winkelmann (1987) 635]. For further references on the mausoleum in medieval sources, see Pohlsander (1995) 151 and Chapter 11.

[15] Wegner (1984) 146.

Fig. 9.2 Porphyry sarcophagus from the Mausoleum of Helena; now at the Vatican Museums, Sala a Croce Greca. © Governatorato SCV—Direzione dei Musei Vaticani. All rights reserved.

It is true that there is no proof Helena had been buried in this coffin. When it was recovered and reused, her bones had already been long gone from the mausoleum and no epitaph survived. Since the mausoleum had been planned as a collective burial place, it is also unclear whether Helena was really the only member of the imperial family laid to rest here, even if Constantine himself was eventually buried in Constantinople. As has been mentioned before, sole occupancy of mausolea was rare for imperial women. The porphyry sarcophagus may therefore have belonged to someone else entirely. It has also been suggested that the sarcophagus had been intended for Constantine originally and then recycled for his mother when he abandoned his plans of burial in Rome. Constantine is even believed to have appropriated the sarcophagus from Maxentius' mausoleum on the Via Appia, as an ultimate humiliation of the usurper.[16] It is however uncertain whether the

---

[16] Maxentius: Johnson (2009) 118. Coarelli (2016) 499 suggests the original occupant was intended to be Maximian. Krautheimer (1959) 202 doubts Helena was buried in the sarcophagus. For the fate of Helena's body, see Pohlsander (1995) 157–66.

usurper Maxentius would have had the opportunity to import porphyry from the imperial quarries at Mons Porphyrites in Eastern Egypt, its only source, unless he recycled materials already in Rome.

Such quests for a male occupant of this porphyry sarcophagus rely on the assumptions that, as a woman, Helena could not have been buried in a coffin with martial imagery or, if she was, that such a coffin could not have been originally intended for her. These assumptions are questionable for several reasons. To begin with, Helena had been publicly associated with masculine and martial values also during her lifetime, especially *securitas*, precisely because it helped Constantine legitimize his origins and his rule. From this perspective, the symbolism on her sarcophagus is not as incongruous as often thought, and certainly no more so than Helena having the same aquiline nose as her former partner Constantius on her coinage. Constantine needed his mother to be as imperial as possible. We also need to remember that sarcophagus decoration was not necessarily personal or biographical, and all the more so because Roman sarcophagi could be used for the burial of multiple bodies, including a mix of male and female, whose individual relationship with the meaning of the outside carvings often remains elusive to the modern observer.[17] As we have seen, there is a strong possibility that at the time of Helena's funeral Constantine anticipated that he would eventually be buried in Rome, too. This may well have extended to the anticipation that his body would be joining his mother's in this very coffin. The solidness of porphyry made its carving a highly skilled, costly, and very difficult technique, which explains why so few carved porphyry sarcophagi exist. Indeed, Helena's is the most accomplished of those surviving. It seems odd, therefore, that Constantine would not have shipped this one to Constantinople if he had already made the plan by the late 320s to be laid to rest there. The only emperor who had departed from co-burial with family members had been Galerius who had even built two separate mausolea for himself and his mother Romula. Although Constantine followed Galerius in honoring his mother in an exceptional way, it is less certain he would have gone so far. When Helena died, Constantine therefore may have still been assuming that the sarcophagus would ultimately be his own.[18]

---

[17] Borg (2013) 203–6. I would like to thank Barbara Borg for discussion of this evidence.

[18] On Helena being associated with *securitas* and having the same nose as Constantius: Chapter 5. It is of note that all known decorated sarcophagi made of imperial porphyry are attributed to women [Helena, Constantina: see Chapter 10, Pulcheria: Johnson (2009) 16]. As it is unlikely that female imperial bodies were valued more highly than male, all these sarcophagi had not been intended for single use. In fact, sarcophagi at the Apostoleion are recorded to have contained both male and female

The silver altar Constantine donated to stand in front of Helena's tomb was not his only gift. Four silver candelabra with golden edgings, twenty silver chandeliers, and one enormous gold one decorated with oil lamps in the shape of dolphins were also among his donations. They would illuminate the mausoleum's interior even further when mourners came to pay their respects.[19] The presence of the altar shows that cult activities were supposed to take place at the grave of the emperor's mother that were separate from those in the basilica, which had received an altar of its own. Given that the cost of the mausoleum's furnishing outweighed those of the funerary basilica, Constantine considered it the more important part of the complex. Since the basilica was as yet not focused on a defined martyr cult, visitors perhaps perceived it in the same way. Constantine also gave liturgical vessels—jewel-encrusted chalices, a paten (low bowl), and pitchers—which indicate that the Eucharist was celebrated at the mausoleum's altar. Altars, however, also played a role in traditional funerary cults, for offerings of food on the anniversary of death or on feast days dedicated to the commemoration of ancestors. Such festivities were also conducted in the adjacent funerary basilica by relatives of the less exalted dead, and increasingly in Christianized forms.

The whole complex on the Via Labicana, accessible to a wide demographic, was therefore geared toward a unique combination of funerary and imperial cult, with the mausoleum enshrining the imperial remains towering over it as its focal point (Fig. 9.3). Statues or busts of the empress may have been erected here.[20] Helena was not deified as previous empresses had been (and Constantine still would be). But the architecture ensured a large number of people filed past her tomb on a continuous basis. Those coming to visit the graves of their loved ones in hope of their salvation would inevitably pray

---

members of the imperial family, see Downey (1959) 30–31; also for the later belief that Constantine and Helena shared a sarcophagus in Constantinople. See also Johnson (2009) 172 for a sarcophagus with two bodies in the Theodosian mausoleum at the Vatican. For the sarcophagus from the Via Labicana as originally intended for Constantine, see, for example, Drijvers (1992a) 75 with an earlier bibliography; Holloway (2004) 88, Diefenbach (2007) 179; Potter (2013) 261; they all argue that Constantine passed it on to his mother for single use.

[19] LP I 182. Upon his death, Constantine also lay in state surrounded by golden candelabra: Eusebius, Vita Constantini 4.66.

[20] Three portraits sometimes attributed to Helena derive from the vicinity of the mausoleum (Museo Torlonia inv. 614 and 615; Pontificia Commissione di Archeologia Sacra inv. 82), although the attributions are very insecure: Giuliani (2016).

Fig. 9.3 Reconstructed lateral view of the complex of basilica and mausoleum "at the two laurel trees" on the Via Labicana. Drawn by Robert Heffron.

for Helena, too.[21] These architectural and liturgical innovations in imperial burial were truly trendsetting. Helena was the first member of an imperial dynasty laid to rest in a mausoleum attached to a church, a practice that would become standard for almost all emperors and their male and female relatives thereafter.[22]

To ensure that the lights at his mother's tomb—and as Constantine may have still thought, his own—would eternally burn, and the buildings retained their sacred aura, Constantine also ordered an annual supply of lamp oil, balsam, and spices for incense, and endowed the building with landed estates. Again, he spared no expense. The lamp oil was to be kept fragrant with spikenard, an expensive perfume imported from Eastern Asia, which also had biblical connotations. The estates, all listed in the sixth-century Book of Pontiffs, were both far-flung, on the island of Sardinia, at Misenum, in Tuscany, and in the Sabina, and close by, in the form of the Fundus Lauretum around the complex itself. The latter was at some point designated as the "possession" of Helena. If genuine, the passage indicates that this estate had been among Helena's resources during her lifetime.[23] It is harder to say whether Helena had owned it outright or had been merely sustained by its revenue and whether the donation consisted in the land itself or again just its annual profits, or when exactly it was consigned to the ecclesiastical complex on the Via Labicana.[24]

---

[21] See Diefenbach (2007) 165–81 about the hierarchy between the basilica and the mausoleum and 208–12 about the meaning of the altar. On Constantine's deification, Cameron, Hall (1999) 348–49. CIL 13.1023, which implies deification of Helena, is probably inauthentic.

[22] Johnson (2009) 111. It is unclear whether the Apostoleion followed the same model of mausoleum-cum-church; see Mango (1990).

[23] For the possibility that it was a later interpolation to the text, see p. 162.

[24] LP I 183. On spikenard Browning (2009), s.v. "spikenard." Oil and estates are listed for the basilica, but must refer to the entire complex as otherwise the mausoleum would have been left without

Eusebius tells us that Helena had composed her will before she died but does not mention any legacies to churches. Instead, he says, she left everything she had "accrued" (hypêrxe) "in the whole world" to her son and her grandsons, the Caesars, in equal parts.[25] Once again, Eusebius was keen to insist that legitimacy flowed through this dynasty right down to the grandsons, just like piety and property. He may therefore have left out other details of Helena's will. She is likely, for example, to have left her jewelry to her granddaughters, Constantina and Helena the Younger, as was customary in elite Roman families. Much later, the panegyrist Claudian intimated that jewels were passed on in the imperial family through the female line.[26] In 360, when Helena the Younger's husband Julian was proclaimed Augustus by his troops in Paris, the soldiers suggested he should be crowned with a necklace or headband from Helena the Younger's jewelry box. Although Julian refused, for the soldiers Helena the Younger's jewels clearly had an official, even sacred association, probably because they had come down to her through the imperial line, and even from her grandmother who had so frequently appeared bejeweled on imperial coinage.[27]

Still, Eusebius is vague about Helena's actual ownership of property, using the ambiguous verb "hypêrxe," and he does not mention bequests to churches. No less ambiguous is the term *possessio* the Book of Pontiffs uses to describe Helena's relationship to the estate around the Via Labicana, which, if taken in its technical sense, did not refer to full ownership, but to the holding or use of goods.[28] All of this reflects the fact that Helena had no inherited patrimony of her own, but that all her possessions had been allocated to her from the *res privatae*, that is, in effect from Constantine, and now reverted to him, or to the causes he specified. Like a dutiful son, he specified the cause to be commemoration of his mother, "placing votive gifts" at Helena's mausoleum "out of love of his mother and in veneration of the martyrs," as the

---

maintenance and in the dark; see Diefenbach (2007) 174. All estates from Helena's budget: Davis (2010) xxxiv; for properties in Sardinia rather than the whole of Sardinia, see LP I 199.

[25] Eusebius, Vita Constantini, 3.46: καθ'ὅλης ὑπῆρξε τῆς οἰκουμένης.
[26] On the transmission of jewelry between women Berg (2003) 51; Claudian, Epithalamium of Honorius and Maria 10.10.
[27] Ammianus Marcellinus, 20.4.17–18. Zonaras, Epit. hist. 13.10 also recounts the soldiers' idea of fashioning a diadem from a woman's necklace, but without mentioning Helena. I would like to thank Nicola Ernst, Guy Halsall, Christian Rollinger, and Michael E. Stewart for an inspiring discussion about this scene.
[28] On the legal meaning of the term *possessio*, see Heumann, Seckel (1971) 436–41. The technical term for ownership was *dominium*. On the obscure meaning of the term as used in the Book of Pontiffs, Maiuri (2007) 238–39.

Book of Pontiffs tells us.[29] Since the estates described in the Book of Pontiffs were all situated in the Western empire, some scholars believe that the endowment was made before Constantine's conquest of the East in 324 and hence many years prior to Helena's death.[30] Such an early transfer of income from the Fundus Lauretum from Helena to the basilica on the Via Labicana would however mean that the empress had been deprived of it at a time when she had been residing in Rome at the neighboring Sessorium. It seems more plausible therefore that the revenue from the Fundus Lauretum at least had been diverted from her maintenance onto that of the cult complex only after she had died or had left Rome. It is also possible that only the rents from the estates (amounting to a staggering 3,754 solidi per annum) were then ceded on an annual basis, much like the annual supply of lamp oil that would have certainly been organied by the Count of the Sacred Largesse. The endowment lists in the Book of Pontiffs are notoriously hard to interpret, but if this is true, the estate at the Via Labicana, and the cult complex situated upon it, remained in imperial ownership for the time being. The later designation of the area as *sub-augusta* does indeed suggest a continued link with the imperial family, as does the report that the emperor Valentinian III was murdered here in 455. Keeping it in imperial ownership would have assured that the buildings were used as Constantine had intended, for the memory of his imperial dynasty.[31]

Constantine also arranged splendid and expensive forms of commemoration for Helena outside of Rome. In Palestine, he embellished the two churches whose foundation Helena had facilitated. Here, Constantine donated silver and golden vessels and precious tapestries, to "eternalise the memory of his mother."[32] In Constantinople, public spaces were filled with images of Helena. The *Parastaseis*, an eighth-century catalog of the monuments of Constantinople, lists nine representations of Helena in sculpture, painting, or mosaic form, while the tenth-century *Patria of Constantinople*, a body of similar texts, adds another two. Admittedly, most of these artworks do not date back to Constantinian times, but were erected or commissioned later, to

---

[29] LP I 183: *in quo loco et pro amorem matris suae et ueneratione sanctorum posuit dona uoti sui.* Compare to Constantius who also embellished his father's tomb to repay a debt: Julian, Or. 1.16C.

[30] See, for example, Drijvers (1992a) 31; Brandenburg (2004) 58.

[31] On continuous imperial ownership of the ground on which the Constantinian basilicas stood, Thacker (2007) 32. On the term *sub-augusta*, Deichmann, Tschira (1957) 69, who also believe that the Fundus Lauretum passed to the basilica only after Helena's death (75–76). On Valentinian: Prosper Tiro, Chron. Continuatio Codicis Reichenauensis 455.

[32] Eusebius, Vita Constantini 3.41: τῆς αὐτοῦ μητρός ... διαιωνίζων τὴν μνήμην.

honor Helena's legendary status as finder of the True Cross.[33] But a handful, some made again of costly porphyry and located at key locations along Constantinople's main ceremonial route, the Mese, may have already been erected by Constantine and his sons. One of these locations, where Helena's statue stood atop a porphyry column, was the Augusteion, a ceremonial square southwest of the Hagia Sophia in front of the imperial palace's monumental entrance that was allegedly even named after the Augusta. And at least one other statue of Helena in the city, located in the Senate House at the Forum of Constantine, was part of a dynastic group, in which she appeared alongside Constantine and his sons.[34]

To round things off, Constantine renamed a province in Helena's honor, Helenopontus, formerly the province of Diospontus on the southern shore of the Black Sea with its capital at Sinope. Here, he followed the example of Galerius, who had named the province Valeria on the Danube in honor of his wife. A governor of Helenopontus, Flavius Leontius, was mentioned in an inscription from around 335.[35] Constantine also named cities after Helena, again after the model of Galerius who had named his birthplace Romuliana after his mother, but also that of sundry other monarchs since Hellenistic times. According to the church historian Sozomen, there were two: one of which was in Palestine, the other one in Bithynia. The former may have been a town in Galilee, today's Kfar Kama, that Helena had visited, supposedly prompting the inhabitants to embrace Christianity.[36] The latter, as other reports confirm, was Helenopolis, the former village of Drepanon, which, as we have seen, was Helena's most likely birthplace. It was awarded city status and exemption from taxes. Probably on this occasion, city walls, a church,

---

[33] This is the case for Parastaseis 16, Patria 2.16, 2.102 (statue group of Constantine and Helena, with a cross between them, at the Forum of Constantine); Parastaseis 34, Patria 2.29 (statues of Constantine and Helena with a cross on an arch at the Milion); Parastaseis 52 (statues or other images of Constantine and Helena with a cross at the Forum Bovis) Parastaseis 53, Patria 2.66 (mosaic in the church of the Theotokos); Patria 2.35 (mosaic in the church of St. John Diippion, commissioned by Phokas). See also Suda s.v. Helena; for further comment, Schade (2003) 230–32; Cameron, Herrin (1984) 37 and 3–8 for these texts in general.

[34] Augusteion: Patria 2.15; also Malalas, Chron. 13.8; Chronicon Paschale 328 (Dindorf, p. 529); John the Lydian, De mensibus 4.138 (also on the naming). Others: Porphyry statue seen at Hagia Sophia: Parastaseis 11, Patria 2.96 (also lists an ivory statue for Helena and a silver mosaic image on a bronze column, but these are unlikely to be from the fourth century); statue in the Senate House at the Forum of Constantine: Parastaseis 43; statue at Philadelphion (square where the Mese bifurcated): Parastaseis 58. See Pohlsander (1995) 143–44; Gehn, Ward-Perkins (2016) 143.

[35] Justinian, Nov. 28.1 (535); PLRE I Leontius 23, 503. On the province of Valeria, see Chapter 4. On the practice of renaming cities, Lenski (2016) 131–64.

[36] Sozomen, Hist. eccl. 2.2. On Kfar Kama, see Chapter 8. Another more obscure tradition suggests that Constantine renamed a place in Spain after Helena, too; see p. 19, n. 20.

and a new road through the Drakon valley to Nicaea were also built to mark its elevation.[37]

It is possible that some of these public honors may have already been conferred on Helena during her lifetime, commensurate with Constantine's keen desire to publicly promote his dynasty from 324, and after 326, his mother in particular. The foundation rituals of Constantinople took place shortly after the emperor's defeat of Licinius, on November 8, 324, the same day that his son Constantius was proclaimed Caesar, and Helena and Fausta Augustae. The city began to be monumentalized and furnished as an imperial residence from then onward.[38] These works in Constantinople may have included a palace for Helena. In the sixth century, a neighborhood in the southwestern part of the city was known as the Helenianai, which also housed baths of that name. This may show that Constantine hoped Helena would settle in Constantinople but does not necessarily mean that Helena ever lived there. She would, in any case, not have done so for any length of time due to her tight engagement schedule between 325 and 329. This putative project would rather show that Constantine was seeking to build up his new foundation as a dynastic stage, emulating Diocletian's building of palaces for his wife Prisca and daughter Valeria in Nicomedia, in which at least Valeria cannot have resided for much time either.[39]

The renaming of cities and provinces in her honor may also have taken place during Helena's lifetime, as we know occurred, once again, in the case of Valeria. To be sure, we can discard the report by the heterodox fifth-century church historian Philostorgius that Helena had founded Helenopolis herself, as she did not have the power to confer civic rights onto communities. Her legendary status again overshadowed reality here. But Helenopolis' foundation is dated by other sources to January 7, the feast day of the martyr Lucian who was also honored by the elevation of Drepanon, in either 327 or 328, when, by our reckoning, Helena was still alive.[40] If this was so, Helena cannot

---

[37] See Chapter 1. Church: Eusebius, Vita Constantini 4.61; Socrates, Hist. eccl. 1.39; Sozomen, Hist. eccl. 2.34. City walls: Vita Luciani 20. There is no archaeological evidence for a church or walls.

[38] Records of statues for Fausta and Crispus (Parastaseis 43; Parastaseis 7; Patria 2.93) suggest that honors for members of the imperial family were commissioned in Constantinople before 326. On the foundation of Constantinople, see Barnes (2014) 111–12.

[39] Procopius, Bell. Pers. 1.24.30. Baths: Victor of Tunnuna, Chron. 498; see Angelova (2015) 141. On Diocletian's palaces for Prisca and Valeria in Nicomedia, see Chapter 4. There were many Byzantine monasteries and churches in Constantinople with a spurious tradition of having been founded by Helena, including the Apostoleion; see Pohlsander (1995) 140 for bibliographical references.

[40] Philostorgius, Hist. eccl. 2.12–13; the Vita Luciani 20, drawing on Philostorgius adds the even more dubious details that Helena resettled the inhabitants from the surrounding countryside. On January 7, 327 or 328 as foundation day: Jerome, Chron. 327; Chronicon Paschale 327 (Dindorf,

have attended any inauguration ceremonies, as she was traveling elsewhere on both occasions. Still, the inconsistency in their dating undermines the reliability of these claims, especially as Sozomen clearly implies the naming of cities occurred after Helena's death, to strengthen her memory. The same must apply to Helena's porphyry column in the renamed Augusteion in Constantinople, if the record is historic. The architectural arrangement of a square around an honorary monument, like the Fora of Augustus or of Trajan in Rome, or indeed of Constantine in Constantinople, was an unprecedented (and unrepeated) honor to bestow on an empress.[41] It is doubtful that Helena was awarded such an unusual tribute during her life.

Helena's celebration, posthumous or not, laid out a circumscribed topography of remembrance: Rome, Constantinople, the Holy Land, and Bithynia-Pontus, where Nicomedia and Helenopolis were situated. It was at these key imperial locations that Constantine sought to propel his mother into his subjects' collective memory, to create an imagined map of a unified, divinely instituted empire. This was to eternalize Helena's image as the most Christian and legitimate ancestress of his dynasty. Constantine repaid his debt to Helena as his mother, as was customary, but also to her as an imperial protector, who had now departed to become, as Eusebius said, closer to God than any human could hope. But beyond his wish to project his power, the sheer variety of the forms of commemoration, their expense and, especially in the case of her ceremonial square in Constantinople, their uniqueness, suggest that Constantine was also gripped by a profound feeling of loss and grief.

Helena would not be forgotten; quite the contrary. But these attempts to instill her positive memory initially stalled. Constantine's enormous efforts to ensure her sustained presence in the minds of his subjects only fully paid off decades later. With one, unique exception, to which we will presently turn, her immediate descendants did not link themselves overtly back to Helena. She was not mentioned again in Constantinian self-representation after the late 330s. Most fourth-century authors who wrote after Eusebius—at least in the form in which their works have come down to us—either ignored Helena or dwelled on the more unsavory aspects of her life. In a Christian context, as we have seen, ambiguity around the orthodoxy and commitment to the

p. 527). Either date has also been used as a *terminus ante quem* for Helena's death; see Barnes (1981) 221–22.

[41] Angelova (2015) 141.

Nicene faith of Constantine and especially Helena's grandson Constantius II helps to explain such silence or hostility. The deaths of Crispus and Fausta also cast a long shadow over Constantine's and therefore Helena's memory.[42] Above all, Helena's mid-fourth-century image reflects the continuing fissures in the Constantinian dynasty created by Constantius I's two sexual relationships back in the third century. After Helena's death, Constantine proceeded to repair it. This move already shifted attention away from Helena. In addition, the divisions between Constantine's line and that of his half-siblings were exacerbated again by the bloody events following Constantine's death, to which we will now turn. Despite Eusebius' efforts in the *Life of Constantine* to downplay these divisions, they were written up by pagan writers eager to cheer on Theodora's grandson, the pagan Julian. It was in this context that Helena's image as an evil "stepmother" emerged and would linger on for the better part of the fourth century.

Rebranching the Tree

At some point in the early 330s Constantine decided to build stronger links to his half-siblings than he had ever done before. Something of a rapprochement since the execution of his sister Anastasia's husband in 316 had already occurred around Constantine's Vicennalia in 326, when his brothers, probably Julius Constantius and Flavius Dalmatius, had joined the emperor in Rome.[43] A few years later Julius Constantius married Basilina, daughter of Julius Julianus, Licinius' former Praetorian prefect and Constantine's consul of 325. His previous wife, the Roman aristocrat Galla, had passed away shortly after giving birth to their son Gallus, in 326, also leaving behind at least one other daughter and son.[44] Like Galla, Julius Constantius' new wife Basilina was from a grand and cultured family, with property in Bithynia and throughout Asia Minor.[45] This marriage shows how Constantine used his half-siblings to bind Eastern elites to the imperial family, just as he had used them much earlier to do the same with the senatorial aristocracy in Rome.[46] Both brothers were honored with the consulate, too, Flavius Dalmatius in

---

[42] On Constantine's image in the mid-fourth century, Lieu (1998) 140.
[43] The third, Hannibalianus, may have already been dead by this point.
[44] On the daughter, see the discussion that follows here.
[45] Vanderspoel (1999).
[46] On Constantine's half-brothers at the Vicennalia, see Chapter 7, and on the rift around 316, Chapter 5.

333 and Julius Constantius in 335, and with the respective titles of *censor* and *patricius*. Flavius Dalmatius also received a military commission based in Antioch.[47] Around the same time, Constantine began to reside more frequently in Constantinople, having only visited intermittently before. The city's consecration ceremony was solemnly conducted in the presence of the emperor on May 11, 330. The emperor's gradual shift of attention from Rome and the West generally toward his new foundation and the East has often been commented on and linked, in particular, to his alleged troubles with the traditionally minded old senatorial aristocracy and people of Rome, which came to a head during his visit in 326. It is difficult to establish what Constantinople really meant to Constantine, for there are few contemporary sources on its early history, but it is notable that we can place him more firmly in the city only after Helena's death.[48] With the departure of the old Augusta who had resided in Rome for so long, a strong familial link to the old capital had also disappeared. At the same time, his half-siblings now connected the emperor to new networks in the East and the wider Propontis region, which was, of course, also his mother's home region.

In December 333, meanwhile, Constantine elevated his own and Fausta's youngest son Constans to the rank of Caesar. All his surviving sons now held this title, creating the tripartite design for succession so extolled by Eusebius in the *Life of Constantine*. Yet, less than two years later, Constantine revised this plan—if it had ever existed—by forming a new imperial college that also included the sons of Flavius Dalmatius, who had lately distinguished himself by crushing an attempted usurpation in Cyprus, by Calocaerus, a military official. Dalmatius' eponymous elder son was now made a fourth Caesar, while the younger one, Hannibalianus the Younger, was awarded the titles *nobilissimus* (as the tetrarchic Caesars had been) and the more peculiar "king of kings and of the Pontic people," with responsibility for Armenia and allied client kingdoms.[49] Hannibalianus's appointment must be viewed in the context of Constantine's plans to campaign against Persia, whose šāh Shapur likewise laid claim to the title of king of kings (*šāhanšāh*) and influence in Armenia. He had indeed abducted Armenia's original king, Diran, whom Hannibalianus the Younger replaced.[50]

---

[47] PLRE I, Constantius 7, 226; Dalmatius 6, 240–41.
[48] On the relationship between Constantine and Constantinople, see Grig, Kelly (2012) 6–12.
[49] On Hannibalianus' titles, Origo Const. 6.35: *regem regum et Ponticarum gentium*; Ammianus Marcellinus, 14.1: "king" (*rex*); Epitome de Caesaribus 41.20: *Armeniam nationesque circumsocias*; Zosimus, Hist. nea 2.39.2: νωβελίσσιμος.
[50] Barnes (1981) 259; (2014) 165–67; Potter (2013) 289.

This burst of promotions was accompanied with a flurry of intradynastic weddings and betrothals. Again, this was not dissimilar to the days of the tetrarchy, but this time, many of the brides and grooms were already blood relatives, producing "marriages that were no marriages," as Constantine's nephew Julian would later say (see the Family Tree).[51] Constantine's second-eldest, Constantius II, married his cousin (also, through his mother Fausta, his niece), Julius Constantius' and Galla's daughter, whose name is lost to us. Their union was celebrated with many banquets in 336, Constantine's tricennalian year. As Eusebius of Caesarea was pleased to report, these were strictly gender-segregated and therefore thoroughly Christian affairs.[52] The year before, presumably on the occasion of his promotion, Hannibalianus had already married Constantius' sister Constantina, marking the first appearance of Constantine's elder daughter, who had been born around 320, in the historical record. The fifth-century church historian Philostorgius maintains that Constantine also awarded Constantina the title of Augusta and the right to wear a diadem. Constantine may have tried in this way to boost the position of Hannibalianus the Younger, who was not a Caesar, but it seems more likely that Philostorgius anachronistically imposed a status and insignia onto Constantina that were more common for fifth-century empresses.[53] At around the same time as Constantina's marriage, Constantine's eldest son Constantine II had also acquired a wife. Her identity is unknown, but it is reasonable to assume that she was another cousin-niece.[54] Constantine and Fausta's younger children, Constans and Helena, seem not yet to have reached marriageable age, but at least Constans was nonetheless included in the emperor's dynastic strategies. He was betrothed to Olympias, the daughter of Ablabius, Constantine's powerful Praetorian prefect. Perhaps Constantine was running out of girls on his siblings' side, or Olympias' mother was a Constantinian relative or the emperor was simply seeking to assure Ablabius' loyalty. Finally, Constantine's youngest child, Helena, born around 325, may have been betrothed to the Caesar Flavius

---

[51] Julian, Or. 7.228C–D.

[52] Eusebius, Vita Constantini 4.49. The wedding may have taken place in Nicomedia or Constantinople.

[53] Ammianus Marcellinus, 14.1.2; Origo Const. 6.35; Philostorgius, Hist. eccl. 3.22, 3.28. Although her name is sometimes given as Constantia or even Constantiniana, her own autograph was Constantina, which should be the preferred spelling: ILCV 1768; see also CIL 6.40790. See Busch (2015) 31 on the Augusta title.

[54] Vanderspoel (2020) 42, Tougher (2020) 195, and discussion that follows. Barnes (2014) 165 argues she was the daughter of Flavius Optatus, whom he takes to be a relative of Helena.

Dalmatius the Younger, completing a reasonably full balance of ties between the two branches of the dynasty.[55]

The intricacies of these spousal and successional tactics show that Constantine was serious about his plans to integrate his relatives into a new imperial college. To keep things tidy, in 336 he even eliminated Licinius' last remaining son, one of the few lingering dynastic threats from the past.[56] This son, whom Licinius had fathered with a concubine, had perhaps owed his survival of the upheaval in the mid-320s to his stepmother Constantia. But by 336 she had died, like Helena in the presence of Constantine, probably in Nicomedia.[57] Constantine now issued a law ordering that this "son of Licinianus" be stripped of the rank his father had conferred upon him, bound in fetters, whipped, and reduced to his "original status at birth," and that his property be confiscated. The man managed to escape. Three months later, Constantine issued another law that considerably tightened the rules around the illegitimacy of children. Almost in passing, the emperor remarked that the "son of Licinianus" had been caught and was to be condemned to forced labor at a weaving mill in Carthage. This was a doubly humiliating punishment, as weaving was considered women's work.[58] While the timing of this imprisonment could be purely accidental, this was a critical period of Constantine's reign for dynastic planning, as the emperor was advancing in age. It is notable that Constantine did not kill this son of Licinius as he had killed his legitimate one, perhaps because he was only the son of a concubine, but he still did not leave much to chance. Galerius' illegitimate son Candidianus, killed by Licinius himself, shows that emperors feared the dynastic potency of their rivals' offspring in whatever form it might come, and Constantine himself was, of course, the best example that illegitimacy was not necessarily an impediment to imperial power.

The exact motivations behind Constantine's designs for his succession remain a mystery. The emperor returned to the experiments of the tetrarchic era, perhaps for administrative and military reasons, perhaps to heal the divisions in his family and eliminate the danger of usurpation, or perhaps because he believed his own sons were too young to rule alone. Modern scholars are also prone to speculate that it had only been Helena who had

---

[55] PLRE I Flavius Ablabius 4, 3–4; Olympias 1, 642. On the dynastic marriages of 335–336, Barnes (2014) 165. Chausson (2007) 150–52 suggests that Olympias' mother was a Constantinian relative.
[56] Although one should note that Crispus' children may still have been alive, see Chapter 7.
[57] On the date and circumstances of Constantia's death, probably in the early 330s, Hillner (2017b).
[58] CTh 4.6. 2 (April 336); 4.6.3 (July 336); Evans Grubbs (1995) 284–86. For the law, see also Chapter 2.

previously impeded Constantine's half-siblings' inclusion in the regime. This is possible but lacks evidence. More significant may have been the influence, during Constantine's last years, of leading Eastern officials now connected to the emperor by kinship ties, such as Ablabius, who supported the cause of the emperor's half-brothers.[59] Whatever Constantine had aimed to achieve through Helena's commemoration, it clearly did not lead to him prioritizing his own bloodline. He also dangerously failed to establish or delayed implementing a clear scheme of seniority within the college he created. In its absence, all four Caesars, and their respective supporters, must have expected they would advance to the status of Augustus upon Constantine's death. His demise came to pass, relatively suddenly, at Pentecost in 337 (May 22). Upon falling ill in Constantinople, the emperor took a boat across the Propontis to the spa near Helenopolis, and then traveled to his mother's city and its church to prepare for baptism. Having reconnected with Helena in this way, he moved to an imperial villa outside Nicomedia, where he was baptized and died.[60] Immediately, the unresolved question of succession came to a head. The crisis that now engulfed the Constantinian dynasty had fatal consequences for the majority of its adult men, but most of the women again survived, with significant consequences for future dynastic politics.

Coming through Slaughter

A few months after Constantine's death, during the summer of 337, a series of coins began to be issued by the mints in Trier, Rome, and Constantinople, the key cities in the respective territories of each of Constantine's sons (Figs. 9.4 and 9.5).[61] They were commemorative coins showing their grandmother Helena and Theodora, the grandmother of Constantine's fourth Caesar, Dalmatius the Younger, who had been allotted Moesia, Thrace, and Greece. The captions addressed both in the dative case, presenting the coins as an offering to these women and therefore indicating that Theodora, too, was deceased. The captions also styled both women as "Augusta," even though Theodora had never received this title during her lifetime. The women

---

[59] Helena's influence, for example, Burgess (2008) 8. Ablabius: Harries (2012) 187–88.
[60] On Constantine's death, see Burgess (1999). The imperial villa where he died was later named as Acyron/Achyron.
[61] RIC VIII Treveri 42, 43, 47, 48, 55, 56, 63–65, 78, 79, 90, 91; Rome 37, 28, 53, 54; Constantinople 33–36, 38, 48–51.

Fig. 9.4 Bronze follis showing Helena with caption *Fl(aviae) Iul(iae) Helenae Aug(ustae)* on the obverse; *pax publica* on the reverse (RIC VIII Treveri 63). Courtesy of the American Numismatic Society.

Fig. 9.5 Bronze follis showing Theodora with caption *Fl(aviae) Max(imae) Theodorae Aug(ustae)* on the obverse; *pietas Romana* on the reverse (RIC VIII Treveri 65). Courtesy of the American Numismatic Society.

appeared with their full names, Flavia Iulia Helena—the first time Helena appeared as such on coinage—and Flavia Maxima Theodora, recalling the full name of her sister, Fausta. With Helena marking a line of descent from Constantius I, Theodora was distinguished as Maximian's daughter. This would be the last time her immediate descendants mentioned Helena.

What appears as a message of harmony and an optimistic embracing of the different branches that made up the Constantinian dynasty, in reality, obscured a horrendous truth. Shortly before the coins were minted, not only her grandson Flavius Dalmatius the Younger, but seven further male descendants of Theodora had been killed.

As with any violent episodes in Constantine's family, the details of what happened in the summer of 337 are murky, beginning with the identity of those present at Constantine's deathbed.[62] To the distress of Eusebius of Caesarea, so fond of death scenes with immediate kin, all of Constantine's sons were absent. The only person directly attested as in attendance was the bishop Eusebius of Nicomedia, who baptized Constantine. Constantine's brother Julius Constantius must have been nearby, not only because he was Eusebius' relative by marriage, but because he resided in Constantinople or somewhere in the Propontis region.[63] Nonetheless, later claims that Constantine's "real" will had to be hidden from his half-siblings for fear of tampering, that palace eunuchs suppressed the news of his death for fear of usurpation, or that Constantine's brothers had tried to poison the emperor because he had changed his mind about the fourfold succession are false.[64] Despite Eusebius of Caesarea's retrospective insistence that Constantine "bestowed as a father's estate the inheritance of Empire" exclusively onto his sons, there is no sign that Constantine did not hold onto his long-standing and more elaborate plans until the end.[65]

When the dead emperor's son Constantius arrived from Antioch, all that was left for him to do was to arrange the funeral, which was not attended by his brothers. Sometime after, and before late June, when he departed for Sirmium to meet with his brothers, Constantius fell out with his uncles and cousins. Constantine's sons had been unhappy with their father's succession plans for some time, as is exemplified by the fact that they had not minted gold and silver coins for the Caesar Flavius Dalmatius the Younger in their allotted parts of the empire. They may have been worried about Dalmatius'

---

[62] I largely follow Burgess (2008), who lists a previous bibliography. More recent interventions include Woods (2011); Maraval (2013) 23–37; Marcos (2014). Modern scholars have called the assassinations a "summer of blood" or "massacre of the princes." In the fourth century, the event was known as "slaughter," φόνος; see Libanius, Or. 18.10.

[63] On Eusebius of Nicomedia and the baptism of Constantine, see Barry (2019). The fifth-century church historians also allude to an "Arian" presbyter and former friend of Constantia present at Constantine's death, who was, however, a later fabrication; see Hillner (2019a). On Eusebius' network, see Chapter 8.

[64] Hidden will and palace eunuchs: Rufinus, Hist. eccl. 10.12; Poison: Philostorgius 2.16.

[65] Vita Constantini 63.3; 68.3, 69.2.

popularity in military circles or about whether their right to rule would be called into question due to their mother Fausta's disgrace. In fact, like their rivals, they descended from Maximian and Constantius, but could not fully claim this pedigree.[66] By September 9, when the three brothers were finally proclaimed Augusti by the Danubian troops, the Caesar Dalmatius had been murdered, along with his brother, the *rex* Hannibalianus the Younger, their father Flavius Dalmatius, their uncle Julius Constantius, and four other male relatives. These last remain nameless, but must be further offspring of Julius Constantius' siblings, as his son Julian called them his "cousins."[67] Unrelated high-ranking aristocratic supporters of their cause also died, including the former tutor of Constantia's dead son and consul of 334, Flavius Optatus, and the Praetorian prefect Ablabius, Constans' father-in-law to be, as well as "many nobles."[68]

The first official version of what had happened suggested that Constantine's half-brothers Julius Constantius and Flavius Dalmatius had tried to usurp power. Constantius confiscated Julius Constantius' property, and the Caesar Dalmatius the Younger's name was erased from official inscriptions. In his part of the empire, Italy and Illyria, Constans began minting coins with the caption *securitas reipublicae*, as previously used on the issues of his grandmother Helena, intimating that the empire had been saved from (internal) enemies. But this version of events was soon dropped in favor of a story that the army had instigated the assassinations in fear of usurpation against Constantine's sons' sole succession, but without their complicity. In reality, Constantius at least would have known about this scheme, even if he had not actively encouraged it.[69]

Whoever was specifically responsible, the summer of 337 conveniently relieved Constantine's sons of most of their rivals for imperial rule. The killings were not totally unprecedented, of course. They replicated Licinius' elimination of tetrarchic progeny in 313, and Constantine's extermination of Licinius' line.[70] But they were simultaneously more ruthless, being directed against numerous kin, and less rigorous, as they spared not only women, but also small children, as Constantine had not always done. Among the

---

[66] Vanderspoel (2020) 39.
[67] Julian, Epistula ad Athenienses 270D: ἀνεψιοί.
[68] Jerome, Chron. 338: *multi nobilium occisi*. For their possible identity, see Barnes (1981) 398 n. 10 and 11.
[69] As already observed by Eutropius, Brev. 10.9.1 (based on the so-called Enmannsche Kaisergeschichte, a mid-fourth-century now lost text).
[70] For Licinius' killings, see Chapter 4.

survivors were the widow of Hannibalianus the Younger, Constantina, and Flavius Dalmatius the Younger's presumed fiancée, Helena. Constans broke off his engagement to Olympias upon her father's murder, but she, too, was left alive. Of Constantius and Constantine II's own unnamed cousins-nieces-wives, not much further is known. Perhaps they had already passed away, but if not, it seems unlikely that they were among those killed, given the example of Olympias and the silence of Julian on this point. It has been suggested that Constantius repudiated his wife, but we cannot be sure.[71] Nor were this wife's young brothers Julian and Gallus, at this point about 5 and 11 years old, put to death. Julian and Gallus' cousin Julius Nepotianus, son of Constantine's half-sister Eutropia the Younger and the Roman aristocrat Virius Nepotianus, was also spared, as were his mother and perhaps even his aunt, Anastasia. At least one of their female cousins must also have survived the blood bath, as we shall see.

The question remains why all of these relatives were allowed to live. In some cases, such as that of Constantina and Helena it is not surprising, as they were the full sisters of Constantine's sons. It was more beneficial to claim them back for the dynasty, as in the former case of Constantine's sister Constantia. Constantine II and Constantius' wives, in turn, reinforced their husbands' and prospective children's links to the emperors of old, Constantius I and Maximian. Even Olympias was deemed more useful alive than dead, and her dynastic value and dependency on the imperial court's clemency after her father's murder eventually proved useful. In 354 Constantius married Olympias to Arsaces, the king of Armenia, to seal an alliance with Constantius. She was clearly a coveted imperial prize, becoming the first Roman imperial woman married to a foreign leader.[72]

Male children were more dangerous than female relatives as they could grow into imperial rivals rather than imperial tools. This was deemed not to apply to Nepotianus, who was descended through a female line, which also indicates that the four unnamed cousins Julian mentions as killed were his uncles' rather than his aunts' children. The survival of Julian and Gallus is more peculiar. It may have come down to the intervention by influential people such as Eusebius of Nicomedia, Julian's maternal relative, who did

---

[71] Vanderspoel (2020) 43–44 speculates that Constantius' wife may have been the woman named in the Book of Pontiffs as living in Rome at St. Agnes (taking the term "germana" as meaning cousin and assuming a divorce), but this seems improbable. See more on this in p. 287, n. 33.

[72] Ammianus Marcellinus, 20.11.3; Athanasius, Historia Arianorum 69, blaming Constantius for marrying Olympias to a "Barbarian," reflecting the unprecedented nature of this move. She was later poisoned at the Armenian court; see PLRE, Olympias 1, 642.

indeed become his guardian.[73] Julian and Gallus, however, may also have never been a target for assassination in the first place. Keeping male spares with a prestigious pedigree and of malleable age around, but at arm's length, was useful to the new and still heirless Augusti as they set out to order their empire. Constantine had at first done the same with his siblings, before he had sired his own sons. Stories of others' intervention do not preclude such a strategic move, as it suited Constantine's sons to present themselves as magnanimous, clement, and Christian in the face of manifest guilt.[74] The subsequent treatment of the boys, especially from the early 340s when they were moved to the tightly controlled imperial estate of Macellum in Cappadocia, giving the impression of internal exile, ensured that an aura of ancestral criminality always surrounded them.[75]

Constantine II, Costantius, and Constans had learned from their father the benefits of pruning the family tree, even if they did it their way. They also drew on his methods in reshaping it for popular consumption. To be sure, they rarely followed his example by refashioning the public image of their living wives, or of the aunts or cousins whose male relatives they had killed. None of the brothers awarded their wives the title of Augusta, which marked a return to the dynastic strategy of the earlier tetrarchy. It reflects a concern that the promotion of wives would create imbalance in the imperial college, especially if some wives so honored were themselves of imperial lineage, while others were not.[76]

Constantine's sons found it safer to resurrect dead women, Helena and Theodora. The coins bearing their portraits that they minted after the killings offer a spectacular repackaging of imperial women reminiscent of Constantine's pairing of Helena and Fausta, but entirely unique in their focus on deceased relatives. As had been often the case under Constantine, the women's portraits appeared on bronze issues, ensuring their wide circulation among the population. Anyone contemplating both coins

---

[73] On Eusebius of Nicomedia taking in Julian: Ammianus Marcellinus, 22.9. Zonaras, Epit. hist. 13.10 claimed that his parents had entrusted Julian to Eusebius for his education. Eunapius, Lives of the Sophists 7.15 claimed that Julian had been spirited away by palace eunuchs and Gregory of Nazianzus, Or. 4.91.5–7 that the bishop Mark of Arethusa had intervened for him. See also Tougher (2020) 195.
[74] Frakes (2005) 99.
[75] Move to Macellum: Julian, Epistula ad Athenienses 271B–C. He calls it exile.
[76] Tougher (2020) 210 speculates that the absence of Augusta titles under Constantine's sons was due to the absence of sons, but many examples from Roman imperial history show that the production of sons was not the key prerequisite for women being awarded the title. See also Chapters 4, 5, and 11 here.

together would, however, have noticed some differences. Helena's portrait was paired, on the coins' reverse, with the figure of *pax* (Peace) holding a palm branch and a long scepter ending in a sphere, surrounded by a slogan proclaiming, "Public Peace" (*pax publica*). The reverse of Theodora's coins showed a woman nursing a child—recalling the iconography on some of Fausta's coins—identified as "Roman Piety" (*pietas Romana*), a very feminine virtue. Theodora was extolled for her maternal qualities, a strikingly cynical move given that almost all her male descendants had just been murdered. Conversely, Helena was partnered with a male imperial concept, even more so than had been the case with her former *securitas reipublicae* allegory under Constantine, for it was exclusively the emperor(s) who brought about and guaranteed peace. The iconography compounded this difference: while both women wear the braid-wreath hairstyle most closely associated with Helena, only Helena's appears studded with pearls and only she wears a ceremonial mantle with an embroidered rim. To the viewer, the coins established a clear hierarchy between the two grandmothers. While it is difficult to confirm if these coins were ever viewed together, they were conceived together with that theoretical possibility in mind.

The coins were first minted in Trier, where Constantine II was based, and were also most vigorously produced there. The mints in Rome and Constantinople began such issues only in September 337 and with much smaller distributions. Unsurprisingly, Helena's portrait was minted more often than Theodora's in Constantinople, where Constantius was based. The series terminated when Constantine II died in 340. It seems therefore that it had been Constantine who had taken the initiative as the most senior of the three brothers. As the emperor who benefited least from the division of the Caesar Flavius Dalmatius the Younger's allotted territory, he was probably also the most unhappy with rumors about his complicity in his relatives' murder.[77] But if this was so, he still managed to persuade his brothers to follow suit, suggesting that the coinage scheme was appealing to them, too. Celebrating Theodora expressed their grief and helped to deflect blame for the extermination of her line away from all three of them. Giving her the title of "Augusta" showed that they would have honored their relatives' rights to succession, had they only been given a chance to do so by their rampaging soldiers. Making Theodora visible in this way also established an ancestral link to Maximian, one that the brothers could less easily make through

---

[77] Burgess (2008) 22–24.

their own disgraced mother Fausta. This link was especially valuable for Constantius and Constantine who were married to her granddaughters (the coinage, incidentally, is the best proof that these women were still alive).[78] At the same time, lest anyone still had misgivings about her background, Helena's more official appearance ensured that no one would have doubts about her grandsons' legitimacy and their ability to bring peace to the imperial realm.

* * *

Going forward, Helena's lineage would intermittently attempt to strengthen its ties with Theodora's once again. The tools through which this was accomplished were Helena's two granddaughters, Constantina and Helena the Younger, in time married to their cousins Gallus and Julian, respectively.[79] At the same time, Theodora's surviving female descendants were not considered entirely without dynastic potential of their own either. They would give hope to usurpers and, as it turned out, to later-fourth-century emperors keen to establish Constantinian credentials. The lives of mid-fourth-century Constantinian women therefore continued to be shaped by the fraught relationship between their female ancestors, even if these were no longer directly referenced. At the same time, these women defined what it meant to be an imperial woman after Helena, in an increasingly Christianized empire. In this way, they also came to shape Helena's posthumous image, when, at the end of the fourth century, ecclesiastical writers rediscovered Helena as a useful figure through whom to pass judgment on imperial power. It is therefore, again, important to spend time with these women.

---

[78] Theodora's link to Maximian claimed in the absence of Fausta: Vanderspoel (2020) 39–40. The coinage of Theodora underscoring the prestige of the imperial wives: Woods (2011). On the coins and the meaning of the attributes, see also Longo (2009) 97.

[79] Chausson (2007) 115–16 suggests that Constantine had a third daughter, from a third marriage, due to Philostorgius, Hist. eccl. 3.22, claiming Constantina was the "oldest" of Constantine's daughters. For a critique of this suggestion, see Barnes (2014) 152.

10
Silence of the Empress

Today's visitors to the room known as the Sala a Croce Greca in the Vatican Museums are confronted with two massive porphyry sarcophagi facing each other. Following the prescribed route, they pass on their left the sarcophagus discussed in the previous chapter, which came originally from the imperial mausoleum next to the basilica "at the two laurel trees" on the Via Labicana and may have contained Helena's body. Opposite stands another one, richly decorated with vintage scenes of putti harvesting grapes (Fig. 10.1). It is generally believed to have housed the body of Helena's granddaughter Constantina, and perhaps also that of Constantina's sister, the younger Helena, although this latter Helena may also have been buried in another porphyry sarcophagus now reused as a reliquary in the basilica of St. Peter. These last two coffins had been removed in the early seventeenth and late eighteenth century, respectively, from a mausoleum that stood next to the church of St. Agnes founded by Constantina on the Via Nomentana, 3 kilometers northeast of Rome (Map 8, n. 1).[1]

The current arrangement of Helena's sarcophagus opposite that of her granddaughter(s) perpetuates early modern ideas of a harmonious Constantinian past, but their proximity obscures their diverging geographical provenance, from the east and north of the city of Rome, respectively. These different provenances, in turn, reflect at least in part the persistent violent divisions in the Constantinian family created by Constantius I's relationships with Helena and Theodora back in the late third century, and the diminution of Helena's role in the minds of her immediate descendants. As we shall see, in the mid-fourth century, the imperial mausoleum on the Via Nomentana was a space over which both Helena's and Theodora's offspring competed in the aftermath of yet more conflict and bloodshed. In the process, Helena herself was marginalized. Instead, her grandchildren rediscovered their mother

---

[1] On the second sarcophagus, sometimes believed to be Helena the Younger's, now in St. Peter's, see Delbrueck (1932) 168. It was incorporated into the altar of Sts. Simeon and Jude in the south transept of St. Peter's. When the porphyry sarcophagus now at the Vatican Museums was opened in the eighteenth century, it contained more than one body; see Rasch, Arbeiter (2007) 10, 29.

Fig. 10.1 Porphyry sarcophagus from the Mausoleum of Constantina; now at the Vatican Museums, Sala a Croce Greca. © Governatorato SCV—Direzione dei Musei Vaticani. All rights reserved.

Fausta, and even their maternal grandmother Eutropia, as more suitable ancestresses. Further political events then ensured that, rather than Helena's progeny, it was "Theodoran" women, her great-granddaughter Justina and Justina's own daughter Galla the Younger, descendants of one of Theodora's children, who became the carrier of dynastic legitimacy and, at least at first, the embodiment of the Constantinian past (see the Family Tree).

This is not to deny Helena's role in forging a path for these women toward spheres in which they could act. Helena's image as the face of the dynasty, imperial delegate, church patron, imperial mother, and player in theological disputes shaped these later women's roles and representation.[2] But observations of such impact can only be based on parallels with the later women's actions, aided by the occasional textual reference to them, rather than on hard data of direct influence. Even later Constantinian women

---

[2] See Brubaker (1997), although she does not consider why Helena was rarely mentioned as a direct model for fourth-century imperial women.

refrained from situating themselves into a tradition that had started with Helena. Furthermore, the various elements of Helena's image shaped the lives and representation of the women who came after her rather differently. Where it came to being a delegate, church patron, and loyal defender of family interests, it was Helena's older granddaughter Constantina who picked up the trail her grandmother had laid in the last decade of her life. The contours of her agency are, however, a lot clearer than Helena's. Constantina had her own voice, her own resources for a defined Christian project, and left a clear written record of her political influence. This impression may come down to uneven source transmission but was also a consequence of personal circumstances and historical contingency, especially the progressive Christianization of the empire. Powerful discourses emerged around widowhood, virginity, and celibacy, which, in combination with the expansion of a Christian church looking for patrons, gave Constantina more room for maneuvering than Helena had enjoyed.

As time moved on and the male Constantinian line died out, the divisions between the "Helenian" and "Theodoran" branches of the Constantinian dynasty and therefore also the celebration or rejection of Helena as the dynasty's "ancestress" became ever less meaningful. What lingered with contemporaries was an awareness that surviving female descendants of the Constantinian dynasty presented a powerful link to the past whatever their actual line of descent. In addition, imperial women's visibility as Christian patrons that had started with Helena and further increased with her granddaughter Constantina turned them into more sustained targets within the great theological debates of the time. In an ironic twist of historical development, Helena's negative mid-fourth-century assessment in an ecclesiastical source, Athanasius' *History of the Arians*, foreshadowed that of Theodora's descendant Justina, who, although a "Theodoran," became the Constantinian link to not only one, but two subsequent dynasties, and to a usurper besides (see the Family Tree). The progeny of two emperors (Constantius I and Maximian), an imperial wife twice over (of Magnentius and then Valentinian I), a dowager empress, a mother of a child emperor (Valentinian II), and mother-in-law of yet another emperor (Theodosius I), Justina combined several existing and also some startlingly new female imperial roles. She did so in a changed empire, which had seen the consolidation of even more robust Christian institutions, especially the bishop's office, and a deeper sectarian climate than Helena had ever known. Where Helena's spat with a bishop had been a minor episode in her life, almost lost from the historical record,

Justina's conflict with a bishop became the defining feature of her memory and provided one of the defining frameworks for Helena's resurrection in legend.

Extending Helena: Constantina

Sometime between 337 and 340 Helena's granddaughter Constantina came to Rome.[3] She arrived there from the East. Born in Serdica or Sirmium around 320, she had probably been brought up in the imperial palace at Nicomedia, in surroundings that had little in common with her grandmother's early life in the same region.[4] Whether Constantina and her younger sister Helena ever met their grandmother is unknown, since after 320 Helena may have only passed through Bithynia once and briefly. When it came to role models, the sudden disappearance of their mother Fausta during their childhood may have left a greater impression, teaching the imperial girls that within their family a moral misstep could have life-threatening consequences.

Constantina was soon to find out that such danger could even emanate from simply having the wrong ancestry. In 335, she married her "Theodoran" cousin Hannibalianus the Younger, the "king of kings and the Pontic people." They resided in Constantinople or Nicomedia, despite Hannibalianus' supposed duties in Armenia, although he may also have spent some time away leading a military campaign against Persia.[5] Two years later, however, Hannibalianus was murdered in Constantinople during the massacre of "Theodoran" relatives following Constantine's death. Constantina was made a widow, at just 16 years of age or so. Her marriage had remained childless. If she had been an aristocratic girl, Constantina would have reentered the marriage market.[6] At the imperial level, however, where girls carried dynastic potency, the pool of suitable husbands who were not deemed a threat to their male relatives' right to rule was always very small, and even smaller if the preference was for intrafamilial marriages, as was usually the case in the Constantinian house. At this moment in time, there was clearly no urgency for Constantina to remarry. Like that of her grandmother's decades before, Constantina's life was therefore driven off course. Unlike Helena,

---

[3] Suggested by CIL 6.40790, on which see the text that follows.
[4] On Constantina's birthdate and place, see Hillner (2018).
[5] Isaac (1997) 437.
[6] On marriage as the end goal of a Roman elite girl's life, see Caldwell (2015) 17–44.

however, we know what Constantina subsequently did, partly through her own words. Her actions show both striking parallels to her grandmother's life and changed circumstances within which imperial women could express their agency.

It is unlikely that Constantina's appearance in Rome so soon after the troublesome events in Constantinople came down to her own choice. As a woman, an orphan, and a minor, she had to have a guardian. Normally, uncles assumed this role, but Constantina's had all just been killed.[7] Her guardianship was therefore probably assumed by her brothers, the new Augusti, even though they were also still underage, who determined her movements. All three Constantinian brothers benefited from having an imperial presence in Rome at this time, but especially Constans and Constantius. Rome was in Constans' territory, but he never visited, residing instead in his father's birth city of Naissus and elsewhere, in order to avoid being drawn into civic ceremonials that would have compromised his apparently rather fervent Christian beliefs.[8] At the same time, Constans relied on an exclusive group of members of old aristocratic families, predominantly pagans, to fill both high imperial positions in Rome and at court until at least 348. As a woman, Constantina was free from traditional expectations to partake in sacrifice and could therefore interact with the largely pagan aristocracy on more neutral and less public terms than her male relatives. However, since Constantina came to Rome from the East, it must have been Constantius who initially suggested she take up her residence there. Constantius was no less keen on maintaining or rather repairing good relationships with Roman aristocrats, some of whose relatives had just been murdered under his watch or (in the case of his cousin Gallus) were under his control. Among these, Gallus' powerful maternal uncle, Vulcacius Rufinus, was particularly prominent. He soon made a stellar career, becoming Constantius' "Count of the East" (*comes per orientem*) in Antioch in 342 and a member of his imperial council (*consistorium*), while then progressing to the Praetorian prefecture of Italy (344–347) and Illyria (347–352). In time, Constantius may have also wanted an imperial presence in Rome to keep check on Constans himself, who in 340 had killed their oldest brother Constantine and thereby tightened his grip on the West. Constantina fit the bill of imperial delegate perfectly, for Constantine II's marriage had ended with his death—if he even had

---

[7] On guardians Arjava (1996) 115.
[8] Of Constantine's sons, only Constans was baptized before his deathbed; see Moser (2017) 46.

a wife at this point—while Constans never married. Even though widowed, Constantina was the most senior woman of the Constantinian dynasty in the West throughout the 340s.⁹

Constantina therefore was continuing the tried and tested role of her grandmother Helena, who had also arrived in Rome following a brutal fall-out within the Constantinian dynasty, to mediate imperial authority and patronage in the ever-important imperial capital, including with people close to Theodora's descendants. Her mission of projecting imperial unity and strengthening the image of her side of the family is also amply demonstrated by a public honor she received within a short time of her arrival. As had happened to Helena, an equestrian supervisor of imperial property (*praepositus rerum privatarum*), Flavius Gavianus, erected a bronze statue for Constantina, the marble base of which was found just west of the Lateran basilica (see Map 8).¹⁰ The inscription that Gavianus had carved into it praised Constantina in familiar terms, as "our lady" (*domina nostra*) and, importantly, "noble and venerable" sister of the Augusti, "sprung from divine stock (*prosapia*)." The phrasing followed the customary trend in Constantinian epigraphy of foregrounding ancestry and direct bloodlines and of reclaiming women for the dynasty, this time to obscure Constantina's disastrous marriage to a disgraced man. It does not mention, however, that Constantina carried the title of Augusta, awarded by her father upon marriage to Hannibalianus the Younger, as would be claimed later in the fifth century. She either had never received the title to begin with, or it was now quietly dropped, and Constantina herself folded back into a dynastic hierarchy dominated by her brothers.¹¹

Much later, hagiographical accounts, written in the sixth century, told of Constantina's palace eunuchs, the *praepositus* John and the *primicerius* Paul.

---

⁹ On the role of Constantina, Harries (2014); Dirschlmayer (2015) 58. Moser (2018) 85–118 on the relationship between the brothers, Constantius' interest in Rome, and both brothers' collaboration with Roman senators. On Constans and Rome, see also Moser (2017). On Constans' residences, McEvoy (2020) 282. On Vulcacius Rufinus, PLRE I Rufinus 25, 782–83.

¹⁰ CIL 6.40790: *Divina prosapia ab / auctore Rom[ani] / imperii procrea[tae] / filiae divi Consta[ntini] / pii, maximi, sororiqu[e] / dominor(um) nostrorum / Constanti et Constantis / perpetuorum Auggg(ustorum) / d(ominae) n(ostrae) Fl(aviae) Constantinae nob(ili) / ac venerabili / Fl(avius) Gavianus v(ir) p(erfectissimus) p(rae)p(ositus) rer(um) / privatar(um) semper vester.* The inscription originally identified Constantina as the sister of the three Augusti, so must date to 337–340, and was altered after her eldest brother Constantine II was killed in early 340. Several portrait heads deriving from Rome have been identified as Constantina, but none convincingly. See Calza (1972) 334–39; Wegner (1984) 155. It is possible that a statue for Constantina's sister Helena the Younger was erected here, too; see Cerrito (2019).

¹¹ On Constantina's possible Augusta title, see Chapter 9. On the wording of the inscription, also Moser (2016) 1237–38.

The story detailed their endeavors to look after the poor on the Caelian hill, just south of the Lateran, using the fortunes that Constantine's daughter—here called Augusta—had left them, including a house (Map 8, n. 2). Another hagiographical text, the Passion of Gallicanus, imagines Constantina within the imperial palace, where she fostered and converted the aristocratic daughters of the protagonist, the pagan general Gallicanus. While these accounts are fictional, they show that Constantina's presence not only in Rome, but also in the southeastern part of Rome, where the Sessorian Palace and—still closer to the find spot of her inscription—her mother's former residence "in the Lateran area" were situated, had left a deep mark on local memory. Constantina was remembered as having dealt with a similar circle of people as her grandmother had while in Rome—palace officials, managers of imperial domains, and the female relatives of Roman aristocrats—and having moved in the same spaces.[12]

As had been the case with Helena, circumstances thus gave Constantina a rather unusual and even official visibility, despite her status as a spare and unmarried imperial sister. Yet, Constantina managed to move beyond the mere inheritance of Helena's role in Rome. She increased her visibility substantially by associating herself with a powerful emerging feature of Christian devotion in Rome, the cult of the Roman martyrs. This is the reason why she appears so frequently in hagiography written in and for the city of Rome, far more frequently than Helena herself. While Constantina was resident in Rome, Christian church building there continued apace. Several churches commonly linked with Constantine, among them St. Peter in the Vatican, were only completed or initiated during the reigns of his sons.[13] Like Helena before her, we can imagine Constantina was involved in these projects. In addition, but unlike Helena, Constantina is recorded as a founder of a church in Rome in her own right, the aforementioned funerary basilica dedicated to the martyr St. Agnes, on the Via Nomentana. Some of its 100-meter-long walls, circus-shaped like those of the basilica "at the two laurel trees" on the Via Labicana, are still visible today (Fig. 10.2).

The sixth-century Book of Pontiffs traces the familiar process of church founding involving an imperial woman that we have already witnessed in the case of Helena and Eutropia in Palestine. It states that it had been Constantine "who built the basilica of the holy martyr Agnes at the request of his daughter

---

[12] Passio Iohannis et Pauli 1, 3 (the foundation legend of the Titulus Pammachii/Sts. John and Paul on the Caelian hill); Passio Gallicani 2; see also Chapter 6. On the house of Fausta, Chapter 3 and 6.

[13] On the chronology of the Constantinian basilicas, see p. 155, n. 44.

Fig. 10.2 Panoramic view from the south over the complex of St. Agnes, Via Nomentana, Rome. On the left, remains of the funerary basilica; on the right, the circular mausoleum of Constantina, now S. Costanza. Courtesy of santagnese.org, Creative Commons License (CC BY-SA 2.0).

and a baptistery in the same place, where his sister Constantia was baptized along with the emperor's daughter by bishop Silvester [d. 335]."[14] The chronology here is clearly muddled, for Constantina could not have formed a plan to found a church in Rome before 335, when she was still very young and in the East. Neither could her aunt Constantia, who died in the East in the early 330s, have been baptized at St. Agnes. The archaeological remains of St. Agnes have been dated to the 340s, and no traces of a fourth-century baptistery found.[15] Nonetheless, the entry in the Book of Pontiffs probably reflects that Constantina asked for permission for the foundation, either from her father or, given the dating, more likely from her brother Constans. The church was to be erected on imperial land that, like the estate on which the basilica

---

[14] LP I 180: *Eodem tempore fecit basilicam sanctae martyris Agnae ex rogatu filiae suae et baptisterium in eodem loco, ubi et baptizata est soror eius Constantia cum filia Augusti a Siluestrio episcopo*. Constantia's appearance here probably resulted from confusion over homonymous naming patterns in the Constantinian dynasty. The story is somehow related to Constantine's own alleged baptism by Silvester; see Diefenbach (2007) 107 n. 105, 156 n. 290. It is also in some form of dialogue with the sixth-century Passio of Agnes, which depicts Constantina asking her father and brothers for support to build a church for the martyr, whose intervention helped her to heal from leprosy: Conti, Burrus, Trout (2020) 21, and see Passio Agnetis et Emeritianae 16.

[15] On the basilica of St. Agnes, see Frutaz (1969); Brandenburg (2004) 69–86; Rasch, Arbeiter (2007); Dirschlmayer (2015) 58–63.

"at the two laurel trees" had risen, contained the graves of earlier periods. Just north of the church sprawled extensive catacombs, which continued to be used. The church building itself destroyed a necropolis of the Praetorian Guard and of imperial freedmen. Like the *equites singulares*, the Praetorian Guard had fought for Maxentius at the Milvian Bridge and had been dismantled by Constantine. The decision to deconsecrate their burial ground was therefore not a difficult one, but it had to be made by an emperor.[16]

So far Constantina's actions mirror those of her grandmother, especially in Palestine. But in Constantina's case, we have a record that shows how, on this occasion, it was not a simple matter of an imperial woman fulfilling her male relatives' will. A late antique visitor to the church was greeted by a monumental marble inscription, affixed on the church's southern wall or its apse, proudly proclaiming, in fourteen stylish hexameters, Constantina as its founder:

> I, Constantina, venerating God and dedicated to Christ,
> having devoutly provided all the expenses,
> with divine inspiration and Christ's great help,
> consecrated this temple of Agnes, victorious virgin,
> because she has prevailed over the temples of all earthly works
> where now the loftiest roofs gleam with gold.
> Christ's name is celebrated at this site,
> who alone could defeat the Tartarean death
> after he ascended to heaven and alone brought forward triumph,
> restoring the name of Adam and the body and all its members,
> lifted from dark deaths and the blind night.
> You, the martyr devoted to Christ, will hold this worthy gift
> from our own riches for long centuries;
> oh joyous virgin Agnes of memorable name.[17]

---

[16] On these former burials, Styger (1933) 208–10.

[17] ILCV 1768 = ICUR 8.20752: *Constantina d(eu)m venerans Christoq(ue) dicata / omnibus impensis devota mente paratis / numine divino multum Christoq(ue) iuvante / sacravi templum victricis virginis Agnes / templorum quod vincit opus terrenaq(ue) cuncta / aurea quae rutilant summi fastigia tecti / nomen enim Christi celebratur sedibus istis / tartaream solus potuit qui vincere mortem / invectus caelo solusq(ue) inferre triumphum / nomen Adae referens et corpus et omnia membra / a mortis tenebris et caeca nocte levata / dignum igitur munus martyr devotaq(ue) Christo / ex opibus nostris per s(a)ecula longa tenebris (sic) / o felix virgo memorandi nominis Agnes / Constantina deo.* The actual inscription is lost, and the text only survives in manuscript; see Conti, Burrus, Trout (2020) 283–84.

These classicizing verses echoed the language of contemporary imperial monuments, with a focus on conquest, victory, and triumph. These achievements were attributed to Agnes and ultimately Christ. Still, it was Constantina who presented them to the world, drawing an elegant visual link between herself and Agnes through the first and last word of the inscription giving their respective names, and framing the entire poem with a vertical acrostic spelling "Constantina, for God" (CONSTANTINA DEO). Its reader learns almost nothing about Agnes other than that she was a "victorious virgin" and a martyr, but comes away with a clear impression of Constantina as profoundly pious, deeply erudite, and unmistakably imperial, if not even imperious.[18]

Even though Helena is often credited with this honor, it is Constantina's poem that offers our earliest unequivocal record of an imperial woman as an independent Christian church founder. It is, of course, entirely possible that founder epigrams had been commissioned for other Constantinian churches in Rome or elsewhere and that we are simply missing earlier evidence, including for Helena. It has indeed been suggested that Constantina had been directly inspired by the pious activities of her grandmother, whether in Rome or Palestine.[19] This may well be the case, although she does not say so. The expressive skill in any case bears the hand of an erudite person. Although we cannot be entirely sure that Constantina had composed the poem herself, it is not inconceivable. Perhaps unlike her grandmother, as an imperial girl, Constantina would have not only learned to read and write in the first place, but even acquired an advanced level of literacy. Constantine's court had been an exceedingly cultured one, employing famous intellectuals, at least for the education of the Caesars, Constantina's brothers.[20]

In addition to being a remarkable record of a female imperial voice, the inscription also contains valuable information on Constantina's involvement in church foundation, which again reveals significant differences with her grandmother's patronage activities. The beginning and the end of Constantina's poem make it clear that, even if she had to ask permission to use the ground on which the church rose, the building itself was financed by her own money, her "riches" (*opes*). Helena, by contrast, had always been

---

[18] Trout (2014) 221–23; Harries (2014) 266–67. It should be noted that some manuscripts render verbs in the inscription in the third-, rather than the first-person singular; see ICUR 8.20752.
[19] Brubaker (1997) 59; Jones (2007) 119.
[20] On elite girls' education, Caldwell (2015) 17–44. One of the tutors may have been the Gallic poet Aemilius Magnus Arborius, who was possibly also killed in the massacre of 337; PLRE I, Arborius 4, 98.

presented as using official imperial funds for official imperial purposes. Given her background, she had no independent means to do otherwise. But Constantina, as we know, was an heiress, having received her share of her father's inheritance.[21] Constantina must certainly have had ample funds for her church. St. Agnes was the biggest of all the funerary basilicas erected in Rome in the first half of the fourth century. It presented an architectural challenge due to the steep slope on which it was erected, which necessitated enormous and expensive substructures under the apse. Constantina also may have endowed the church with liturgical vessels (gold and silver patens, chalices, and chandeliers) and landed income, so it could last "for centuries." The church's rents, documented in the Book of Pontiffs, were not as extensive as those of other Constantinian basilicas (only 695 solidi annually), and they all came from estates situated near Rome, especially around the Via Salaria just to the north of the complex. This incongruence between the landed income and the size of the basilica suggests that Constantina relied on her own funds in endowing it, concentrated, as possibly her mother's had been, in and around Rome, rather than drawing on far-flung imperial domains owned by her brothers. These funds were by necessity more limited, not least because as a girl, her share in her father's inheritance may have been smaller than that of her brothers.[22]

The modest nature of the endowment probably contributed to the massive church falling into disuse relatively soon, after little more than two centuries.[23] Nonetheless, for Constantina herself, her financial independence meant she was not beholden to imperial wishes in choosing where to direct her patronage. In the case of Helena, we can only speculate what she thought about the cults she patronized, whether that be of Lucian of Antioch or of the Virgin Mary. It is even unclear who was venerated in the basilica "at the two laurel trees" next to the mausoleum in which she was buried. Helena did not have her own voice to communicate her personal piety. By contrast, Constantina's attachment to Agnes was palpable. Although she gives little away, Constantina knew, and was aware her audience knew, an oral version of Agnes' story, which must have contained elements of the written version from the later fourth century that has come down to us. This describes how

---

[21] On Constantine dividing his inheritance among his sons and daughters: Julian, Or. 7.227D.
[22] LP I 180–181. On the differences between daughters' and sons' shares in inheritance, see Arjava (1996) 62–73.
[23] It was replaced in the early seventh century, also because changed patterns of devotion demanded a building on top of Agnes' tomb.

Agnes had been a young aristocratic girl courted by the son of a pagan urban prefect at a time when Christians were still persecuted. She had remained steadfast in her Christian determination to preserve her virginity, angering the slighted boy's father who had put her through a series of tortures—including a spell in a brothel where her suitors were struck blind—and ultimately to death.[24] The origins of Agnes' cult are obscure. It is not known in which persecution she was supposed to have died, but Agnes' feast day, celebrated on the Via Nomentana on February 21, was already mentioned in a liturgical calendar drawn up in the 330s, just before Constantina arrived in Rome. The widow's interest may have been awakened due to the emerging popularity of Agnes' cult or the eroticized melodrama of the story, but surely also because she discovered that a martyr's tomb was situated on imperial land, in the vicinity of her own landholdings.[25]

What is more, the very first line in Constantina's poem shows that, for her, Agnes was not just an object of devotion, but of emulation. Constantina describes herself as "dedicated to Christ" (*Christo dicata*), a phrase that hints at the consecration of Christian virgins. Of course, Constantina, having already been married, could not claim to be a virgin, but she could claim the spiritual authority of Christian widowhood, an esteemed status in the Christian church, not quite, but almost as prized as virginity.[26] Given the fluidity of the ascetic movement in the early fourth century, the term *dicata* may in any case describe a private vow rather than any formal consecration.[27] Its use in Constantina's poem shows that she was fully aware of Christian ideals of celibacy. She may have been so from a young age, since her father Constantine had begun legislating in favor of such lifestyles, abolishing the age-old penalties for refusals to marry or remarry.[28] But more importantly, just at the time when Constantina was residing in Rome, more concrete ideas about Christian asceticism were beginning to circulate in the city. They were facilitated by the arrival of Athanasius of Alexandria, who Constantius had banished from his see and who sought protection from his friend Julius, the bishop of Rome, from 339 to 343. Athanasius and his

---

[24] On the development of the written versions of Agnes' story, see Jones (2007) 123–24. On the unknown martyrs venerated at the basilica "at the two laurel trees," see Chapter 6.
[25] Agnes' feast day is mentioned in the liturgical calendar included in the Codex Calendar of 354 (LP I, 11). This list may have been drawn up in 336; see Dirschlmayer (2015) 62.
[26] On the ambiguous category of Christian widows, see Methuen (1997).
[27] On the flexibility around the status of virginity in the fourth century and the vagueness of terminology, Undheim (2017) 13–14.
[28] On Constantine's "celibacy" legislation, see Evans Grubbs (1995) 118–31.

entourage were hosted by none other than Constantina's half-aunt Eutropia the Younger, probably the wife or widow of the Roman aristocrat and consul of 336 Virius Nepotianus. They spread ideas about Christian asceticism, virginity, and widowhood to a captivated female audience through stories about the great Egyptian holy men Antony and Pachomius. Constantina may well have reconnected with Eutropia, after all, also the full aunt of her murdered husband, and come into contact with these religious ideas, or at least had them reinforced, in this way. This at least happened to other female relatives of Eutropia, the young sisters Marcella and Asella, who were so inspired by the Egyptian visitors that they decided to dedicate themselves to an austere Christian lifestyle.[29] The language Constantina uses in her poem is an astonishing insight into how an imperial woman made sense of the interrupted nature of her life that we completely lack for her grandmother Helena. Although it is perfectly possible that Helena converted to Christianity during her obscure years, and found meaning in doing so, more public and imperially endorsed Christian discourses and the martyr Agnes' example of resilience now gave Constantina the opportunity to turn her situation of temporary marital ineligibility into a statement of virtue.[30]

Constantina thus explicitly departed from Helena's and Fausta's female imperial virtues of fertility and motherhood in her self-representation, foregrounding an alternative Christian lifestyle and focusing on Christian rather than traditional civic patronage. She may also have extended Christian largesse from the *suburbium* to the center of Rome. Just a few minutes' walk north from the residence with frescos of the Constantinian family that we visited in previous chapters lie the remains of a chapel that potentially bear traces of Constantina's intervention (Map 8, n. 3). Established in the fourth century, it was redecorated in the fifth with a painting that represents Christ crowning two women, one in imperial dress and the other in a grey *palla* pulled over her head. The base of Constantina's statue sponsored by the imperial supervisor Gavianus was found built into the walls of a room on an upper story above this chapel, alongside an honorary inscription for the fifth-century empress Licinia Eudoxia, the wife of Valentinian III, commissioned

---

[29] On Eutropia the Younger's Christian "salon" in Rome, Hillner (2017a). On the Egyptian delegation's influence on spreading ideas about asceticism to elite women in Rome Palladius, Historia Lausiaca 1.4; Undheim (2017) 14–15. On Marcella's family, Chausson (2002) 149. She was probably related to the Constantinian family through her maternal kinship with the Nummii family, into which Constantine's half-sister Anastasia had married. Marcella's imperial in-laws (*regalis affinitas*) are mentioned in Ps.-Jerome, Exhortatio ad Marcellam 2.

[30] On Constantina's inspiration by Agnes, see also Conti, Burrus, Trout (2020) 39.

by yet another imperial official. They had probably originally stood in a courtyard in front of the chapel and were then reused at some later date when the site was falling into disrepair. It seems plausible that it was Constantina who had founded this chapel and Eudoxia who redecorated it, eager to connect herself to a Constantinian past and its pious imperial women. If this is true, the two women in the painting may represent Eudoxia herself and Constantina dressed in ascetic clothes, or perhaps Agnes and Constantina, with the martyr taking on the imperial appearance that she would later assume in her depiction at the ecclesiastical complex on the Via Nomentana.[31] It is intriguing to imagine that, while Helena had still followed civic traditions by gifting a bath outside her palace to the people of Rome, Constantina now sponsored a place of Christian worship.

Of course, Constantina was neither Augusta, or at least not anymore, nor the wife or mother of a reigning emperor, so there was no immediate need for her to make a dynastic statement through her acts of patronage, as there had been for Helena.[32] In her spiritual quest she also benefited from knowledge and practices that had not yet been fully available to Helena. Equipped with this new Christian wisdom, Constantina may well have planned to live out the rest of her life as a widow and imperial delegate in Rome, a role for which she was still remembered in the city in the sixth century.[33] By the end of the 340s, however, a political crisis engulfing the reigns of her brothers meant Constantina's more traditional qualities were again required. Like her grandmother after the dynastic murders of 326, Constantina now resumed a more active and mobile imperial lifestyle in support of her male relatives, though the focus of her loyalty at some point shifted from her brother to her new husband.

In January 350, Constans was ousted by one of his generals in Gaul, the *comes rei militaris* Magnentius, who declared himself emperor. The fleeing Constans was murdered in a town called Helena (Elne near Perpignan),

---

[31] On this site, the so-called Cappella dell'Angelo under the Ospale dell'Angelo, now within the complex of the Ospedale S. Giovanni-Addolorata, see Yamada, Cerrito (2015) 687–93; (2020) 275–321. The frescoes are now stored within the Ospedale dell'Angelo. On their identification as imperial figures, Morretti (2006) 419–24, although note that Yamada, Cerrito (2020) disagree. Agnes appears in imperial clothes also in the apse mosaic of her seventh-century church on the Via Nomentana. On Constantina's statue, see previous discussion.

[32] Dirschlmayer (2015) 61.

[33] See LP I, 207 and its confused story of a sister of Constantius called Constantia, living at the cemetery of St. Agnes in 358 and mediating between Constantius and bishop Liberius. Although it cannot be historical, as Constantina was already dead in 358, it reflects how Constantina was remembered in Rome. For Constantina's later remembrance as a virgin, rather than a widow, see also Burrus (2020).

fulfilling a prophecy, according to the much later Byzantine historian Zonaras, that he would die in his grandmother Helena's arms.[34] Less than two months later, on March 1, Constantina proclaimed as Caesar in the West a man called Vetranio, the infantry commander (*magister peditum*) of the Danubian troops. Constantina, we are told, informed her brother by letter about this decision. Constantius was on the frontier with Persia at this time and in no position to argue. He accepted and later in the summer even conferred on Vetranio the title of Augustus. Once Constantius was back in the Balkans in the autumn, however, he promptly deprived Vetranio of the imperial purple. The two men appeared in front of their armies at Naissus, a place of deep symbolic meaning for the Constantinian dynasty, and Vetranio publicly agreed to retire to Bithynia.[35]

It has been argued that Constantina had promoted Vetranio in order to marry and rule beside him. This would have been an astonishingly ambitious, and also, given her ascetic activities in Rome, surprising move. Furthermore, Constantinian children had for decades been accustomed to marrying their equals, and it would have been an unprecedented decision for a woman to end this habit. It also seems inconceivable that Constantius would not have reproved his sister publicly had she planned a power grab. It is therefore more likely that Constantina acted in support of Constantius, to prevent Magnentius from gaining access to the vitally important Illyrian armies, giving a distant Constantius time to prepare his next moves. This is not to say that Vetranio's uprising was purely a tactical ploy rather than a real usurpation. Nonetheless, it was shaped by those around him, particularly the aforementioned Praetorian prefect of Illyria, Vulcacius Rufinus, Constantius' and Constantina's senatorial kinsman by marriage. Rufinus knew that Vetranio's endorsement by a member of the imperial house would stabilize the general's position, as well as binding his soldiers' loyalties to the Constantinian dynasty that had conferred on him the position of Caesar. The selection of Constantina to play this legitimizing role is unsurprising, because at the time she was not only the most senior member of the Constantinian dynasty in the West, but also, as Constantius was by now unmarried, the most senior imperial woman in the whole empire.[36] Constantina therefore probably

---

[34] Zonaras, Epit. hist. 13.6.
[35] Constantina's proclamation of Vetranio: Philostorgius, Hist. eccl. 3.22; Passio Artemii 11; Chronicon Paschale 350 (Dindorf, p. 539). On the events: Harries (2012) 194–99; Maraval (2013) 88–92; Potter (2014) 462.
[36] This also explains Magnentius' petition to marry her, which was refused. See the discussion that follows.

traveled to the Balkans from Rome at Rufinus' behest early in 350 to provide an alleviating presence. She probably consented to this plan, because service to the dynasty was, after all, what she had been trained for.[37]

Picking up this service again after nearly fourteen years of widowhood, Constantina was also soon to become a bride once again, wed to a man more than five years her junior. Rufinus, as we shall see later, was playing a double game between Magnentius and Constantius. One of the Praetorian prefect's objectives had been to bolster his own family's position at court by carving an imperial role out of the chaos for his nephew Gallus, still in internal exile in Cappadocia.[38] Constantius duly recalled Gallus from his isolation at the imperial villa at Macellum, elevated him to Caesar, and arranged his marriage to Constantina. The wedding was held at Sirmium on March 15, 351, a city well used to imperial dynastic events, having witnessed the births of several imperial children, including Constantius himself.[39] Several reasons had persuaded Constantius to bring back his nephew into the imperial fold. Gallus reached the legal age of 25 in 350 or 351, so was less easily controlled starting then.[40] Constantius' first marriage had, moreover, not produced any living children. As the only male survivor among his brothers, he needed to showcase the strength of the dynasty and the availability of heirs. Magnentius had just made his own brother Caesar for the same reason. The Vetranio affair had also confirmed that ruling the empire from a single base was difficult, particularly since Constantius expected to be preoccupied with Magnentius for some time, as indeed proved to be the case. Gallus' marriage to Constantina also signaled Constantius' rejection of any deal with Magnentius who had asked for her hand in marriage as part of peace negotiations in 350 and been refused.[41]

The new couple initially stayed in Sirmium, while at nearby Mursa Constantius defeated Magnentius, who remained in control of all Western territories outside the Balkans. It was clear that Constantius had to press further West, thereby depriving the East of an imperial presence for a prolonged period. To act as cover, Gallus and Constantina were sent to Antioch,

---

[37] For Constantina's belief that she was acting in Constantius' interest, see Drinkwater (2000); Harries (2014) 197–98; as acting in her own interest: Bleckmann (1994); Maraval (2013) 91; Vanderspoel (2020) 79–80. Vetranio's "usurpation" as a ploy by Rufinus: Potter (2014) 462.
[38] Moser (2018) 179. Rufinus became Praetorian prefect in Gaul in 354, after the final defeat of Magnentius.
[39] See p. 118.
[40] Age of majority: Huebner, Ratzan (2009) 16–17.
[41] Petrus Patricius, frg. 16.

arriving in the autumn of 351 in the city where Helena had wintered more than two decades earlier. Here, Constantina gave birth to a daughter, whose name is not recorded. This girl was Helena's first posthumous and first great-grandchild since the birth of Crispus' children twenty years earlier.[42] In Antioch, Constantina therefore returned her body to the fulfilment of the traditional tasks assigned to imperial women.

It was also in the city on the Orontes that Constantina morphed into the proverbial woman of malign influence. In this guise, she left a mark in fourth-century historiography like no other Constantinian woman before, far exceeding the attention it had ever paid to Helena. Gallus was, by all accounts, an inexpert and cruel Caesar.[43] Some sources maintained that Constantina was complicit in Gallus' conduct, or even its main inspiration. If we are to believe the fourth-century historian Ammianus Marcellinus, for example, it was the bloodthirsty, greedy, and fire-starting Constantina who continuously incited her husband to ever more cruel acts, even interfering in the male business of imperial justice.[44] It is not easy to understand to what extent such assessments provide real insight into Constantina's character or actions, as they were primarily employed to pass judgments on the men in her life.[45] Nonetheless, the frequency of Constantina's appearance in a variety of specific stories concerning Gallus' judicial activity in Antioch suggests that criticism of her interference in her husband's business may, at least to some extent, have been grounded in fact.[46] Whether it was as brutal, ill-advised, and challenging to her own brother as portrayed is, however, debatable. Constantina did what everyone expected of a dutiful Roman wife: supporting her husband. Where Ammianus saw backroom scheming—as in his tale of a noble woman who asked Constantina for help by giving her a necklace—others would have seen an empress's daily routine of receiving the visits of women, which habitually included the exchange of gifts.[47] Even so, Constantina must have gone about such business in a way that was visible enough to disquiet some ancient commentators. Unlike her grandmother, she was certainly a woman not afraid of transgressing conventional boundaries of female

---

[42] Constantina's daughter: Julian, Epistula ad Athenienses 272 D.
[43] On Gallus in Antioch, Harries (2012) 198–99; Potter (2014) 464–66; Moser (2018) 180–83.
[44] Ammianus Marcellinus, 14.1, 7.4, 9.3, 11.22. Philostorgius, Hist. eccl. 3.28 maintains Constantina ensured the execution of officials sent by Constantius to check on Gallus. Passio Artemii 13 records the story of Constantius' officials' execution without mentioning Constantina; see also Zonaras, Epit. hist. 13.8–9.
[45] Wieber-Scariot (1999) 74–195.
[46] Leppin (2011) 185–202.
[47] Ammianus Marcellinus, 14.1.3. On empresses' audiences, see Chapter 6.

imperial behavior. Again unlike Helena, this confidence may have derived from her pedigree, seniority, and superior prestige to her husband. But it also drew on her political experiences that she had accrued in Rome in following Helena's model.

Constantina's confidence would perhaps in theory have been sufficient to save her husband's life. By 354, having finally defeated Magnentius, Constantius had enough of Gallus' mismanagement of the East and was growing suspicious he might be planning an usurpation. In an attempt of conventional peacemaking, Constantina traveled to court to plead for Gallus, but never reached her brother. She died on the way of a sudden fever while crossing the Anatolian peninsula, at Caeni Gallicani, an imperial post station in Bithynia. As such, she ended her life in the same region and environment in which her grandmother is believed to have begun hers. Gallus did not survive much longer. He was executed at Pola in Istria, just as his cousin Crispus had been many years before.[48] We do not know what became of the couple's daughter, Helena's great-grandchild.

Burying Empresses, One More Time

Constantina died in Bithynia, but was buried in Rome, next to her church foundation of St. Agnes.[49] The sacred complex on the Via Nomentana had been transformed since the late 340s, when Constantina had left it to return to court. Just off the southern end of the basilica's narthex, to the left of the church's entrance, now stood a circular mausoleum that still stands today, having been converted into the church of St. Costanza by the seventh century (see Fig. 10.2). Surrounded by an external marble portico and accessed through a vestibule, it featured a light-flooded and domed central space separated by a circle of columns from a darker ambulatory punctuated with fifteen niches. The interior of the mausoleum was (and in part still is) richly decorated with mosaics that depicted scenes from the Old and New Testaments in the focal areas of the dome, while the ambulatory's

---

[48] Ammianus Marcellinus, 14.11.6; Passio Artemii 14; Philostorgius, Hist. eccl. 4.1, Zonaras, Epit. hist. 13.9. Gallus' execution at Pola, like Crispus: Ammianus Marcellinus, 14.11.20–23.
[49] Ammianus Marcellinus, 21.1.5.

Fig. 10.3 Detail of the mosaic ceiling of the ambulatory, S. Costanza, Rome. Courtesy of MM @ Wikimedia, Creative Commons License (CC BY-SA 3.0).

vaults featured an array of geometrical, floral, and pastoral patterns typical of Roman funerary art (Fig. 10.3).[50]

This circular mausoleum replaced a triconch structure (a space with three apses) of petite size, which had been built already at the time of the basilica's original construction. The purpose of this earlier structure is not entirely clear, but it may have been intended already by Constantina as her future resting place.[51] Again, similarities with Helena's mausoleum on the Via Labicana can be noted, but here the relationship of the basilica to the mausoleum was very different from that of the complex at the Via Labicana. In the latter, the imperial mausoleum was clearly the focal point, whereas at the Via Nomentana the—initially very modest—imperial tomb was tucked away to the side of the church. Nor did it receive any separate endowment. The focus of this layout had moved away from imperial commemoration to the cult of

---

[50] On the architectural history of the mausoleum: Rasch, Arbeiter (2007); Johnson (2009) 139–56. Two central male and female bust portraits in the sections displaying vintaging putti have at times been identified as Constantina and Hannibalianus the Younger, but this is very unlikely.

[51] Stanley (1994) argues that the triconch may have contained Agnes' relics, but this has been refuted.

the martyr Agnes. On the Via Nomentana, Constantina had wanted her imperial burial to be subsumed into a larger funerary space that was orientated, as her poem made clear, toward the hope that all the faithful resting here would find salvation with Christ through Agnes' intercession and the celebration of the Eucharist.[52]

It was from the circular mausoleum that replaced the triconch structure that in the early modern period the two porphyry sarcophagi now at the Vatican Museums and at St. Peter's, respectively, were retrieved. The presence here of sarcophagi made from porphyry, a stone under exclusive imperial control, indicates that, despite the spiritual focus that Constantina had planned, the site's potential for dynastic imperial commemoration was not forgotten. The same is suggested by the rebuilding of the triconch on a more monumental scale. Although this rebuilding cannot be precisely dated, it is likely that it—and the commissioning of the corresponding sarcophagi—happened on Constantius' initiative, instigated by Constantina's death. The extant mausoleum's stunning "double-shell" architecture resembles several other imperial churches built or rebuilt by Constantius in the 350s, including the Anastasis at the Holy Sepulchre in Jerusalem.[53] The sarcophagus with the vintage scenes commonly believed to be Constantina's was one of a matching pair, with its counterpart sent to the Apostoleion in Constantinople, where in 360 Constantius' second wife Eusebia and then again a year later he himself would be buried.[54] Whatever Constantina had intended for her mausoleum, by the time of her death or very shortly afterward, it had been incorporated into a dynastic burial topography that bound together the two capitals.

It is striking that, following Constantina's example, Constantius also did not associate himself with the "imperial tombs" their father had built on the Via Labicana, where their grandmother already rested. This meant that, within a generation the focus of Constantinian dynastic commemoration in Rome had migrated across the city, from the Via Labicana to the Via Nomentana. This was partly due to the strength of Agnes' cult, the popularity of which Constantius may have personally witnessed during his famous visit

---

[52] Diefenbach (2007) 174.

[53] Kleinbauer (2006). Brubaker (1997) 59 speculates about Constantina's interest in the Holy Sepulchre design due to its connection with Helena, but this connection had not yet been made in the mid-fourth century; see Chapters 8 and 11. The Passio Agnetis et Emeritianae 16 maintains that Constantia had ordered the building of the mausoleum herself.

[54] Kelly (2003) 590. Again, the two may have been buried in one sarcophagus, perhaps this one. Only a fragment survives, with similar carvings as the one on the sarcophagus in the Vatican Museums [now in the Archaeological Museum in Istanbul inv. 806; see Bardill (2012), 183–87].

to Rome in 357. Beyond popular devotion, however, there was also an imperial context to this spatial shift in commemoration, revolving around who chose to remember what and where. It is revealing of his attitudes toward the Constantinian legacy in Rome that, when it came to stressing links to the old capital through female relatives, Constantius did not select his paternal grandmother, who was buried there, but his and his sisters' mother Fausta, who had been born there, as well as Fausta's mother Eutropia, his maternal grandmother. These relationships and the stellar ancestry they alluded to were extolled in a panegyric that his cousin Julian, who had become his Caesar in 355, composed for Constantius' visit to Rome in 357. Julian described Fausta here as "the daughter of one emperor, the wife of another, the sister of a third, and the mother not of one emperor, but of several." Whatever Fausta had done in the past, thirty years after her death it no longer affected her capacity to confer legitimacy. In the same panegyric, Julian also connected Constantius through his mother to Rome itself. Fausta's birth and childhood in the city, he argued, had turned Rome into Constantius' "mother and nurse." A few moments later Julian went so far as cite Fausta's and Theodora's mother Eutropia, Constantius' "grandmother . . . on the mother's side" as the source of his Eastern background.[55] Despite her unimpeachable connections both to Rome and the East, and to Constantius' father Constantine, Helena was not mentioned anywhere. Perhaps all of these references were Julian's choices, but, given the panegyric format, they must have been choices that Constantius was happy to hear.[56] By 357, the emperor had clearly given up on commemorating Helena as the "ancestress" of his line.

This remarkable development was perhaps attributable to continuing rumors about Helena's background, rumors that Julian, after he had fallen out with Constantius and usurped imperial power in 360, was equally happy to feed, painting Helena as his own father's wicked stepmother of low repute.[57] Constantius' mother Fausta may have been disgraced at some point, but at least she had the right pedigree. But in the specific context of Rome, another reason for Constantius to cover Helena with a blanket of silence and to

---

[55] Julian Or. 1.9B–C: τοῦ μὲν εἶναι παῖδα, γαμετὴν δὲ ἑτέρου, καὶ ἀδελφὴν ἄλλου, καὶ πολλῶν αὐτοκρατόρων, οὐχὶ δὲ ἑνὸς μητέρα; 1.5C–D: μήτηρ οὖσα σὴ καὶ τροφὸς and 6A: τὸν τοῦ μητροπάτορος τοῦ σοῦ προπέμψαι γάμον.

[56] The Constantinian brothers had already advertised descent from Maximian since the late 330s, although without mentioning their mother: ILS 730, 732.

[57] See Julian's *Letter to the Corinthians*, written from Naissus in 361, a fragment of which is preserved in Libanius, Or. 14.29–30; Tougher (2020) 193 n. 18. Julian's views on Helena can also be reconstructed from the writings of other pagan writers; see Chapter 1.

highlight Fausta and Eutropia, Maximianic women with strong connections to the city, was that in the mid-350s Rome was still full of his "Theodoran" and therefore also "Maximianic" relatives. This situation had to be handled with care, since it could turn very dangerous indeed, as Constantius had recently experienced.

During the usurpation of Magnentius, loyalties in Rome had fluctuated, but political action in the city—whether for or against Constantius—had often crystallized around the emperor's "Theodoran" aristocratic relatives.[58] Some of these relatives had, as we have seen, been early supporters of Constantius' cause, especially his wife's uncles Vulcacius Rufinus and Naeratius Cerealis, who became the emperor's first urban prefect after Magnentius lost control of the city in 352. The emperor's urban prefect in 353–355 and in 357–359, Memmius Vitrasius Orfitus, was a further member of this group. Orfitus was married to a Constantia, probably another product of one of Constantine's siblings' senatorial marriages.[59] However, another, less loyal "Theodoran" branch of the Constantinian dynasty, also based in Rome, became active in the months of uncertainty that followed Magnentius' usurpation. In January 351, another of the boys who had survived the massacre of 337, Constantine's nephew Julius Nepotianus, by now grown up, was proclaimed Augustus in Rome. He was supported by some senators as well as sections of the populace and was able to put together some sort of army, partly consisting of gladiators. Nepotianus' mother was Eutropia the Younger, Constantine's half-sister, who was not only of imperial descent, but also, as we have seen, well connected with Rome's aristocracy and emerging ecclesiastical establishment. Nepotianus' links therefore reached deep into vital urban institutions: the Senate, the clergy, and the entertainment industry.[60] Although Magnentius' master of offices Marcellinus suppressed his uprising within a month, this was not achieved without protracted guerrilla fighting in the streets of Rome, during which many died, including sundry nobles and Eutropia the Younger herself.[61]

---

[58] See also Humphries (2020) 165–71.
[59] PLRE I, Cerealis 2, 197–99; I Orfitus 3, 651–52. On Orfitus' wife, see Cameron (1996) 301.
[60] On Nepotianus' usurpation, see Ehling (2001). The uprising is usually dated to June 350, but Bleckmann (2003b) 46 n. 7 shows it took place in January 351, following the proclamation of Magnentius' brother Decentius as Caesar in Milan.
[61] Suppression within a month: Epitome de Caesaribus 42.3; Zosimus, Hist. nea 2.43.2–4, among others; street fighting: Aurelius Victor, Caes. 42.6–8. Death of nobles and Magnentius' proscription of aristocratic supporters: Eutropius, Brev. 10.11; John of Antioch frg. 200. Killing of Eutropia the Younger: Athanasius, Apologia ad Const. 4.

In 354, shortly after Constantius had finally defeated the usurper Magnentius, he dispatched his new wife Eusebia, whom he had probably married the year before, to Rome. Eusebia's host was the aforementioned urban prefect Orfitus, probably another "Theodoran" kinsman of the emperor, who organized a splendid official *adventus* for the empress.[62] Eusebia's visit foreshadowed her husband's grand trip to Rome in 357 during which he celebrated the defeat of Magnentius. But in 354, Constantius was detained by a military campaign on the Rhine. The fact that he sent his wife as a vanguard shows how crucial he considered an imperial presence in Rome to be at this time, not least because of the fraught situation left by the massacre of Nepotianus and his supporters. Even though Nepotianus had been his cousin, who had perhaps hoped that Constantius would choose him as an imperial partner in the West to counter the threat of Magnentius, at the time the emperor had considered him just another usurper, left him to face Magnentius on his own, and in this way condoned the ensuing bloodshed among his "Theodoran" relatives. In addition, Constantius had just executed Gallus, another relative of the "Theodoran" group in the capital or was about to do so. He clearly felt that he had to rebuild trust in Rome, and it must therefore have been Eusebia's brief to project harmony and peace after such a period of crisis. As we know, using an imperial woman for this purpose had precedent in the Constantinian family. Constantius' attempts to rewrite his facilitation of the massacre in Rome are also evident in another panegyric delivered by Julian in 358, where Magnentius was accused of having killed "almost all who were connected with the imperial family" in the city, even, shockingly, unprecedentedly, "women."[63]

Eusebia's presence in Rome to ease the aftermath of dynastic violence also provides the context for the burial in Rome of Constantina, widow of not only one, but two murdered "Theodoran" men, even though she had died far away in Bithynia and could more practically have been interred with her father in Constantinople.[64] For, given the date of her death, the empress Eusebia, the urban prefect Orfitus, and possibly Rome's new bishop Liberius must together have received the body of Constantina and organized her funeral on the Via Nomentana, thereby ceremonially affirming the unity of

---

[62] On the *adventus* Julian, Or. 3.129C and Chapter 6. On the date and Eusebia's person, PLRE I Eusebia, 300. She was the daughter of Fl. Eusebius, consul in 347.
[63] Julian, Or. 2.58C-D: φόνων τε ἀδίκων ἀνδρῶν καὶ γυναικῶν, πολλῶν μὲν ἰδιωτῶν, πάντων δὲ σχεδὸν ὁπόσοι τοῦ βασιλείου γένους.
[64] Moser (2018) 288.

the Constantinian dynasty. The dynastic meaning of Constantina's burial, in turn, explains another imperial funeral at the same site that occurred six years later. In late 360, Julian sent the corpse of his wife Helena, Constantius' younger sister, who had passed away during the year, to Rome, to be buried next to Constantina. The two had married in 355, shortly after Julian had been appointed Constantius' Caesar, taking his executed brother Gallus' place. Although Constantius was profoundly suspicious of his cousin, he had sent the pair to Gaul to provide an imperial presence in this troublesome province. Here, Julian had played ball for a while, distinguishing himself on the military front, until he confirmed his cousin's suspicions by usurping imperial power in February 360.[65]

Julian's decision to bury his wife in Rome, where the Senate was hostile to his usurpation, and in a Christian space, despite his well-known rejection of the faith he had inherited from his family, would be puzzling if it was not for the deep significance that the site on the Via Nomentana held for Constantius.[66] It was an opportunity for Julian to claim an imperial space recently fêted by Constantius, shortly after his usurpation and shortly after Constantius' own empress, Eusebia, had been buried in Constantinople. The dynastic nature of Helena the Younger's burial clearly comes across in the account of Ammianus, a profound admirer of Julian. Ammianus tells us that Julian dispatched Helena's body to Rome while he was celebrating his five-year anniversary (dated from his appointment as Caesar that was also the date of his marriage to Helena) by holding games in Vienne in southern Gaul. The Quintennalia and burial were therefore linked as two imperial occasions and Helena the Younger's coffin must have been escorted to Rome in a ceremonial procession. Ammianus also pointedly reminded his readers that Julian's late empress was now resting with her sister Constantina, formerly the wife of Gallus, Julian's brother. He deliberately failed to mention, on this occasion, that both were also Constantius' sisters, foregrounding their relations to Julian's side of the family.[67] Later, Ammianus suggested that Julian should have been buried in Rome, too, rather than at Tarsus where he finally came to rest.[68] In Ammianus' literary corner at least, the mausoleum on the

---

[65] On the background: Harries (2012) 296–317; Potter (2014) 470–72, 487–507.
[66] On the Senate's hostility, see Moser (2018) 310. For this reason, it can be doubted that Julian was behind the rebuilding of the mausoleum on the Via Nomentana, as suggested by Mackie (1997) due to its "dionysiac" decorations.
[67] Ammianus Marcellinus 21.1.5.
[68] Ammianus Marcellinus, 25.10.5. A late Byzantine source, Symeon Logothete, Chronicon 90.3 claims that Helena the Younger's body was later transferred to the Apostoleion in Constantinople, to rest with Julian whose own body had been brought here from Tarsus later in the fourth century.

Via Nomentana was a decidedly "Theodoran," or even "Julianist" place of memory.

Between the latest rapprochement of the two branches of the Constantinian family in the 350s and Julian's attempts to stir up divisions again in 360, Constantine's splendid commemorative complex on the Via Labicana, where Helena rested, lay disregarded. Although Helena had been the first Constantinian woman to visit Rome in order to rebuild relations after a falling-out with "Theodoran" relatives, setting a model first for Constantina, after the massacre of 337, and then for Eusebia, after the further massacre in 351 and Gallus' downfall in 354, the old Augusta was now seen as an obstacle to such endeavors, and considered to be best ignored or even vilified.

Countering Helena: Justina

Julian was correct when he claimed in his second panegyric on Constantius, delivered in 358, that not all, but only "almost all connected with the imperial family," had been killed during the suppression of Nepotianus' usurpation in early 351.[69] Apart from the "Theodoran" male in-laws who had wisely sided with Constantius, there was indeed a little girl among the survivors, called Justina. She was the daughter of Justus, a scion of the aristocratic Vettii family. The names of Justina's brothers, Cerealis and Constantianus, and her own later daughter, Galla the Younger, suggest Justina's mother was related both to the Constantinian family and to the Naeratii, the Roman family of Julius Constantius' first wife Galla and her brothers, Vulcacius Rufinus and Naeratius Cerealis (see the Family Tree). Perhaps her mother had been another daughter of Julius Constantius and Galla, or even the widow of Constantine II, who had returned to Rome after his death to marry into the senatorial aristocracy.[70] On account of this Constantinian heritage, even

---

[69] In fact, aristocratic descendants from Constantine's siblings' marriages into the Roman aristocracy are recorded in Rome until well into the fifth century; see ILCV 1758, 1759 and perhaps ILCV 66; Chausson (2007) 138–41.

[70] On Justina's ancestry, Rougé (1958); Chausson (2002) 135. The most detailed account of her life was provided by Chausson (2007) 97–187. On Justus, PLRE I Iustus 1, 490. Justina's Constantinian kinship is amply proven by her continuous desirability as an imperial bride, although it should be noted that it is seldom explicitly stated in late antique sources, apart from Themistius, Or. 3.43B, who calls hers a bastard and spurious dynastic line; see also Woods (2004) 325–27 (who argues Justina descended from Crispus, which can be excluded due to the nomenclature of her relatives). This silence is likely the result of active suppression given, first, Justina's descent from Theodora, and, second, her later reputation as an "Arian" empress; see the discussion that follows.

though only "Theodoran" in nature, the little girl Justina would become one of the most coveted imperial brides of the fourth century, providing her, eventually, with unprecedented visibility as the mother of a child emperor, Valentinian II. She would, however, also grow into one of the most maligned empresses of her time on account of her support for opponents to the Council of Nicaea, even more maligned than her earlier relative Constantina. Justina's representation in our sources reflects familiar anxieties—if on a much grander scale—about an empress's influence on Christian policy that we have already encountered with Helena's alleged role in the banishment of the bishop Eustathius of Antioch. Justina's portrait therefore echoed earlier literary techniques of transforming imperial women into religious schemers from which Helena's had already, briefly, suffered. At the same time, the full-blown depiction of Justina as an arch-heretic led to Helena decisively shedding this earlier reputation. To counter Justina's model, Helena's "Arian" past was forgotten and she was discovered as a significant figure and beacon of Christian orthodoxy from the Constantinian past.

To understand Justina's spheres of action that shaped her and eventually Helena's representation, we must begin by tracing her early life as a female member of the Constantinian dynasty. Justina survived the massacre in Rome because she either had been or was about to be married to the usurper Magnentius. How this marriage came about is rather obscure. It appears that Justina had not been Magnentius' first choice, unsurprisingly, as she was a Constantinian only through a secondary and female line. Justina's likely kinship with the Naeratii raises questions about the involvement in her marriage arrangements of the group supposedly loyal to Constantius, especially Vulcacius Rufinus and Naeratius Cerealis. As we have seen, Rufinus was behind the redirection of Vetranio's usurpation into support for Constantius, but Vetranio himself had also negotiated with Magnentius, to the extent that he and Magnentius had sent a common embassy to Constantius in the autumn of 350.[71] It was led by Vulcacius Rufinus, who therefore knew of or had perhaps even brokered their relationship, as a safety net for the eventuality that Magnentius would not be easily defeated. As explored earlier, Magnentius' delegates proposed double marriage plans to Constantius, between the emperor and Magnentius' daughter, and between Constantina

---

[71] Zonaras, Epit. hist. 13.7.18; Petrus Patricius, frg. 16.

and Magnentius himself.[72] Constantius refused, leaving Magnentius to hunt around for another Constantinian woman to boost his legitimacy. It is not inconceivable that it was Rufinus, aware of the rebuttal, who brought his relative Justina into the equation. Justina's father Justus may equally have acted on his own account, backing the man who now ruled the West, because, as was later reported, he dreamt of imperial descendants. Justus was in any case rewarded with the governorship of Picenum but paid a hefty price when Constantius had him executed, clearly holding him solely responsible for his daughter's shameful marriage.[73] However it came about, we can be sure that Justina's consent to this marriage was not sought, for she may only have been a few years old in 350.[74]

Justina's Constantinian pedigree also explains why she was not killed after the defeat of her husband Magnentius either. Like so many imperial women before her, her life was merely interrupted and, as in similar cases, took a turn away from the public eye, at first leaving little record. All we know is that she stayed in the orbit of the imperial court, doubtlessly so she could in time be used as a negotiating tool, like Constans' former bride Olympias, another orphan whose relatives had been killed by an emperor, leaving her financially dependent on the court. Her youth and gender meant that Justina still needed guardians, and these may well have been found among her maternal relatives at court. It seems that Justina turned into a lady-in-waiting, living in enforced celibacy, first for Eusebia and then for Constantius' last wife, Faustina, who was perhaps a relative of Constantius' urban prefect Memmius Vitrasius Orfitus.[75] But then she was inherited by another empress, of a different dynasty, who unwittingly returned her to the limelight.

The Constantinian dynasty had a remarkable ability to produce sons, but this ability also engendered deadly competition among its men. When Constantius died in 361, Julian was the only heir left who had descended through a male line. Two years later, he tragically died in battle at Samarra against the Persians, leaving the army and the Eastern frontier in disarray. Eventually, the reins of the empire were taken over by a new imperial college,

---

[72] On the embassy and Rufinus' role, Bleckmann (1994) 50–57, although he thinks that Magnentius was already married to Justina before his usurpation, which is unlikely, especially given Justina's very young age.

[73] Socrates, Hist. eccl. 4.31, including on Justus' dream. See PLRE I Iustus 1, 490 for dating Justus' governorship to Magnentius' rule in Italy, rather than Constantius' as claimed by Socrates. See also Rougé (1974).

[74] On Justina being underage in 350, John of Antioch, frg. 212. Chausson (2007) 161 argues she may have been born as late as 345.

[75] Chausson (2007) 112. John of Antioch, frg. 212 describes Justina as a celibate widow at this time.

comprising the former tribune Valentinian and his brother Valens. The new Augusti, who originally hailed from Pannonia, traveled to Naissus, where in Constantine's villa at Mediana they divided the empire between themselves. Valentinian took control of the Western empire including Illyricum, and Valens of the East. Their meeting place at Naissus was chosen, as it had been many times before, to underscore continuity from the Constantinian past.[76]

But such continuity from the Constantinian past was ensured by more than choice of venues, at least on Valentinian's side. He sought to tie his family more directly—and twice over—to the Constantinian house. This was in reaction to a bold attempt to usurp imperial power by Procopius, a maternal relative of Julian. Procopius had served in Julian's army and allegedly been appointed by the late emperor as his successor. It was also Procopius who had taken Julian's body back from Persia for burial in Tarsus, next to the tomb of Maximinus Daza, in accordance with Julian's instructions. Valentinian and Valens were sufficiently worried about him that they looked to have him arrested at this residence in Cappadocia, but he escaped. On September 28, 365, Procopius appeared in Constantinople, where loyalty to the Constantinian dynasty was strong, to assert his right to the throne. While Valens was away in Antioch, Procopius had himself proclaimed Augustus by soldiers stationed in the city in front of the Baths of Anastasia.

The choice of monument, named after Constantine's sister, was no coincidence. But Procopius did not confine himself to vague toponymic connections or rely purely on his cognate kinship links to Julian. He was able to brandish to an awed audience the empress Faustina, Constantius II's widow, and her 5-year-old daughter Constantia the Younger, and received the imperial "insignia" in their presence. Quite how Faustina and her daughter had ended up in his entourage is unclear. Constantius may have entrusted them to Julian upon his death when he confirmed him as Augustus. If this is true, Justina, who was probably also Julian's niece, must also have been part of this female group, particularly as we also find her brother Constantianus in Julian's service, as a military tribune and commander of the fleet on the Euphrates. Julian will have passed these women on to Procopius in the full knowledge that they needed protection from any new emperor outside the dynasty, but also conscious of the symbolic power they could confer. We are reminded of the attempted transfer of Galerius' widow Valeria to Licinius back in 311. Indeed, Procopius kept Faustina and Constantia the Younger

---

[76] Potter (2014) 505–9. Meeting in Naissus: Ammianus Marcellinus, 26.5.1–3.

about as talismans during his subsequent conflict with the Valentinians, even carrying mother and daughter onto the battlefield in a litter. Many soldiers and their officers, especially among the Gothic federate troops, fondly remembered Constantinian rule and chose to support Procopius as its legitimate heir. He quickly took control of the whole of Bithynia, Julian's home region.[77]

Eventually, it was not enough, for military supremacy still trumped dynastic legitimacy as a route to imperial succession. Procopius' uprising was suppressed. But Valentinian and Valens were sufficiently rattled by his ability to marshal the past and manipulate the present through Constantinian women to look to emulate it. Valens quickly reassociated the baths in Constantinople that had provided the setting for Procopius' usurpation with his own daughter, also called Anastasia.[78] Valentinian proceeded to an even more tried and trusted technique, by turning these women into "Valentinianic" ones. It helped that Procopius had not married any of them, or if he had, then that information was deliberately concealed. But marriage was now chosen as a way to harness their potential. The infant Constantia the Younger was betrothed to Valentinian's son Gratian, then 8 years old, eventually marrying him c. 372.[79] Meanwhile, Justina had joined Valentinian's court some time before, becoming a lady-in-waiting to Valentinian's wife Severa (sometimes also called Marina), just after Severa's son Gratian had been made Augustus, in 367. According to the fifth-century church historian Socrates, Severa described Justina's beauty to her husband after seeing her naked at the baths. Gripped by lust, the emperor decided to marry Justina, but, since he was a Christian, without divorcing Severa. To accomplish this, he allegedly drew up a law that allowed him to have two wives at once. No trace can be found of Valentinian's supposed legalization of bigamy. Instead, this story was a fabrication to make sense of Valentinian's remarriage to a woman who was by Socrates' time considered a heretic.[80]

---

[77] Lenski (2002) 97–104; McEvoy (2016) 159–63. Ammianus Marcellinus, 26.7.10: Baths of Anastasia; Procopius shows around Constantia; Faustina's presence when Procopius received imperial insignia. Ammianus Marcellinus, 26.9.3 for the litters on the battlefield. On Valeria, see Chapter 4. On Constantianus, PLRE I Constantianus 1, 221.

[78] Zosimus, Hist. nea 5.9.3.

[79] Ammianus Marcellinus, 29.6.7; she is recorded as married in 374, when she was 14, AE 1913, 227.

[80] Socrates, Hist. eccl. 4.31. Cf. Malalas, Chron. 13.31; Jordanes, Romana, 310–11; John of Nikiu, Chron. 82.9–14; Chronicon Paschale 369 (Dindorf, p. 559), who all report she was banished because of a property fraud. PLRE I Severa 2, 828; for interpretation, Barnes (1998) 123–26; Woods (2006). On fourth-century divorce law, see Arjava (1996) 177–80.

The story also shows that the decision of a Christian emperor to divorce and remarry, and to a widow to boot, caused great moralizing concern and a real risk to Valentinian's reputation. Constantine had outlawed unilateral divorce except in the case of the most egregious criminal behavior by the dismissed spouse. Even though Julian had relaxed this law, Christian attitudes toward divorce were still strict, as they were about the remarriage of widows. Linking himself to the Constantinian past at whatever cost must therefore have mattered a great deal to Valentinian, who was poorly networked with his leading military and administrative officials. His son Gratian felt the same. When his wife Constantia the Younger died in 383, he sent her for burial at the Apostoleion in Constantinople (where his father Valentinian then already lay), to assert his claim to this Constantinian space, in a striking parallel to Julian's dispatching of his wife Helena's body to Rome for burial.[81] The appropriation of both Constantia, Helena's granddaughter, and Justina, Theodora's great-granddaughter, reveals that whatever division between the "Helenian" and the "Theodoran" branch might still have existed a few years before, had evaporated for Valentinian. Any Constantinian woman was good enough.[82] Whatever Justina, and indeed Severa, felt about all this is unknown. But Justina's stepson Gratian apparently kept in touch with his mother's whereabouts, as Constantine had, and brought her back to his court after his father's death.[83] This is a striking parallel to Constantine's treatment of Helena.

In November 375, Valentinian I suddenly died of a stroke at Brigetio in Pannonia. At the time, Justina was living in the vicinity, at an imperial villa located further south near Sirmium, together with her 4-year-old son Valentinian and presumably also her daughters, Galla the Younger, Iusta, and Grata.[84] It is from this moment on that Justina becomes immensely visible in the written record, assuming a role that had not been available to any Constantinian woman before, that of mother of a child emperor. Although Valentinian left a brother Valens and a grown-up son Gratian, who were both Augusti, Valentinian's army in Pannonia now proclaimed Justina's nearby

---

[81] Chronicon Paschale 383 (Dindorf, p. 563). McEvoy (2016) 167–71. Constantia was the last member of a Western imperial family transferred to Constantinople.
[82] Valentinian may even have awarded Justina the title Augusta [see CJ 6.22.7 (371)], although the evidence is inconclusive. See Lenski (2002) 103 n. 214. Malalas, Chron. 13.31 records the title Augusta for Severa and Jordanes, Romana 314 for Valens' wife Domnica, respectively, but both may be anachronistic; see Holum (1982) 31 n. 91.
[83] Chronicon Paschale 378 (Dindorf, p. 560); Ammianus Marcellinus, 28.1.57.
[84] Ammianus Marcellinus, 30.10.4. The villa, unlocated, was called Murocincta.

infant son Valentinian as a third Augustus. This move seems to have been manipulated by Justina's brother Cerealis, who exploited the unwillingness of senior military officials in Illyria to submit to the authority of the adult Augusti Gratian and Valens. While this looks like a power grab, Justina and her family may also have been motivated by the knowledge—grounded in the memory of so much dynastic bloodshed in the preceding decades—that the offspring of an emperor's second relationship was exceedingly vulnerable. They may well have thought that being Augustus did not only confer power onto Valentinian but also provided safety for all of them.[85]

Valentinian II and his mother soon relocated from Sirmium to Milan, following the disastrous defeat of Valens by formerly allied Gothic troops at the battle of Adrianople in Thrace in 378 and Gratian's proclamation of the general Theodosius as Eastern Augustus in nearby Thessalonica in 379. In 383, Gratian was himself murdered by supporters of a new Western usurper, the general Magnus Maximus in Gaul, who may have been married to yet another descendant of Constantine, perhaps via Crispus.[86] The 12-year-old Valentinian thus became senior Augustus in perilous circumstances. To make matters worse, Valentinian, Justina, and their court now entered into a heated conflict with Milan's bishop Ambrose over the use of the city's churches for the court's large contingent of non-Nicene worshippers. This episode underscores how over the course of the fourth century the office of the bishop—especially if occupied by a man of Ambrose's background—had emerged as an important factor in imperial and urban politics, with consequences that extended to the role and representation of imperial women, and of the image of Helena.

Our understanding of the events in this so-called basilica conflict is distorted by our access to only Ambrose's side of it. In January 386, Valentinian II had passed a law that allowed non-Nicene Christians to worship in public. Since the time of Constantine, the theological debates about the relationship between God and Christ had intensified and had been acerbated by different emperors taking different sides. While Constantius II and Valens had supported opponents of Nicaea—with Constantius even sponsoring an anti-Nicene theological formula, the so-called Homoian creed of Rimini—the new

---

[85] Ammianus Marcellinus, 30.10.4; Philostorgius, Hist. eccl. 9.16, see also A7.46, 46a, 46b. Cf. Potter (2014) 530, who suggests Justina was "interested in exercising power in her own right."

[86] Liebeschuetz (2005) 11–12; McLynn (1994) 122. For Valentinian's proclamation, McEvoy (2013) 54–55. Magnus Maximus' wife, unnamed in contemporary sources (Sulpicius Severus, Dial. 2.6), was named as "Helena" in later Welsh legend; see Harbus (2002) 52–63.

Eastern Augustus Theodosius in 381 had outlawed all but Nicene Christians within cities. Valentinian II's law of 386 was in clear defiance of this order. For the celebration of Holy Week that year, Valentinian then commanded, not for the first time, that Ambrose release several Milanese churches to the bishop of the city's non-Nicene community, Auxentius. When Ambrose refused, Valentinian's soldiers occupied two churches and besieged a third. Eventually, the court backed down, partly because the usurper Magnus Maximus threatened to invade Italy in support of Ambrose.[87] Maximus invaded anyway in 387, forcing Valentinian and his family to flee and take refuge at Thessalonica. Here, they managed to persuade Theodosius, who had hitherto sought to maintain an equilibrium by accepting both Valentinian and Maximus as co-emperors, to take on the latter. According to the pagan historian Zosimus, it was Justina—alone among the courtiers at Thessalonica—who pleaded with Theodosius to intervene against Maximus in 387, even deploying her tearful daughter Galla the Younger. Galla was so young and beautiful that Theodosius, who had just been widowed, fell passionately in love with her and agreed to Justina's plan.[88] The story of the politically shrewd dowager empress and the love-struck Theodosius is romantic, but Justina again knew that what she was offering in the person of Galla was something that she had been taught was a guarantee of survival: a connection not only to Valentinian, but also to Constantinian heritage. For Theodosius, the ardent Nicene, this was attractive enough for him to disregard his bride's family's anti-Nicene sympathies.[89] Having married Galla, Theodosius defeated Magnus Maximus in 388 and restored Valentinian to power.

In Ambrose's account of the "basilica conflict," it is Justina who again assumes a larger-than-life quality. In criticizing Valentinian II's mother, the bishop of Milan redirected Athanasius' image of an emperor's mother as an adversary of churchmen from Helena to Justina, and in so doing decisively shaped the subsequent memory of empresses who crossed bishops. Whereas Helena's sparring with the "orthodox" Eustathius of Antioch back in the winter of 327–328 had left a subdued record in Nicene literature, in Ambrose's hands Justina became the quintessential "Arian," even though he gives few details of what she actually did. In a letter to his sister Marcellina,

---

[87] The conflict is described in Ambrose, Epp. 75, 75a, and 76. The law passed is CTh 16.1.4 (386). For chronology, I follow Liebeschuetz (2011) 124–28; see for a possible topography, Lenox-Conyngham (1982).
[88] Zosimus, Hist. nea 4.43.1–3, 4.44.1–4.
[89] On Theodosius' motivations: Holum (1982) 43–46; Busch (2015) 36.

a consecrated virgin in the Roman church, clearly intended for wider consumption, Ambrose paints Justina, "that woman," as his persecutor. She was like Eve who led men astray, like Jezebel who had persecuted Elijah, like Herodias who had demanded the head of John the Baptist. Ambrose also referenced Jezebel in a sermon he preached during this period.[90]

Although Ambrose's framing of Justina as an "Arian" was a slur, the bishop could draw on acknowledged ideas of her religious sentiments. Justina probably had been brought up at Constantius' non-Nicene court, so it would hardly be surprising if she considered the Homoian creed of Rimini to be orthodoxy. Homoian Christianity was also strongly favored in Sirmium, where Justina had been residing. Indeed, its Homoian community had approached her for support during a coup led by none other than Ambrose of Milan to ordain a Nicene, Anemius, as bishop in 378.[91] Ambrose's biographer Paulinus described Justina's intervention in the episcopal election in Sirmium as the first clash between empress and bishop, ahead of the major one in Milan a few years later.

Even so, it is highly unlikely that Justina was the main driver of religious policy, or any policy, at her son Valentinian's court.[92] The "basilica conflict" was a high-risk strategy. Under no circumstances would the powerful men at Valentinian's court—including the Frankish *magister militum* Bauto—have allowed an empress's personal beliefs to dictate such events without good cause, even if we might imagine that she had strong feelings on the matter. But there were many good reasons for the court to want to establish places of Homoian worship in Milan. Since Magnus Maximus controlled the majority of the Western army, Valentinian relied on the recruitment of Gothic allied forces, many of whom were non-Nicene. Ambrose caricatured these as Justina's followers, who were accustomed to living "in wagons," but they were, first of all, Valentinian's soldiers, even if some of them may have formed Justina's bodyguard. The civil population in Milan also included many

---

[90] Ambrose, Ep. 76.12: *femina ista*, 18; Ep. 75a.17. Justina's negative religious influence on her son is also mentioned in Ep. 53.2 to Theodosius after Valentinian's death. Later commentators on the "basilica conflict" eagerly lap up the story about Justina's influence: Paulinus of Milan, Vita Ambrosii 12; Rufinus, Hist. eccl. 11.15–16; Socrates, Hist. eccl. 5.11; Sozomen, Hist. eccl. 7.13; Gaudentius of Brescia, Serm. praef. 5. Note that Socrates and Sozomen place the events before the murder of Gratian. In Theodoret, Hist. eccl. 5.13 Justina appears, but stays more in the background as Valentinian's "Arian" teacher.

[91] On Homoians in Illyricum, Lenski (2002) 234–42. On the Nicene coup in Sirmium Paulinus of Milan, Vita Ambrosii 11; McLynn (1994) 97. Sulpicius Severus' claim that Justina (called "Arriana") prevented the holy man Martin from seeing Valentinian seems a fabrication in hindsight of the "basilica conflict" (Dial. 2.5).

[92] McEvoy (2013) 9–12, 125.

non-Nicene Christians, partly due to an influx of refugees from the Danubian regions after the battle of Adrianople, but also because the Milanese church had been presided over by a Homoian bishop for almost two decades before Ambrose assumed control. Valentinian's residence city was therefore hardly the stronghold of Nicene beliefs that Ambrose made it out to be, and the young emperor was in desperate need of connecting with loyal audiences on an urban ceremonial stage outside the palace.[93]

Ambrose's focus on Justina as a patron of Homoian groups in Milan was therefore only partially true but offered him a way to divert attention from these wider political considerations. It reduced the conflict to a timeless if unspecific battle between an irrational woman and a holy man, in the manner already attempted by Athanasius with regard to Helena and other imperial women in his *History of the Arians*. This heightened Ambrose's own status as a latter-day prophet, but also allowed him to make comments on other men, especially his adversary, the non-Nicene bishop Auxentius, who had chosen to attach himself to female impurity. It also, cautiously, exonerated the emperor himself from responsibility, while at the same time delineating clear boundaries between church and state, and bishop and court that, in Milan, were in very close physical proximity.[94]

Still, the construction of Justina as an evil and heretical empress also created serious problems for Ambrose. With Theodosius' reinstallation of Valentinian in the West, the court at Milan was here to stay, and with it imperial women. Justina by that time had passed away, and Valentinian soon followed, dying in mysterious circumstances in 392.[95] Theodosius again had to intervene in the West, suppressing the ensuing usurpation of Valentinian's master of offices Eugenius through his victory at the famous battle of the Frigidus. Shortly before his death, in 395, Theodosius then installed his own 9-year-old son Honorius as Augustus of the West in Milan, under the guardianship of the *magister militum* Stilicho and his wife, Theodosius' niece and adopted daughter Serena.

Although this superficially established an entirely new dynasty, many connections to the old regime remained. Theodosius was wed to Justina's daughter Galla the Younger, the mother of his daughter Galla Placidia, and

---

[93] McLynn (1994) 170–74; Maier (1994); Humphries (2000) 132; Dirschlmayer (2015) 73–74.
[94] This stands in contrast to later church historians, who give Valentinian a greater role in the conflict, undoubtedly, to distinguish between the Valentinian and Theodosian dynasties; see Washington (2015) 184.
[95] For the date of Justina's death, see PLRE I, Iustina, 489. For Valentinian's mysterious death and the installment of Honorius, see McEvoy (2013) 96–97, 136–37.

his older son Arcadius would soon be married to Bauto's daughter Eudoxia. Valentinian's other sisters, Iusta and Grata, meanwhile remained in residence at the court in Milan.[96] More importantly, Ambrose would have known that it was only a matter of time until a new empress-consort for Honorius arrived in the city. The bishop of Milan was well aware that this world of Theodosian women needed a better role model than the "Arian" schemer he had recently caricatured. This is how Helena at last returned as a new model empress.

---

[96] For Eudoxia's background, Busch (2015) 60. For Iusta and Grata in Milan: Ambrose, ob. Val. 2.35–38.

11
New Model Empress

On February 25, 395, the third Sunday of Lent, members of the imperial court, the clergy, the civic community, and the emperor Theodosius' and the defeated usurper Eugenius' armies assembled to hear Ambrose of Milan speak. The occasion was a service led by the bishop to commemorate Theodosius' death of dropsy on January 17. Now, after a forty-day wake, Ambrose, who had perhaps been appointed as the eulogist by the dying emperor himself, recited a funeral oration.[1] This oration contains our first fully extant record of someone praising Helena since the days of Eusebius of Caesarea, and only the second incident of a late antique author presenting her as the legendary finder of relics of the True Cross.

Despite Ambrose's praise, the emergence of Helena as an exemplary Christian empress would take a meandering route throughout the fifth and sixth centuries. Sometimes, following Helena's example was empowering for imperial women of this period, especially when it occurred in connection with church founding and travel. However, Helena's integration into imperial ceremonial—from echoes of her coin image in imperial iconography to the appearance of her name in imperial acclamations—also imposed on empresses certain expectations of behavior. These expectations were concerned above all with the empress's role as half of an imperial pair, complementing the emperor as a new Constantine. Helena's potential to serve as a more independent model of and for female behavior was only realized outside the empire, particularly at the hands of two remarkable women, Radegund of Poitiers and her biographer, the nun Baudonivia.

Ambrose's Helena

Ambrose began his funeral oration for Theodosius on a legal note, reminding those present that Theodosius had died without much to leave his two sons

---

[1] See McLynn (1994) 357–60; Liebeschuetz (2005) 174–203; McEvoy (2013) 145–47.

Helena Augusta. Julia Hillner, Oxford University Press. © Oxford University Press 2023.
DOI: 10.1093/oso/9780190875299.003.0012

Arcadius and Honorius—because he had already given them everything during his lifetime: "the empire, his power, the name of Augustus" (De ob. Th. 5: *regnum, potestatem, nomen Augusti*). His last will simply placed them under the protection of "a relative," whom Ambrose leaves unnamed, but who can only be Theodosius' supreme military commander Stilicho. This was of course, as Ambrose says, because the new emperors were underage, especially the infant Honorius, whom the bishop had asked to assist him at the altar. But, as Ambrose reminded the soldiers in the audience, it was their faith that would "perfect" Honorius' age (De ob. Th. 6: *fides militum imperatoris perfecta est aetas*).

For, Ambrose continued, it was not just worldly goods that Theodosius had left his sons. His was also an "inheritance of faith" (De ob. Th. 9: *haereditas fidei*), which had secured him victory at the battle of the Frigidus, uniting the warring armies. Ambrose moved next to itemizing Theodosius' achievements and virtues, a conventional element of funerary speeches, but here constructed around the exegesis of Psalm 114: "I have loved because the Lord has heard the voice of my prayer." Ambrose's oration, of course, doubled as a sermon, part of a Christian service in which this psalm had been read.[2] Theodosius' virtues accordingly were mercy (especially for the supporters of Eugenius), humility, and a willingness to repent. All of these qualities may have been unusual in an emperor, but secured him entry into heaven, in Ambrose's account a decidedly royal space. There, Theodosius encountered his former co-Augustus, Gratian, his "fellow in mercy" (De ob. Th. 39: *misericordiae suae consortio*), his own father, his wife Flaccilla, his two children who had predeceased him, Pulcheria and Gratian, and, finally, Constantine. It was from Constantine that Theodosius, and other subsequent emperors, had received the "inheritance of faith" that Theodosius now passed onto his sons (De ob. Th. 40: *haereditatem fidei principibus dereliquit*), fulfilling the prophecy of Zechariah: "on that day will be holy to the Lord what is upon the horse's bridle" (Zech. 14:20: *In illo die erit, quod super frenum equi, sanctum Domino*).

It is at this point that Helena makes her entry, taking the audience on a trip that filled about a fifth of Ambrose's speech (De ob. Th. 41–51). Here, Helena emerges as nothing less than the founder of the Christian empire, through her discovery of the signs of the Lord's Passion, the wood and nails of the True Cross. Whatever had brought the historical Helena to the East in

---

[2] Lunn-Rockliffe (2008) 197.

the first place, in Ambrose's account her visit is confined to the Holy Land, where she had hurried in order to "search for the manger of the Lord" and to "scrutinize the site of the Lord's passion" (*scrutata est locum Dominicae passionis... praesepe domini requisivit*). Inspired by the Holy Spirit, and after an impassioned speech against the devil who had hidden the sacred objects, she began to dig, quickly revealing three crosses. From her gospel reading she knew, according to Ambrose, that the True Cross would bear an inscription, purely so it could be identified by posterity, as Helena duly did. Not yet satisfied, she went on to search for the nails. No further detail is given of how she found them. Instead, Ambrose dwells on what Helena did with the nails: from one she had a bridle made (*frenum*), the other she incorporated into a diadem (*diadema*). She sent these to Constantine, who "used them both and transmitted his faith to subsequent kings" (*Utroque usus est Constantinus, et fidem transmisit ad posteros reges*). Thus was Zechariah's prophecy fulfilled and persecution ended.

Ambrose's digression away from his subject, Theodosius, to the accomplishments of an entirely different character, and a woman, was peculiar for a funerary speech. Yet, the excursus' message, in essence an exegesis of Zech. 14:20, tallies exactly with the wider points Ambrose was making about hereditary Christian rule and the importance of imperial humility.[3] Legitimacy flowed through the succession of Christian emperors, from the first who had ended the persecutions to the child standing at the altar. It was passed on through their faith—orthodox, of course—and embodied in the holy objects that emperors protected, and that in turn protected the empire. It was, however, not in the conversion of an emperor that this legitimacy had its origin, but from the quest of a humble woman "who preferred to be esteemed as dung in order to win Christ" (De ob. Th. 32: *quae maluit aestimari stercora, ut Christum lucrifaceret*). In this way was the "arrogance" (*insolentia*) of pagan emperors, those who "did not have a holy thing upon their bridle" defeated (*quibus non fuit sanctum super frenum*; De ob. Th. 50).

Despite her prominence, it is not Helena who is the protagonist here. Ambrose takes effort to let us know that, as a woman (*ut mulier*), she would usually have been hesitant, but that she was filled with the Holy Spirit to do her duty, to aid her son, the empire, and therefore humankind, like the Virgin

---

[3] Borgehammar (1991) 60–66; Drijvers (1992a) 109–13; Bojcov (2009). It has also been suggested that the excursus was a later addition inserted by Ambrose upon publication of the speech; see, first, Favez (1932). For the debate, see Drijvers (1992a) 109–10.

Mary had been. And Ambrose's Helena was not a church founder. Ambrose makes no mention of any church founded in the Holy Land, nor is he particularly interested in the wood of the cross. His attention is on the nails, which "rule the entire globe" (*qui totum regit orbem*), and what Helena did with them so that they came to sit on the emperor's head and the reins of his horse.[4] This is because his audience's attention was on the dead emperor in front of them, and his living son, who either was wearing or would wear a diadem, just like Honorius (so Ambrose implied) would one day ride his horse into battle at the head of the army that was now listening. It is usually assumed that Ambrose delivered his funeral oration in the cathedral of Milan. It is more likely, however, that the service was held at one of the churches outside the city, where the soldiers could assemble outside. From here, as Ambrose tells us, Theodosius' body would be dispatched for burial in Constantinople immediately after the service had ended (De ob. Th. 54–55). The plan was for Honorius to escort his father for some of the way, so his horse, or rather pony, may well have been waiting outside, too.[5]

It was therefore the precariousness of the situation, with a child inheriting the Western empire as well as a defeated army in the fraught aftermath of a civil war, and the materiality of imperial ceremonial, in which well-known physical objects played a significant role, which combine to explain Ambrose's Helena excursus. It is possible that these objects really contained relics that were believed to be pieces of the cross, but this is a moot point.[6] Ambrose described them as such in order to concentrate everyone's minds on what was at stake at this moment in time: pull the diadem from Honorius' head, or the reins from his horse, and the Christian empire would crumble. The physical shape of these imperial trappings helped to foster the impression of sacrality. Since the later years of Constantine's reign, the emperor's diadem had featured a row of jewels, either pearls or rosettes made of larger stones, on a metal band. This is exactly what Ambrose described when he claimed that Constantine's diadem was "inlaid with jewels, which are connected by the even more precious jewel of divine redemption embedded in the iron."[7] Equestrian ornaments, likewise, included bejeweled breastplates or

---

[4] Koenen (1996) 174–75.

[5] See Bojcov (2009) 32–33 who argues the service was held at the basilica Palatina, later S. Lorenzo, although the basilica Prophetarum (S. Dionigi) is also a possibility, as it was situated on the road to Aquileia and the East. On the presence of actual objects, see also Borgehammar (1991) 60–64.

[6] On the possibility that Honorius' diadem contained a cross relic, see Sordi (1993) (for), Koenen (1996) (against).

[7] Ambrose, De ob. Th. 47: *misit . . . diadema gemmis insignitum quas pretiosior ferro innexa crucis redemptionis divinae gemma conecteret*. Ambrose seems to imply the nail was inserted into the metal

headbands that could be connected easily with the nail that Helena had allegedly intended "for the decoration" of the emperor's horse.[8] Ambrose depersonalized imperial rule, locating its power in the cross's nails, but at the same time personalized it anew, because Honorius (a humble child protected by the Holy Spirit) had inherited it and wore the nails.

Even though Helena was therefore merely a tool in his argument, it is unlikely that Ambrose would have invoked her had her story been completely unfamiliar to his audience. Instead, it seems clear that he expected them to have conflicting information and views about her. As we shall see, stories of her relic finds in the Holy Land, including the nails she had allegedly sent to Constantine, were already in circulation at this time, especially in the East.[9] His audience also seems to have known about Helena's infamous, even distasteful origins, which was information perhaps particularly likely to be current at an imperial court of which descendants of Theodora were still members. Right at the start of his excursus, Ambrose confronted this problem head-on and turned it into a virtue (De ob. Th. 42). Yes, Helena's background was in hospitality, and yes, this was where Constantine's father had met her, resulting in a relationship that may not have been entirely legitimate. Ambrose initially keeps it open that such stories were mere gossip ("they say," *asserunt*). But he soon takes them as fact (implying that he thought them true) and grounds them, as we have seen, in biblical images of good "inn-keeping."[10] Helena was born into dung, but raised to royalty through Christ (*illam Christus de stercore levavit ad regnum*). She was therefore, just like the Virgin Mary, a useful figure for Ambrose "to think with" about the workings of the Holy Spirit through a humble woman, who was "pious," not "arrogant" (De ob. Th. 48: *non insolentia ista, sed pietas est*), even though mother of a supreme being.

Ambrose's main worry following Theodosius' death was the loyalty of fickle soldiers to a new child emperor. He was also concerned, however, about the complicated makeup of the imperial court, and the role of women

---

band. There is no evidence, however, that Constantine's or Honorius' diadem has survived as the so-called iron crown now in Monza.

[8] Ambrose, De ob. Th. 47: *ad decorem*. It was only by the sixth century that the nail was believed to be in the bit of the emperor's horse; see Bojcov (2009) 63. For the decoration of the fourth-century emperor's horse, see, for example, the Missorium of Kerch, Hermitage, St. Petersburg.

[9] On Ambrose's audience's knowledge of Helena, Georgiou (2013) 604. On her legend, see the discussion that follows.

[10] See Chapter 1.

within it.[11] Ambrose is rather vague about Stilicho's claim that he had been appointed guardian to Honorius, let alone his older brother Arcadius.[12] Perhaps he had doubts about Stilicho's intentions. Stilicho was married to Serena, Theodosius' niece, who must herself have been present at the service, together with Theodosius' 3-year-old daughter Galla Placidia.[13] As well as acting as a surrogate mother to Honorius, Serena was also the biological mother of Stilicho's son Eucherius. Placidia, born of Theodosius' marriage to Galla the Younger, was the last surviving imperial descendant of the Valentinian and Constantinian dynasties. Both women therefore carried a potential threat to Honorius' rule, for different reasons: Serena because she was ideally placed to push the interests of her own offspring, and Placidia because her dynastic potential could give hope to suitors. In time, it was easy to imagine that her cousin Eucherius would be among the latter.[14]

Ambrose may therefore have hoped that the image of the pious Helena would resonate with these women, too (or would be instilled over time in the toddler Placidia), although decidedly not in relation to imperial legitimacy. Helena is not among those whom Theodosius meets in heaven, whereas his first wife, Honorius' mother Flaccilla, a "soul faithful to God" (*fidelis anima Deo*), pointedly is. Although Helena was the mother of an emperor, Ambrose does not mention either that she was Augusta, or the powers that Constantine had conferred on her according to Eusebius of Caesarea, and, as we shall see, later authors. Instead, Ambrose made it clear from the outset that Helena was "a mighty woman" because "she gave something that was greater than anything she could receive from the emperor" (*Magna femina . . . multo amplius . . . quod imperatori conferret quam quod ab imperatore acciperet*; De ob. Th. 41). Rather than pursuing her own interests, she worked tirelessly for the good of the Christian empire: "How fortunate was Constantine with such a mother!" (*Beatus Constantinus tali parente!*). This was the lesson Ambrose's Helena was supposed to impart to the imperial women of his time.[15]

It is hard to imagine that Ambrose was not also thinking of another recently deceased emperor here, Valentinian II, who, by Ambrose's own

---

[11] Georgiou (2013) 605–8 argues that Ambrose addressed Serena, Stilicho's wife, specifically but does not consider the danger of suggesting an imperial mother as model to a woman who should not be one. On this problem, see Bojcov (2009) 9.

[12] McEvoy (2013) 142–44.

[13] For Placidia's birthdate, estimated between 388 and 392, see Busch (2015) 86 n. 3 and 87 for her presence in Milan.

[14] In fact, this is what Stilicho and Serena seem to have planned only a few years later; see McEvoy (2013) 161.

[15] Angelova (2015) 251.

reckoning, had not been so fortunate in his mother Justina, the grandmother of the infant Placidia. Justina's daughter and Placidia's mother Galla the Younger, while also deceased, is also strikingly absent from the relatives with whom Ambrose's Theodosius is so joyously reunited in heaven, even though Theodosius' dead son Gratian, whom he does meet, had been Galla's, too (see the Family Tree).[16] Galla the Younger's erasure may be due to her dubious religious credentials and because Christians frowned on second marriages, but for Ambrose she was also an unwanted distraction from the lineage that ran to Honorius. Even so, Justina herself did make an oblique appearance in Theodosius' funeral oration, specifically within its Helena excursus. Ambrose lambasted "Arians" for diminishing Christ's power, even though "emperors carry the nail of his cross on their diadem." Their behavior, he said, was even worse than that of the Jews, who at least recognized this power, even if they had tried to hide it. The unfavorable comparison between Arians and Jews picked up on a theme already prevalent in Ambrose's writings about the "basilica conflict," where Justina had appeared as the leader of such "Arians."[17]

This narrative power of the contrast between Justina and Helena implied in the funeral oration occurred to Ambrose again when he came to assemble his writings for publication a few years later. Although it was not a letter, he famously included the funeral oration for Theodosius in his epistolary collection, finding a special place for it, as the penultimate document in its last book, and therefore the entire work. What is more, he inserted the oration between the letters detailing the so-called basilica conflict and the letter to his sister Marcellina about his own discovery, on June 17, 386, of the relics of the martyrs Gervasius and Protasius, which concludes the collection.[18] He had found these martyrs, hitherto unknown, shortly after the basilica conflict near the tombs of Milan's more well-known martyrs Felix and Nabor and then translated their remains into his brand-new basilica, later known as Ambrosiana (today's S. Ambrogio).

---

[16] On Ambrose's difficult relationship with Justina, see Chapter 10. She was also largely absent from the funeral oration Ambrose gave on the death of her son Valentinian, bar a brief mention in the context of his mission to Magnus Maximus; see Ambrose, De ob. Val. 28.

[17] Ambrose, De ob. Th. 49: *Clavum crucis eius diademati suo praeferunt imperatores, et Ariani postatem eius imminuunt?*; compare with Ep. 75a.31. Of course, many of the soldiers present may have been Homoians, but they would have hardly recognized themselves as "Arians," let alone heretics, and it is unlikely that Ambrose wanted to draw attention to them. On Goths, Gothic soldiers, and the term *Arianism*, see Schäferdiek (2014).

[18] This order of the documents appears in all manuscripts and is therefore considered to have been Ambrose's own choice; see Liebeschuetz (2005) 176. On the "basilica conflict," see Chapter 10.

The funeral oration's curious positioning within the letter collection has been explained by its "mirror-of-princes" quality that fits well with the overarching theme of the last book, the Christian emperor. Helena's discovery of the relics of the Passion lending authority to emperors also neatly led to the next and last letter, on Ambrose's own discovery of relics, that underscored his authority as bishop.[19] But Ambrose's relic-find was also closely connected to the "basilica-conflict" that had just taken place in the spring of the very same year. The relics' authenticity and the legality of their translation had at that time been questioned by members of the imperial court, including, apparently, Justina. Such doubts had given Ambrose another opportunity to rail against "Arians" worse than Jews, as detailed in his letter to Marcellina about his discovery.[20] His letter, and the collection as a whole, end with this standoff, leaving the matter unresolved. We know from other sources, however, that the court backed down. As the eyewitness Augustine of Hippo tells us, God had interfered not only "to repress the fury of a woman, but of an empress." Despite this, he adds, Justina did not turn to the "soundness of believing."[21] This unsettled score may have been only one factor among several that encouraged Ambrose to insert the funeral oration with the Helena excursus between his accounts of the "basilica conflict" proper and of the discovery of relics. But it must have given him great satisfaction to highlight in this way the example of an imperial mother, Helena, who did believe.[22]

Helena's name would not recur in an imperial context again until nearly sixty years after Ambrose's speech. It is therefore not easy to assert any direct influence of Ambrose's image of Helena on the actual or expected behavior of imperial women of his and the next generation. Nonetheless, it is clear from his oration that it had taken the advent of a new, Theodosian, dynasty, to render Helena newly attractive on the imperial stage. We can also trace her renewed appeal in Theodosian self-representation, although initially only in the appearance of empresses, which harked back to Constantinian women in general.

---

[19] Liebeschuetz (2005) 107 n. 7, 177.

[20] Ambrose, Ep. 77.18. The identity of the "Arians" here as members of the imperial court is confirmed by Paulinus of Milan, Vita Ambrosii 15.2. McLynn (1994) 209–19 expertly reconstructs events and the imperial mood.

[21] Augustine, Conf. 9.7: *ad coercendam rabiem femineam, sed regiam . . . inde illius inimicae animus etsi ad credendi sanitatem non applicatus.*

[22] More mysterious is Ambrose's involvement of a basilica Faustae, adjacent to the Ambrosiana (Ep. 77.2), in this story. On the basilica Faustae, see also Chapter 6.

Reviving Helena's Look: Flaccilla and Thermantia

When, on January 19, 379, Gratian had appointed Theodosius as Augustus with authority over the East, the new emperor, born in Spain and Latin-speaking, faced a situation not dissimilar from that which had confronted Constantine in the twilight months of 324. Theodosius was an unfamiliar face to his new subjects and poorly networked with Eastern elites, who were also in the grip of entrenched sectarian conflict. To deal with this situation, Theodosius employed methods that echoed some of Constantine's or were designed to look as if they did. Constantine had left behind a mixed legacy in terms of his religious policies, but his memory commanded enormous respect, especially in the East. Theodosius duly promoted Constantinople as his imperial residence where Valens had preferred Antioch. He gladly agreed to receive the body of Gratian's widow Constantia the Younger, Constantine's granddaughter, for burial in the Apostoleion in late 383, as it offered a ceremonial occasion on which he could associate himself with the first Christian emperor in his own city. He also—allegedly in the tradition of Constantine—fervently embraced Nicene Christianity, enshrining the Nicene creed in imperial law and calling an ecumenical council to Constantinople in 381, where the bishops fell dutifully into line.[23] The stabilization of religious unity, in turn, did much to restore Constantine's image as the founder of Nicene Christianity. But in terms of dynastic self-representation in the Constantinian vein, Theodosius' most striking act was to award his wife Flaccilla the title of Augusta, probably in the same ceremony in which he elevated their 5-year-old son Arcadius to Augustus, held at Hebdomon just outside Constantinople on his own *dies imperii* in 383. Afterward, Theodosius began issuing coins with Flaccilla's portrait, in both bronze and gold, and from all the Eastern mints.[24]

The parallel with how Constantine had treated his women in 324 is palpable. Although Helena and Fausta had not been the last imperial women to be presented as Augustae—for at least Theodora had been after 337—they were clearly the point of reference, as women who had received the title in

---

[23] On Theodosius' problems and his solutions, and Theodosius' fondness for "Constantinian" self-advertisement, Leppin (2003) 54–86, 231. On the meaning of Constantia's burial for Theodosius, McEvoy (2016) 171.

[24] RIC IX, Alexandria 17, Antioch 43, 54, 61–62, 64, Constantinople 48, 49, 55, 61, 72, 76, 81–82, Cyzikus 24, Heraclea 13, 17, 23, 25, Nicomedia 36, 42–43, Siscia 34–35, Thessalonica 46–47. On the elevation, Holum (1982) 29–30; Busch (2015) 29.

Fig. 11.1 Gold solidus showing Aelia Flaccilla Augusta, with pearled diadem and forehead jewel, shoulder brooch and *paludamentum* on the obverse; Victory inscribing the Christogram onto a shield and caption *salus reipublicae* on the reverse (RIC IX Constantinople 48). Courtesy of the American Numismatic Society.

their lifetimes and not, like Theodora, posthumously.[25] Like Galerius and Constantine, Theodosius tried to signal the beginning of a new era, in doing so breaking, once again, the unspoken rules of the imperial college against singling out individual dynastic lines in this way.[26] His actions confirmed the pattern that, in the fourth century, an emperor's need to boost his credentials in relation to fellow or rival emperors was the main reason for turning imperial women into Augustae.

Nonetheless, Theodosius also put his own unique stamp on this kind of propaganda. The coinage he minted for Flaccilla curiously merged some of the features that Constantine had assigned to Helena and Fausta, while also departing from them in others. As in the case of Fausta, the captions of Flaccilla's coins stressed that she guaranteed the "Welfare of the State" (*salus reipublicae*), a concept clearly linked to her fertility and motherhood of imperial heirs. Flaccilla's appearance, however, assumed a much more official character than either Helena's or Fausta's had done (Fig. 11.1). Like Helena and sometimes Fausta, she was depicted wearing a diadem. But whereas the earlier women's hair ornament had been feminine decoration, Flaccilla's

---

[25] In addition to Theodora, Julian's wife Helena the Younger may also have been made Augusta posthumously; see Vida (2014) 171–77.

[26] Flaccilla's Augusta title was, tellingly, ignored by Theodosius' co-emperor Gratian.

more closely resembled that of the emperor, a row of pearls or jewels tied with ribbons at the back, and a large jewel on the forehead, set on a hairstyle more reminiscent of third-century empresses' reverse plait. This diadem was a natural consequence of the growing awareness that the empress's jewelry imparted majesty, as we have already seen in the case of Helena the Younger, whose jewelry had played a role in her husband's Julian's usurpation.[27] What is more, Flaccilla was shown enrobed in the (in real-life purple) emperor's military mantle, the *paludamentum*, fastened on one shoulder with a bejeweled brooch. She was also usually paired with a personification of Victory, hitherto a supremely male attribute. This was now accompanied, as on Theodosius' own coins, by a Christogram, another allusion to Constantinian tradition, but hitherto seen only on coins with portraits of men. While Constantinian coins had stressed gender difference, Theodosian coins therefore assimilated imperial men and women, thereby elevating the status of the empress.[28] To be sure, both Helena and Fausta had somewhat signaled the way here. Helena had already been paired with an allegory usually connected to the emperor's military might, the "Security of the State," while Fausta's coin portrait had sometimes sported the *trabea triumphalis*. But this was not yet comparable with the *koinonia* ("partnership") of the emperor and empress invoked in Theodosian ideas of rulership. The Theodosian empress was not just decorated; she bore her own insignia, which were passed on when she died.[29] These concepts were now sometimes projected back onto Helena, too.[30]

It was therefore more Constantinian iconographic practice, in general, that shaped Flaccilla's image, rather than Helena's own specific coin portrait. This is not surprising, for Helena's role in Constantine's material self-advertisement had been exceptional, dictated by her son's need to define his dynastic line within the larger Constantinian family. Theodosius' goal was the more traditional one of projecting dynastic hope for the future, and therefore focused mostly on his wife and her fertility. Theodosius' mother Thermantia, a Spanish aristocrat, did not appear on his coinage and was not

---

[27] Note also that Ambrose (De ob. Val. 2.37) is adamant that Valentinian II's sisters had not been given jewelry, which reflects rising anxiety about female imperial jewelry's legitimizing imperial authority. On Helena the Younger's jewelry, see Chapter 9.

[28] Holum (1982) 33–34; Brubaker, Tobler (2000) 578–79; Schade (2003) 56.

[29] This is stressed by Gregory of Nyssa in the funeral oration for Flaccilla, In Flaccillam 486–87; see Busch (2015) 34.

[30] Sulpicius Severus and Paulinus projected the idea back to Helena in the Holy Land; see pp. 204–205. On Theodosian *koinonia*: Busch (2015) 27; Angelova (2015) 183–84; it is also referenced by Themistius, Or. 19.288a.

awarded the Augusta title, an omission entirely in accordance with custom. It is notable, however, that a statue of Thermantia was erected posthumously in Rome in the Forum area, probably on the occasion of Theodosius' visit to the city in 389. On the accompanying inscription, she was styled as "nobilissima femina," a title that Fausta, Helena, and Constantia had all carried before her. She was also styled as mother of the Augustus and grandmother of the Caesars, as Helena had been in Rome, and as "enhancing the divine stock," like Constantina before.[31] As in the case of Flaccilla's coinage, this was an amalgamation of features associated with various Constantinian women. It also served a specific purpose for a specific audience, namely the representation of the Theodosian dynasty to the aristocracy of Rome. In the Western empire it was vividly remembered that Theodosius' father, Theodosius the Elder, had been executed for treason in 376. The inscription on Thermantia's statue contested this by pointedly referring to her husband as "divine" (*divus*).[32] The statue was itself probably part of a dynastic group that included Theodosius the Elder, commissioned to erase this stain on the memory of Theodosius' dynasty. Thermantia's primary role here was therefore that of a wife, a feature almost absent from Helena's epigraphy, especially in Rome. Once again, therefore, Constantinian framing was adapted to make a dynastic point peculiar to the Theodosian family. It may have been chosen by the man who erected the statue, the urban prefect Albinus, who must have been familiar with Constantinian epigraphic conventions in Rome. Even so, it must have pleased the emperor to be set within a Constantinian tradition. Theodosius himself continued to apply this tradition elsewhere, by naming palaces in Constantinople after his wife Flaccilla and his daughter Placidia, a custom instigated by Diocletian in Nicomedia and carried on by Constantine for his mother in Constantinople. And eventually, of course, Theodosius married a descendant of the Constantinian dynasty, Galla, the mother of the same Placidia.[33]

---

[31] On the title *nobilissima femina*, see pp. 99–100; on the wording of Helena's and Constantina's inscriptions, pp. 197–199 and p. 279.
[32] CIL 6.36960. On the demise of Theodosius the Elder, see Leppin (2003) 32.
[33] Notitia Urbis Constantinopolitanae Regio I and Regio XI; statues of Flaccilla were also erected at the Senate in Constantinople and in (at least) Ephesus, Aphrodisias, and Antioch; see Schade (2003) 234. For Constantine naming a palace after his mother in Constantinople, see p. 260.

Reviving Helena in Action

Whereas Helena made only implicit appearances in material dynastic trappings, her memory was more directly referenced in discourses emerging during the Theodosian age around the ideal behavior of the empress. Eventually, this gave her a much clearer exemplary profile. When Flaccilla died in 386, her funeral oration was delivered by Gregory, the bishop of Nyssa, who had been one of the main Nicene protagonists at the recent Council of Constantinople.[34] Gregory developed a programmatic image for the orthodox Theodosian empress, one that Flaccilla had, of course, fulfilled, but also one against which later empresses would be measured.[35] In many ways, and unsurprisingly, it resonated with Theodosius' strategies in presenting Flaccilla. She had been a loving wife, who had left behind her sons to be "pillars" (*éreisma*) of the empire, and she had shared not only her husband's life, but also his "kingship" (*basileía*) and "authority" (*archḗ*).[36] She also had many of the qualities customarily associated with the good imperial wife: modesty, accessibility, and a mitigating influence on her husband in matters of justice.[37] But when it came to her Christian virtues, Gregory took a leaf out of Eusebius of Caesarea's book. Like Helena as depicted in the excursus in the *Life of Constantine*, Flaccilla had been supremely pious, but, above all, humble and personally charitable. She had visited her subjects and the oppressed, freed prisoners, fed the hungry, clothed the poor. In this way she was "a column of the church, an ornament of the altars, the wealth of the poor, the blessed right hand and the refuge of the oppressed."[38] And, like Eusebius' Helena, she received her reward for these virtues already in this life, when, like Ambrose's Helena, she rose through humility to greatness.[39]

Gregory seems to have been aware of Eusebius' praise of Helena, or, as Eusebius had perhaps been, of her own funeral oration.[40] Gregory, however,

---

[34] He had also held the funeral oration on Theodosia's small daughter Pulcheria, who had died a few months before. See Busch (2015) 27–30.

[35] Holum (1982) 24.

[36] Gregory of Nyssa, In Flaccillam 478.20–479.1; 488.7–9; 488.7; 488.19. Flaccilla's love for justice was also mentioned by the pagan Themistius, Or. 18.225b–c

[37] Gregory of Nyssa, In Flaccillam 479.2.

[38] Gregory of Nyssa, In Flaccillam 480, 15–23: ὁ τῆς ἐκκλησίας στῦλος, ὁ τῶν θυσιαστηρίων κόσμος, ὁ τῶν πενομένων πλοῦτος, ἡ πολυαρκὴς δεξιά, ὁ κοινὸς τῶν καταπονουμένων λιμήν. Flaccilla gives food and clothes to the poor: 487.13–17, frees prisoners: 487.13–17.

[39] Gregory of Nyssa, In Flaccillam 499.12–14: ἡ μὲν ἀρετῆς ἄθλον εἶχε τὸν τῆς οἰκουμένης προτεταγμένον . . . διὰ τῆς προσκαίρου ταπεινοφροσύνης τὸ ἀληθινὸν ὕψος ἐμπορευσαμένη. For Eusebius, see Vita Constantini 3.43.

[40] Holum (1982) 23, 26; Drijvers (1993) 86; McEvoy (2021) 118, 123 note the similarities.

both universalized and narrowed down Helena's example. The historical Helena had traversed a landscape in the aftermath of civil war under exceptional circumstances. Although Eusebius did his best to extract a general message from her actions, it is clear that they had been aimed at mitigating Constantine's new Christian subjects' recent experiences of "persecution." Helena's had therefore been an exceptional form of charity. Gregory's Flaccilla was presented instead as an empress for whom Christian charity was a quotidian duty and an integral part of her role, in accordance with the gospel maxim that the poor, the prisoners, and the oppressed were the "body of Christ" (Matthew 25:36). In addition, Flaccilla's sphere of action was very much focused on the city of Constantinople whose inhabitants were Gregory's enthralled listeners: the urban poor, the holy virgins, orphans, and clerics whom he imagined as the primary mourners among his audience.[41] Flaccilla was an empress who had not only cared for communities throughout the empire, as Helena had done, but especially for the city in which the imperial court had finally come to a halt. This underscored the new dynasty's special link to their new imperial capital where they presented themselves as God's humble delegates on earth.[42] Piety and humility, expressed among other ways by a willingness to mingle with the crowd—as Helena had in the Holy Land—as well as the care for the destitute and sick would remain the hallmarks of Theodosian imperial women.[43]

Like Ambrose's Helena, Gregory's Flaccilla was not, however, a church patron. This kind of activity had clearly not yet entered the Christian empress's catalog of virtues, despite Helena's example as detailed by Eusebius, and Constantina's somewhat idiosyncratic replication of it. Imperial church building was on the whole still the emperor's domain, as Eusebius had himself also intimated in reference to Helena's foundations in the Holy Land. Still, a change already came with the next generation of Theodosian women. Arcadius' wife Eudoxia (d. 404) was the first imperial woman since Constantina who is known to have founded a church, in the city of Gaza in

---

[41] Gregory of Nyssa, In Flaccillam 480.24–481.2. It should be noted that Flaccilla's piety was also referenced in honors she received in the provinces; see, for Aphrodisias, ILS 9466, and, for Ephesus, AE 1966, 434.

[42] Dirschlmayer (2015) 113. For the special link between the Theodosian dynasty and "urban" Christianity, especially in Constantinople, see also Pfeilschifter (2014) 41–54.

[43] On Helena walking, see Chapter 8. Eudoxia was praised by John Chrysostom for taking off her insignia to walk in a Christian procession (John Chrysostom, Homiliae dictae postquam reliquiae martyrum 2.2). Galla Placidia joins the crowd welcoming the holy man Germanus to Ravenna: Constantius of Lyon, Vita Germani 7.35. On imperial women looking after the poor, for example, Pulcheria: Sozomen, Hist. eccl. 9.1.10.

Palestine. She had been approached by the local bishop, Porphyrius, to secure the emperor's consent to the closure of pagan temples. To seek access to the emperor through an imperial woman was, as we have seen many times, not an unusual or illegitimate thing to do. The novelty was that, after persuading the emperor to destroy the pagan shrines, Eudoxia proceeded personally to finance the building of a church on top of the Temple of Jupiter, as well as endowing it with holy vessels and a guesthouse.[44]

There are several reasons why empresses suddenly reemerged as church founders, and at first in Palestine. In Eudoxia's case, it may have again been significant that she had independent financial means acquired from her birth family. Like Constantina, she may have jumped at the chance to monumentalize her piety and thereby her name (the church was called Eudoxiana).[45] More importantly, the official and public conceptualization of the empress as a Christian patron with a specific concern for urban populations that had emerged with Flaccilla opened new, legitimate spaces of agency for imperial women. This agency was furthered by the progressive "de-militarization" of imperial rule during the Theodosian period, which grounded imperial legitimacy not only in military victory, but also in supreme piety and charity, virtues that could be manifested by imperial men and women alike. But it was women in particular, since they operated outside the traditional government sphere who came to embody these new imperial qualities. The provision of spaces for worship, with annexes for charitable purposes, reflected this special bond between imperial power and God, but was also an expression of imperial reverence for their subjects as fellow Christians.[46]

Another development gave this role and form of self-representation of specifically imperial women a significant boost. This was the increased circulation of legendary stories about Helena, as mother of the first Christian emperor and as founder of one of the most important sites of the Christian empire, the Holy Sepulchre in Jerusalem, erected on the site where she had discovered the True Cross. Eudoxia's church in Gaza, completed in 407, was suggestively cross-shaped.[47]

---

[44] Mark the Deacon, Vita Porphyrii, 36, 41, 53, 75; Busch (2015) 66–68; Holum (1982) 54–56. It should be noted that Serena had already decorated a church in Milan at this point: CIL 5.6250 (S. Nazaro).

[45] Eudoxia's father was the Frankish general Bauto, who had died in 388, after which she came under the guardianship of the *magister militum* Promotus. Her wedding preparations involved the exchange of gifts: Zosimus, Hist. nea 5.3.

[46] Busch (2015) 218–19.

[47] Angelova (2015) 223–24.

A few years before Ambrose's funeral oration for Theodosius, another bishop had already written about Helena's trip to the Holy Land. Around the time of Gregory of Nyssa's funeral oration for Flaccilla, Gelasius of Caesarea, a nephew of Bishop Cyril of Jerusalem, composed a continuation of the church history of his famous predecessor Eusebius, taking up the narrative from 324, when Eusebius' work had ended, up to his own day. This extended church history now survives only in fragments incorporated into later works, but we know that it included the story of Helena's discovery of the True Cross. Where Ambrose's version is the first complete written record of this alleged episode, Gelasius' fragment is the earliest. From what we can reconstruct of his account, Gelasius claimed that a vision inspired Helena to visit Jerusalem to search for the cross. In her quest she was assisted by the bishop of Jerusalem, Macarius. It was Macarius who performed a healing miracle on a sick woman in order to identify the True Cross among the three that had been found. Helena, for her part, put the pieces of the cross into a silver box, fashioned a helmet for Constantine and a bridle for his horse out of the nails, founded the church of the Holy Sepulchre over the place where the relics had been unearthed, and summoned the holy virgins of Jerusalem to a banquet, ministering to them herself.[48]

Even though Gelasius was its first chronicler, he was not the inventor of Helena's discovery of the cross either. In fact, even as Helena's currency had been declining on the imperial stage around the mid-fourth century, in Palestine it had been steadily growing in conjunction with the rising importance of Holy Land pilgrimages and the liturgy of the church of Jerusalem where the cross relic had been found in the days of Constantine. By the 380s, the celebration of the "invention of the cross" was firmly integrated into Jerusalem's church calendar during the feast of the Holy Sepulchre's consecration (the eight-day long *encaenia* that culminated on September 14). Cross relics were also shown to the faithful in a silver reliquary on Good Friday. Many individuals, especially in the Eastern Mediterranean, also kept pieces of the cross as personal devotional items, such as Macrina, the sister of Gregory of Nyssa, who wore one as part of her necklace.[49] Christian pilgrimage had become brisk business in Palestine, and it is hardly surprising

---

[48] Gelasius, Hist. eccl. frg. 20. On his version of the Helena legend, see Drijvers (1992a) 96–98. Gelasius' text was written, at the latest, in 386.

[49] Drijvers (1992a) 81–93. On Macrina: Gregory of Nyssa, Vita Macrinae 30. Pieces of the cross as part of jewelry are also reported for Antioch by John Chrysostom, Contra Iudaeos et Gentiles 10, for men and women; and by Jerome, Commentarii in Matthaeum 4, for women.

that stories began to circulate revolving around one of the most sacred of the objects that pilgrims came to see, touch, and ideally even take home a piece of. Local recollections of the empress who had come in pomp to Jerusalem around the time the relics of the cross had first appeared were surely no less appealing in this context, and eventually allowed Helena's own memory to burst back onto the imperial stage.[50] The intrusion of holy virgins into the story of Helena's discovery of the cross may indicate that female convents in the city were particularly instrumental in its dissemination. Many of these had sprung up on the Mount of Olives since Helena's foundation of a church there, and some of their members, like the monastic founder Melania the Elder, owned their own pieces of the cross.[51] By the time Gelasius was writing in the mid-380s, a written version of this legend perhaps already existed that the Jerusalem clergy could read out during the *encaenia*.

Since many pilgrims to the Holy Land belonged to the highest levels of the elite, this legend must have reached hearers, and female hearers, at the Theodosian court. One possible route of transmission was through the Lady Salvina, who had married Flaccilla's nephew Nebridius around 392. Salvina came from a prominent Berber family in Mauretania Caesariensis and her grandparents may already have owned a relic of the True Cross in the mid-fourth century.[52] Another courtier who would have known the story was Poemenia, the lady who had undertaken a lengthy journey to Egypt and Palestine *c.* 384 through 392. She was perhaps also a member of the Theodosian dynasty, since she was "famous by lineage and by wealth" and able to draw on travel passes and local hospitality. She built a church on the summit of the Mount of Olives at the place from which Christ was believed to have ascended into heaven. This church, perhaps as Poemenia herself intended, quickly became associated with Helena, even though the empress's own foundation had been located further down the hill. Like Silvia, a slightly later female visitor and the sister-in-law of Theodosius' Eastern Praetorian

---

[50] See Heid (1989) for the local origins of the Helena legend; also Hunt (1982) 39–40; Borgehammar (1991) 57–60; Drijvers (1992a) 139–40. Stories without Helena circulated, too: see John Chrysostom, Homiliae LXXXVIII in Iohannem 85.1; and the curious Protonike legend, preserved in the Doctrina Addia, the foundation text of the church of Edessa, which attributed the discovery of the cross to a legendary wife of emperor Claudius; see Drijvers (1997) 288–315. From Edessa also originated the story that Helena had been born here; see Chapter 1.

[51] Melania the Elder received the relic from John, the bishop of Jerusalem: Paulinus of Nola, Ep. 31. Helena was later believed to have founded one of these monasteries herself, Suda s.v. Hestiades.

[52] CIL 8.9255: a dedicatory inscription of a Christian basilica founded by Flavius Nuvel and his wife Monnica or Nonnica to house their relic of the True Cross in Rusguniae. See Moderand (1998) 31–34.

prefect, Poemenia was also in touch with Melania the Elder, the founder of a monastery on the Mount of Olives. Melania, for her part, shortly after meeting these women, traveled to Italy with a cross relic and the Helena story in her luggage. There, she gifted a piece of the cross to her friends, the ascetics Paulinus and Therasia of Nola, and also told them the story of Helena, which Paulinus passed on to further friends in Gaul, the Christian scholar Sulpicius Severus and his mother-in-law.[53]

It is impossible for us to tell which version of the legend Theodosian women heard or knew, of which there were several in circulation by now. As we have seen, Ambrose adapted his source material to his agenda, which was, uniquely, to highlight the role of the nails in the foundation of the Christian Roman empire.[54] Gelasius of Caesarea's version, on the other hand, predictably foregrounded the story's local and ecclesiastical elements: the discovery of the wood, Bishop Macarius' miracle, the founding of the Holy Sepulchre, and Jerusalem's holy virgins. Gelasius' church history was a narrative of Nicene triumphalism. His aim was to bind the Holy Land's sacred sites, objects, and people to the empire in an indissoluble and orthodox union that resonated with Theodosian ideas of Christian imperial rulership.[55] The Nicene church historians who followed his lead in the first half of the fifth century each included the Helena passage, too, while also making their own modifications to it.[56] During the fifth century the legend also evolved in other directions, and particularly into the one that would become known as the *Inventio Crucis*, which lent it a fiercely anti-Jewish tone, picking up on Eusebius of Caesarea's claim that Constantine had built the "New Jerusalem." Here, Helena rounded up all the Jews of Judaea and submitted them to repeated questioning regarding the whereabouts of the cross, until she found a knowledgeable one. She had this man, Judas, imprisoned for seven days, after which he obligingly revealed the hiding place and converted, taking the

---

[53] On Silvia and Poemenia, Hunt (1982) 159–63. On Poemenia's church, see Chapter 8. The quote about Poemenia is from John Rufus, Life of Peter the Iberian 43. Melania's trip to Italy, dated to 400, and the further circulation of the relics and stories she offered to Paulinus: Paulinus of Nola, Ep. 31.

[54] Ambrose's spotlight on the nails is unique and he is also the only one who mentioned a diadem (rather than a helmet) as the reliquary. For discussion on which version of the story Ambrose may have heard, see Drijvers (1992a) 109–11, 123–24.

[55] Winkelmann (1966); Drijvers (1992a) 131. Where Eusebius may still have hesitated to promote the see of Jerusalem in this way (see Chapter 8), Cyril of Jerusalem's nephew Gelasius had no problem with such a strategy.

[56] For references, see p. 233, n. 94. For example, Socrates and Ps.-Gelasius claim that a piece of the cross's wood was enclosed in Constantine's column in Constantinople, while Sozomen is the only one who does not attribute the Holy Sepulchre to Helena, but to Constantine. On the church historians' different versions, Drijvers (1992a) 99–107.

name Cyriacus and becoming bishop of Jerusalem.[57] But whatever direction they took, all these stories stressed Helena's agency and power, describing her as far more independent, spiritually and politically, than she had ever been in real life.[58] This reflected the increased visibility and authority of Roman empresses of their time, while simultaneously enhancing it further.

However, the Nicene church historians, at least, also took pains to inject a note of warning into their narrative. Their versions of Helena's story were invariably followed, only a few chapters later and usually in the same book, by the sobering tale of Constantine's sister Constantia who had allegedly facilitated the intrusion of an "Arian" presbyter, and therefore heresy, into the imperial household, and then by the appalling example of the "Arian" Justina.[59] As Ambrose had similarly pointed out, the unpredictability of womanhood meant that good and bad empresses, or the same empress behaving well and badly, were always in close proximity. The presence of female fickleness could threaten to throw the entire Nicene project off the rails, especially if the authority of bishops was not respected. Outside the tradition of ecclesiastical history, even Helena herself was not entirely immune from such considerations. In another fifth-century text, the so-called *Actus Silvestri* detailing the life and deeds of the Roman bishop Silvester, Helena appears as a delaying factor in the story of Christian salvation. Here, Helena is depicted as a Jewish convert who tries to win Constantine over to Judaism. Luckily (according to the *Actus*), the emperor has the sagacity to arrange a debate between twelve Jewish elders and Silvester, at the conclusion of which everyone present, the erratic Helena included, converted to Christianity.[60] Due to the power of the

---

[57] The *Inventio Crucis* story was already known to (but dismissed by) Sozomen, Hist. eccl. 2.1. On this Helena legend, later the most popular one in medieval Europe (also known as Judas Cyriacus legend), see Drijvers (1992a) 165–85, who places its origins in early-fifth-century Syria; Heid (1989) sees it in Jerusalem. See also Drijvers (2011) 159–67 for further developments of the legend in Syriac.

[58] Georgiou (2013) 614–16. The church historians each had their "favourite" empress: for Socrates, it was Eudocia; for Sozomen, it was Pulcheria; for Theodoret, Flaccilla.

[59] Rufinus, Hist. eccl. 10.7–8 (Helena), 10.12 (Constantia), 11.15 (Justina); Socrates, Hist. eccl. 1.17, 1.25, 5.11; Sozomen, Hist. eccl. 2.1–2, 2.27, 8.13; Theodoret, Hist. eccl. 1.17, 2.2, 5.13; Ps.-Gelasius of Cyzikus, Hist. eccl. 3.6–7, 3.13. Ps.-Gelasius believed Helena and Constantia were mother and daughter and that Constantia's misstep resulted from her inconsolable state after the loss of her deeply pious mother. On the origins of Constantia's supposedly "Arian" credentials, see Chapter 8, and on what the church historians made of it, Hillner (2019a).

[60] On the *Actus Silvestri*, see Canella (2013). The *Actus*' earliest version survives in Latin, but the story circulated widely in Greek and Syriac also and may have Eastern origins. Some manuscripts contain the story of the discovery of the True Cross (the Judas Cyriacus legend), but only in an appendix. The *Actus Silvestri* seem to have been known to Zosimus who, of course< also suspected Helena of interfering in the Fausta affair; another stain on the empress's reputation. Helena's Jewishness may stem from her confusion with Helena of Adiabene who had visited Jerusalem in the first century and alleviated a famine there, as described by Eusebius, Hist. eccl. 2.12.

True Cross story (not mentioned in the original *Actus*), the Nicene church historians ignored such suspicions, and also the allegations that at one time Helena had herself tried to undermine the Nicene project itself, by ensuring the banishment of a bishop, Eustathius of Antioch.[61] For them, such danger was now firmly located in the person of the sinister Constantia, widow of a pagan emperor, depicted as having laid the groundwork for "Arian" empresses to follow, including the hated Justina.

Emulating Helena: Galla Placidia and Eudocia

The Constantinian past therefore continued to furnish a variety of examples of appropriate and inappropriate female imperial comportment. From an imperial perspective, it was important for Theodosian empresses to be seen as engaging with the positive traditions allegedly begun by Helena. This was especially so because they themselves often acquired a reputation for meddling in religious affairs, or, worse, for being new Jezebels with a penchant for persecuting orthodox bishops.[62] Two roughly contemporary imperial women who stand out as particular embodiments of these expectations are the Western Augusta Galla Placidia (421–450), the mother of Valentinian III, and her Eastern counterpart, Aelia Eudocia (423–460), the wife of Theodosius II (see the Family Tree). In both cases, their engagement with the memory of Helena came in response to crisis and helped the imperial center to project a message of political unity and religious righteousness. At the same time, while it is always difficult to assess how much say imperial women had in their own representation, it is also clear that in these two cases each woman associated her actions with Helena in order to bolster her own profile, taking advantage of specific political circumstances. While one did so in full conformity with the imperial center, the other found independence in the model of Helena.

We previously met Placidia as a toddler at the funeral of her father Theodosius, where she had undoubtedly been exhibited because she was the last dynastic link between the Theodosian and Valentinianic houses, as well as the last imperial descendant of the Constantinian family. This link became crucial again several decades later. In the meantime, Placidia had spent

---

[61] See Chapter 8.
[62] On the Jezebel slur, see Stebnicka (2012).

turbulent years. After having been taken captive during the sack of Rome by the Goths in 410 and then married off to their king Athaulf, she had returned as a widow to Honorius' court only to be forced to marry his leading general and later co-Augustus Constantius III. After the latter's death and a falling out with her brother, she went into exile in Constantinople with her two children, Honoria and Valentinian. While she was there, Honorius died and the Roman Senate proclaimed an outsider, the civil servant John, as emperor. After some deliberation, Theodosius II, the Eastern emperor and the son of Eudoxia and Arcadius, intervened to remove John and installed his cousin Valentinian III as the rightful heir to the Western throne. In October 425, the 6-year-old Valentinian was proclaimed Augustus in Rome and Theodosius II confirmed Placidia's title of Augusta, which Honorius had awarded her in 421, but at that time without acknowledgment from the East.[63]

During this ceremony in Rome and the rebuilding of relationships with Italian elites that followed, the long imperial pedigree that Placidia had passed down to her son was a particular asset, as neither Valentinian III nor his father Constantius had been "born into the purple."[64] This imbalance increased Placidia's status, importance, and agency, especially in comparison to that of her grandmother Justina, another mother of a child emperor, but whose small son had enjoyed paternal imperial heritage.[65] Allusion back to the Constantinian past—and hence imperial and Christian orthodox legitimacy—were made not only through an emphasis on what were in reality indirect bloodlines, however, but also through the exhibition of public behavior. Placidia was by no means a passive transmitter of dynastic legitimacy, but fully grasped the importance of a Christian public relations campaign that would stabilize her son's reign. Again unlike her grandmother Justina, she was lucky to find bishops who were willing to help upon her return to Italy in 425. Placidia became an avid church patron, especially in Ravenna during the episcopacy of Peter Chrysologus, where the imperial court mostly resided. In this context, Placidia associated herself closely with the True Cross, to which one of the churches she founded in Ravenna was dedicated. It was flanked by a cross-shaped chapel, the so-called Mausoleum

---

[63] McEvoy (2013) 274 on the importance of Rome. Busch (2015) 93, 96 on Placidia's title.

[64] McEvoy (2013) 139; Busch (2015) 99. It is notable that it was recorded that Constantius III's birthplace was Naissus (Olympiodorus, Frg. 39), which together with his name may have been meant to boost his profile. Placidia's triple lineage (Constantinian, Valentinian, Theodosian) was displayed on a mosaic in the church of St. John in Ravenna that she founded: CIL 11.276 = ILS 818 = ILCV 20; Dirschlmayer (2015) 92–93.

[65] On the difference between Placidia and Justina, see also Sivan (2011) 113–14.

of Galla Placidia that still survives, which she may originally have intended for her own burial or for that of her older son Theodosius, who had died as a child.[66]

But Placidia also turned her attention to Rome, Helena's Italian base. Here, she did not build, but revisited the spaces of her ancestors, embellishing some of the churches, the origins of which were believed to date back to Constantine's time. In Rome Galla Placidia also associated herself directly with Helena, with whom she shared imperial motherhood.[67] When her son Valentinian was crowned in Rome in 425, Placidia may have made a formal visit to the church at the Sessorian Palace, where Helena had resided, later commemorated on the so-called Pola Casket, a carved ivory reliquary produced in Rome c. 440.[68] The Sessorian Palace may have already been Placidia's home when she had spent time in Rome during her youth, and it was certainly one of the imperial residences in use in the 440s when Valentinian's court visited the city more frequently to benefit from Rome's special symbolic importance amidst the crumbling imperial world of the mid-fifth century.[69] Placidia therefore had ample opportunity to absorb memories of Helena at this site. She did her best to update them, too, in order to link the fraught present to the recent and rather more glorious Christian past. Toponyms of palace buildings referencing Helena started to appear for the first time during this period. Galla Placidia also embellished a chapel connected with the church situated within the grounds of the palace, possibly by adding a mosaic showing Helena with the cross (Map 5, n. 12). This chapel, behind the church's apse, may already have been believed to house a relic of the cross, deposited here by Constantine, or indeed it perhaps even did. But it was only in the inscription that Placidia had affixed to the adornments she had financed that the whole church was, for the first time, described as the "Holy Church of Hierusalem."[70] Placidia made sure to mention her children Valentinian and his sister Honoria, too, inserting her own lineage into a

---

[66] Delyannis (2010), 71–85; Sivan (2011) 161; McEvoy (2013) 275–76; Busch (2015) 104–5.
[67] Brubaker (1997) 61; Angelova (2015) 164. Another church Placidia decorated was St. Paul outside the walls that had been built by Theodosius and Honorius; see Brandenburg (2004) 124–25.
[68] Sivan (2011) 117 and n. 96.
[69] Humphries (2007) 39–43.
[70] De Rossi, ICUR IIa.435: "The kings of the earth and all the princes of the people and all judges of the earth praise the name of the Lord. Valentinian, Placidia and Honoria fulfil this vow to the Holy Church of Hierusalem (*Reges terrae et omnes populi principes et omnes iudices terrae laudent nomen Domini. sanctae ecclesiae Hierusalem Valentinianus Placidia et Honoria votum solverunt*). See Brandenburg (2004) 108; for the motif of the decorations, Klein (1988) 367. A basilica Heleniana at the Sessorian Palace is mentioned with reference to the time of Valentinian III in the early sixth century: Gesta de Xysti purgatione 4.

Constantinian success story allegedly begun by an Augusta who was both of venerable antiquity and, in Rome, close in space.

While the Eastern empress Eudocia could not claim kinship with Helena, she also reconnected with the famous Augusta through spatial memory.[71] Having been married to Theodosius II since 421, and styled as Augusta since 423, Eudocia made a trip to the Holy Land in the spring of 438, shortly after her daughter Licinia Eudoxia had married Valentinian III. She was the first empress, and first imperial person, to visit the holy places since Helena, and the contours of her journey were shaped almost exactly around those of the earlier visit as it was known and understood in the mid-fifth century. Eudocia touched on Helena's same way stations, halting for some time in Antioch, where she delivered a speech to the city council while sitting on a golden throne. All the churches that lay on her route were embellished and showered with lavish gifts. The empress humbly paid respect to monks and holy virgins in Palestine, especially those of the monasteries founded by Melania the Younger, granddaughter of the elder Melania. She herself founded a church dedicated to the proto-martyr Stephen at the biblical site of his martyrdom just north of Jerusalem. Finally, Eudocia returned from the Holy Land laden with relics, including some of St. Stephen's, whose remains had been discovered some twenty years earlier. These were eventually deposited in the church of St. Lawrence in Constantinople.[72]

Gerontius' contemporary *Life of Melania* insists Eudocia undertook this journey out of personal piety, encouraged by its holy protagonist. Other authors record that Eudocia traveled to give thanks for her daughter Licinia Eudoxia's marriage, and her consequent hope of grandchildren. This was similar to the reasons Eusebius of Caesarea had given for Helena's trip, in thanksgiving for her son and grandsons. But Eudocia's voyage was undoubtedly also as much an imperial public relations campaign as Helena's had been.[73] Like Helena's, it came in the aftermath of a bruising church council, held in Ephesus in 431, which had deeply divided Christians in the Eastern empire. The council had deposed the bishop of Constantinople, Nestorius, for his teaching that Christ's divine and human nature were distinct and for his denial of the title Theotokos (God-bearer) to the Virgin Mary. Although

---

[71] Brubaker (1997) 62.
[72] This trip is described or mentioned by Socrates, Hist. eccl. 7.47.1–3; Gerontius, Vita Melaniae 58–59; Vita Barsaumae 83; John Rufus, Life of Peter the Iberian 49; Marcellinus comes, Chron. a. 439; Evagrius, Hist. eccl. 1.20–21; Chronicon Paschale 444 (Dindorf, p. 585); John of Nikiu, Chron. 87.18–22; Theophanes, Chron. AM 5927. Hunt (1982) 229–33; Busch (2015) 150–57.
[73] Socrates, Hist. Eccl. 7.47; Gerontius, Vita Melaniae 58–59; Destephen (2018) 45–46.

Nestorius had initially been allowed to retire to a monastery at Antioch, Theodosius had banished him to Petra and then the Egyptian desert in 435 for fear of further dissension. Many of his followers also lost their sees. The bishops John of Antioch and Juvenal of Jerusalem had both attracted criticism for abandoning Nestorius.[74] Eudocia's visit to their sees demonstrated imperial support for them and the council, especially as Theodosius had himself backed Nestorius at first. In Jerusalem, Eudocia was joined by Cyril of Alexandria, Nestorius' main adversary. They appeared together at the dedication of the church of St. Stephen, and, on the next day, at the deposition of relics in a shrine that Melania the Younger had erected on the Mount of Olives.[75] Eudocia's reenactment of Helena's "pilgrimage" to the Holy Land following the Council of Nicaea was thus also calculated to cast the Council of Ephesus and its decisions in the Nicene tradition.

Despite the official nature of her trip, however, Eudocia also managed to exploit the image of an empress on pilgrimage to expand her personal agency, more than Galla Placidia or any other empress before her had managed, and certainly far more than Helena. Having hitherto been overshadowed by her sister-in-law Pulcheria, another Augusta, she now acquired a more public profile.[76] Only a short while later, in 442 or 443, she left Constantinople again, to return to Palestine, but this time for good. As so often with the inner workings of the late Roman imperial court, what really happened to cause this defies reconstruction. Rumors about Eudocia's treasonous adultery with the *magister officiorum* Paulinus, or alternatively her complicity in the undeserved execution of the emperor's dearly loved friend, or simply about jealousy between the emperor's female relatives abounded.[77] All this has clear echoes of how Constantine's wife Fausta had been and was still talked about. Eudocia's memory would, however, acquire a decidedly different dimension from that of her supposedly pagan forebear, because of her success in casting herself as a female imperial pilgrim, again in the wake of Helena. She lived out the rest of her life in the Holy Land, in a conspicuously pious manner, building a great many more churches and expanding the church of St. Stephen in which she would be buried, as well as sponsoring monasteries,

---

[74] On the Council of Ephesus and its aftermath, see Schor (2011) 81–109.

[75] John Rufus, Life of Peter the Iberian 49. On Eudocia's and Theodosius' earlier support of Nestorius, see Holum (1982) 158.

[76] It is perhaps after her return that she founded the church of St. Polyeuktos in Constantinople; see Dirschlmayer (2015) 151. For Pulcheria, see the discussion that follows here.

[77] On the rumors and difficulties to reconstruct what really happened, Holum (1982) 193–94; Busch (2015) 157–62.

hospitals, and hostels, including one at the Holy Sepulchre. In achieving all this, it also helped that Eudocia was independently wealthy.[78]

Eudocia's return to Palestine had much to do with her personal networks in the region, built up in particular through her old friendship with Melania the Younger (who had died in 439) and with the ascetic leader Peter the Iberian. In these circles there was much resistance to further imperial impositions of Christological doctrines. Eudocia was suspected of supporting Palestinian monks who violently rebelled against the theological decisions taken at the Council of Chalcedon in 451, and even of having killed an imperial agent herself. Nonetheless, there was little attempt by the imperial court to shut down her activities, block her access to resources, or revoke her title.[79] It was, on the whole, deemed to be more beneficial to the imperial regime to have an Augusta in the Holy Land, just as the first Christian emperor had done. Eudocia's presence in this unruly province could even be employed to de-escalate tense situations, as her successful intervention with the emperor Marcian, who had succeeded her husband Theodosius in 450, for banished monks and bishops in the aftermath of Chalcedon shows.[80] Her emulation of Helena also increased Eudocia's own power base in Palestine, for admiration for the finder of the True Cross cut across sectarian divides. John Rufus, an anti-Chalcedonian writer who composed a *Life of Peter the Iberian* toward the end of the fifth century, approvingly noted not only the empress Eudocia's wish to dwell close to and worship at the sites of the Lord's Passion, but also Helena's divine zeal in discovering instruments of the Passion and erecting a church here, which had made such worship possible.[81]

---

[78] On Eudocia's second stay in Palestine and the role Helena played in her self-advertisement, see Hunt (1982) 237–48; Lenski (2004); Novembri (2008). Her munificence is detailed most extensively by Cyril of Scythopolis, Vita Euthymii 35. On her independent wealth derived from her father, which plays a role in the story of her becoming empress, see Busch (2015) 138–45.

[79] On Eudocia's friendship with Peter the Iberian, Horn (2004). Eudocia's murder of the *comes domesticorum* Saturninus is mentioned by Marcellinus Comes, Chron. ann. 444.

[80] John Rufus, De obitu Theodosii Hierosolymorum et Romani monachi 8–9. It is unclear how much Eudocia was involved in the actual violence of the monks; see Hillner (2019a).

[81] John Rufus, Life of Peter the Iberian 56 and 71. See also John of Nikiu, Chron. 77.63. Over time, such parallels could even lead to confusion or switching of roles in the True Cross discovery story between Helena (and even other women) and Eudocia, as demonstrated by the Coptic legend of "Eudoxia," allegedly a sister of Constantine who discovered the Holy Tomb; see Drake, Orlandi, Pearson (1980) 155–56.

A "New Helena" in Name: Pulcheria

It is notable that in the case of Eudocia and Galla Placidia, their emulation of Helena's model continued to be suggested through textual juxtaposition of deeds, rather than through invoking Helena's name. We do not, for example, find explicit reminders that Eudocia behaved "like Helena." Perhaps this was because, outside the dynastic kinship group, it had never been customary to invoke individual empresses by name as precedents for aspects of the role of the empress, with the notable exception of the founder figure Livia, the first Augusta. This was because being an empress was not an official position that was handed down through the generations. Instead, as we have consistently seen, unrelated empresses had more commonly been connected with each other through the reuse of their attributes, ranging from titles and divine symbols to hairstyles, the reinhabiting of certain spaces and the replication of particular acts.[82]

Nonetheless, at least as far as Helena was concerned, this reluctance to invoke specific female examples in imperial ceremonial contexts slowly began to change, in parallel to the emergence of Constantine as the benchmark for Christian emperors.[83] It is ironic, however, that the first empress to whom the name, rather than the image, of Helena was attached was one who among her contemporaries had seemingly drawn least on the example of Helena. This empress was Pulcheria, the sister of Theodosius II and the wife of his successor, Marcian.

On October 25, 451, Pulcheria and Marcian attended the church council that the emperor had called at Chalcedon, held in the church of St. Euphemia. The council's task was to solve conflicts that had arisen from the teaching of the Constantinopolitan archimandrite (chief-abbot) Eutyches who had claimed that Christ had a single divine nature. This had led, in turn, to the controversial deposition of Flavian, bishop of Constantinople, for having opposed this doctrine as close to the views associated with Nestorius that had been repudiated at Ephesus twenty years earlier. The session that the imperial couple joined, the council's sixth, was convened to announce its definition of faith, that Christ was "one person in two natures." In his speech to

---

[82] This pattern started right at the beginning of the imperial regime, when both Octavia and Livia sponsored a *porticus* within twenty years of each other, as an expression of their pietas for the Roman people; see Cooley (2013) 31. For Livia as a founder figure, see Angelova (2015) 10–13; 66–83. For the invocation of specific empresses within dynastic groups and the Constantinian dynasty itself, see Julian's Panegyric of 358 discussed in Chapter 10.

[83] Dagron (1996) 141–68, esp. 142.

the assembly, Marcian gave assurances that his role was to confirm this definition, but not to direct the council in any way. He was acting, so he said, "according to the example of the religious prince Constantine" who had done the same at Nicaea. After he had finished speaking, the three hundred or more bishops and thirty-eight imperial officials present rose, wished the emperor and empress a long life, and, taking their cue, filled the church with acclamations of the emperor as a "New Constantine." More acclamations to the "New Constantine, the New Paul, the New David" followed the reading of the agreed definition of faith, in a crescendo building from Christian emperors toward biblical models. The acclamations then accumulated even further, encompassing the imperial couple. They ended in the hailing not only of Marcian as the New Constantine, but also of Pulcheria, the pious, the orthodox, the banisher of Nestorius and Eutyches, who as the "New Helena," with "the faith of Helena" and "the zeal of Helena," had even surpassed the original: Helena had found the True Cross, but Pulcheria had "saved" it.[84]

In the decades before Chalcedon, Pulcheria's persona had been carefully curated in ways by now familiar from the examples of other empresses: She had been presented as a charitable founder of churches, monasteries, and hospitals and as a protector of the state's welfare through the discovery of sacred relics. She was allegedly exhorted in a dream vision to dig up the remains of the Forty Martyrs of Sebaste, which she then had translated into the church of St. Thyrsus in the Helenianai neighborhood of Constantinople.[85] Her actions had also more directly picked up on those of Helena, when, around 420, she and the as yet unmarried Theodosius had sent rich gifts to Jerusalem, including a large golden cross, encrusted with jewels. This act marked a renewal of imperial interest in the Holy Land, perhaps ushered in by the ever-growing dissemination of Helena's story. It paved the way for Pulcheria's sister-in-law Eudocia's later visit. All of this furthered the image of the pious imperial household, whose divine blessing (now also exemplified

---

[84] ACO 2.1, 139–40, 155; ACO 2.2, 101, Session 6:2.3.5.11: Μαρκιανὸς νέος Κωνσταντῖνος. Πουλχερία νέα Ἑλένη. Τῆς Ἑλένης τὴν πίστιν σὺ ἐπεδείξω. Τῆς Ἑλένης τὸν ζῆλον σὺ ἐπεδείξω. [The following only appears in the Latin redaction of the Acts] *Crucem Christi tu defendis. Invenit Helena, salvavit Pulcheria.*

[85] For an overview of Pulcheria's charitable work and foundations, including her seven churches, see Dirschlmayer (2015) 126–39. Sozomen, Hist. eccl. 9.2.1–9.2.18 on the Forty Martyrs of Sebaste. Angelova (2015) 142–43 on whether Helena was the model for Pulcheria here. The date probably falls between 434 and 439.

through its strong ties with the sites of the Passion) guaranteed the security of its subjects, especially in Constantinople.[86]

However, Pulcheria's public image went far beyond these by now conventional expectations and therefore also transcended the model furnished by Helena. Her most distinctive authority came from something that Helena did not possess, life-long virginity. As with other imperial girls before her, it had quickly been realized that the prospect of Pulcheria—and for that matter, her two sisters Arcadia and Marina—becoming a bride presented a threat to dynastic stability. This was especially because, when her father Arcadius had died in 408, their brother Theodosius was still underage.[87] In 414, therefore, when Pulcheria, the eldest, was 14 years old, all three girls were consecrated as holy virgins in a public ceremony. Pulcheria was, in addition, awarded the title of Augusta and coins started to be minted bearing her portrait. As well as finding a practical solution to an old problem, this shows how the imperial court was keenly interested in tapping into the enormous, ever-increasing prestige that could be gained from the practice of Christian asceticism. Her vow heightened Pulcheria's status and visibility, in such a way that the church historian Sozomen even claimed that Pulcheria conducted government business on behalf of her younger brother.[88]

In this way, Pulcheria was reminiscent less of Helena than of the latter's granddaughter Constantina, relics of whose favorite saint, the virgin martyr Agnes, were translated from Rome to Constantinople during this period.[89] But Pulcheria found an even more powerful role model in the most holy of virgins, Mary, through the influence of Atticus, bishop of Constantinople and a keen proponent of Marian theology.[90] If we are to believe pro-Nestorian propaganda, Pulcheria's devotion to Mary manifested itself not just in emulation, but in her claim that, due to her virginity, she shared in the motherhood of Christ.[91] This naturally put her in opposition to the teachings of Atticus' successor Nestorius on the Virgin Mary. Through Nestorius' deposition at the Council of Ephesus in 431, Pulcheria gained a reputation as a supreme defender of the orthodox faith. Three of the seven churches

---

[86] Cross to Jerusalem: Theophanes, Chron. AM 5920; see Hunt (1982) 228–29. For the cross on Pulcheria's coinage, for example, RIC X, Theodosius II 214.
[87] For these considerations, Busch (2015) 112.
[88] Sozomen, Hist. eccl. 9.1.3. On the consecration and the Augusta title, Busch (2015) 113–14. See Harries (2012) on the in reality limited extent of Pulcheria's competencies.
[89] Theodore Lector, Hist. eccl. 2.64.
[90] On the influence of Atticus, Holum (1982) 141; Dirschlmayer (2015) 121.
[91] Letter to Cosmas 8. Holum (1982) 153–54; Limberis (1994) 54–55; Angelova (2015) 244.

she subsequently founded in Constantinople were dedicated to Mary. Of course, Helena had herself also been associated with Mary, first obliquely by Eusebius of Caesarea and then more openly by Ambrose. But Helena's qualities as a model Christian empress could not entirely match up the qualities of female holiness in late antiquity, which called either for martyrdom or sexual celibacy, and ideally in the form of life-long virginity. Unless through old age, Helena was never portrayed as having renounced her links to this world.[92] Pulcheria's power, on the other hand, was built on spectacular renunciation. When, after the Council of Ephesus, the people of Constantinople acclaimed Pulcheria, no mention was made of Helena, but the victory of the Virgin Mary was praised, eliding the distinction between the Augusta and the mother of God. In this way, an imperial identity was also projected onto Mary.[93]

Pulcheria's contrasting identification as a "new Helena" at the Council of Chalcedon twenty years later, responded to a further development, at a later stage in her life, which returned her to a more conventional role: her marriage to Marcian in 450. Pulcheria's dynastic potential was abruptly reignited for the purpose of legitimatizing succession, just as Constantina's had been exactly a century before. After Theodosius had died in July without a male heir, the empire had been left in limbo until Marcian, a protégé of the *magister militum* Aspar, was chosen to succeed him.[94] On top of his military credentials, Marcian sought further forms of legitimation. One of these, which also secured his acceptance among the people of Constantinople, came through his union with Pulcheria. She therefore became a wife, at 51 years of age. Pulcheria may have been the one pushing for the calling of the council at Chalcedon, but it can be assumed that Marcian was only too pleased to grasp the opportunity to present himself in the tradition of Constantine, another trusted source of legitimacy.[95] Pulcheria's styling as a "new Helena" by those attending the council therefore acknowledged her role in the preservation of faith (also demonstrated by her attendance at the council, which was in itself unusual), but it did so only through her being one of an imperial

---

[92] Consolino (1995) 487 comments on the difficulty for women who did not fall within this remit to acquire a reputation for sanctity in late antiquity. See also Brubaker (1997) 63; Harbus (2002) 22.

[93] Kraatz (1904) 49–55. On Pulcheria enhancing the cult of Mary with an imperial dimension. see Limberis (1994) 60–61.

[94] Burgess (1993–94) on the various motivations behind Marcian's elevation.

[95] On Pulcheria's role in calling the council, Holum (1982) 211–12, and her continued vow of virginity 209; on Marcian, Pulcheria, and the tradition of Constantine Schwartz (1927). Although the council was also originally scheduled to be held at Nicaea, it was moved to Chalcedon for administrative reasons.

pair. Pulcheria was not just the "new Helena"; she was the "new Helena" to Marcian's "new Constantine," in an indication of how these acclamations were carefully orchestrated by the imperial court itself. They also acknowledged that, like Constantine and Helena, Marcian and Pulcheria were an unusual imperial pair, because Pulcheria had only agreed to the marriage on the condition that her virginity be preserved. But without her marriage to Marcian, and based on her own reputation alone, Pulcheria would not have attained the honor of being called "Helena."

The acclamations at Chalcedon reflect how by the mid-fifth century, Constantine and his mother had become the ultimate Christian couple on earth, having progressed from historical fallibility to mythical status, almost mapping the relationship between Christ and Mary.[96] In Constantinople, their model image was furthered by the erection of many statues across the urban landscape presenting this imperial pair, usually framing a cross.[97] At the same time, the acclamations at Constantinople also honored Marcian and Pulcheria as outshining even the revered examples of Constantine and Helena. Marcian was presented as the culmination of God's plan begun with David, and Pulcheria as outdoing Helena who, after all, had only "found" the cross. Salvation had not been attained at the time of Constantine and Helena, but was to be reserved for Marcian and Pulcheria's age.

The events at Chalcedon also show that the "title" of Helena was used, if not exactly to rein in the empress's agency, then to harness the power that came from this association not for her own benefit, but for the wider imperial good.[98] We see the latter technique applied again only a few decades after Chalcedon, in 474–475, during the messy succession to the emperor Leo (Marcian's successor). Leo's widow, Verina, was suspected of having promoted the imperial claims of her lover Patricius against those of her son-in-law Zeno, husband to her daughter Ariadne. But in the end, it was not Patricius, but Verina's brother Basiliscus, who usurped power. During his coronation ceremony at Hebdomon, the crowd, led by the circus factions who backed Basiliscus, erupted into acclamations, including the hailing of Verina as "the orthodox Helena." While Verina's true role in all these events cannot be reconstructed, it is clear that casting her as a new Helena once

---

[96] Angelova (2015) 134–35.
[97] Schade (2003) 231–32.
[98] Holum (1982) 216 comments that the acclamations "did not do justice to [Pulcheria's] work." Brubaker (1997) 62 notes that as soon as the name Helena became part of the imperial ceremony, it lost its potency for the agency of imperial women.

again conferred on her brother the status of a new Constantine. This gave him a legitimacy that transcended his kinship with the dowager empress as well as tying his (apparently somewhat unruly) sister into his imperial project.[99]

In the subsequent century, and beyond, the invocation of the empress as a "new Helena" was applied to more conventional imperial consorts, becoming a standard feature of public imperial ceremony. Justin and his wife Euphemia were acclaimed as the new Constantine and new Helena by the crowd in the Hippodrome upon Justin's ascent to the throne in July 518.[100] At the dedication ceremony of the Hagia Sophia in 537, rebuilt after a fire during the Nika riot, Justinian and his wife Theodora were associated with Constantine and Helena, the builders of the Holy Sepulchre, in a hymn written for the occasion by Romanos Melodos. Here again, Romanos eagerly made the point that the imperial pair superseded the earlier one, because they started work straight after a disaster, rather than hundreds of years later. Later in the sixth century, the emperor Tiberius' wife Anastasia was also hailed as the new Helena upon being proclaimed Augusta in 578. But the true reference point of all these tributes continued to be the emperor, who was frequently acclaimed as a "new Constantine" without any female counterpart.[101] Meanwhile, there was a marked decrease in the circulation of the story of Helena's trip to Jerusalem and discovery of the True Cross in Eastern narrative sources through the sixth century.[102] The famous Augusta was mostly reduced to her relationship with her son, to encourage the image of the empress as a complement to the emperor. The status of "new Helena" did not necessarily grant the bearer of the title the increased scope of action that the emulation of Helena's deeds had once provided for Eudocia.

Being Helena: Radegund

It was in the post-Roman West, and through a woman who entirely shed her wifely duties and another woman who wrote of her life, that the model

---

[99] Parastaseis 29.
[100] ACO 3, Collectio Sabbaitica 72 (bis), 74, 75, 86.
[101] Romanos Melodos, On Earthquakes and Fires 22. Theodora is also recorded as sending a pearled cross to Jerusalem, Malalas, Chron. 17.19; Anastasia: John of Ephesus, Hist. eccl. 3.10. For acclamations of the emperor as a new Constantine on his own, Angelova (2015) 3–4.
[102] Georgiou (2013) 616–17. See the cross discovery legend by Alexander Monachos that may be dated to the mid-sixth century and seriously downplays Helena's role in favor of Constantine and above all bishop Macarius: Drijvers (2011) 167–74.

of Helena took a new direction. The Western empire had been dying a slow death since the days of Galla Placidia, but by the later sixth century everyone in its former territory found themselves in a decidedly post-imperial world. Nonetheless, diplomatic and religious ties with the surviving empire in the East remained in place. In 568, an embassy was sent by Sigibert, king of Metz, from Merovingian Gaul to Constantinople. Its mission was to request a cross relic from the emperor Justin II for the convent of Sigibert's stepmother Radegund, in the city of Poitiers.

Radegund had founded her monastic community after leaving her husband, Sigibert's father Clothar. Originally a Thuringian princess, Radegund had been captured by Clothar as war booty during a raid of Thuringian lands in 531, but he was later persuaded to renounce her and even endowed her convent shortly before his death in 561. Radegund sought relics to enhance her foundation's sanctity further and to secure it from outside interference. She clearly did not settle for second best. Her petition to the emperor followed an earlier request to the bishop of Jerusalem for a piece of the cross, which had been turned down. Her appeal to the imperial court, where cross relics were believed to be housed since Helena had allegedly sent them to Constantine, was more successful.[103]

Radegund's friend, the Italian panegyrist Venantius Fortunatus, subsequently composed a poem of thanksgiving to Justin and his wife Sophia. The poem, undoubtedly proclaimed aloud by the messenger on arrival in Constantinople, addressed the unity of the imperial couple, conventionally praising the emperor as the "new Constantine" and Sophia as the "new Helena." Fortunatus' lines here echo, once again, the acclamations of Pulcheria at the Council of Chalcedon, with Sophia now taking the place of Pulcheria. For where Helena had found the cross, Sophia "scatters salvation everywhere." This expansion of Pulcheria's role was an allusion to the imperial couple's stated intent to uphold the Chalcedonian definition of faith, which Fortunatus summarizes in the poem's introduction. By giving a piece of the cross to Radegund, Sophia had even exceeded Pulcheria's example, because now salvation had arrived as far as "barbarian" Gaul.[104]

---

[103] On Radegund's relic mission, see Moreira (1993) 285–305; Noga Banai (2019) with the previous literature. See Cameron (1976) for Justin's motivations in granting Radegund her wish. For beliefs in Gaul that pieces of the cross were in Constantinople, see Gregory of Tours, Liber in gloria mart. 5. On Radegund's biography, Dailey (2015) 68–72.

[104] Venantius Fortunatus, Ad Iustinum et Sophiam Augustos 67–69: *illa invenit opem, tu spargis ubique salutem*.

Fortunatus was clearly well acquainted with Eastern court protocol, probably from his training in Ravenna, the seat of the Byzantine administration of Italy, but also with Western doctrinal concerns. There was much correspondence on the issue of Chalcedon between Rome and Constantinople in the sixth century, as opposition to the council continued to simmer away in the Eastern empire.[105] In such letters, Roman bishops habitually reminded Eastern empresses of their duties as defenders of the Chalcedonian faith, usually triangulating between the roles of Helena, of Pulcheria, and of their addressee. The bishops had clearly read the council's acts and delighted in the examples of imperial orthodoxy that they offered. In 519, for example, Pope Hormisdas implored the wife of Justin I, Euphemia, to "stimulate your spouse's piety," as "you will surpass the honours of the one through whom the unity of the church found the cross," because "through you it will be saved." By not even naming Helena, Hormisdas emphasized Euphemia's identification with Pulcheria, who had "saved the cross," through their common defense of Chalcedon.[106] Less than a century later, another pope, Gregory the Great, in corresponding with an incoming empress, Leontia, wife of Phokas, articulated his hope that God "gives to you in your piety the clemency of Pulcheria Augusta, who for her zeal for the Catholic faith was called in the holy synod [of Chalcedon] the new Helena."[107] Leontia had probably just been acclaimed the New Helena by the people of Constantinople, but Gregory was keen to remind her what this really meant. Helena was only important here insofar as she had shaped the persona of the Chalcedonian empress, Pulcheria, who was presented as the true model of behavior. Fortunatus praised Sophia in very similar vein, as an orthodox empress enhanced by, but also in competition with, the examples of Helena and Pulcheria. For her part, Radegund was presented as the simple beneficiary of such blessed and age-old imperial competition, which made prayers to the cross "swell in distant lands."[108]

Radegund's own community soon forced a change of perspective on their founder and her relationship with Helena. In the early seventh century, Baudonivia, a sister in Radegund's convent, wrote on the life of the queen-turned-nun, who had died in 587. In her writings, she described in detail

---

[105] Sotinel (2005).
[106] Collectio Avellana n. 156: *ut per vos . . . mariti vestri pietas amplius incitetur . . . superabitis quin immo illius merita, quia ecclesiae unitas per illam suum invenit signum, per vos est habitura remedium.* On the background of Hormisdas' correspondence, Hillner (2019b) 224–35.
[107] Gregory the Great, Ep. 13.42 (603): *Sed dat nobis in vestra pietate Pulcheriae Augustae clementiam, quae pro zelo catholicae fidei in sancta synodo Helena nova vocata est.*
[108] Venantius Fortunatus, Ad Iustinum et Sophiam Augustos 86: *facis extremis crescere vota locis.*

what had happened when the relic of the cross arrived in Poitiers. The bishop of the city, Maroveus, was less than pleased, fearing that the convent's possession of a holy object of supra-regional attraction would challenge his own spiritual authority. He refused to open the city gates, so Radegund had to ask the king for a royal order of enforcement and invited the bishop of nearby Tours to preside over the relic's deposition. In this way, as Baudonivia puts it, "what Helena did in Eastern lands, Saint Radegund did in Gaul!"[109] This was an original take on the by now familiar comparisons between Helena's deeds and those of more recent empresses, said to have even surpassed their forbears. Perhaps inspired by Fortunatus' poem, a copy of which must have been kept in the monastery, Baudonivia made Radegund assume the role of the Eastern empress in the equation. It was not through Sophia, but through Radegund's zeal, that the "salvation of the world" that had been found by Helena was able to come to the city of Poitiers.

Yet, Baudonivia adopted another, much more powerful subtext, too. Through their behavior, she explained, Maroveus and his entourage, "satellites" of the devil, had "played the role of the Jews." This was a clear allusion not only to the Passion in the Gospels, but also to the Helena legend known as the *Inventio Crucis*, famous in Gaul, in which Helena's quest had also been resisted by the Jews of Palestine.[110] Where earlier Radegund had assumed the role of Sophia, now she played the role of Helena herself, wrestling the cross from those who wanted to keep it hidden out of pure "envy." Unlike Eastern empresses, who had expanded on Helena's work, Radegund quite literally became Helena, spiritually discovering the cross and therefore the secret of salvation anew, despite attempts to hinder her.[111] As Baudonivia explained, liberally borrowing from the *Inventio Crucis* legend, this discovery came upon Radegund through a vision that inspired her to seek out her relic. In this vision, Radegund "like Saint Helena, imbued with wisdom, full of the fear of God, glorious with good works, eagerly sought to salute the wood" and "when she found it, she clapped both hands ... she knelt on the ground adoring the Lord." In the *Inventio Crucis*, it had been the Jew Judas who had

---

[109] Baudonivia, Vita Radegundis 2.16: *Quod fecit illa [Helena] in Orientali patria, hoc fecit beata Radegundis in Gallia.* Baudonivia had just named Helena.

[110] Baudonivia, Vita Radegundis 2.16: *aliud pro alio adserentes Iudaico ordine*; McNamara, Whatley, Halborg (1992) 98 n. 118; Hahn (2006) 271. The *Inventio Crucis* legend is also referenced in Gregory of Tours, Decem Libri Hist. 1.36, who was close to both Radegund and Venantius Fortunatus. See also Gregory of Tours, Decem Libri Hist. 9.40 for Radegund's difficulty with Maroveus, although he does not mention that her relic mission involved a piece of the cross or indeed Helena in this context.

[111] On Radegund's spiritual discovery of the cross, see Hahn (2006).

performed these gestures of delight and worship, but he, too, was cast aside to highlight Radegund's reincarnation of the saintly Augusta.[112] All of this may not have been entirely Baudonivia's own invention. Radegund had most likely furthered her identification with Helena herself, by enclosing the True Cross in a silver box, as Helena had supposedly done in Jerusalem, and perhaps even by modeling the chapel in which the True Cross relic was housed in Poitiers on the relic chapel in the Hierusalem church at the Sessorian Palace in Rome.[113]

In none of the Eastern stories about her or acclamations invoking her example had Helena ever been called a saint, or at least not in her own right. Of course, Eusebius of Caesarea had employed conventional hagiographic language when describing Helena as "thrice-blessed," but his main objective had been to elevate Constantine into the realm of holiness, a project in which, at least at first, he had little success.[114] The church historian Gelasius, as far as we can tell from Rufinus of Aquileia's Latin translation of his work, had described Helena as "a woman matchless in faith and devotion, and of singular generosity." But the miracle that led to the identification of the cross was, in this version of the story, performed not by Helena, but by the bishop of Jerusalem, Macarius.[115] The Eastern church historians followed in this vein, celebrating Helena as the mother of the first Christian emperor and therefore an exemplary Augusta, whose humility, charity, piety, and zeal had allowed her to become witness to a miracle that unlocked the prospect of salvation for the entire empire. But, neither in her lifetime, nor through her bodily remains, had she been portrayed as performing miracles, nor was she invoked as a focus of intercessory appeal to God on behalf of the faithful.

In the West, the situation was different. Ambrose, who, among late antique writers had most vigorously associated Helena with the Virgin Mary, had already called her "of holy memory." In Rome, a cult around Helena's body developed from at least the sixth century. It followed the emergence in Rome of more sustained devotion to the True Cross, which is visible from the fifth century and was promoted further by Galla Placidia. By the sixth

---

[112] Baudonivia, *Vita Radegundis* 2.16: *Ut sicut beata Helena sapientia inbuta, timore Dei plena, bonis operibus gloriosa lignum salutare, ubi precium mundi pro nostra salute appensum fuerat . . . ita ut invento ambabus manibus plauderet et, in terra genu flexo, Dominum adoraret.* On Baudonivia drawing verbally on the *Inventio Crucis* and the conflation of Helena and Judas to raise Helena's and therefore also Radegund's profile, see Whatley (1993) 81–91.
[113] Noga Banai (2019) 197–98.
[114] Coon (1997) 97; Harbus (2002) 19.
[115] Rufinus, Hist. eccl. 10.7: *femina incomparabilis fide et religione animi, ac magnificentia singulari.*

century, Rome celebrated a unique feast day of the cross on May 3rd, based on the *Inventio Crucis* story, which dated Helena's discovery to that day. The city had also acquired further cross relics and associated sacred spaces, including at St. Peter's in the Vatican.[116] These developments had almost certainly, in turn, led to renewed interest in the empress buried outside the city. The sixth-century Book of Pontiffs calls Helena a "saint" (*beata*) when describing her burial "at the two laurel trees" on the Via Labicana. By the seventh century pilgrims came from far and wide to see the empress's tomb or even "the church of the holy Helena," located by pilgrim guides on the Via Labicana.[117] By the end of that century, two Greek monks had left a touching graffito on the apse of the crypt in the catacombs attached to her mausoleum in which they sought the intercessory prayers "of the holy martyrs and of Saint Helena" for their salvation.[118]

In all this Western devotion, there is little trace of Constantine. Even Ambrose had treated the emperor as a far more subdued figure than Helena. This was either due to Constantine's religious past, still considered checkered, or because the Milanese bishop's aim was to locate the origins of imperial humility, and the emperor's humble mother served this purpose far better than Constantine himself. In Rome, the holy Helena no longer needed an emperor at all to underscore her status and achievements, and certainly not by the seventh century. Those who venerated her here did not seek her out as an example for the behavior of empresses, but as an aid to obtain the grace of God. There were, of course, no more empresses in Rome or elsewhere in Western Europe by this time. To be sure, Helena and Constantine did continue to be used to exhort kings and queens to correct behavior also in the post-Roman West. Around the time that Baudonivia was writing her *Life of Radegund*, for example, Gregory the Great implored Bertha, the Christian queen of Kent, to convert her husband Æthelberht, by following the example of Helena, mother of Constantine, through whom God "had inflamed the hearts of the Romans to the Christian faith."[119] Yet the much less stable lines of continuity

---

[116] De Blaauw (1997) 68; De Blaauw (2014) 150.

[117] LP I 182; the author also knew the *Inventio Crucis*. Notitia ecclesiarum urbis Romae, Via Labicana: *pausant sancti martyres . . . et sancta Helena in sua rotunda*; De locis sanctis martyrum, Via Labicana-Prenestina: *Iuxta viam vero Lavicanam ecclesia est Sanctae Elenae ubi ipsa corpore iacet*; Itinerarium Malmesburiense, Septima Porta: *via Lauicana quae ad beatam Helenam tendit*. See Pohlsander (1995) 186–89.

[118] ICUR 6.15965.

[119] Gregory the Great, ep. 11.35. On Bertha's role in conversion, see MacCarron (2017) 650–70. Gregory clearly expected Bertha to know Helena's story, not surprisingly as she was originally a princess from Merovingian Gaul. On "imitatio Helenae" of early medieval queens, often refracted through an "imitatio Radegundis," see McNamara (1996) 61–80.

from the first Christian emperor to the royal courts of the post-Roman world meant that here Helena could also become a Christian figure independent from imperial men.

Baudonivia was not in the business of administering advice to earthly wives of kings, and, unsurprisingly, Constantine receives no mention in her *Life of Radegund*. Baudonivia's focus was on the life of a female monastic founder, who, according to Gregory, bishop of neighboring Tours, was "great among the people" on account of her conspicuous asceticism. Gregory was another of Radegund's friends who had perhaps even delivered her funeral oration. Elsewhere he also associated Radegund with Helena, both queens (*reginae*) "comparable in merit and faith," but he described neither of the women as saintly on this occasion. Instead, he called Helena "Augusta," thereby also enhancing Radegund's royal status.[120] Baudonivia, writing with a longer and monastic perspective, more forcefully pushed the image of sanctity, emphasizing not only Radegund's qualities as a pious and charitable queen who progressed to fervent nun and then to the provider of holy relics. Baudinivia's Radegund was more. She was a miracle worker herself, and already during her lifetime.[121] She could dispel demons just by making the sign of the cross.[122] Venantius Fortunatus, who had also written his own *Life of Radegund* shortly after her death, had entertained similar themes, but had mentioned neither Radegund's cross relic nor Helena.[123] His aim was to detach the image of Radegund's sanctity from that of the cross and thereby heighten her personal holiness.[124] Baudonivia may have had similar qualms about the relic stealing Radegund's limelight. Even so, the True Cross, kept within her monastic community and as such enhancing it, mattered greatly to her, too. Baudonivia was also, more than Fortunatus, interested in Radegund's royal history, as it elevated the status of her monastery.[125] Baudonivia's insistence that Radegund's actions overlapped with those of the Christian empress Helena bound the sanctity of the cross tightly

---

[120] Gregory of Tours, Decem Libri Hist. 3.7: *ut magna in populis haberetur*; Gregory of Tours, Liber in gloria mart. 5: *merito et fide Helenae conparanda regina Radegundis*; Gregory of Tours, Liber in gloria conf. 104. For Gregory, greater certainty of Radegund's sanctity was only established upon her death, when demoniacs who witnessed the funeral procession started to shout, as such confirming the presence of the holy; see Effros (1990) 44–45.

[121] See, for example, Baudonivia, Vita Radegundis 2.11.

[122] Baudonivia, Vita Radegundis 2.18.

[123] See, for example, Venantius Fortunatus, Vita Radegundis 1.11 for Radegund freeing prisoners through intercessory prayers.

[124] Effros (1990) 42.

[125] Baudonivia, Vita Radegundis 2.10 details Radegund's continuous diplomatic work. See Scheibelreiter (1979).

to Radegund's personal sanctity as a Christian queen. This merged both the cross and Radegund into a single focus of devotion, both within the convent and beyond. Baudonivia's Helena, therefore, served to shape Radegund's specific holiness, and with it that of her monastery. It also meant that Helena was neither in competition with Radegund nor superseded by her, as was the case with Eastern empresses. If Radegund was Helena, Helena was also Radegund, and in the process she became a saint herself.

Epilogue

By the eleventh century, Helena had acquired two feast days in the Christian calendar.[1] In the orthodox churches, Helena was and still is jointly venerated with Constantine on May 21, commemorating the emperor's date of death. In the Catholic Church, her feast day falls on August 18, and is separate from that of Constantine who was never recognized as a saint in the West. These medieval expressions of devotion were a result of centuries of organic growth of Helena's cult. Their twofold nature has its roots in late antiquity and was at least partly linked to how late antique royal women were meant to interact, and did interact, with Helena's memory.

The rediscovery of Helena as an imperial role model followed decades of silence, punctuated by bouts of negativity surrounding her name. It came about as a result of a combination of factors: the emergence of the Theodosian dynasty and their need for legitimacy especially given the prevalence of child emperor succession; receding memories of the historical Constantine and his increasing mythologization as a founder of the Nicene Christian empire; and the progressive materialization of Christian devotion in and deriving from the Holy Land, which only Helena and no Christian emperor had visited. Constantine's hugely experimental step to promote his obscure mother—at the time, a decision based on specific historical circumstances not all related to his new-found Christian faith—finally paid off. It did so because subsequent Christian writers and rulers rediscovered what Eusebius had already realized: Helena's visit to the Holy Land fit very neatly into a narrative of the founding of the Christian empire.

Helena's success as a figure of Christian devotion also reflects popular reverence for the True Cross relics, the Holy Sepulchre, and the Virgin Mary. In late antiquity, it also reflects the imperial court's ability to bend this devotion back onto contemporary imperial women who behaved toward holy objects, places, and people in similar ways to those allegedly manifested by Helena, and therefore back onto itself. From the fifth century, each imperial couple became the mirror image of the first Christian emperor and his

---

[1] Klein (1988) 372–73; Pohlsander (1995) 194.

mother, a resplendent earthly likeness of the ultimate divine couple of Christ and Mary. This was Helena's route to sanctity in the Eastern or "Byzantine" empire, where her veneration continued to be shackled to Constantine's and, like that of the emperor himself, emerged only slowly.[2]

The model of Helena increased Byzantine empresses' status because of heightened acknowledgment of their role as imperial consorts. This certainly increased their power, too, but it is important to remember that the source of this power continued to rest with the emperor. The case of Theodosius II's estranged wife Eudocia shows that the model of Helena could confer agency independent of the emperor, but in the Eastern empire this remained an exceptional case, at least in late antiquity. At the imperial center, it was quickly countered by the harnessing of Helena's name for empresses who did dutifully submit to the role of female imperial counterpart, be this as wife, like Pulcheria, or sister, like Verina.

Under these circumstances, it is not surprising that the more innovative image of Helena as a saint, and independent of Constantine, developed outside the empire, and in dialogue with an unconventional woman, Radegund, who used to be a queen, but was not a mother nor, really, a wife. Even so, judged by the historical evidence, Helena's Eastern reincarnation as an adjunct saint of Constantine is not an inaccurate reflection of her relationship with her son during her lifetime. Largely due to her ordinary background, this relationship had always been one of dependency and loyalty, if surely also of maternal love. With the emergence of Helena as the sovereign Western royal saint we leave this historical Helena firmly behind.

---

[2] The earliest hagiographic lives of Constantine were compiled in the ninth century, although they may have drawn on pre-sixth-century material; see Kazhdan (1987); Georgiou (2013) 624.

Ancient Sources

Acta Synhodi a. DI, ed. Th. Mommsen, MGH AA 12, Berlin: Weidmann, 1894.
Actus Silvestri, ed. B. Mombritius, *Sanctuarium seu Vitae Sanctorum*, vol. 2, Hildesheim: Olms, 1978.
Almann of Hautvillers, Vita seu potius homilia de S. Helena, ed. P. Dräger, Trier: Kliomedia, 2007.
Ambrose, Epistulae, ed. M. Zelzer, CSEL 82.3, Vienna: Hoelder-Pichler-Tempsky, 1982.
Ambrose, De obitu Theodosii, ed. V. Zimmerl-Prangl, CSEL 196, Berlin: De Gruyter, 2021.
Ambrose, De obitu Valentiniani, ed. V. Zimmerl-Prangl, CSEL 196, Berlin: De Gruyter, 2021.
Ammianus Marcellinus, Res gestae, ed. W. Seyfarth, Leipzig: Teubner, 1978.
Anonymus Valesianus, pars posterior, ed. J. C. Rolfe, *Ammianus Marcellinus*, vol. 3, LCL, Cambridge, MA: Harvard University Press, 1939.
Athanasius, Apologia ad Constantium, ed. H. C. Brennecke, U. Heil, A. von Stockhausen, *Athanasius: Werke*, vol. 2.8, Berlin: De Gruyter, 2006.
Athanasius, Historia Arianorum, ed. H. G. Opitz, *Athanasius: Werke*, vol. 2.1, Berlin: De Gruyter, 1934.
Augustine, Confessiones, ed. L. Verheijen, CCSL 27, Turnhout: Brepols, 1981.
Aurelius Victor, Liber de Caesaribus, ed. F. Pichlmayer, R. Gruendel, Leipzig: Teubner, 1970.
Baudonivia, Vita Radegundis (De vita sanctae Radegundis liber II), ed. B. Krusch, MGH SRM 2, Hannover: Hahn, 1888.
Bede, Chronica maiora, ed. Th. Mommsen, MGH AA 13, Berlin: Weidmann, 1898.
Bede, Historia ecclesiastica gentis anglorum, ed. B. Colgrave, R. A. B. Mynors, 2nd edn., Oxford: Clarendon, 1992.
Cades, Tommaso, *Impronte gemmarie dell'Istituto/Der 'große' Cades*, 78 vols., Daktyliotheca now in Rome, German Archaeological Institute, 1831–1868.
Cades, Tommaso, *Raccolta di ritratti di uomini illustri greci e latini*, Daktyliotheca now in Bonn, Akademisches Kunstmuseum.
Canons Ascribed to Maruta of Maipherqat and Related Sources, ed. A. Vööbus, CSCO 139/140, Script. Syr. 191/192, Louvain: Peeters, 1982.
Cassiodorus, Chronica, ed. Th. Mommsen, MGH AA 11, Berlin: Weidmann, 1894.
Cassius Dio, Historiae Romanae, ed. E. Cary, LCL, Cambridge, MA: Harvard University Press, 1954–1955.
Chronica Gallica a. 511, ed. Th. Mommsen, MGH AA 9, Berlin: Weidmann, 1892.
Chronicon Paschale, ed. L. Dindorf, Bonn: Weber, 1832.
Chronicle of Seert, ed. Scher Addai, *Histoire nestorienne inédite. Chronique de Séert*, PO 4, Paris: Firmin Didot, 1908.
Claudian, ed. M. Platnauer, LCL, 2 vols., Cambridge, MA: Harvard University Press, 1956.
Collectio Avellana, ed. O. Guenther, CSEL 35.2, Vienna: Gerold, 1895.
Constantius of Lyon, Vita Germani, ed. R. Borius, Sources Chrétiennes 112, Paris: du Cerf, 1965.

Consularia Constantinopolitana, ed. Th. Mommsen, MGH AA 9, Berlin: Weidmann, 1892.
Cyprian, Epistulae, ed. W. Hartel, CSEL 3.2., Vienna: Tempsky, 1871.
Cyril of Jerusalem, Catecheses mystagogicae, ed. A. Piédagnel, Sources Chrétiennes 126, Paris: du Cerf, 1988.
Cyril of Scythopolis, Vita Euthymii, ed. E. Schwartz, *Kyrillos von Skythopolis*, Leipzig: Hinrichs, 1939.
De locis sanctis martyrum, ed. R. Valentini, G. Zucchetti, *Codice topografico della città di Roma*, vol. 2, Rome: R. Istituto storico italiano per il medio evo, 1942.
Depositio martyrum, ed. R. Valentini, G. Zucchetti, *Codice topografico della città di Roma*, vol. 2, Rome: R. Istituto storico italiano per il medio evo, 1942.
Egeria, Itinerarium, ed. E. Franceschini, R. Weber, CCSL 175, Turnhout: Brepols, 1965.
Epitome de Caesaribus, ed. F. Pichlmayer, R. Gruendel, Leipzig: Teubner, 1970.
Eunapius, Lives of the Sophists, ed. W. C. Wright, LCL, Cambridge, MA: Harvard University Press, 1921.
Eusebius of Caesarea, Demonstratio evangelica, ed. I. A. Heikel, GCS 23, Leipzig: Hinrichs, 1913.
Eusebius of Caesarea, Historia ecclesiastica, ed. E. Schwartz, GCS 9.1–2, Leipzig: Hinrichs, 1903–1909.
Eusebius of Caesarea, Martyrs of Palestine, ed. G. Bardy, Sources Chrétiennes 55, Paris: du Cerf, 1967.
Eusebius of Caesarea, Onomasticon, ed. R. S. Notley, Z. Safrai, Boston, Leiden: Brill, 2005.
Eusebius of Caesarea, Tricennalian Oration/Laus Constantini, ed. I. A. Heikel, GCS 7, Leipzig: Hinrichs, 1902.
Eusebius of Caesarea, Vita Constantini, ed. F. Winkelmann, GCS 57, Berlin: Akademie Verlag, 1991.
Eutropius, Breviarium ab urbe condita, ed. C. Santini, Leipzig: Teubner, 1979.
Eutychius of Alexandria (Sa'id ibn Batiq), Annales, ed. M. Breydy, CSCO 471–472, Scriptores Arabici 44–45, Leuven: Peeters, 1985.
Evagrius, Historia ecclesiastica, ed. A. Hübner, Turnhout: Brepols, 2007.
Firmicus Maternus, Mathesis, ed. W. Kroll, F. Skutsch, 2 vols., Leipzig: Teubner, 1897–1913.
Fredegar, Chronica, ed. B. Krusch, MGH SRM 2, Hannover: Hahn, 1888.
Gaudentius of Brescia, Sermones, ed. A. Glueck, CSEL 68, Vienna: Hölder-Pichler-Tempsky, 1936.
Gelasius of Caesarea, Historia ecclesiastica, ed. M. Wallraff, J. Stutz, N. Marinides, GCS N.F. 25, Berlin: De Gruyter, 2017.
Gerontius, Vita Melaniae, ed. D. Gorce, Sources Chrétiennes 90, Paris: du Cerf, 1962.
Gesta de Xysti purgatione, ed. E. Wirbelauer, *Zwei Päpste in Rom. Der Konflikt zwischen Laurentius und Symmachus (498–514)*, Munich: Tuduv, 1993.
Gregory of Nazianzus, Orationes, ed. J. Mossay, Sources chrétiennes 270, Paris: du Cerf, 1980.
Gregory of Nyssa, In Flaccillam, ed. A. Spira, *Gregorii Nysseni opera*, vol. 9: Sermones, Leiden: Brill, 1967.
Gregory of Nyssa, Vita Macrinae, ed. V. W. Callahan, *Gregorii Nysseni opera*, vol. 8: Opera ascetica, Leiden: Brill, 1952.
Gregory of Tours, Decem libri historiarum, ed. B. Krusch, W. Levison, MGH SRM 1.1, Hannover: Hahn, 1951.

Gregory of Tours, Liber in gloria martyrum, ed. B. Krusch, MGH SRM 1.2, Hannover: Hahn, 1884.
Gregory of Tours, Liber in gloria confessorum, ed. B. Krusch, MGH SRM 1.2, Hannover: Hahn, 1884.
Gregory Thaumaturgus, Epistolae canonicae, ed. J. P. Migne, PG 10, Paris: Migne, 1857.
Gregory the Great, Epistulae, ed. D. Norberg, CCSL 140, 140A, Turnhout: Brepols, 1982.
Hamza ibn-al-Hasan (Hamza al-Isfahani), Annales, transl. U. M. Daudpota, *The Annals of Hamzah al-Isfahani*, Bombay: K.R. Cama Oriental Institute, 1932.
Hierocles, Synecdemus, ed. J. P. Migne, PG 113, Paris: Migne, 1864.
Historia Augusta, ed. D. Magie, LCL, Cambridge, MA: Harvard University Press, 1921–1932.
Itinerarium Burdigalense, ed. P. Geyer, O. Cuntz, CCSL 175, Turnhout: Brepols, 1965.
Itinerarium Malmesburiense, ed. R. Valentini, G. Zucchetti, *Codice topografico della città di Roma*, vol. 2, Rome: R. Istituto storico italiano per il medio evo, 1942.
Jerome, Chronicon, ed. R. Helm, GCS Eusebius Werke 7, Berlin: Akademie Verlag, 1984.
Jerome, Commentarii in Matthaeum, ed. D. Hurst, M. Adriaen, CCSL 77, Turnhout: Brepols, 1969.
Jerome, De viris illustribus, ed. W. Herding, Leipzig: Teubner, 1889.
Jerome, Epistulae, ed. J. Labourt, 8 vols., Paris: Les Belles Lettres, 1949–1963.
John Chrysostom, Ad viduam, ed. B. Grillet, H. Ettinger, Sources Chrétiennes 138, Paris: du Cerf, 1968.
John Chrysostom, Adversus Iudaeos, ed. J. P. Migne, PG 48, Paris: Migne, 1862.
John Chrysostom, Contra Iudaeos et Gentiles, quod Christus sit Deus, ed. J. P. Migne, PG 48, Paris: Migne, 1862.
John Chrysostomus, Homiliae XV in Epistolam ad Philippenses, ed. J. P. Migne, PG 62, Paris: Migne, 1862.
John Chrysostom, Homiliae XXI de statuis, ed. J. P. Migne, PG 49, Paris: Migne, 1862.
John Chrysostom, Homiliae dictae postquam reliquiae martyrum, ed. J. P. Migne, PG 63, Paris: Migne, 1862.
John Chrysostom, Homiliae LXXXVIII in Iohannem, ed. J. P. Migne, PG 59, Paris: Migne 1862.
John of Antioch, ed. S. Mariev, *Ioannis Antiocheni Fragmenta Quae Supersunt Omnia*, Berlin: De Gruyter, 2008.
John of Ephesus, Historia ecclesiastica, ed. E. W. Brooks, CSCO 105, Leuven: Peeters, 1935–1936.
John of Nikiu, Chronicle, transl. R. H. Charles, London, Oxford: Williams and Norgate, 1916.
John Rufus, Life of Peter the Iberian, transl. C. B. Horn. R. R. Phenix, Atlanta: Society of Biblical Literature, 2009.
John Rufus, De obitu Theodosii et Romani monachi, transl. C. B. Horn. R. R. Phenix, Atlanta: Society of Biblical Literature, 2009.
John the Lydian, De mensibus, ed. R. Wünsch, Leipzig: Teubner, 1898.
Jordanes, Romana, Getica, ed. Th. Mommsen, MGH AA 5.1, Berlin: Weidmann, 1882.
Julian, Epistulae, ed. W. C. Wright, LCL, Cambridge, MA: Harvard University Press, 1923.
Julian, Epistula ad Athenienses, ed. J. Bidez, *L'Empereur Julien. Oeuvres complètes*, vol. 1.1, Paris: Les Belles Lettres, 1932–1964.
Julian, Misopogon, ed. Ch. Lacombrade, *L'Empereur Julien. Oeuvres complètes*, vol. 2.2, Paris: Les Belles Lettres, 1932–1964.

Julian, Orationes, ed. J. Bidez, *L'Empereur Julien. Oeuvres complètes*, vol. 1.1, Paris: Les Belles Lettres, 1932–1964.
Justinian, Novellae, ed. R. Schoell, W. Kroll, Corpus Iuris Civilis, vol. 3, Berlin: Weidmann, 1954.
Lactantius, De mortibus persecutorum, ed. J. L. Creed, Oxford: Oxford University Press, 1995.
Letter to Cosmas/La Lettre à Cosme, ed. F. Nau, *Documents pour servir à l'histoire de l'Église nestorienne*, PO 13.2, Paris: Firmin-Didot, 1916.
Libanius, Orationes, ed. R. Foerster, *Libanius: Opera*, Leipzig: Teubner, 1903–1927.
Libellus de Constantino Magno eiusque matre Helena, ed. G. Giangrasso, Firenze: Gismel, 1999.
Malalas, Chronographia, ed. J. Thurn, Berlin: De Gruyter, 2000.
Marcellinus Comes, Chronica, ed. Th. Mommsen, MGH AA 11, Berlin: Weidmann, 1894.
Mark the Deacon, Vita Porphyrii Episcopi Gazensis, ed. Soc. Phil. Bon. Sodal., Leipzig: Teubner, 1895.
Merobaudes, Carmina, ed. F. Vollmer, MGH AA 14, Berlin: Weidmann, 1905.
Nikephoros, Historia ecclesiastica, ed. J. P. Migne, PG 100, Paris: Migne, 1863.
Notitia ecclesiarum urbis Romae, ed. R. Valentini, G. Zucchetti, *Codice topografico della città di Roma*, vol. 2, Rome: R. Istituto storico italiano per il medio evo, 1942.
Notitia urbis Constantinopolitanae, ed. O. Seeck, *Notitia dignitatum, accedunt notitia urbis Constantinopolitanae et Laterculi Provinciarum*, Frankfurt am Main: Minerva, 1962.
Optatus, Against the Donatists, ed. K. Ziwsa, *S. Optati Milevitani Libri VII*, CSEL 26, Vienna: Tempsky, 1893.
Origo Constantini Imperatoris (Anonymi Valesiani Pars Prior), ed. J. Moreau, *Excerpta Valesiana*, Leipzig: Teubner, 1961.
Orosius, Historiarum adversum paganos libri septem, ed. K. Zangemeister, CSEL 5, Hildesheim: Olms, 1967.
Palladius, Dialogue sur la vie de Jean Chrysostome, ed. A. M. Malingrey, Sources Chrétiennes 341, Paris: du Cerf, 1988.
Palladius, Historia Lausiaca, ed. G. J. M. Bartelink, Milan: Mondadori, 1974.
Panegyrici Latini, ed. R. A. B. Mynors, Oxford: Oxford University Press, 1964.
Parastaseis syntomoi chronikai, ed. T. Preger, *Scriptores Originum Constantinopolitarum*, vol. 1, Leipzig: Teubner, 1901.
Passio Agnetis et Emeritianae, ed. B. Mombritius, *Sanctuarium seu Vitae Sanctorum*, vol. 1, Hildesheim: Olms, 1978.
Passio Artemii, ed. B. Kotter, in *Johannes von Damaskos: Die Schriften. Band 5: Opera homiletica et hagiographica*, Berlin: De Gruyter, 1988.
Passio Gallicani, ed. B. Mombritius, *Sanctuarium seu Vitae Sanctorum*, vol. 1, Hildesheim: Olms, 1978.
Passio Iohannis et Pauli, ed. B. Mombritius, *Sanctuarium seu Vitae Sanctorum*, vol. 1, Hildesheim: Olms, 1978.
Patria of Constantinople, ed. T. Preger, *Scriptores Originum Constantinopolitarum*, vol. 2, Leipzig: Teubner, 1907.
Pauli Sententiae, ed. J. Baviera, Fontes iuris Romani anteiustiniani, vol. 2, 2nd edn., Florence: Barbèra, 1940.
Paulinus of Milan, Vita Ambrosii, ed. A. A. R. Bastiaensen, in C. Mohrmann (ed.), *Vite dei Santi*, vol. 3, Milan: Mondadori, 1975.

Paulinus of Nola, Epistulae, ed. G. de Hartel, M. Kamptner, CSEL 19, 2nd edn., Vienna: Verlag der Österreichischen Akademie der Wissenschaften, 1999.
Peter the Patrician, Fragments, ed. K. Müller, *Fragmenta Historicorum Graecorum*, Vol. 4, Paris: Didot, 1841–1870 (available at http://www.dfhg-project.org/).
Philostorgius, Historia ecclesiastica, ed. J. Bidez, F. Winkelmann, GCS 21, Berlin: Akademie Verlag, 1981.
Pliny, Historia naturalis, ed. H. Rackham, W. H. S. Jones, D. E. Eichholz, LCL, Cambridge, MA: Harvard University Press, 1949–1954.
Plutarch, Life of Alexander, ed. B. Perrin, *Plutarch: Lives*, vol. 7, LCL, Cambridge, MA: Harvard University Press, 1919.
Procopius, De bello Persico, ed. J. Haury, G. Wirth, Leipzig: Teubner, 1962.
Procopius, De aedificiis, ed. J. Haury, G. Wirth, Leipzig: Teubner, 1964.
Prosper Tiro, Epitoma Chronicon, ed. Th. Mommsen, MGH AA 9, Berlin: Weidmann, 1892.
Prosper Tiro, Epitoma Chronicon. Continuatio Codicis Reichenauensis, ed. Th. Mommsen, MGH AA 9, Berlin: Weidmann, 1892.
Ps.-Gelasius of Cyzikus, Historia ecclesiastica, ed. G. C. Hansen, GCS N.F. 9, Berlin: Akademie Verlag, 2002.
Ps.-Jerome, Exhortatio ad Marcellam, ed. J. P. Migne, Patrologia Latina 30, Paris: Migne, 1863.
Romanos Melodos, On Earthquakes and Fires, ed. P. Maas, C. A. Trypanis, Sancti Romani Melodi Cantica, vol. 1, Oxford: Clarendon Press, 1963.
Rufinus, Historia ecclesiastica, ed. E. Schwartz, Th. Mommsen, GCS Eusebius Werke 2.2, Leipzig: Hinrichs, 1908.
Sidonius Apollinaris, Epistulae et Carmina, ed. C. Lütjohann, MGH AA 8, Berlin: Weidmann, 1961.
Socrates, Historia ecclesiastica, ed. G. C. Hansen, GCS N.F. 1, Berlin: Akademie Verlag, 1995.
Sozomen, Historia ecclesiastica, ed. G. C. Hansen, Turnhout: Brepols, 2004.
Suda, Lexicon, ed. A. Adler, Leipzig: Teubner, 1928–1938.
Sulpicius Severus, Dialogi, ed. J. Fontaine, Sources Chrétiennes 510, Paris: du Cerf, 2006.
Sulpicius Severus, Chronica, ed. G. de Senneville-Grave, Sources Chrétiennes 441, Paris: du Cerf, 1999.
Symeon Logothete, Chronicon, ed. S. Wahlgren, Berlin: De Gruyter, 2006.
Synesius of Cyrene, Epistulae, ed. R. Hercher, Amsterdam: Hakkert, 1965.
Tertullian, Apologeticus, ed. H. Hoppe, CSEL 69–70, Vienna: Hoelder-Pichler-Tempsky, 1939–1942.
Themistius, Orationes, ed. W. Dindorf, Leipzig: Teubner, 1961.
Theodoret, Historia ecclesiastica, ed. L. Parmentier, F. Scheidweiler, GCS 44, Berlin: Akademie Verlag, 1954.
Theodor Lector, Historia ecclesiastica, ed. G. C. Hansen, GCS 57, Berlin: Akademie Verlag, 1971.
Theophanes, Chronographia, ed. K. De Boor, Leipzig: Teubner, 1883–1885.
Urkunden, ed. H. G. Opitz, *Athanasius Werke*, vol. 3.1, Berlin, Leipzig: De Gruyter, 1934–1935.
Venantius Fortunatus, Ad Iustinum et Sophiam Augustos, ed. F. Leo, MGH AA 4.1, Berlin: Weidmann, 1881.
Venantius Fortunatus, Vita Radegundis (De vita sanctae Radegundis liber I), ed. B. Krusch, MGH SRM 2, Hannover: Hahn, 1888.

Victor of Tunnuna, Chronica, ed. Th. Mommsen, MGH AA 11, Berlin: Weidmann, 1894.
Vita Barsaumae, ed. F. Nau, "Résumé de Monographies Syriaques. Histoire de Barsauma de Nisibie," *Revue de l'Orient chrétien* 18 (1913) 270–76, 379–89; 19 (1914) 113–34, 278–89.
Vita Luciani, ed. J. Bidez, *Philostorgius, Historia ecclesiastica*, Anhang 6, GCS 21, Leipzig: Hinrichs, 1913.
Zonaras, Epitome historiarum, ed. M. Pinder, Bonn: Weber, 1897.
Zosimus, Historia nea, ed. F. Paschoud, 3 vols., Paris: Les Belles Lettres, 1971–1989.

Modern Studies

Annetta Alexandridis (2000), "Exklusiv oder bürgernah? Die Frauen des römischen Kaiserhauses im Bild," in Kunst, Riemer, 9–18.

Andreas Alföldi (1955), "Zur Erklärung der konstantinischen Deckengemälde in Trier," *Historia* 4, 131–50.

Maria R. Alföldi (1959–1960), "Helena nobilissima femina: Zur Deutung der Trierer Deckengemälde," *Jahrbuch für Numismatik und Geldgeschichte* 10, 79–90.

Maria R. Alföldi (1963), *Die constantinische Goldprägung. Untersuchungen zu ihrer Bedeutung für Kaiserpolitik und Hofkunst*, Mainz: Verlag des römisch-germanischen Zentralmuseum Mainz/Rudolf Habelt.

Géza Alföldy (2014), *The Social History of Rome*, London: Routledge (rev. English transl. of 3rd German edn., 1984).

Eugenio Alliata, Rosario Pierri (2002), "Il Monte degli Ulivi nella Demonstratio evangelica di Eusebio di Cesarea," *Liber Annuus: Annual of the Studium Biblicum Franciscanum Jerusalem* 52, 307–20.

Diliana N. Angelova (2015), *Sacred Founders: Women, Men, and Gods in the Discourse of Imperial Founding, Rome through Early Byzantium*, Oakland: University of California Press.

F. P. Arata (1993), "La statua seduta dell'imperatrice Elena nel Museo Capitolino. Nuove considerazioni conseguenti il recente restauro," *Mitteilungen des deutschen archäologischen Instituts. Römische Abteilung* 100, 185–200.

Antti Arjava (1996), *Women and Law in Late Antiquity*, Oxford: Oxford University Press.

Pascal Arnaud (2005), *Les routes de la navigation antique: Itinéraires en Méditerranée*, Paris: Éditions Errance.

Linnea Åshede (2016), "A Demanding Supply: Prostitutes in the Roman World," in S. L. Budin, J. MacIntosh Turfa (eds.), *Women in Antiquity, Real Women Across the Ancient World*, London: Routledge, 923–41.

Roger S. Bagnall, Raffaella Cribiore (2006), with contributions by Evie Ahtaridis, *Women's Letters from Ancient Egypt, 300BC–800AD*, Ann Arbor: University of Michigan Press.

Nicholas Baker-Brian, Shaun Tougher (eds.) (2020), *The Sons of Constantine, AD 337–361: In the Shadows of Constantine and Julian*, Cham: Palgrave MacMillan.

Mariarosaria Barbera, Marina Magnani Cianetti (2016), "Costantino all'Esquilino: Il Sessorium e il cd. Tempio di Minerva Medica," in Brandt, Castiglia, Fiocchi Nicolai, 361–76.

Jonathan Bardill (2012), *Constantine, Divine Emperor of the Christian Golden Age*, Cambridge, UK: Cambridge University Press.

Timothy D. Barnes (1978), "Emperor and Bishops, A.D. 324–344: Some Problems," *American Journal of Ancient History* 3, 53–75.

Timothy D. Barnes (1981), *Constantine and Eusebius*, Cambridge, MA: Harvard University Press.

Timothy D. Barnes (1982), *The New Empire of Diocletian and Constantine*, Cambridge, MA: Harvard University Press.
Timothy D. Barnes (1987), "Himerius and the Fourth Century," *Classical Philology* 82, 206–25.
Timothy D. Barnes (1989), "Panegyric, History and Hagiography in Eusebius' Life of Constantine," in R. Williams (ed.), *The Making of Orthodoxy: Essays in Honour of Henry Chadwick*, Cambridge, UK: Cambridge University Press, 94–123.
Timothy D. Barnes (1993), *Athanasius and Constantius: Theology and Politics in the Constantinian Empire*, Cambridge, MA: Harvard University Press.
Timothy D. Barnes (1998), *Ammianus Marcellinus and the Representation of Historical Reality*, Ithaca, NY, and London: Cornell University Press.
Timothy D. Barnes (1999), "The Wife of Maximinus," *Classical Philology* 94, 459–60.
Timothy D. Barnes (2004), "The Date of the Martyrdom of Lucian of Antioch," *Zeitschrift für Antikes Christentum* 8, 350–53.
Timothy D. Barnes (2010), "The Letter of Eusebius to Constantia (CPG 3503)," *Studia Patristica* 46, 313–17.
Timothy D. Barnes (2014), *Constantine. Dynasty, Religion and Power in the Later Roman Empire*, Malden, MA: Wiley-Blackwell.
Jennifer Barry (2019), *Bishops in Flight. Exile and Displacement in Late Antiquity*, Oakland: University of California Press.
Elizabeth Bartman (2001), "Hair and the Artifice of Roman Female Adornment," *AJA* 105, 1–25.
F. L. Bastet (1968), "Die grosse Kamee in Den Haag," *Bulletin Antieke Beschaving* 43, 2–22.
Alicia Batten (2009), "Neither Gold nor Braided Hair (1 Timothy 2.9; 1 Peter 3.3): Adornment, Gender and Honour in Antiquity," *New Testament Studies* 55, 484–501.
Roger Beck (1999), "The Astronomical Design of Karakush, a Royal Burial Site in Ancient Commagene: An Hypothesis," *Culture and Cosmos* 3, 10–34.
Klaus Belke (2020), *Tabula Imperii Byzantini, Vol. 13: Bithynia und Hellespont*, Vienna: Verlag der Österreichischen Akademie der Wissenschaften.
Ria Berg (2003), "Wearing Wealth. *Mundus Muliebris* and *Ornatus* as Status Markers for Women in Imperial Rome," in P. Setälä, R. Berg, R. Hälikkä, M. Keltanen, J. Pölönen, V. Vuolanto (eds.), *Women, Wealth and Power in the Roman Empire*, Rome: Acta Instituti Romani Finlandiae, 15–73.
Marianne Bergmann (1977), *Studien zum römischen Porträt des 3. Jahrhunderts n. Chr.*, Bonn: Habelt.
Marianne Bergmann (1989), "Die Nase der Fausta und Flavia Maxima Theodora?," in N. Başgelen, M. Lugal (eds.), *Festschrift für Jale Inan: Armağani*, Istanbul: Arkeoloji ve Sanat Yayinlari, 327–36.
Markus Beyeler (2011), *Geschenke des Kaisers. Studien zur Chronologie, zu den Empfängern und zu den Gegenständen der kaiserlichen Vergabungen im 4. Jahrhunder n. Chr.*, Berlin: Akademie Verlag.
Martin Biddle (2000), "The History of the Church of the Holy Sepulchre," in M. Biddle (ed.), *The Church of the Holy Sepulchre*, New York: Rizzoli, 23–62.
Ernest Bihain (1973), "L'Épître de Cyrille de Jérusalem à Constance sur la vision de la croix (BHG³ 413)," *Byzantion* 43, 246–96.

Mette Birkedal Bruun, Louis Hamilton (2016), "Rites for Dedicating Churches," in H. Gittos, S. Hamilton (eds.), *Understanding Medieval Liturgy: Essays in Interpretation*, London: Routledge, 177-204.
Bruno Bleckmann (1994), "Constantina, Vetranio und Gallus Caesar," *Chiron* 24, 29-68.
Bruno Bleckmann (2002), "Die severische Familie und die Soldatenkaiser," in Temporini-Gräfin Vitzhum 2002b, 265-339.
Bruno Bleckmann (2003a), "Die Vita BHG 365 und die Rekonstruktion der verlorenen Kirchengeschichte Philostorgs. Der Kampf zwischen Konstantin und Licinius," *JAC* 46, 7-16.
Bruno Bleckmann (2003b), "Gallus, César de l'Orient?," in F. Chausson, E. Wolff (eds.), *Consuetudinis amor: Fragments d'histoire romaine (IIe-VIe siècles) offerts à Jean-Pierre Callu*, Rome: L'Erma di Bretschneider, 45-56.
Hanswulf Bloedhorn (1995), "Die Eleona und das Imbomon in Jerusalem: Eine Doppelkirchanlage auf dem Ölberg?," in E. Dassmann, J. Engemann (eds.), *Akten des XII. Internationalen Kongresses für christliche Archäologie, Bonn, 22.-28. September 1991*, Münster: Aschendorff, 568-71.
Mary T. Boatwright (1991), "The Imperial Women of the Early Second Century AD," *The American Journal of Philology* 112, 513-40.
Michail A. Bojcov (2009), "Der Heilige Kranz und der heilige Pferdezaum des Kaisers Konstantin und des Bischofs Ambrosius," *Frühmittelalterliche Studien* 42, 1-69.
Giorgio Bonamente, Noël Lenski, Rita Lizzi Testa (eds.) (2012), *Costantino prima e dopo Costantino = Constantine Before and After Constantine*, Bari: Edipuglia.
Barbara Borg (2013), *Crisis and Ambition. Tombs and Burial Customs in Third Century CE Rome*, Oxford: Oxford University Press.
Stephan Borgehammar (1991), *How the Holy Cross Was Found: From Event to Mediaeval Legend*, Stockholm: Almqvist & Wiksell International.
Elisabetta Borgia, Donato Colli, Sergio Palladino, Claudia Paterna (2008a), "Horti Spei Veteris e Palatium Sessorianum: Nuove acquisizioni da interventi urbani 1996-2008," Part I, *The Journal of Fasti Online* (available at www.fastionline.org/docs/FOLDER-it-2008-124.pdf).
Elisabetta Borgia, Donato Colli, Sergio Palladino, Claudia Paterna (2008b), "Horti Spei Veteris e Palatium Sessorianum: Nuove acquisizioni da interventi urbani 1996-2008," Part II, *The Journal of Fasti Online* (available at www.fastionline.org/docs/FOLDER-it-2008-125.pdf).
Laura Bottiglieri, Donato Colli, Sergio Palladino (2016), "Il comprensorio archaeologico di S. Croce in Gerusalemme a Roma: Nuovi interventi di riqualificazione e recenti scoperte (2013-2014)," *Bollettino di Archeologia Online* 7 (available at https://bollettino diarcheologiaonline.beniculturali.it/).
Glen W. Bowersock (2002), "Peter and Constantine," in Carrié, Lizzi Testa, 209-17.
Kim Bowes (2008), *Private Worship, Public Values and Religious Change in Late Antiquity*, Cambridge, UK: Cambridge University Press.
Alan Bowman, Averil Cameron, Peter Garnsey (eds.) (2005), *Cambridge Ancient History, Vol. 12: The Crisis of Empire, A.D. 193-337*, 2nd edn., Cambridge, UK: Cambridge University Press.
Jan Bouzek, Denver Graninger (2015), "Geography," in J. Valeva, E. Nankov, D. Graninger (eds.), *A Companion to Ancient Thrace*, Chichester, UK: Wiley-Blackwell, 12-21.
Hugo Brandenburg (1985), "Zur Deutung der Deckenbilder aus der Trierer Domgrabung," *Boreas* 8, 143-89.

Hugo Brandenburg (2004), *Die frühchristlichen Kirchen Roms vom 4. bis zum 7. Jahrhundert. Der Beginn der abendländischen Kirchenbaukunst*, Regensburg: Schnell + Steiner.

Ulrich Brandl, Miloje Vasić (eds.) (2007), *Roms Erbe auf dem Balkan. Spätantike Kaiservillen und Stadtanlagen in Serbien*, Mainz: Zabern.

Olof Brandt, Gabriele Castiglia, Vincenzo Fiocchi Nicolai (eds.) (2016), *Acta XVI Congressus Internationalis Archaeologiae Christianae: Romae (22.-28.9.2013): Costantino e i Costantinidi: l'innovazione costantiniana, le sue radici e i suoi sviluppi* (Vol. 1-2), Vatican City: Pontificio Istituto di Archeologica Cristiana.

Jan N. Bremmer (1999), "Pauper or Patroness. The Widow in the Early Christian Church," in J. Bremmer, L. van den Bosch, *Between Poverty and Pyre: Moments in the History of Widowhood*, London: Routledge, 31–57.

Beat Brenk (1987), "Spolia from Constantine to Charlemagne: Aesthetics versus Ideology," *DOP* 41, 103–9.

T. Corey Brennan (2018), *Sabina Augusta: An Imperial Journey*, Oxford: Oxford University Press.

W. R. F. Browning (2009), *A Dictionary of the Bible*, 2nd edn., Oxford: Oxford University Press.

Leslie Brubaker (1997), "Memories of Helena: Patterns in Imperial Female Matronage in the Fourth and Fifth Centuries," in Liz James (ed.), *Women, Men and Eunuchs: Gender in Byzantium*, London: Routledge, 52–73.

Leslie Brubaker, Helen Tobler (2000), "The Gender of Money: Byzantine Empresses on Coins (324–802)," *G&H* 12, 572–94.

Gerda Bruns (1948), *Staatskameen des 4. Jahrhunderts nach Christi Geburt*, Berlin: De Gruyter, 29–31.

Patrick Bruun (1961), *Studies in Constantinian Chronology*, New York: The American Numismatic Society, 1–75.

Patrick Bruun (1966), "General Introduction," in id. *Roman Imperial Coinage, Vol. 7: Constantine and Licinius*, London: Spink & Son.

Patrick Bruun (1997), "The Victorious Signs of Constantine: A Reappraisal," *NC* 157, 41–59.

Richard Burgess (1993–1994), "The Accession of Marcian in the Light of Chalcedonian Apologetic and Monophysite Polemic," *Byzantinische Zeitschrift* 86-87, 47–68.

Richard Burgess (1999), "ΑΧΥΡΩΝ or ΠΡΟΑΣΤΕΙΟΝ? The Location and Circumstances of Constantine's Death," *JTS* n.s. 50, 153–61.

Richard Burgess (2008), "The Summer of Blood: The 'Great Massacre' of 337 and the Promotion of the Sons of Constantine," *DOP* 62, 5–51.

Richard Burgess, Witold Witakowski (1999), *Studies in Eusebian and Post-Eusebian Chronography*, Stuttgart: Franz Steiner.

Virgina Burrus (2020), "Remembering Constantina at the Tomb of Agnes and Beyond," in Y. R. Kim, A. T. McLaughlin (eds.), *Leadership and Community in Late Antiquity: Essays in Honour of Raymond Van Dam*, Turnhout: Brepols, 165–88.

Anja Busch (2015), *Die Frauen der theodosianischen Dynastie. Macht und Repräsentation kaiserlicher Frauen im 5. Jahrhundert*, Stuttgart: Franz Steiner.

Lauren Caldwell (2015), *Roman Girlhood and the Fashioning of Feminity*, Cambridge, UK: Cambridge University Press.

Jean-Pierre Callu (2002), "Naissance de la dynastie constantinienne: le tournant de 314–316," in Carrié, Lizzi Testa, 131–40.

Raissa Calza (1972), *Iconografia romana imperiale da Carausio a Giuliano (287–363 d.C.)*, Rome: L'Erma di Bretschneider.
Nenad Cambi (2004), "Tetrarchic Practice in Name Giving," in A. Demandt (ed.), *Diokletian und die Tetrarchie. Aspekte einer Zeitenwende*, Berlin: De Gruyter, 38–46.
Nenad Cambi (2007), "Das frühe Christentum," in M. Sanander (ed.), *Kroatien in der Antike*, Mainz: Zabern, 121–36.
Nenad Cambi, Josip Belamarić, Tomislav Marasović (eds.) (2009), *Dioklecijan, Tetrarhija i Dioklecijanova Palača. O 1700 Obljetnici Postojanja/Diocletian, Tetrarchy and Diocletian's Palace. On the 1700th Anniversary of Existence*, Split: Književni krug Publishers.
Alan Cameron (1996), "Orfitus and Constantia: A Note on Roman Gold-Glasses," *JRA* 9, 295–301.
Averil Cameron (1976), "The Early Religious Policies of Justin II," *Studies in Church History* 13, 51–67.
Averil Cameron (1997), "Eusebius' Vita Constantini and the Construction of Constantine," in M. Edwards, S. Swain (eds.), *Portraits: Biographical Representations in the Greek and Latin Literature of the Roman Empire*, Oxford: Clarendon, 145–74.
Averil Cameron, Stuart Hall (1999), *Eusebius: Life of Constantine*, Oxford: Clarendon.
Averil Cameron, Judith Herrin (1984), *Constantinople in the Eighth Century. The Parastaseis Syntomoi Chronikai*, Leiden: Brill.
Tessa Canella (2013), "Gli Actus Silvestri tra Oriente e Occidente. Storia e diffusione di una leggenda costantiniana," in A. Melloni, P. Brown, J. Helmrath, E. Prinzivalli, S. Ronchey, N. Tanner (eds.), *Costantino I. Enciclopedia costantiniana sulla figura e l'immagine dell'imperatore del cosiddetto Editto di Milano 313–2013*, Rome: Istituto della Enciclopedia Italiana Treccani, 241–58.
Filippo Carlà (2012), "Le iconografie monetali e l'abbandono del linguaggio tetrarchico: l'evoluzione dell'autorappresentazione imperiale (306–310 d. C.)," in Bonamente, Lenski, Lizzi Testa, 59–84.
Bernard Carra de Vaux (1896), *Maçoudi. Le livre de l'avertissement et de la revision*, Paris: Imprimerie Nationale.
Jean Michel Carrié, Rita Lizzi Testa (eds.) (2002), *"Humana sapit": Études d'Antiquité tardive offertes à Lellia Cracco Ruggini*, Turnhout: Brepols.
Maureen Carroll (2018), *Infancy and Earliest Childhood in the Roman World: "A Fragment of Time,"* Oxford: Oxford University Press.
Alessandra Cerrito (2019), "Un inedito frammento di iscrizione onoraria proveniente dal comprensorio dell'Ospedale di San Giovanni-Addolorata," *Mitteilungen des Deutschen Archäologischen Instituts, Römische Abteilung*, 125, 289–311.
Henry Chadwick (1948), "The Fall of Eustathius of Antioch," *JTS* 49, 27–35.
Edward Champlin (1982), "St. Gallicanus (Consul 317)," *Phoenix* 36, 71–76.
André Chastagnol (1960), *La préfecture urbaine à Rome sous le Bas-Empire*, Paris: Presses universitaires de France.
François Chausson (2002), "Une Sœur de Constantin: Anastasia," in Carrié, Lizzi Testa, 129–53.
François Chausson (2007), *Stemmata aurea: Constantin, Justine, Théodose. Revendications généalogiques et idéologie impériale au IVe siècle*, Rome: L'Erma di Bretschneider.
Robert Cioffi (2016), "Travel in the Roman World," *Oxford Handbooks Online* (available at https://www.oxfordhandbooks.com/view/10.1093/oxfordhb/9780199935 390.001.0001/oxfordhb-9780199935390-e-110).

Elizabeth Clark (1990), "Patrons not Priests: Gender and Power in Late Ancient Christianity," *G&H* 2, 253–74.

Gillian Clark (1993), *Women in Late Antiquity: Pagan and Christian Lifestyles*, Oxford: Clarendon.

Manfred Clauss (2002), "Die Frauen der diokletianisch-konstantinischen Zeit," in Temporini-Gräfin Vitzhum 2002b, 340–69.

Frank Clover (1971), *Flavius Merobaudes: A Translation and Historical Commentary*, Philadelphia: American Philosophical Society.

Filippo Coarelli (1986), "L'urbs e il suburbio," in A. Giardina (ed.), *Società romana e impero tardoantico, Vol. 2: Roma-politica, economia, paesaggio urbano*, Rome, Bari: Laterza, 1–58.

Filippo Coarelli (2016), "Mausolei imperiali tardoantichi: le origini di un tipo architettonico," in Brandt, Castiglia, Fiocchi Nicolai, 493–508.

Antonio Maria Colini (1955), "Horti Spei Veteris, Palatium Sessorianum," *Atti della Pontificia Accademia Romana di Archeologia. Memorie* 8, 137–77.

Donato Colli (1996), "Il Palazzo Sessoriano nell'area archeologica di S. Croce in Gerusalemme: Ultima sede imperiale a Roma?," *Mélanges de l'École française de Rome/Antiquité* 109, 771–815.

Franca Ela Consolino (1995), "La 'santa' regina da Elena a Galla Placidia nella tradizione dell'Occidente latino," in R. Raffaelli, *Vicende e figure femminili in Grecia e a Roma*, Ancona: Commissione per le pari opportunità tra uomo e donna della Regione Marche, 467–92.

Franca Ela Consolino (2001), "Helena Augusta. From Innkeeper to Empress," in A. Fraschetti (ed.), *Roman Women*, Chicago: Chicago University Press, 141–59.

Marco Conti, Virginia Burrus, Dennis Trout (2020), *The Lives of Saint Constantina*, Oxford: Oxford University Press.

Alison Cooley (2013), "Women Beyond Rome: Trend-Setters or Dedicated Followers of Fashion?," in E. Hemelrijk, G. Woolf (eds.), *Women and the Roman City in the Latin West*, Leiden, Boston: Brill, 23–46.

Lynda Coon (1997), *Sacred Fictions: Holy Women and Hagiography in Late Antiquity*, Philadelphia: University of Pennsylvania Press.

Kate Cooper (1992), "Insinuations of Womanly Influence: An Aspect of the Christianization of the Roman Aristocracy," *JRS* 82, 150–64.

Kate Cooper (1996), *The Virgin and the Bride: Idealized Womanhood in Late Antiquity*, Cambridge, MA: Harvard University Press.

Kate Cooper (2007a), "Closely Watched Households: Visibility, Exposure and Private Power in the Roman Domus," *Past & Present* 197, 3–33.

Kate Cooper (2007b), *The Fall of the Roman Household*, Cambridge, UK: Cambridge University Press.

Kate Cooper (2013), *Band of Angels: The Forgotten World of Early Christian Women*, New York: Overlook Press.

Kate Cooper, Julia Hillner (eds.) (2007), *Religion, Dynasty and Patronage in Early Christian Rome, 300–900*, Cambridge, UK: Cambridge University Press.

Simon Corcoran (2012), "Grappling with the Hydra: Co-ordination and Conflict in the Management of Tetrarchic Succession," in Bonamente, Lenski, Lizzi Testa, 3–16.

Simon Corcoran (2017), "Maxentius: A Roman Emperor in Rome," *AnTard* 25, 59–74.

Mats Cullhed (1994), *Conservator urbis Romae: Studies in the Politics and Propaganda of the Emperor Maxentius*, Stockholm: Paul Åströms Ferlög.

John Curran (2000), *Pagan City and Christian Capital: Rome in the Fourth Century*, Oxford: Oxford University Press.
Gilbert Dagron (1996), *Empereur et prêtre: Étude sur le 'césaropapisme' byzantine*, Paris: Éditions Gallimard.
Erin T. Dailey (2015), *Queens, Consorts, Concubines: Gregory of Tours and the Women of the Merovingian Elite*, Leiden, Boston: Brill.
Caillan Davenport (2017), "Rome and the Rhythms of Imperial Life from the Antonines to Constantine," *AnTard* 25, 23-39.
Raymond Davis (2010), *The Book of Pontiffs: The Ancient Biographies of the First Ninety Bishops to AD 715*, 3rd edn., Liverpool: Liverpool University Press.
Sible de Blaauw (1997), "Jerusalem and the Cult of the Cross," in R. L. Colella (ed.), *Pratum Romanum: Richard Krautheimer zum 100. Geburtstag*, Wiesbaden: Reichert, 55-73.
Sible de Blaauw (2014), "Translations of the Sacred City between Jerusalem and Rome," in J. Goudeau, M. Verhoeven, W. Weijers (eds.), *The Imagined and Real Jerusalem in Art and Architecture*, Leiden, Boston: Brill, 136-66.
Friedrich Wilhelm Deichmann, Arnold Tschira (1957), "Das Mausoleum der Kaiserin Helena und die Basilika der Heiligen Marcellinus und Petrus an der via Labicana," *Jahrbuch des Deutschen Archäologischen Instituts* 72, 44-110.
Richard Delbrueck (1932), *Antike Porphyrwerke*, Berlin: De Gruyter.
Richard Delbrueck (1933), *Spätantike Kaiserporträts: Von Constantinus Magnus bis zum Ende des Westreichs*, Berlin: De Gruyter.
Roland Delmaire (1989), *Largesses sacrées et res privata: L'aerarium impérial et son administration du IVe au VIe siècle*, Rome: École Française de Rome.
Paolo Delogu (2011), "Costantino, Elena e il mausoleo sulla via Labicana," in Vendittelli 2011a, 12-29.
Deborah Mauskopf Delyannis (2010), *Ravenna in Late Antiquity*, New York: Cambridge University Press.
Alexander Demandt, Josef Engemann (eds.) (2007), *Konstantin der Grosse. Imperator Caesar Flavius Constantinus: Ausstellungskatalog*, Mainz: Zabern.
Eric De Sena (2014), "Constantine in the Imperial Palace in Serdica," in Nenad Lemajić (ed.), *International Symposium on Constantine, Sirmium and Early Christianity (Proceedings)*, Sremska Mitrovica: Institute for the Protection of Cultural Monuments, 7-24.
Sylvain Destephen (2018), "En représentation et par délégation: La souveraine chrétienne sur les routes au Bas-Empire," in F. Chausson, S. Destephen (eds.), *Augusta, Regina, Basilissa: La souveraine de l'Empire romain au Moyen Âge*, Paris: De Boccard, 37-58.
Steffen Diefenbach (2007), *Römische Erinnerungsräume: Heiligenmemoria und Kollektive Identitäten im Rom des 3. bis 5. Jahrhunderts n. Chr.*, Berlin: De Gruyter.
Margherita Di Mattia (2003), "L'imperatrice Eusebia fra tradizione storiografica, tecnica, retorica e funzioni narrative," *Siculorum Gymnasium* 56, 327-49.
Lucietta Di Paola (2016), "Mansiones e stathmoi nelle fonti letterarie tardoantiche: Destinazione d'uso, equipaggiamento, immagini," in P. Basso, E. Zanini (eds.), *Statio amoena: Sostare e vivere lungo le strade romane*, Oxford: Archaeopress, 9-18.
Michaela Dirschlmayer (2015), *Kirchenstiftungen römischer Kaiserinnen vom 4. bis zum 6. Jahrhundert. Die Erschließung neuer Handlungsspielräume*, Münster: Aschendorff.
Suzanne Dixon (2001), *Reading Roman Women: Source, Genres and Real Life*, London: Duckworth.

Glanville Downey (1959), "The Tombs of the Byzantine Emperors at the Church of the Holy Apostles in Constantinople," *JHS* 79, 27–51.

Harold A. Drake (1985), "Eusebius on the True Cross," *JEH* 36, 1–22.

Harold A. Drake, Tito Orlandi, Birger Pearson (1980), *Eudoxia and the Holy Sepulchre: A Constantinian Legend in Coptic*, Milan: Cisalpino-Goliardica.

Vlastimil Drbal (2014), "Die christliche und pagane Pilgerfahrt in der Zeit Konstantins des Großen: die heilige Helena vs. Nikagoras von Athen," in E. Juhász (ed.), *Byzanz und das Abendland II: Studia Byzantino-Occidentalia*, Budapest: Eötvös József Collegium, 119–34.

Jan Willem Drijvers (1992a), *Helena Augusta: The Mother of Constantine the Great and the Legend of Her Finding the True Cross*, Leiden: Brill.

Jan Willem Drijvers (1992b), "Flavia Maxima Fausta. Some Remarks," *Historia* 41, 500–506.

Jan Willem Drijvers (1993), "Helena Augusta: Exemplary Christian Empress," *Studia Patristica* 24, 85–90.

Jan Willem Drijvers (1997), "The Protonike Legend, the Doctrina Addai and Bishop Rabbula of Edessa," *Vigiliae Christianae* 51, 288–315.

Jan Willem Drijvers (2001), "Marutha of Maïpherqat on Helena Augusta, Jerusalem and the Council of Nicaea," *Studia Patristica* 34, 51–64.

Jan Willem Drijvers (2011), "Helena Augusta. Cross and Myth: New Reflections," *Millennium: Yearbook on the Culture and History of the First Millennium C.E.* 8, 125–74.

Jan Willem Drijvers (2016), "Helena Augusta and the City of Rome," in M. Verhoeven, L. Bosman, H. van Asperen (eds.), *Monuments & Memory: Christian Cult Buildings and Constructions of the Past: Essays in Honour of Sible de Blaauw*, Turnhout: Brepols, 149–55.

John F. Drinkwater (2000), "The Revolt and Ethnic Origin of the Usurper Magnentius (350–353) and the Rebellion of Vetranio," *Chiron* 30, 131–59.

John F. Drinkwater (2005), "Maximinus to Diocletian and the 'Crisis,'" in Bowman, Cameron, Garnsey, 28–66.

John F. Drinkwater (2007), *The Alamanni and Rome 213–496: Caracalla to Clovis*, Oxford: Oxford University Press.

Richard P. Duncan-Jones (1977), "Age-Rounding, Illiteracy and Social Differentiation in the Roman Empire," *Chiron* 7, 333–53.

Ejnar Dyggve, Frederik Weilbach (1933), *Recherches à Salone*, Vol. 2, Copenhagen: J.H. Schultz.

Bonnie Effros (1990), "Images of Sanctity: Contrasting Descriptions of Radegund by Venantius Fortunatus and Gregory of Tours," *UCLA Historical Journal* 10, 38–58.

Bonnie Effros (2002), *Caring for Body and Soul: Burial and Afterlife in the Merovingian World*, University Park: Pennsylvania State University Press.

Kay Ehling (2001), "Die Erhebung des Nepotianus in Rom im Juni 350 n. Chr. und sein Programm der urbs Roma christiana," *Göttinger Forum für Altertumswissenschaft* 4, 141–58.

Simon Ellis (2000), *Roman Housing*, London: Duckworth.

Jaś Elsner, Ian Rutherford (2005), "Introduction," in id. (eds.), *Pilgrimage in Graeco-Roman and Early Christian Antiquity: Seeing the Gods*, Oxford: Oxford University Press, 1–38.

Wilhelm Enßlin (1930), "Maximianus (1)," *RE* 14, no. 2, 2486–516.

Chris Entwistle, Noël Adams (eds.) (2011), *"Gems of Heaven": Recent Research on Engraved Gemstones in Late Antiquity, c. AD 200–600*, London: British Museum.
Thomas Etzemüller (2012), *Biographien: Lesen—Erforschen—Erzählen*, Frankfurt, New York: Campus Verlag.
Judith Evans Grubbs (1995), *Law and Family in Late Antiquity: The Emperor Constantine's Marriage Legislation*, Oxford: Oxford University Press.
Rebecca Stephens Falcasantos (2017), "Wandering Wombs, Inspired Intellects: Christian Religious Travel in Late Antiquity," *JECS* 25, 89–117.
Charles Favez (1932), "L'épisode de l'invention de la Croix dans l'oration funèbre de Théodose par St. Ambroise," *Revue des études latines* 10, 423–29.
Jane Fejfer (2008), *Roman Portraits in Context*, Berlin: De Gruyter.
Snežana Ferjančič (2013), "History of the Roman Provinces in the Territory of Modern Day Serbia during the Principate," in Popović, Borić-Brešković, 16–25.
Erica Filippini (2016), *"Felix progenies Constantini Aug*: Alcune osservazioni intorno a *RIC* VII, Treviri, 442," in Neri, Girotti, 225–38.
Klaus Fittschen, Paul Zanker (1983), *Katalog der römischen Porträts in den Kapitolinischen Museen und den anderen kommunalen Sammlungen der Stadt Rom, Vol. 3: Kaiserinnen- und Prinzessinenbildnisse*, Mainz: Zabern.
Sandra Ann Fortner, Andrea Rottloff (2000), *Auf den Spuren der Kaiserin Helena: Römische Aristokratinnen pilgern ins Heilige Land*, Erfurt: Alan Sutton.
Fabiola Fraioli (2012), "Region V. Esquiliae," in A. Carandini, P. Carafa (eds.), *The Atlas of Ancient Rome: Biography and Portraits of the City*, 2 vols., Princeton, NJ: Princeton University Press, 323–41.
Robert M. Frakes (2005), "The Dynasty of Constantine Down to 363," in Lenski 2005, 91–208.
Monika Frass (2006), *Antike römische Gärten: Soziale und wirtschafliche Funktionen der Horti Romani*, Horn: Berger.
Amato Pietro Frutaz (1969), *Il complesso monumentale di Sant'Agnese e di Santa Costanza*, 2nd edn., Vatican City: Tipografia poliglotta vaticana.
Elisabetta Gagetti (2011), "Three Degrees of Separation: Detail Reworking, Type Updating and Identity Transformation in Roman Imperial Glyptic Portraits in the Round," in Entwistle, Adams 135–48.
Marcello Gaggiotti (2010), "La gens Neratia," in G. De Benedittis (ed.), *La Villa dei Neratii: Campagne di scavo 2004–2010*, Campobasso: Palladino, 14–32.
Osvaldo Garbarino (2005), "Il Santo Sepolcro di Gerusalemme: Appunti di ricerca storico-architettonica," *Liber Annuus: Annual of the Studium Biblicum Franciscanum* 55, 239–314.
Patrick Geary (2006), *Women at the Beginning. Origin Myths from the Amazons to the Virgin Mary*, Princeton, NJ: Princeton University Press.
Ulrich Gehn, Bryan Ward Perkins (2016), "Constantinople," in Smith, Ward Perkins, 136–44.
Andriani Georgiou (2013), "Helena: The Subversive Persona of an Ideal Christian Empress in Early Byzantium," *JECS* 21, 597–624.
Stephen Gero (1981), "The True Image of Christ: Eusebius' Letter to Constantia Reconsidered," *JTS*, n.s., 32, 460–70.
Roy Gibson (2020), *Man of High Empire: The Life of Pliny the Younger*, Oxford: Oxford University Press.

Karl-Josef Gilles (1986), "Eine unbekannte Hochzeitsprägung der Fausta aus Trier," *Funde und Ausgrabungen im Bezirk Trier* 18, 44-47.
Judith Ginsburg (2006), *Representing Agrippina: Constructions of Female Power in the Early Roman Empire*, Oxford: Oxford University Press.
Klaus-Peter Goethert, Marco Kiessel (2007), "Trier--Residenz in der Spätantike," in Demandt, Engemann, 304-11.
Walter Goffart (1980), *Barbarians and Romans, AD 418-584: The Techniques of Accommodation*, Princeton, NJ: Princeton University Press.
Ittai Gradel (2002), *Emperor Worship and Roman Religion*, Oxford: Clarendon Press.
Lucy Grig, Gavin Kelly (2012), "Introduction: Rome and Constantinople in Context," in L. Grig, G. Kelly (eds.), *Two Romes. Rome and Constantinople in Late Antiquity*, Oxford: Oxford University Press, 3-30.
Miriam J. Groen-Vallinga, Laurens E. Tacoma (2017), "The Value of Labour: Diocletian's Price Edict," in K. Verboven, C. Laes (eds.), *Work, Labour and Professions in the Roman World*, Leiden: Brill, 104-32.
Tziona Grossmark (2006), "The Inn as a Place of Violence and Danger in Rabbinic Literature," in H.A. Drake, *Violence in Late Antiquity: Perceptions and Practices*, Aldershot, UK: Ashgate, 57-68.
Maria Cristina Gualandi Genito (1975), "Ritratti tardo-imperiali su lucerne cristiane," *Felix Ravenna. Rivista di Antichità Ravennati, Cristiane e Bizantine* 109-110, 79-95.
Raffaella Giuliani (2016), "Un ritratto ritrovato dell'Augusta Elena dal complesso *ad duas lauros*," in Brandt, Castiglia, Fiocchi Nicolai, 879-93.
Margherita Guarducci (1972), "Nuove testimonianze per la 'domus Faustae'?," *Archeologia Classica* 24, 386-92.
Serena Guglielmi (2016), "Un gruppo statuario di età costantiniana dal *Sessorium*," in Brandt, Castiglia, Fiocchi Nicolai, 1337-58.
Michelangelo Guidi (1908), *Un Bios di Costantino*, Rome: Tipografia della R. Accademia dei Lincei.
Federico Guidobaldi (1999), "Sessorium," *LTUR* 4, 304-8.
Jean Guyon (1987), *Le cimetière aux deux lauriers: Recherches sur les catacombes romaines*, Rome: École Française.
David Gwynn (2007), *The Eusebians: The Polemic of Athanasius of Alexandria and the Construction of the "Arian controversy,"* Oxford: Oxford University Press.
Cynthia Hahn (2006), "Collector and Saint: Queen Radegund and Devotion to the Relic of the True Cross," *Word and Image* 22, 268-74.
Ruud Halbertsma (2015), "Nulli tam laeti triumphi—Constantine's Victory on a Reworked Cameo in Leiden," *BABESCH* 90, 221-36.
Guy Halsall (1998), "Burial, Ritual and Merovingian Society," in J. Hill, M. Swan (eds.), *The Community, the Family, and the Saint: Patterns of Power in Early Medieval Europe*, Turnhout: Brepols, 325-38.
Guy Halsall (2014), "Two Worlds Become One: A 'Counter-Intuitive' View of the Roman Empire and 'Germanic' Migration," *German History* 32, 515-32.
R. P. C. Hanson (1988), *The Search for the Christian Doctrine of God: The Arian Controversy 318-38*, Edinburgh: T&T.
Antonina Harbus (2002), *Helena of Britain in Medieval Legend*, Cambridge, UK: D.S. Brewer.
Jill Harries (2012), *Imperial Rome AD 284-363: The New Empire*, Edinburgh: Edinburgh University Press.

Jill Harries (2013), "Men Without Women: Theodosius' Consistory and the Business of Government," in C. Kelly (ed.), *Theodosius II: Rethinking the Roman Empire in Late Antiquity*, Cambridge, UK: Cambridge University Press, 67–89.

Jill Harries (2014), "The Empress Tale, AD 300–360," in Harrison, Humfress, Sandwell, 197–214.

Carol Harrison, Caroline Humfress, Isabella Sandwell (eds.) (2014), *Being Christian in Late Antiquity: A Festschrift for Gillian Clark*, Oxford: Oxford University Press.

Elizabeth Hartley, Jane Hawkes, Martin Henig, Frances Mee (2006), *Constantine the Great: York's Roman Emperor*, York, UK: York Museums and Gallery Trust.

Stefan Heid (1989), "Der Ursprung der Helenalegende im Pilgerbetrieb Jerusalems," *JAC* 32, 41–71.

Stefan Heid (2001), "Die gute Absicht im Schweigen Eusebs über die Kreuzauffindung," *Römische Quartalschrift* 96, 37–56.

Heinz Heinen (1995), "Helena, Konstantin und die Überlieferung der Kreuzesauffindung im 4. Jahrhundert," in E. Arentz (ed.), *Der Heilige Rock zu Trier: Studien zur Geschichte und Verehrung der Tunika Christi*, Trier: Paulinus Verlag, 83–117.

Heinz Heinen (1998), "Konstantins Mutter Helena: De stercore ad regnum," *Trierer Zeitschrift* 61, 227–40.

Heinz Heinen (2008), "Konstantins Mutter Helena: Geschichte und Bedeutung," *Archiv für Mittelrheinische Kirchengeschichte* 60, 9–29.

Olivier Hekster (2015), *Emperors and Ancestors: Roman Rulers and the Constraints of Tradition*, Oxford: Oxford University Press.

Monica Hellström (2016), "On the Form and Function of Constantine's Circiform Funerary Basilicas in Rome," in Salzman, Sághy, Lizzi Testa, 291–313.

Emily A. Hemelrijk (2015), *Hidden Lives, Public Personae: Women and Civic Life in the Roman West*, New York: Oxford University Press.

Martin Henig (2006), "N. 76, Cameo," in Hartley, Hawkes, Henig, Mee, 138–39.

Karen K. Hersch (2010), *The Roman Wedding: Ritual and Meaning in Antiquity*, Cambridge, UK: Cambridge University Press.

Hermann Gottlieb Heumann, Emil Seckel (1971), *Handlexikon zu den Quellen des römischen Rechts*, 11th edn., Graz: Akademische Druck- und Verlagsanstalt.

Julia Hillner (2015), *Prison, Punishment and Penance in Late Antiquity*, Cambridge, UK: Cambridge University Press.

Julia Hillner (2017a), "A Woman's Place: Imperial Women in Late Antique Rome," *AnTard* 25, 75–94.

Julia Hillner (2017b), "Constantia, Half-Sister of Constantine and Wife of Licinius," *Oxford Classical Dictionary Online* (available at https://doi.org/10.1093/acrefore/ 9780199381135.013.8065).

Julia Hillner (2018), "Constantina, Daughter of Constantine, Wife of Gallus Caesar, and Patron of St. Agnes at Rome," *Oxford Classical Dictionary Online* (available at https:// doi.org/10.1093/acrefore/9780199381135.013.8066).

Julia Hillner (2019a), "Imperial Women and Clerical Exile in Late Antiquity," *SLA* 3, 369–412.

Julia Hillner (2019b), "Preserving Female Voices: Female Letters in Late Antique Letter Collections," in R. Lizzi Testa, G. Marconi (eds.), *A Late Antique Experiment in Canon Law: The Collectio Avellana and its Revivals*, Cambridge, UK: Cambridge Scholars, 210–44.

Julia Hillner (2019c), "Empresses, Queens and Letters: Finding a 'Female Voice' in Late Antiquity?," *G&H* 31, 353–82.

Julia Hillner, Máirín MacCarron, Ulriika Vihervalli (2022), "The Politics of Female Namelessness Between Late Antiquity and the Early Middle Ages," *JLA* 15.2.

Alfred Hirt (2015), "Centurions, Quarries, and the Emperor," in P. Erdkamp, K. Verboven, A. Zuiderhoek (eds.), *Ownership and Exploitation of Land and Natural Resources in the Roman World*, Oxford: Oxford University Press, 289–314.

R. Ross Holloway (2004), *Constantine and Rome*, New Haven, CT, and London: Yale University Press.

Kenneth Holum (1982), *Theodosian Empresses: Women and Imperial Dominion in Late Antiquity*, Berkeley and Los Angeles: University of California Press.

Kenneth Holum (1990), "Hadrian and St. Helena: Imperial Travel and the Origins of Christian Holy Land Pilgrimage," in R. Ousterhout (ed.), *The Blessings of Pilgrimage*, Urbana and Chicago: University of Illinois Press, 1990, 66–81.

Cornelia Horn (2004), "Empress Eudocia and the Monk Peter the Iberian: Patronage, Pilgrimage, and the Love of a Foster-Mother in Fifth-Century Palestine," *Byzantinische Forschungen* 28, 197–214.

Sabine Huebner (2007), "'Brother-Sister' Marriage in Roman Egypt: A Curiosity of Humankind or a Widespread Family Strategy?," *JRS* 97, 21–49.

Sabine Huebner (2013), *The Family in Roman Egypt: A Comparative Approach to Intergenerational Solidarity and Conflict*, Cambridge, UK: Cambridge University Press.

Sabine Huebner, David M. Ratzan (2009), "Fatherless Antiquity? Perspectives on 'Fatherlessness' in the Ancient Mediterranean," in id. (eds.), *Growing Up Fatherless in Antiquity*, Cambridge, UK: Cambridge University Press, 3–28.

Franz Humer (2014), *Carnuntum. Wiedergeborene Stadt der Kaiser*, Mainz: Zabern.

Caroline Humfress (2020), "'Cherchez la femme!' Heresy and Law in Late Antiquity," *Studies in Church History* 56, 36–59.

John H. Humphrey (1986), *Roman Circuses. Arenas for Chariot Racing*, Berkeley and Los Angeles: University of California Press.

Mark Humphries (2000), *Communities of the Blessed: Social Environments and Religious Change in Northern Italy, AD 200–400*, Oxford: Oxford University Press.

Mark Humphries (2007), "From Emperor to Pope? Ceremonial, Space and Authority at Rome from Constantine to Gregory the Great," in Cooper, Hillner, 21–58.

Mark Humphries (2020), "The Memory of Mursa: Usurpation, Civil War and Contested Legitimacy under the Sons of Constantine," in Baker-Brian, Tougher, 157–83.

Anne Hunnell Chen (2018), "Omitted Empresses: The (Non-)Role of Imperial Women in Tetrarchic Propaganda," *JLA* 11, 42–82.

Edward David Hunt (1982), *Holy Land Pilgrimage in the Later Roman Empire*, Oxford: Clarendon Press.

Edward David Hunt (1997), "Constantine and Jerusalem," *JEH* 48, 405–24.

Frauke Hutmacher (2010), "Von der Ehefrau zur Mutter. Die Bedeutung des Herrscherwechsels für die Person der Kaiserin im frühen Prinzipat," *Potestas* 3, 53–68.

Oded Irshai (2006), "From Oblivion to Fame: The History of the Palestinian Church (135–303 CE)," in Limor, Stroumsa, 91–140.

Benjamin Isaac (1997), "The Eastern Frontier," in Bowman, Cameron, Garnsey, 437–60.

Andrew S. Jacobs (2016), *Epiphanius of Cyprus: A Cultural Biography*, Oakland: University of California Press.

Liz James (2001), *Empresses and Power in Early Byzantium*, London: Leicester University Press.
Liz James (2013), "Ghosts in the Machine: The Lives and Deaths of Constantinian Imperial Women," in L. Garland, B. Neil (eds.), *Questions of Gender in Byzantine Society*, London: Routledge, 93-112.
Jasna Jeličić-Radonić (2009), "Diocletian and the Salona urbs orientalis," in Cambi, Belamarić, Marasović, 307-33.
Gordana Jeremić, Aleksandra Filipović (2016), "Traces of Early Christianity in Naissus," in Brandt, Castiglia, Fiocchi Nicolai, 1743-58.
Mark J. Johnson (2005), "Architecture of Empire," in Lenski 2005, 278-97.
Mark J. Johnson (2009), *The Roman Imperial Mausoleum in Late Antiquity*, Cambridge, UK: Cambridge University Press.
Hannah Jones (2007), "Agnes and Constantina: Domesticity and Cult Patronage in the Passion of Agnes," in Cooper, Hillner, 115-39.
Sandra Joshel (1992), *Work, Identity and Legal Status at Rome: A Study of the Occupational Inscriptions*, Norman: University of Oklahoma Press.
Heinz Kähler (1962), *Die Stiftermosaiken in der Konstantinischen Südkirche von Aquileia*, Cologne: M. Dumont Schauberg Verlag.
Mika Kajava (1985), "Some Remarks on the Name and the Origin of Helena Augusta," *Acta Philologica Fennica* 19, 41-54.
Ioli Kalavrezou (2012), "Light and the Precious Object, or Value in the Eyes of the Byzantines," in J. K. Papadopoulos (ed.), *The Construction of Value in the Ancient World*, Los Angeles: Cotsen Institute of Archaeology at UCLA, 354-69.
Dayna S. Kalleres (2005), "Cultivating True Sight at the Center of the World: Cyril of Jerusalem and the Lenten Catechumenate," *Church History* 74, 431-59.
Max Kaser (1971), *Das römische Privatrecht*, Vol. 1, 2nd edn., Munich: C.H. Beck.
Alexander Kazhdan (1987), "Constantin imaginaire: Byzantine Legends of the Ninth Century about Constantine the Great," *Byzantion* 57, 196-250.
Christopher Kelly (2006), *Ruling the Later Roman Empire*, Cambridge, MA, London: Harvard University Press.
Gavin Kelly (2003), "The New Rome and the Old: Ammianus Marcellinus' Silences on Constantinople," *Classical Quarterly* 53, 588-607.
Theodor Kempf (1950), "Konstantinische Deckenmalereien aus dem Trierer Dom," *Trierer Zeitschrift für Geschichte und Kunst des Trierer Landes und seiner Nachbargebiete* 19, 45-51.
Theodor Kempf (1977), "Die konstantinischen Deckenmalereien aus dem Trierer Dom," *Archäologisches Korrespondenzblatt* 7, 147-60.
Theodor Kempf (1978), "Das Haus der heiligen Helena," in *Neues Trierisches Jahrbuch: Beiheft*, Trier: Paulinus-Druckerei, 3-16.
J. P. C. Kent (1981), "Historical Survey," in id., *The Roman Imperial Coinage*, Vol. 8, London: Spink & Son, 5-18.
Bente Kiileric (2014), "Defacement and Replacement as Political Strategies in Ancient and Byzantine Ruler Images," in K. Kolrud, M. Prusac (eds.), *Iconoclasm from Antiquity to Modernity*, Farnham, UK: Ashgate, 57-73.
Young Richard Kim (2015), *Epiphanius of Cyprus. Imagining an Orthodox World*, Ann Arbor: University of Michigan Press.
Mark Kinkead-Weekes (2002), "Writing Lives Forwards," in P. France, W. St Clair (eds.), *Mapping Lives: The Uses of Biography*, Oxford: Oxford University Press, 235-52.

Richard Klein (1988), "Helena II (Kaiserin)," in *Reallexikon für Antike und Christentum*, Vol. 14, Stuttgart: Hiersemann, 355–75.
W. Eugene Kleinbauer (2006), "Antioch, Jerusalem, and Rome: The Patronage of Emperor Constantius II and Architectural Invention," *Gesta* 45, 125–45.
Ulrike Koenen (1996), "Symbol und Zierde auf Diadem und Kronreif spätantiker und byzantinischer Herrscher und die Kreuzauffindungslegende bei Ambrosius," *JAC* 39, 170–99.
Anne Kolb (ed.) (2010a), *Augustae: Machtbewusste Frauen am römischen Kaiserhof*, Berlin: Akademie Verlag.
Anne Kolb (2010b), "Augustae. Zielsetzung, Definition, Prosopographischer Überblick," in Kolb 2010a, 11–38.
Frank Kolb (2007), "Das kaiserliche Zeremoniell," in Demandt, Engemann, 173–78.
Wilhelm Kraatz (1904), *Koptische Akten zum Ephesinischen Konzil vom Jahre 431*, Leipzig: Hinrichs.
Richard Krautheimer (1937), "S. Croce in Gerusalemme," CBCR 1, 165–94.
Richard Krautheimer (1959), "SS. Marcellino e Pietro on the Via Labicana," CBCR 2, 191–204.
Richard Krautheimer, Spencer Corbett, with R. E. Malmstrom (1977), "S. Giovanni in Laterano," CBCR 5, 1–92.
Antje Krug (2011), "The Belgrade Cameo," in Entwistle, Adams, 188–91.
Mathew Kuefler (2015), "The Merry Widows of Late Roman Antiquity: The Evidence of the Theodosian Code," *G&H* 27, 28–52.
Michael Kulikowski (2007), *Rome's Gothic Wars. From the Third Century to Alaric*, Cambridge, UK: Cambridge University Press.
Christiane Kunst (2010), "Patronage/Matronage der *Augustae*," in Kolb 2010a, 145–61.
Christiane Kunst, Ulrike Riemer (2000), *Grenzen der Macht. Zur Rolle der römischen Kaiserfrauen*, Stuttgart: Franz Steiner.
Donald G. Kyle (1998), *Spectacles of Death in Ancient Rome*, London, New York: Routledge.
Bertrand Laçon, Tiphaine Moreau (2012), *Constantin. Un Auguste chrétien*, Paris: Armand Colin.
Christian Laes (2011), *Children in the Roman Empire: Outsiders Within*, Cambridge, UK: Cambridge University Press.
Alice Landkron (2006), "Zur Gewandstatue im Museum Carnuntinum," *Forum Archaeologiae. Zeitschrift für klassische Archäologie* 38 (available at http://farch.net).
Julie Langford (2013), *Maternal Megalomania. Julia Domna and the Imperial Politics of Motherhood*, Baltimore: Johns Hopkins.
Last Statues of Antiquity Database, available at http://laststatues.classics.ox.ac.uk/
Jacob A. Latham (2016), *Performance, Memory and Processions in Ancient Rome: The Pompa Circensis from the Late Republic to Late Antiquity*, Cambridge, UK: Cambridge University Press.
Patrick Laurence (2002), "Helena, mère de Constantin: Métamorphoses d'une image," *Augustinianum* 42, 75–96.
Irving Lavin (1967), "An Ancient Statue of the Empress Helena Reidentified," *Art Bulletin* 49, 58.
Bill Leadbetter (1998), "The Illegitimacy of Constantine and the Birth of the Tetrarchy," in Lieu, Montserrat, 74–85.
Bill Leadbetter (2009), *Galerius and the Will of Diocletian*, London: Routledge.

Douglas Lee (2007), *War in Late Antiquity: A Social History*, Maiden, MA, and Oxford: Blackwell.
Hermione Lee (2009), *Biography: A Very Short Introduction*, Oxford: Oxford University Press.
Andrew Lenox-Conyngham (1982), "The Topography of the Basilica Conflict of A.D. 385/6 in Milan," *Historia* 31, 353–63.
Noel Lenski (2002), *Failure of Empire: Valens and the Roman State in the Fourth Century A.D.*, Berkeley: University of California Press.
Noel Lenski (2004), "Empresses in the Holy Land: The Creation of a Christian Utopia in Late Antique Palestine," in L. Ellis, F. L. Kidner (eds.), *Travel, Communication and Geography in Late Antiquity*, Farnham, UK: Ashgate, 113–124.
Noel Lenski (ed.) (2005), *The Cambridge Companion to the Age of Constantine*, Cambridge, UK: Cambridge University Press.
Noel Lenski (2016), *Constantine and the Cities: Imperial Authority and Christian Politics*, Philadelphia: University of Pennsylvania Press.
Hartmut Leppin (2003), *Theodosius der Große: Auf dem Weg zum Christlichen Imperium*, Darmstadt: Primus.
Hartmut Leppin (2011), "Das Bild des Gallus bei Philostorg: Überlegungen zur Traditionsgeschichte," in D. Meyer (ed.), *Philostorge et l'historiographie de l'Antiquité tardive*, Stuttgart: Steiner, 185–202.
Barbara Levick (2014), *Faustina I and II. Imperial Women of the Golden Age*, Oxford: Oxford University Press.
Blake Leyerle (2009), "Mobility and the Traces of Empire," in P. Rousseau (ed.), *A Companion to Late Antiquity*, Malden, MA: Blackwell, 110–24.
Wolf Liebeschuetz (2005), *Ambrose of Milan: Political Speeches and Letters* (Translated Texts for Historians), Liverpool: Liverpool University Press.
Wolf Liebeschuetz (2007), "Was There a Crisis of the Third Century?," in O. Hekster, G. de Kleijn, D. Slootjes (eds.), *Crises and the Roman Empire*, Leiden: Brill, 11–20.
Wolf Liebeschuetz (2011), *Ambrose and John Chrysostom: Clerics between Desert and Empire*, Oxford: Oxford University Press.
Samuel N. C. Lieu (1998), "From History to Legend and Legend to History: The Medieval and Byzantine Transformation of Constantine's Vita," in Lieu, Montserrat, 136–76.
Samuel N. C. Lieu, Dominic Montserrat (1998), *Constantine. History, Historiography and Legend*, London, New York: Routledge.
Richard Lim (1999), "In the Temple of Laughter: Visual and Literary Representations of Spectators at Roman Games," *Studies in the History of Art* 56, 342–65.
Vasiliki Limberis (1994), *Divine Heiress, the Virgin Mary and the Creation of Christian Constantinople*, London: Routledge.
Ora Limor (2014), "Mary in Jerusalem: An Imaginary Map," in B. Kühnel, G. Noga-Banai, H. Vorholt (eds.), *Visual Constructs of Jerusalem*, Turnhout: Brepols, 11–22.
Ora Limor, Guy G. Stroumsa (eds.) (2006), *Christians and Christianity in the Holy Land: From the Origins to the Latin Kingdoms*, Turnhout: Brepols.
Jeanette Lindblom (2019), *Women and Public Space: Social Codes and Female Presence in the Byzantine Urban Society of the 6th to the 8th Centuries*, Helsinki: Unigrafia.
Paolo Liverani (1990), "L'ambiente nell'antichità," in C. Pietrangeli (ed.), *San Giovanni in Laterano*, Florence: Nardini, 22–37.
Paolo Liverani (2004), "L'area lateranense in età tardoantica e le origini del Patriarchio," *MEFR/Antiquité* 116, 17–49.

Paolo Liverani (2015), "Old St. Peter's and the Emperor Constans? A Debate with G. W. Bowersock," *JRA* 28, 485–504.
Paolo Liverani (2020), "The Evolution of the Lateran: From the Domus to the Episcopal Complex," in L. Bosman, I. Haynes, P. Liverani (eds.), *The Basilica of Saint John Lateran to 1600*, Cambridge, UK: Cambridge University Press, 6–24.
Alastair Logan (2011), "Constantine, the Liber pontificalis and the Christian Basilicas of Rome," *Studia Patristica* 50, 31–53.
Yannis Lolos (2007), "Via Egnatia after Egnatius: Imperial Policy and Intra-Regional Contacts," *Mediterranean Historical Review* 22, 273–93.
Katia Longo (2009), *Donne di potere nella tarda antichità: Le Augustae attraverso le immagini monetali*, Reggio Calabaria: Falzea Editore.
Hans Peter L'Orange (1984), *Das spätantike Herrscherbild von Diokletian bis zu den Konstantin-Söhnen 284–361 n. Chr.*, Berlin: Gebr. Mann Verlag.
Maria Losito (2010), "Novità archeologiche sul Santo Sepolcro a Gerusalemme: Aelia Capitolina e la nascita dell'Anastasis costantiniana (I parte)," *Arte cristiana: Rivista internazionale di storia dell'arte e di arti liturgiche* 98, 59–69.
Sophie Lunn Rockliffe (2008), "Ambrose's Imperial Funeral Orations," *JEH* 59, 191–207.
Sabine Mac Cormack (1976), "Latin Prose Panegyric: Tradition and Continuity in the Later Roman Empire," *Revue d'études augustiniennes et patristiques* 22, 29–77.
Máirín MacCarron (2017), "Royal Marriage and Conversion in Bede's Historia Ecclesiastica Gentis Anglorum," *JTS* n.s. 68, 650–70.
Christopher S. Mackay, "Lactantius and the Succession to Diocletian," *Classical Philology* 94 (1999), 198–209.
Gillian Mackie (1997), "A New Look at the Patronage of Santa Costanza, Rome," *Byzantion* 67, 383–406.
Harry O. Maier (1994), "Private Space as the Social Context of Arianism in Ambrose's Milan," *JTS* n.s. 45, 72–93.
Marco Maiuro (2007), "Archivi, amministrazione del patrimonio e proprietà imperiali nel Liber Pontificalis: la redazione del libellus copiato nella vita Sylvestri," in D. Pupillo (ed.), *Le proprietà imperiali in Italia romana: Economia, produzione, amministrazione*, Florence: Le Lettere, 235–58.
Pierre-Louis Malosse (2001), "Noblesse, sottise et tragédie. Le regard porté par Julien sur sa propre famille," *Quaderni di storia (Bari)* 54, 41–67.
Cyril Mango (1990), "Constantine's Mausoleum and the Translation of Relics," *BZ* 83, 51–62.
Cyril Mango (1994), "The Empress Helena, Helenopolis, Pylae," *Travaux et Mémoires* 12, 143–58.
Pierre Maraval (2002), "The Earliest Phase of Christian Pilgrimage in the Near East (before the 7th Century)," *DOP* 56, 63–74.
Pierre Maraval (2013), *Les fils de Constantin*, Paris: CNRS Éditions, 2013.
Moysés Marcos (2014), "Constantine, Dalmatius and the Summer of A.D. 337," *Latomus* 73, 748–74.
Adrian B. Marsden (1999), "Imperial Portrait Gems, Medallions and Mounted Coins: Changes in Imperial *donativa* in the 3rd Century AD," in M. Henig, D. Plantzos (eds.), *Classicism to Neo-Classicism: Essays dedicated to Gertrud Seidmann*, Oxford: Archaeopress, 89–103.
Jules Maurice (1908), *Numismatique constantinienne, Vol. 1: Iconographie et chronologie. Description historique des émissions monétaires*, Paris: Ernest Leroux.

Jules Maurice (1914), "Potraits d'impératrices de l'époque constantinienne," *NC* 14, 314–29.
Anne McClanan (2002), *Representations of Early Byzantine Empresses: Image and Empire*, New York: Palgrave.
Meaghan McEvoy (2013), *Child Emperor Rule in the Late Roman West, AD 367–455*, Oxford: Oxford University Press.
Meaghan McEvoy (2016), "Constantia. The Last Constantinian," *Antichthon* 50, 154–79.
Meaghan McEvoy (2020), "Imperial Cities under the Sons of Constantine," in Baker-Brian, Tougher, 275–307.
Meaghan McEvoy (2021), "Orations for the First Generation of Theodosian Imperial Women," *JLA* 14, 117–41.
Susanna McFadden (2013), "A Constantinian Image Program in Rome Rediscovered: The Late Antique Megalographia from the So-Called Domus Faustae," *MAAR* 58, 83–114.
Thomas A. J. McGinn (1991), "Concubinage and the Lex Iulia on Adultery," *TAPhA* 121, 335–75.
Thomas A. J. McGinn (1997), "The Legal Definition of Prostitute in Late Antiquity." *MAAR* 42, 73–116.
Thomas A. J. McGinn (1998), *Prostitution, Sexuality, and the Law in Ancient Rome*, New York, Oxford: Oxford University Press.
Thomas A. J. McGinn (2002), "The Augustan Marriage Legislation and Social Practice: Elite Endogamy versus Male 'Marrying Down,'" in J.-J. Aubert, B. Sirks (eds.), *In Speculum Iuris: Roman Law as a Reflection of Social and Economic Life in Antiquity*, Ann Arbor: University of Michigan Press, 46–93.
Thomas A. J. McGinn (2004), *The Economy of Prostitution in the Roman World: A Study of Social History and the Brothel*, Ann Arbor: University of Michigan Press.
Anne McGowan, Paul F. Bradshaw (2018), *The Pilgrimage of Egeria: A New Translation of the Itinerarium Egeriae with Introduction and Commentary*, Collegeville, MN: Liturgical Press.
Paul McKechnie (2019), *Christianizing Asia Minor: Conversion, Communities and Social Change in the Pre-Constantinian Era*, Cambridge, UK: Cambridge University Press.
Neil B. McLynn (1994), *Ambrose of Milan: Church and Court in a Christian Capital*, Berkeley: University of California Press.
Neil B. McLynn (2006), "The Transformations of Imperial Churchgoing in the Fourth Century," in M. Edwards, S. Swain (eds.), *Approaching Late Antiquity: The Transformation from Early to Late Empire*, Oxford: Oxford University Press, 235–70.
Jo Ann McNamara (1996), "Imitatio Helenae: Sainthood as an Attribute of Queenship in the Early Middle Ages," in S. Sticca (ed.), *Saints: Studies in Hagiography*, Binghamton, NY: MRTS, 61–80.
Jo Ann McNamara, E. Gordon Whatley, and John E. Halborg (eds.) (1992), *Sainted Women of the Dark Ages*, Durham, NC: Duke University Press.
Aristotelis Mentzos (2010), "Reflections on the Architectural History of the Tetrarchic Palace Complex at Thessalonikē," in L. Nasrallah, C. Bakirtzis, S. J. Friesen (eds.), *From Roman to Early Christian Thessalonikē: Studies in Religion and Archaeology*, Cambridge, MA: Harvard Divinity School, 333–59.
Joseph F. Merriman (1977), "The Empress Helena and the Aqua Augustea," *Archeologia Classica* 29, 436–46.
Charlotte Methuen (1997), "The 'Virgin Widow': A Problematic Social Role for the Early Church?," *Harvard Theological Review* 90, 285–98.

Fergus Millar (1971), "Paul of Samosata, Zenobia and Aurelian: The Church, Local Culture and Political Allegiance in Third-Century Syria," *JRS* 61, 1–17.

Gordana Milosević (2013), "The Architecture of the Residential Complex in Mediana," in Popović, Borić-Brešković, 118–25.

S. C. Mimouni (1990), "La synagogue 'judeo-chrétienne' de Jerusalem au Mont Sion," *Proche-Orient Chrétien* 40, 215–34.

Miroslava Mirković (2007), *Moesia superior: Eine Provinz an der mittleren Donau*, Mainz: Zabern.

Dragana Mladenović (2009), "Astral Path to Soul Salvation in Late Antiquity? The Orientation of Two Late Roman Imperial Mausolea from Eastern Serbia," *AJA* 113, 81–97.

Yves Moderand (1998), "Gildon," *Encylopédie Berbère* 20, 3134–36.

Isabel Moreira (1993), "Provisatrix Optima: St Radegund of Poitiers' Relic Petitions to the East," *Journal of Medieval History* 19, 285–305.

Francesca Romana Morretti (2006), "I pannelli dipinti della Cappella 'Cristiana' nell'area dell'Ospedale S. Giovanni," in M. Andaloro (ed.), *L'orizzonte tardoantico e le nuove immagini, 312–468*, Vol. 1, Rome: Jaca Book, 419–24.

Muriel Moser (2016), "Le concept de dynastie d'après les inscriptions de Constantin et des Constantinides," in Brandt, Castiglia, Fiocchi Nicolai, 1235–43.

Muriel Moser (2017), "Ein Kaiser geht auf Distanz: Zur Rompolitik Constans' I," *AnTard* 25, 41–58.

Muriel Moser (2018), *Emperor and Senators in the Reign of Constantius II: Maintaining Imperial Rule Between Rome and Constantinople in the Fourth Century AD*, Cambridge, UK: Cambridge University Press.

René Mouterde (1908–1909), "Notes épigraphiques." *Mélanges de l'Université Saint-Joseph Beyrouth (Faculté Orientale)* 3, 535–55.

Jakob Munk Højte (2000), "Imperial Visits as Occasion for the Erection of Portrait Statues?," *ZPE* 133, 221–35.

Geoffrey Nathan (2000), *The Family in Late Antiquity: The Rise of Christianity and the Endurance of Tradition*, London, New York: Routledge.

Gerard Nauroy (2016), "The Letter Collection of Ambrose of Milan," in Watts, Storin, Sogno, 146–60.

Isabel Lasala Navarro (2009a), *Helena Augusta: Una biografía histórica*, dissertation, Universidad de Zaragoza.

Isabel Lasala Navarro (2009b), "Epigrafia Helenae, compendio, analisis y conclusiones," *Epigraphica: Periodico Internazionale di Epigrafia* 71, 241–61.

Valerio Neri, Beatrice Girotti (eds.) (2016), *La famiglia tardoantica: Società, diritto, religione*, Milan: Edizioni Universitarie LED.

Caitríona Ní Dhúill (2020), *Metabiography: Reflecting on Biography*, Cham: Palgrave Macmillan.

C. E. V. Nixon, Barbara Saylor Rodgers (1994), *In Praise of Later Roman Emperors: The Panegyrici Latini*, Berkeley and Los Angeles: University of California Press.

Galit Noga Banai (2019), "Relocation to the West: The Relic of the True Cross in Poitiers," in S. Esders, Y. Fox, Y. Hen, L. Sarti (eds.), *East and West in the Early Middle Ages: The Merovingian Kingdoms in Mediterranean Perspective*, Cambridge, UK: Cambridge University Press, 189–201.

Johannes Nollé (1993), *Side im Altertum: Geschichte und Zeugnisse*, Bonn: Habelt.

Valeria Novembri (2008), "Elena e le altre. Imperatrici e regine sulla via di Gerusalemme tra IV e VI secolo," *Vetera Christianorum* 45, 301-22.

David Noy (2011), "Goodbye Livia: Dying in the Roman Home," in V. Hope, J. Huskinson (eds.), *Memory and Mourning: Studies on Roman Death*, Oxford: Oxbow, 1-20.

Charles Matson Odahl (2004), *Constantine and the Christian Empire*, London: Routledge.

Konstantin Olbrich (2010), "Kaiser in der Krise. Religions- und rechtsgeschichtliche Aspekte der 'Familienmorde' des Jahres 326," *Klio. Beiträge zur alten Geschichte* 92, 104-17.

Adrastos Omissi (2018), *Emperors and Usurpers in the Later Roman Empire: Civil War, Panegyric, and the Construction of Legitimacy*, Oxford: Oxford University Press.

Fatih Onur (2006), "Some Late Roman Inscriptions from Side," *Gephyra: Zeitschrift für die Geschichte und Kulturen des Antiken Östlichen Mittelmeerraums* 3, 103-200.

Dafne Oosten (2016), "The Mausoleum of Helena and the Adjoining Basilica Ad Duas Lauros: Construction, Evolution and Reception," in M. Weijers, L. Bosman, H. van Asperen (eds.), *Monuments & Memory: Christian Cult Buildings and Constructions of the Past. Essays in Honour of Sible de Blaauw*, Turnhout: Brepols, 131-43.

Hans-Georg Opitz (1934), "Die Vita Constantini des Codex Angelicus 22," *Byzantion* 9, 535-93.

Silvia Orlandi (2016), "Elena e S. Croce in Gerusalemme," in T. Canella (ed.), *L'impero constantiniano e i luoghi sacri*, Bologna: il Mulino, 273-91.

Sergio Palladino (1996), "Le terme eleniane a Roma," *MEFR/Antiquité* 108, 855-71.

Fabrizio Paolucci (2012-2013), "La statua di Elena seduta della Galleria degli Uffizi alla luce dei recenti restauri," *Atti della Pontificia Accademia Romana di Archeologia*, ser. 3, Rendiconti 85, 415-32.

Arietta Papaconstantinou (2015), "Introduction," in A. Papaconstantinou, N. McLynn, D. L. Schwartz (eds.), *Conversion in Late Antiquity: Christianity, Islam and Beyond*, Farnham, UK: Ashgate, xv-xxxvii.

Elio Paparatti (2011), "Ipotesi ricostruttiva del sistema decorativo marmoreo," in Vendittelli 2011a, 92-99.

Tim Parkin (2003), *Old Age in the Roman World*, Baltimore: Johns Hopkins University Press.

Sara Parvis (2006), *Marcellus of Ancyra and the Lost Years of the Arian Controversy*, Oxford: Oxford University Press.

François Paschoud (2003), "Introduction," in id., Zosime, *Histoire nouvelle*, Vol. 1, Paris: Les Belles Lettres, vii-cxi.

Joseph Patrich (2006), "Early Christian Churches in the Holy Land," in Limor, Stroumsa, 355-99.

Matthew J. Perry (2014), *Gender, Manumission and the Roman Freedwoman*, New York: Cambridge University Press.

Rene Pfeilschifter (2014), *Der Kaiser und Kontantinopel: Kommunikation und Konfliktaustrag in einer spätantiken Metropole*, Berlin: De Gruyter.

Sara E. Phang (2004), "Intimate Conquests: Roman Soldiers' Slave Women and Freedwomen," *Ancient World* 35, 207-37.

Paul Plass (1995), *The Game of Death in Ancient Rome: Arena Sport and Political Suicide*, Madison: University of Wisconsin Press.

Hans A. Pohlsander, "Crispus: Brilliant Career and Tragic Death," *Historia* 33 (1984) 79-106.

Hans A. Pohlsander (1995), *Helena: Empress and Saint*, Chicago: Aries.

Ivana Popović (1998), "Golden Jewellery from the Imperial Mausouleum at Šarkamen (Eastern Serbia)," *AnTard* 6, 287–312.
Ivana Popović (2007), "Sirmium (Sremska Mitrovica)—Residenzstadt der römischen Kaiser und Stätte der frühen Christen," in Brandl, Vasić, 17–32.
Ivana Popović (2013a), "Jewellery as an Insigne of Authority, Imperial Donation and as Personal Adornment," in Popović, Borić-Brešković, 188–95.
Ivana Popović (2013b), "Sirmium and Naissus as Centres for the Manufacture, Thesauration and Distribution of Objects Made of Precious Metals," in Popović, Borić-Brešković, 162–73.
Ivana Popović, Bojana Borić-Brešković (eds.) (2013), *Constantine the Great and the Edict of Milan 313: The Birth of Christianity in the Roman Provinces on the Soil of Serbia*, Belgrade: National Museum in Belgrade.
Miodrag Popović, Miodrag Tomović (2005), *Šarkamen: A Tetrarchic Imperial Palace, the Memorial Complex*, Belgrade: Archaeological Institute.
David Potter (1993), "Martyrdom as Spectacle," in R. Scodel (ed.), *Theater and Society in the Classical World*, Ann Arbour: University of Michigan Press, 53–88.
David Potter (2009), "Constantine and Fausta," in P. Harvey, C. Conybeare (eds.), *Maxima Debetur Magistro Reverentia: Essays on Rome and the Roman Tradition in Honor of Russell T. Scott*, Como: New Press Edizioni, 137–53.
David Potter (2010), "The Unity of the Roman Empire," in S. McGill, C. Sogno, E. Watts (eds.), *From the Tetrarchs to the Theodosians: Later Roman History and Culture, 284–450CE*, Cambridge, UK: Cambridge University Press, 13–32.
David Potter (2013), *Constantine the Emperor*, Oxford: Oxford University Press.
David Potter (2014), *The Roman Empire at Bay, AD 180–395*, 2nd edn., London: Routledge.
Kim Power (1992), "Sed unam tamen: Augustine and His Concubine," *Augustinian Studies* 23, 49–76.
Markus Prell (1997), *Sozialökonomische Untersuchungen zur Armut im antiken Rom: von den Gracchen bis Kaiser Diokletian*, Stuttgart: Steiner.
Simon Price (1987), "From Noble Funerals to Divine Cult: The Consecration of Roman Emperors," in D. Cannadine, *Rituals of Royalty: Power and Ceremonial in Traditional Societies*, Cambridge, UK: Cambridge University Press, 56–105.
Stefan Priwitzer (2010), "Dynastisches Potential von Kaiserfrauen im Prinzipat am Beispiel der Faustina minor: Tochter, Ehefrau und Mutter," in Kolb 2010a, 237–51.
Marina Prusac (2011), *From Face to Face: Recarving of Roman Portraits and the Late-Antique Portrait Arts*, Brill: Leiden.
Anna Maria Ramieri (1989), "Ritratti femminili conservati presso la Pontificia Commissione di Archeologia Sacra," in *Quaeritur inventus colitur: Miscellanea in onore di Padre Umberto Maria Fasola*, Vatican City: Pontificio Istituto di Archeologia Cristiana, 605–24.
Lars Ramskold (2011), "Coins and Medallions Struck for the Inauguration of Constantinopolis, 11 May 330," in M. Rakocija (ed.), *Niš and Byzantium, Ninth Symposium, Niš, 3–5 June 2010*, Niš: NKC, 125–53.
Lars Ramskold (2013), "Constantine's Vicennalia and the Death of Crispus," in M. Rakocija (ed.), *Niš and Byzantium, Eleventh Symposium, Niš, 3–5 June 2012*, Niš: NKC, 409–56.
Jürgen Rasch (1998), *Das Mausoleum der Kaiserin Helena in Rom und der "Tempio della Tosse" in Tivoli*, Mainz: Zabern.

Jürgen Rasch, Achim Arbeiter, Friedrich Wilhelm Deichmann, Jens Rohmann (2007), *Das Mausoleum der Constantina in Rome*, Mainz: Zabern.
Beryl Rawson (1974), "Roman Concubinage and Other De Facto Marriages," *TAPhA* 104, 279–305.
Éric Rebillard (1999), "Les formes de l'assistance funéraire dans l'Empire romain et leur évolution dans l'Antiquité tardive," *AnTard* 7, 269–82.
Annette Yoshiko Reed (2017, February 15), "Two New Books on Epiphanius: Biography and Its Limits for Late Antiquity," *Ancient Jew Review* (available at https://www.ancie ntjewreview.com/read/2017/2/10/two-new-books-on-epiphanius-biography-and-its-limits-for-late-antiquity).
Giuseppe Restaino (2017), "S. Croce in Gerusalemme: dagli 'Horti Spei Veteris' al 'Palatium Sessorianum,'" *Rivista di Archeologia Cristiana* 93, 457–503.
Lawrence Richardson Jr. (1992), *A New Topographical Dictionary of Ancient Rome*, Baltimore: Johns Hopkins University Press.
R. T. Ridley, "Anonymity in the Vita Constantini," *Byzantion* 50 (1980), 241–58.
James B. Rives (1999), "The Decree of Decius and the Religion of Empire," *JRS* 89, 135–54.
Louis Robert (1949), "Inscriptions de la région de Yalova en Bithynie," *Hellenica* 7, 30–44.
Marco Rocco (2013), "Fausta, Costantino e lo 'stuprum per vim,'" *Rivista storica dell'antichità* 43, 243–60.
Marco Rocco (2018), "Intolerance at the Court of Constantine? The Case of Fausta and Helena," in D. Dainese, V. Gheller (eds.), *Beyond Intolerance: The Milan Meeting in AD 313 and the Evolution of Imperial Policy from the Age of the Tetrarchs to Julian the Apostate*, Turnhout: Brepols, 105–27.
Christian Rollinger (forthcoming), "Specie dominationis: Praetorians, Germans, and the City of Rome," in M. Hebblewhite, C. Whately (eds.), *Brill's Companion to Bodyguards in the Ancient Mediterranean World*.
Marice Rose (2006), "The Trier Ceiling: Power and Status on Display in Late Antiquity," *Greece & Rome* 53, 92–109.
Klaus Rosen (2013), *Konstantin der Große. Kaiser zwischen Machtpolitik und Religion*, Stuttgart: Klett-Cotta.
Jean Rougé (1958), "La Pseudo-Bigamie de Valentinien Ier," *Cahiers d'histoire* 3, 5–15.
Jean Rougé (1974), "Justine, la belle Sicilienne," *Latomus* 33, 676–79.
Jean Rougé (1980), "Fausta, femme de Constantin: Criminelle ou victime," *Cahiers d'histoire* 25, 3–17.
Ze'ev Rubin (1982), "The Church of the Holy Sepulchre and the Conflict Between the Sees of Caesarea and Jerusalem," in L. Levine (ed.), *The Jerusalem Cathedra: Studies in the History, Archaeology, Geography and Ethnography of the Land of Israel*, Vol. 2, Detroit, MI: Wayne State University Press, 79–105.
Richard P. Saller (1982), *Personal Patronage under the Early Empire*, Cambridge, UK: Cambridge University Press.
Benet Salway (1994), "What's in a Name? A Survey of Roman Onomastic Practice from c. 700 B.C. to A.D. 700," *JRS* 84, 124–45.
Michele Salzman (2016), "Constantine and the Roman Senate: Conflict, Cooperation and Concealed Resistance," in Salzman, Sághy, Lizzi Testa, 11–45.
Michele Salzman, Marianne Sághy, Rita Lizzi Testa (2016), *Pagans and Christians in Late Antique Rome*, New York: Cambridge University Press.
Mirjana Sanader (2007), *Dalmatia. Eine Römische Provinz an der Adria*, Mainz: Zabern.

Marco Sannazaro (2016), "Milano e i Costantinidi," in Brandt, Castiglia, Fiocchi Nicolai, 405–29.
Teresa Sardella (2016), "La famiglia cristiana: il fidanzamento nella costruzione di una identità religiosa (IV-V secolo)," in Neri, Girotti, 79–100.
Kathrin Schade (2000), "Die bildliche Repräsentation der römischen Kaiserin zwischen Prinzipat und Byzanz," in Kunst, Riemer, 41–55.
Kathrin Schade (2003), *Frauen in der Spätantike—Status und Repräsentation: Eine Untersuchung zur römischen und frühbyzantinischen Bildniskunst*, Mainz: Zabern.
Kathrin Schade (2016) "Women," in Smith, Ward Perkins, 249–58.
Knut Schäferdiek (2014), "Ulfila und der sogenannte Gotische Arianismus," in G. M. Berndt, R. Steinacher, *Arianism: Roman Heresy and Barbarian Creed*, Farnham, UK: Ashgate, 21–44.
Georg Scheibelreiter (1979), "Königstöchter im Kloster. Radegund (†587) und der Nonnenaufstand von Poitiers (589)," *Mitteilungen des Instituts für Österreichische Geschichtsforschung* 87, 1–37.
Walter Scheidel (1995), "The Most Silent Women of Greece and Rome: Rural Labour and Women's Life in the Ancient World," *Greece & Rome* 42, 202–17.
Walter Scheidel (2005), "Marriage, Families, and Survival in the Roman Imperial Army: Demographic Aspects," *Princeton/Stanford Working Papers in Classics* (available at https://www.princeton.edu/~pswpc/pdfs/scheidel/110509.pdf).
Walter Scheidel, Elijah Meeks, "ORBIS," *The Stanford Geospatial Network Model of the Roman World* (available at https://orbis.stanford.edu/).
Adam M. Schor (2011), *Theodoret's People: Social Networks and Religious Conflict in Late Roman Syria*, Berkeley: University of California Press.
Walter Schumacher (1986), "Das Baptisterium von Alt-St. Peter und seine Probleme," in O. Feld (ed.), *Studien zur spätantiken und byzantinischen Kunst: Friedrich Wilhelm Deichmann gewidmet*, Bonn: Habelt, 215–33.
Eduard Schwartz (1927), "Die Kaiserin Pulcheria auf der Synode von Chalkedon," in *Festgabe für Adolf Jülicher zum 70. Geburtstag, 26. Januar 1927*, Tübingen: JCB Mohr, 203–12.
Valnea Santa Maria Scrinari (1989), "Contributo all'urbanistica tardo antica sul campo laterano," in *Actes du XIe congrès international d'archéologie chrétienne*, Rome: École Française de Rome, 2201–20.
Valnea Santa Maria Scrinari (1991), *Il Laterano imperiale*, Vol. 1, Vatican City: Pontificio Istituto di archeologia Cristiana, 1991.
Deborah Sebag, Yossi Nagar (2007), "Fouilles dans le jardin de l'Éléona à Jérusalem (Pl I-II)," *Revue Biblique* 114, 427–46.
Otto Seeck (1901), "Constantius 1," *RE* 4.1, 1040–43.
Otto Seeck (1912), "Helena 2," *RE* 7, no. 2, 2820–22.
Kristina Sessa (2007), "Christianity and the Cubiculum: Spiritual Politics and Domestic Space in Late Antique Rome," *JECS* 15, 171–204.
Kristina Sessa (2018), *Daily Life in Late Antiquity*, Cambridge, UK: Cambridge University Press.
Erika Simon (1986), *Die konstantinischen Deckengemälde in Trier*, Mainz: Zabern.
Hagith Sivan (2008), *Palestine in Late Antiquity*, Oxford: Oxford University Press.
Hagith Sivan (2011), *Galla Placidia: The Last Roman Empress*, Oxford: Oxford University Press.

Michael Slusser (2003), "The Martyrdom of Lucian of Antioch," *Zeitschrift für Antikes Christentum* 7, 329-37.

Julie Ann Smith (2007), "'My Lord's Native Land': Mapping the Christian Holy Land," *Church History* 76, 1-31.

R. R. R. Smith (1997), "The Public Image of Licinius I: Portrait Sculpture and Imperial Ideology in the Early Fourth Century," *JRS* 87, 184-85.

R. R. R. Smith, Bryan Ward Perkins (2016), *The Last Statues of Antiquity*, Oxford: Oxford University Press.

Claudia Sode, Paul Speck (2004), "Ikonoklasmus vor der Zeit? Der Brief des Eusebios von Kaisareia an Kaiserin Konstantia," *Jahrbuch der Österreichischen Byzantinistik* 54, 113-34.

Marta Sordi (1993), "Dall'elmo di Constantino alla corona ferrea," in G. Bonamente, F. Fusco (eds.), *Costantino il grande*, Vol. 2, Macerata: Università di Macerata, 883-982.

Claire Sotinel (2005), "Popes and Emperors in the Sixth Century," in M. Maas (ed.), *The Cambridge Companion to the Age of Justinian*, Cambridge, UK: Cambridge University Press, 267-90.

Pat Southern (2007), *The Roman Army: A Social and Institutional History*, Oxford: Oxford University Press.

Thomas Späth (2010), "Augustae zwischen modernen Konzepten und römischen Praktiken der Macht," in Kolb 2010a, 293-308.

Jeffrey Spier (2007), *Late Antique and Early Christian Gems*, Wiesbaden: Reichert.

Dragoslav Srejović (1995), "Diva Romula, Divus Galerius," in id., *The Age of Tetrarchs. A Symposium Held from the 4th to the 9th October 1993*, Belgrade: Serbian Academy of Sciences and Arts, 295-310.

Dragoslav Srejović, Miodrag Tomović, Čedomir Vasić (1996), "Šarkamen. Tetrarchical Imperial Palace," *Starinar* 47, 231-43.

Dragoslav Srejović, Čedomir Vasić (1994), *Imperial Mausolea and Consecration Memorials in Felix Romuliana (Gamzigrad, East Serbia)*, Belgrade: Centre for Archaeological Research.

David J. Stanley (1994), "New Discoveries at Santa Costanza," *DOP* 48, 257-61.

Krystyna Stebnicka (2012), "Jezebel and Eudoxia: Reflections on the History of the First Conflict Between John Chrysostom and Empress Eudoxia," *Palamedes: A Journal of Ancient History* 7, 143-54.

Janet Stephens (2008), "Ancient Roman Hairdressing: On (Hair) Pins and Needles," *JRA* 21, 110-32.

Paul Stephenson (2009), *Constantine: Unconquered Emperor, Christian Victor*, London: Quercus.

Paul Stephenson (2015), "A Note on the Constantinian Cameo, Now in Leiden," *BABESCH* 90, 237-40.

Frank Stini (2011), *Plenum exiliis mare: Untersuchungen zum Exil in der römischen Kaiserzeit*, Stuttgart: Steiner.

Ann M. Stout (1995), "Jewelry as a Symbol of Status in the Roman Empire," in J. L. Sebesta, L. Bonfante (eds.), *The World of Roman Costume*, Madison: University of Wisconsin Press, 77-100.

Paul Styger (1933), *Die römischen Katakomben: Archäologische Forschungen über den Ursprung und die Bedeutung der altchristlichen Grabstätten*, Berlin: Verlag für Kunstwissenschaft.

C. H. V. Sutherland, R. A. G. Carson (1967), "General Introduction," in id., *Roman Imperial Coinage*, Vol. 6, London: Spink & Son, 1–112.

Laurens Tacoma (2016), *Moving Romans: Migration to Rome in the Principate*, Oxford: Oxford University Press.

Joan E. Taylor (1993), *Christians and the Holy Places: The Myth of Jewish-Christian Origins*, Oxford: Oxford University Press.

Sergey A. Temeryazev, Tetiana P. Makarenko (2017), *The Coinage of Roman Empresses*, 2 vols., CreateSpace Independent Publishing.

Hildegard Temporini-Gräfin Vitzhum (2002a), "Die Frauen der 'Adoptivkaiser' von Traian bis Commodus," in Temporini-Gräfin Vitzhum 2002b, 187–264.

Hildegard Temporini-Gräfin Vitzhum (ed.) (2002b), *Die Kaiserinnen Roms: Von Livia bis Theodora*, Munich: Beck.

Alan Thacker (2007), "Rome of the Martyrs: Saints, Cults and Relics, Fourth to Seventh Centuries," in Éamonn Ó Carragáin (ed.), *Roma felix: Formation and Reflections of Medieval Rome*, Farnham, UK: Ashgate, 13–50.

Hans Georg Thümmel (1984), "'Eusebios' Brief an Kaiserin Konstantia," *Klio. Beiträge zur alten Geschichte* 66, 210–22.

Hans Georg Thümmel (1992), *Die Frühgeschichte der ostkirchlichen Bilderlehre: Texte und Untersuchungen zur Zeit vor dem Ikonoklasmus*, Berlin: De Gruyter.

Miodrag Tomović (2009), "Šarkamen (East Serbia). An Imperial Tetrarchic Palace, Mausoleum and Memorial Complex," in Cambi, Belamarić, Marasović, 411–67.

Shaun Tougher (2008), *The Eunuch in Byzantine History and Society*, London: Routledge.

Shaun Tougher (2011), "Imperial Blood: Family Relationships in the Dynasty of Constantine the Great," in M. Harlow, L. Larsson Loven (eds.), *Families in the Roman and Late Antique World*, London: Continuum, 181–98.

Shaun Tougher (2020), "Eusebia and Eusebius: The Roles and Significance of Constantinian Imperial Women and Court Eunuchs," in Baker-Brian, Tougher, 185–220.

Dennis Trout (2014), "'Being Female': Verse Commemoration at the Coemeterium S. Agnetis (Via Nomentana)," in Harrison, Humfress, Sandwell, 215–34.

Yoram Tsafrir (1993), "Ancient Churches in the Holy Land," *Biblical Archaeology Review* 19, 26–39.

Sissel Undheim (2017), *Borderline Virginities: Sacred and Secular Virgins in Late Antiquity*, London: Routledge.

Rebecca Usherwood (2022), *Political Memory and the Constantinian Dynasty: Fashioning Disgrace*, Cham: Palgrave Macmillan.

Raymond Van Dam (2007), *The Roman Revolution of Constantine*, Cambridge, UK: Cambridge University Press.

Raymond Van Dam (2011), *Remembering Constantine at the Milvian Bridge*, Cambridge, UK: Cambridge University Press.

John Vanderspoel (1999), "Correspondents and Correspondence of Julius Julianus," *Byzantion* 69, 396–478.

John Vanderspoel (2020), "From the Tetrarchy to the Constantinian Dynasty: A Narrative Introduction," in Baker-Brian, Tougher, 23–55.

John Vanderspoel, Michelle L. Mann (2002), "The Empress Fausta as Romano-Celtic Dea Nutrix," *NC* 162, 350–55.

Cornelis R. Van Tilburg (2007), *Traffic and Congestion in the Roman Empire*, London: Routledge.

Eric R. Varner (2001), "Portraits, Plots and Politics: Damnatio Memoriae and the Images of Imperial Women," *MAAR* 46, 41–93.
Eric R. Varner (2004), *Mutilation and Transformation: Damnatio Memoriae and Roman Imperial Portraiture*, Leiden, Boston: Brill.
Eric R. Varner (2020), "Innovation and Orthodoxy in the Portraiture of Constantine and His Sons," in Baker-Brian, Tougher, 97–132.
Miloje Vasić (2007), "Mediana—Die kaiserliche Villa bei Niš," in Brandl, Vasić, 96–107.
Miloje Vasić (2013), "Cities and Imperial Villae in Roman Provinces in the Territory of Present-Day Serbia," in Popović, Borić-Brešković, 76–101.
Miloje Vasić, Miodrag Tomović (2005), "Šarkamen (East Serbia): An Imperial Residence and Memorial Complex of the Tetrarchic Period," *Germania* 83, 257–305.
Laura Vendittelli (ed.) (2011a), *Il mausoleo di Sant'Elena*, Rome: Mondadori Electa.
Laura Vendittelli (2011b), "Il territorio inter duas lauros," in Vendittelli 2011a, 8–11.
Laura Vendittelli (2011c), "Lo scavo del mausoleo," in Vendittelli 2011a, 30–50.
István Vida (2014), "The Coinage of Flavia Maxima Helena," in *Dissertationes Archaeologicae ex Instituto Archaeologico Universitatis de Rolando Eötvös nominatae* 3, 171–77.
Louis-Hugues Vincent, Félix-Marie Abel (1914–1926), *Jérusalem Nouvelle*, Vol. 2: *Jerusalem: Recherches de topographie, d'archéologie et d'histoire*, Paris: J. Gabalda.
Nina von Zimmermann (2005), "Zu den Wegen der Frauenbiographikforschung," in C. von Zimmermann, N. von Zimmermann (eds.), *Frauenbiographik. Lebensbeschreibungen und Porträts*, Tübingen: G. Narr, 17–32.
Byron L. Waldron (2018), *Diocletian, Hereditary Succession and the Tetrarchic Dynasty*, dissertation, University of Sidney.
Wolfgang Waldstein (1964), *Untersuchungen zum römischen Begnadigungsrecht: Abolitio-Indulgentia-Venia*, Innsbruck: Universitätsverlag Wagner.
P. W. L. Walker (1990), *Holy City, Holy Places? Christian Attitudes to Jerusalem and the Holy Land in the Fourth Century*, New York: Clarendon.
Henry Beauchamp Walters (1926), *Gem/Catalogue of Engraved Gems & Cameos, Greek, Etruscan & Roman in the British Museum*, London: British Museum Press.
Bryan Ward Perkins (2016), "Statues at the End of Antiquity: The Evidence of the Inscribed Bases" in Smith, Ward Perkins, 28–42.
Belinda Washington (2015), *The Roles of Imperial Women in the Later Roman Empire, A.D. 306–455*, dissertation, University of Edinburgh.
Edward J. Watts, Bradley K. Storin, Cristiana Sogno (eds.) (2016), *Late Antique Letter Collections: A Critical Introduction and Reference Guide*, Berkeley: University of California Press.
Evelyn Waugh (1950), *Helena: A Novel*, New York, Boston, London: Back Bay Books.
Winfried Weber (2000), *Constantinische Deckengemälde aus dem römischen Palast unter dem Dom*, 4th edn, Trier: Bischöfliches Dom- und Diözesanmuseum.
Barbara Weber Della Croce (2010), "Der spätantike Kameo des Ada-Evangeliars: Überlegungen zur Deutung und Datierung," *Kurtrierisches Jahrbuch* 50, 21–33.
Barbara Weber Della Croce (2016), "Die konstantinischen Deckenmalereien unter dem Trierer Dom - eine Neubetrachtung," in Brandt, Castiglia, Fiocchi Nicolai, 1505–19.
Max Wegner (1984), "Die Bildnisse der Frauen und des Julian," in H. P. L'Orange (ed.), *Das spätantike Herrscherbild von Diokletian bis zu den Konstantin-Söhnen 284–361 n. Chr.*, Berlin: Gebr. Mann Verlag.

Shlomit Weksler-Bdolah (2019), *Aelia Capitolina—Jerusalem in the Roman Period: In Light of Archaeological Research*, Leiden, Boston: Brill.
E. Gordon Whatley (1993), "An Early Literary Quotation from the *Inventio S. Crucis*: A Note on Baudonivia's *Vita Radegundis* (*BHL* 7049)," *Analecta Bollandiana* 111, 81–91.
C. R. Whittaker (2004), *Rome and Its Frontiers: The Dynamics of Empire*, London: Routledge.
Anja Wieber-Scariot (1999), *Zwischen Polemik und Panegyrik: Frauen des Kaiserhauses und Herrscherinnen des Ostens in den Res gestae des Ammianus Marcellinus*, Trier: Wissenschaftlicher Verlag.
John J. Wilkes (1969), *Dalmatia*, London: Routledge.
John J. Wilkes (2005), "Provinces and Frontiers," in Bowman, Cameron, Garnsey, 212–68.
R. J. A. Wilson (2018), "Roman Villas in Sicily," in A. Marzano, G. P. R. Métraux, *The Roman Villa in the Mediterranean Basin: Late Republic to Late Antiquity*, Cambridge, UK: Cambridge University Press, 195–219.
Fridhelm Winkelmann (1966), "Charakter und Bedeutung der Kirchengeschichte des Gelasios von Kaisareia," *Byzantinische Forschungen* 1, 346–85.
Fridhelm Winkelmann (1987), "Die älteste erhaltene griechische hagiographische Vita Konstantins und Helenas (BHG Nr. 365z, 366, 366a)," in J. Dummer, J. Irmscher (eds.), *Texte und Textkritik: eine Aufsatzsammlung*, Berlin: Akademie Verlag, 623–38.
Philip Wood (2017), "Constantine in the Chronicle of Seert," *SLA* 1, 150–72.
David Woods (1991), *The Christianisation of the Roman Army in the Fourth Century*, dissertation, Queen's University of Belfast.
David Woods (1998), "On the Death of the Empress Fausta" *Greece & Rome* 45, 70–86.
David Woods (2004), "The Constantinian Origin of Justina (Themistius, Or.3.43b)," *Classical Quarterly* 54, 325–27.
David Woods (2006), "Valentinian I, Severa, Marina and Justina," *Classica et Mediaevalia* 57, 173–87.
David Woods (2011), "Numismatic Evidence and the Succession to Constantine I," *NC* 171, 187–96.
Greg Woolf (2000), "Literacy," in A. Bowman, P. Garnsey, D. Rathbone (eds.), *Cambridge Ancient History*, Vol. 11, 2nd edn., Cambridge, UK: Cambridge University Press, 875–97.
Ulrike Wulf-Rheidt (2007), "Residieren in Rom oder in der Provinz?," in Brandl, Vasić, 59–79.
Jun Yamada, Alessandra Cerrito (2015), "Nuovi scavi e ricerche sulle prime fasi insediative cristiane nel complesso degli Horti Domitiae Lucillae e della 'Domus Annii' (Comprensorio ospedaliero S. Giovanni-Addolorata, Roma)," in R. Martorelli, A. Piras, P. G. Spanu (eds.), *Isole e terraferma nel primo cristianesimo: Identità locale ed interscambi culturali, religiosi e produttivi*, Cagliari: PFTS, 687–93.
Jun Yamada, Alessandra Cerrito (2020), "Scoperta di nuove pitture nell'oratorio paleocristiano sotto l'Ospedale dell'Angelo (Complesso ospedaliero S. Giovanni-Addolorata, Roma)," *Atti della Pontificia Accademia Romana di Archeologia*, Ser. 3, Rendiconti 91, 275–321.

Ann Marie Yasin (2012), "Reassessing Salona's Churches: Martyrium Evolution in Question," *JECS* 20, 59–112.

Fikret Yegül (1992), *Baths and Bathing in Classical Antiquity: An Architectural History*, Cambridge, MA: MIT.

Annie Zadoks-Josephus Jitta (1966), "Imperial Messages in Agate II," *BABESCH* 41, 91–104.

Erika Zwierlein-Diehl (2007), *Antike Gemmen und ihr Nachleben*, Berlin: De Gruyter.

Index

For the benefit of digital users, indexed terms that span two pages (e.g., 52–53) may, on occasion, appear on only one of those pages.

Figures are indicated by *f* following the page number

Ablabius, Praetorian prefect, xvii, 193n.38, 264–66, 268–69
Abraham, biblical patriarch, 219–20, 238
Acacius, *comes*, 238–39
Ada Cameo, 119–22, 121*f*, 135, 179–80
Adonis, god, 241
adoption, 61, 62–63, 65, 68, 104–5, 117n.18, 198–99, 307
Adrianople, city in Thrace, xvi, 114–15, 122–24, 304, 306–7
adultery, 29–30, 31n.59, 74–75, 106–7, 189–90, 192–93, 194n.39, 239, 332–33
Aegean Sea, 44, 118–19, 215–16, 248
Aeneas, mythical founder of Rome, 198–99
Agnes, martyr, 282–83, 284–87, 292–94, 336–37
Agrippina, mother of Nero, 94, 157n.50, 178–79
Albinus (Ceionius Rufius), urban prefect, 319–20
Alemanni, 23–24, 60, 248
Alexander the Great, 91–92, 129, 131
Almann of Hautvillers, monk and author of a *Life of Saint Helena*, 7–8
Alpinius Magnus, governor of Lucania et Bruttii, 34, 153–54
Ambrose, bishop of Milan, 24–25, 28–29, 30–31, 138n.75, 304–8, 309–16, 318–19, 324, 326–27, 336–37, 343–45
    and basilica conflict, xviii, 304–7, 314–15, 316
    and funeral oration on Theodosius I, 309–16, 324

Ammianus Marcellinus, historian, 290–91, 297–98
Anastasia, daughter of Valens, 302
Anastasia, empress, wife of Tiberius, 339
Anastasia, half-sister of Constantine, xxi, xxvi*f*, 41–43, 50n.55, 61–62, 73, 77, 116–17, 153, 202, 262–63, 269–70, 286n.29
Anastasis (Resurrection). *See* Christianity
Anastasius IV, pope, 252
Ancyra, capital of Galatia I, 219
Anemius, bishop of Sirmium, 306
Antioch, imperial residence city, xvi, 66n.32, 76–77, 100–1, 103, 106, 107–8, 125–26, 127–28, 137, 138–39, 185, 214n.29, 218–21, 223–25, 226–28, 238n.111, 247, 262–63, 268–69, 278–79, 289–91, 301, 317, 320n.33, 324n.49, 331–32
Apollonia, city in Palaestina, 230
Aquileia, imperial residence city, 59, 65–66, 74–75, 80, 167n.77, 175–76, 216, 312n.5
Arcadia, daughter of Arcadius, xxvi*f*, 336
Arcadius, emperor, xviii, xxvi*f*, 307–8, 309–10, 313–14, 317, 336
architecture, palatial, 114, 150–53, 217–18, 234–35
Ariadne, empress, wife of Zeno, 338–39
Arians, Arianism. *See* Christianity
Arius, priest in Alexandria, 182–83, 184, 207, 225–27
Armenia, kingdom, 263, 270, 277–78
arrogatio, 40–41

Asia Minor (Anatolian peninsula), 18, 24–27, 58n.2, 95, 99–100, 214–16, 248, 262–63
Aspar, *magister militum*, 337–38
Athanasius, bishop of Alexandria, 148n.22, 206, 207–8, 213–14, 224–29, 243, 270n.72, 276–77, 285–86, 295n.61, 305–6, 307
Athaulf, Gothic king, xviii, xxvi*f*, 328–29
Atticus, bishop of Constantinople, 336–37
Augustine, bishop of Hippo, 35–36, 39–41, 43, 316
Augustus, emperor, 46, 91–92, 94, 94n.35, 99–100, 104–5, 120*f*, 178–79, 198–99
Aurelian, emperor, xv, 26–27, 28–29, 32–33, 39–40, 44, 45–46, 58–59, 60–61, 100–1, 120*f*, 144–45
Auxentius, Non-Nicene bishop of Milan, 304–5, 307

Balkans, xv, xxx*f*, 17, 22–23, 26–27, 43, 44–45, 83, 95–96, 113, 187, 215–16, 222n.57, 287–90
banishment, xvi, 3, 107–8, 141–42, 153, 182, 183n.10, 184, 207–9, 210–11, 224–29, 270–71, 285–86, 289, 298–99, 302n.80, 327–29, 331–32, 333, 334–35
Basilina, mother of Julian, xxi, xxvi*f*, 19–20, 225–27, 228, 262–63
Basilinopolis, city in Bithynia, 19–20
Basiliscus, usurper, 338–39
Bassianus, husband of Anastasia, Constantine's half-sister, xvi, xxvi*f*, 41–42, 73–74, 116–17, 140–42, 153, 181–82
Baudonivia, author of a *Life of Radegund*, 1n.2, 309, 341–43, 344–46
Bauto, *magister militum*, 306–7, 323n.45
Bethlehem, 28, 218–19, 240–42, 247
cave and church of the Nativity, 234–35, 237, 240–42
betrothal. *See* marriage
Bithynia (Bithynia-Pontus), Roman province, xvii, 18, 19–20, 24–25, 26–27, 28–29, 32–33, 259–60, 261, 277, 287–88, 291–92, 296–97, 301–2

Book of Pontiffs (*Liber pontificalis*), 159–62, 165n.69, 252, 256, 257–58, 280–82, 343–44
Bordeaux Pilgrim, traveler to Jerusalem, 220, 234n.96, 235–36, 242–43
Bosphorus, 24–25, 26–27, 44, 118, 122–23, 153, 215–16
Byzantium, city on the Bosphorus, 33, 45, 118, 122–23. *See also* Constantinople

Caeni Gallicani, post station in Bithynia, 29n.50, 291
Caesarea, capital of Palaestina I, 219, 229–30. *See also* Eusebius, bishop of Caesarea; Gelasius, bishop of Caesarea.
Calocaerus, usurper, 263
Campania, Roman province, 158, 192n.34, 215
Candidianus, son of Galerius, xvi, xxvi*f*, 99, 104–5, 106–8, 265
Cappadocia, Roman province, 124n.39, 183n.10, 289, 301
Carnuntum, capital of Pannonia Superior, xvi, 71, 96–97, 97n.45, 98*f*, 99–100, 101, 103, 106
Carrhae, city in Mesopotamia, 219–20
Cerealis (Naeratius), urban prefect, 295, 298–300
Cerealis, brother of empress Justina, xxvi*f*, 298–99, 303–4
child of Crispus, xvi, xxvi*f*, 190–91, 265n.56, 289–90, 304
Christianity
    Anastasis (Resurrection), 232
    Arians, Arianism, 147–48, 183n.8, 191, 193, 224–29, 298–99, 298n.70, 305–6, 307–8, 314–15, 316, 327–28
    asceticism, 152–53, 275–76, 284–86, 288–89, 336–37, 345–46
    conversion, 4–5, 19–20, 72, 78–79, 193, 241–43, 311, 344–45
    Homoians, 19, 304–7, 315n.17
    homoousian formula, 184
    martyrdom, martyrs, 18–19, 47, 76, 78–79, 152–53, 163–64, 165–66, 225–26, 228, 229–30, 255, 257–58, 280–85, 315, 331, 335–37, 343–44

INDEX

persecutions, xv, 18–24, 25, 26–27, 76, 78–79, 93, 148–49, 163–64, 182, 184, 229–30, 284–85, 310–11, 321–22
pilgrimage, xix, 3–4, 27, 209, 214, 219–20, 232, 234–35, 242–43, 324–26, 331–33, 343–44
relics, 7–8, 18–19, 76, 225–26, 228, 247, 292n.51, 315–16, 331–32, 335–37, 340, 345–46 (*see also* Christianity, True Cross)
sanctity, 336–37, 343–46, 347–48
Trinity, 206, 225, 228, 236–37, 240n.117
True Cross, 1–2, 6, 7–8, 18n.12, 159–61, 167–68, 200–1, 204, 232–34, 250n.9, 258–59, 309, 311–13, 314–15, 323–28, 329–31, 333, 334–36, 339–44, 345–46, 347–48
Virgin Mary, 10, 96, 138n.75, 241–42, 284, 312–13, 331, 336–38, 343, 347–48
women as church founders, 165–66
Claudia, fictional niece or daughter of Claudius Gothicus, 26, 178
Claudian, panegyrist, 257
Claudius Gothicus, emperor, xv, 24–25, 26, 71–72, 73–75, 112n.4, 120*f*, 325n.50
Clothar, Merovingian king, 340
concubinage, xxvi*f*, 5–6, 34–37, 39–41, 43, 48, 50, 66–67, 99, 114–15, 116n.17, 185, 188, 265
Constans, emperor, son of Constantine and Fausta, xvi, xxvi*f*, 17n.8, 19n.20, 120–22, 132–33, 149n.28, 159n.53, 180–81, 185, 263–65, 268–70, 271, 278–79, 280–82, 287–88, 300
Constantia, city. *See* Maiuma
Constantia, half-sister of Constantine, wife of Licinius, xvi, xxvi*f*, xxxii*f*, 41–43, 50n.55, 61–62, 113–17, 118, 122, 123–24, 128–29, 147–48, 167–68, 180–81n.5, 183–87, 191, 192–93, 195–98, 196*f*, 200–3, 213–14, 216–17, 222–23, 227–28, 242, 265, 268–69, 268n.63, 270, 280–82, 319–20, 327–28
Constantia, posthumous daughter of Constantius II, xviii, xxvi*f*, 301–3, 317
Constantianus, brother of empress Justina, xxvi*f*, 298–99, 301–2

Constantina, daughter of Constantine, xvi, xxvi*f*, xxxiii*f*, 3, 28–29, 42n.34, 149n.28, 254–55n.18, 257, 264–65, 269–70, 273, 274, 275–94, 275*f*, 281*f*, 296–300, 319–20, 322–23, 336–38
Constantine, emperor, *passim*
 and attitude to Rome, 72–75, 140–42, 194–95, 201
 and birth and childhood, 39–41
 and church foundation, 145–46, 154–55, 162–65, 231–32, 238–41
 and conversion, 57–58, 77–79, 189, 193, 327–28
 and death, 266–67, 268
 and dynastic representation, 56–57, 73–75, 95–96, 118–22, 178–81, 185–87, 195–98
 and family crisis of 326, 187–94
 and Nicene Christianity (*see* Council of Nicaea)
 and succession plans, 116–17, 179–80, 262–65
Constantine II, emperor, xvi, xxvi*f*, 17n.8, 116–17, 118, 120–22, 268–73, 278–79
Constantinople, *passim*
 Augusteion, 259–61
 Apostoleion, 249, 250, 259–61, 260n.39, 293, 297n.68, 303, 317
 baths of Anastasia, 157n.50, 301, 302n.77
 column of Constantine, 232–34, 326n.56
 dedication ceremony, xvii, 262–63
 forum of Constantine, 258–59
 foundation, xvii, 187, 201, 260, 262–63
 Hagia Sophia, 258–59, 339
 Hebdomon, 317, 338–39
 Helenianai, 260, 335–36
 Hippodrome, 339
 Mese, 258–59
 palaces named after imperial women, 260, 319–20
 St. Lawrence, 331
 St. Thyrsus, 335–36
 See also Byzantium
Constantius I, emperor, *passim*
 and death, 63–64
 and origins, 26–27

Constantius I, emperor, *passim* (*cont.*)
  and relationship with Helena, 36–39, 40–41
  and relationship with Theodora, 60–62
  as ancestor, 71–72, 73–74, 200, 270
Constantius II, emperor, xvi, xxvi*f*, 12n.30, 17n.8, 118, 120–22, 124, 130n.53, 261–62, 264–65, 268–73, 278–79, 287–91, 293–98, 299–300, 301–2, 304–5, 306
Constantius III, emperor, xix, xxvi*f*, 328–29, 329n.64
Constantius, ambassador in 315, 41–42, 43
Constantius (Flavius Constantius), Praetorian prefect, 42n.33, 201
Council of Ephesus (431), xix, 331–32, 336–37
Council of Chalcedon (451), xix, 333, 334–36, 337–39, 340
Council of Nicaea (325), xvii, 76–77, 182–83, 184, 185, 187, 191, 204, 206, 207, 212–13, 219, 225–27, 228–29, 231, 298–99, 331–32, 337n.95
Council of Nicomedia (327/8), 207, 212–13, 224–25
Council of Rimini (359), 207
Count of the Sacred Largesses, 223
Crispus, Caesar, son of Constantine and Minervina, xv, xxvi*f*, 17n.8, 37–38, 66–67, 116, 117n.22, 118, 120–23, 124, 125–26, 133–35, 150n.31, 169, 178–82, 178n.1, 185, 187–94, 196–98, 208–9, 210, 212, 215, 239, 260n.38, 261–62, 265n.56, 289–90, 291, 298n.70, 304
Cyprian, bishop of Carthage, 28–29
Cyprus, island, 214–15, 248, 263
Cyril, bishop of Alexandria, 331–32
Cyril, bishop of Jerusalem, 232–34, 324, 326n.55

Daburiyya, town in Galilee, 219
Dacia Ripensis, Roman province, 26, 82, 87, 88–89, 90–91, 118, 252
Dalmatius, half-brother of Constantine, xxi, xxvi*f*, 61–62, 117, 141n.5, 141n.6, 195–96, 213n.28, 262–63

Dalmatius the Younger, Caesar, xvii, xxvi*f*, 263–65, 266–70, 272–73
damnatio memoriae, 187–88, 192
Danube, river, xviii, 17, 22–23, 25–26, 26n.42, 32–33, 44, 59, 60, 61, 71, 90, 96–97, 103, 114–15, 259–60
Dardania, region in the central Balkans, 26
daughter of Gallus and Constantina, 289–90, 291
Decius, emperor, xv, 22–25
dependency, 11–12, 20, 73–74, 90–91, 149, 270, 300, 348
Dioclea, mother of Diocletian, 87
Diocletian, emperor, xv, xxvi*f*, 49–50, 59–60, 61–64, 76–77, 83, 84–85, 87–89, 91–92, 93, 94, 95, 96–100, 104, 154–56, 196–97, 260, 319–20
divorce, 5–6, 48, 303
Dracilianus, deputy of Praetorian prefect, 231–32
Drepanon, xv, 18–20, 24–25, 27–28, 32–33, 76–77, 225–26, 228, 259–61. *See also* Helenopolis

Edessa, capital of Osrhoëne, xv, 17–18, 25–26, 219–20, 325n.50
Egeria, pilgrim, 1n.2, 219–20, 222–23, 232–34, 235–36, 239n.116, 248
Elias, prophet, 225–26
Emmaus, biblical site, 230
empress (general)
  and appearance, 101–3
  and apotheosis, 89
  and arrival ceremonies, 143–44, 221–22
  and Augusta title, 99–100, 124, 317–18
  and Christian charity, 321–22
  and church foundations, 165–67, 238, 240, 322–23
  and courtiers, 149
  and formal audiences, 147–49
  and imperial mausolea, 94
  and *mater castrorum* title, 99–100
  and motherhood, 93–94
  and *nobilissima femina* title, 99–100, 104, 119, 187, 198, 319–20
  and *trabea triumphalis*, 102, 135, 180–81, 318–19
  as "New Helena," 338–39, 348

Ephesus, city in Lydia, 220, 228, 320n.33, 322n.41, 334–35
Epiphanius, bishop of Salamis in Cyprus, 12
equites singulares, 145–46, 162, 280–82
Eucherius, son of Stilicho and Serena, xxvif, 313–14
Eudocia, empress, wife of Theodosius II, xix, xxvif, 218–19, 220, 223–24, 247, 331–34, 339, 348
Eudoxia, empress, wife of Arcadius, xviii, xxvif, 157–58, 222n.56, 307–8, 322–23, 328–29
Eudoxia, legendary sister of Constantine, 333n.81
Eugenius, usurper, xviii, 307, 309, 310
eunuchs. *See* slavery
Euphemia, empress, wife of Justin I, 339, 341
Euphrates, river, 23, 25–26, 32–33, 76, 219–20, 301–2
Eusebia, empress, second wife of Constantius II, xvii, xxvif, 12n.30, 143–44, 147–48, 148n.23, 220–21, 222–23, 293, 296–98, 300
Eusebius, bishop of Caesarea, *passim*
 and death of Constantius I, 63–64
 and discovery of Christ's tomb, 231–34
 and Helena excursus in the *Life of Constantine*, 206–8, 235–37
Eusebius, bishop of Nicomedia, xxii, 184–85, 225–29, 268, 270–71
Eusebius, eunuch, 147–48
Eustathius, bishop of Antioch, 224–26, 227, 229, 298–99, 305–6, 327–28
Eutropia, empress, wife of Maximian, xxii, xxvif, xxxiif, 50n.55, 57–59, 60, 65, 65n.28, 73–74, 140–41, 146, 195–96, 202, 222–23, 238–42, 274–75, 280–82, 293–94
Eutropia the Younger, half-sister of Constantine, xxi, xxvif, 41–42, 50n.55, 61–62, 73, 153, 227, 269–70, 285–86, 295
Eutropius, bishop of Adrianople, 225–27
Eutropius, historian, 37–38, 58n.2, 269n.69

Fausta, wife of Constantine, *passim*
 and appearance on coinage, 80–113, 125–31, 132–35, 318–19
 and appearance on glyptic art, 119–22, 135–37, 178–80
 and appearance in sculpture, 135
 and appearance on terracotta lamps, 137
 and church patronage, 148–49, 165–66
 and disappearance, 192
 and role in family crisis of 326, 189–90
 and role in Maximian's downfall (*see* Maximian, plot against Constantine)
 and Rome, 60, 284–85, 293–95
 and *trabea triumphalis*, 135
 and wedding, 65–70
 as Augusta, 124–25
 as *nobilissima femina*, 69–70, 119
Faustina the Younger, wife of Marcus Aurelius, 111, 131, 157n.50
Faustina, empress, third wife of Constantius II, xviii, xxvif, 300, 301–2
Felix Romuliana (Gamzigrad), imperial villa in Dacia Ripensis, 83–84, 89
Flaccilla, empress, wife of Theodosius I, xviii, xxvif, 143–44, 153n.36, 250–51, 310, 314, 317–24, 318n.26, 318f, 327n.58
Flavian, bishop of Constantinople, 334–35

Galerius, emperor, xv, xxvif, 2n.5, 34n.2, 48n.48, 49, 50, 59, 62–64, 65, 68–69, 72, 73–74, 76, 83–107, 108n.83, 113–14, 118–19, 131, 132, 137–38, 164–65, 200, 254, 259–60, 265, 317–18
Galilee, region, 219, 237, 239–40, 259–60
Galla, wife of Julius Constantius, xxii, xxvif, 73, 195–96, 227, 262–63, 264–65, 298–99
Galla the Younger, sister of Valentinian II, xviii, xxvif, 274–75, 298–99, 303–5, 307–8, 313–15, 319–20
Galla Placidia, daughter of Theodosius I and mother of Valentinian III, xviii, xxvif, 150–52, 167–68, 307–8, 313–15, 319–20, 322n.43, 328–31, 332–33, 334, 339–40, 343–44
Gallicanus, martyr, 152–53

388 INDEX

Gallicanus (Ovinius), urban prefect, 155–56
Gallienus, emperor, xv, 26–27, 46, 47, 76, 120f
Gallus, Caesar and cousin of Constantius II, xvii, xxvif, 58n.2, 195–96, 262–63, 269–71, 273, 278–79, 289–91, 296–98
Gaul, region, xvii, 27, 59, 60–61, 70, 71, 96–97, 116–17, 184, 188, 226–27, 249, 287–88, 289n.38, 296–98, 304, 325–26, 339–40, 340n.103, 341–43, 344n.119
Gavianus (Flavius), *praepositus rerum privatarum*, 150, 279, 286–87
Gaza, city in Palaestina, 214–15, 242, 248 basilica Eudoxiana, 322–23. *See also* Maiuma
Gelasius, bishop of Caesarea, 42, 324–25, 326–27, 343
Gerontius, author of the *Life of Melania*, 150n.32, 218–19, 331–32
glyptic art, 119–22, 135–37
Goths, xv, 22–25, 26–27, 90, 248, 301–2, 304, 306–7, 315n.17, 328–29
Grata, sister of Valentinian II, xxvif, 303–4, 307–8, 319n.27
Gratian, emperor, xviii, xxvif, 153n.37, 302–4, 306n.90, 310, 314–15, 317, 318n.26
Gregory, bishop of Neocaesarea, 24–25, 90
Gregory, bishop of Nyssa, 222n.55, 250–51, 318–19, 321–23, 324–25
Gregory, bishop of Tours, 342n.110, 345–46
Gregory the Great, bishop of Rome, 341, 344–45
Gypasius (Valerius), *curator*, 153–54

Hadrian, emperor, 120f, 144–45, 210, 220, 223–24, 230
Hague Cameo, 124n.40, 178–79, 179f, 180–82
Hannibalianus, half-brother of Constantine, xxii, xxvif, 57–58, 61–62, 262–63
Hannibalianus the Younger, son of Flavius Dalmatius, xvii, xxvif, 263–65, 268–70, 277–78, 279, 292n.50
Helena, mother of Constantine, *passim*
and age, 20–21
and "Arianism," 225–29, 307, 314–15
and baptism, 247–48
and birth place, 17–20
and burial (*see* Rome, Mausoleum of Helena)
and Christian worship, 167–68
and church foundation, 158–67, 234–37, 240–41, 283–84
and clothes, 135, 168, 175, 180–81, 272–73
and coinage, 111–13, 125–32, 169–70, 180–81, 266–68, 271–73, 318–20
and conversion, 76–79, 241–42
and courtiers, 149–50, 222–23, 279–80
and death, 247–49
and diadem, 129–31
and discovery of True Cross, 232–34, 310–11, 324–28, 340–41, 342–43
and epigraphy, 197–201, 319–20
and glyptic art, 119–22, 135–36
and hairstyles, 111, 128–31, 168–69, 173–75
and imperial commemoration, 258–62, 293–95
and imperial travel, 215–16, 220–24
and literacy, 20–21
and motherhood, 40–43
and name, 16–17, 126–27, 198, 266–67
and original social status, 15–17
and patronage of civic buildings, 156–58
and prostitution, 27–32, 229
and relationship with Constantius (*see* Constantius I)
and role in family crisis of 326, 189–94
and sanctity, 336, 343–46, 347–48
and sculpture, 170–76
and terracotta lamps, 137
and will, 257–58
as Augusta, 124, 317–18
as *genetrix*, 198–201
as *nobilissima femina*, 119
as imperial delegate, 149, 150–57, 158, 210–14, 232
Helena, wife of Crispus, xvi, xxvif, 50n.55, 111n.1, 190–91, 202

Helena the Younger, daughter of Constantine and Fausta, xiv, xxvi*f*, 50n.55, 124, 222–23, 257, 264–65, 269–70, 274, 279n.10, 297–98, 318–19, 318n.25
Helenopolis, 18–20, 32–33, 221n.46, 259–61, 265–66. *See also* Drepanon
Helenopontus, province, 19–20, 259–60
Homoians. *See* Christianity
homoousian formula. *See* Christianity
Honorius, emperor, xviii, xxvi*f*, 152–53, 307–8, 309–10, 311–15, 328–29
Hormisdas, bishop of Rome, 341

Illyria, 22–23, 87, 269, 288–89, 303–4
Inventio Crucis legend, 326–27, 342–44
Ioppa, city in Palaestina, 230
Iulius, gentile name, 16–17, 116–17, 150, 156–57, 188, 196–97, 198
Iusta, sister of Valentinian II, xxvi*f*, 303–4, 307–8, 319n.27

Jerome, priest and ascetic, 18–19, 153, 191, 295n.60
Jerusalem, 155, 159–60, 204, 210, 218–20, 223–24, 230, 232–34, 235n.100, 238, 239–40, 242–43, 247, 324–25, 326–27, 331–32, 335–36, 339, 342–43
  Eleona, 234–36, 235*f*, 237, 240–41
  Golgotha, 231–32, 233n.94
  Holy Sepulchre, 231–35, 237, 247n.1, 293, 323–25, 326–27, 332–33, 339, 347–48
  Inbomon, 237
  Mount of Olives, 234–35, 237, 240–41, 247, 324–26, 331–32
  Mount Zion, 231–32
  Roman colony Aelia Capitolina, 230, 232, 242–43
  St. Stephen, 247, 331–33
jewelry, 80, 82, 83, 85–87, 101–3, 105, 119–22, 128–32, 135, 168, 223, 255, 257, 312–13, 318–19, 318*f*, 324n.49, 335–36
Jezebel, biblical queen, 225–26, 229, 305–6, 328
John, bishop of Antioch, 331–32
John and Paul, martyrs, 279–80
John, usurper, 328–29

John Chrysostom, priest in Antioch and bishop of Constantinople, 202, 212–13
John Rufus, author of the *Life of Peter the Iberian*, 333
Joseph of Tiberias, Jewish convert, 237
Judaea, region, 326–27
Julia Domna, empress, wife of Septimius Severus, 93–94, 133–34, 133n.65, 148n.23
Julia Maesa, sister of Julia Domna, 93–94, 131
Julia Mamaea, mother of emperor Severus Alexander, 22, 93–94, 131
Julia Soaemias, mother of emperor Elagabalus, 93–94, 131
Julian, son of Julius Constantius and cousin of Constantius II, xviii, xxvi*f*, 19–20, 30–31, 58, 58n.2, 65–66, 141, 143–44, 148n.23, 149, 157–58, 193n.37, 222–23, 227n.75, 257, 261–62, 264–65, 268–71, 273, 293–95, 296–99, 300–2, 303, 318–19
Julius, bishop of Rome, 285–86
Julius Constantius, half-brother of Constantine, xxiii, xxvi*f*, 41–42, 61–62, 73, 116, 117, 117n.18, 141–42, 195–96, 225–26, 227, 262–63, 264–65, 268–69, 298–99
Julius Julianus, Praetorian Prefect, 227, 262–63
Juno, goddess, 68–70, 74–75, 89n.20, 131, 200–1
Justin I, emperor, 339, 341
Justin II, emperor, 157–58, 339–40
Justina, empress, second wife of Valentinian I, xvii, xxvi*f*, 202n.55, 274–75, 276–77, 298–308, 314–16, 327–28, 329–30
Justinian I, emperor, 18, 235n.100, 339
Juvenal, bishop of Jerusalem, 331–32

Lactantius, Christian rhetor, 37–38, 62–63, 71–72, 84–85, 90–93, 95–96, 97–99, 104–5, 106–8, 113–14, 117
Leo I, emperor, 338–39
Leontia, empress, wife of Phokas, 341
Leontius, governor of Helenopontus, 259–60

Libanius of Antioch, orator, 28–29, 30–31, 40–41, 183–84
Licinia Eudoxia, empress, wife of Valentinian III, xix, xxvif, 286–87, 331–32
Licinianus, Caesar, son of Licinius and Constantia, xvi, xxvif, 114–15, 118, 123–24, 181–82, 183–84, 185–87, 191–93, 196–97, 216
Licinius, emperor, *passim*
  killed by Constantine, 183, 193
  and killing of imperial women, 107–8
  and marriage to Constantia, 113–14, 116–24, 185–87
  and origins, 87
  and Sirmium, 115
  and succession plans, 116–17
  as reason for Helena's travels, 210–12
Livia, empress, second wife of Augustus, 9n.24, 99–100, 104–5, 178–79, 178n.1, 198–99, 334
Lucian of Antioch, martyr, xvi, 18–19, 76–78, 225–26, 227–28, 260–61, 284–85

Macarius, bishop of Jerusalem, 155, 230–34, 237–38, 324, 326–27, 339n.102, 343
Macellum, imperial villa in Cappadocia, 270–71, 289
Macrina, sister of Gregory of Nyssa, 324–25
Magna Mater, goddess, 89
Magnentius, usurper, xvii, xxvif, 276–77, 287–90, 291, 299–300
Magnia Urbica, empress, wife of Carus or Carinus, 70n.44, 102–3, 131, 180–81
Magnus Maximus, usurper, xviii, 304–5, 306–7, 315n.16
Maiuma, port of Gaza, 242, 248
Mamertinus, orator, 60–61, 68
Mamre, biblical site, 238–41
Marcellina, sister of Ambrose of Milan, 305–6, 315–16
Marcellus, bishop of Ancyra, 225–26
Marcian, emperor, xix, xxvif, 333, 334–35, 337–38
Marina, daughter of Arcadius, xxvif, 336
Maris, bishop of Chalcedon, 184
marriage, 15–38, 40–41, 66–68, 70–71, 87, 116–17, 277–78
Marutha, bishop of Maïpherqat in Mesopotamia, 17–18

Maxentius, usurper, xv, xxvif, 55–56, 58, 60, 62–63, 65, 68, 71–75, 79, 84–85, 87, 96–97, 108, 113–14, 122–23, 140, 145–46, 148–49, 154–55, 162–63, 178, 185, 194–96, 253–54, 280–82
Maximian, emperor, *passim*
  and origins, 87
  and paternity of Theodora, 57–58
  and plot against Constantine, 71–72, 149, 183, 193
  and Rome, 59–60, 140–41
  as ancestor, 73–74, 266–67, 270
  as *paterfamilias*, 62–63
Maximilianus (Iulius), *comes*, 150, 156–57, 199f
Maximinus Daza, emperor, xv, xxvif, 18–19, 37–38, 62–63, 76, 83–91, 92–93, 95–97, 103, 104–5, 106–8, 113–15, 118, 123–24, 125–26, 164–65, 200, 223–24, 239, 252, 301
Mediana, imperial villa in Moesia Superior, 44–45, 45f, 217–18, 218f, 300–1
Mediterranean Sea, 214–15
Melania (the Elder), Roman noblewoman and ascetic, 324–26, 331
Melania (the Younger), Roman noblewoman and ascetic, 150n.32, 152–53, 219, 331–33
Mesopotamia, region, 17–18, 22, 61, 219–20
Milan, imperial residence city, xvi, 40n.23, 59, 113–15, 165–66, 216, 222n.57, 295n.60, 304–8, 313, 315, 323n.44, *See also* Ambrose, bishop of Milan
Minervina, mother of Crispus, xv, xxvif, 50n.55, 66–68, 133–34, 178–79, 181–82
Mints, 70, 100–1, 103, 111–13, 118–19, 125, 129, 130–31, 223, 266–67, 272–73, 317
Mithraism, 89–90, 97
Moesia Superior, Roman province, 17, 22–23, 26, 90–91, 215–16, 266–67
mother of Maximinus Daza, 50n.55, 83–87, 88–91, 95, 97, 102, 200, 252

Naeratii, aristocratic family, xxii, xxvif, 58–59, 141–42, 298–300
Naissus, city in Moesia Superior, 17, 24–25, 26, 39–41, 43–45, 61, 85–86, 137–38, 176, 187, 217–18, 278–79, 287–88, 294n.57, 300–1, 329n.64

Nantes medallion, 180–82, 200–1
Nepotianus (Iulius), usurper and cousin of Constantius II, xvii, xxvi*f*, 270–71, 295–96, 298–99
Nepotianus (Virius), consul, xxiii, xxvi*f*, 269–70, 285–86
Nestorius, bishop of Constantinople, 331–32, 334–35, 336–37
Nicene creed. *See* Council of Nicaea
Nicomedia, imperial residence city, xv, 18–19, 24–25, 26–27, 32–33, 60, 75–77, 78–79, 84–85, 93, 97–99, 100–1, 103, 106–8, 118, 122–24, 129n.50, 132n.64, 170n.84, 176, 182, 183–84, 187, 215–16, 218–19, 220, 228, 249n.5, 260, 261, 264n.52, 265, 266–67, 277–78, 319–20. *See also* Council of Nicomedia; Eusebius of Nicomedia
Nikiupolis, city in Egypt, 223–24
Non-Nicene Christians. *See* Christianity: Homoians
Nummii, aristocratic family, xxi, 73–74, 116, 286n.29

Olympias, fiancé of Constans, xvii, xxvi*f*, 264–65, 269–70, 300
Olympias, mother of Alexander the Great, 91–92
Optatianus Porfyrius, poet, 117
Optatus (Flavius), consul, 30–31, 37, 183–84, 264n.54, 268–69
Origo Constantini, 16–17, 41–42, 117
Orfitus, urban prefect, 295–97, 300
Orontes, river, 107, 223–24
Orosius, church historian, 191, 193
Osrhoëne, Roman province, 17–18, 22, 219–20
Ossius of Cordoba, bishop, 148–49
Otacilia Severa, empress, wife of Philip the Arab, 24*f*

paganism, 6, 25, 76, 106, 108, 140, 162, 165–66, 183, 185, 193, 194–95, 202–3, 228, 238, 241, 261–62, 278–79, 284–85, 311, 322–23, 327–28. *See also* Mithraism; Juno, goddess; Magna Mater, goddess; Venus, goddess
Palestine, region, xvii, xxxii*f*, 1, 4–5, 6, 19–20, 155–56, 204–5, 206–7, 212–13, 214–16, 218–21, 229–43, 247, 256,
258–60, 269n.67, 280–82, 322–23, 324–26, 331, 332–33, 342–43
Pannonia, region, 22–23, 96–97, 103, 113–14, 215–16, 301, 303–4
Parastaseis, catalogue of monuments, 258–59
Patria, catalogue of monuments, 258–59
patria potestas, 62–63, 65, 74–75, 106–7, 187–88
Patricius, Master of the Offices and lover of empress Verina, 338–39
Paul, apostle, 248, 334–35
Paulinus, bishop of Nola, 204–5, 325–26
Paulinus, friend of Theodosius II, 332–33
Paulinus of Milan, hagiographer, 306
Persia, xviii, 17–18, 22, 27–28, 219–20, 263, 277–78, 287–88, 301. *See also* Sasanians
Peter and Marcellinus, martyrs, 154–55n.44, 163–64
Peter the Iberian, ascetic leader, 333
Philip the Arab, emperor, 22–23, 24*f*
Philostorgius, church historian, 18–19, 30–31, 260–61, 264–65
Phoenice, Roman province, 219
Pistius (Flavius), *praepositus rerum privatarum*, 150
plague, 23–24
Poemenia, pilgrim, 215n.32, 223–24, 237, 325–26
Poitiers, city in Gaul, 339–40, 341–43
Pola, city in Istria, xvii, 187–88, 291
Pola Casket, 330–31
porphyry, 82, 252, 253–54, 253*f*, 258–59, 260–61, 274, 275*f*, 293
poverty, 17–18, 31–32, 33, 35, 36–38, 212–13, 221–22, 280, 321–22
Praetorian guard, 22, 45, 280–82
pregnancy, 27–28, 39–40, 41, 43, 189–90, 238, 241–42
Prisca, empress, wife of Diocletian, xvi, xxvi*f*, 50n.55, 60, 84–85, 94, 97–100, 106–7, 108, 118–19, 123–24, 153, 260
Privernum, city in Campania, 158, 192n.34
Procopius, historian, 18–20
Procopius, usurper, xviii, 301–2
Propontis, sea, xv, 18, 20, 22–23, 24–25, 32–33, 39, 43, 44, 262–63, 265–66, 268. *See also* Drepanon; Helenopolis

protectores, military unit, 26–27, 32–33, 36–37, 39–40
Ps.-Gelasius of Cyzikus, church historian, 42, 327n.59
Pulcheria, daughter of Theodosius I, xxvi*f*, 310, 321n.34
Pulcheria, empress, daughter of Arcadius, xix, xxvi*f*, 322n.43, 327n.58, 332–33, 334–38, 340–41, 348
Pythia, thermal baths in Bithynia, 32–33

Radegund of Poitiers, queen and nun, 309, 339–43, 345–46, 348
Ravenna, imperial residence city, 80n.2, 322n.43, 329–30, 341
Rhine, river, 59, 71, 248, 296
Romanos Melodos, hymnographer, 339
Rome, *passim*
  Aurelian wall, 146–47, 161
  Basilica ad duas lauros (= of Sts. Peter and Marcellinus), 154–55n.44, 161–65, 250, 256*f*, 274, 280–82, 284–85, 343–44
  Basilica Heleniana, 150–52, 159–60, 330n.70
  Basilica of the Apostles, 154–55n.44, 158–59
  Basilica of St. Agnes, 154–55n.44, 270n.71, 274, 280–85, 281*f*, 287n.33, 291–92
  Basilica of St. Paul, 154–55n.44, 330n.67
  Basilica of St. Peter, 153, 154–55n.44, 160–61, 274, 280, 293, 344–45
  baths of Helena, 156–58, 157*f*
  burial in cemeterial basilicas, 163–64, 255–56, 284–85, 292–93
  Caelian hill, 74–75, 144, 279–80
  Capitoline Museums, 74n.61, 171*f*, 173–75, 196*f*
  Cappella Cristiana (Ospedale S. Giovanni), 286–87
  catacombs, 162, 163–64, 170n.86, 280–82, 344–45
  Circus Maximus, 143–44, 146, 194–95
  Domus Faustae, 60, 75n.63, 140–41, 148–49, 279–80
  Fundus Lauretum, 161–62, 165–66, 256, 257–58
  Horti Spei Veteris, 144
  Lateran basilica, 55, 145–46, 149, 150, 162–63, 164–65, 179n.2, 252, 279, 280
  Mausoleum of Constantina (S. Costanza), 274–75, 275*f*, 281*f*, 291–93, 296–98
  Mausoleum of Helena, xvii, 7n.20, 164–66, 249, 250–56, 251*f*, 256*f*, 257–58, 274, 284–85, 343–44
  Porta Labicana (Porta Maggiore, Porta Sessoriana), 144, 145–46, 161, 250–51
  residence under INPS, 55–57, 74–75, 192, 195n.41
  S. Croce in Gerusalemme, 150–52, 150n.29, 150n.31, 154–55n.44, 159–60, 160*f*, 167–68, 199*f*, 200–1
  Sessorian Palace, xvi, xxxi*f*, 141–42, 147*f*, 149–53, 151*f*, 158n.52, 159–61, 167–68, 176, 199*f*, 232–34, 250, 251–55, 257–58, 279–80, 330–31, 342–43
  Vatican Museums, 156n.48, 253*f*, 274, 275*f*, 293
  Via Flaminia, 143–44
  Via Labicana, 144, 145–46, 157–58, 161 (*see also* Basilica ad duas lauros; Mausoleum of Helena)
  Via Nomentana (*see* Agnes martyr; Mausoleum of Constantina)
  Via Praenestina, 161
  Villa of Maxentius, 146, 253–54
Romula, mother of Galerius, xv, xxvi*f*, 50n.55, 83, 84–85, 88–96, 88*f*, 103, 105, 119, 131, 137–38, 200, 254
Rufinus, church historian, 42, 202, 343
Rufinus (Vulcacius), Praetorian prefect, xxii, 278–79, 288–89, 295, 298–300

Sabina, empress, wife of Hadrian, 175–76, 215n.35, 220
Saepinum, city in Samnium, 141–42
Salerno (Salernum), city in Lucania et Bruttii, 153–54
Salona, capital of Dalmatia, xv, 46–47, 47*f*, 49, 78–79, 88–89, 100n.54, 107n.79, 108n.83, 176
Salvina, Theodosian courtier, 325–26
Samosata, city in Commagene, 76

Šarkamen, site of imperial villa in Dacia Ripensis, 82–84, 85–86, 85*f*, 86*f*, 88–90, 91, 95, 97, 106, 252
Sasanians, 17–18, 22, 26–27, 235n.100, 248. *See also* Persia
Seleucia, city in Pamphylia, 248
Senate, 22, 59, 89, 93, 143–44, 146n.20, 183, 258–59, 295, 297–98, 328–29
Senecio, brother of Bassianus, 116–17
Septimius Severus, emperor, 22, 93n.34, 120*f*
Serdica, city in Thrace, 44–45, 91n.25, 100–1, 103, 118, 187, 217–18, 248–49, 277
Serena, niece of Theodosius I, xxvi*f*, 152–53, 307, 313–14, 323n.44
Severa (or Marina), empress, first wife of Valentinian I, xviii, xxvi*f*, 303–4
Severianus, son of emperor Severus, xvi, 107
Severus, emperor (tetrarchy), xv, 50n.55, 62–63, 65, 67–68, 87, 96–97, 107
Severus Alexander, emperor, 22, 93–94, 120*f*, 131
Side, city in Pamphylia, 215, 220–21, 248
Sigibert, Merovingian king, 339–40
Silvester, bishop of Rome, 155, 280–82, 327–28
Silvia, pilgrim, 325–26
Sirmium, imperial residence city, xvi, 22–23, 58–59, 87, 113–15, 116–17, 118, 125n.45, 128–29, 135, 187, 216, 217–18, 268–69, 277, 289–90, 303–4, 306
slavery, xvii, 16–17, 29–30, 31–32, 35–37, 39, 40–41, 42–43, 71, 87, 99, 106–7, 114–15, 146–48, 149, 150–52, 155–56, 168, 185, 193, 198, 222–24, 268, 279–80
Socrates, church historian, 42, 302, 326n.56, 327n.58
son of Licinius, illegitimate, 41n.28, 114–15, 185, 265
Sophia, empress, wife of Justin I, 157–58, 340–43
Sozomen, church historian, 42, 219, 259–61, 327n.58, 336
Split (Spalatum), Diocletian's place of retirement, 88–89, 108n.83

Stilicho, *magister militum*, xxvi*f*, 307, 309–10, 313–14
Sulpicius Severus, chronicler, 204–5, 319n.30, 325–26
Surrentum, city in Campania, 158, 192–93, 195
Syria, region, xxii, 58–59, 106, 107–8, 214–15, 219, 222–24, 327n.57

Tacitus, emperor, 49, 120*f*
Tarsus, capital of Cilicia, 107, 297–98, 301
tetrarchy, xv, xxx*f*, 4–5, 9, 17n.8, 49–50, 55–56, 59–60, 62–63, 65–66, 68–71, 74–75, 76–77, 79, 82, 84–87, 89, 92–93, 97–100, 102, 104, 114–15, 118, 119, 137–38, 146–47, 187, 213–14, 219, 263–66, 271
Thecla, martyr, 248
Theodora, empress, wife of Constantius I, xxi, xxvi*f*, 5–6, 8n.21, 9–10, 41–42, 49, 50n.55, 56–65, 56*f*, 70, 71–72, 74–75, 97–99, 118, 141, 178, 181–82, 185, 190–91, 193–94, 195–96, 266–68, 267*f*, 271–73, 274–75, 298n.70, 313, 317–18
Theodora, empress, wife of Justinian I, 9n.24, 339
Theodoret, church historian, 42, 229, 232–34, 327n.58
Theodosius I, emperor, xviii, xxvi*f*, 28, 143–44, 153n.36, 250–51, 276–77, 304–5, 306n.90, 307–8, 309–15, 317–21, 324, 325–26, 328–29, 330n.67
Theodosius II, emperor, xviii, xxvi*f*, 218–19, 247, 328–29, 331–32, 333, 334, 335–36, 337–38, 348
Theodosius the Elder, father of Theodosius I, 319–20
Theodosius, son of Galla Placidia, 329–30
Theognis, bishop of Nicaea, 184
theophany. *See* Christianity
Thermantia, mother of Theodosius I, 319–20
Thessalonica, imperial residence city, xvi, 102*f*, 103–4, 106–7, 108, 111, 112*f*, 113, 115–16, 118–20, 122, 123–24, 125–26, 125n.45, 127–29, 137, 138–39, 185, 215–16, 217–18, 248, 304–5
Thomas, apostle, 219–20

394 INDEX

Thrace, region, xv, 17, 20, 23–24, 25–27, 33, 39, 103, 118, 122–23, 187, 215–16, 248, 266–67, 304
Trajan, emperor, 23, 100–1, 120*f*, 124, 261
Trier, imperial residence city, x, 1–2, 7–8, 27, 59, 60–61, 64, 65, 68–69, 70, 75–76, 114, 119–20n.29, 121*f*, 125n.45, 132–34, 150–53, 179–80, 187–88, 248–49, 266–67, 272–73
  Trier ceiling, 80–82, 81*f*, 85–86, 105, 128–29, 135
Trinity. *See* Christianity
True Cross. *See* Christianity

Ulpia Severina, empress, wife of Aurelian, 45, 97, 101

Valens, emperor, xviii, 300–2, 303–5, 317
Valentinianus bar Qustus, legendary emperor, 25–26
Valentinian I, emperor, xviii, xxvi*f*, 25–26, 202n.55, 276–77, 301–4
Valentinian II, emperor, xviii, xxvi*f*, 276–77, 298–99, 304–8, 314–15, 319n.27
Valentinian III, emperor, xix, xxvi*f*, 150–52, 167–68, 257–58, 286–87, 328–31
Valeria (Galeria), empress, wife of Galerius, xi–xii, xvi, xxvi*f*, 50n.55, 60, 84–85, 95, 97–108, 116–17, 118–19, 123–24, 126–27, 128–29, 130–32, 133–35, 149–50, 153, 169–70, 180–81, 197–99, 213–14, 239, 259–61, 301–2

Valeria Maximilla, wife of usurper Maxentius, xxiv, xxvi*f*, 50n.55, 65n.29, 73–74, 84–85, 99–100, 123–24
Valerian, emperor, xv, 23, 26–27, 94n.36, 120*f*
Venantius Fortunatus, author of a *Life of Radegund*, 340, 342n.110, 345–46
Venus, goddess, 68–70, 100–1, 102*f*, 131, 151*f*, 175, 198–99, 230–31, 232–34
Verina, empress, wife of Leo I, 338–39, 348
Vetranio, co-emperor of Constantius II, xvii, 287–89, 299–300
Via Egnatia, 215–16
Via Maris, 229–30
Virgin Mary. *See* Christianity
Virii Nepotiani, aristocratic family, 73
Volusianus (Rufius), urban prefect, 117

Waugh, Evelyn, 8–9
wedding. *See* marriage
wife of Constantine II, xvii, xxvi*f*, 264–65, 269–70, 272–73, 298–99
wife of Constantius II, daughter of Julius Constantius, xvii, xxvi*f*, 264–65, 269–70, 272–73
wife of Maximinus Daza, xvi, xxvi*f*, 50n.55, 83, 106–7, 123–24, 126–27, 200, 223–24

York (Eboracum), city in Britannia, xv, 63–64

Zenobia, queen of Palmyra, xv, 26–27
Zosimus, historian, 30–31, 183, 189, 193–95, 305–6

www.ingramcontent.com/pod-product-compliance
Lightning Source LLC
Chambersburg PA
CBHW052115070325
23148CB00004B/173